LUKE CAGE, POWER MAN

VOL. 2

POWER MAN #28-49 & ANNUAL #1

POWER MAN #28
WRITER: **DON MCGREGOR**
PENCILER: **GEORGE TUSKA**
INKER: **VINCE COLLETTA**
LETTERER: **DAVE HUNT**

POWER MAN #29
WRITER: **BILL MANTLO**
PENCILER: **GEORGE TUSKA**
INKER: **VINCE COLLETTA**
LETTERER: **KAREN MANTLO**

POWER MAN #30
WRITER: **DON MCGREGOR**
PENCILER: **RICH BUCKLER & ARVELL JONES**
INKER & LETTERER: **KEITH POLLARD**

POWER MAN #31
WRITER: **DON MCGREGOR**
PENCILER: **SAL BUSCEMA**
INKER: **"CRUSTY BUNKERS"**
LETTERER: **JEAN HIPP**

POWER MAN #32
WRITER: **DON MCGREGOR**
PENCILER: **FRANK ROBBINS**
INKER: **VINCE COLLETTA**
LETTERER: **KAREN MANTLO**

POWER MAN #33
WRITER: **DON MCGREGOR**
PENCILER: **FRANK ROBBINS**
INKER: **VINCE COLLETTA**
LETTERER: **KAREN MANTLO**

POWER MAN #34
WRITER: **DON MCGREGOR**
PENCILER: **FRANK ROBBINS**
INKER: **FRANK SPRINGER**
LETTERER: **IRVING WATANABE**

POWER MAN #35
PLOT: **MARV WOLFMAN**
SCRIPT: **DON MCGREGOR**
PENCILER: **MARIE SEVERIN**
INKERS: **JOE GIELLA & FRANK GIACOIA**
LETTERER: **KAREN MANTLO**

POWER MAN #36
EDITOR'S NOTE: POWER MAN #36 REPRINTS A STORY ORIGINALLY FEATURED IN HEROES FOR HIRE #12

POWER MAN ANNUAL #1
WRITER: **CHRIS CLAREMONT**
PENCILER: **LEE ELIAS**
INKER: **DAVE HUNT**
LETTERER: **DENISE WOHL**

POWER MAN #37
WRITER: **MARV WOLFMAN**
PENCILER: **RON WILSON**
INKER: **AUBREY BRADFORD**
LETTERER: **MICHELLE WOLFMAN**

POWER MAN #38
PLOT: **MARV WOLFMAN**
SCRIPT: **BILL MANTLO**
PENCILER: **BOB BROWN**
INKER: **JIM MOONEY**
LETTERER: **JOE ROSEN**

POWER MAN #39
PLOT: **MARV WOLFMAN**
SCRIPT: **BILL MANTLO**
PENCILER: **BOB BROWN**
INKER: **KLAUS JANSON**
LETTERER: **DENISE WOHL**

POWER MAN #40
WRITER: **MARV WOLFMAN**
PENCILER: **LEE ELIAS**
INKER: **FRANK GIACOIA**
LETTERER: **DENISE WOHL**

POWER MAN #41
WRITER: **MARV WOLFMAN**
PENCILER: **LEE ELIAS**
INKER: **TOM PALMER**
LETTERER: **IRVING WATANABE**

POWER MAN #42
WRITER: **MARV WOLFMAN**
PENCILER: **LEE ELIAS**
INKER: **ALEX NIÑO**
LETTERER: **JOHN COSTANZA**

HATE TO *MESS UP* YOUR PLANS, JACK--

--BUT YOU AIN'T KILLING *NOBODY* TONIGHT... MUCH LESS ME!

NOW WHYN'T YOU JUST PUT *DOWN* THAT *GUN*-- 'CAUSE A *PIECE* LIKE THAT MAKES ME...

...LOSE...

...MY *COOL!*

I *DON'T* THINK YOU'RE *LISTENING*... ...SO WE'LL KEEP ON *TRYING* THIS TILL YOU GET IT *RIGHT.*

YOU *STILL* STANDING?

SINCE I TOOK THAT BATH IN THOSE BIO-CHEM-ICALS... I'M USED TO A MAN STAY-ING *DOWN* WHEN I HIT HIM.

I'M NOT ONLY *NOT* DOWN... BUT I'M STILL HOLDING ONTO *"JOSH"* HERE. YOU GOT YOURSELF SOME BIG WORDS, AND YOU BACKED 'EM UP *PRETTY WELL,* BUT IT'D TAKE MORE THAN THEM TO SEPARATE ME AN' *"JOSH".*

SOMMA THEM *SHRINKS,* YOU KNOW, DOWN ON THE *WEST SIDE,* THEY MIGHT THINK IT KINDA *WEIRD* THAT I GAVE *"JOSH"* A NAME... BUT *"JOSH"* AN' ME... WE BEEN *THROUGH* SOME THINGS TOGETHER. *TIGHTER'N* I'VE BEEN WITH MOST *PEOPLE!*

NAME'S *ROACH,* TOUGH-GUY. *COCKROACH HAMILTON!* AND YOU MADE YOURSELF A *BAAADD* MISTAKE BUTTIN' IN ON THIS *KILL*--

--'CAUSE *"JOSH"* AN' I JUST PUT YOU ON OUR *LIST!*

POWER MAN #43
WRITER: **MARV WOLFMAN**
PENCILER: **LEE ELIAS**
INKER: **ALEX NIÑO**
LETTERER: **JOHN COSTANZA**

POWER MAN #44
PLOT: **MARV WOLFMAN**
SCRIPT: **ED HANNIGAN**
PENCILER: **LEE ELIAS**
INKER: **TOM PALMER**
LETTERER: **JOE ROSEN**

POWER MAN #45
WRITER: **MARV WOLFMAN**
ARTIST: **LEE ELIAS**
LETTERER: **IRVING WATANABE**

POWER MAN #46
PLOT: **MARV WOLFMAN**
SCRIPT: **ROGER SLIFER**
ARTIST: **LEE ELIAS**
LETTERER: **DENISE WOHL**

POWER MAN #47
WRITER: **CHRIS CLAREMONT**
PENCILER: **GEORGE TUSKA**
INKER: **BOB SMITH**
LETTERER: **HOWARD BENDER**

POWER MAN #48
WRITER: **CHRIS CLAREMONT**
PENCILER: **JOHN BYRNE**
INKER: **DAN GREEN**
LETTERER: **ANNETTE KAWECKI**

POWER MAN #49
WRITER: **CHRIS CLAREMONT**
PENCILER: **JOHN BYRNE**
INKER: **DAN GREEN**
LETTERER: **ANNETTE KAWECKI**

REPRINT CREDITS

MARVEL ESSENTIAL DESIGN:
JOHN "JG" ROSHELL OF COMICRAFT
FRONT COVER ART:
DAVE COCKRUM
BACK COVER ART:
GIL KANE
COVER COLORS:
TOM SMITH
COLLECTION EDITOR:
MICHAEL SHORT
ASSOCIATE EDITORS:
MARK D. BEAZLEY & JENNIFER GRÜNWALD
SENIOR EDITOR, SPECIAL PROJECTS:
JEFF YOUNGQUIST

PRODUCTION:
JERRON QUALITY COLOR
VICE PRESIDENT OF SALES:
DAVID GABRIEL
CREATIVE DIRECTOR:
TOM MARVELLI
EDITOR IN CHIEF:
JOE QUESADA
PUBLISHER:
DAN BUCKLEY
SELECT ART RECONSTRUCTION:
DALE CRANE
SPECIAL THANKS TO
POND SCUM, MIKE FICHERA & STUART VANDAL

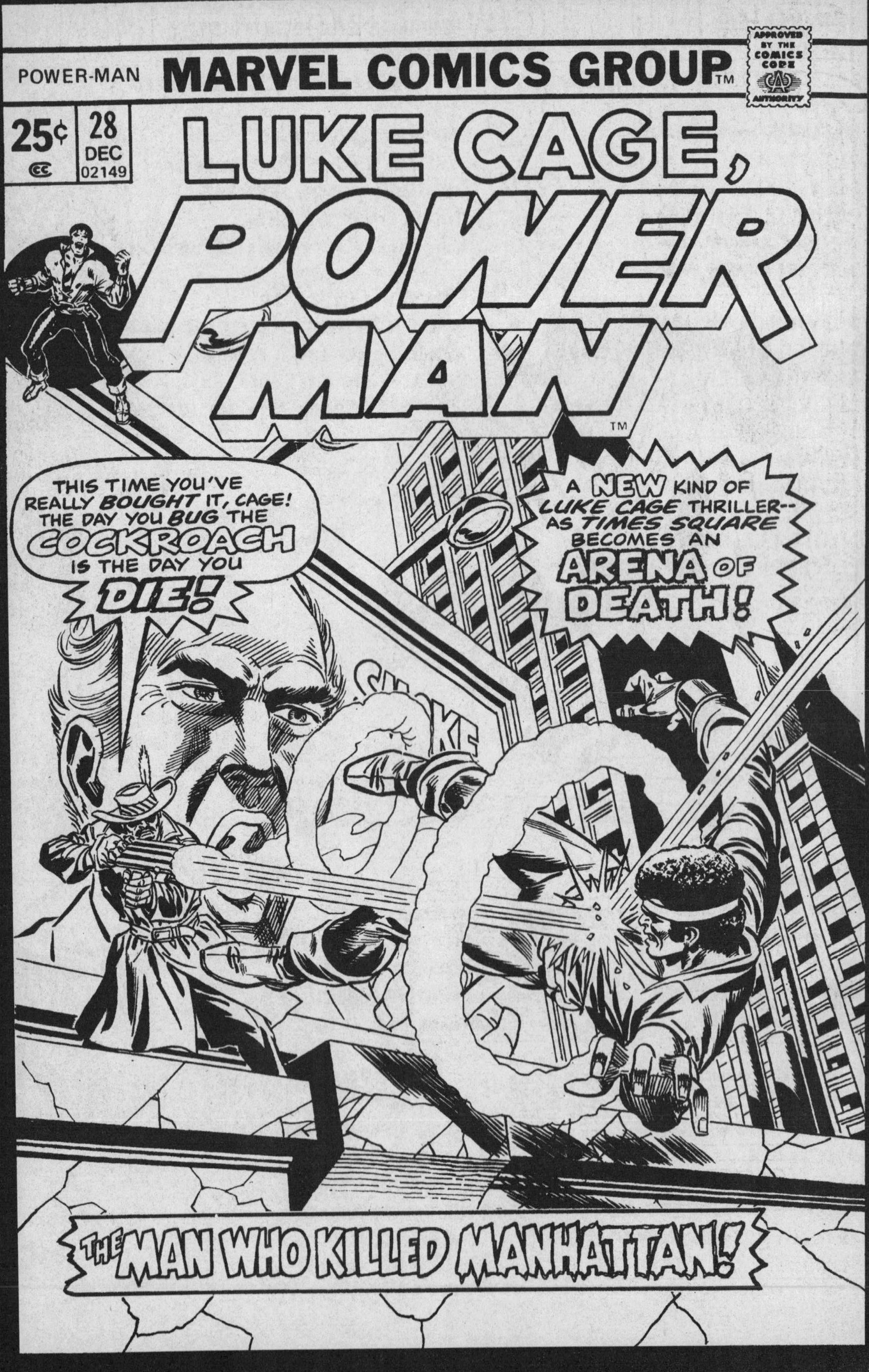

POWER-MAN
MARVEL COMICS GROUP
APPROVED BY THE COMICS CODE AUTHORITY
25¢
28 DEC 02149
LUKE CAGE, POWER MAN
THIS TIME YOU'VE REALLY BOUGHT IT, CAGE! THE DAY YOU BUG THE COCKROACH IS THE DAY YOU DIE!
A NEW KIND OF LUKE CAGE THRILLER-- AS TIMES SQUARE BECOMES AN ARENA OF DEATH!
THE MAN WHO KILLED MANHATTAN!

Stan Lee PRESENTS: LUKE CAGE, POWER MAN

THE MAN WHO KILLED JIMMY CRICKET!

MANHATTAN AT BROADWAY AND TIMES SQUARE. 2 A.M. THE RESTLESS HOUR, WHEN IT SEEMS THERE NEVER WAS ANYTHING CALLED DAWN!

PUT UP THE FANCY SHOTGUN, MISTER...

...OR I'M COMIN' RIGHT THROUGH YOU!

I GOT MYSELF A TARGET TO WASTE TONIGHT, HERO--

--DON'T MATTER NONE TO ME WHETHER I KILL ONE... OR TWO... AND YOU JUST ELECTED TO BE THE FIRST!

DON McGREGOR
WRITER

GEORGE TUSKA AND VINNIE COLLETTA
ARTISTS

DAVE H.
LETTERER

MARV WOLFMAN
EDITOR

PETRA GOLDBERG
COLORIST

THE JUNKIES NOD ON THE SIDEWALKS, MURMURING THEIR "IN" SLANG. THE HUSTLERS BECOME A BIT MORE DESPERATE TO MAKE THEIR HIT FOR THE NIGHT.

THE BROKEN PEOPLE, THE DREAMLESS DREAMERS, STAGGER ABOUT, THEIR EYES THE COLOR OF THE NEON SIGNS THEY PASS AS THEY SEEK A SUBWAY STAIRWELL FOR A NIGHT'S LODGINGS.

AND, THE WINSTON SIGN STILL PUFFS ITS STEAM INTO THE SOOT-GREY SKY, DESPITE THE FACT THAT LUKE CAGE COMES BATTERING THROUGH IT.

FOR CAGE, THE NIGHT HAS JUST BEGUN--

--BUT THE MAN WITH THE SIX-BARRELED SHOTGUN IS DETERMINED TO END IT... ABRUPTLY!

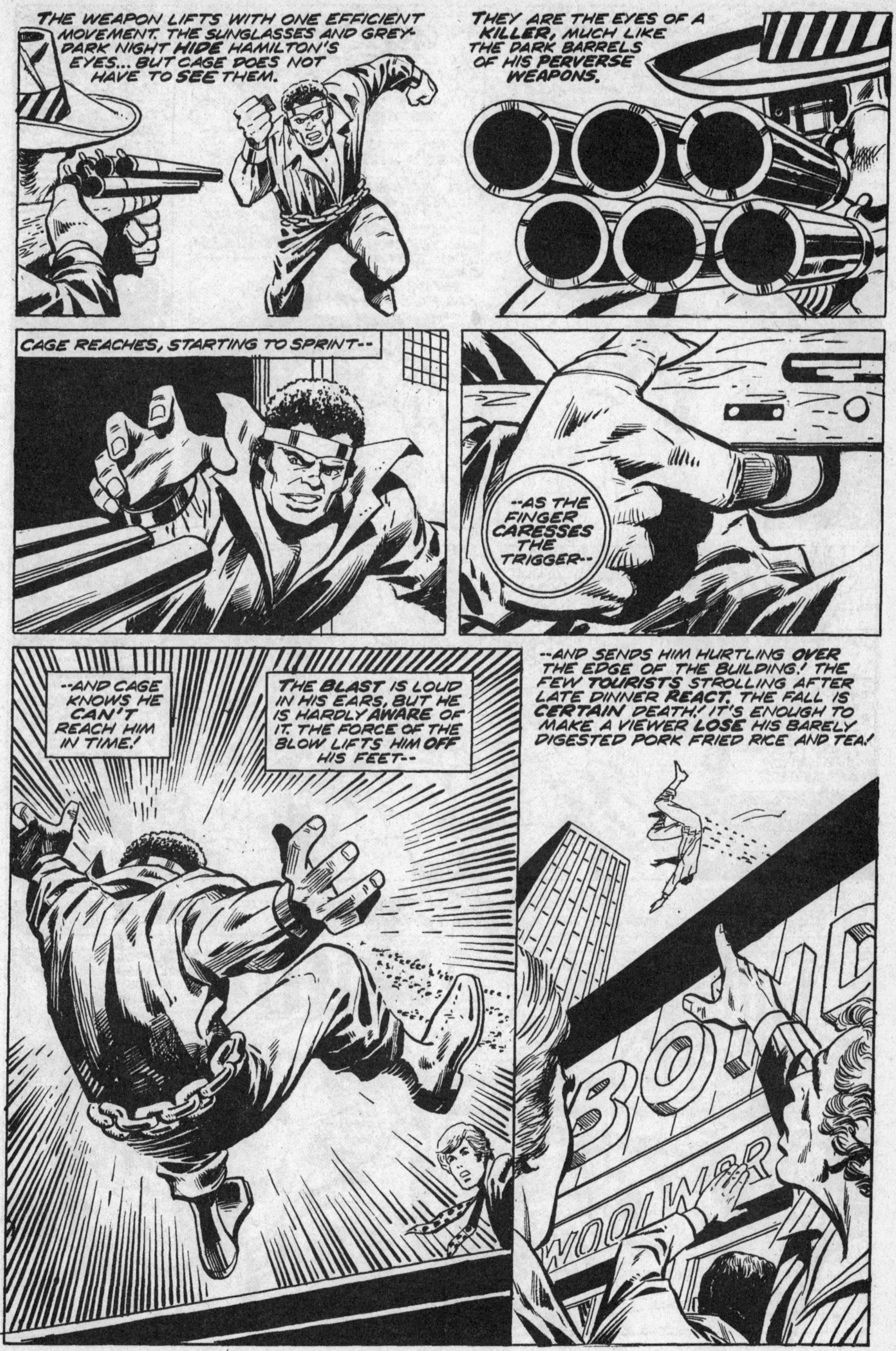

THE WEAPON LIFTS WITH ONE EFFICIENT MOVEMENT. THE SUNGLASSES AND GREY-DARK NIGHT HIDE HAMILTON'S EYES... BUT CAGE DOES NOT HAVE TO SEE THEM.
THEY ARE THE EYES OF A KILLER, MUCH LIKE THE DARK BARRELS OF HIS PERVERSE WEAPONS.
CAGE REACHES, STARTING TO SPRINT--
--AS THE FINGER CARESSES THE TRIGGER--
--AND CAGE KNOWS HE CAN'T REACH HIM IN TIME!
THE BLAST IS LOUD IN HIS EARS, BUT HE IS HARDLY AWARE OF IT. THE FORCE OF THE BLOW LIFTS HIM OFF HIS FEET--
--AND SENDS HIM HURTLING OVER THE EDGE OF THE BUILDING! THE FEW TOURISTS STROLLING AFTER LATE DINNER REACT. THE FALL IS CERTAIN DEATH! IT'S ENOUGH TO MAKE A VIEWER LOSE HIS BARELY DIGESTED PORK FRIED RICE AND TEA!

THE WIDE SIDEWALKS WAIT TO RECEIVE HIS BODY. BEFORE THE NEW WORKDAY, THE BRIGHT RED THAT GIVES BLOOD ITS VIBRANT MESSAGE OF LIFE WILL HAVE TURNED A DULL BROWN!

THE REST OF THE UNFORTUNATE MESS WILL HAVE TO BE OBLITERATED BY THE NIGHT DENIZENS THAT PROWL MANHATTAN... THE SANITARY TRUCKS TRYING TO WASH AWAY YESTERDAY'S MISTAKES.

WORDS PASS BY CAGE'S EYES... "COCA COLA"... "COLONEL SANDERS"... "ALLIED CHEMICAL" ...THEY CONTINUE THEIR NEON CALLIGRAPHY, A GAY EPITAPH, GAUDY WITH THE PROMISE OF FULFILLMENT!

THE BUILDING EDGE GIVES CAGE THE CHANCE TO KEEP READING THOSE PROMISES!

A SIREN SCREAMS! THERE IS NOTHING ALIEN ABOUT THIS SOUND.

IT IS A MODERN SCREAM, OFTEN IN THE BACKGROUND, DAY OR NIGHT--

HEY, WAIT A MINUTE! DON'T YOU KNOW WHO I AM?

--ACCOMPANIED BY FLASHING RED..OR SOMETIMES BLUE ...LIGHTS THAT SPEAK OF URGENCY.

I'M HARRY WENTWORTH... WENTWORTH! I'M THE GUY YOUR BOSS MADE THE DEAL WITH. YOUR CONTACT!

WENTWORTH! WITHOUT ME, YOU GUYS WOULDN'T HAVE ANYTHING. I JUST GAVE YOU EVERYTHING YOU NEED.

CAGE'S SHOULDER THROBS, ECHOING THE PANICKED MAN'S VOICE... AND HE KNOWS THAT NEITHER HE NOR THE URGENT SIRENS WILL BE ABLE TO OFFER THE MAN... DELIVERANCE!

THAT'S WHO I AM! WENTWORTH!

I'M...

...IMPRESSED...

...BUT NOT MUCH!

YOU WANTA SAY "HI" TO "JOSH"--

--'FORE HE SAYS "GOODBYE" TO YOU?

LOOK...I WAS JUST LOOKING FOR A WAY TO GET *AHEAD*, YOU KNOW?

I MEAN, TO HELP PAY THE BLASTED *CAR INSURANCE* AND THOSE MONSTER *CON ED* BILLS, YOU KNOW?

GIVE MYSELF A CHANCE TO SEE HOW *MY LIFE* GOT TO *THIS*... THIS *GRIND*, YOU KNOW?

NO...

...I DON'T KNOW.

BLAM

HARRY WENTWORTH TURNS, TRYING TO *OUT-RUN* THE BLAST. WHEN THE SHELLS HIT, IT *ROBS* HIM OF CONTROL OF HIS LIMBS, PICKS HIM UP IN AN *ANGRY* GESTURE...AND TOSSES HIM LIMP AND BLOODIED OVER *7TH* AVENUE.

NO *HARD FEELINGS*, THOUGH...

....MR. WENTWORTH.

CAGE SHOUTS--

--BUT THE WORDS ARE *LOST* AND *USELESS!* CAGE HAS SEEN TOO MUCH OF THIS OF *LATE.* MEN *WITHOUT* CONSCIENCES... PREDATORS STALKING THEIR KILL IN *PLUSH RESTAURANTS* AND AIR-CONDITIONED OFFICES, AND MORE TRADITIONAL PLACES...LIKE THIS ROOFTOP!

BOND

SHEEE-OOOOTT'!

I KNEW THEM THERE *NAVY* BOYS WAS *RECRUITIN'*--

--BUT THAT AIN'T THE KINDA *MESSAGE* GONNA GET 'EM ANY *NEW RECRUITS.* NO WAY!

DEATH BENEATH THE WINSTON SIGN. THE OUT-OF TOWNERS GET THEIR MONEY'S WORTH ...A MOVIE-EYE-VIEW OF *SIN-CITY.*

IT RECONFIRMS THEIR *FAITH* IN THE *BIG CITY MYTH*...A *MUGGER* IN *EVERY ALLEY-WAY.* IT'S NICE TO KNOW *NEIL SIMON* WAS RIGHT.

THE GORDON'S BOTTLE STILL POURS ITS *ELECTRIC GIN*...A TOAST TO THE SPECTATORS...UNWITNESSED BY THE CORPSE. THE CROWD STIRS. TIME TO BE *GETTIN ON!*

ESPECIALLY IF YOU'RE GOING TO *SCORE* BEFORE THE *MORNING.*

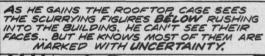

AS HE GAINS THE ROOFTOP CAGE SEES THE SCURRYING FIGURES *BELOW* RUSHING INTO THE BUILDING. HE CAN'T SEE THEIR FACES... BUT HE KNOWS MOST OF THEM ARE MARKED WITH *UNCERTAINTY.*

THEY HAVE *NO WAY* OF KNOWING WHAT THEY WILL MEET UP WITH ON THIS *ROOFTOP*--

--AND ONE *WRONG* MOVE ON HIS PART COULD START ANOTHER SHOOTING GALLERY CONTEST ...WITH *HIM* AS THE TARGET!

KEEP *COOL,* MEN--

--I'M WITH THE *GOOD GUYS!*

DETECTIVE *CHASE*...HE SEEMS TO BE THE ONLY ONE UP HERE.

THAT'S FINE, SERGEANT...TAKE TWO OF YOUR MEN AND HAVE THEM *SPREAD OUT* OVER THE ROOFTOP... SEE IF YOU CAN FIND WHERE THE *THIRD MAN* MADE HIS *EXIT* TO THE STREET.

YOU'RE *FAST* ON THE UPTAKE.

I HOPE YOU HAVE AS MUCH *STEEL* ON THAT TRIGGER *FINGER* AS YOU DO IN YOUR EYES, M'MAN--

--NOT THAT BULLETS HURT ME ALL THAT *MUCH*... BUT I'VE GOT ME *ENOUGH* PAIN FOR THE MOMENT. THAT JAMES BOND *ANTIQUE* SHOTGUN NEAR SHOT MY *ARM* CLEAN OFF!

BY THE WAY... IF YOU CHECK THE GUY *BELOW* YOU'LL SEE HE WAS *ALSO* BLASTED AWAY BY THAT SHOT- GUN... SAME ONE THAT *TORE* MY THREADS... AND ME!

AN' I DON'T *USUALLY* GO 'ROUND TRYIN' TO PUT HOLES IN MYSELF.

NICE SPEECH, CAGE--

--BUT *HUMPHREY BOGART* DID IT *BETTER* THIRTY YEARS AGO.

COME ON, CAGE... WE'LL *CHECK* THAT CORPSE TOGETHER.

TOGETHERNESS... AN' WE HAVEN'T *EVEN* BEEN INTRODUCED YET.

MY, MY. I'LL TAKE ODDS YOU KEEP A *CASSETTE RECORD-IN'* OF THE *POLICE STORY* THEME MUSIC IN YOUR SQUAD CAR SO YOU CAN SWITCH IT *ON* WHEN YOU GO INTO ACTION.

THE NAME'S DE-TECTIVE 2ND GRADE *QUENTIN CHASE* TO YOU, CAGE--

--AND THAT'S *NOT* ACTION, CAGE. THAT'S A PIECE OF *DEAD MEAT* OVER THERE THAT *ONCE* HAD A HISTORY ...THAT *WAS* A LOT *MORE* THAN DEAD MEAT ONLY FIFTEEN MINUTES AGO.

SO *KNOCK OFF* THE CUTE TALK.

I'VE GOT SOME *QUES-TIONS* FOR YOU, CAGE. YOU BETTER HAVE SOME *GOOD* ANSWERS.

WHY ARE YOU COMING ON SO *STRONG*, CHASE? YOU MADE YOUR *POINT* ABOUT THE VICTIM.

BECAUSE *YOU'RE* COMING ON TOO STRONG, CAGE.

CAGE LOOKS AWAY FROM CHASE'S *GREY EYES* AND OUT TO THE PO-LICE PERIMETERS. THE PRETZEL VENDORS DROP LUKEWARM FIG-URE EIGHTS INTO LITTLE BAGS.

NEARBY, A JEWELRY HUCKSTER MAKES *CHANGE* FOR A FIVE.

HE HAS SEEN SOMETHING IN THOSE *GREY DEPTHS* THAT SCARES HIM... THEY ARE THE EYES OF A MAN WHO HAS BEHELD MANY *COMPASSION-LESS ACTS*--

--A MAN WHO IS *SADDENED* BY THE SADISMS THE HUMAN MIND CAN CON-JURE. SOME PEOPLE *NEVER BECOME IMMUNE*.

SINCE YOU OPENED YOUR OFFICE...YES, I *KNOW* ABOUT YOU, CAGE... IT COMES TO MY ATTENTION THERE HAVE BEEN *NO LESS* THAN *FOUR* DEAD BODIES--

--AND MAYBE *MORE* WE AREN'T AWARE OF--

--ALL LEFT LYING DEAD AT *YOUR* FEET!

IF YOU'RE ON TOP OF IT...YOU KNOW I *DIDN'T* KILL THEM.

I'LL *GIVE* YOU THAT... BUT THAT'S *WAY* TOO MANY BODIES, CAGE... SOMEBODY'S GOT TO *START* ASKING QUESTIONS.

THAT'S *ME.*

FOR OPENERS... IS THAT LAST NAME ...CAGE... FOR *REAL?*

WITH A NAME LIKE CHASE YOU GOT YOURSELF SOME *BRASS* ASKIN' A QUESTION LIKE *THAT.*

I'LL CHECK IT OUT, CAGE. I WANT YOU TO *KNOW* THAT. MAYBE YOU'D BETTER COME DOWN TO THE *PRECINCT* WITH US... AND WE'LL TALK ABOUT THE *FACTS* OF LIFE.

IF I *HAVE* TO LEARN 'EM, CHASE ...I HOPE I LEARN 'EM FROM SOMEONE A LOT MORE *DESIRABLE* THAN YOU.

ANY QUESTIONS YOU GOT, I CAN ANSWER 'EM *RIGHT HERE--*

--OR I CAN HAVE *CHARLTON GRUNDGE* --RECOGNIZE THE NAME? --OF *ADONIS CHEMICAL* GIVE YOU THE SAME ANSWERS--

--BUT WITH A LOT MORE *POWER* THAN I COULD... *POWER MAN* OR NO!

NEDICKS

POLICE

THOSE ARE SOME PRETTY *HEAVY* NAMES YOU'RE THROWING AROUND, CAGE. YOU *GAMBLING* I WON'T RUFFLE THEIR FEATHERS?

THE DEAD MAN IS *HARRY WENTWORTH.* HARRY WORKED FOR *ADONIS CHEMICAL*... BUT IT WAS A *GIG* HE WASN'T TOO PLEASED WITH.

HARRY STARTED *RIPPING OFF* PLANS FOR SOME *CHEMICAL SHIPMENTS.*

MR. GRUNDGE... HE'S THE *REPRESENTATIVE* FROM ADONIS THAT'S PAYIN' MY *TAB*... WANTED TO KNOW *WHO* THE PLANS WERE GOING TO.

I *FOLLOWED* HARRY... AN' HE MET UP WITH A MAN WITH A CASE OF THE *UGLIES*... CALLS HIMSELF COCKROACH HAMILTON.

I TRIED TO *STOP* IT ...BUT THIS ROACH IS *BADDER'N* LISTER-INE... AN' OFF HIS *NUT* TO BOOT.

GORD

BON *Clothing*

OKAY, CAGE. WE'LL CHECK IT OUT. *COUNT ON IT.*

I'M NOT TRYING TO *HASSLE* YOU, CAGE--

--IF YOU'RE ON THE *LEVEL*, THEN WE'RE *SQUARE*... BUT IF YOU'RE *NOT*--

--I'LL FIND OUT... AND I'LL BE COMING *BACK* FOR YOU.

CAGE IS OBLIVIOUS TO THE *NOMADIC* FIGURES LINING 42ND STREET.

CHASE CAN BE *RELENTLESS*... THAT'S OBVIOUS.

AND ENOUGH *PROBING* COULD REVEAL THAT LUKE CAGE IS REALLY AN ESCAPED CONVICT.

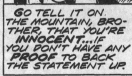

GO TELL IT ON THE MOUNTAIN, BRO- THER, THAT YOU'RE INNOCENT...IF YOU DON'T HAVE ANY *PROOF* TO BACK THE STATEMENT UP.

HEY, D.W., WHATTA THEY *SHOWIN'* TONIGHT?

ARTHUR PENN'S CLASSIC FILM, *"THE LEFT-HANDED GUN."*

--BUT LUKE, I WOULDN'T--

--USE--

--THAT--

--MACHINE.

THAT'S JUST WHAT I NEEDED TO *CAP OFF* A NIGHT GOIN' STEADILY *DOWNHILL*...

--AND STILL *DROPPIN'*.

HATE TO ADD TO THE LAST SLOPE, BUT MY *UNCLE* SAYS YOUR *LEASE* IS *UP* AND HE WANTS TO *RAISE* THE RENT.

FOR THAT *RATHOLE*? IS HE *KIDDING*?

NO, I DON'T SUPPOSE HE *IS*.

LOOK, THIS SHOULDER OF MINE IS REALLY *ACTIN'* UP... I'M GOING *UP-TOWN* TO NOAH BUR-STEIN'S STORE-FRONT CLINIC. GOOD THING HE SLEEPS IN.

I'LL CATCH YOU LATER, D.W.

THE FIGURES ON THE SIDE-WALK SEEM YANKED FROM DIFFERENT LANDSCAPES, BUT THEY DO HAVE COMMON TRAITS. THEY HAVE SOMETHING TO SELL... A WAY... THEMSELVES ...TRINKETS.

THE EMPTY SUBWAY STATION AIR BATTERS CAGE'S SENSES--

--BUT THE HUDDLED FIGURE WRAPPED IN RAGS DOES NOT NOTICE.

CAGE STANDS IN SOLITUDE AND WONDERS HOW SHE CAME TO THIS NIGHT--

--AND REMEMBERS HARRY WENTWORTH, NEATLY DRESSED, ASKING THE SAME QUESTION.

THE ONE OTHER FIGURE IN THE CAR GLARES AT CAGE INTENSELY... AS IF THEY SHARE SOME SECRET NIGHT INSANITY.

CLINIC

CAGE STEPS OUT INTO THE QUIETER EN-VIRONS OF 116TH ST., JUST OUTSIDE MORNINGSIDE PARK.

THE INTENSE SCRUTINY HAS LEFT HIM FEELING HAUNTED INSIDE.

NOAH...I KNOW THIS IS KINDA LATE AT NIGHT TO BE COMIN' 'ROUND.

LUCAS!

WHAT'S THE MATTER, NOAH? SOMETHIN' WRONG?

IT'S...IT'S NOTHING, LUCAS.

COME IN. COME IN. I WAS UP ANYWAY. MOTHER BROUGHT HER CHILD OVER ABOUT FIVE MINUTES AGO.

YOU SURE NOTHING'S WRONG?

YES, LUCAS--

--I'M SURE.

PLEASE BE QUIET
SMOKING

YOU THAT... POWER MAN FELLA?

THAT'S ME.

YOU TALK RIGHT UP... THAT'S GOOD.

I SEEN YOU 'ROUND. YOU AIN'T AFRAID OF NOTHIN', ARE YA?

I'M AFRAID OF SOME THINGS...

SOMETIMES.

HEY! WHATTA YOU TRYIN' TO DO T'ME, NOAH? THIS ISN'T A MASSAGE PARLOR.

DID YOU FORGET THAT?

THE FORCE OF THE BLAST DISLOCATED YOUR SHOULDER, LUKE. I'LL HAVE TO SET IT.

NOW?

NOW.

NOAH, I NEVER DID DIG YOUR SENSE OF HUMOR. NOT A'TALL.

AND DON'T MAKE THE KID AFRAID OF DOCTORS. COULD WARP HIM FOR LIFE.

HOW'D IT HAPPEN?

I'D RATHER KNOW WHAT YOU WERE SHOT WITH THAT COULD MESS YOU UP LIKE THAT.

WELL, IT WASN'T A MATTEL FANNER '50, YOU CAN MAKE BOOK ON THAT.

THE MOTHER LOOKS AT CAGE... PERHAPS TRYING TO SEE THE **HERO** HER SON SEES...

...BUT IF SHE **DOES**... IT DOES NOT **REGISTER** ON HER FACE.

ADULTS LOVE TO RAISE KIDS ON **MYTHS**, LUKE THINKS, REMEMBERING HIS CHILDHOOD. AS IF THEY **WISH** THE MYTHS WERE REAL BUT CAN'T LIVE UP TO THE **CONCEPT**.

WHY IS THAT? HE WONDERS, WINCING.

THIS ISN'T GOING TO BE **EASY**, LUCAS.

DOES IT... **HURT?**

IS IT SO THEY CAN GO OUT INTO THE WORLD, ARMED ONLY WITH MYTHS FOR PROTECTION? UNTIL THEY LEARN THAT ALL THE LITTLE MYTHS AREN'T NECESSARILY **TRUTHS**.

LUKE LOOKS UP INTO THE **YOUNG** WATCHING EYES... AND KNOWS THEY WILL REFLECT ENOUGH **PAIN** SOME DAY... NO NEED TO **ADD** TO IT NOW. PERHAPS **THAT'S** THE **REASON** FOR THE MYTHS.

WELL, I WOULDN'T MAKE A **HABIT** OF THIS, IF YOU KNOW WHAT I MEAN?

YOU'RE DOING FINE, LUCAS. THAT'S A GREAT SMILE.

NOAH...YOU... ...ARE ENJOYING THIS... ...TOO MUCH!

AN' ONE OF **THESE** DAYS ...I'LL **GET** YOU FOR IT!

THE **JOKE** GOES...I'LL GET **YOU**... WHEN YOU RECEIVE MY **BILL**.

DAYLIGHT.

THERE IS NO DAWN, AS IF THE 2 A.M. HOUR'S QUESTION OF ITS EXISTENCE WERE CORRECT.

ADONIS CHEMICAL

THE SKIES MERELY LIGHTEN TO A GREY THAT IS ALMOST NONEXISTENT--

--A BLEACHED BACKDROP WITHOUT ANY HINT OF LIFE.

WAKE UP, CAGE! GET ON WITH IT. MOVE ON OUT!

DON'T BOTHER ASKING WHY-- YOU PROBABLY WON'T LIKE THE ANSWER.

HE BROWSES THROUGH HELEN GURLEY BROWN'S PARODY OF LIFE--

COSMOPOLITAN

--UNTIL CHARLTON GRUNDGE'S RECEPTIONIST RETURNS, LOOKING LIKE A REAL-LIFE PARODY OF THE WOMEN IN THE MAGAZINE.

CHARLTON GRUNDGE LOOKS AT CAGE. THE MOTTO OF ADONIS CHEMICAL IS INDELIBLY STAMPED ON HIS FACE: ADONIS CHEMICAL... WE'RE MAKING A BEAUTIFUL WORLD ...FOR YOU!

IT IS A LIE GRUNDGE CAN SPEAK WITH UTTER CONVICTION.

WELL, CAGE ...I SEE THE MORNING HEADLINES SAY YOU WEREN'T VERY... SUCCESSFUL.

WHAT THE HEADLINES DON'T SAY IS THAT YOU LIED TO ME, GRUNDGE.

YOU DIDN'T REALLY TELL ME WHAT WAS GOIN' DOWN IN THIS CASE...EXACTLY WHAT HARRY WENTWORTH WAS TAKIN' OUTTA THIS JOINT!

ADONIS CHEMICAL IS HARDLY A JOINT.

COUPLE OF PEOPLE SET ME STRAIGHT. THIS WHOLE SCENE CONCERNS A SHIPMENT OF GAS CANNISTERS... RIGHT, MR. GRUNDGE?

A GAS SO DEADLY THAT IF A LEAK WERE TO HAPPEN IN THIS CITY AND CONTAMINATE THE AIR--

--OVER HALF THE POPULATION OF MANHATTAN COULD BE INFECTED WITH LUNG CANCER! ISN'T THAT RIGHT... MR. GRUNDGE?

TH...THAT'S NEVER BEEN *PROVEN*... CONCLUSIVELY.

HOW *MANY* OF YOUR *RESEARCHERS* GOTTA *WARN* YOU BEFORE YOU START *LIS'NIN*?

WE'VE TAKEN *PRECAUTIONS*...SO GET OFF YOUR HIGH HORSE.

I'M NO *PUNK KID* ON THE *STREET* THAT YOU CAN MANHANDLE LIKE THIS!

WE CAN *MAKE* ...OR *BREAK* YOU ...IN THIS CITY, CAGE.

THAT'S BEEN TRIED *BEFORE*, GRUNDGE...*YOU* WANTA *TRY* IT?

RIGHT *NOW*? RIGHT *HERE* AN' NOW?

NO ANSWER, HUH? THAT'S NOT YOUR *STYLE*, IS IT, GRUNDGE?

YOUR STYLE...*ADONIS CHEMICAL'S* STYLE ...IS TO *PROJECT* A *GOOD IMAGE* TO THE *PEOPLE*...CONTRIBUTE *FUNDS* TO PUBLIC T.V. ...*SPONSOR* A CLEAN-UP PROGRAM...BUT LET'S NOT *RUSH* IT, BOYS.

AN' THIS *GAS* WE'RE RAPPIN' ABOUT ...IT'S BEIN' FLOWN IN TO *KENNEDY AIRPORT*...RIGHT, BABY? ...UNLOADED ONTO SPECIALLY DESIGNED TRUCKS AND SHIPPED *THROUGH* MANHATTAN TO YOUR *CONNECTICUT* PLANT ...*RIGHT*?

THERE IS *NO RISK!* WE'VE GONE THROUGH EVERY *EXPENSE*...THAT'S SOMETHING I DON'T EXPECT *YOU* TO UNDERSTAND, CAGE...*EVERY EXPENSE* TO MAKE THE *TRANSPORTATION* OF THESE--

--SOMEWHAT *TOXIC* MATERIALS...*SAFE!*

TOXIC! THAT'S A REAL CUTE WORD, GRUNDGE...BUT WHAT YOUR TONGUE *FORGOT* TO SAY IS THAT A *FREAK ACCIDENT* COULD *BREAK OPEN* THOSE CANNISTERS!

THE ODDS *AGAINST* THAT... ARE PHENOMENAL... OR THAT AN ACCIDENT...IF ONE *DID* OCCUR...WOULD AFFECT THE CANNISTERS.

EVEN A 1% CHANCE IS A *STUPID THREAT* TO PEOPLE'S LIVES! AN' *ANOTHER* THING YOU *FORGOT* TO MENTION... IS THAT HARRY WENTWORTH STOLE THE *MAPS* OF THE *TRANSPORTATION ROUTE* FOR THOSE CHEMICALS--

--AND THAT THEY'RE NOW IN THE *HANDS* OF WHOEVER HE GOT THEM FOR!

IT WAS *YOUR JOB* TO FIND THE MAN. YOU'RE THE ONE THAT *BLEW IT!*

YOU'RE *SOMETHING ELSE*, JACK! HOW'D YOU *DO* IT?

DO WHAT?

KILL YOUR CONSCIENCE ...YOU MUSTA *PLUGGED* IT SQUARE BETWEEN THE EYES...OR DON'T YOU *BELIEVE* IN JIMINY CRICKET?

CAGE SEES THE LOOK COME INTO GRUNDGE'S EYES...THE MUSTERING OF ANGER THAT *FORETELLS* GRUNDGE'S ATTACK SECONDS BEFORE HE *LAUNCHES* HIMSELF AT CAGE!

GRUNDGE *RUNS* RIGHT INTO CAGE'S FIST AS IT LIFTS FROM THE FLOOR--

--AND THE *IMPACT* LIFTS HIM OFF THE FLOOR, OVER HIS DESK, PAST HIS THRONE-LIKE OFFICE CHAIR--

--AND *THROUGH* THE *MAHOGANY* PANELLING OF HIS CLOSET DOOR!

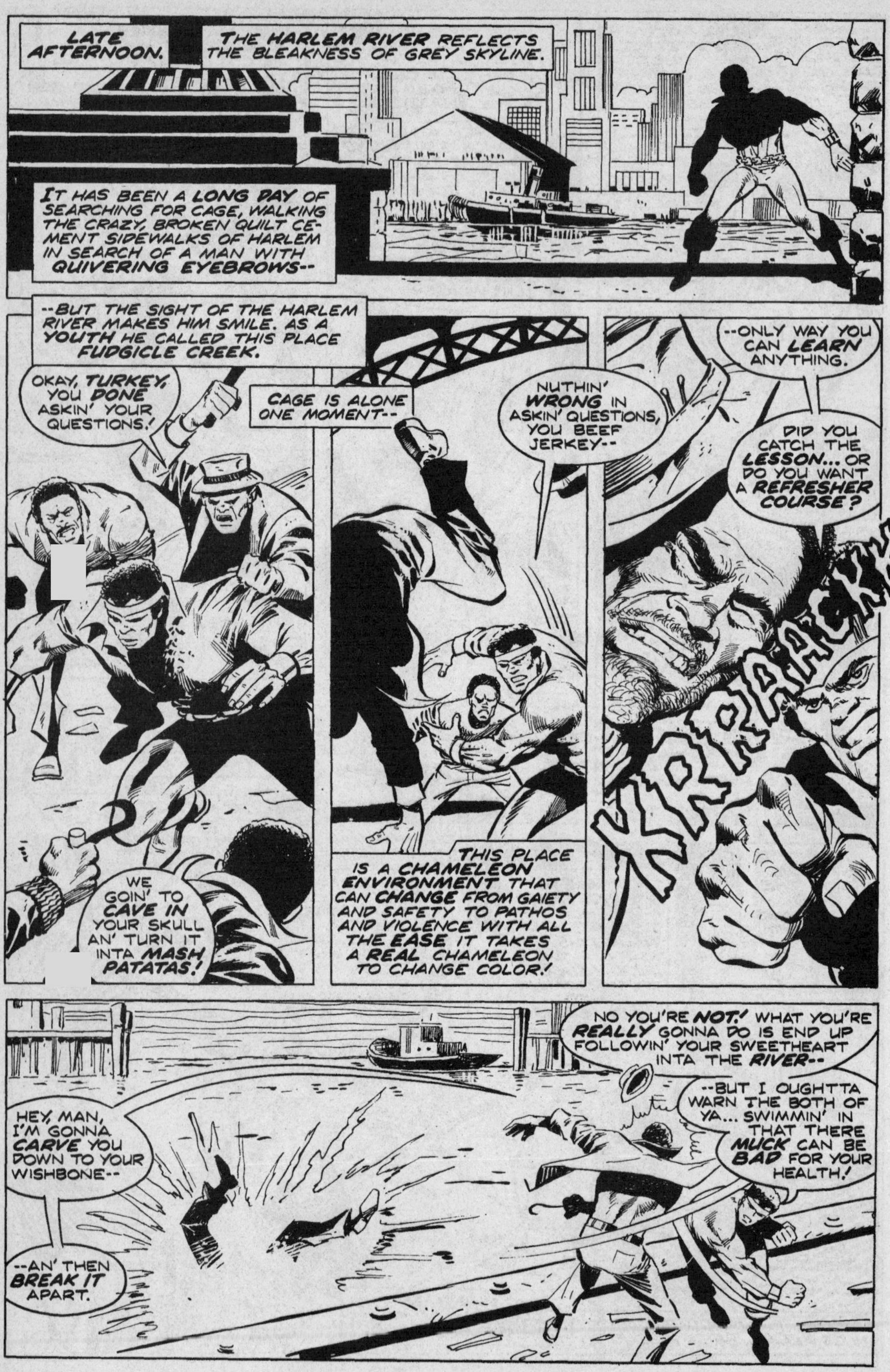
LATE AFTERNOON.
THE HARLEM RIVER REFLECTS THE BLEAKNESS OF GREY SKYLINE.
IT HAS BEEN A LONG DAY OF SEARCHING FOR CAGE, WALKING THE CRAZY, BROKEN QUILT CEMENT SIDEWALKS OF HARLEM IN SEARCH OF A MAN WITH QUIVERING EYEBROWS--
--BUT THE SIGHT OF THE HARLEM RIVER MAKES HIM SMILE. AS A YOUTH HE CALLED THIS PLACE FUDGICLE CREEK.
OKAY, TURKEY, YOU DONE ASKIN' YOUR QUESTIONS!
WE GOIN' TO CAVE IN YOUR SKULL AN' TURN IT INTA MASH PATATAS!
CAGE IS ALONE ONE MOMENT--
NUTHIN' WRONG IN ASKIN' QUESTIONS, YOU BEEF JERKEY--
THIS PLACE IS A CHAMELEON ENVIRONMENT THAT CAN CHANGE FROM GAIETY AND SAFETY TO PATHOS AND VIOLENCE WITH ALL THE EASE IT TAKES A REAL CHAMELEON TO CHANGE COLOR!
--ONLY WAY YOU CAN LEARN ANYTHING.
DID YOU CATCH THE LESSON... OR DO YOU WANT A REFRESHER COURSE?
KRRAACKK
HEY, MAN, I'M GONNA CARVE YOU DOWN TO YOUR WISHBONE--
--AN' THEN BREAK IT APART.
NO YOU'RE NOT! WHAT YOU'RE REALLY GONNA DO IS END UP FOLLOWIN' YOUR SWEETHEART INTA THE RIVER--
--BUT I OUGHTTA WARN THE BOTH OF YA... SWIMMIN' IN THAT THERE MUCK CAN BE BAD FOR YOUR HEALTH!

WHEN YOU'RE DONE *CRAWLING* BACK ONTO THE WHARF, WE'LL LET YOU BLOW YOUR *NOSE*--

--AN THEN YOU'RE GOIN' TO TELL ME WHERE THIS ROACH FELLER IS *HANGING OUT.*

IS THAT WHAT YOU'RE SO *UPTIGHT* ABOUT? *NO KIDDIN'*?

WELL HERE I AM, JACK, IN THE *FLESH*--

--AN' ME AN' JOSH, WE GOT US A *SURPRISE* FOR YA!

CAGE TRIES TO *RECOIL* FROM THE *GAS* THAT CLINGS ABOUT HIM.

IT INVADES HIS NOSTRILS WITH A TICKLING AND NAUSEOUS SENSATION. THE MIND *NUMBS*, MUSHROOMING INTO *SURREALISM.*

SURVIVAL IS *OVERCOME*. CAGE'S POWERFUL LUNGS *RELAX*, BREATHING RYTHMICALLY.

LET ME AT HIM, ROACH. I'M GONNA *BUST* HIS *KNEE-CAPS* FOR 'IM. LET 'EM MAKE SOME *LIP* ABOUT THAT.

YOU AIN'T GOIN' TO DO NUTHIN' OF THE *KIND*. THE MAN'S GOTTEN HISSELF OUTTA *LINE*...AN' HE'S GOT *MORE* TO WORRY ABOUT THAN HIS KNEECAPS.

A *LOT* MORE!

THE BEGINNING OF DUSK.

THE SKY TRIES TO TURN BLACK BUT SUCCUMBS TO A DARKER SHADE OF GREY.

CAGE *AWAKENS.* AND IS IMMEDIATELY AWARE THAT SOMETHING IS *WRONG!* SURVIVAL ADRENALIN FIGHTS OFF THE REMAINING EFFECTS OF THE *DRUG.*

GOOD TO SEE YA *WAKIN' UP,* BROTHER.

ROACH WAS AFRAID YOU WAS GONNA *MISS* THIS WHOLE THING.

YOU HAVE YOURSELF A *NICE TIME* DOWN HERE, *HEAR?*

COME BACK HERE, YOU MOTHERLESS--

THE SOUND OF AN APPROACHING BOAT CUTS CAGE *SHORT.* HIS MIND *EXPLODES* WITH EPITHETS THAT BODE ILL WILL TO THE MEN WHO HAVE LEFT HIM HERE.

EXACTLY *WHERE* IS HERE?

HE IS *CHAINED...* MANACLED TO SOME SORT OF STRUCTURE.

A *BRIDGE!* AND SUDDENLY HE KNOWS WHICH ONE. THE *HARLEM RIVER BRIDGE.*

THE *TUGBOAT HORN* INTRUDES UPON HIS THOUGHTS INSISTENTLY AND THEN THERE IS *ANOTHER SOUND.*

THE GRINDING OF *GEARS!*

THE BRIDGE IS ABOUT TO *OPEN* TO LET THE BOAT PASS THROUGH. AND THE FULL IMPLICATION OF THE *TRAP* HITS HIM.

HIS LEGS ARE *MANACLED* TO ONE HALF OF THE BRIDGE... HIS *WRISTS* TO THE OTHER. WHEN THE DRAWBRIDGE BEGINS TO RISE...

...IT WILL TEAR HIM IN HALF!

NEXT: RICH BUCKLER AND DON McGREGOR ARE BACK-- AND LUKE CAGE HAS GOT THEM-- IN *"LOOK WHAT THEY'VE DONE TO OUR LIVES, MA!"* --AND INTRODUCING *PIRANHA JONES...* HIS BITE IS WORSE THAN HIS BARK!

POWER-MAN
MARVEL COMICS GROUP
APPROVED BY THE COMICS CODE AUTHORITY
25¢
29
FEB
02149
LUKE CAGE,
POWER MAN
HERE HE IS! THE MOST FRIGHTFUL VILLAIN EVER!
YOU SHOULDN'T MAKE JOKES ABOUT MY LOOKS, CAGE!
NOBODY LAUGHS AT MR. FISH!

LUKE CAGE: Wrongly convicted and sentenced to prison—reborn in a freak experiment there that gave him *steel-hard skin* and *strength beyond belief*—a man who hides his identity as an escaped convict in the role of a HERO FOR HIRE!

Stan Lee PRESENTS: **LUKE CAGE, POWER MAN!**™

BOISTEROUS BILL MANTLO *Script* / GORGEOUS GEORGE TUSKA *art* / VENTURESOME VINCE COLLETTA *Inks* / KITTENISH KAREN M. *Lettering* / DANDY DON W. *Colorist* / MARVELOUS MARV WOLFMAN *Editor*

AS MUCH AS WE HATE TO *SAY* IT, PILGRIMS, WE HAVE TO INFORM YOU THAT THE DREADED *DEADLINE DOOM* HAS STRUCK AGAIN-- THIS TIME MAKING POWER MAN ITS VICTIM RIGHT IN THE *MIDDLE* OF OUR CLIFF-HANGING SAGA BEGAN *LAST* ISSUE. BELIEVE US, MARVEL MANIACS, *NO ONE* REGRETS IT MORE THAN US.

HOWEVER, WHILE YOU'RE WAITING FOR THE CONTINUATION OF *THAT* TITANIC TALE, GLOM YOUR EYES ON THIS BRAND NEW BLOCKBUSTER!

WHAT A *CRUMMY* WAY TO SPEND A SATURDAY NIGHT!

IF DOC BURSTEIN HADN'T GONE OUTTA HIS *WAY* RECOMMENDING THIS GUY *JAKE* TO ME, I NEVER WOULDA OFFERED TO PLAY *SENTRY-BOY* OVER HIS FLEET OF BLASTED *TRUCKS.*

BUT *SOMEBODY'S* SABOTAGIN' HIS GIG, AND *NITRO* AIN'T SOMETHIN' HE COULDA HANDLED *HIMSELF!*

ELSE HE WOULDN'T'VE CALLED ON *ME!*

HUDSON Truck

NO ONE LAUGHS AT MR. FISH!

KNOCK OFF THE COMPLAININ', BRO'.

BORING OR NOT-- THIS IS STILL HELPIN' YOU PAY OFF THE RENT--

--AN' ANYTHING THAT DOES THAT AIN'T SOMETHIN' TO SNEEZE AT--

--SPECIALLY WHEN YOU'RE AS FAR BEHIND ON IT AS I--

HEY!

COULDA SWORE I SAW SOMETHIN' MOVE UP THERE!

NUTHIN'!

YOU'RE ACTIN' LIKE A SCARED KID, LUCAS --JUMPIN' AT SHADOWS!

BUT SHADOWS DON'T MAKE NOISE!

TRAM

AN' THEY SURE AS BLAZES DON'T KNOCK OVER SHIPPING-CRATES!

IT SOUNDED LIKE IT CAME--

--FROM BEHIND ME!

SOMEBODY THREW SOMETHIN' TOWARDS THE TRUCKS!

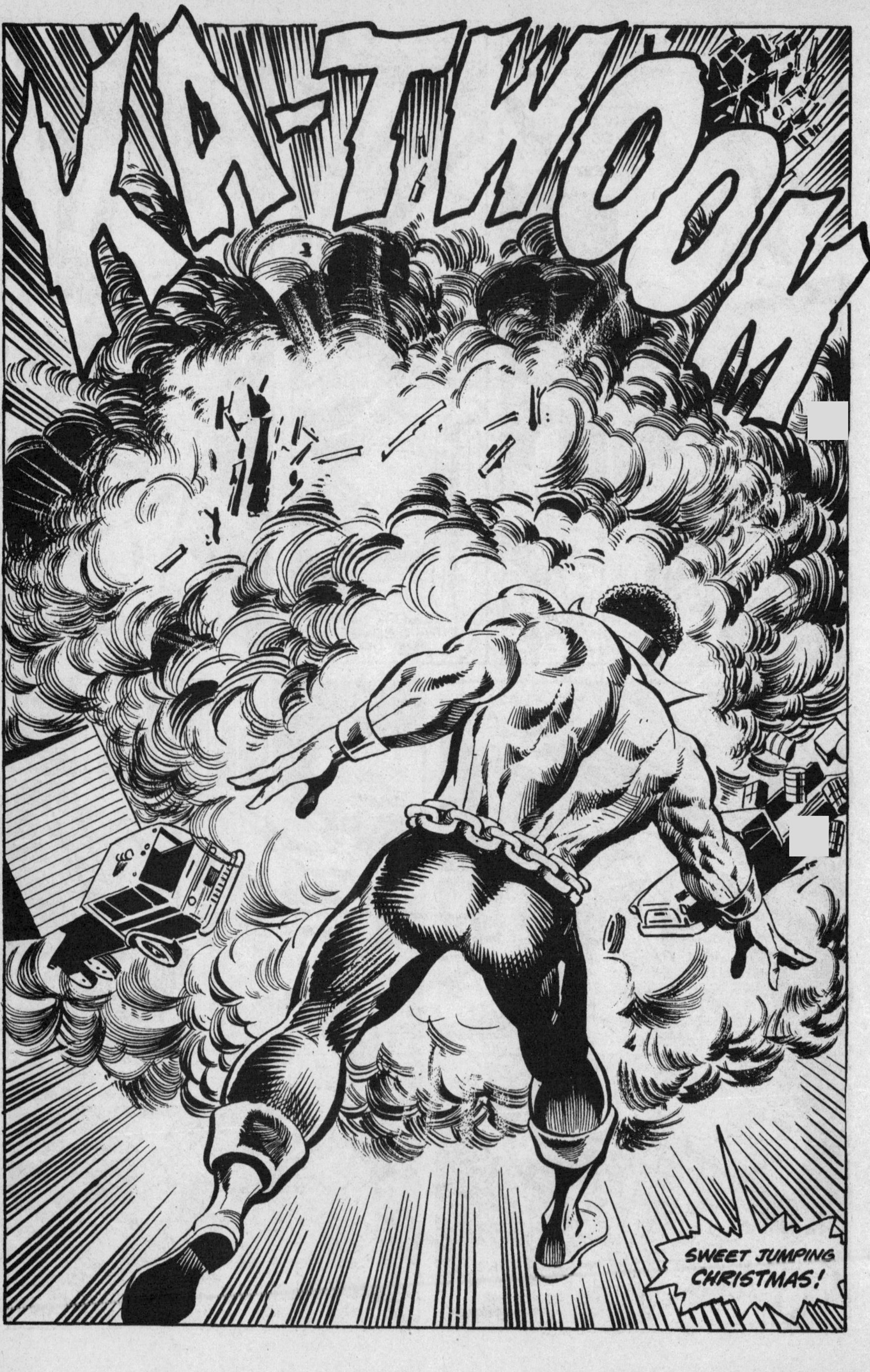
KA-THOOM
SWEET JUMPING CHRISTMAS!

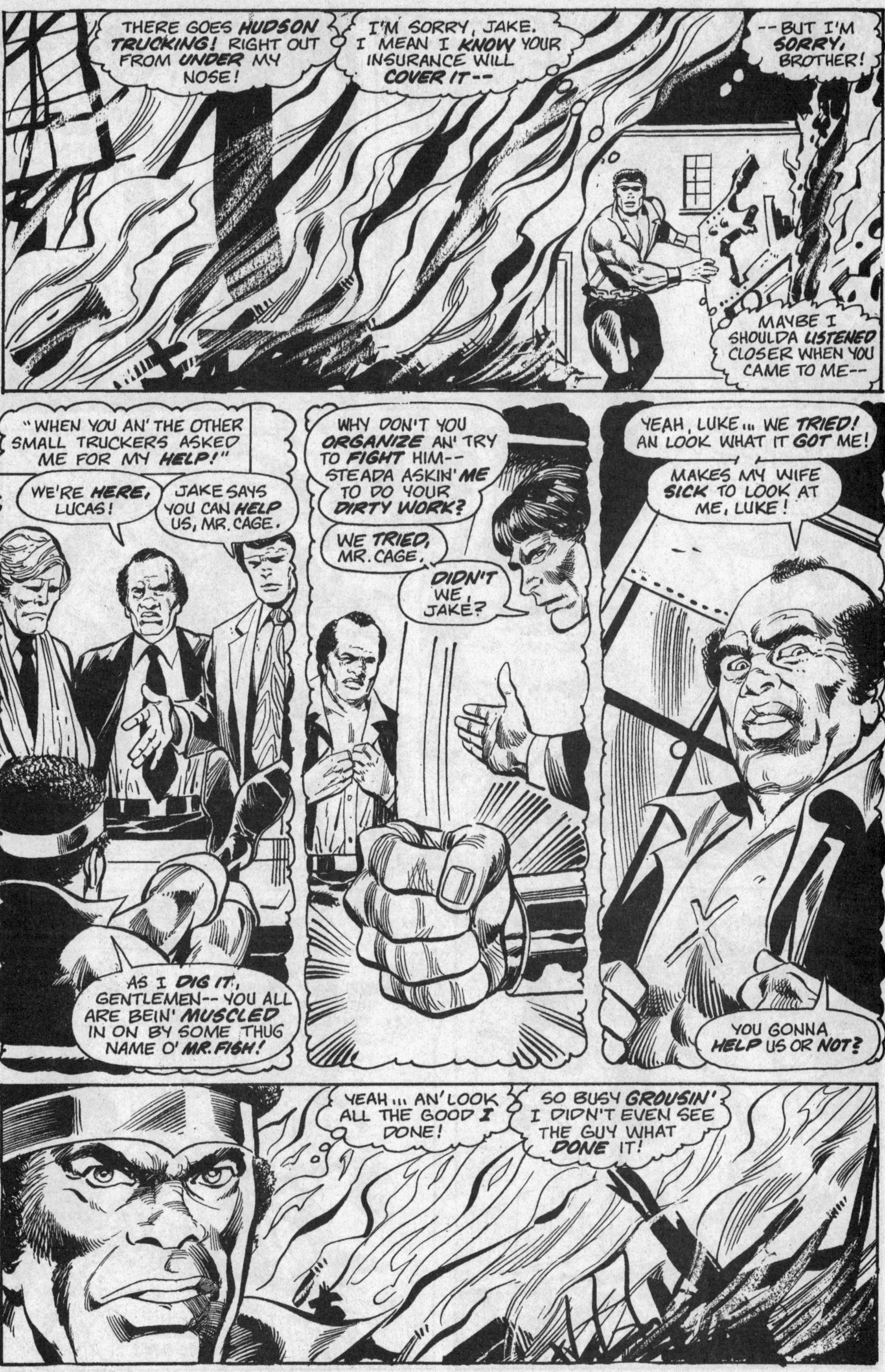

THERE GOES HUDSON TRUCKING! RIGHT OUT FROM UNDER MY NOSE!
I'M SORRY, JAKE. I MEAN I KNOW YOUR INSURANCE WILL COVER IT--
--BUT I'M SORRY, BROTHER!
MAYBE I SHOULDA LISTENED CLOSER WHEN YOU CAME TO ME--
"WHEN YOU AN' THE OTHER SMALL TRUCKERS ASKED ME FOR MY HELP!"
WE'RE HERE, LUCAS!
JAKE SAYS YOU CAN HELP US, MR. CAGE.
AS I DIG IT, GENTLEMEN-- YOU ALL ARE BEIN' MUSCLED IN ON BY SOME THUG NAME O' MR. FISH!
WHY DON'T YOU ORGANIZE AN' TRY TO FIGHT HIM-- STEADA ASKIN' ME TO DO YOUR DIRTY WORK?
WE TRIED, MR. CAGE.
DIDN'T WE, JAKE?
YEAH, LUKE... WE TRIED! AN LOOK WHAT IT GOT ME!
MAKES MY WIFE SICK TO LOOK AT ME, LUKE!
YOU GONNA HELP US OR NOT?
YEAH... AN' LOOK ALL THE GOOD I DONE!
SO BUSY GROUSIN' I DIDN'T EVEN SEE THE GUY WHAT DONE IT!

SO WHAT AM I GONNA SAY TO JAKE IN THE *MORN*--

HOLD YOUR *HORSES*, LUCAS!

THERE GOES THE SUCKER, *NOW!*

MOVIN' LIKE A *BAT* OUTTA *HELL!*

BUT HE'S GONNA HAVETA *STOP* AT THAT *DEAD-END* UP AHEAD!

GONE! WHERE THE #$%%#!

RIGHT BEHIND YA, HERO!

KRAKK!

THE NIGHT ERUPTS INTO *NEON STARS* IN LUKE CAGE'S HEAD...

CRIPES! YOU STILL *STANDIN'??*

THAT SHOT WOULDA KILLED A NEW YORK *COP*-- AN' YOU DIDN'T EVEN *BLINK!*

... BUT HE THRUSTS THEIR BRILLIANCE *AWAY* AS HE STRUGGLES TO RISE TO HIS UNSTEADY *FEET.*

YOU SHOULDN'T'VE *TALKED*, BRO'--CAUSE NOW THEIR AIN'T *NO WAY* I'M EVER GONNA FORGET YOUR *VOICE!*

WON'T DO YOU NO *GOOD*, HERO-MAN--

--YOU AIN'T *NEVER* GONNA HEAR IT *AGAIN!*

THAT'S WHAT YOU THINK, BROTHER!

AIN'T NO *FENCE* BUILT THAT'S GONNA KEEP ME AWAY FROM--

SWEET LORD!

THERE AIN'T NOWHERE TO *GO* ON THE OTHER SIDE O' THIS FENCE BUT--

--DOWN!!

THE SUCKER *KNEW* I'D DO THAT!

HE *LURED* ME RIGHT INTO IT!

STILL ALIVE, CAGE? YOUR HEAD MUST BE AS THICK AS *CEMENT*, BOY!

DON'T CROW YET, FRIEND!

I AIN'T *DONE* WITH YOU!

OH YES YOU *ARE*, MR. CAGE!

QUITE DONE!

WHO--?

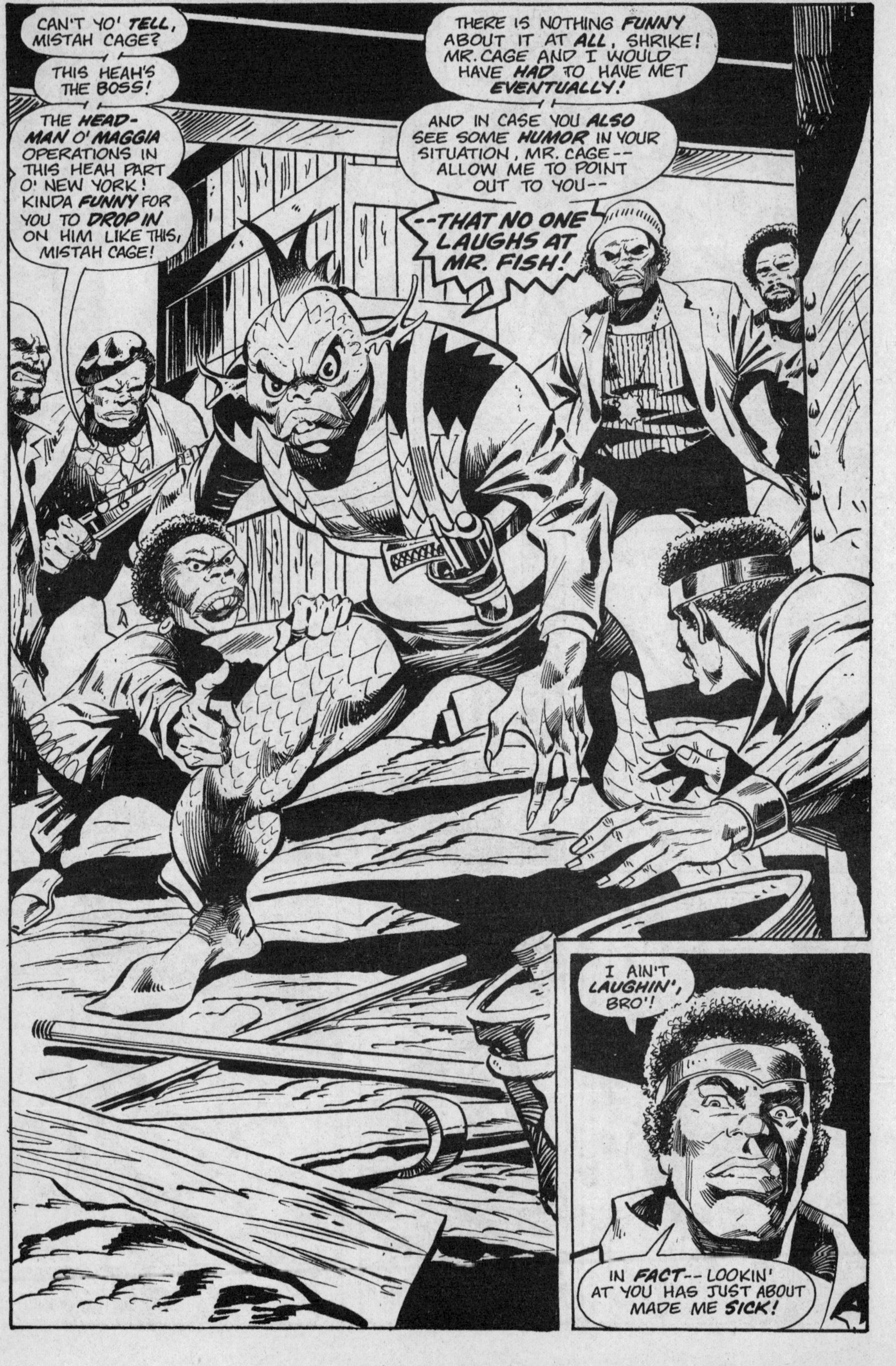
CAN'T YO' TELL, MISTAH CAGE?
THIS HEAH'S THE BOSS!
THE HEAD-MAN O' MAGGIA OPERATIONS IN THIS HEAH PART O' NEW YORK! KINDA FUNNY FOR YOU TO DROP IN ON HIM LIKE THIS, MISTAH CAGE!
THERE IS NOTHING FUNNY ABOUT IT AT ALL, SHRIKE! MR. CAGE AND I WOULD HAVE HAD TO HAVE MET EVENTUALLY!
AND IN CASE YOU ALSO SEE SOME HUMOR IN YOUR SITUATION, MR. CAGE-- ALLOW ME TO POINT OUT TO YOU--
--THAT NO ONE LAUGHS AT MR. FISH!
I AIN'T LAUGHIN', BRO'!
IN FACT-- LOOKIN' AT YOU HAS JUST ABOUT MADE ME SICK!

YOU ARE AS **ARROGANT** AS I WAS **INFORMED** YOU'D BE, CAGE!

AND BOTH YOUR **ARROGANCE** AND YOUR **PRESENCE** ARE MUCH TOO **TIME-CONSUMING,** THUS--

--I MUST GIVE MY MEN THAT WHICH THEY **DESIRE** AND ALLOW THEM TO **DESTROY** YOU!

NOW YOU'RE **TALKIN'** MR. FISH!

TOK!

TCHOK

ZZISSST!

THESE MAGGIA WEAPONS'LL PAY YOU **BACK** FOR A LOT O' FOLKS IN **PRISON** ON ACCOUNTA YOU, CAGE!

UNHHHH! THE SLUGS AIN'T **PENETRATIN'**--

ZTRAKT!

--BUT THE **IMPACT** IS ALMOST MORE'N I CAN **BEAR!**

STILL **ALIVE,** CAGE? THAT'S **TOO BAD!**

NOW YOU'RE JUST GONNA HAVE TO **WORK** AT DYIN'!

PTOW

THAT'S WHAT **YOU** SAY, SUCKER!

NOW GIMME THAT **POP GUN** BEFORE YOU **HURT** SOMEBODY FOR **REAL!**

LORDY! HE --HE **CRUSHED** MY RIFLE!

YEEOWWW

YOU'RE LUCKY I DIDN'T CRUSH YOUR **SKULL,** M'MAN!

BUT ALL YOU JOKERS DON'T MEAN A **THING!**

IT'S **MR. FISH** I WANT-- AND YOU'RE JUST IN THE **WAY!**

THAT MAY *BE*, MISTAH CAGE! BUT YO' *STILL* GOTS TO GO THROUGH *US* FIRST!

IT'S *ME*, MISTAH CAGE! *SHRIKE!*

JUST KEEPIN' YO' *BUSY* 'TILL THE *BOSS* GETS HIS STUFF *TOGETHER!*

HE DON'T *HURT*--BUT HE'S *MOVIN'* SO BLAMED *FAST* I CAN'T GRAB HIM TO GET HIM *OFF!*

WHAT THE--??

MY *STUFF* IS *READY*, SHRIKE!

AND MR. CAGE IS A *DEAD MAN!*

FTASHT!

THIS SIDE

JUMP, SHRIKE! NOW!

I'S *JUMPIN'*, MR. FISH!

ARRGGGG

YOU--YOU *COOKED* HIM, MR. FISH!

FRIED 'IM LIKE A *FLOUNDER!*

YET STILL HE *LIVES!*

BUT NOT FOR *LONG!*

UNNH! THIS DUDE WEIGHS A TON!

AT A GESTURE FROM THE MYSTERIOUS MR. FISH, LUKE CAGE IS HOISTED AND CARRIED TOWARD A WAITING ELEVATOR...

...AND LIT BY THE BLUE OF STREET LIGHTS AND THE YELLOW OF THE MOON...

...HE IS BORNE UP THE SIDE OF A SKELETAL STRUCTURE OF STEEL RIB-WORK AND CONCRETE MUSCLE...

...TWENTY-FIVE STORIES UP!

SOON, SHRIKE... SOON WE WILL NOT HAVE MR. CAGE TO WORRY ABOUT ANY LONGER!

AND ONCE HE IS OUT OF THE WAY-- WHO IS THE MAGGIA TO TELL ME WHAT MY TERRITORY MUST BE?

·WARNING· DO NOT LIFT GATE

CAGE IS A MEAN ONE, MISTAH FISH!

"YOU ALL BETTAH FINISH HIM FAST-LIKE... AFORE HE WAKES UP-- IF YOU ALL KNOWS WHAT I MEAN!"

AND AGAIN CAGE IS LIFTED... OUT ONTO THE GIRDERS THAT SWAY IN THE WINDS OVER MANHATTAN.

TIE HIM **GOOD,** FLY!

PRETTY BOY IS WAKIN' **UP!**

DANGER

UNHHH--

YOU ARE ABOUT TO **DIE,** MR.CAGE--YET YOU STILL DO NOT KNOW WHO **I AM!**

I **HATE** HAVING A MAN DIE WITH A **QUESTION** IN HIS MIND!

HEY, FRIEND! I COULD CARE **LESS**-- UNHHH!

NOBODY **ASKED** YO' MISTAH CAGE!

"THANK YOU, SHRIKE! I WAS STRICTLY **SMALL-TIME,** MR.CAGE--PENNY-ANTE **BURGLARY**--"

"--UNTIL ONE NIGHT DOWN AT THE **DOCKS** ON **FULTON** STREET..."

THAT'S **IT!** THE TRUCK THAT'S S'POSED TO BE CARRYING THE **ISOTOPE** THE MAGGIA **WANTS!**

"THE **DRIVER** WAS SO CAUGHT UP IN HIS **FUNNY-BOOK** HE DIDN'T EVER HEAR ME **COMIN'**--

PLAY BOY

"--'TILL IT WAS **TOO LATE!**"

STROW!

EEYAGGHH!

IT'S IN ONE O' THEM **CRATES,** BROTHERS!

OUR TICKET TO **PARADISE!**

DANGER

"WE BUSTED IN THERE AND **TORE** AT THE BOXES--

"--AND **I** WAS THE FIRST TO LOCATE THE **ISOTOPE!**"

HEY, MAN! IT'S--IT'S **GLOWIN'**!

WONDER IF IT'S POISON?? I--I FEEL KIND O' DIZZY!

KINDA HOT!

I'M BURNING UP!

CAN'T STAND IT! GOTTA GET OUT!

"THE OTHERS FLED AS I-- GLOWING FROM THE CONTAMINATING ISOTOPE --DOVE INTO THE FILTHY WATERS OF THE EAST RIVER!

SPLASH!

"AND THOUGH I STAYED BENEATH THE WATER FOR WHAT SEEMED LIKE HOURS--"

HEY! PULL CLOSER, CHARLEY!

SOMETHING'S MAKIN' THE WATER BOIL OVER YONDER!

"--STILL I BURNED FROM WITHIN! MY ENTIRE BEING AFLAME AS I--"

"--CHANGED!"

I CAN FEEL SOMETHIN' SLIMY MOVIN' AROUND UNDER THE BOAT, CHARLEY--

--OH!

OH MY LORD!

"THEY FLED FROM ME, AND ALTHOUGH I DIDN'T UNDERSTAND WHY AT THE TIME--"

"--I KNEW INSTINCTIVELY THAT I WOULD NEVER BE THE SAME AGAIN!"

THAT WAS ALL REAL *INTERESTIN'*, FISH-FACE!

NOW--IF YOU DON'T *MIND*, THAT IS-- I'D LIKE TO *DIE* BEFORE I HAVE TO LISTEN TO ANOTHER ONE O' YOUR *BORIN'* STORIES!

YOUR *WORDS* HAVE SEALED YOUR *FATE*, CAGE!

TAKE HIM!

C'MON, BOYS-- YOU *HEARD* THE MAN! TAKE ME!

YOU *ASKED* FOR THIS WISE-GUY--

-- AND YOU'RE GONNA *GET IT!*

JUST WHAT I *HOPED* THEY'D DO!

I COULDN'T DO *NOTHIN'* AS LONG AS FISH HAD HIS *BLASTER* ON ME AN' I. WAS *SURROUNDED* BY HIS TOUGHS--

--SO I HAD TO *GAMBLE* ON THEM FINISHIN' ME OFF *THIS* WAY!

SNAP!

THIS *CABLE* THEY TRUSSED ME UP WITH IS THE *EASY PART*--

--BUT *EVERYTHIN'* HINGES ON ME GRABBIN' THAT *BEAM* STICKIN' OUT DOWN THERE--

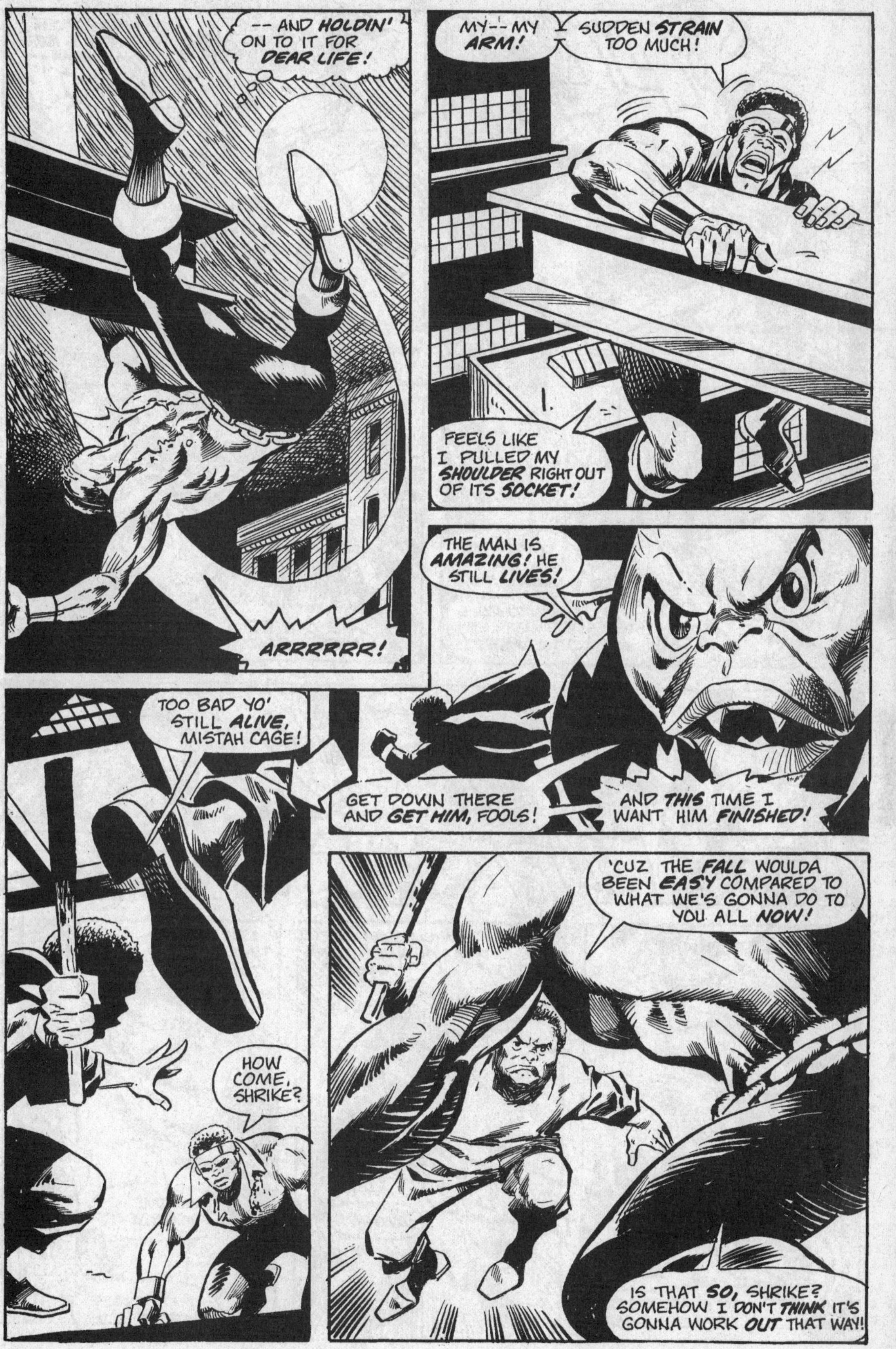
-- AND HOLDIN' ON TO IT FOR DEAR LIFE!
ARRRRRR!
MY-- MY ARM!
SUDDEN STRAIN TOO MUCH!
FEELS LIKE I PULLED MY SHOULDER RIGHT OUT OF ITS SOCKET!
THE MAN IS AMAZING! HE STILL LIVES!
GET DOWN THERE AND GET HIM, FOOLS!
AND THIS TIME I WANT HIM FINISHED!
TOO BAD YO' STILL ALIVE, MISTAH CAGE!
HOW COME, SHRIKE?
'CUZ THE FALL WOULDA BEEN EASY COMPARED TO WHAT WE'S GONNA DO TO YOU ALL NOW!
IS THAT SO, SHRIKE? SOMEHOW I DON'T THINK IT'S GONNA WORK OUT THAT WAY!

SPLANG!

TOWW!

AN' EVEN WITH A *BUM ARM*--

MR. FISH! DO SOMETHIN'!

'CAUSE THE WAY YOU'RE *COMIN'* AT ME--

--ALL I GOT TO *DO* IS STEP ASIDE AND LET *YOU* DO THE *REST!*

--I CAN *STILL* WASTE YOU CLOWNS!

HE'S GONE *CRAZY!*

STRAMMM

CRAZY OR *NOT*--

--MY BLASTER STOPPED HIM ONCE *BEFORE*--

--IT WILL STOP HIM *AGAIN!*

ZISST!

UNGHH!

NOT *THIS* TIME, FISH!

THIS TIME IS *DIFFERENT!*

IT-- IT DIDN'T *AFFECT* YOU!!

YOU CATCH ON QUICK, FISH!

NOW GIVE ME THAT *TOY O'* YOURS--

SMASH!

--AN' *SMILE*-- WHILE I PASTE YOUR *FACE* ALL OVER *NEW YORK!*

WHAMM

NO! I'M NOT DONE YET!

YOU ARE NOT THE *ONLY* ONE POSSESSING POWER, CAGE!

AND YOU ARE NOT THE *ONLY* ONE WHO KNOWS HOW TO *USE* IT!

OOOFFFF!

BA-THAMM!

AND WHILE YOU *SAVED* YOURSELF FROM THE FALL THE *FIRST* TIME--

--I *DOUBT* WHETHER YOU CAN DO SO *TWICE!*

ESPECIALLY WITH ONLY *ONE* GOOD *ARM!*

HE'S PUSHIN' ME TOWARDS THE *EDGE!!* GOTTA *STOP* HIM!

ONE ARM'S ALL I NEED FOR THE LIKES OF *YOU,* SLIMY!

POW!

AN' I'VE HAD JUST ABOUT *ENOUGH* O' THIS SICK LITTLE *GAME* O' YOURS!

YOUR *BOYS* HAVE SPLIT-- AN' BY NOW THE MAGGIA MUST KNOW THAT YOU *BLEW IT!*

YOU'RE *FINISHED,* MR. FISH! PRETTY *FUNNY,* HUH?

NO!

NOT YET, CAGE!

MY ARM!

WRAMM

WAVES OF BLINDING PAIN SWEEP THROUGH LUKE CAGE...

NOT AS LONG AS YOU *LIVE!*

"...AND HE STRUGGLES TO SEE THROUGH PAIN GLAZED EYES, KNOWING THAT HIS FOE IS ALMOST UPON HIM..."

"...MOVING AT THE LAST MOMENT, MORE OUT OF INSTINCT THAN ANYTHING ELSE..."

NO! YOU WEREN'T SUPPOSED TO *MOVE!*

GOODBYE, MR. FISH!

CRUMMY WAY TO GO, MAN--

--BUT IT'S THE SAME AS WHAT YOU WANTED FOR *ME*, SO I CAN'T FEEL *TOO BAD* ABOUT IT!

I MEAN YOU JUST SPENT ONE WHOLE SATURDAY NIGHT *SURROUNDED* BY KILLERS, CORRUPTION AN' *FREAKS*--

BUT WHAT WAS IT ALL *FOR*, CAGE?

--IT'S *BOUND* TO MAKE A *DIFFERENCE* IN THE WAY YOU *FEEL*!

ELEVATOR

BOUND TO MAKE YOU *WONDER* WHY THE BLAZES YOU'RE IN THIS GIG IN THE *FIRST PLACE*!

CAN'T BE THE *MONEY*-- 'CAUSE I NEVER SEEM TO MAKE ANY!

CAN'T BE THE *FAME*-- 'CAUSE THERE'S EVEN *LESS* O' THAT!

BUT THERE'S JUST *GOT* TO BE *SOMETHIN'* IN IT!

I THINK.

NEXT

A *RETURN* TO OUR PIRANHA JONES ADVENTURE IN WHICH THE MUSICAL QUESTION IS ASKED... *LOOK WHAT THEY'VE DONE TO OUR LIVES MA!*

POWER-MAN
MARVEL COMICS GROUP
APPROVED BY THE COMICS CODE AUTHORITY
25¢
30 APR 02149
LUKE CAGE, POWER MAN
YOU'RE CORNERED, HERO! NOW GIVE US WHAT WE'VE COME FOR--OR
DIE!
YOU WANT THIS STUFF, CREEPS--YOU'LL HAVE TO TAKE IT OFF MY CORPSE!
YOU KEEP STANDIN' THERE, CAGE--AN THAT'S JUST WHAT WE'RE GONNA DO!
BUCKLER & JANSON
INTRODUCING! THE MALEVOLENT MENACE OF THE MAN THEY CALL... PIRANHA!

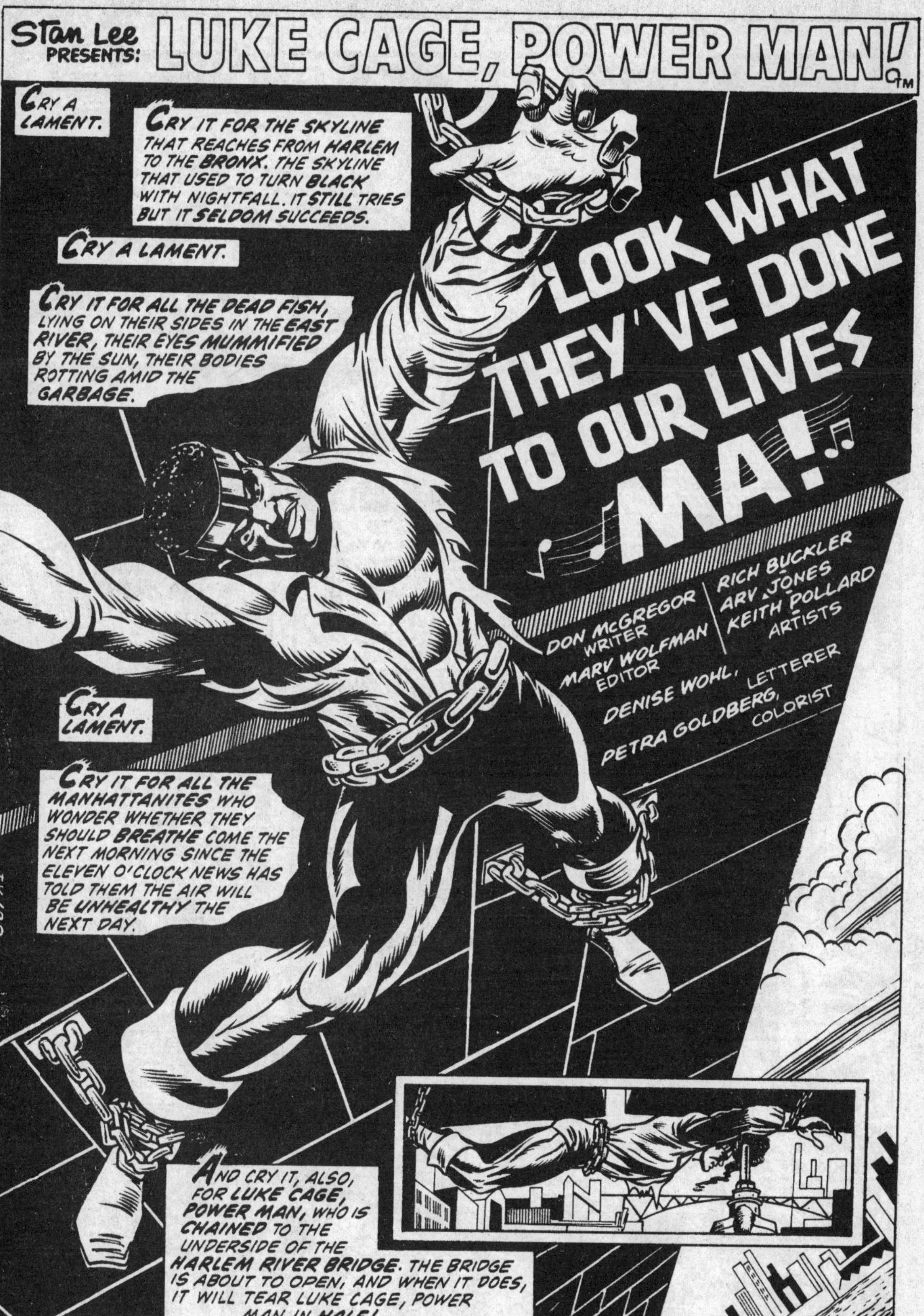

Stan Lee PRESENTS: LUKE CAGE, POWER MAN! TM
CRY A LAMENT.
CRY IT FOR THE SKYLINE THAT REACHES FROM HARLEM TO THE BRONX. THE SKYLINE THAT USED TO TURN BLACK WITH NIGHTFALL. IT STILL TRIES BUT IT SELDOM SUCCEEDS.
CRY A LAMENT.
CRY IT FOR ALL THE DEAD FISH, LYING ON THEIR SIDES IN THE EAST RIVER, THEIR EYES MUMMIFIED BY THE SUN, THEIR BODIES ROTTING AMID THE GARBAGE.
LOOK WHAT THEY'VE DONE TO OUR LIVES MA!
DON McGREGOR WRITER
MARV WOLFMAN EDITOR
RICH BUCKLER ARV JONES KEITH POLLARD ARTISTS
DENISE WOHL, LETTERER
PETRA GOLDBERG, COLORIST
CRY A LAMENT.
CRY IT FOR ALL THE MANHATTANITES WHO WONDER WHETHER THEY SHOULD BREATHE COME THE NEXT MORNING SINCE THE ELEVEN O'CLOCK NEWS HAS TOLD THEM THE AIR WILL BE UNHEALTHY THE NEXT DAY.
JV 129
AND CRY IT, ALSO, FOR LUKE CAGE, POWER MAN, WHO IS CHAINED TO THE UNDERSIDE OF THE HARLEM RIVER BRIDGE. THE BRIDGE IS ABOUT TO OPEN, AND WHEN IT DOES, IT WILL TEAR LUKE CAGE, POWER MAN, IN HALF!

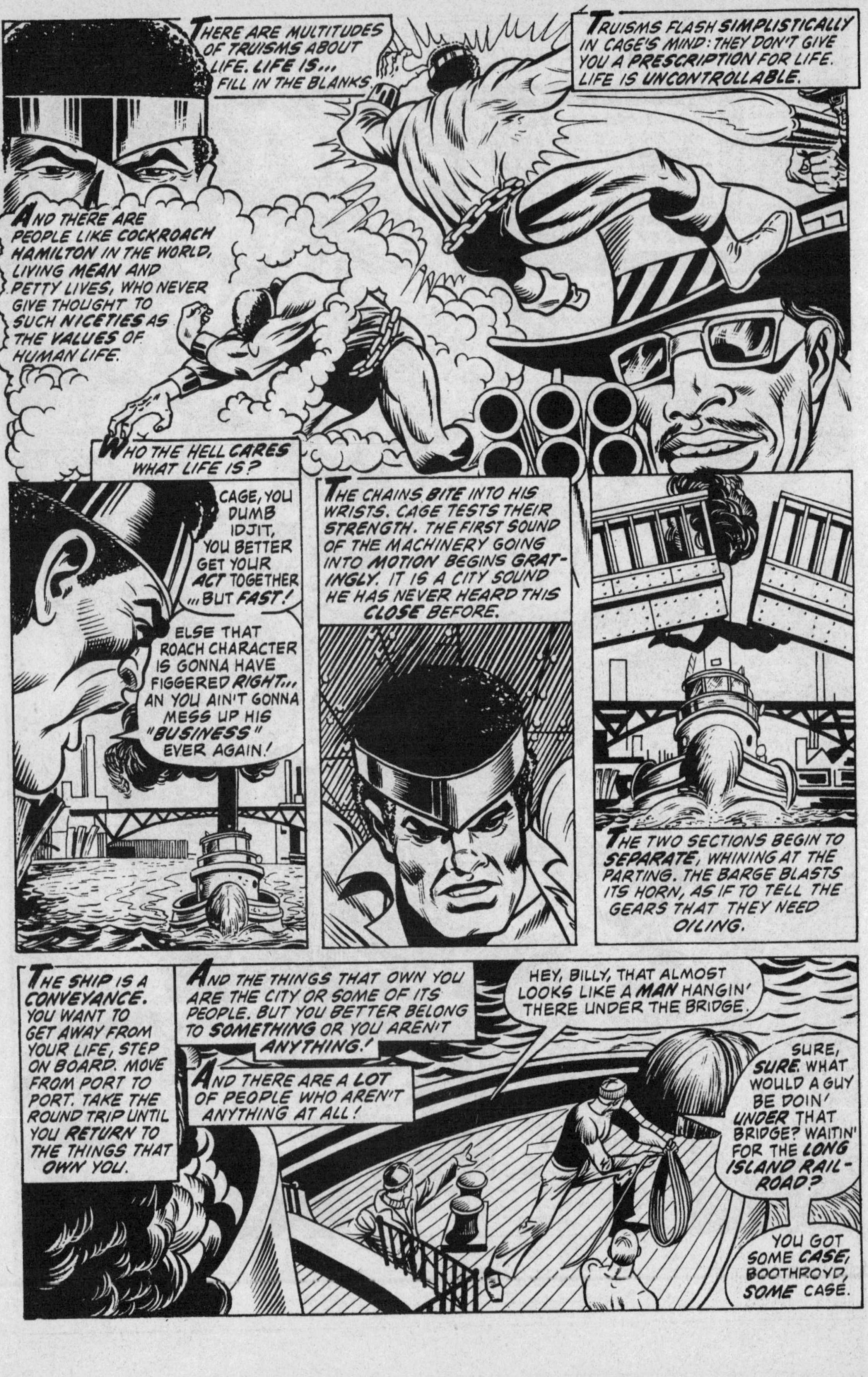

THERE ARE MULTITUDES OF TRUISMS ABOUT LIFE. LIFE IS... FILL IN THE BLANKS.
TRUISMS FLASH SIMPLISTICALLY IN CAGE'S MIND: THEY DON'T GIVE YOU A PRESCRIPTION FOR LIFE. LIFE IS UNCONTROLLABLE.
AND THERE ARE PEOPLE LIKE COCKROACH HAMILTON IN THE WORLD, LIVING MEAN AND PETTY LIVES, WHO NEVER GIVE THOUGHT TO SUCH NICETIES AS THE VALUES OF HUMAN LIFE.
WHO THE HELL CARES WHAT LIFE IS?
CAGE, YOU DUMB IDJIT, YOU BETTER GET YOUR ACT TOGETHER ...BUT FAST!
ELSE THAT ROACH CHARACTER IS GONNA HAVE FIGGERED RIGHT... AN YOU AIN'T GONNA MESS UP HIS "BUSINESS" EVER AGAIN!
THE CHAINS BITE INTO HIS WRISTS. CAGE TESTS THEIR STRENGTH. THE FIRST SOUND OF THE MACHINERY GOING INTO MOTION BEGINS GRATINGLY. IT IS A CITY SOUND HE HAS NEVER HEARD THIS CLOSE BEFORE.
THE TWO SECTIONS BEGIN TO SEPARATE, WHINING AT THE PARTING. THE BARGE BLASTS ITS HORN, AS IF TO TELL THE GEARS THAT THEY NEED OILING.
THE SHIP IS A CONVEYANCE. YOU WANT TO GET AWAY FROM YOUR LIFE, STEP ON BOARD. MOVE FROM PORT TO PORT. TAKE THE ROUND TRIP UNTIL YOU RETURN TO THE THINGS THAT OWN YOU.
AND THE THINGS THAT OWN YOU ARE THE CITY OR SOME OF ITS PEOPLE. BUT YOU BETTER BELONG TO SOMETHING OR YOU AREN'T ANYTHING!
AND THERE ARE A LOT OF PEOPLE WHO AREN'T ANYTHING AT ALL!
HEY, BILLY, THAT ALMOST LOOKS LIKE A MAN HANGIN' THERE UNDER THE BRIDGE.
SURE, SURE. WHAT WOULD A GUY BE DOIN' UNDER THAT BRIDGE? WAITIN' FOR THE LONG ISLAND RAIL-ROAD?
YOU GOT SOME CASE, BOOTHROYD, SOME CASE.

CAGE PULLS THE LENGTH OF THE CHAIN TO ITS LIMIT! HIS FLESH GIVES.

THE MASONRY AT THE OTHER END HOLDS FIRM!

THE BARGE CLEAVES THE WATER, CHURNING UP MACDONALD'S WRAPPERS AND CHICKEN DELIGHT CONTAINERS.

AND THE TWO HALVES OF THE BRIDGE... DISCONNECT!

THE CHAINS RIP UP CAGE'S WRISTS, STRAINING TO CRUSH THROUGH THE HANDS.

AND THE TUGBOAT BLISSFULLY DRAWS CLOSER.

ITS HORN IS BUOYANT LIKE THE SOUND OF BEGINNING LOVERS SWEARING THAT LOVE NEVER ENDS.

CRY A LAMENT.

CRY IT FOR ALL THE LOVERS WHO WERE WRONG!

CRY IT FOR ALL THE TUGBOATS THAT NEVER MADE IT!

CRY IT FOR ALL THE TORN FLESH THROUGH THE AGES!

CAGE'S EYES CLOSE, LOCKING IN THE AGONY.

HIS EYES OPEN WIDE, FILLED WITH THE KNOWLEDGE THAT HE IS NOT IMMUNE TO SUCH INTENSE PAIN AND HURT.

ROACH, YOU GOT YOURSELF A *PROBLEM.* A *REAL* PROBLEM. 'CAUSE YOU DIDN'T MAKE THESE THINGS *STRONG ENOUGH* TO HOLD OLD LUKE CAGE.

AND IF I GET OUT OF THIS, I'M GONNA BRING SO MUCH *GRIEF* DOWN AROUND YOUR SHOULDERS--

--YOU'LL *SUFFOCATE* IN IT!

ON THE **OTHER** HAND, I COULDA FIGURED THIS **WRONG!**

THE IMAGE OF A **POSTER** SELLING ON BROADWAY SNAPS INTO CAGE'S MIND: A **KITTEN** CHINNING HIMSELF AND TRYING TO LOOK ADORABLE AT THE SAME TIME AND THE CUTE CLINCHER, "HANG IN THERE, BABY." PRINTED UNDERNEATH.

SOME PEOPLE WILL BUY ANYTHING!

CAGE HANGS FROM THE BRIDGE, AND THE SHOULDER THAT WAS **DISLOCATED** BY COCKROACH HAMILTON UPON THEIR FIRST MEETING THROBS BRUTALLY.

CAGE DOES NOT LOOK AS ADORABLE AS THE KITTEN IN THE POSTER.

HE IGNORES THE FACT THAT HIS FINGERS ARE **SLIPPERY** FROM THE BLOOD COURSING FROM HIS WRISTS AND **WRENCHES** AT THE CHAINS--

-- WRENCHES AT THEM **SAVAGELY** --

-- AND FEELS HIS STEEL-HARD FLESH **TEAR** UNDER THE STRAIN.

THE CHAINS ALSO **BREAK!** BONDAGE BROKEN AT THE COST OF BLOOD!

ISN'T IT ALWAYS THE WAY?

YOU DIDN'T *BELIEVE ME,* RIGHT? WELL WHATTA YOU THINK THAT *IS?* THE FLYING NUN?

GET *OUTTA* THE WAY! GET OUTTA THE *WAY!*

HE'S GONNA *LAND* RIGHT ON *TOP* OF US!

IT'S SOME NUTTY *PUBLICITY STUNT,* THAT'S WHAT IT IS. *GOTTA* BE.

*C*AGE HURTLES THRU THE COPPER SKIES. SOMEWHERE IN THE DISTANCE, THE BRONX IS *BURNING,* FLAMES AND SMOKE ADDING A LITTLE COLOR TO THE GREY.

*C*AGE FAILS TO SEE IT!

HEY, YOU GUYS WANTA KEEP IT *DOWN?* SOME OF US ARE TRYING TO GET SOME...

SLEEP..?

THAT'S ALL RIGHT. DON'T BOTHER GETTING *UP* ON MY ACCOUNT.

I ONLY *DROPPED BY* FOR A MOMENT.

*G*IVE THEM THE *COOL PARTING LINE,* BUT THE PAIN FROM THE WOUNDS AT HIS ANKLES AND WRISTS AND SHOULDER THROW HIS TIMING OFF.

NO, I'M AFRAID I REALLY CAN'T *STAY.*

*H*IS BODY SHAKES SLIGHTLY FROM THE *ORDEAL.* ANOTHER *LIFE TRUISM* HITS HIM: LIFE *ISN'T* A SERIES OF ONE LINERS.

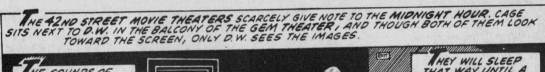

THE SOUNDS OF AMPLIFIED DEATH FROM THE SCREEN LULLS THE SLEEPERS WHO ARE CAREFUL NOT TO KICK THEIR PLAIN BROWN PAPER BAGS. THERE MIGHT BE A GULP OR TWO OF WINE LEFT.

THEY WILL SLEEP THAT WAY UNTIL A PATROLMAN SLAPS THE SOULS OF THEIR FEET WITH A NIGHTSTICK, AND THEN THEY WILL PROMPTLY RETURN TO THEIR NIGHT'S REST WHEN HE HAS WALKED AWAY.

ADONIS CHEMICAL HIRED ME TO FOLLOW ONE OF THEIR EMPLOYEES... A HARRY WENTWORTH. SEEMS HE WAS STEALING MAP ROUTES OF DEADLY CHEMICALS THAT ADONIS CHEMICAL WAS SHIPPING RIGHT THRU FUN CITY.

LET THAT GAS INTO THE AIR IN MANHATTAN AND YOU GOT A MASS EPIDEMIC OF LUNG CANCER ON YOUR HANDS.

WAY I HEARD IT, LUCUS, THEY'RE STILL ARGUING ABOUT SHIPPING RADIOACTIVE STUFF THRU HERE. WHY NOT THIS JUNK?!

THIS ROACH CHARACTER... I TELL YOU D.W., HE LOOKS JUST LIKE A COCKROACH... GOT THE MAPS FROM WENTWORTH...

...AND BLEW HIM AWAY WITH THAT SIX BARRELED SHOTGUN OF HIS.

IT ALSO FIRES GAS. I FOUND THAT OUT BEFORE HE LET ME HAVE IT. WOKE UP STRAPPED TO THE UNDERSIDE OF THE HARLEM RIVER BRIDGE.

I'VE BEEN IN PLEAS-ENTER PLACES.

YEAH, WELL MY UNCLE WANTS TO UP YOUR RENT BY $40.00 A MONTH.

HE CAN'T DO THAT. IT'S AGAINST THE LAW.

TELL HIM THAT.

PROBLEM WITH YOUR UNCLE IS, HE'S NEVER PUTTIN' ME ON WHEN HE SAYS THOSE THINGS.

--THAT SODA MACHINE YOU'RE USING--

HEY, WAIT UP, LUKE--

--IT'S STILL NOT--

--FIXED.

THAT FIGURES. Y'KNOW, D.W., THIS ROACH *SICKIE* MIGHT GET *HIS* SOMEDAY... JUST LIKE I'M GONNA GET THIS *MONEY HUNGRY MACHINE* SOMEDAY... BUT WHO MAKES ADONIS CHEMICAL PAY?

WHO MAKES *THEM* PAY FOR WHAT THEY'RE *DOIN'* TO OUR *LIVES*?

AT THE MOVIES

YOU SURE YOU NEVER BELONGED TO ONE OF THEM *DEFUNCT* RADICAL MOVEMENTS OF THE 60'S?

NOT ME, MAN. I HAVE *ENOUGH* TROUBLES BEIN' *RESPONSIBLE* FOR WHAT I DO. I'M JUST TRYIN' TO *GET ON THROUGH*!

I THINK SOMEBODY'S TRYIN' TO GET YOUR *ATTENTION*, D.W... ELSE YOU'VE JUST BEEN *PROPOSITIONED*.

YOU *ALWAYS* WERE A *FAN* OF THE... "ARTS".

THIS IS *WINNIE*, LUKE. SHORT FOR *WINIFRED*, BUT SHE LIKES TO BE CALLED *WIN*. SHE'S AN ART STUDENT AT *HUNTER COLLEGE*.

WE'D *HANG* WITH YOU, LUKE, BUT WE WANTA CATCH *DICK SUMMER* DOING ONE OF HIS *LOVING TOUCH SENSITIVITY TUNE-UP* ON THE RADIO.

WHAT'S THAT, A *DISEASE*?

IF IT IS, I HOPE IT'S *CATCHING*!

WHILE THE *PORTABLE RADIOS* ISSUE FORTH THE VOICE OF A *SULTRY WOMAN* URGING THE *AUDIENCE* TO SPEND THE NIGHT WITH DICK SUMMER--

--THE *FUNKIER STATIONS* RAISE URGENT SUMMONS TO THE *STARLESS SKIES* ABOVE HARLEM.

COCKROACH HAMILTON STRIDES UP *143RD STREET*.

THE *FRENTIC ENERGY* POUNDED INTO THE *BONGO DRUMS* EARLIER HAS *SOFTENED*... AS IF THE BEAT AND ITS DRUMMER HAVE BOTH RECOGNIZED *DAWN'S* APPROACH.

PASSIONATE SHOUTS FOLLOW THE ROLL OF A PAIR OF *DICE*. FOR THE INSTANT, ALL OF LIFE HINGES ON THE *OUTCOME* OF THOSE TINY CUBES.

45 LENOX

BABY MIGHT NOT HAVE A PAIR OF *SHOES*... OR ANYTHING ELSE COME MORNING.

COCKROACH HAS HEARD THE LATE NIGHT SOUNDS OF HARLEM ALL HIS LIFE. AS A CHILD, THEY *FRIGHTENED* HIM, BUT NOW THEY ARE *COMFORTING*.

STRANGE HOW THINGS *CHANGE*.

HE ENTERS HIS APARTMENT, SLIPPING THE *POLICE LOCK BAR* INTO THE DOOR AND FLOORING--

--AND THERE IS JUST *HIM*... AND HIS SHOTGUN *"JOSH"*... AND THE *COCKROACHES*... AND THE *NIGHT-TIME SOUNDS*.

THE PLASTER IS CRACKED. THE ROACHES SCURRY AWAY FROM THE REFRIGERATOR'S LIGHT.

HAMILTON MOVES CASUALLY.

THIS IS THE ONLY PLACE IN THE WORLD WHERE ROACH HAMILTON MOVES CASUALLY.

OKAY, "JOSH", WE GOT US SOME TIME TO *KILL*, 'TIL PIRANHA GETS IN *TOUCH* WITH US.

REAL ROACHES SCAMPER FRANTICALLY OVER THEIR FOOD *TREASURE*--

--BUT THEIR *QUIVERING ANTENNAE* DO NOT DISTURB HAMILTON--

--THESE CREATURES ARE THE MOST FAMILIAR *LIVING* THINGS IN HIS LIFE.

COME ON! GET YOUR *SKINNY* LITTLE BUTTS OUTTA MY *CHEESE SNIPS.*

RRINNGG!!

TAKE A GUESS WHO THAT IS, "JOSH".

YEAH, THIS IS ME, *PIRANHA.*

YOU WANT ME TO *WHAT*?

WHEN? ...NOW!?

OKAY, BOSS...*YOU'RE* THE BOSS. I'LL PACK UP "JOSH" AN' WE'LL *MAKE IT* TO YOUR PLACE WITHIN THE HOUR.

THE EAST SIDE HAS CLOSED DOWN FOR THE NIGHT, WAITING FOR THE MORNING TO BRING IT *TUMULTUOUSLY ALIVE* AGAIN WITH CARS AND BUSES AND TAXIS AND *SMARTLY CHIC* PEOPLE AND *FRENCH POODLES* WITH BOWS.

ONE PENTHOUSE IS ALIVE.

THE PENTHOUSE IS AN *OASIS*--

--AN OASIS OF *EXOTIC PLANTS*--

--IN THE MIDST OF A *DESERT* OF STEEL AND CEMENT--

--AND SITTING IN THE CENTER OF IT IS *PIRANHA JONES.*

YOU MADE *REMARKABLE* TIME, ROACH.

CAUGHT THE *TRAINS* JUST *RIGHT!*

IT STILL *AMAZES* ME THAT YOU CAN RIDE IN THOSE *DEATH-TRAPS.* AH, WELL, TO EACH HIS *OWN!*

YOU SURE KEEP THESE *FLUNKIES* HUSTLIN'... THEY KEEP MESSIN' WITH THOSE *FLOWERS* MORE'N THEY DO WITH THE FURNITURE.

BUT OF COURSE... THE FLOWERS ARE MUCH MORE *DELICATE* THAN THE FURNITURE.

I'M HAVING THESE NEWEST SPECIMENS... *PERUVIAN BLOSSOMS*... MOVED INTO THE HOTHOUSE. THE *AIR* IN MANHATTAN COULD NEVER *SUSTAIN* THEM.

DO YOU KNOW, ROACH, THAT THE *TREES* ALONG THE *GRAND CONCOURSE* IN THE *BRONX* DO NOT TURN COLORS DURING THE *FALL*? NO? I DON'T EXPECT THAT WAS *EVER* A CONCERN OF YOURS.

YOU'RE RIGHT!

IT WASN'T!

NEVERTHELESS, *I* WAS FASCINATED. I SUSPECT THAT THIS *ODDITY* OCCURS BECAUSE THERE SIMPLY IS NOT ENOUGH *OXYGEN* IN THE BRONX AIR TO ALLOW THE LEAVES TO *PERFORM* THEIR NATURAL FUNCTION.

AND JUST A FEW *DECADES AGO*, THE BRONX HAD THE *LAST FARMLANDS* IN NEW YORK CITY. THAT'S SOMETHING YOU SHOULD *PONDER*.

YEAH, MAYBE I'LL DO *THAT*... AFTER THEY *FISH* THAT *CAGE TURKEY* OUTTA THE *HARLEM RIVER!*

BUT NOW, YOU DIDN'T HAUL MY *CARCASS* OUT HERE TO TALK ABOUT NO *LILLIES* AND WHAT NOT!

ROACH, YOU ARE *WITHOUT TACT*... BUT BLUNT. *AND CORRECT!*

I NOTICE YOU KEEP YOUR *DISTANCE* FROM THE *POOL*. AFRAID OF MY *PETS?* AH, WELL, I'M NOT *OVERLY FOND* OF THE ROACHES THAT INFEST *YOUR DEN*, EITHER.

I'VE HAD A CHANCE TO *STUDY* THE TRANSPORTATION MAPS YOU GOT FROM *WENTWORTH*... AND I WANTED YOU TO KNOW THAT... *THE RAID*... IS STILL *ON*... FOR TOMORROW MORNING!

ADONIS CHEMICAL WILL MAINTAIN *SECURE* IN THEIR *ARROGANCE*... THAT THERE IS NO *REAL THREAT* TO THEIR SHIPMENT.

AFTER ALL... HOW CAN... ANYONE *HIJACK* SUCH A HUGE CONVOY? TOMORROW MORNING... *THEY'LL FIND OUT!*

MORNING IS ABRUPT ON 42ND STREET. CAR HORNS SCREAM FOR BLOOD! THE NEON SIGNS DIE! KNUCKLES POUND ON WOOD LIKE A FIST TO THE TEETH.!

NOK! NOK!

CAGE WAKES IMMEDIATELY. THE SHEETS CLING TO HIM LIKE FORGOTTEN DREAMS, AND HIS WOUNDS ACHE AS REMINDERS OF YESTERDAYS FOLLIES.

OKAY, OKAY, WHOEVER YOU ARE. SAVE YOURSELF SOME WEAR AND TEAR, I'M COMING.

BUT YOU'D BETTER HAVE YOURSELVES TWENTY GOOD REASONS FOR WAKIN' A MAN THIS EARLY.!

YOU'RE LUKE CAGE?

YEAH! I DON'T RECOGNIZE YOU, BUT YOU'RE FRIEND THERE WITH THE WIRE THROUGH HIS TEETH IS OUT OF HIS ELEMENT.!

MORNING MR. GRUNDGE. SURE ADONIS CHEMICAL CAN SPARE SUCH A BIG WHEEL AS YOURSELF AWAY FROM THE OFFICE?

THAT'LL BE ENOUGH, MR. CAGE. MY CLIENT DID NOT COME ALL THIS WAY TO BE INSULTED.!

WE ARE IN THE PROCESS OF FILING CRIMINAL CHARGES AGAINST YOU!

FOR WHAT? HAVING A CONSCIENCE!

ASSAULT AND BATTERY, MR. CAGE.!!

SSSAAT'S RIIGHH!

YOU SOUND BETTER THIS WAY, GRUNDGE!

THIS ISN'T EXACTLY THE TAJ MAHAL I'M LIVIN' IN, HERE.

NOW LOOK, PERRY MASON.... WHAT'S HE GONNA GET BY TAKIN' ME INTO COURT?

MY NAME IS MOSS. GRASSY MOSS. NOT PERRY MASON. AND YOUR SURROUNDINGS DON'T MEAN THAT ADONIS CHEMICAL OR MR. GRUNDGE ARE LETTING YOU GET AWAY WITH ASSAULT.

MAYBE HE FORGOT TO TELL YOU, HE GOT HOT AND BOTHERED 'BOUT SOME THINGS I SAID.... AND HE... ATTACKED ME!

UUU...FILSSSY ...SONSA

KEEP COOL, GRUNDGE...YOU'RE SOUNDING MORE DELIRIOUS THAN EVER.

NORMALLY, MR. MOSS, THEY CALL WHAT I DID TO MR. GRUNDGE--

-- I MEAN IN THE TRADE, YOU KNOW--

THEY CALL WHAT I DID, SELF-DEFENSE. YOU MIGHT'VE HEARD OF THE WORD.

NOW IF YOU... "GENTLEMEN"... ARE FINISHED... I'VE GOT SOME COFFEE TO BREW... TO TAKE AN UNPLEASANT TASTE OUTTA MY MOUTH.

WE ARE NOT FINISHED, MR. CAGE. MR. GRUNDGE ALSO WANTS ME TO INFORM YOU OFFICIALLY, THAT YOU ARE NO LONGER HIRED BY ADONIS CHEMICAL.

YEAH, AN' THAT I'M OFF THE CASE. UNOFFICIALLY, YOU CAN TELL MR. GRUNDGE WHAT HE CAN DO WITH HIS OFFICIAL STATEMENT.

AND I HOPE HE FINDS IT UNPLEASANT.

SSSAT'S NUFF SISSEEPECTT!

NOW, NOW, MR. GRUNDGE. WE DON'T WANT YOU HURTING YOURSELF AGAIN. YOU DO SEEM TO HAVE TO HAVE A HABIT OF DOING THAT.

SSETT ME SOO! SILL' U!!

NOW LOOK HOW CARELESS YOU ARE, FALLING DOWN ON THE FLOOR THAT WAY.

HE REALLY IS CLUMSY, MR. MOSS. ADONIS CHEMICAL OUGHTTA GIVE HIM A PHYSICAL... CATCH THESE ILLNESSES EARLY AN' YOU CAN NIP 'EM IN THE BUD.

IN REAL LIFE YOU CAN'T GET AWAY WITH SUCH SIMPLISTIC SOLUTIONS, MR. CAGE. IN FACT, YOUR KIND IS A DANGER TO SOCIETY... A PRIME EXAMPLE OF THE FASCIST MENTALITY.

TAKING THE LAW INTO YOUR OWN HANDS... PERCEIVING JUSTICE AND REAL LIFE IN YOUR OWN WARPED IMAGINATION.

YOU GONNA SAY WORDS LIKE THAT TO ME, MOSS, IN MY OWN PLACE, THEN YOU BETTER TAKE OFF THOSE ONE WAY GLASSES.

I WANT TO SEE THE EYES OF A MAN WHO CAN DEFEND THE VERY THINGS THAT'RE KILLIN' US... THOUGH I DOUBT THERE'S MUCH TA SEE!

IF GUYS LIKE GRUNDGE AND YOU KEEP GOING THE WAY YOU ARE...

...THERE MIGHT NOT BE MUCH "REAL" LIFE LEFT!

SNAP!

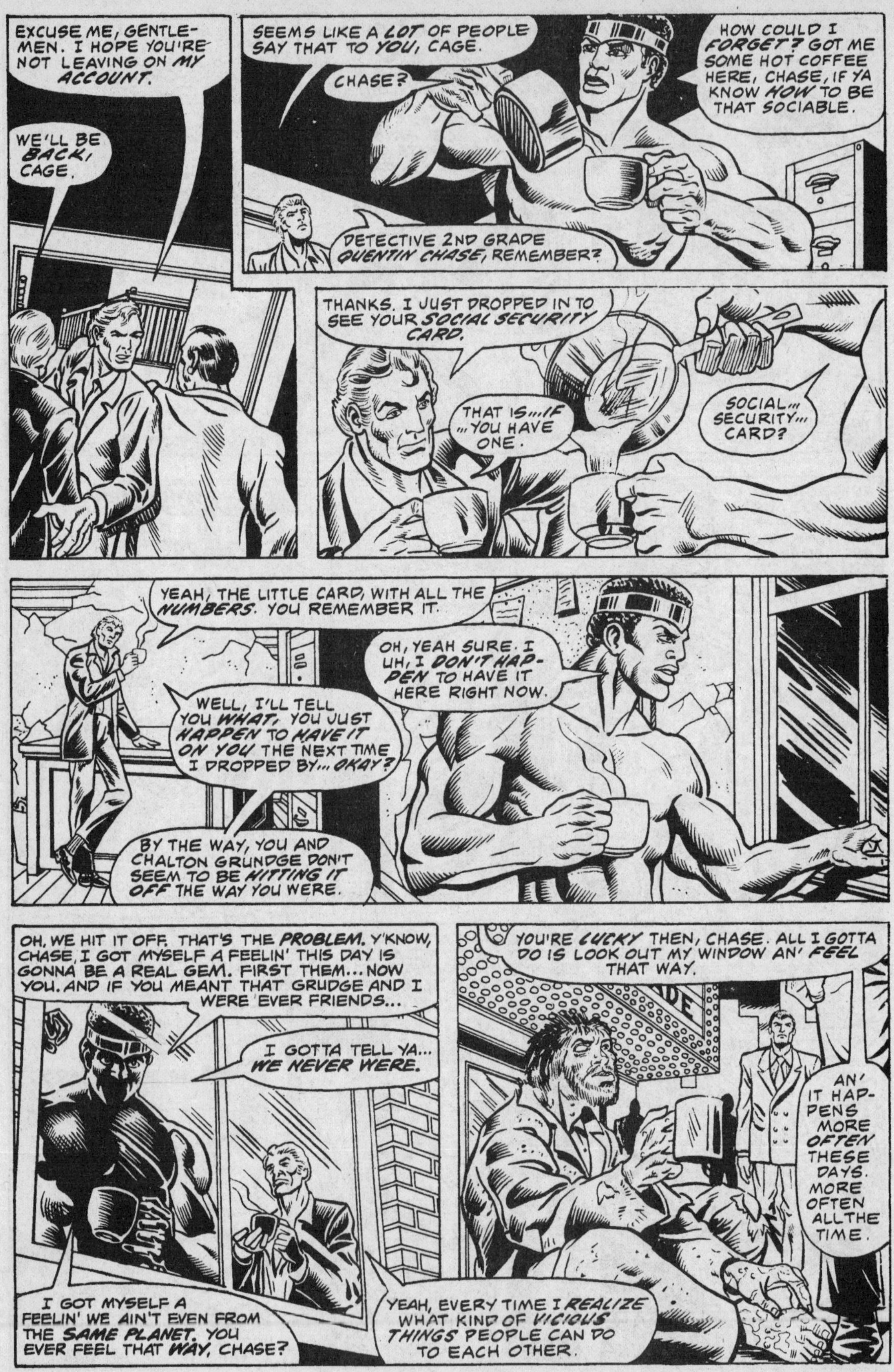

EXCUSE ME, GENTLEMEN. I HOPE YOU'RE NOT LEAVING ON MY ACCOUNT.
WE'LL BE BACK, CAGE.
SEEMS LIKE A LOT OF PEOPLE SAY THAT TO YOU, CAGE.
CHASE?
DETECTIVE 2ND GRADE QUENTIN CHASE, REMEMBER?
HOW COULD I FORGET? GOT ME SOME HOT COFFEE HERE, CHASE, IF YA KNOW HOW TO BE THAT SOCIABLE.
THANKS. I JUST DROPPED IN TO SEE YOUR SOCIAL SECURITY CARD.
THAT IS...IF ...YOU HAVE ONE.
SOCIAL... SECURITY... CARD?
YEAH, THE LITTLE CARD, WITH ALL THE NUMBERS. YOU REMEMBER IT.
OH, YEAH SURE. I UH, I DON'T HAPPEN TO HAVE IT HERE RIGHT NOW.
WELL, I'LL TELL YOU WHAT. YOU JUST HAPPEN TO HAVE IT ON YOU THE NEXT TIME I DROPPED BY... OKAY?
BY THE WAY, YOU AND CHALTON GRUNDGE DON'T SEEM TO BE HITTING IT OFF THE WAY YOU WERE.
OH, WE HIT IT OFF. THAT'S THE PROBLEM. Y'KNOW, CHASE, I GOT MYSELF A FEELIN' THIS DAY IS GONNA BE A REAL GEM. FIRST THEM... NOW YOU. AND IF YOU MEANT THAT GRUDGE AND I WERE EVER FRIENDS...
I GOTTA TELL YA... WE NEVER WERE.
I GOT MYSELF A FEELIN' WE AIN'T EVEN FROM THE SAME PLANET. YOU EVER FEEL THAT WAY, CHASE?
YOU'RE LUCKY THEN, CHASE. ALL I GOTTA DO IS LOOK OUT MY WINDOW AN' FEEL THAT WAY.
AN' IT HAPPENS MORE OFTEN THESE DAYS. MORE OFTEN ALL THE TIME.
YEAH, EVERY TIME I REALIZE WHAT KIND OF VICIOUS THINGS PEOPLE CAN DO TO EACH OTHER.

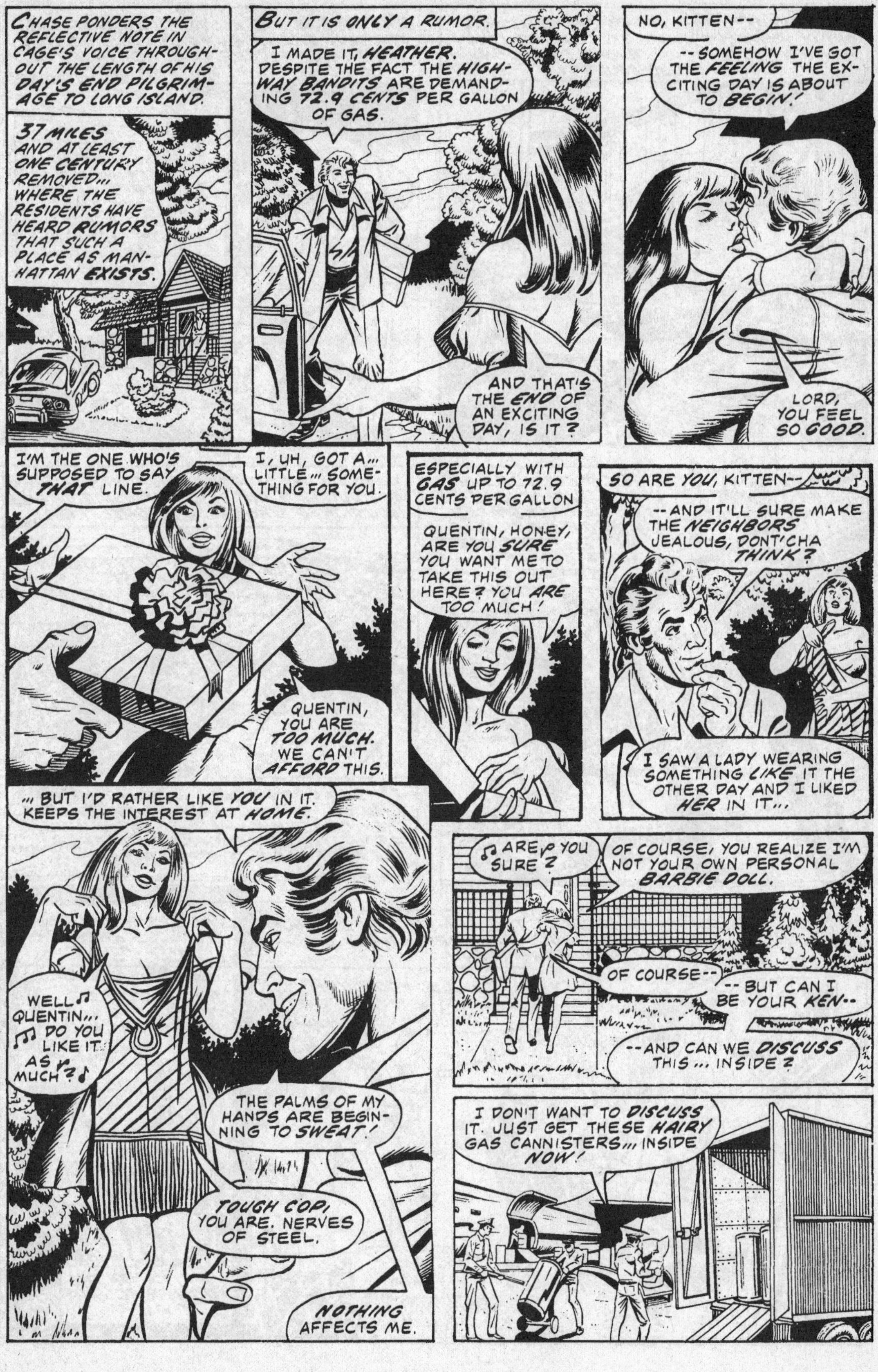
CHASE PONDERS THE REFLECTIVE NOTE IN CAGE'S VOICE THROUGHOUT THE LENGTH OF HIS DAY'S END PILGRIMAGE TO LONG ISLAND.
37 MILES AND AT LEAST ONE CENTURY REMOVED... WHERE THE RESIDENTS HAVE HEARD RUMORS THAT SUCH A PLACE AS MANHATTAN EXISTS.
BUT IT IS ONLY A RUMOR.
I MADE IT, HEATHER. DESPITE THE FACT THE HIGHWAY BANDITS ARE DEMANDING 72.9 CENTS PER GALLON OF GAS.
AND THAT'S THE END OF AN EXCITING DAY, IS IT?
NO, KITTEN--
--SOMEHOW I'VE GOT THE FEELING THE EXCITING DAY IS ABOUT TO BEGIN!
LORD, YOU FEEL SO GOOD.
I'M THE ONE WHO'S SUPPOSED TO SAY THAT LINE.
I, UH, GOT A... LITTLE... SOMETHING FOR YOU.
QUENTIN, YOU ARE TOO MUCH. WE CAN'T AFFORD THIS.
ESPECIALLY WITH GAS UP TO 72.9 CENTS PER GALLON
QUENTIN, HONEY, ARE YOU SURE YOU WANT ME TO TAKE THIS OUT HERE? YOU ARE TOO MUCH!
SO ARE YOU, KITTEN--
--AND IT'LL SURE MAKE THE NEIGHBORS JEALOUS, DONT'CHA THINK?
I SAW A LADY WEARING SOMETHING LIKE IT THE OTHER DAY AND I LIKED HER IN IT...
...BUT I'D RATHER LIKE YOU IN IT. KEEPS THE INTEREST AT HOME.
WELL♫ QUENTIN... ♫ DO YOU LIKE IT AS MUCH?♪
THE PALMS OF MY HANDS ARE BEGINNING TO SWEAT!
TOUGH COP, YOU ARE. NERVES OF STEEL.
NOTHING AFFECTS ME.
♫ARE YOU SURE?
OF COURSE, YOU REALIZE I'M NOT YOUR OWN PERSONAL BARBIE DOLL.
OF COURSE--
--BUT CAN I BE YOUR KEN--
--AND CAN WE DISCUSS THIS... INSIDE?
I DON'T WANT TO DISCUSS IT. JUST GET THESE HAIRY GAS CANNISTERS... INSIDE NOW!

THE CONVOYS FROM ADONIS CHEMICAL PULL OUT OF KENNEDY AIRPORT, LOOKING LIKE ANY OTHER CONVOY OF TRUCKS DELIVERING GOODS CROSS-COUNTRY!

THE DRIVERS ARE ALL FAMILIAR WITH THE TERRAIN. THE TRIBOROUGH BRIDGE HAS LOST ITS GRANDEUR FOR THEM, AND THEY SCARCELY CONSIDER THEIR CARGO.

THE TRANSPORTATION OF THESE DEADLY CHEMICALS IS LESS IMPORTANT THAN THE EFFECT THE JOUNCING CAB IS HAVING ON THEIR KIDNEYS.

MANHATTAN... THE WEST SIDE.

THE SECTION OF THE CITY THAT OFFERS ITS OWN NEWSPAPER, WISDOM'S CHILD, AS A GUIDE TO THE WEST SIDE'S CULTURAL STATUS--

-- AND A HOST OF PSYCHIATRISTS AT $25.00 AN HOUR FOR THE CHIC POPULACE OR DIS-ILLUSIONED WHO CAN AFFORD THEM.

UNTANGLE MY PAST, PLEASE, AND TELL ME WHO I AM!

IT IS UNDER DEBATE WHETHER OR NOT THEY CAN UNTANGLE IDENTITIES ... BUT THEY CERTAINLY CAN'T DO ANYTHING ABOUT THE NETS WHICH DROP FROM THE ROOFTOPS OF BROADWAY.

AND THE COMMANDO TACTICS OF THE ARMED FORCES WHICH FOLLOW THE DESCENT OF THE WIRE MESH ARE HARDLY CANDIDATES FOR GROUP THERAPY!

JACKSON, YOU LEAD YOUR UNIT TO THE TRUCKS AT THE END OF THE CONVOY!

YOU GOT IT, MY MAN.

THE RUSH HOUR TRAFFIC GOES BERSERK WITH SOUND.

AND INSIDE THE TRUCKS, THE GAS CANNISTERS WAIT--

--WAIT WITH THE POWER TO END IT ALL!

 ONE OF THE CANNISTERS, SNAPPED FROM ITS SECURING LINES--

--FALLS--

 --BOUNCES ONTO THE MACADAM--

 --AND COLLIDES WITH A STAINED FIRE HYDRANT.

 THE EVENT GOES UNNOTICED FROM THE ROOFTOPS.

PIRANHA, YOU PULL OFF A DEAL LIKE THIS, IT'S GONNA BLOW THE MAN'S MIND TILL IT'S BENT ALL OUTTA SHAPE!

NOT ONLY THAT, BUT IT'S GONNA BUY "JOSH" AN' ME A WHOOOLE LOTTA CHEESE SNIPS!

YOU EAT SUCH GARBAGE, ROACH. HAVN'T YOU THE FAINTEST IDEA HOW BAD THAT STUFF IS FOR YOUR SYSTEM?

 IT'S ALL PRESERVATIVES... CHEMICALS.

LIKE THAT JUNK DOWN THERE, HUH?

OH, NO. THOSE PRESERVATIVES ARE MUCH... SLOWER. YOU DID INSTRUCT THE MEN TO BE CAREFUL WHILE LOADING THOSE CANNISTERS ONTO OUR WAITING VEHICLES? THAT CHEMICAL MIXTURE IS EXTREMELY VOLATILE!

 THAT'S AS GOOD AN ENTRANCE CUE AS ANY!

HEADS UP, BROTHERS AND SISTERS--

--AN' YOU TWO MAKE AS UGLY A PAIR OF BOBSEY TWINS THAT'S EVER MADE ANY SCENE.

 THE WEST SIDE CLOTHING SHOPS AND TRINKET PALACES RUSH UP AT CAGE--

B-KOW!

--UNTIL HE HITS THE WIRE NETTING AND USES IT AS A TRAMPOLINE TO SMASH HIMSELF RIGHT INTO THE CENTER OF THE COMMANDO UNITS...

WHAT'S UP, DOC?

BETTER TAKE CARE OF THAT NOSE THERE. THAT'S ONE NASTY NOSEBLEED YOU GOT YOURSELF, FRIEND!

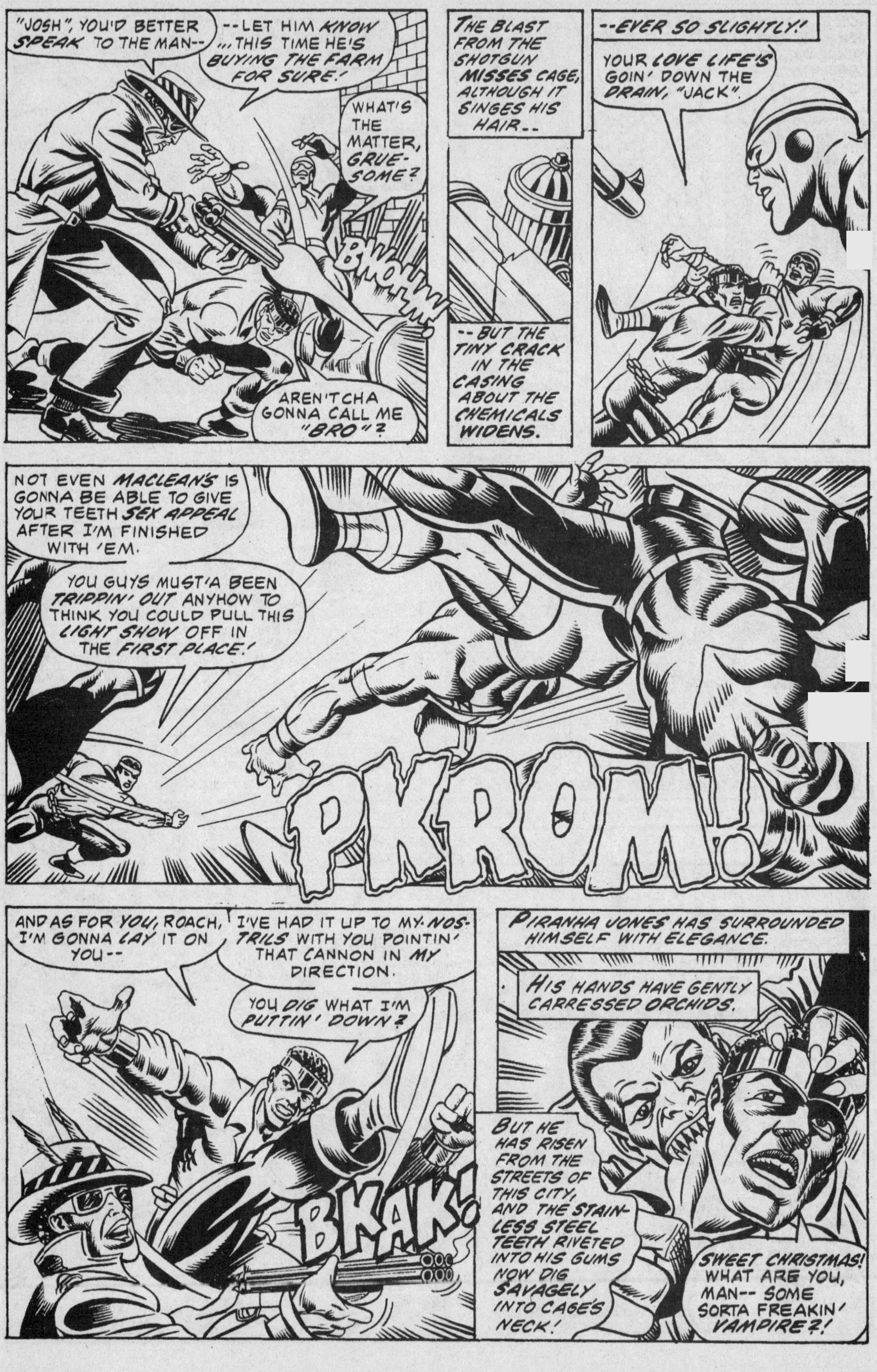
"JOSH", YOU'D BETTER SPEAK TO THE MAN--
--LET HIM KNOW ...THIS TIME HE'S BUYING THE FARM FOR SURE!
WHAT'S THE MATTER, GRUE-SOME?
BWOWW
AREN'TCHA GONNA CALL ME "BRO"?
THE BLAST FROM THE SHOTGUN MISSES CAGE, ALTHOUGH IT SINGES HIS HAIR--
--BUT THE TINY CRACK IN THE CASING ABOUT THE CHEMICALS WIDENS.
--EVER SO SLIGHTLY!
YOUR LOVE LIFE'S GOIN' DOWN THE DRAIN, "JACK".
NOT EVEN MACLEAN'S IS GONNA BE ABLE TO GIVE YOUR TEETH SEX APPEAL AFTER I'M FINISHED WITH 'EM.
YOU GUYS MUST'A BEEN TRIPPIN' OUT ANYHOW TO THINK YOU COULD PULL THIS LIGHT SHOW OFF IN THE FIRST PLACE!
PKROM!
AND AS FOR YOU, ROACH, I'M GONNA LAY IT ON YOU--
I'VE HAD IT UP TO MY NOS-TRILS WITH YOU POINTIN' THAT CANNON IN MY DIRECTION.
YOU DIG WHAT I'M PUTTIN' DOWN?
BKAK!
PIRANHA JONES HAS SURROUNDED HIMSELF WITH ELEGANCE.
HIS HANDS HAVE GENTLY CARRESSED ORCHIDS.
BUT HE HAS RISEN FROM THE STREETS OF THIS CITY, AND THE STAIN-LESS STEEL TEETH RIVETED INTO HIS GUMS NOW DIG SAVAGELY INTO CAGE'S NECK!
SWEET CHRISTMAS! WHAT ARE YOU, MAN-- SOME SORTA FREAKIN' VAMPIRE?!

DON'T MATTER *WHAT* YOU ARE, MISTER--IT WILL TAKE *STRONGER* TEETH THAN YOURS TO PUNCH THRU *LUKE CAGE'S* SKIN!

CAGE HURLS THIS NEW AT-TACKER FROM HIM!

HE IS REPULSED!

LUKE CAGE HAS SEEN AND HEARD AND FELT A LOT OF THINGS, BUT NEVER A MAN *SAVAGING* HIS NECK LIKE SOME *BLOOD CRAZED BEAST!*

SILENTLY BUT FEARFULLY, HIS MIND ASKS WHAT SORT OF A HUMAN BEING HE CAN BE FIGHTING!?

I GOT ME A FEELING YOU'RE THE *JOKER* IN THE DECK!

YOU ARE *WRONG,* CAGE. WITHOUT *ME,* THE DECK DOESN'T *EXIST!*

THEN I'M *SCATTERIN'* YOUR CARDS TO THE *WINDS,* MISTER!

WE'LL LET SOMEBODY PICK UP YOUR *PIECES* LATER!

JACKSON, THE ADONIS CHEM-ICAL SECURITY GUARDS NEED *NEUTRALIZING!*

DON'T WORRY... THEY ARE AS GOOD AS *WASTED!*

IT'S YOUR PIECES THEY'LL BE PICKING UP, CAGE.

AND YOU HAVE *DISRUPTED* OUR TIME SCHEDULE. THE POLICE ARE ALREADY *APPROACHING--*

--AND OUR *EXIT* MUST BE *EXECUTED* BEFORE THEY ARRIVE.

PIRANHA'S GREY TEETH CUT JAGGEDLY DOWN THE LENGTH OF CAGE'S ARM--

--AND CAGE PAINFULLY JERKS IT BACK INTO THE CANNIS-TER OVER WHICH ALL THE DAYS MAYHEM HAS BEEN COMMITTED!

PIRANHA RETALIATES, AND THE FORCE OF HIS ATTACK SURPRISES CAGE.

THEY CRASH INTO THE CANNISTER... AND THE TINY CRACK IS SUDDENLY NOT QUITE SO TINY!

FRAK!

PIRANHA'S HEAD DESCENDS, AND THE STEEL TEETH FINDS CAGE'S JUGULAR!

CAGE SEES THE SKINNY BLACK KID, A BREATHING SKELETON MAINLINING SKAG INTO WHAT IS LEFT OF HIS BODY...THE KID WHO CLUED HIM INTO THE "WEIRD NUMBER HAPPENIN' ON THE WEST SIDE."

AND CAGE WISHES THAT HIS TEN SPOT HAD ALSO BOUGHT THE NAME OF THE MAN WHO HAS COME CLOSE TO ENDING HIS LIFE.

AND HE ALSO WISHES HE COULD FORGET THE BREATHING SKELETON'S DEAD EYES.

AND THEN HE DOES FORGET!

AND PIRANHA AND COCKROACH HAMILTON HALT THEIR ATTACK!

SHEE--OOT! HEY, MAN, IF THAT GAS IS AS BAD AS YOU SAID IT WAS ...

IT IS, ROACH!

IT IS!!

AND THAT MEANS YOU AND ADONIS CHEMICAL HAVEN'T ONLY KILLED US...

...BUT THE CITY OF NEW YORK AS WELL!

NEXT: THE EPIC CONCLUSION OF OUR PIRANHA JONES AND COCKROACH HAMILTON TRILOGY... AND PERHAPS OF LUKE CAGE AND NEW YORK AS WELL!

OVER THE YEARS, THEY MURDERED THE STARS!

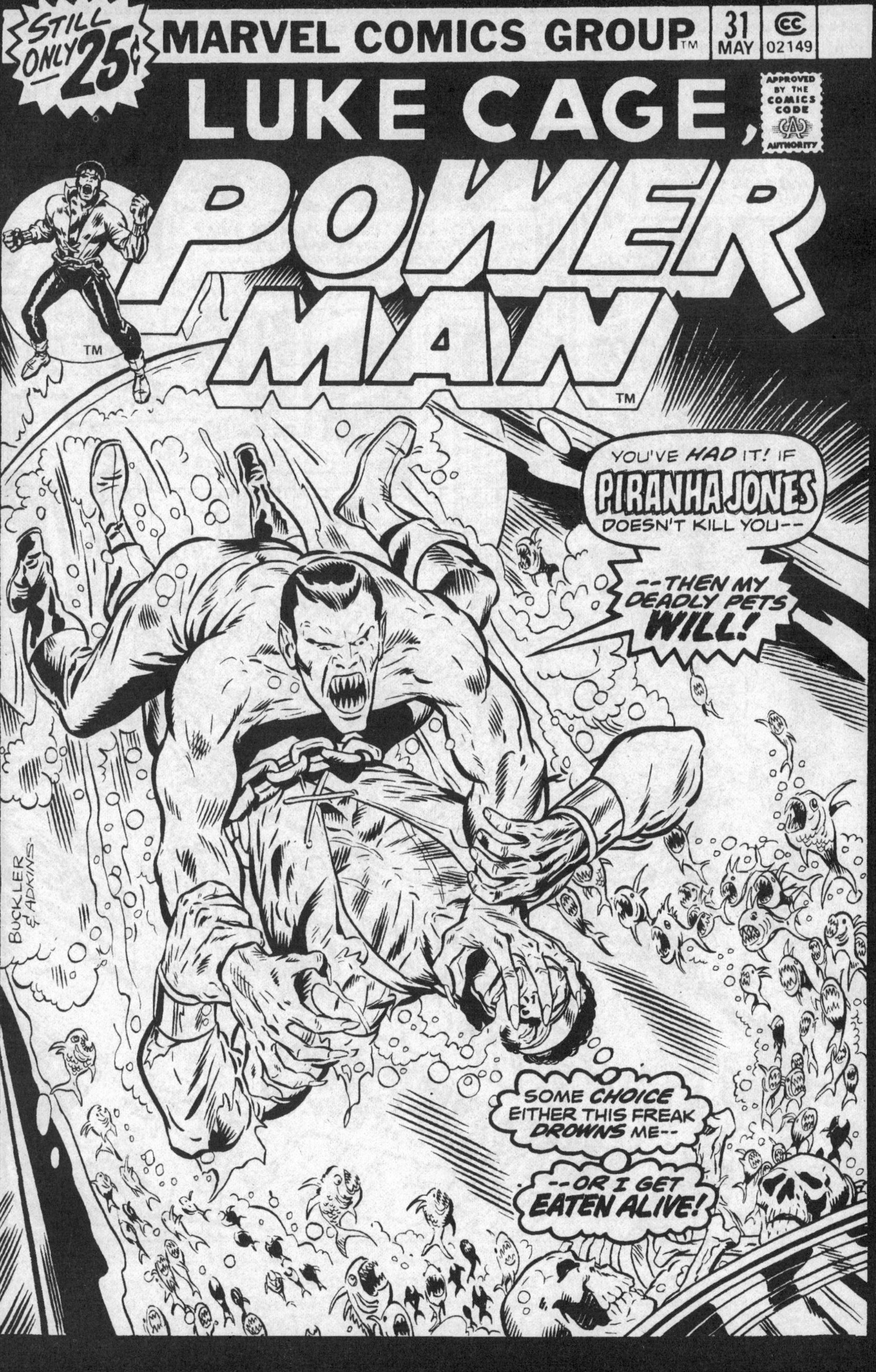
STILL ONLY 25¢
MARVEL COMICS GROUP
31 MAY
CC 02149
APPROVED BY THE COMICS CODE AUTHORITY
LUKE CAGE, POWER MAN
YOU'VE HAD IT! IF PIRANHA JONES DOESN'T KILL YOU--
--THEN MY DEADLY PETS WILL!
SOME CHOICE EITHER THIS FREAK DROWNS ME--
--OR I GET EATEN ALIVE!
BUCKLER & ADKINS

LUKE CAGE: Wrongly convicted and sentenced to prison—reborn in a freak experiment there that gave him ***steel-hard skin*** and ***strength beyond belief***—a man who hides his identity as an escaped convict in the role of a ***HERO FOR HIRE!***

Stan Lee PRESENTS: LUKE CAGE, POWER MAN!™

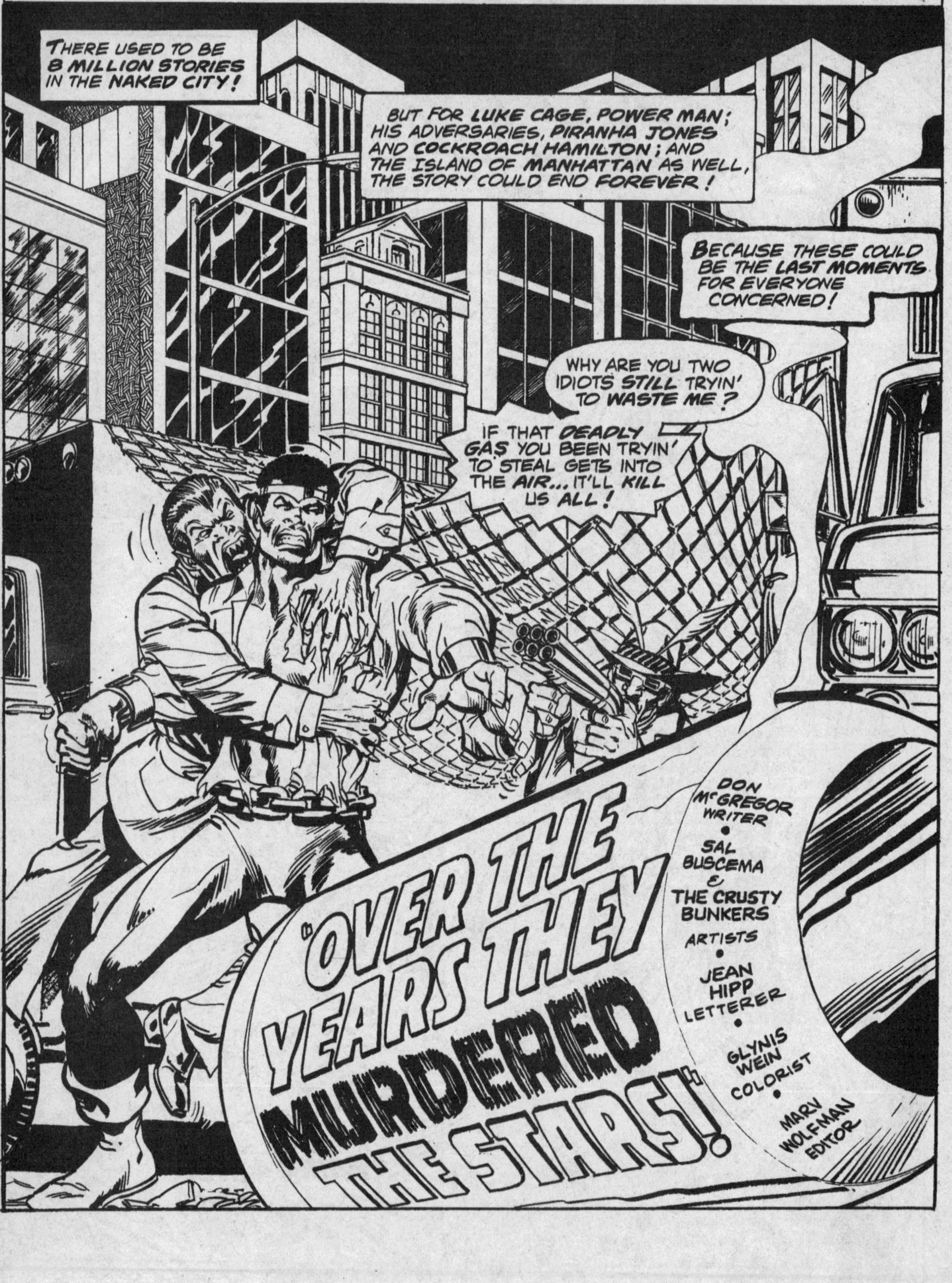
THERE USED TO BE 8 MILLION STORIES IN THE NAKED CITY!
BUT FOR LUKE CAGE, POWER MAN; HIS ADVERSARIES, PIRANHA JONES AND COCKROACH HAMILTON; AND THE ISLAND OF MANHATTAN AS WELL, THE STORY COULD END FOREVER!
BECAUSE THESE COULD BE THE LAST MOMENTS FOR EVERYONE CONCERNED!
WHY ARE YOU TWO IDIOTS STILL TRYIN' TO WASTE ME?
IF THAT DEADLY GAS YOU BEEN TRYIN' TO STEAL GETS INTO THE AIR... IT'LL KILL US ALL!
"OVER THE YEARS THEY MURDERED THE STARS!"
DON McGREGOR WRITER
SAL BUSCEMA & THE CRUSTY BUNKERS ARTISTS
JEAN HIPP LETTERER
GLYNIS WEIN COLORIST
MARV WOLFMAN EDITOR

YOU'RE *SLOW* ON THE UPTAKE, PIRANHA!

DON'T YOU *GET IT,* YET?

WHOM

BROK!

YOU MIGHT BE A *MASTERMIND* WITH *ELITIST COMMANDOES*--

--AND YOU MIGHT HAVE *STEEL TEETH* THE BIG BAD WOLF WOULD BE *PROUD* TO CLAIM--

--BUT YOUR *HEIST* HAS GONE DOWN THE *TUBES!*

WE'RE *ALL* LOSERS... INCLUDING *ADONIS CHEMICAL* AND ITS *WHEELS* WHO SCREWED UP IN THE FIRST PLACE WHEN THEY HATCHED THEIR *"BRILLIANT"* PLAN TO SHIP THESE GAS CAN-NISTERS DOWN THE *WEST SIDE!*

MAYBE SO, CAGE--

--BUT ME AND *"JOSH"* HERE, WE GOT SOME LAST MINUTE *"WORDS"* WITH YOU.

AND *"JOSH"* HAS GOT A *VOICE* THAT'S GOTTA BE *HEARD!*

VOOOM!

CAGE SLAMS HIS FIST UP-WARDS AS THE FIRST BARREL OF *SIX* ERUPTS. THE BLAST SEARS THE SIDE OF HIS FACE.

IT ALSO *BLINDS* CAGE--

--BUT HE STILL *STRIKES OUT,* HIS FIST FINDING *FLESH!*

DEATH DRIFTS ON THE AIR, ALMOST *LAZILY.* A PRETTY PINK RIBBON SPIRALING UPWARD--

--AND BEGINNING TO *SPREAD!*

COME ON, LUCAS, THIS AIN'T NO PENNY-ANTE GAME OF *STICKBALL*! MAKE SOME *TIME*!

A TRACE OF *BLEACHED SUNSET* PEEKS THROUGH THE APARTMENT BUILDINGS LINING THE *JERSEY PALISADES*, A CURIOUS SPECTATOR THAT HAS JUST BEGUN TO PIERCE THE *HAZE* AND WITNESS THE ARRIVAL OF NEW PARTICIPANTS TO THE *MADNESS*.

*O*NE OF PIRANHA'S COMMANDOES LIFTS A *WEAPON*...AND IT IS SLIGHTLY MORE SOPHISTICATED THAN A *SATURDAY NIGHT SPECIAL*.

ZZAM

--AND QUENTON CHASE HAS FACED A FEW OF THOSE HOME-MADE WEAPONS IN HIS TIME--

TRUE, A SATURDAY NIGHT SPECIAL CAN *KILL* A HUMAN BEING IF THE VICTIM IS *CLOSE ENOUGH*--

AN' YOU BETTER COME UP WITH SOMETHIN' *DYNAMITE*, REAL QUICK--

--BUT *THIS* ARMAMENT *TWISTS* METAL AS EASILY AS IT *SHATTERS* GLASS! THE TAX-PAYERS WON'T CARE MUCH FOR THE IDEA, EITHER!

*C*HASE STEADIES HIS AIM AND FIRES HIS .357 MAGNUM..

BDAM!

*H*E KNOWS WHAT THIS GUN CAN DO TO A MAN, AND IT IS NOT *PLEASANT* KNOWLEDGE.

*C*HASE IS DUE FOR A *SHOCK*, BECAUSE THIS TIME, THE BULLET HAS *LITTLE EFFECT*...AND HIS ATTACKER IS LEFT *UNHARMED* AND READY TO RENEW HIS ATTACK!

--OR IT'S *ALL* SHE WROTE!

THIS CANNISTER, DWARFED BY HIS HUGE HANDS, CAN'T REALLY BE *THAT* DEADLY, CAN IT? HE DOESN'T HAVE AN ANSWER... BUT HE *HOLDS* HIS BREATH. MAYBE HIS LUNGS COULD *SURVIVE* THAT INSIDIOUS PINK RIBBON... AND THEN AGAIN, MAYBE THEY *CAN'T!*

THE GAS SEEPS ENTICINGLY THROUGH HIS FINGERS AS CAGE THINKS TO HIMSELF: "LOOK, YOU TURKEY-- DID YOU REALLY THINK YOU COULD PLUG THE LEAK THAT EASILY AND MAKE LIKE THAT PUNK IN THE *STORY BOOKS* STICKING HIS FINGER IN THE DIKE, WHO HELD BACK THE FLOOD?"

"AND HOW *LONG* DO YOU THINK YOU COULD HOLD THE GAS *BACK?* UNTIL QUENTIN CHASE AND HIS COHORTS MANAGE TO MAKE THE *SCENE?*

"AND WHAT THEN? WHAT COULD THEY DO?"

CAGE RAISES A *FIST.*

HE HAMMERS AT THE CANNISTER... AND *HOPES* TO HELL THIS ACTION WILL *WORK!*

PIRANHA JONE'S *VOICE* IS IN HIS EARS. IT IS SPEAKING TO COCK-ROACH HAMILTON AND THE VOICE *REPEATS* THE SAME WORDS OVER AND OVER AGAIN... LIKE AN *ECHO* THAT REFUSES TO *DIE!*

BOM!

"THAT CHEMICAL MIXTURE IS *EXTREMELY VOLATILE.*"

BOM!

"...EXTREMELY VOLATILE."

"...EXTREMELY VOLATILE."

"...EXTREMELY VOLATILE."

BOM!

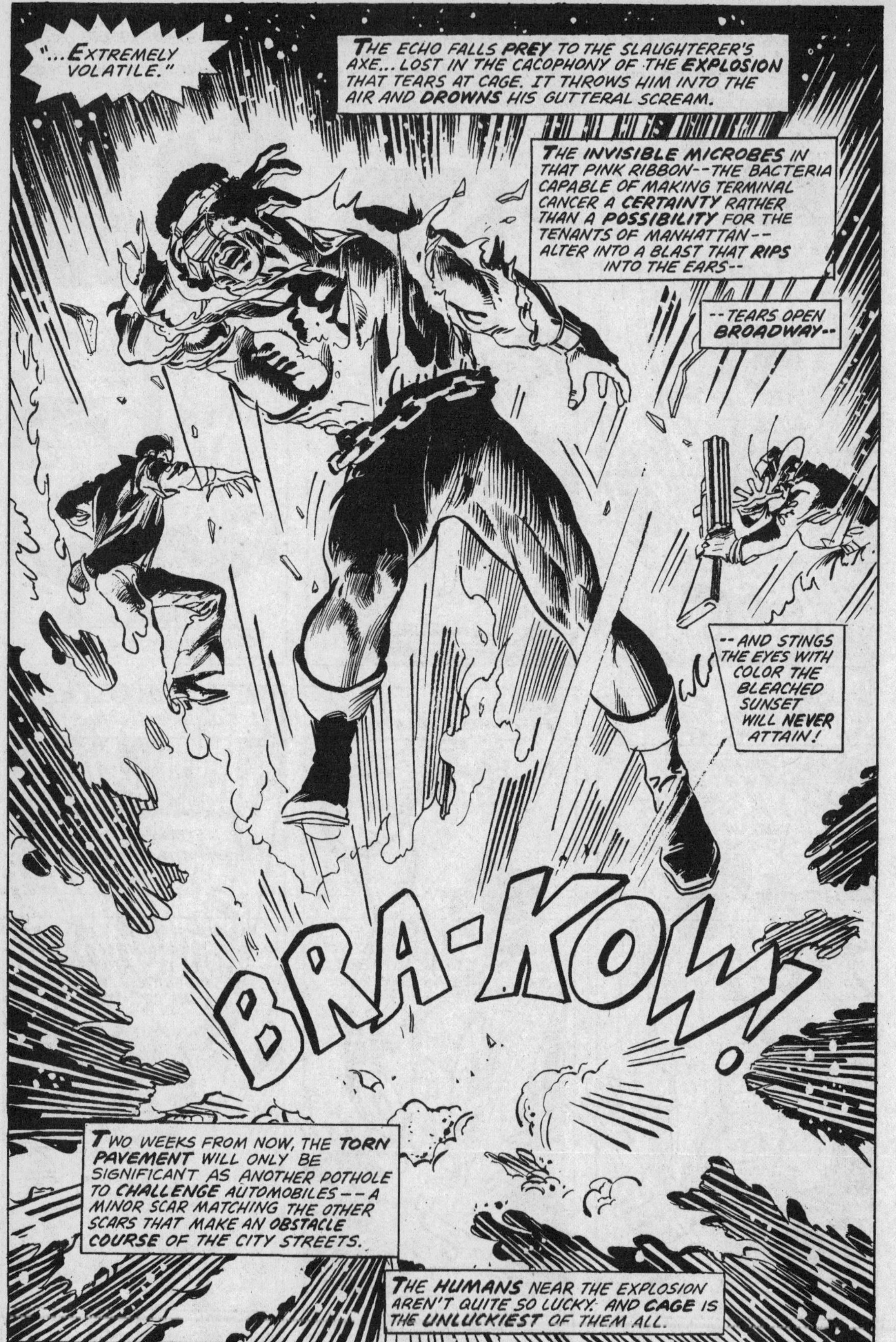
"...EXTREMELY VOLATILE."
THE ECHO FALLS PREY TO THE SLAUGHTERER'S AXE... LOST IN THE CACOPHONY OF THE EXPLOSION THAT TEARS AT CAGE. IT THROWS HIM INTO THE AIR AND DROWNS HIS GUTTERAL SCREAM.
THE INVISIBLE MICROBES IN THAT PINK RIBBON--THE BACTERIA CAPABLE OF MAKING TERMINAL CANCER A CERTAINTY RATHER THAN A POSSIBILITY FOR THE TENANTS OF MANHATTAN--ALTER INTO A BLAST THAT RIPS INTO THE EARS--
--TEARS OPEN BROADWAY--
--AND STINGS THE EYES WITH COLOR THE BLEACHED SUNSET WILL NEVER ATTAIN!
BRA-KOW!
TWO WEEKS FROM NOW, THE TORN PAVEMENT WILL ONLY BE SIGNIFICANT AS ANOTHER POTHOLE TO CHALLENGE AUTOMOBILES--A MINOR SCAR MATCHING THE OTHER SCARS THAT MAKE AN OBSTACLE COURSE OF THE CITY STREETS.
THE HUMANS NEAR THE EXPLOSION AREN'T QUITE SO LUCKY. AND CAGE IS THE UNLUCKIEST OF THEM ALL.

VERY *INTUITIVE*, MR. CAGE. YOU *ALTERED* THE COMPOSITION OF THOSE *UNSTABLE* ELEMENTS--

--AND THEREBY *SAVED* US ALL. HOWEVER, I FIND IT *FASCINATING* THAT *YOU*...ARE STILL MOVING.

YEAH... PIRANHA, *HE'S* IMPRESSED--

--BUT ME AND "*JOSH*", WE BEEN AROUND A BIT *MORE'N* HIM--

--AND WE AIN'T NOWHERE *NEAR* AS IMPRESSED.

YOU GET THE *MESSAGE*, MR. STREET-TOUGH BLACK?

WHUUDDKK!

ROACH, I'M *GONNA*--

SPLUCT!

YOU'RE GONNA *WHAT?*

HEY, "*JOSH*", HOW *ABOUT* THAT? STREET-TOUGH BLACK'S STILL *GAME.*

NOW, I CALLS THAT *CLASS*. *REAL* CLASS.

YOU *ENJOY* YOURSELF ROACH--

--'CAUSE IF I *GET MY HANDS* AROUND YOUR--

CRUSSK!

YOU AIN'T GETTIN' YOUR HANDS 'ROUND *NUTHIN'*! HOW ABOUT THAT "*JOSH*"-- I THINK HE'S *FINALLY* GOT THE MESSAGE.

THAT WAS AN *OVERLY* VIOLENT DISPLAY, ROACH.

WHA'CHU *TALKIN'* 'BOUT, PIRANHA? I SEEN WHAT YOU CAN DO WITH THEM THERE *STEEL TEETH* OF YOURS.

I OUGHTTA MUSH CAGE'S *BRAINS* FOR HIM.

EASY, ROACH. *EASY.* LET US NOT ACT SO *EMOTIONALLY.* WE MAY HAVE NEED OF A *HOSTAGE*, SINCE IT'S EVIDENT WE MUST *RETREAT.*

AND PERHAPS MR. CAGE CAN BE...*PERSUADED*...TO CHANGE ALLEGIANCES--AND IF HE *CAN'T* BE PERSUADED...WELL, MY *PETS* DESERVE A--

--*BANQUET.*

QUENTIN CHASE HUGS THE MACADAM, HOPING IT WILL ABSORB HIM.

STRANGELY ENOUGH, RALPH NADER'S NAME SURFACES IN HIS THOUGHTS: "HEY, NADER, LATCH ONTO THIS...THE DETROIT AUTOMOTIVE INDUSTRY SHOULD BLUSH WHEN THEY HEAR THAT THESE BULLETS TORE THROUGH THIS CAR DOOR AS IF IT WERE MADE OF TIN."

THE THOUGHT IS DROWNED-- SUBMERGED BY INSTINCTIVE MOVEMENT.

YOU FORCE ALL THOUGHT FROM THE MIND. THREE SECONDS OF CONTEMPLATION CAN COST YOU YOUR LIFE... AND YOU DON'T ALWAYS HAVE SUCH A FLAMBOYANT ATTACK AS A WARNING THAT YOUR LIFE IS IN DANGER.

THE SOUND OF IMPACT IS ABRUPT--

-- AND FINAL!

YOU SAD, SORRY SON...

AHHH, FORGET IT.

IT ALWAYS ENDS THIS WAY... AND IT NEVER MAKES ANY SENSE!

HE SHOULD BE USED TO IT BY NOW. DEATH SHOULD NOT CONTINUE TO WRACK HIM UP EACH TIME HE HAS TO VIEW IT.

THREE SECONDS OF CONTEMPLATION--

-- NEARLY THREE SECONDS TOO LONG!

CHASE ROLLS BEHIND HIS CAR AND RETURNS FIRE. IT HASN'T ENDED YET, BUT IT STILL DOESN'T MAKE ANY SENSE.

DON'T THEY REALIZE THAT IT'S OVER?

THREE FIGURES SEEK THE ALLEYWAYS, LABORING UNDER CAGE'S 300 LBS. THREE FIGURES WHO REALIZE THAT THIS ACT... HAS, INDEED, FINISHED, BUT THAT THE NIGHT WILL CONTINUE.

OKAY, MISTER, OUR MEN HAVE THE REST OF THOSE TRIGGER-HAPPY COMMANDOES UNDER *WRAPS.* THE *EXPLOSION* TOOK THE FIGHT OUT OF THEM.

NOW MAYBE YOU'LL TELL ME WHO *YOU* ARE. YOU'RE NOT FROM THIS *PRECINCT.*

THAT *COULD* HAVE BEEN A *VERY BAD MISTAKE* YOU JUST MADE THERE, *PATROL-MAN.*

WHAT'S THAT?

COMING UP BEHIND ME AND GRABBING AT ME WITHOUT *IDENTIFYING* YOURSELF.

YOUR MISTAKE... COULD HAVE MADE *ME* MAKE A BAD MISTAKE. THAT'S A LESSON YOU'D BETTER LEARN... *QUICK!*

I STILL WANT TO KNOW WHY YOU'RE *HERE.*

I'M *CHASE,* DETECTIVE-SECOND OUT OF *MANHATTAN-SOUTH.* CALL CAME IN DESCRIBING LUKE CAGE AS ONE OF THE PARTICIPANTS IN THIS *GRAND-STAND HEIST.*

AND LUKE CAGE *IS* MY CONCERN.

NO KIDDING, YOU AND HIM *BROTHERS* OR SOMETHING?

TWINS, THAT'S RIGHT. EXCEPT I WAS BORN FIVE MINUTES *EARLIER...* AND HE'S A LITTLE BIT *TALLER* THAN ME.

ONLY WAY YOU CAN TELL US *APART.*

THIS CAPER ALSO TIES IN WITH A *MURDER* THAT TOOK PLACE IN OUR *JURISDICTION.* ONE OF ADONIS CHEMICAL'S EMPLOYEES WAS BLOWN AWAY DOWN THERE.

WELL, THAT *CAGE* CHARACTER TORE LOOSE HERE. THE *DESK SERGEANT* WILL PROBABLY BE *SWAMPED* WITH CALLS FROM IRATE CITIZENS WITH *FRENCH POODLES* THAT'VE HAD *NERVOUS BREAKDOWNS.*

YOU BETTER HAVE YOUR MEN *STRIP* THOSE COMMANDOES OUT OF THEIR UNIFORMS. THOSE CHEST-PIECES ARE *BULLET-PROOF!*

WE'LL BE ALL RIGHT UP HERE *WITHOUT* YOUR HELP, CHASE.

BUT MAYBE NOT WITHOUT *CAGE'S* HELP. I'VE GOT A FEELING HE JUST *SAVED* OUR HASH.

ALL OF US!

AND I DON'T *SEE* HIM ANYWHERE AMONG THE GROUP YOUR GUYS HAVE *LINED UP.*

WHICH, *KNOWING* CAGE, COULD MEAN HE'S *DEAD MEAT!*

EARLY MORNING. THE **EAST SIDE** IS QUIETER THAN ITS UPTOWN NEIGHBOR, HARLEM. THE **2 A.M.** SOUNDS ARE MORE MUTED. THE DESPERATION IS MORE SUBTLE. THE LAUGHTER IS MORE ARTIFICIAL.

THE RENT IS PHENOMENALLY HIGHER-- THOUGH RESIDENTS CAN CLAIM THAT THEY LIVE IN THE SAME AREA **PAUL SIMON** ONCE DID, IF THAT'S THE KIND OF THING THAT TURNS THEM ON.

PIRANHA JONES' PENTHOUSE OFFERS A VIEW OF THE **CARL SHURZ PARK** AND THE **EAST RIVER.** SOMEWHERE ON THE RIVER'S EDGE, LOVERS SIT AND SEE ONLY **THEMSELVES** AND WISH THEY HAD SUCH A PENTHOUSE FOR THEIR **RENDEZVOUS.**

IT IS NOT QUITE SO ROMANTIC **INSIDE** THE PENTHOUSE.

WELCOME, MR. CAGE.

YOU **RECUPERATE** WITH STARTLING RAPIDITY.

I SEE YOU ADMIRE MY **ORCHIDS.** HERE, MR. CAGE, LET ME **GRACE** YOU WITH ONE OF THEM.

YES. YES. THAT'S QUITE SUITABLE. OFFERS THE **PERFECT** CONTRAST. A MAN WITHOUT A TASTE FOR BEAUTY **ADORNED** BY NATURE'S MOST **FRAGILE** DELICACY.

PIRANHA... GET YOUR HANDS... OFF ME

NOW, NOW, MR. CAGE. LET'S NOT BE SO **TEMPERAMENTAL.**

IT WAS ONLY **MY** INTERVENTION THAT KEPT YOU **ALIVE...** ALBEIT, A BIT BATTERED.

GIVE ME A MINUTE.... AND I'LL THANK YOU.

PROPERLY.

ROACH, HE'S ALMOST AS **COLORFUL** AS YOU ARE. AND HIS **RESOURCEFULNESS** IS SOMETHING TO PONDER.

OH, I RECALL, MR. CAGE, THAT WE HAVE NOT BEEN **FORMALLY** INTRODUCED. I AM... PIRANHA JONES.

ACTUALLY, MY MOTHER NEVER NAMED ME PIRANHA... BUT IT'S A NAME I LOOK ON WITH **AFFECTION.**

LOOK AT THIS CITY-- THAT IS, IF YOU CAN LIFT YOUR HEAD, MR. CAGE. ADMITTEDLY, IT IS **TERRIBLY** FILTHY... AND YET, ALSO **ELECTRIC!**

THE MOST EXCITING CITY IN THE WORLD... LOS ANGELES, MONTE CARLO,... THEY **DON'T** COMPARE.

TIMES SQUARE IS IN A STATE OF TRANSITION. THE CROWD THAT DRIFTS ALONG 42nd STREET DOES NOT SEE THE HORDE OF NIGHT-FIGURES WHO CLIMB LADDERS IN A SEEMINGLY ENDLESS ROW... AND, FROM A DISTANCE THESE FIGURES SEEM TO LACK NOT ONLY INDIVIDUALITY--

--BUT ALSO SUBSTANCE.

BUS STOP

THIS ARMY OF COLORLESS ELVES STRIPS THE MARQUEES. AND BY MORNING, THE NEW POSTERS AND BOLD LETTERS WILL APPEAR TO HAVE MIRACULOUSLY CHANGED THEMSELVES.

THE ADVERTISEMENTS WILL PROMISE THAT THIS WEEK'S PROGRAM IS MORE EXCITING, MORE PROVOCATIVE THAN LAST WEEK'S EXCITING PROVOCATIVE FEATURES--

--EVEN THOUGH MANY OF THE FILMS WILL HAVE MERELY MOVED DOWN TO THEIR NEIGHBORING THEATER.

I HATE TO INTERRUPT A MAN SO HARD AT WORK... BUT YOU'RE D.W., AREN'T YOU?

YOU'RE A FRIEND OF CAGE'S, RIGHT?

YEAH, LUKE AND I HAVE SPENT SOME TIME TOGETHER.

BUT I'M NOT SURE YOU'RE A FRIEND OF HIS.

ARE YOU?

THAT'S DEBATABLE. I'M WITH THE POLICE DEPARTMENT.

YOU DIDN'T HAVE TO TELL ME, IT WASN'T HARD TO FIGURE OUT.

D.W., THAT'S NOT NICE.

SORRY, WIN. I'M TRYING TO PROTECT MY IMAGE.

YEAH, AND WHAT KIND OF IMAGE IS THAT?

NEVER MIND, IT'S NOT IMPORTANT, AND THE QUESTION DOESN'T NEED AN ANSWER.

AND RIGHT NOW, JUST FOR YOUR INFORMATION, I'M NOT TRYING TO HASSLE CAGE. I'M TRYING TO OFFER HIM SOME PROTECTION.

AND NOT JUST FOR HIS IMAGE-- BUT HIS LIFE! BUT YOU KEEP ON PROTECTING YOUR IMAGE, D.W... HOPE IT COMES IN HANDY SOMEDAY.

THE MEAL IS A SUMPTUOUS *FARCE*... A DRAWING ROOM SCENE FROM AN ANTIQUATED BROADWAY PLAY. THE FIREPLACE IS MORE *REAL*, BURNING SOOTHINGLY IN THE *BACKGROUND*--

--BUT IT DOES NOT *DULL* THE FACT THAT ALL *SIX BARRELS* OF ROACH'S SHOTGUN ARE *AIMED* AT CAGE'S DIGESTIVE TRACT.

TO *CONTINUE* MY THESIS, MR. CAGE-- AND I HOPE I AM NOT *BORING YOU*-- I HAD ALMOST HOPED THE CITY *WOULD* DEFAULT.

THE FACT IS, I REALIZE, AND *YOU* SHOULD ALSO, THAT THE CITY WOULD NOT FACE *FINANCIAL DISASTER* IF ITS PUBLIC SERVANTS *CUT* THEIR GRAFT AND CORRUPTION, OH, BY 5%.

BUT THEN, WHO WANTS TO TAKE A *LOSS*? CERTAINLY, NOT I. IN THE CITY'S CASE, PERHAPS I COULD HAVE *TAKEN OVER* IF IT HAD DEFAULTED. WHAT A *STIMULATING* IDEA.

YEAH, TO *YOU* MAYBE.

LOOK, PIRANHA, YOU GOT SOME *REAL FOOD* A MAN CAN PUT IN HIS GUTS?

HOW'S ABOUT A BAG OF *CHEESE SNIPS*?

I HAVE THE *DISTINCT FEELING* YOUR BODY WOULD *REJECT* REAL FOOD, ROACH, IF YOU GAVE IT *HALF* THE OPPORTUNITY TO SAMPLE SOME.

BUT COME NOW, MR. CAGE. PLEASE *SPEAK* YOUR MIND. YOU'VE BEEN AWFULLY *SULLEN*.

YOU DON'T *WANTA* KNOW WHAT I'VE BEEN THINKING. TAKE MY *WORD* FOR IT.

AH, A *SUPERB DISPLAY* OF ANIMOSITY, MR. CAGE. I WON'T DELUDE MYSELF INTO THINKING YOU WILL *CHANGE* YOUR ATTITUDE AND CONSIDER JOINING US.

AND THAT, MR. CAGE... IS YOUR *DEATH SENTENCE*!

ROACH, SEEING AS YOU FIND THE MEAL SO *REPREHENSIBLE*, WOULD YOU MIND HITTING THE *SWITCH* FOR MY LITTLE... *AQUARIUM?*

I SEE YOU *ALREADY* GUESSED THE NEXT EXHIBITION, ROACH, AND PUT MY LITTLE DISPLAY INTO *MOTION*.

IT COST ME A *FORTUNE* TO INSTALL THIS *SLIDE-AWAY FLOOR*, MR. CAGE... BUT I THINK IT WAS *WORTH* THE PRICE, DON'T YOU?

IT'S GOT MORE *CLASS* THAN ITS *OWNER*... I'LL GIVE IT THAT.

PLEASE *JOIN* ME, MR. CAGE. I'D LIKE YOU TO *OBSERVE* MY PETS AT *CLOSE RANGE*.

WHY DON'T YOU JUMP IN WITH THE REST OF THE *CARNIVORES*...IT'D BE HARD TO TELL YOU *APART*.

HEY, NOW, MR. STREET-TOUGH BLACK. PIRANHA TOLD YOU TO *HUSTLE* YOUR HIDE OVER THERE, SO LET'S GET *WITH IT*--

--ELSE "JOSH" AN' ME ARE GONNA HAFTA DO SOME *SURGERY*. TAKE YOUR *TONSILS* OUT FOR YOU, NO SWEAT AT ALL.

THAT'S IT, MR. STREET-TOUGH BLACK. NOW DON'T *TWITCH*. WE WOULDN'T WANT THE TOP'A YOUR HEAD ALL OVER THE *CEILING*, WOULD WE, HUH?

ROACH, DON'T LET THAT *WEAPON* FOOL YOU, INTO THINKING YOU'RE A MAN. YOU'D BE *WRONG*.

QUENTIN CHASE **LISTENS** TO HIS DAUGHTER, AND HER VOICE IS FILLED WITH **WONDER.**

HE SHOULDN'T HAVE AWAKENED HER, BUT HERE IN THIS ROOM OF ROCKING HORSES AND SESAME STREET PUPPETS, THE **MEMORY** OF A MAN BLEEDING ONTO THE CITY STREETS **RECEDES.** HE KNOWS IT WILL **RETURN.** LIKE A PLAGUE.

YOU KNOW THEM **PENS** WHAT MOMMY GAVE YOU?

THE RED AND GREEN **ONES,** HONEY?

I CAN MAKE **COLORS** PRETTY AS YOURS. RIGHT, MOMMY?

SHE COLORS **INSIDE** THE LINES, QUENT. YOU SHOULD SEE.

I'LL LOOK AT THEM **TOMORROW,** BABY. SEE IF I **DON'T.**

YOU GET SOME **SLEEP** NOW.

G'NIGHT.

GOOD-NIGHT, WHAT?

GOOD-NIGHT, DADDY. GOOD-NIGHT, MOMMY.

I'M GLAD OUR LITTLE GIRL IS GOING TO GROW UP WITH PARENTS WHO **STILL** LAUGH AND TOUCH. I DON'T SEE MUCH OF IT **OUT THERE.**

YOU **ALWAYS** THINK YOU'RE SUCH A **ROMANTIC,** QUENTIN.

I THINK **YOU** ARE, TOO, CHRISTIE.

I GUESS...AT LEAST... **ONCE** UPON A TIME.

I THINK YOU **STILL** ARE.

PIRANHA STANDS DANGEROUSLY CLOSE TO THE POOL'S EDGE. HE GRINS, REVEALING STEEL TEETH OF SILVERED DEATH. THE PIRANHA FISH BELOW SEEM TO RETURN THE GRIN.

CAGE WATCHES... AND, AT THE SAME TIME, FLEXES HIS WRISTS. SINCE THIS DÉTENTE BEGAN, HE HAS BEEN REPEATING THE SAME MOTION.

AND HE HAS LOST COUNT OF HOW MANY TIMES HE HAS TRIED TO BREAK HIS CHAINS.

THIS TIME, THE EFFORT WORKS!

QUITE DRAMATICALLY!

BRASK!

ROACH, YOU CAN'T SCURRY AWAY FAST ENOUGH--

--TO STOP YOU AN' "JOSH" FROM HAVIN' A LOVER'S QUARREL.

THIS IS YOUR LAST CARESS.

THE END TABLE COST $395.00 PLUS 8% SALES TAX.

THE LAMP COST $125.50, THE LITTLE OLD 8% INCLUDED.

THEY TURN TO VERY EXPENSIVE FIREWOOD AND SHARDS OF BROKEN GLASS.

YOU BEEN SHOVIN' THIS THING IN MY FACE SINCE I FIRST MET UP WITH YOU, ROACH.

NOW I DON'T WANT TO GIVE YOU THE IMPRESSION THAT I'M FED UP TO HERE WITH YOU AN' YOUR GUN--

-- BUT LET ME SHOW YOU HOW I FEEL ABOUT IT.

SCRUNCH!

KROK!

AM I GETTIN' THROUGH TO YOU, ROACH?

PING!

CLINK!

STOP IT, YOU UGLY MOTHER!

YOU PUT "JOSH" DOWN, CAGE!

PIRANHA, YOU FIGGER YOU GOT ALL THE *ANGLES* COVERED. TAKE ADVANTAGE OF EVERYTHING AT EVERYBODY'S *EXPENSE.* MAN, *CHARLTON GRUNDGE* AND HIS *BOY-LAWYER, GRASSY MOSS,* CAN *BUST ME* FOR TAKIN' THEM ON, BUT *YOU'RE* GONNA HAVE TROUBLE SWEARIN' A *COMPLAINT.*

YOU ALSO GOT A *TOUCH* THAT'LL *WILT* ORCHIDS. YOU *READ ME?*

YOU'VE WREAKED ENOUGH *HAVOC* TONIGHT, CAGE. YOU'RE TRYING TO TAKE IT ALL *AWAY*--

-- BUT YOU HAVE *OVERPLAYED* YOUR HAND.

WHAT THE --?!

THERE IS AN *ODD* TRAIT ABOUT PIRANHA FISH. THEY DON'T *ALWAYS* BITE.

SPLASH!

A BATHER CAN BE IN THEIR MIDST FOR *HOURS* AND ESCAPE WITHOUT A *SCRATCH.*

THE PROBLEM *IS,* WHEN THEY *DO* BITE... THEY AREN'T JUST OUT FOR A *SNACK.*

A SCHOOL OF PIRANHA CAN *DEVOUR* A HUMAN BEING IN THE TIME IT TAKES TO RUN AN ANACIN COMMERCIAL. THE RESULT IS A RAVENOUS BLOOD-BATH THAT IS *BASIC* AND *PRIMITIVE* AND FILLED WITH EMOTION ONLY ON ITS HUMAN VICTIM'S *BEHALF.*

THE PIRANHA, FROM ALL APPEARANCES, ARE PURELY *OBJECTIVE* ABOUT IT.

I'LL *LET* 'EM TEAR YOUR ROTTEN HEART OUT, CAGE!

STAK!

VMMMMMMM

YOU AIN'T GETTIN' YOUR TAIL OUTTA *THIS ONE,* YOU--!!

PIRANHA JONES RAKES CAGE'S THROAT WITH HIS STEEL TEETH.

HE LOST HIS REAL TEETH WHEN HE WAS FIFTEEN. THEY TURNED TO DECAY AND THEN THEY PAIN-FULLY ROTTED AWAY.

PIRANHA WAS **DESTITUTE** AT THE TIME, AND HIS MOTHER HAD **DIED** IN A FACTORY ACCIDENT.

HIS FATHER HAD TAKEN **PERMANENT RESIDENCE** AT THE RIVER'S EDGE BAR... THAT IS, UNTIL FUNDS **RAN OUT.**

A DECADE AND A HALF **LATER,** PIRANHA HAD THESE SPECIAL INCISORS STITCHED INTO HIS GUMS... **WITHOUT ANESTHETIC!**

PIRANHA IS ABOUT TO LOSE SOME **MORE** TEETH.

WOOSH-OCK!

A WISP OF BLOOD **TRAILS** FROM PIRANHA'S OPEN MOUTH.

WILL ONE TRACE OF BLOOD DRIVE THE PIRANHA INTO A **FRENZY,** WONDERS CAGE--

-- OR IS IT ONLY **BARRACUDA** THAT ARE **THAT** INJUDICIOUS?

CAGE DECIDES NOT TO **WAIT** FOR AN ANSWER.

THE WATER PRESSURE **PULLS** AT HIM.

PIRANHA JONES **WEIGHS** HIM DOWN.

BUT CAGE STILL COMES CRASHING THROUGH THE BARRIER!

YOU *LOST*, PIRANHA. YOU HAD IT *RIGHT*... IT'S ALL TAKEN AWAY. BUT YOU GOT IT WRONG, IF YOU THINK I *WON*.

NOBODY DID!

ADONIS CHEMICAL WILL SHIP MORE'A THAT *JUNK* NEXT MONTH. SO WE *LOSE*, UNTIL THOSE *SOUL- LESS MOTHERS* AT ADONIS PANIC WHEN *THEY* START DYIN' CAUSE'A THEIR *IDIOCIES.*

HEY, PIRANHA, ARE YOU *LIS'NIN'*?

UNTIL THAT TIME, THE CHARLTON GRUNDGE'S AND GRASSY MOSS'S ARE GONNA GO *SCOT FREE.*

CAN'T TOUCH 'EM.

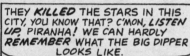

THEY *KILLED* THE STARS IN THIS CITY, YOU KNOW THAT? C'MON, *LISTEN UP*, PIRANHA! WE CAN HARDLY *REMEMBER* WHAT THE BIG DIPPER LOOKS LIKE.

AH, SHOOT PIRANHA, MAYBE YOUR *READ* CAN *BUY* AS MUCH *JUSTICE* AS CHARLTON GRUNDGE CAN?

THAT, YOU C'N *HASSLE OUT* WITH QUENTIN CHASE...

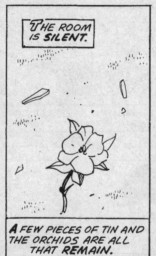

THE ROOM IS SILENT.

A FEW PIECES OF TIN AND THE ORCHIDS ARE ALL THAT *REMAIN.*

PIRANHA--

--LET'S CALL IT NIGHT.

THE WOMAN AND THE IRISH TERRIER ARE DEFINITELY EAST SIDE INHABITANTS --

--THEY *BOTH* HAVE THAT SLEEK, WELL- BRED LOOK.

THROUGH THE ROOFTOPS THERE IS A GLIMPSE OF THE CORPSE-REMAINS OF A STAR.

VERY FAINT... BUT *ENCOURAGING.*

EXCUSE ME... I THINK *YOU'D* LOOK BETTER WITH THIS THAN ME.

AND YOU KNOW *WHAT*... I *OWE* YOU MORE'N THAT--

--CAUSE YOU JUST MADE ME REALIZE WE'RE *STILL ALIVE*, LADY.

AND RIGHT NOW, LET'S BE *GLAD* JUST FOR *THAT.*

NEXT: THE MOST CONTROVERSIAL CAGE SAGA EVER --AS DON McGREGOR TEAMS UP WITH FRANK ROBBINS TO PRODUCE...

WILDFIRE AND *THE FIRE NEXT TIME!*

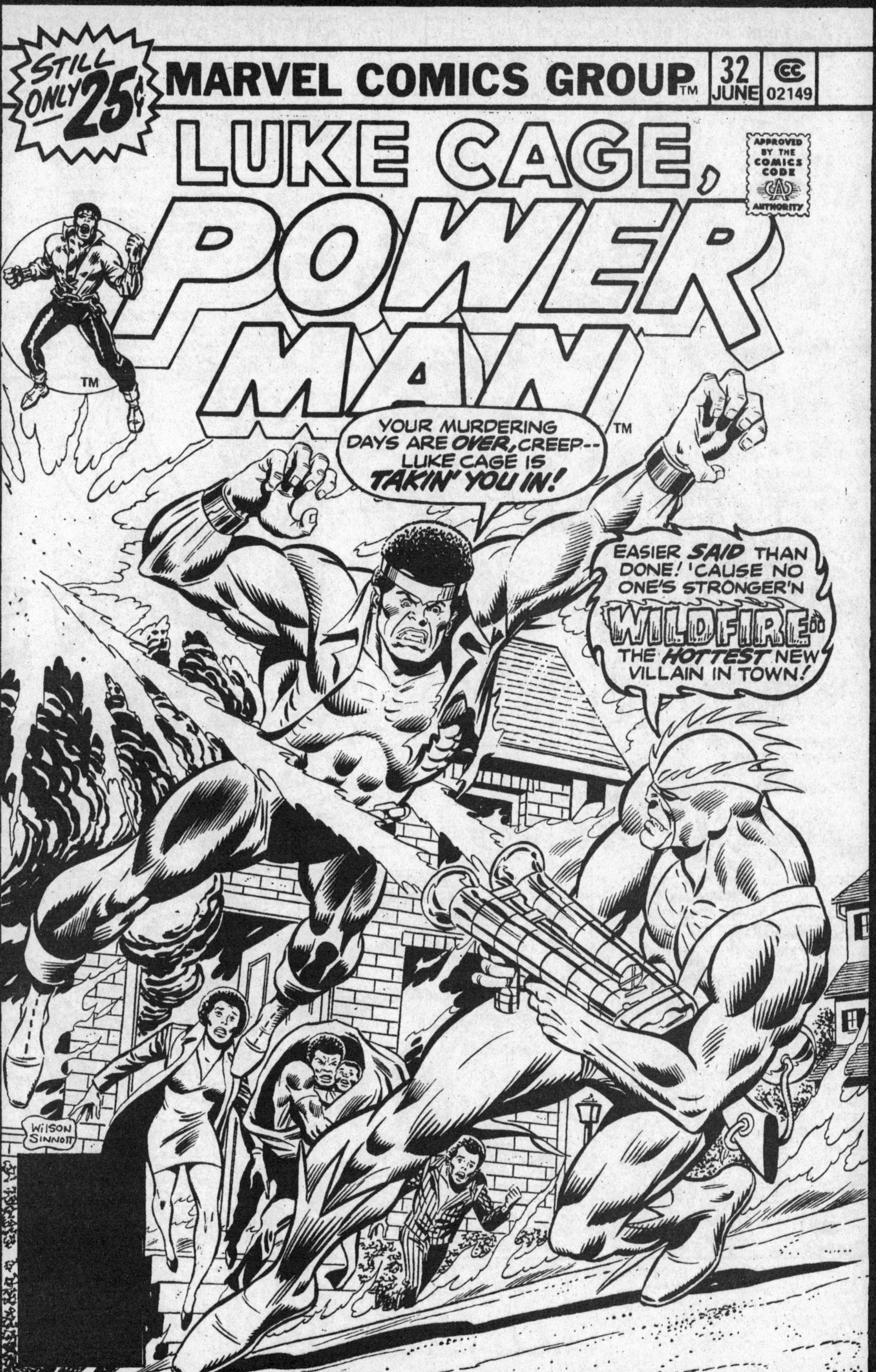
STILL ONLY 25¢
MARVEL COMICS GROUP™
32 JUNE
CC 02149
LUKE CAGE, POWER MAN™
APPROVED BY THE COMICS CODE AUTHORITY
YOUR MURDERING DAYS ARE OVER, CREEP-- LUKE CAGE IS TAKIN' YOU IN!
EASIER SAID THAN DONE! 'CAUSE NO ONE'S STRONGER'N WILDFIRE.. THE HOTTEST NEW VILLAIN IN TOWN!
WILSON SINNOTT

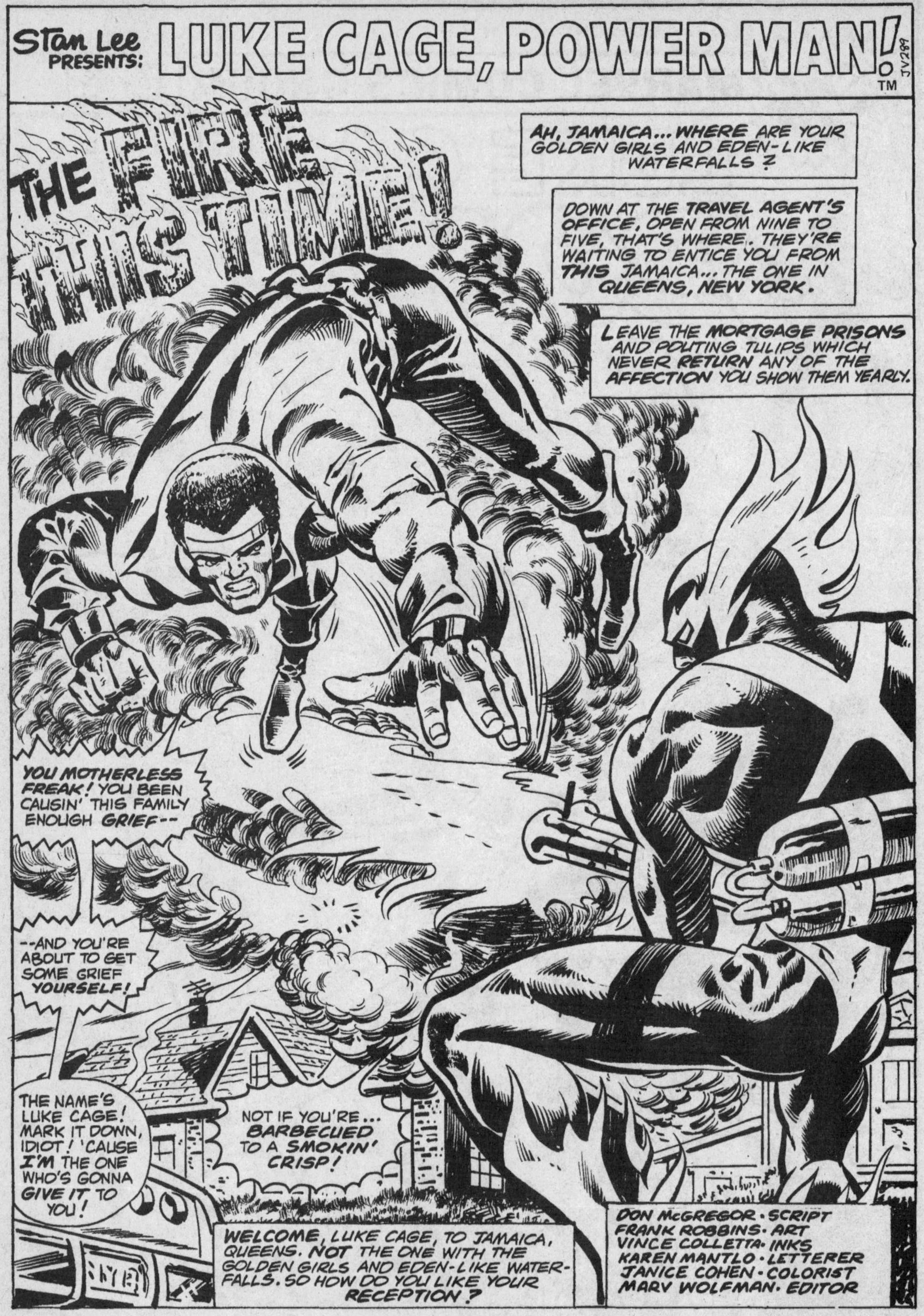
Stan Lee PRESENTS: LUKE CAGE, POWER MAN!™
JV289
THE FIRE THIS TIME!
AH, JAMAICA... WHERE ARE YOUR GOLDEN GIRLS AND EDEN-LIKE WATERFALLS?
DOWN AT THE TRAVEL AGENT'S OFFICE, OPEN FROM NINE TO FIVE, THAT'S WHERE. THEY'RE WAITING TO ENTICE YOU FROM THIS JAMAICA... THE ONE IN QUEENS, NEW YORK.
LEAVE THE MORTGAGE PRISONS AND POUTING TULIPS WHICH NEVER RETURN ANY OF THE AFFECTION YOU SHOW THEM YEARLY.
YOU MOTHERLESS FREAK! YOU BEEN CAUSIN' THIS FAMILY ENOUGH GRIEF--
--AND YOU'RE ABOUT TO GET SOME GRIEF YOURSELF!
THE NAME'S LUKE CAGE! MARK IT DOWN, IDIOT! 'CAUSE I'M THE ONE WHO'S GONNA GIVE IT, TO YOU!
NOT IF YOU'RE... BARBECUED TO A SMOKIN' CRISP!
WELCOME, LUKE CAGE, TO JAMAICA, QUEENS. NOT THE ONE WITH THE GOLDEN GIRLS AND EDEN-LIKE WATER-FALLS. SO HOW DO YOU LIKE YOUR RECEPTION?
DON McGREGOR · SCRIPT
FRANK ROBBINS · ART
VINCE COLLETTA · INKS
KAREN MANTLO · LETTERER
JANICE COHEN · COLORIST
MARV WOLFMAN · EDITOR

YOU OUGHTTA GET A **KICK** OUTTA THAT BARBECUED LINE, BOY...

NOT AS MUCH A KICK AS WHEN I KNOCK YOUR TAIL **CLEAR ACROSS THE STREET!**

YOU'RE NOT GOING TO GET THAT **CLOSE.**

SO THE **SIMMONS** FAMILY GOT ONE OF THEIR **OWN KIND** TO WATCH OUT FOR ME, HUH?

WHAT WAS IT...? THAT THEY KNEW I'D BE **BACK?**

YOU BETTER **BELIEVE** I'LL BE BACK. UNTIL THEY'RE **GONE!**

AND YOU THINK YOU'RE THE **ONLY ONE** THAT'S GOT A **NAME?**

WELL, YOU'RE **WRONG!** I'VE GOT ONE, TOO!

IT'S **WILDFIRE**, CAGE-- YOU **GOT** THAT? ...**WILDFIRE!**

FOOSH!

THE FLAMES BURST AROUND HIM IN A TORRENT THAT **SCORCHES** CAGE'S CHEST AS HE SLAMS INTO THE CAREFULLY TENDED FRONT LAWN.

WHOMP

THE TULIPS DON'T OFFER ANY CONSOLATION.

YOU KEEP TWISTING AND TURNING, MISTER. BUT THIS ISN'T A **FOOTBALL FIELD**--

--OR A **BASEBALL DIAMOND**--

--OR THE **OLYMPICS**, WHERE YOU CAN **SHOW OFF!**

I MIGHT BE **WHITE**, BUT I CAN MOVE AS FAST AS YOU...**MAYBE FASTER** ...AND THAT'S GOING TO **BURN** YOUR SUPERIORITY ACT TO A **CINDER!**

LIGHTS FLARE IN *NEIGHBORING* HOUSES. FIGURES APPEAR IN THE DOORWAYS AND WINDOWS.

IT NEVER *FAILS,* MADELYN... THOSE *SECURITY PATROL CARS* THAT'RE SUP-POSED TO KEEP *UNDESIRABLES* OFF OUR SIDEWALKS AFTER DARK...

I KNOW, GEORGE... ARE *NEVER* AROUND WHEN YOU *NEED* THEM.

GEORGE DOES NOT REPLY AS TO *WHICH* FIGURE HE CONSIDERS THE MOST UNDESIRABLE.

YOU'RE LETTIN' YOUR *MOUTH* GET THE *REST 'A YOU* IN MORE TROUBLE THAN YOU'RE READY TO *DEAL* WITH!

YOU'RE *WRONG* ABOUT THAT! *DEAD WRONG!*

IS THE AIR SWEETER OUT HERE, CAGE, THAN IN MANHATTAN?

CAN YOU ACTUALLY GLIMPSE A FEW *STARS* IN THE NIGHT HEAVENS?

NO, *YOU'RE* THE ONE WHO'S WRONG, MISTER.

I AIN'T SURE I'VE CAUGHT YOUR *DRIFT* YET...BUT IF IT'S WHAT I *THINK* IT IS...

PERHAPS. BUT THE FEAR AND HATE ARE JUST AS *STRONG,* MERELY HIDDEN B'A *PICTURESQUE* FACADE.

...YOU'RE *SICKER'N* MY *CLIENTS* THOUGHT.

I DON'T KNOW WHAT YOUR *HANG UP* IS...

...BUT I *DO* KNOW YOU HADDA BE *AWARE* THAT THE SIMMONSES HAVE *TWO KIDS* IN THAT HOUSE--

--AND YOU WERE STILL READY TO PUT THE *TORCH* TO IT!

AND THAT MEANS YOU'RE ON LUKE CAGE'S *LIST,* MADMAN--

--ON MY *BAD* LIST!

AUGGIE SIMMONS: "I SEEN 'EM FROM THE WINDOW. POWER MAN WAS ALL OVER THE PLACE, I MEAN IT, NO KIDDIN'... THAT GUY WITH THE FIRE-GUN... WILDFIRE ...HE DIDN'T COME NOWHERE CLOSE TO HITTIN' POWER MAN!"

"DADDY AND MOMMY CAME AN' GOT ME AND LITTLE BETH... AN' I WAS KINDA SCARED!"

"...BUT NOT TOO SCARED!"

ALEX... THE HOUSE... THE HOUSE IS GOING UP IN FLAMES!

NO, AUGGIE... DON'T YOU RUN OFF ...YOU STAY RIGHT WITH ME, YOU UNDERSTAND?

OH, ALEX, WHAT'LL WE DO NOW?

AUGGIE SIMMONS: "MY MOMMY RAN OUT ONTO THE SIDEWALK... BUT I WAS AHEAD'A HER 'CAUSE'N I CAN RUN FASTER.

"THERE WAS LOTSA PEOPLE ALL OVER, AN' MOMMY WAS CRYIN! I DON'T LIKE TO SEE MOMMY CRY LIKE THAT."

SOMEBODY... PLEASE... OH, GOD... PLEASE CALL THE FIRE DEPARTMENT!

WHAT'S THE MATTER? ARE YOU ALL DEAF? ARE YOU ALL BLIND?!!

LOOK, THE MAN THAT SET OUR HOUSE ON FIRE IS TRYING TO KILL MR. CAGE!

AUGGIE SIMMONS: "IT WAS KINDA WEIRD. THEY LOOKED LIKE ZOMBIES IS WHAT THEY LOOKED LIKED."

"NOBODY MOVED... BUT I DON'T KNOW WHAT MOMMY WAS SO UPSET ABOUT... 'CAUSE POWER MAN CAN TAKE CARE OF HIMSELF."

DIDJA SEE THAT? WOW! THE FLAME CAT IS GONNA KNOCK THE OTHER GUY'S TEETH DOWN HIS THROAT.

THIS IS WHAT I THINK OF YOUR LIST, MISTER!

CHAK!

THE YOUNG VOICE SOUNDS THRILLED. THERE HASN'T BEEN THIS MUCH EXCITEMENT SINCE RUDI MALOX BLOODIED CHARLIE HERNANDEZ' MOUTH IN THE BOY'S LAV AT SCHOOL.

MAN, THIS HAS BEEN A DYNAMITE YEAR!

CAGE HURTLES BACKWARD. THERE ARE BRICKS *CONCEALED* IN THE TULIP BEDS.

YOU GOT IT ALL *WRONG* IF YOU THINK ONE SWIPE WITH YOUR TINKER-TOY IS GONNA *TAKE ME* OUTTA THE PICTURE.

WHICH FIGURES, THINKS CAGE, MORDANTLY.

TINKER-TOY!?

YOU WANNA KNOW THE *HOURS* I PUT INTO *BUILDIN'* THIS THING?

TIME *WASTED*, THEN ... THAT COULD'A BEEN PUT TO A LOT *BETTER* USE!

THAT'S YOUR *LAST* PUT-DOWN, MISTER. I'M NOT LETTING PEOPLE RUN OVER ME ANYMORE, YOU *GOT* THAT?

YOU AND YOUR *HAH!*..."BROTHERS" ...CALL *ME* SICK DO YA? WELL, LET'S SEE YOU "SHUFFLE" OUT OF THE WAY THIS TIME!

NOT SO *ARROGANT* NOW, HUH? *SQUIRMING* A BIT! THEY'LL BE READING YOUR *OBITUARY* IN THE "DAILY NEWS" TOMORROW.

LET THEM CRY *THEN*. YOU AND YOUR FRIENDS ALREADY HAVE THOSE BLEEDING-HEART NEWSPAPER BUMS MAKING *ME* OUT THE *VILLAIN!*

THEY DO THE *SAME THING* ON ALL THEM BLASTED T.V. SHOWS! YOU THINK BECAUSE YOU'RE *BLACK* YOU'RE THE ONLY ONES THAT GOT ANY *RIGHTS!* WELL, *WE* GOT 'EM TOO, UNDERSTAND?

YOU KEEP SHOWING US AS *ARCHIE BUNKERS* --BURPING BEER, "HONKIES" ...THAT'S THE WORD YOU *USE*, RIGHT?

WELL, THIS IS *ONE DUMB* "HONKIE" THAT'S GONNA *FRY* YOUR HIDE!

THE WORD YOU'RE USIN'S OUTTA *DATE*, MAN! JUST LIKE *YOU'RE* OUTTA DATE.

AUGGIE SIMMONS: "LITTLE BETH WAS *BAWLIN'*... BUT SHE'S ONLY A BABY. SHE'S NOT *TOUGH* LIKE ME.

"BUT MOMMY DIDN'T HAVE NO TEARS OR *NUTHIN'* NO MORE. SHE HAD THIS KIND'A LOOK LIKE WHEN SHE AND DADDY ARE GONNA *YELL* AT EACH OTHER."

ALEX, WHAT ARE YOU GOING TO *DO?*

WHAT THOSE OTHERS *WON'T!*

CAGE MIGHT BE JUST A *HIRED* MAN... BUT HE PUT HIMSELF ON THE *LINE* FOR US--

--AND THIS TIME THAT *MANIAC* ISN'T GOING TO GET *AWAY!*

ALEX MOVES STEALTHILY, THE WAY *MOVIE HEROES* MOVE... BUT HE HAS NEVER SMELT *NERVOUS SWEAT* COMING FROM A MOVIE HERO'S ARMPITS--

-- NOR HAS HE HAD TO FIGHT THE *FEAR* THAT THREATENS TO *PARALYZE* HIM.

TAKE A *QUICK LOOK* OUT THERE. THEY'RE *ALL* LOOKING AT ME, MISTER--

-- YOU WANT'A *BET* ON HOW MANY OF THEM ARE *WAITING* FOR ME TO PULL THIS TRIGGER?

I'LL *PASS*... BUT I'M HOPIN' IT'S ONLY 'CAUSE THEY DON'T KNOW WHAT TO *DO* IN A SITUATION LIKE THIS THAT LEAVES 'EM *STANDING* THERE.

AUGGIE SIMMONS: "I WANTED TO *JOIN* DADDY... BUT MOMMY GAVE THAT *LOOK* THAT MEANT I'D GET IT *REAL GOOD* IF'N I MOVED."

"I DON'T LIKE IT *MUCH* WHEN SHE LOOKS LIKE THAT!

"BUT YOU *SHOULD'A* SEEN THAT GUN. *BIGGEST* GUN I EVER SEEN. EVEN BIGGER'N A *CANNON!*"

YOU THINK I'M GONNA KEEP WAITIN' FOR YOU TO MAKE YOUR *PLAY*, JACK, YOU GOT IT *ALL WRONG!*

AN' YOU'RE *SOMETHIN'* ELSE, MAN, CRYIN' 'BOUT HOW NOBODY SEES *YOU* AS A PERSON--!

WHAT D'YOU THINK *YOU'VE* BEEN DOIN' TO THE SIMMONSES?

OH, YOU'RE GONNA *GET IT.* I JUST WANTED YOU TO KNOW *WHY.*

MY KIDS COME HOME FROM *SCHOOL*, AND THEY FEED ME THAT KIND OF *TRIPE* YOU'RE SPOUTING, *MY OWN KIDS!* THEY'RE TURNING MY OWN KIDS *AGAINST* ME!

WELL, THERE'S A *HERO* TO REPRESENT US, SEE--

--AND I'M IT!

STALL, CAGE! *STALL!* ALEX SIMMONS DOESN'T HAVE A *CHANCE* IF WILDFIRE CATCHES SIGHT OF HIM!

ANOTHER MINUTE AND HE'LL MAKE IT.

EXCEPT NEITHER CAGE, NOR ALEX, HAVE ANOTHER MINUTE.

WILDFIRE! WATCH OUT! *BEHIND YOU!*

IT DOESN'T MATTER *WHY* SHE SCREAMED. THE FACT IS, SHE *DID!*

ALEX SPRINGS AND LUKE CAGE IS ABRUPTLY *AFRAID*. ALEX SIMMONS DOES NOT HAVE BIO-CHEMICALLY ALTERED FLESH TO OFFER HIM ANY PROTECTION, AND FLAMES WHIP ON THE WIND *TOWARD* HIM!

YOU'RE *SOMETHIN'* ALRIGHT, WILDFIRE--

--BUT I *WOULDN'T* CALL IT A HERO!

BTOW

KEEP MOVIN', ALEX! THIS IS *NO TIME* TO STOP!

I GOT HIM, CAGE! I GOT...

GET *OUTTA* THE WAY, ALEX! LET *ME* TAKE HIM OUT!

SEEING AS THE *TWO* OF YOU ARE SO MUCH IN *LOVE* WITH EACH OTHER--

--I DON'T THINK YOU SHOULD BE KEPT *APART!*

THAT WASN'T A *BAD LINE,* WAS IT?

WHAT'S THE MATTER... *"BROTHERS"...* CAT GOT YOUR TONGUES?

AUGGIE SIMMONS: "WIL'FIRE MUST'A HEARD THE *FIRE ENGINES* OR SOMETHIN'... 'CAUSE THAT'S WHEN HE STARTED TO *RUN*... AN' MOMMY SCREAMED WORDS AT HIM I NEVER *EVER* HEARD HER SAY BEFORE.

"MOMMY SHOULD'VE LET ME AT HIM... I'DA *FIXED* HIM!"

WATCH OUT! HE'S COMING THIS WAY!

GEORGE, HE'S NOT GOING TO *SHOOT* THAT THING, IS HE?

HE'LL *KILL* US ALL!

HEY, MISTER-- YOU BETTER *LET HIM GO!* HE'LL FIRE RIGHT INTO THIS *CROWD!*

MAN, I'M BURNIN' A *REAL ANGER* RIGHT NOW... IF I *THOUGHT* YOU WERE PROTECTIN' THAT *BASKET CASE*--

--I'D *FORGET* THAT YOU REALLY AREN'T *UP* TO FACING THE WAY I'D LAY INTO YOU!

AUGGIE SIMMONS: "THERE MUST'A BEEN A MILYUN FIREMEN, AN' THERE WERE RED SPARKS ALL OVER THE SKY. REAL PRETTY... BUT I DIDN'T LIKE THE SMOKE. THAT WAS ICKY."

ALEX, THAT WAS A GUTSY THING YOU DID BACK THERE. IT TOOK A LOTTA...

LUKE!

OH, YEAH. RIGHT. THE KIDS.

YOU KNOW, BACK IN '71, CAGE, I CAME UP HERE WITH A WHITE FRIEND OF MINE WHO WAS LOOKIN' FOR A PLACE TO LIVE. I WAS TAKING HIM AROUND BECAUSE HE DIDN'T KNOW THE CITY.

REAL ESTATE AGENT WOULDN'T EVEN LET ME RIDE WITH THEM WHEN THEY WENT TO HOUSES. I FOOLED MYSELF INTO THINKING THINGS HAD CHANGED IN FOUR YEARS.

FIREMEN SAY IT COULD HAVE BEEN WORSE... THE HOUSE'LL SMELL OF SMOKE... AND THE MAIN PORTION IS WATERLOGGED.

BUT I'M NOT LEAVING. THEY ARE... NOT... GOING TO... DRIVE ME OUT!

DON'T GET THICK, ALEX. IT COULD BE WORSE NEXT TIME.

AND WHERE DO YOU SUGGEST WE GO, SANDY?

I'M SORRY. BUT I'M NOT RUNNING. YOU'RE THE ONE WHO GOT ME TO STAY WITH THAT INSURANCE JOB UNTIL WE MADE ENOUGH TO AFFORD THIS PLACE.

OKAY, WE SQUEAK BY... AND FINALLY MAKE IT. AND WE DON'T HAVE ENOUGH LEFT TO PACK IT UP AND LEAVE. AND I WON'T LET THEM DEFEAT ME!

MEN! YOU'VE ALWAYS GOT TO PROVE SOMETHING!

THINK IT'LL PROVE ANYTHING IF YOUR KIDS ARE DEAD WHEN IT ENDS?

DON'T MAKE ME OUT TO BE A GUTLESS WOMAN, ALEX-- I'M NOT THAT AND YOU KNOW IT! WE'LL STAY...'CAUSE YOU'RE RIGHT... WE DON'T HAVE ANYPLACE ELSE TO GO!

BUT IT DOESN'T MATTER WHO STARTED THE WAR, ALEX...IF YOU LOSE EVERYTHING JUST TO WIN A POINT.

YOUR LADY SPEAKS HER MIND.

TELL YOU SOMETHING, LUKE, IF I HAD THE BREAD I'D SEND HER AND THE KIDS AWAY.

COMES A TIME, THOUGH, WHEN YOU GOT TO MAKE A STAND.

AND I GUESS MY TIME HAS COME!

TIMES SQUARE AT NOON. THE MOVIE HOUSES HAVE REOPENED AFTER FIVE HOURS OF SILENCE, AND THE HOUSES WITH LIVE ENTERTAINMENT ARE VYING FOR THEIR CLIENTELE.

DETECTIVE 2ND GRADE QUENTIN CHASE STARES AT CAGE OVER THE FOAMHEAD OF A CUP OF ORANGE JULIUS AND THE INTERROGATION BEGINS--

--CASUAL, AND YET, AT THE SAME TIME, DEADLY!

I SEE THE NEWSPAPERS ARE SHOUTING ABOUT YOUR NEW CASE...

...WHICH BRINGS TO MIND THE FACT THAT YOU STILL HAVEN'T PRODUCED A SOCIAL SECURITY CARD TO PROVE LUKE CAGE IS STRICTLY LEGIT.

THAT SUSPICIOUS NATURE OF YOURS IS GONNA RUIN YOUR PERSONALITY, CHASE--

I'M SURPRISED TO SEE YOU ON THE DAY SHIFT, CHASE--

--I WAS STARTIN' TO BELIEVE YOU WERE A VAMPIRE AND SLEPT IN A COFFIN.

I USED TO... BUT MY WIFE FOUND IT TOO UNCOMFORTABLE.

BUT IF YOU SQUINT REAL HARD I THINK YOU'LL SEE WHAT YOU'VE BEEN HOUNDIN' ME FOR.

THIS FOR REAL?

NOW, CHASE, WOULD I LAY A JIVE RAP ON YOU?

UP ONE WALL AND DOWN ANOTHER. I CAN CHECK AND SEE IF THIS IS VALID.

AHH, YOU DON'T HAVE TO GO OUT OF YOUR WAY ON MY ACCOUNT.

HEY! HEY! A CUP! SO FAR SO GOOD!

AND ICE, YET! WE'RE GONNA--

--GO--

--ALL THE--

--WAY.

YIICH! HOW DO YOU DRINK THAT STUFF?

NORMALLY, I DON'T GET THE CHANCE

HELLO, CHRISTIE?... HEY KITTEN, THIS IS QUENT... OH... YOU KNOW THAT... I'M, UH, I'M GOING TO BE A BIT LATE TONIGHT... I WANT TO LOOK INTO THIS WILDFIRE PSYCHO CASE... UNOFFICIALLY.

YOU DON'T SPEND ENOUGH TIME WORKING THAT YOU FEEL YOU HAVE TO TAKE ON UNOFFICIAL CASES AS WELL?

I HAD PLANS FOR YOU AND I TONIGHT.

KEEP THEM IN MIND. YOU'VE ALREADY INTRIGUED ME. AND, KITTEN, I LOVE YOU.

GOOD-BYE, QUENT.

NIGHTTIME IN JAMAICA: A DARK FIGURE *FLIRTS* WITH THE SHADOWS UNDER THE PINE TREE. THIS FIGURE DOES NOT HOLD A DOG ON A *LEASH*, NOR ARE THE EYES AS *BORED* WITH THE SAME *PAMPERED* GARDENS AND CARS THAT HAVE BEEN ON THIS ROAD FOR YEARS.

AND STILL, THE FIGURE IS TAKEN BY *SURPRISE!*

CHASE!

MAN, YOUR MOTHER NEARLY HAD *ONE LESS SON!*

WHAT'RE YOU *DOIN'* OUT HERE?

RUININ' MY *MARRIAGE.*

I'VE GOTTA BE OUT OF MY *HEAD* SPENDING THE NIGHT BESIDE YOU WHEN I'VE GOT A *WARM WOMAN* WAITING AT HOME.

I'M CRAZIER THAN THIS *PYRO-MANIAC* YOU'RE CHECKING OUT.

WHEN I TOLD HEATHER THIS AFTER-NOON THAT I'D BE *LATE* LOOKING INTO THIS ... I DIDN'T MEAN FROM A *DESK.*

CHASE... YOU ARE THE *STRAIGHTEST* COP I'VE RUN INTO. I'M NOT SURE *YOU'RE FOR REAL.*

I'M ONLY *OUT HERE* BECAUSE OF *YOU,* CAGE. YOU HAVE A TENDENCY TO LEAVE *CORPSES* DECO-RATING SIDEWALKS WHEN YOU'RE DONE WITH A *JOB.*

Y'KNOW WHAT *I THINK,* CHASE? *I THINK* YOU DON'T DIG THIS WILDFIRE ANY MORE THAN I DO. I THINK YOU'RE DOIN' THIS 'CAUSE YOU KNOW HOW THE SIMMONSES HAVE BEEN *HURTIN'.*

THAT'S *SOME* IMAGINATION YOU'VE GOT, CAGE. WHY, I'VE NEVER EVEN *MET* THESE PEOPLE.

SURE, CHASE ...ANYTHING YOU SAY.

HAROLD AND ETHYL PAPRIKA SELDOM SAY *ANYTHING* TO EACH OTHER.

ON WEEKENDS, HAROLD POLISHES THE CAR UNTIL IT *GLEAMS*--IT'S THE MOST *PASSIONATE* THING HAROLD DOES IN THIS GUISE--BUT HE STARES RIGHT THROUGH HIS REFLECTION.

THEY *TOUCH* AS *STRANGERS* WHO HAVE CHOSEN THE SAME *DWELLING* TO LIVE OUT THEIR LIVES.

AND REMEMBER, *THURSDAY* IS MY *W.A.M.* MEETING.

ON WEEKNIGHTS, ETHYL SWITCHES CHANNELS DURING COMMERCIALS... AND THE GREY LIGHT FROM THE SET *DIMS* THEIR LIVES.

OH, HAROLD... BEFORE YOU LEAVE... REMEMBER, I HAVE AN *ENCOUNTER SESSION* TOMORROW... SO YOU'LL HAVE TO STAY WITH THE *KIDS.*

OKAY... OKAY... THEY BETTER KEEP THAT STEREO TURNED *DOWN* OR I'LL BREAK IT OVER THEIR *HEADS.*

WHAM?

W.A.M.

WOMEN ARE MEN.

THEY *ARE?*

DEFINITELY.

REMEMBER, I EXPLAINED THE WHOLE *THEORY* TO YOU LAST NIGHT AFTER YOU RETURNED FROM THAT *RIDICULOUS* CLUB SHOOT OF YOURS.

MS. RACHEL SOBRIETY IS ITS *FOUNDER.* ONCE SHE DISCOVERED SHE WAS A MAN SHE REALIZED *ALL SISTERS* WERE MEN.

YEAH... YEAH... IT ALL *COMES BACK,* ETHYL... SKIP THE LECTURE... THE MEAT-LOAF'S ALREADY *REPEATING* ON ME.

HAROLD PAPRIKA ENTERS THE GARAGE AND HIS HANDS ARE *SHAKING.* HARDLY ANYTHING MAKES *SENSE* ANYMORE. NOT ETHYL. NOT THE *KIDS.*

NOT THE WORLD.

RACHEL SOBRIETY... WHERE DOES ETHYL MEET UP WITH THESE *LOSERS?*

WOMEN...

...ALMOST AS *BAD* AS THEM *BLACKS!*

27

THEY SIT UNCOMFORTABLY ON THE TREE BRANCHES, *ANTAGONISTS* RELUCTANTLY RESPECTING ONE ANOTHER.

THEY SHARE EXHAUSTION. THE SENSES BECOME *LESS* ALERT.

CAGE, I'M GOING TO GET *OUT* OF HERE AND HOPE CHRISTIE HASN'T *FORGOTTEN* THE PLANS SHE HAD.

OR IF SHE HAS, I'LL TRY TO *REMIND* HER.

ANYHOW, IT LOOKS LIKE WILDFIRE'S GOING TO *COOL IT,* AT LEAST FOR--

--TONIGHT!!

FOOM!

CHASE, YOU AIN'T EXACTLY *SHERLOCK HOLMES!*

BUT WE BETTER *MOVE IT,* 'CAUSE HE'S GOT HIS SIGHTS *LOCKED IN* ON US--

--AND I GOT ME A FEELIN' HE DON'T CARE NONE THAT *SMOKEY THE BEAR* AIN'T GONNA APPROVE OF THAT *FANCY MATCHSTICK* AND WHAT HE'S *DOIN'* WITH IT!

CAGE...

...WHERE DO YOU... UUHH...

...FIND THE *BREATH* TO TALK...ARGH...

CHASE *CRASHES* THROUGH THE TIMBERS BURNT THE NIGHT BEFORE AND *KNOWS* HE ISN'T GOING TO REACH *ANY* WARM BEDS TONIGHT.

CAGE HITS THE SHINGLES WITH ALL *300 LBS*--

--AND HE FEELS THE ROOF *GIVE* UNDER HIS BOOTS--

--*BUCKLING* AS IF IT WERE *SHEET GLASS!*

THERE ARE TIMES WHEN THAT *EXTRA WEIGHT* CAN BE A *DISADVANTAGE.*

AUGGIE SIMMONS: "I WAS ALREADY AWAKE WHEN POWER MAN, HE CAME RIGHT THROUGH THE ROOF. I COULDN'T SLEEP CAUSE MY NOSE WAS ALL STUFFED UP FROM THE SMOKE."

HI, *POWER MAN*, I DON'T THINK DADDY'S GONNA LIKE THE WAY YOU CAME THROUGH THE *ROOF*.

HE SAYS THE HOUSE ISN'T NO *BARN*.

BUT I DON'T THINK HE'LL *YELL* TOO MUCH AT *YOU*.

WHAT KIND'A *GAME* ARE WE PLAYIN'?

THERE'S *NOTHING* TO BE SCARED OF, SON--!

YOU GET YOUR MOM AND DAD *UP*, OKAY? I'M GOIN' DOWNSTAIRS RIGHT NOW TO PUT AN *END* TO ALL THIS.

HE RACES DOWN THE STAIRS, FOUR STEPS AT A TIME--

--BUT HE STILL FAILS TO *REACH* THE DOOR BEFORE SHEETS OF FLAME CUT *THROUGH* IT.

THE HEAT IS SO INTENSE THAT WHEN HE BREATHES, IT *SCORCHES* HIS LUNGS.

BUT THAT DOESN'T *STOP* CAGE!

AND NEITHER DOES THE *DOOR*!

MAN, YOU BETTER START *PRAYING!* CHASE HAS BEEN LAYIN' SOME *HEAVY STUFF* AT MY FEET ABOUT CORPSES--

--AND YOU BETTER HOPE YOU KNOW A PRAYER THAT'LL MAKE ME STOP HITTING YOU WHILE YOU'RE *STILL BREATHING!*

YOU AND *ETHYL* OUGHT TO GET TOGETHER ... YOU *BOTH* GIVE ME HEARTBURN!

BUT THAT'S JUST WHAT YOU'D *LIKE*, ISN'T IT? TO GET NEXT TO *ETHYL!*

ETHYL??

DON'T YOU *KNOW?!* WOMEN ARE *MEN!*

AS CAGE GOUGES UP THE GRASS UNDER HIS IMPACT, HE WONDERS IF HE HAS HEARD INFERNO *CORRECTLY.*

AND THEN CAGE REALIZES INFERNO IS *CHARGING* INTO THE HOUSE, AND HE RECALLS A LITTLE BOY'S LIQUID EYES OF *WONDER*--

--AND ALSO REALIZES THAT HE DOESN'T EVEN *KNOW* THE KID'S NAME!

YET, THE KID HAD SAID SOMETHING *ODD* WHEN HE WENT RACING THROUGH THAT ROOM.

SOMETHING VERY ODD

THEY'RE AT IT *AGAIN,* ALEX. WE WERE BETTER OFF *SHARING ROOMS* WITH ROACHES AND RATS!

C'MON, HONEY. WE'VE GOT TO GET *OUT OF HERE.* MOMMA KNOWS YOU'RE *TIRED.*

WHERE'S *AUGGIE?*

AUGGIE SAID IT'S A *GAME,* MOMMY. *IS* IT, MOMMY?

AUGGIE SIMMONS: "LITTLE BETH LIKES GAMES, TOO, THOUGH SHE ALWAYS *BAWLS* WHEN WE PLAY *BOOGIE MAN.*

"BUT SHE LOVES *HIDE* AND SEEK AND ALWAYS GIGGLES WHEN SHE HIDES.

"I CAN *ALWAYS* FIND HER THAT WAY, BUT MOMMY AN' DADDY'LL NEVER FIND *ME!* 'CAUSE I CAN HIDE REAL GOOD!"

ONE THING *WRONG* ABOUT DRESSIN' UP LIKE A *PEACOCK* ON THE MAKE, WILDFIRE--

IT POW!

-- IT MAKES YOU EASY TO *FIND*!

ALEX! THE STAIRWAY'S *AFIRE*! WE CAN'T GET DOWN OR *OUT*!

BLANKETS! WE NEED BLANKETS!

ALEX!

WHATTA YOU PEOPLE *DOIN'* STILL UP THERE?!

YOU AIN'T GOT *TIME* FOR BLANKETS, MAN!

DROP HER TO ME, ALEX! TRUST ME, MAN!

ALEX HESITATES. LITTLE BETH SNUGGLES *TRUSTINGLY* IN HIS ARMS

THE CLIMBING FLAMES GIVE HIM LITTLE *CHOICE*. HE HAS TO TRUST CAGE.

GET YOUR *ROBE* UP OVER YOUR *HAIR*, SANDRA!

WE'RE GOING ON *THROUGH*!

LUKE, WHERE'D YOU *PUT* AUGGIE? *OUTSIDE*?

AUGGIE! YOU MEAN THE *BOY*? LAST I SEEN 'IM, HE WAS *UPSTAIRS*!

OH GOOD LORD! HE MUST *STILL* BE UP THERE! I'M *GOING* BACK UP, LUKE. STAY HERE, SANDRA!

NO YOU DON'T, WILDFIRE! YOU'RE NOT GOIN' *ANYWHERE* THAT I DON'T SEND YOU!

MORE *VENGEANCE*, LUKE? YOU *COPYING* HIS STYLE?

STAY *OUTTA* THIS, CHASE...OR I'LL TAKE YOU ON, TOO!

KTOW

GO AHEAD, LUKE. MAKE HIM THINK *HIS WAY* WAS RIGHT ALL ALONG!

CAGE STOPS, BUT IT IS NEITHER WILDFIRE NOR CHASE WHO STOP HIM. IT IS THE SOBBING SOUNDS RIPPED FROM A MAN WHO DOES NOT CRY.

SANDY, I'VE GOT HIM, SANDY!

BUT HE'S... HE'S NOT BREATHING, SANDY!

IT MUST'VE BEEN THE SMOKE, SO THICK IN THERE... AND FLAMES AT THE DOORWAY!

HEY, I'M SORRY, MISTER, I DIDN'T WANT TO KILL A KID!

JEEZ, THAT WASN'T WHAT I WAS TRYING TO DO!

SORRY--

--ISN'T GOOD ENOUGH!

BOM

ALEX AND SANDRA SIMMONS WATCH HELPLESSLY, AND LISTEN TO THE SOUND OF OXYGEN MONOTONOUSLY HISSING INTO THE AIR.

A LIFE SOUND THAT NOW SPEAKS OF GRAVE-SIDES AND GRIEVING AND WASTE.

GO AHEAD, CHASE. TELL ME HOW THE GOOD GUYS WON! HOW WE GOT OUR MAN. TELL ME HOW I SHOULD'A REASONED WITH THAT NUT INSTEAD'A BELTIN' HIM, TELL ME IT'S NOT TOO LATE!

NO, I WON'T TELL YOU THAT, CAGE. SOME PEOPLE LIVE THEIR LIVES NEVER LEARNING THE LESSONS THEY SHOULD'VE BEEN TAUGHT AS KIDS.

AND YOU'RE RIGHT. IT IS TOO LATE! PEOPLE HAVE TO LEARN THE LESSON BEFORE IT COMES TO THIS.

IT'S TOO LATE FOR WILDFIRE... THE MOTHER... THE FATHER... THE FAMILY... AND IF WE DON'T GET WITH IT... SOON... IT'LL BE TOO LATE FOR ALL OF US. THERE WON'T BE A...

...NEXT TIME.

NEXT: STICKS AND STONES WILL BREAK YOUR BONES, BUT SPEARS WILL KILL YOU!

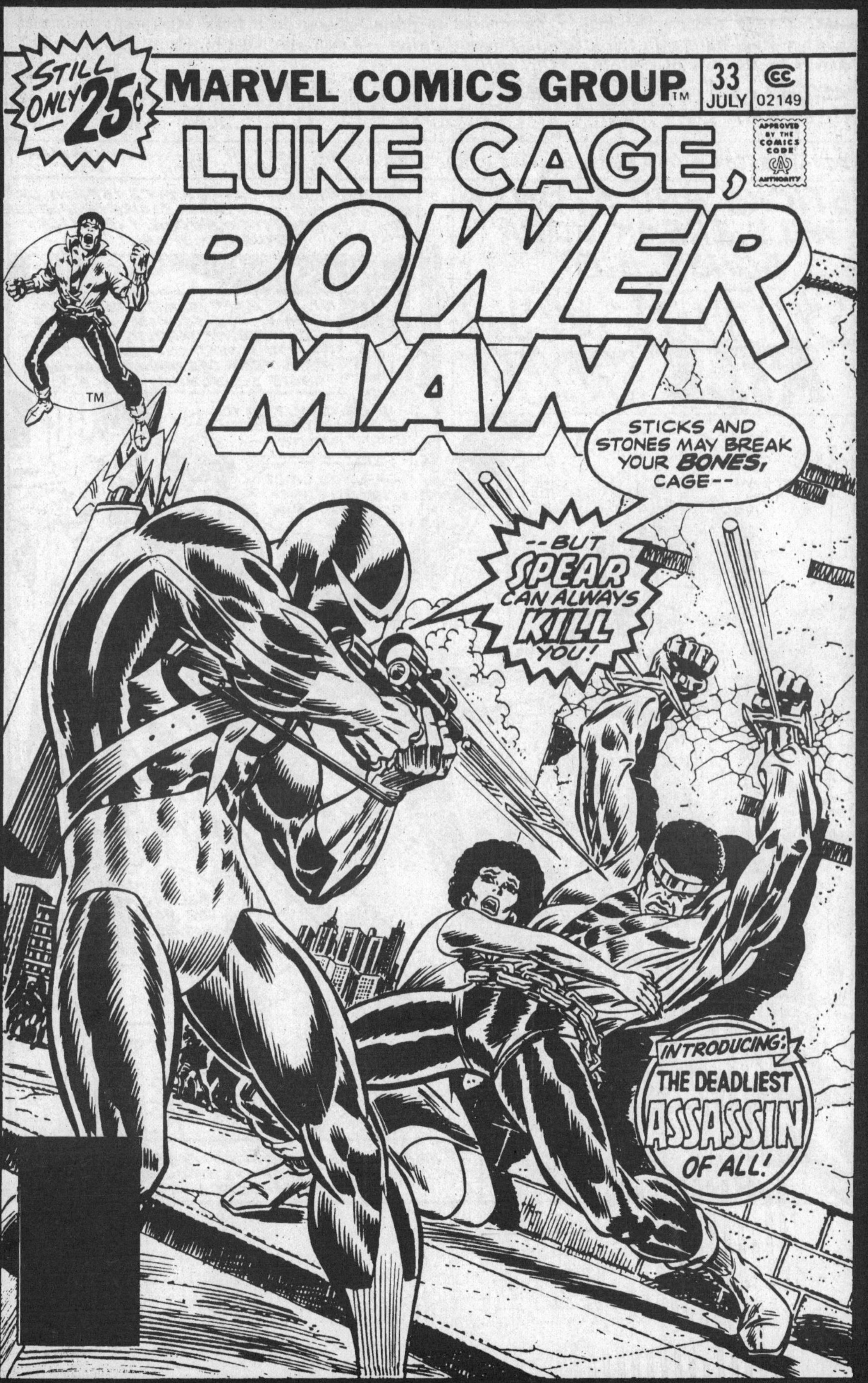
STILL ONLY 25¢
MARVEL COMICS GROUP
33 JULY
CC 02149
APPROVED BY THE COMICS CODE AUTHORITY
LUKE CAGE, POWER MAN
STICKS AND STONES MAY BREAK YOUR BONES, CAGE--
--BUT SPEAR CAN ALWAYS KILL YOU!
INTRODUCING: THE DEADLIEST ASSASSIN OF ALL!

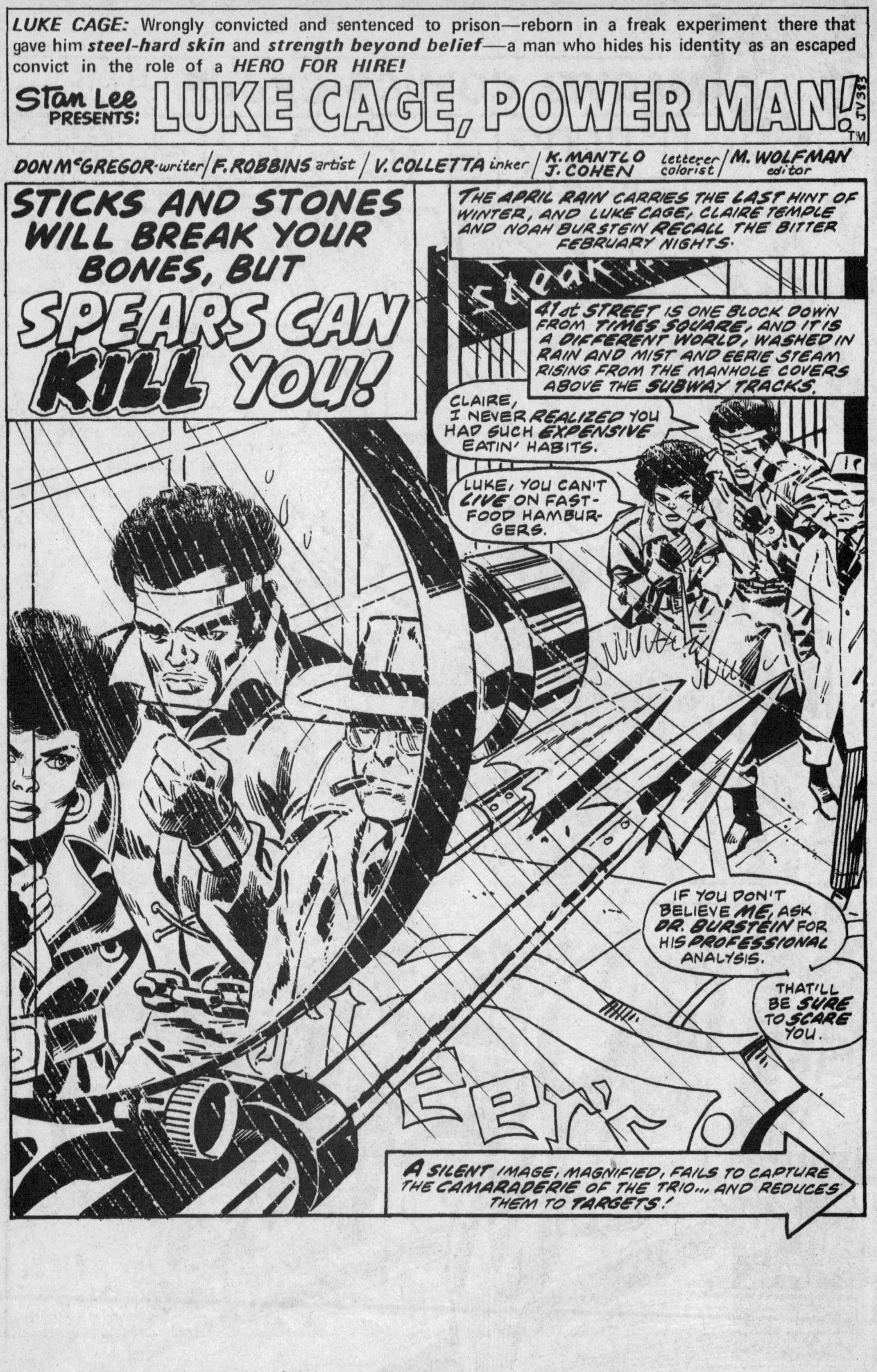
LUKE CAGE: Wrongly convicted and sentenced to prison—reborn in a freak experiment there that gave him steel-hard skin and strength beyond belief—a man who hides his identity as an escaped convict in the role of a HERO FOR HIRE!
Stan Lee PRESENTS: LUKE CAGE, POWER MAN!
DON McGREGOR-writer / F. ROBBINS artist / V. COLLETTA inker / K. MANTLO letterer J. COHEN colorist / M. WOLFMAN editor
STICKS AND STONES WILL BREAK YOUR BONES, BUT SPEARS CAN KILL YOU!
THE APRIL RAIN CARRIES THE LAST HINT OF WINTER, AND LUKE CAGE, CLAIRE TEMPLE AND NOAH BURSTEIN RECALL THE BITTER FEBRUARY NIGHTS.
41st STREET IS ONE BLOCK DOWN FROM TIMES SQUARE, AND IT IS A DIFFERENT WORLD, WASHED IN RAIN AND MIST AND EERIE STEAM RISING FROM THE MANHOLE COVERS ABOVE THE SUBWAY TRACKS.
CLAIRE, I NEVER REALIZED YOU HAD SUCH EXPENSIVE EATIN' HABITS.
LUKE, YOU CAN'T LIVE ON FAST-FOOD HAMBURGERS.
IF YOU DON'T BELIEVE ME, ASK DR. BURSTEIN FOR HIS PROFESSIONAL ANALYSIS.
THAT'LL BE SURE TO SCARE YOU.
A SILENT IMAGE, MAGNIFIED, FAILS TO CAPTURE THE CAMARADERIE OF THE TRIO... AND REDUCES THEM TO TARGETS!

THE SHAFT IS SIX FEET LONG, AND IS EJECTED FROM THE WEAPON WITH HIGH-POWERED VELOCITY.

NO OFFENSE, NOAH, BUT SINCE YOU SET MY SHOULDER STRAIGHT YOU ALREADY SCARE ME.

I BEEN MEANIN' TO TALK TO YOU 'BOUT YOUR BEDSIDE MANNER.

ENOUGH POWER TO SHATTER THROUGH THE COLORFUL DISPLAY SIGN!

THE NEON KALEIDOSCOPE EXPLODES INTO RAZOR EDGED CONFETTI.

IT AIN'T EXACTLY CHAD EVERETT. --WHA--!

LUCAS, I AM BEGINNING TO SUSPECT THAT YOU ARE AFRAID OF ANY DOCTOR.

GET DOWN, NOAH!

KRACK-CHARK

BE CAREFUL, CLAIRE... WE'RE GONNA HIT...

THE MISSILE IMBEDS ITSELF INTO THE CONCRETE, AND REMAINS STANDING, AS IF IT HAS PENETRATED MERE WOOD.

...HARD!

COME ON, CAGE, WHAT ARE YOU WAITING FOR? A FORMAL INVITATION?

I FIGURED I'D HAVE TO DEAL WITH YOU WHEN I WENT AFTER BURSTEIN--

--SO WE MIGHT AS WELL GET IT OVER WITH RIGHT NOW.

THE CHALLENGE SHOULD SOUND ABSURDLY MELODRAMATIC--

--BUT IT DOESN'T!

LUKE, WHAT IS IT?

Y'GOT ME, CLAIRE, BUT THAT CRAZY'S ABOUT READY TO USE US AS PINCUSHIONS AGAIN--

--WHICH DOESN'T LEAVE US TIME TO DISCUSS IT!

IT LEAVES YOU NO TIME AT ALL, CAGE!

YOU AREN'T ANYWHERE NEAR AS QUICK AS SPEAR.

THAT'S ME, CAGE "SPEAR!

AND THE ONLY TIME I MISS MY TARGET IS WHEN IT'S ON PURPOSE.

WHY ME, GOD?

I BEEN GOOD.

CY'S CAFE

WHY DO I HAVE TO MEET UP WITH ALL THE FRUITCAKES?

CAGE'S 300-ODD POUNDS LEAVE A DENT IN THE TRUCK ROOFTOP THAT WILL GIVE THE LOADING DOCK MEN A MYSTERY TO DEBATE OVER THEIR MID-MORNING COFFEE BREAK.

THE ROOF-TOP IS SLICK. THE STONE SEEMS TO HAVE ABSORBED THE NIGHT RAIN, AND FOR A MOMENT CAGE ALMOST TOPPLES BACK ONTO THE STREET--

--BUT HIS MOMENTUM CARRIES HIM OVER THE EDGE.

CAGE STOPS... STUNNED!

THE ROOFTOP IS EMPTY...YET ECHOES WITH SOFT LAUGHTER

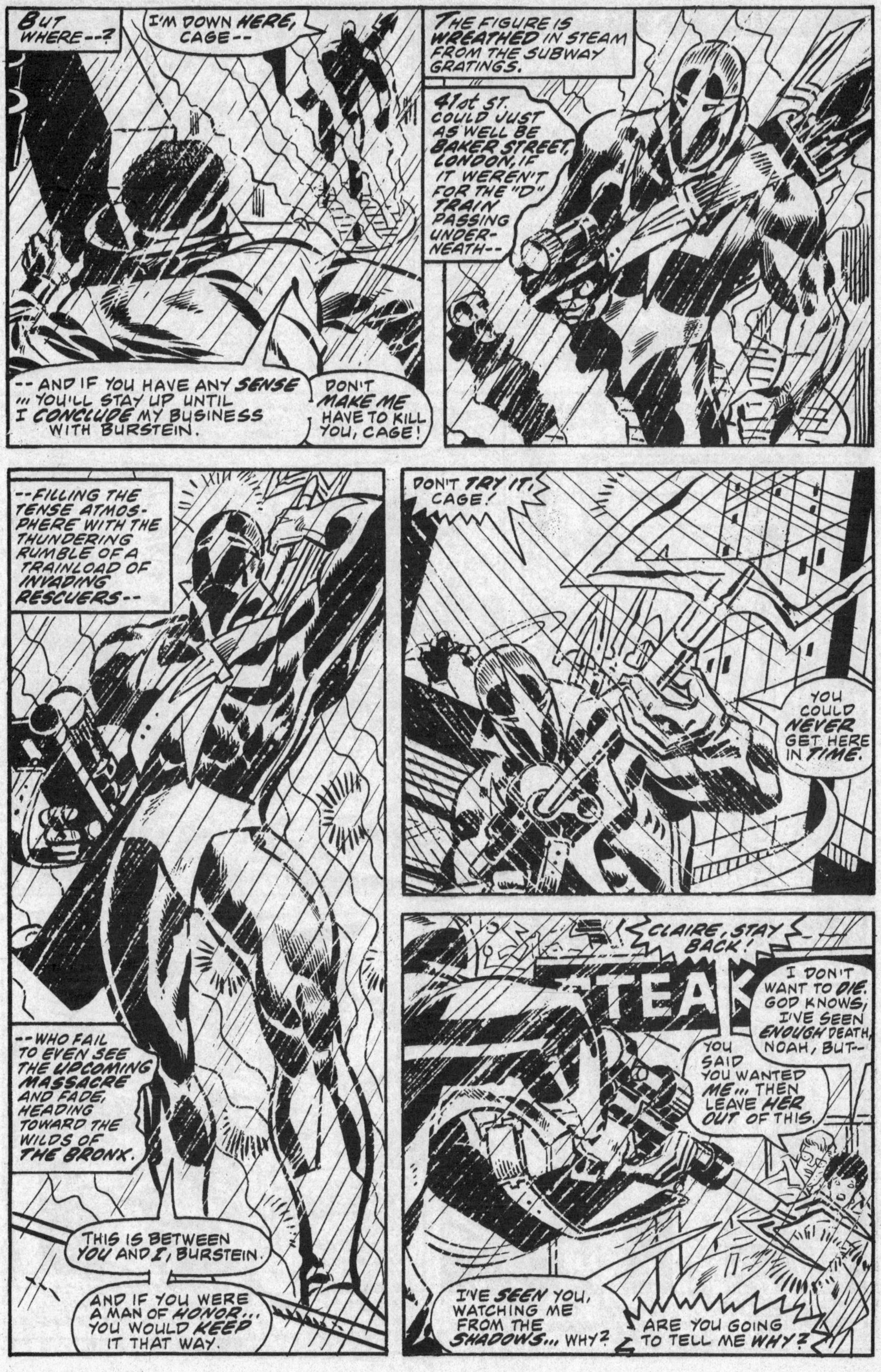
BUT WHERE--?
I'M DOWN HERE, CAGE--
--AND IF YOU HAVE ANY SENSE ... YOU'LL STAY UP UNTIL I CONCLUDE MY BUSINESS WITH BURSTEIN.
DON'T MAKE ME HAVE TO KILL YOU, CAGE!
THE FIGURE IS WREATHED IN STEAM FROM THE SUBWAY GRATINGS.
41st ST. COULD JUST AS WELL BE BAKER STREET, LONDON, IF IT WEREN'T FOR THE "D" TRAIN PASSING UNDERNEATH--
--FILLING THE TENSE ATMOSPHERE WITH THE THUNDERING RUMBLE OF A TRAINLOAD OF INVADING RESCUERS--
--WHO FAIL TO EVEN SEE THE UPCOMING MASSACRE AND FADE, HEADING TOWARD THE WILDS OF THE BRONX.
THIS IS BETWEEN YOU AND I, BURSTEIN.
AND IF YOU WERE A MAN OF HONOR... YOU WOULD KEEP IT THAT WAY.
DON'T TRY IT, CAGE!
YOU COULD NEVER GET HERE IN TIME.
CLAIRE, STAY BACK!
TEAK
I DON'T WANT TO DIE. GOD KNOWS, I'VE SEEN ENOUGH DEATH, NOAH, BUT--
YOU SAID YOU WANTED ME... THEN LEAVE HER OUT OF THIS.
I'VE SEEN YOU, WATCHING ME FROM THE SHADOWS... WHY?
ARE YOU GOING TO TELL ME WHY?

CHEERS-STEAK HOUSE

CAGE WIPES FRANTICALLY AT THE RAIN THAT DISTORTS HIS VISION.

IS THAT MANIAC GOING TO SHOOT EVEN IF HE DOESN'T ATTACK?

YOU PLAY THE *PROTECTOR* NOW, NOAH BURSTEIN. *HOW GALLANT!*

IT IS A *DIFFERENT ROLE* THAN YOU'VE PLAYED IN THE *PAST!*

HE WANTS TO *SCREAM* FOR CLAIRE AND NOAH, THE WAY HE SCREAMED FOR LITTLE AUGIE SIMMONS.

AND HE KNOWS THE SCREAM WON'T *CHANGE* THE OUTCOME.

AS A DOCTOR, BURSTEIN... YOU ARE A *HYPOCRITE!* WHEN YOU HEAL A PATIENT THESE DAYS, DOES IT *SALVE* YOUR CONSCIENCE?

AND EVEN IF YOUR MEDICAL DEVOTION WERE *SINCERE*... WHICH I DOUBT... EVEN IF YOU HAD TRULY *REPENTED* AND SOUGHT DELIVERANCE...

I DO NOT--

I CANNOT--

--FORGIVE YOU!

JEREMY DRAKE AND HIS WIFE HAVE JUST FINISHED A STEAK, CONSUMED SOME WINE, AND CONDUCTED THEMSELVES WITH *SOPHISTICATED ARROGANCE.*

THE ARROGANCE IS STRIPPED FROM THEM THE MOMENT THEY SPOT THE *MISSILE* HEADING TOWARD THEM.

OF COURSE, JEREMY DRAKE HAS NO IDEA WHAT THE MISSILE *IS* THAT SLAMS INTO HIS *THROAT* AND DRIVES HIM *BACK* INTO THE DOOR.

BUT IT *KILLS* ALL HIS LIFE-TIME ILLUSIONS IN LESS THAN FIVE SECONDS.

HANG IT UP, "ACTION-JACKSON!"

WE GOT ENOUGH PEOPLE GOIN' OFF THE DEEP-END IN THIS CITY AN' KILLING OTHERS!

THIS LUNACY STOPS HERE!

KRACK!

AND-- AHHH!

NORMALLY, WHEN YOU ARE HIT IN THE MOUTH, SEVERAL UNPLEASANT ACTIONS OCCUR.

FIRST, YOUR HEAD POUNDS A JOHN PHILIP SOUSA MARCH, COMPLETE WITH CRASHING CYMBALS.

SECOND, YOUR VISION CREATES AWARD-WINNING ABSTRACT PAINTINGS.

AND THIRD, PERHAPS MOST UNPLEASANT, YOUR OWN TEETH BETRAY YOU, CARVING UP THE INSIDE OF YOUR MOUTH. IT WILL REMIND YOU FOR WEEKS THAT YOU SHOULD HAVE DUCKED FASTER.

THAT'S WHAT HAPPENS NORMALLY.

BUT NOT THIS TIME!

OKAY, SUPER-FLY. I DON'T KNOW HOW YOU CAN STOMACH BURSTEIN--

--BUT THAT'S NOT A PROBLEM YOU'LL HAVE TO WORRY ABOUT MUCH LONGER. I'LL BE BACK--

"--AND YOU CAN TELL BURSTEIN HE CAN COUNT ON THAT!"

NOAH? ...YOU OKAY?

IT WAS ME HE WANTED TO KILL, LUCAS, WASN'T IT?

ME.

LUKE, THE POLICE ARE ON THEIR WAY. FOR ONCE, LET THEM DO WHAT THEY'RE PAID TO DO.

JER... JEREMY, PL...PLEASE LET IT BE O-OVER!

AAWWWAAARRRRR

THEY'RE NOT AS INVULNERABLE AS I AM, CLAIRE--

--AN' THEY DON'T HAVE A PERSONAL STAKE IN THIS!

AND THEY'D BE MUCH MORE FORGIVING THAN I WILL!

SPEAR CROSSES 6TH AVENUE RECKLESSLY.

COMPARED TO NEARBY BROADWAY, 6TH AVENUE IS VIRTUALLY COLORLESS AND SILENT. THERE ISN'T A SINGLE COMPUTER-GAME OR SHOOTING-GALLERY IN SIGHT. BUT SPEAR COMES DANGEROUSLY NEAR BEING STRUCK DOWN--

--UNTIL THE DRIVER SWERVES, REALIZING IN ONE STARTLING SECOND THAT HE HAS CAUGHT ANOTHER HUMAN BEING IN HIS HEADLIGHTS.

CAGE!

MAN, AM I GLAD THIS ISN'T A TRACTOR-TRAILER!

--OR THEY'D BE SCRAPING ME OFF THIS STREET FROM HERE TO ROCKE-FELLER CENTER.

THE DARK, AUSTERE OFFICE BUILDINGS SEEM TO SCOWL DIS-APPROVINGLY. THEY HAVE BEEN DESIGNED TO PRESENT A FORMIDABLE IMAGE OF RESPECTABILITY, AS IF DENYING THEIR CLOSE PROXIMITY TO TIMES SQUARE.

I DIDN'T WANT TO HAVE TO KILL YOU, CAGE--

--BUT YOU'RE NOT LEAVING ME ANY CHOICE.

CAGE TAKES THE STEPS INTO WILLIAM CULLEN BRYANT PARK FOUR-AT-A-TIME--

--AND HEARS A STRANGE HISS-ING SOUND. HE CAN'T STOP! AND HIS MOMEN-TUM IS CARRYING HIM RIGHT INTO THE BIZARRE SPEAR!

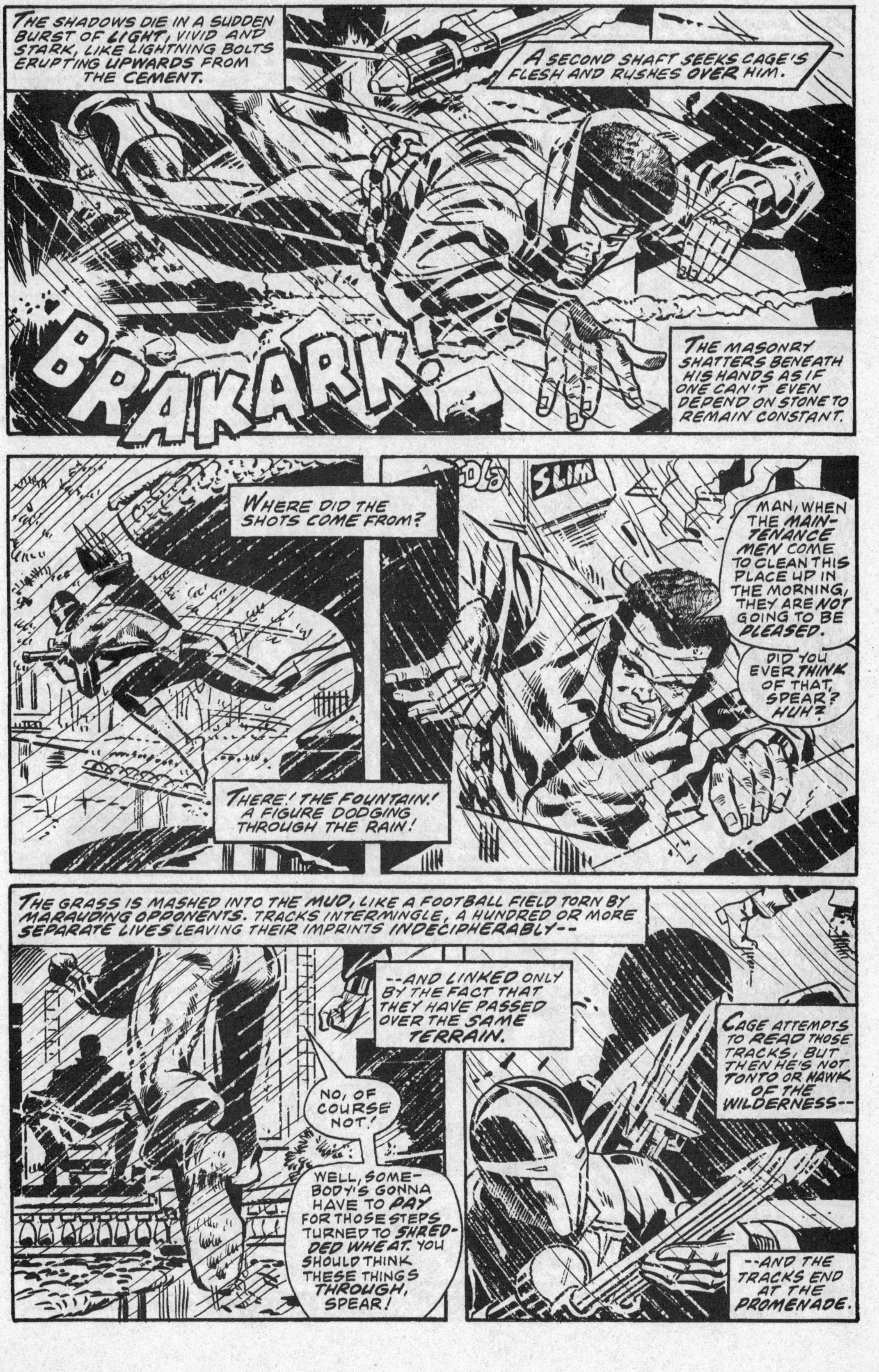

THE SHADOWS DIE IN A SUDDEN BURST OF LIGHT, VIVID AND STARK, LIKE LIGHTNING BOLTS ERUPTING UPWARDS FROM THE CEMENT.
A SECOND SHAFT SEEKS CAGE'S FLESH AND RUSHES OVER HIM.
BRAKARK!
THE MASONRY SHATTERS BENEATH HIS HANDS AS IF ONE CAN'T EVEN DEPEND ON STONE TO REMAIN CONSTANT.
WHERE DID THE SHOTS COME FROM?
THERE! THE FOUNTAIN! A FIGURE DODGING THROUGH THE RAIN!
SLIM
MAN, WHEN THE MAINTENANCE MEN COME TO CLEAN THIS PLACE UP IN THE MORNING, THEY ARE NOT GOING TO BE PLEASED.
DID YOU EVER THINK OF THAT, SPEAR? HUH?
THE GRASS IS MASHED INTO THE MUD, LIKE A FOOTBALL FIELD TORN BY MARAUDING OPPONENTS. TRACKS INTERMINGLE, A HUNDRED OR MORE SEPARATE LIVES LEAVING THEIR IMPRINTS INDECIPHERABLY--
--AND LINKED ONLY BY THE FACT THAT THEY HAVE PASSED OVER THE SAME TERRAIN.
NO, OF COURSE NOT!
WELL, SOMEBODY'S GONNA HAVE TO PAY FOR THOSE STEPS TURNED TO SHREDDED WHEAT. YOU SHOULD THINK THESE THINGS THROUGH, SPEAR!
CAGE ATTEMPTS TO READ THOSE TRACKS, BUT THEN HE'S NOT TONTO OR HAWK OF THE WILDERNESS--
--AND THE TRACKS END AT THE PROMENADE.

FOUR SHAFTS FIRE AS ONE, CLEAVING THROUGH THE RAIN.

THE TREES LINING THE PROMENADE ALL BEND TOWARD 6th AVENUE, A WOOD REGIMENT WHOSE SPIRIT HAS BEEN BROKEN AND FORCED TO PAY HOMAGE TO THE DISTANT STREET LAMPS.

THE FOUR SHAFTS TAKE ON INDIVIDUAL STATUS, LIFT CAGE OFF THE PROMENADE--

--AND SHACKLE HIM TO THE ROW OF TREES!

I'VE ABOUT HAD IT WITH EVERY MICKEY MOUSE SHARP-SHOOTER IN THE FIVE BOR-OUGHS OF NEW YORK USING ME FOR SHOOTING PRACTICE!

Y'HEAR ME, SPEAR?

HE DOESN'T!

CAGE STANDS IN THE RAIN, AND IT FANS HIS ANGER.

HE SEARCHES THE SHADOWS, BUT ONLY THE GRAFFITI REMAINS. THE STATUE OF WILLIAM CULLEN BRYANT CONTINUES TO READ HIS MARBLE BOOK, IGNORING THE GRAFFITI, THE RAIN, AND THE PEOPLE WHO SPEND THE NIGHT IN HIS DOMAIN.

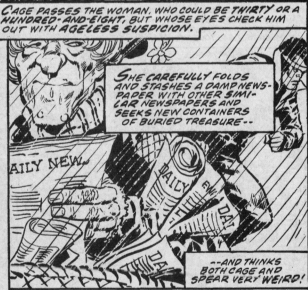

CAGE PASSES THE WOMAN, WHO COULD BE THIRTY OR A HUNDRED-AND-EIGHT, BUT WHOSE EYES CHECK HIM OUT WITH AGELESS SUSPICION.

SHE CAREFULLY FOLDS AND STASHES A DAMP NEWS-PAPER WITH OTHER SIMI-LAR NEWSPAPERS AND SEEKS NEW CONTAINERS OF BURIED TREASURE--

DAILY NEW.

--AND THINKS BOTH CAGE AND SPEAR VERY WEIRD!

DETECTIVE 2ND GRADE QUENTIN CHASE STARES INTO THE HORROR LOCKED IN JEREMY SLATE'S EYES AND REALIZES SLATE CAN'T STOP THE TEARS AND DOESN'T KNOW HOW ELSE TO EXPRESS HIS TERROR.

AND CHASE WONDERS WHEN HE LEARNED HOW TO ACCEPT THE UNACCEPTABLE. OR CAN HE ACCEPT IT? OUTWARDLY, CERTAINLY. BUT INSIDE--?

I COULDN'T BREATHE... COULDN'T...

NOAH BURSTEIN STARES INTO THE BLURRED LENSES OF HIS GLASSES ...AND DOESN'T THINK TO WIPE THEM CLEAN.

TELL US, MR. SLATE... HOW DID IT FEEL AT THE ACTUAL MOMENT OF IMPACT?

WHAT DO YOU THINK THEY SHOULD DO TO THE MAN WHO DID THIS IF THEY CATCH HIM?

MR. SLATE... WERE YOU SCARED?

I... I... COULDN'T BREATHE... COULDN'T...

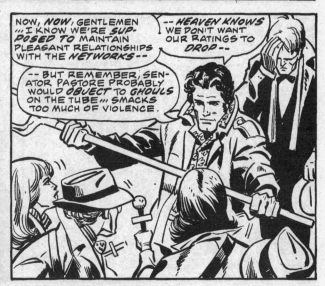

NOW, NOW, GENTLEMEN ...I KNOW WE'RE SUPPOSED TO MAINTAIN PLEASANT RELATIONSHIPS WITH THE NETWORKS--

--BUT REMEMBER, SENATOR PASTORE PROBABLY WOULD OBJECT TO GHOULS ON THE TUBE ...SMACKS TOO MUCH OF VIOLENCE.

-- HEAVEN KNOWS WE DON'T WANT OUR RATINGS TO DROP--

BY THE WAY, DO YOU GUYS THINK WATCHING COP SHOWS HAS WARPED YOUR MINDS?

WHAT I'M GETTING AT IS THAT YOU GUYS SHOULD HAVE A LITTLE HEART. JUST A LITTLE.

WE'RE ONLY DOING OUR JOB, OFFICER. NO NEED BEING SARCASTIC.

SARCASTIC? ME? IS THAT WHAT I WAS BEING?

CAGE STALKS THROUGH THE RAIN, HIS FLESH TAKING THE COLOR OF THE FLASHING RED LIGHTS AND ...SMOULDERING IN HIS EYES!

CAGE... YOU **KNOW** THESE PEOPLE?

WE'VE MET. YOU MADE **GOOD TIME** TONIGHT, CHASE.

IN THE THICK OF IT AGAIN, **RIGHT, CAGE?** IS THERE **ANY** ACT OF VIOLENCE THAT HAPPENS IN THIS CITY YOU **AREN'T** DIRECTLY INVOLVED IN?

WAY **YOU** SPEAK CHASE, A MAN'D THINK **EVERYBODY** IN TIMES SQUARE OR CENTRAL PARK COULDN'T GET THROUGH THE **DAY** WITHOUT GETTIN' MUGGED, MOLESTED--

--OR TICKLED.

FORGIVE ME, CHASE. THAT WASN'T ONE OF MY **BETTER** COMEBACKS, BUT THIS HASN'T BEEN ONE'A MY **BETTER NIGHTS** EITHER.

WHAT WAS ALL THIS **SPEAR**-SHOOTIN' ABOUT, NOAH? IT WAS YOUR **TAIL** HE WAS AFTER.

WHAT IS **IT**, MAN... SOME KINDA **VENDETTA--?**

--OR WHAT?

I DON'T KNOW.

NOAH, THE MAN'S **GOTTA** HAVE A REASON.

YES, LUCAS, YOU'RE **RIGHT.** A MAN WOULDN'T BE **DRIVEN** TO WHAT THIS MAN HAS **DONE** IF HE DIDN'T HAVE A REASON.

I WISH I **KNEW** WHAT COULD MAKE ANOTHER HUMAN BEING WANT SO **DESPERATELY** TO KILL ME.

I COULD **HEAR** IT IN HIS VOICE, LUCAS--

--HEAR THE HATRED OF YEARS...

--AND I **DON'T KNOW HIM--**

--NOR WHY HE SHOULD HATE ME IN A WAY THAT CONSUMES HIS WHOLE LIFE. FORGIVE ME, GENTLEMEN, BUT IF YOU DON'T **NEED** ME ANY FURTHER, I WANT TO RETURN TO THE **CLINIC.**

GOODNIGHT, DETECTIVE CHASE. SAY GOODNIGHT TO **CLAIRE** FOR ME, LUCAS.

NOAH BURNTEIN WATCHES THE TAXI-METER TICK OFF 1/6 MILES AT 10¢ A CLICK. A DIME A *BLOCK*, FROM 41st AND SIXTH TO THE *STOREFRONT CLINIC* IN HARLEM. THE PRICE HAS GONE UP SINCE HARRY CHAPIN SANG HIS SONG ABOUT TAXIS.

YEAH, IT'S THE *KIDS* YOU GOTTA *WATCH OUT* FOR IN HARLEM THESE DAYS.

THEY'RE *ALL* WORKIN' THEIR LITTLE *DODGES.*

'CEPT WHATTA YOU GONNA *DO* WHEN ITS A *KID*?

TELL YA, MISTER, THEY DON'T WANT YOU PACKING A *PIECE.* BUT I FIGGER I GOT A RIGHT TO *PROTECT* MYSELF, *RIGHT*?

YES--

--WHAT *ARE* YOU GOING TO DO?

WHAT AM I GOING TO DO?

DURING THE RIDE *UPTOWN*, HE HAS REVIEWED HIS LIFE TO THE *BEAT* OF DIMES *DEVOURED* BY MILES.

LIKE MOST INTROSPECTIVE MEN, NOAH FINDS HIMSELF *WANTING* IN MANY AREAS--

--AND WISHES THERE WERE *SOMEONE* TO *CONSOLE* HIM THROUGH THE *DARK HOURS* AND NOT CARE THAT HE IS *NOT* PERFECT.

WWUUU-

THE SPEAR THAT TEARS THROUGH THE DOORWAY OF THE CLINIC DOES NOT CONSOLE HIM IN THE LEAST.

AND NEITHER DOES THE MESSAGE THE DEADLY MISSILE HAS DELIVERED.

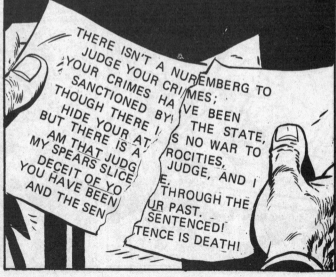

THERE ISN'T A NUREMBERG TO JUDGE YOUR CRIMES; YOUR CRIMES HAVE BEEN SANCTIONED BY THE STATE, THOUGH THERE IS NO WAR TO HIDE YOUR ATROCITIES, BUT THERE IS A JUDGE, AND I AM THAT JUDGE. THROUGH THE DECEIT OF YOUR PAST. YOU HAVE BEEN SENTENCED! AND THE SENTENCE IS DEATH!

THE *GEM THEATER* IS STILL OPEN WHEN CAGE FINALLY ENTERS THE BUILDING. HE SPOTS *D.W.* AND *WIN.*

IN THE BACK GROUND, ROBERT REDFORD AS *JEREMIAH JOHNSON* KILLS HIS FIRST GRIZZLY FOR THE *THIRD* TIME THAT NIGHT. NOT STANDARD FARE FOR THE GRIND-EM-TO-A-PULP MARKET OF *42ND* STREET.

BUT THE *POSTERS* OUTSIDE COULD CONVINCE THE GRIND-EM-TO-A-PULP MARKET *OTHERWISE.*

I'VE TALKED TO A FEW OF THE *STUDENTS* I KNOW FROM *HUNTER* AND THEY SEEM EXCITED ABOUT YOUR FILM PROJECT, *D.W.*

HELLO, *LUKE.* HAVE A *GOOD TIME* TONIGHT?

FANTASTIC. WE ALMOST BECAME THE *MEAL.* WHATCHA GOT THERE?

WHAT DOES IT *LOOK* LIKE, MAN? MY 16MM *BOLEX AIREFLEX.* GONNA MAKE MOVING *PICTURES,* WHAT DO YOU THINK ABOUT THAT? GONNA DO MY *ORSON WELLES* ACT.

SOMETHING WITH *MEANING.* WORKS ON *DIFFERENT LEVELS....* YOU KNOW-- DEPENDS ON HOW YOU *INTERPRET* IT.

HOW SHOULD I INTERPRET THIS *MECHANICAL MONSTER* HERE?

BETTER TALK *NICE* TO IT, *LUKE....* THE MACHINE'S TEMPERAMENTAL.

YEAH, WELL SO AM I, D.W..... *SO AM I*--

--AND THAT'S THE LAST *35¢* THIS *MONEY-HUNGRY MONSTROSITY* GOBBLES UP ON ME!

WHACKETY!

Y'HEAR THAT *MACHINE?*

YOU'VE PUT THE *SCREWS* TO ME ONCE TOO OFTEN. THIS *TIME...* YOU AIN'T GETTIN' OFF *EASY.*

HEY, WAITA-MINNIT NOW--!! NOW *HOLD ON* A SEC!

THAT'S *ENOUGH!* I SAID, *THAT'S ENOUGH.*

SPLOOOSH!

I CAN'T BELIEVE IT. IT'S DOIN' *IT* TO ME AGAIN. C'MON, GIMME A *BREAK!*

THE NEXT DAY IS BRIGHT AND CLEAR, THE SKY A COLOR BLUE SO RICH AND PURE THAT THE MIND HAS TROUBLE BELIEVING IT IS REAL.

STANDING AT THE GRAVESITE FOR AUGGIE SIMMONS, CAGE CURSES THAT RICH AND PURE BLUE. THE SKY SHOULD BE GREY, AS BLEAK AS THE EVENTS IN THIS QUEENS CEMETERY.

PLEASE, LORD, RECEIVE THIS INNOCENT.

INNOCENT, THAT'S RIGHT!

HE LOOKS AT ALEX AND SANDY SIMMONS... AND LITTLE BETH... AND A MENTAL MIRAGE OF ALEX'S FACE WHEN HE FIRST CAME TO THE GEM THEATRE TO HIRE THE "BROTHER" POWER MAN.

HIS SON WAS STILL ALIVE THEN.

POWER ISN'T EVERYTHING. IT DIDN'T STOP A SICK, DISILLUSIONED MAN FROM FULFILLING HIS DESIRE TO DESTROY.

ALEX...WISHED I COULD HELP MAKE IT HURT LESS.

AN' I KNOW I CAN'T. BUT I WISH I COULD.

MAN WHO DID THIS IS IN PRISON, LUKE. WE GOT JUSTICE, ISN'T THAT WHAT WE GOT?

THEY PUT THE MAN AWAY... BUT AUGGIE'S STILL DEAD. I KEEP EXPECTIN' TO HEAR HIM CALL "DAD" IN THAT LITTLE VOICE OF HIS.

I STILL KNOW THE SOUND OF MY SON'S VOICE, LUKE. HE HAD HIS OWN VOICE, LUKE.

MAN WHO DID THIS, WHAT DO YOU THINK..., THINK HE'LL BE ELIGIBLE FOR PAROLE IN THREE YEARS.

ONE THING I DO KNOW..., AUGGIE... WON'T BE BACK IN THREE YEARS.

NOT EVER.

LITTLE BETH DOES NOT CRY.

CAGE WONDERS HOW SHE *SEES* THAT NIGHT... THE NIGHT *WILDFIRE* SET THE HOUSE *ABLAZE*... AND AUGGIE TOLD HER HE WAS PLAYING *HIDE-AND-SEEK.*

SHE HAS *WITHDRAWN,* THE YOUNG EYES ARE STILL *YOUNG*...YET THEY ARE *ALSO OLD.* AND IT *SCARES* CAGE.

LITTLE BETH... HONEY... WOULD YOU LIKE ME TO HOLD YOU? IT'S ME, LUKE.

AUGGIE LIKED TO CALL ME "*THE POWER MAN*" YOU WANTA *TALK ABOUT* AUGGIE, LITTLE BETH?

I KNOW YOU MUSTA *LOVED* AUGGIE *VERY* MUCH.

IT'S *HARD,* LITTLE BETH. HARD TO *LOSE* SOMEONE YOU LOVE.

BUT YOUR MOMMY AND YOUR DADDY, *THEY* LOVE YOU.

CAN YOU *HEAR* ME, LITTLE BETH?

G'BYE, HONEY.

PLEASE... BE OKAY, HUH?

CHARLTON GRUNDGE and GRASSY MOSS SEE THE SECRETARIES WHO HAVE FLOCKED TO THEIR LUNCH-TIME OASIS OUTSIDE CENTRAL PARK, BUT THE PARK ITSELF MIGHT AS WELL BE ANOTHER HOTEL OR RESTAURANT AS FAR AS THEY ARE CONCERNED.

A HOT DOG IS HOW MUCH?

I TOLD 'JA.... 50¢ ALREADY.

BUSES AND HOT DOG STANDS, AND BORED HORSES WITH DYING FLOWERS IN THEIR MANES WHO WAIT TO PULL LOVERS THROUGH THE PARK IN CARRIAGES SUPPOSEDLY REFLECTIVE OF THE GAY 90'S, ALL CROWD THE AREA.

I WANT TO NAIL CAGE! YOU HEAR ME, GRASSY.... I WANT HIM CRUCIFIED!

WELL, YOU'VE CERTAINLY MADE UP FOR THE TIME YOU HAD YOUR MOUTH WIRED SHUT, CHARLTON. AND, YES, CHARLTON, I KNOW IT WAS BECAUSE CAGE HIT YOU THAT YOU HAD YOUR MOUTH WIRED TIGHT.

NOW, YOU LISTEN, I'M A LAW-YER -- A GOOD ONE. YOU SHOULDN'T WORRY A-BOUT WHAT OTHER PEOPLE WILL THINK ABOUT YOU, CHARLTON.... THAT WAY YOU DON'T STOP DOING THINGS AT THEIR EXPENSE.

TAKE CAGE-- HE SPOUTS MORALITY. AND, LIKE EVERYBODY ELSE, TWISTS IT TO FIT HIS OWN TERMS. RIGHT AND WRONG, WHO'S TO DECIDE?

LET A JUDGE DECIDE. HE GETS PAID FOR IT.

WE'LL GET CAGE, CHARLTON. BELIEVE ME.... BUT I'D LIKE TO HELP CAGE HANG HIMSELF.

WE'LL GIVE HIM THE ROPE ... WE'LL GIVE HIM THE TREE LIMB, AND IF HE NEEDS IT --

SLOSH!

CLINK! CLINK!

--THE PUSH!

THE APRIL DAY PASSES. THE FUNERAL ENDS; THE DINNERS ARE FINISHED. CLAIRE TEMPLE WALKS OUT OF THE STOREFRONT CLINIC, AND REALIZES SHE HAS DONE THAT SAME ACTION FOR THE PAST TWO YEARS.

YOU SURE YOU'LL BE ALRIGHT, NOAH?

I CAN'T THINK OF ANY REASON WHY I SHOULDN'T. THERE'S BEEN NO WORD FROM THE MAN WHO ATTACKED US LAST NIGHT!

I PRAY THAT IT'S PAST!

OKAY, NOAH. YOU SLEEP TIGHT. I'D STAY, BUT I HAVE AN IDEA LUKE WILL BE FEELING PRETTY DOWN AFTER THE FUNERAL TODAY.

AND I KINDA NEED HIM, TOO.

NOAH STANDS IN THE DOORWAY UNTIL THE SUBWAY SWALLOWS CLAIRE. HE IS ALONE WITH THE CITY, BREATHING IT AND FEELING IT, WHEN THE FLAMING SPEAR CUTS INTO HIS MEDITATION.

IT IS NOT OVER!

DON'T WORRY, BURSTEIN ... YOU WON'T HAVE TO SWEAT MUCH LONGER!

SOON, YOU'LL BURN IN THE FIRES OF THE HELL YOU CREATED!

AND EVEN CAGE--

--EVEN HE CAN'T STOP YOUR DEATH!

NEXT:

DEATH, TAXES and SPRINGTIME VENDETTAS

THE I.R.S. AFTER CAGE? SPEAR HITS THE TARGET? A NEW VILLAIN CALLED THE MANGLER? YES, TRUE-BELIEVER, ALL THIS AND MORE -- YOU'VE GOT TO BE HERE TO REALLY BELIEVE IT. •

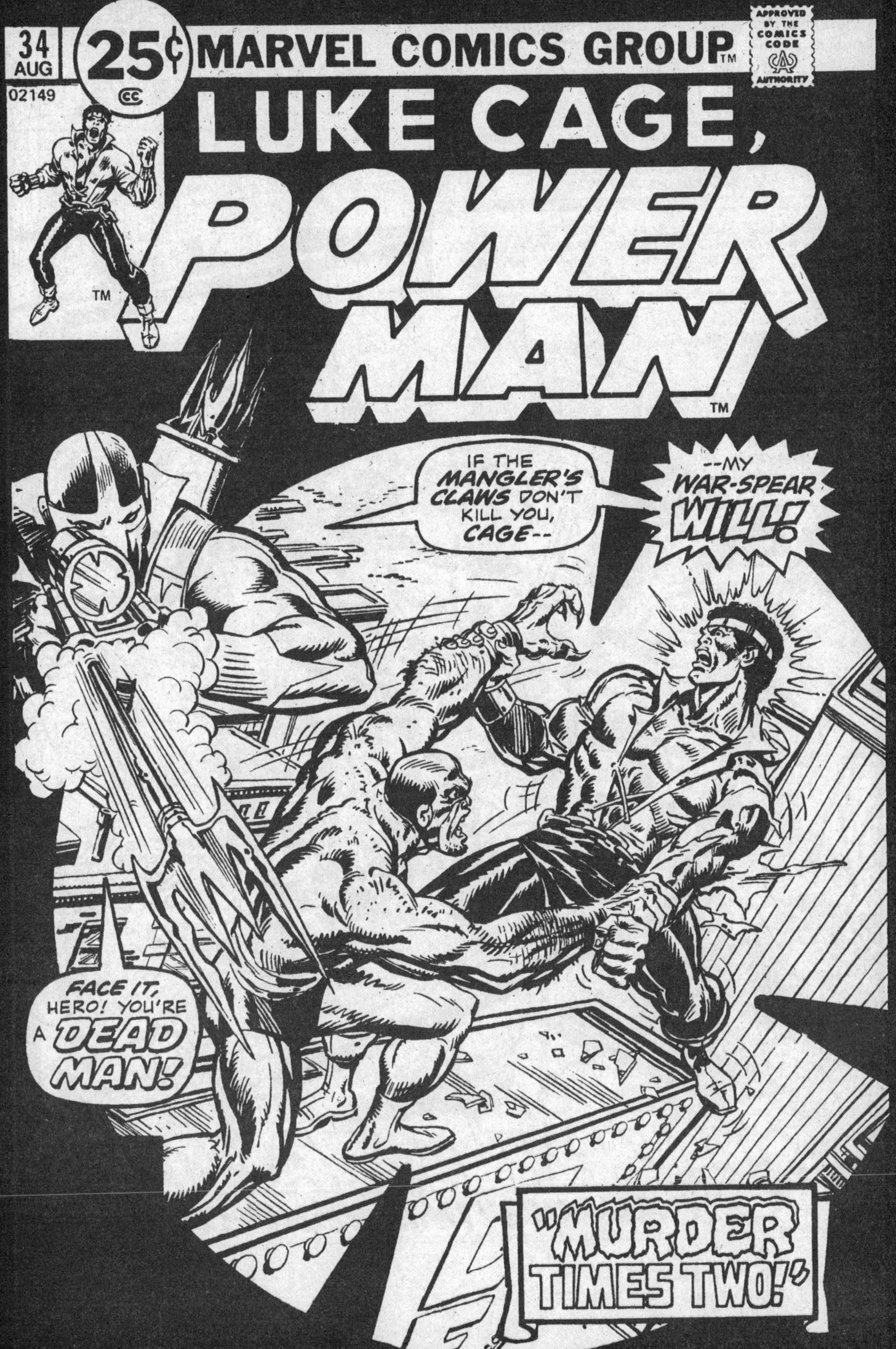
34
AUG
25¢
MARVEL COMICS GROUP
02149
LUKE CAGE,
POWER MAN
IF THE MANGLER'S CLAWS DON'T KILL YOU, CAGE--
--MY WAR-SPEAR WILL!
FACE IT, HERO! YOU'RE A DEAD MAN!
"MURDER TIMES TWO!"

LUKE CAGE: Wrongly convicted and sentenced to prison—reborn in a freak experiment there that gave him *steel-hard skin* and *strength beyond belief*—a man who hides his identity as an escaped convict in the role of a HERO FOR HIRE!

Stan Lee PRESENTS: LUKE CAGE, POWER MAN!

SOMEWHERE IN THE MANHATTAN LAW BOOKS THERE IS A PASSAGE THAT FORBIDS A MAN TO LIVE IN THE SAME QUARTERS HE IS USING AS A BUSINESS OFFICE.

LUKE CAGE EATS, SLEEPS, AND OTHERWISE EXISTS, SUCH AS IT IS, IN HIS CRACKED PLASTER AND SPLINTERY WOOD OFFICE OVER THE GEM THEATER!

CAGE HAS NEVER HEARD ABOUT THE LAW CONCERNING RESIDENCE IN AN OFFICE ON 42ND ST., BUT HE IS VAGUELY AWARE OF THE PASSAGE THAT FROWNS ON BREAKING DOWN DOORS OF SAID OFFICES.

THAT BIT OF LEGAL LEGERDEMAIN WOULD HAVE FORCED SUCH CLASSIC, DOWN-ON-THEIR-LUCK, HARD-BOILED PRIVATE EYES AS RAYMOND CHANDLER'S PHILIP MARLOWE INTO EVEN BLEAKER OUTLOOKS FROM THEIR GRIMY WINDOWS.

NOT THAT THOSE LAWS SEEM TO DO MUCH GOOD WHERE LUKE CAGE IS CONCERNED.

AHHH, COME ON, FOLKS! CUT ME SOME SLACK!

DON'T BE GOIN' AN' BUSTIN' ANOTHER DOOR TO HELL AN' GONE! D.W.'s UNCLE IS ALREADY UPPIN' THE RENT ON THIS HOLE!

DON McGREGOR ·WRITER·
F. ROBBINS ·ARTIST·
F. SPRINGER ·INKER·
IRV WATANABE ·LETTERER·
DON WARFIELD ·COLORIST·
ARCHIE GOODWIN, EDITOR·

DEATH, TAXES, and SPRINGTIME VENDETTAS!

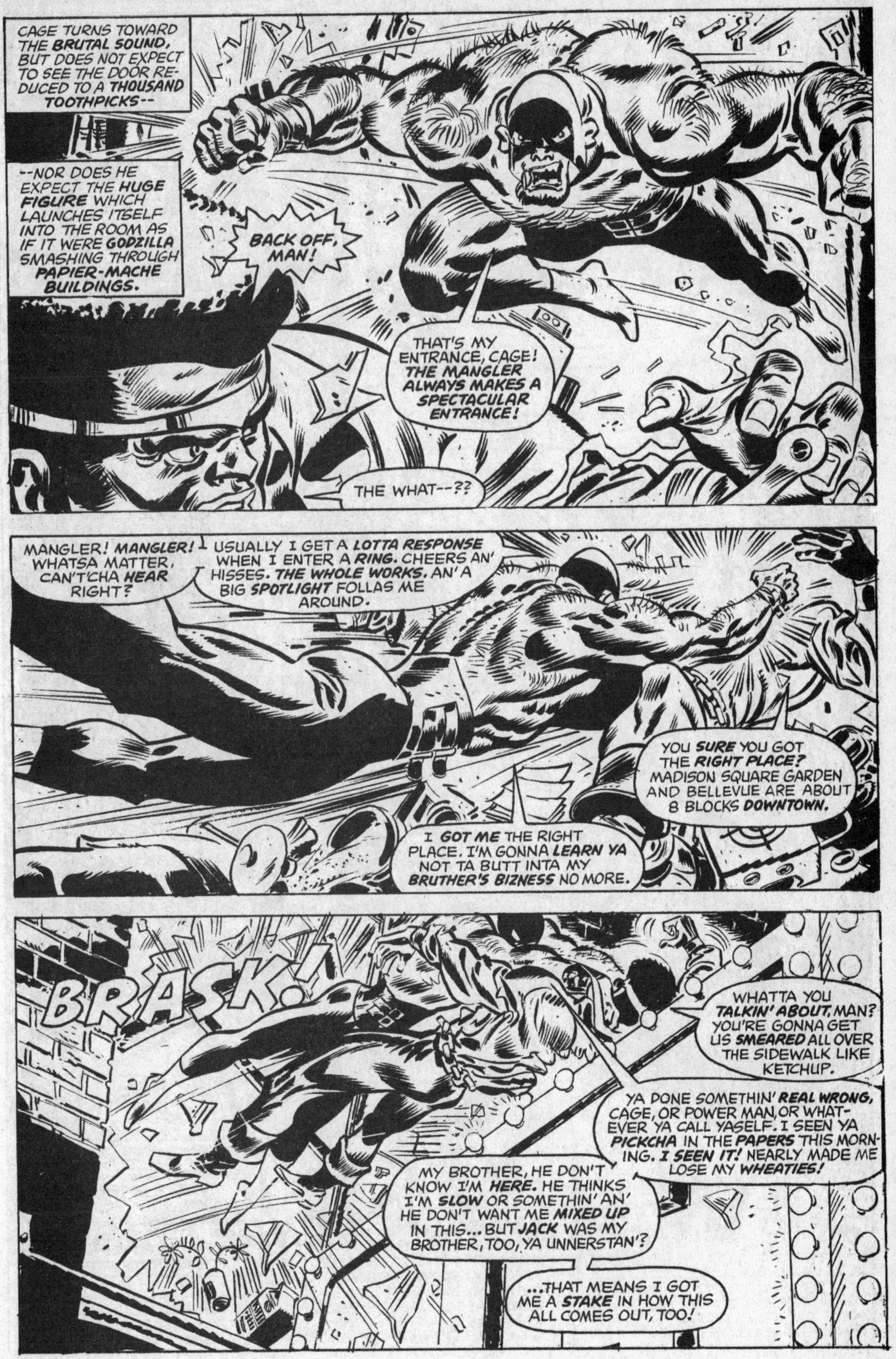
CAGE TURNS TOWARD THE BRUTAL SOUND, BUT DOES NOT EXPECT TO SEE THE DOOR REDUCED TO A THOUSAND TOOTHPICKS--
--NOR DOES HE EXPECT THE HUGE FIGURE WHICH LAUNCHES ITSELF INTO THE ROOM AS IF IT WERE GODZILLA SMASHING THROUGH PAPIER-MACHE BUILDINGS.
BACK OFF, MAN!
THAT'S MY ENTRANCE, CAGE! THE MANGLER ALWAYS MAKES A SPECTACULAR ENTRANCE!
THE WHAT--??
MANGLER! MANGLER! WHATSA MATTER, CAN'T'CHA HEAR RIGHT?
USUALLY I GET A LOTTA RESPONSE WHEN I ENTER A RING. CHEERS AN' HISSES. THE WHOLE WORKS. AN' A BIG SPOTLIGHT FOLLAS ME AROUND.
YOU SURE YOU GOT THE RIGHT PLACE? MADISON SQUARE GARDEN AND BELLEVUE ARE ABOUT 8 BLOCKS DOWNTOWN.
I GOT ME THE RIGHT PLACE. I'M GONNA LEARN YA NOT TA BUTT INTA MY BRUTHER'S BIZNESS NO MORE.
BRASK!
WHATTA YOU TALKIN' ABOUT, MAN? YOU'RE GONNA GET US SMEARED ALL OVER THE SIDEWALK LIKE KETCHUP.
YA DONE SOMETHIN' REAL WRONG, CAGE, OR POWER MAN, OR WHATEVER YA CALL YASELF. I SEEN YA PICKCHA IN THE PAPERS THIS MORNING. I SEEN IT! NEARLY MADE ME LOSE MY WHEATIES!
MY BROTHER, HE DON'T KNOW I'M HERE. HE THINKS I'M SLOW OR SOMETHIN' AN' HE DON'T WANT ME MIXED UP IN THIS... BUT JACK WAS MY BROTHER, TOO, YA UNNERSTAN'?
...THAT MEANS I GOT ME A STAKE IN HOW THIS ALL COMES OUT, TOO!

HEY, HEADS UP! CAGE IS *AT IT* AGAIN!

LOOK, OSWALD RABBIT, I AIN'T FIGURIN' ON BECOMING *PART* OF THE *BILLBOARD DISPLAY*.

YOU WANNA PLAY *SONNY CHIBA*, YOU GO *DO IT* SOME-WHERE ELSE.

PRE-FERABLY BY *YOUR-SELF*.

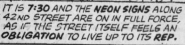

IT IS *7:30* AND THE *NEON SIGNS* ALONG *42ND STREET* ARE ON IN FULL FORCE, AS IF THE STREET ITSELF FEELS AN *OBLIGATION* TO LIVE UP TO ITS *REP*.

THE MANGLER WEIGHS *MORE* THAN CAGE, AND CAGE TIPS THE SCALES AT *300 ODD POUNDS*. THE FIGURE GRASPS AT THE *NEON CASINGS* AS THE FIGURES BELOW *SCRAMBLE* TO GET OUT OF THE WAY. GAS *ERUPTS* INTO THE NIGHT!

THERE ARE PEOPLE WHO *LIVE* AROUND THE *TIMES SQUARE AREA* WHO WOULD *NEVER* SPEAK TO YOU *AGAIN* IF YOU SUGGESTED THERE WAS ANYTHING *NEGATIVE* ABOUT THEIR *CHOSEN LAND*.

AND THERE ARE *OTHERS* WHO AVOID TIMES SQUARE AS IF IT WERE A *LEPER COLONY*. NOT EVEN THE BRIGHT LIGHTS OR MAYOR BEAME'S ASSUR-ANCE THAT HE IS CLEANING UP *THE STRIP* WILL BRING THEM *NEAR* THE AREA.

THE *AVOIDERS* WOULD VIEW THE MANGLER'S *DESCENT* AND SMUGLY CLAIM, *"SEE, I TOLD YOU SO."*

MAN, I GOTTA MEET ALL THE **WINNERS.**

WHAT'S ALL THIS **RAP** ABOUT **BROTHERS?** YOU GONNA LAY A **BRO'** LINE ON ME... HOW YOU AN' ME ARE **BROTHERS--** IS **THAT** IT?

SCOPE-SIGHT IMAGE.

HEY, DON'T GO AWAY **MAD** NOW.

CAGE'S VOICE CARRIES **ACROSS THE STREET.**

YOU AIN'T GOIN' **NOWHERE** TILL WE SET THIS THING--

--STRAI... HUNGH!

THE MANGLER DOESN'T ANSWER, BUT CAGE RECEIVES A **REPLY.**

SPECIAL DELIVERY!

THE **SPEAR** IS FIRED AT **HIGH VELOCITY** AND APPEARS LIKE A **MYSTICAL** SLEIGHT-OF-HAND TRANSFORMATION THAT **DOUG HENNING** PULLS IN THE BROADWAY PLAY, **"THE MAGIC SHOW"** ONLY SIX BLOCKS UPTOWN.

NONE OF THE **SPECTATORS** KNOW WHERE THE **MISSILE** CAME FROM, BUT THEY ALL **GASP** IN AMAZEMENT AS IT DRIVES CAGE BACK THROUGH THE WINDOW.

AND THEY **ASSUME** THE SHOW IS OVER!

THE SHOW ISN'T *COMPLETELY* OVER. THE CURTAIN HAS ONLY BEEN *DRAWN* ON CAGE.

GET *OUT* OF HERE, *BROTHER.* MAKE YOURSELF *SCARCE.*

SPEAR! YOU *HOMICIDAL FRUIT-CAKE!* I'M GONNA MAKE YOU *GARGLE* WITH ONE OF YOUR LITTLE *PIN-STICKERS!*

OKAY, LUCAS, IT'S *TIME* TO MAKE THE BIG *SPRINT.*

I GOT ME A FEELIN' THAT *"BROTHER"* LINE WAS THE *REAL* BLOOD-LINK. BUT WHO'S THIS *"JACK"?* IS SPEAR A *"JACK"* IN *REAL LIFE?*

BUSY NIGHT, LUKE?

BERTHA, I WISH YOU'D *SCREEN* MY CLIENTELE *BEFORE* THEY CLIMB THE STAIRS AND *BUST UP* THE JOINT.

SO *TELL* ME... HOW DO I PICK THE *STRAIGHTS* FROM THE *WEIRDOS?*

HEY, MISTER, YOU SEE AN AMATEUR HAYSTACK CALHOON COME BY HERE?

HUH?

NEVER MIND. I'M BEGINNIN' T' *SOUND* LIKE THE *FREAKS* WHO'VE BEEN COMIN' AT *ME* IN THE *MIDDLE* OF A *CONVERSATION.* I NEVER KNOW *WHAT* THEY'RE TALKIN' ABOUT.

MANGLER!

MANG...UHH...

YOU GOT A *PROBLEM,* BRO'?

UHH...NO, JUST GOT THIS LITTLE *HABIT.* I KEEP *TALKIN'* TO MYSELF.

YOU OUGHTTA GET *HELP* FOR THAT, BRO'!

FEELING LONELY, GOOD LOOKING?

CAGE CLIMBS OUT OF THE SUBWAY AND SEES DETECTIVE 2ND GRADE **QUENTIN CHASE** WAITING FOR HIS ARRIVAL. HE DOESN'T FEEL **LONELY** ANYMORE. THE NIGHT IS **CROWDED** WITH PEOPLE PLAYING **CAMEO ROLES** AND **PASSING** THROUGH HIS LIFE.

HE LEAVES THE STAIRWELL AND BREATHES AGAIN, BUT THE **ODOR** OF THE SUBWAY ENTRANCE **LINGERS**, LIKE THE AIR IN AN **UNSANITARY RESTROOM.**

LET'S **SEE**, DETECTIVE CHASE. YOU HERE TO **PROTECT** LUKE AGAIN?

NO, **D.W.**, THIS TIME I'M MERELY DROPPING BY TO PROTECT **YOUR** REPUTATION.

OH...AND NO **OFFENSE** MEANT... BUT ALSO TO **ASK** MR. CAGE **POLITELY** IF HE CAN'T LET A NIGHT GO BY WITHOUT **DISTURBING** THE PEACE.

I **HEARD** THAT, CHASE. Y'CAN'T **BLAME** ME FOR THE PSYCHOS PLAYIN' **DARTS** IN THIS CITY.

IT WAS THAT **SPEAR-FETISH NUT** AGAIN... AND HE'S GOT SOME **HAIRY APE** WHO OBVIOUSLY **HATCHED** FROM THE SAME **LOONY BIN** WITH HIM. GUY CALLS HIMSELF-- **STEEL** YOURSELF NOW-- **THE MANGLER.**

I'M BEGINNING TO **WORRY** ABOUT THE TYPE OF PEOPLE WE'RE RAISING IN THIS WORLD, CAGE.

YEAH, THEY AIN'T GOT MUCH **HEART**, HAVE THEY?

OF COURSE, THE MAN THIS **SPEAR** IS TRYIN' TO **KILL**--DR. **NOAH BURSTEIN**--MAYBE HE'S GOT TOO MUCH **HEART.**

OR **GUILT.**

GUILT?

THAT'S THE WAY BURSTEIN **STRUCK** ME WHEN THIS "SPEAR" TRIED TO NAIL HIM **TWO NIGHTS** AGO.

BUT **YOU** KNOW THIS BURSTEIN BETTER'N I DO.

WE GO BACK **A WAYS. HEY**, YOU MIND TELLIN' ME HOW YOU **ALWAYS** GET HERE SO QUICK WHEN THINGS GET **SCREWED** UP?

IT'S OUR **NEW, IMPROVED VIDEO MONITORS** IN THE STREET. REAL DICK TRACY STUFF. DON'T YOU JUST **LOVE** IT?

GIVES ME SHIVERS UP MY **SPINE**. SO HOW COME YOU DIDN'T SEE SPEAR LAYIN' FOR ME UP ON THE **ROOFTOPS?**

WE PROBABLY SWITCHED **CHANNELS.**

WE CAN'T STAND TO SEE **UNCENSORED VIOLENCE** DURING **FAMILY VIEWING HOURS.**

D.W., THE **HOT DOGS** IN THIS THEATER TASTE LIKE GROUND-UP **LEATHER.**

I MEAN, I KNOW YOU'RE NO **SIDNEY POITIER**--

THEY **SHOULD**, WIN. THAT'S WHAT MY UNCLE MAX **ORDERS** FROM THE **DELI.**

LUKE, IF I CAN TEAR YOU FROM THE **87TH PRECINCT** THERE, I WANT TO TELL YOU I THINK YOU HAVE ENOUGH **PRESENCE** TO DO A ROLE IN MY **FILM.**

I'M NO **PAM GRIER** EITHER, D.W.

WHAT'RE YOU **CALLIN'** YOUR EXTRAVAGANZA?

"DEATH OF A NATION." LET'S HEAR IT FOR STRAIGHT-FORWARD **PRETENSION.**

HEY! THE **SODA MACHINE--** IT'S **WORKING!**

WIN, DEAR --WHILE WE HAVEN'T HAD A CHANCE TO **TALK,** I WANT TO **THANK** YOU--

--'CAUSE **THIS TIME--**

CLICK!

K·K·KLUP

--I'VE **SEEN** THIS MONSTER **WORK--**

NLURP

--WITH MY **OWN** EYES.

SEE THAT, CHASE? IT'S **PERSISTENCE** THAT COUNTS IN THIS **WORLD.** MACHINE LEARNED ITS **MANNERS** WHEN I **WHACKED** IT **UPSIDE** ITS HEAD THE OTHER NIGHT.

I'M SO GLAD FOR YOU, **CAGE,** THAT SUCH A **MINOR TRIUMPH** CAN **BRIGHTEN** YOUR VIEW OF **LIFE.** NOW COULD WE GET BACK TO **BURSTEIN?** ANY-MORE **THREATS** ON HIS LIFE?

NOT SINCE SPEAR SENT THOSE **FLAMING SPEARS** INTO THE DOOR-WAY OF HIS STORE-FRONT CLINIC LAST NIGHT.

AND HE HAS NO **IDEA** WHO THIS **SPEAR** CHARACTER COULD **BE?**

SO HE **CLAIMS.**

YOU THINK NOAH ACTS **GUILTY**--TO ME, IT'S LIKE NOAH FEELS THE GUY HAS SOME **RIGHT** TO WASTE HIM. I DON'T UND--

WHAT THE--??

THAT MACHINE'S **ALIVE,** I'M TELLING YA! IT'S EVEN GOT THE **CUPS** WORKIN' FOR IT!

D.W., YOU **SURE** YOUR UNCLE MAX DIDN'T GET THIS **MONSTER** FROM THE **TWILIGHT ZONE?**

AHH, FORGET IT! I'M BEGINNIN' TO FEEL LIKE *CHARLIE BROWN.*

TAKE IT *EASY,* CAGE. WOULDN'T WANT TO HAVE TO PULL YOU *IN* FOR DEFACING PUBLIC PROPERTY.

OPERATOR? YEAH, I'D LIKE THE NUMBER FOR THE *ALEX SIMMONS* RESIDENCE.

HELLO? ALEX? THIS IS LUKE CAGE. I HATE TO *DISTURB* YOU, BUT EVER SINCE I WAS AT YOUR SON'S *FUNERAL* WELL, I CAN'T GET *LITTLE BETH* OUTTA MY MIND. HOW IS SHE TAKING IT?

IT'S HARD TO *TELL,* LUKE. BOTH *SANDY* AND I ARE *CONCERNED.* WE LOST OUR LITTLE *BOY...* WE DON'T WANT TO LOSE OUR LITTLE *GIRL,* TOO.

SHE *WON'T* TALK ABOUT THE NIGHT OF THE *FIRE* MUCH. 'COURSE SHE DOESN'T *KNOW* THAT IT WAS SET BY A *MAN.*

ONCE IN AWHILE, SHE'LL *TURN* TO ME AND SAY, "AUGGIE SAID IT WAS *HIDE-AND-SEEK,* DAD." YOU THINK SHE *BLAMES* HERSELF FOR AUGGIE'S *DEATH,* LUKE?

I DON'T KNOW. *MAYBE*--LOTTA *BURDEN* FOR A CHILD TO BEAR.

LISSEN, IF IT'S OKAY WITH YOU AND SANDY, HOW'S ABOUT I TAKE HER TO SEE "*THE BLUE BIRD*" AT *RADIO CITY MUSIC HALL* THIS WEEKEND?

YEAH, I *KNOW* I DON'T *GOTTA* DO THAT. MAYBE I KNOW HOW SHE *FEELS...* 'CAUSE MAYBE I FEEL THE *SAME WAY* SHE DOES. SEE YOU *SATURDAY,* ALEX.

IN *WEST HARLEM,* MORNINGSIDE PARK IS NEARLY *DESERTED.* PEOPLE *SELDOM* WALK ITS PATHS DURING DAYLIGHT, NEVER MIND WHEN *NIGHTFALL* ARRIVES.

THE PEOPLE WHO PASS *MORNINGSIDE PARK* ADMIRE IT FROM A *DISTANCE,* AND THERE IS A *SAYING* THAT, "ONCE YOU ENTER MORNINGSIDE PARK, THERE'S NO *GUARANTEE* YOU'LL LEAVE IT--*ALIVE!*"

THAT'S SOMEWHAT OF AN *EXAGGERATION,* BUT THE GRASS AND TREES STILL REMAIN VIRTUALLY *UNUSED...* AND THE *BIG-CITY MYTH-CURSE* FLOURISHES.

NOW WHAT DID YOU HOPE TO ACCOMPLISH BY *BARGING* INTO CAGE'S OFFICE AND TEARING THE PLACE *APART?* IT WAS A LUCKY THING I WAS *CHECKING* TO MAKE SURE HE HAD NO PLANS TO *SEE* BURSTEIN *TONIGHT.*

I *TOLD* YOU TO STAY OUT OF THIS, *DIDN'T* I?

I KNOW *WHATCHA SAID*, BUT I ALSO SEEN THEM T.V. NEWS SHOWS AND THE PAPERS. I KNEW *YOU* WAS THE *SPEAR CAGE* AND THE POLICE WERE UP IN *ARMS* ABOUT.

DIDN'T WANT THIS CAGE *STOPPIN' YOU* FROM GETTIN' BURSTEIN LIKE HE DID THE *OTHER NIGHT.* FIGURED I'D TAKE HIM *OUT* FOR YOU.

CAGE *DIDN'T* STOP ME FROM KILLING BURSTEIN. BURSTEIN WAS AS GOOD AS *DEAD* IF I'D *WANTED* IT THAT WAY. I WANT BURSTEIN TO *LIVE* WITH THE KNOWLEDGE HE'S ABOUT TO *DIE.*

I WANT BURSTEIN'S *DEATH* TO BE AS *CLOSE* TO JACK'S AS...

HEY...KEEP IT DOWN...THAT'S HIM, AIN'T IT?

YEAH, THAT'S *HIM.* DOESN'T LOOK A WHOLE LOT *DIFFERENT* FROM THE *DAYS* WHEN HE WAS *DOCTORING* AT THE *PRISON*, DOES HE?

HE'S DOING HIS *SHOPPING.* SAME ROUTINE EVERY TUESDAY AND THURSDAY NIGHT.

HE LIVES LIKE A *MONK* IN THAT *STORE-FRONT CLINIC.* COOKS HIS OWN MEALS.

PABLO'S BODEGA MA

BODEGA

GOYA BEANS

BARATO!

PAN

WELL, WOULD YOU *LOOK* AT *THIS?* OLD DR. BURSTEIN HAS SOMEONE *ELSE* KEEPING *TABS* ON HIM.

WHERE?

ACROSS THE *STREET.* IN THE ALLEY WAY. *IT'S CAGE!*

YOU WANTED TO MAKE YOURSELF *USEFUL*-- TELL YOU WHAT YOU *DO.* GO DOWN THE *BLOCK* AND ENTER THAT ALLEY FROM THE *OTHER SIDE.*

I WANT YOU TO OCCUPY CAGE'S TIME WHILE I SHOW BURSTEIN THAT HE'S *NOT SAFE*--

--ANYWHERE!

THE ALLEY-WAY IS NOT *EMPTY.* IT IS FULL OF *DEBRIS,* AND SOME OF IT *MOVES* EVEN THOUGH MOST EVERYTHING IN THESE SHADOWS HAS BEEN *DISCARDED.*

HEY, MAN, WHA'CHU *DOIN'* IN *MY* ALLEY?

GO WAN'... GET YOUR *TAIL* OUTTA MY ALLEY! THIS IS MY *TURF,* SEE?

ALL MINE.

HEY, YOU *LIS'NIN'* T' ME?

HOLD IT UP A *MINNIT,* "JIM." WHAD IS *THIS*?

A CON-VENTION OR WHAT?

DID'N I *TELL* YOU GUYS? THIS HERE'S *MY* ALLEY!

LOOK, MAN, KEEP IT *DOWN,* WILL--

NO ONE'S EVER *BROKEN* THIS HOLD! THIS IS THE MANGLER'S *SPECIAL DEATH-GRIP.*

YOU AS GOOD AS *DAID,* CAGE-- AS DAID AS THAT *JUNKIE!*

Y'CAN *FORGET* HIM, CAGE, I GOT MY ARMS *LOCKED* ABOUT YOUR *THROAT.*

THE LITTLE STORE SMELLS OF MEAT AND FRUIT AND SAWDUST. A LITTLE BELL TINKLES AS THE DOOR IS SWUNG **OPEN**...AND IT SIGNALS SPEAR'S **ENTRANCE**.

GOOD EVENING, BURSTEIN.

REMEMBER ME?

GUAVA

YOU DIDN'T THINK I'D **FORGOTTEN** YOU? I'D **NEVER** DO THAT, BURSTEIN...NOT EVEN AFTER I'VE **KILLED** YOU.

NOW? IS NOW THE **TIME?**

NOT YET...IT CAN'T END SO QUICKLY. IT DIDN'T END QUICKLY FOR JACK.

JACK?

YOU WANT TO TELL ME HOW IT **FEELS**, BURSTEIN...THE WAY JACK **TOLD** ME WHILE **HE** WAITED FOR **DEATH?**

YOU AREN'T **SAFE** ANYWHERE. NOT AT THE **CLINIC**, OR A **GROCERY STORE**. YOU'RE FAIR GAME.

ANYWHERE ...AND ANYTIME!

WHARR

SHRED!

NOAH BURSTEIN LIES IN THE SAWDUST, AND **LISTENS** TO THE LITTLE BELL SIGNAL SPEAR'S **DEPARTURE**.

LONG SECONDS **PASS** BEFORE HE BEGINS TO **BREATHE** AGAIN.

THE JUNKIE IS OUTRAGED, AS IF THIS OUTSIDE INDIGNITY RIVALS THE DEGRADATION HIS LIFE HAS BECOME.

FIGHT BACK... A DECEPTIVE DEFIANCE THAT HAUGHTILY CLAIMS THAT EVERYTHING HAS NOT YET BEEN LOST.

MANGLER, WHAT IS IT WITH YOU, HUH?

YOU FEEL YOU GOTTA LIVE UP TO YOUR NAME, OR WHAT?

HEY, THAT HURT, CAGE!

CHARK!

YEAH, NO KIDDIN'.

THEN CHECK THIS OUT.

SHUU-WHANCK!

AND WHILE YOU'RE AT IT, GET DOWN ON THIS, TOO!

HEY, DIDN' I TELL YOU GUYS ...I DON' HAFTA SHARE THIS HERE ALLEY WITH YOU FREAKS.

WHAT'S WID YOU? YOU NODDIN' ON ME, HUNH?

YOU AN' THE OTHER CREEP, Y' KNOW EACH OTHER, HUNH?

WHATSA MATTER? Y' WON'T TALK TA ME?

WHADDYA THINK? YOU'RE TOO GOOD F' ME?

NOAH, HAS SPEAR--?

NEVER MIND, I SEE HE'S *BEEN* HERE.

LUCAS! WHERE'D *YOU* COME FROM?

SHARING THE *ALLEY-WORLD* WITH A *PERMANENT* RESIDENT AND ONE *PART-TIME VISITOR* WITH AN OPTION TO *BUY.* I'VE BEEN ON YOUR *TAIL,* HOPIN' TO MAKE SURE WHAT *HAPPENED*--

WHAT IS HAPPENING TO *MY LIFE,* LUCAS? A MAN WANTS TO *KILL ME*...AND NOW MY EVERY ACTION IS *WATCHED!* PRIVACY--

--WOULDN'T.

PRIVACY? WHAT'S *THAT,* NOAH?

DIDN'T THEY PASS AN AMENDMENT *AGAINST* THAT OR SOMETHIN'?

DON'T GET *CUTE* WITH ME, LUCAS. MY NERVES COULDN'T *TAKE* THAT. *WAIT!* WHERE ARE WE--

HERE, NOAH. ONE OF THE *DYNAMIC DUO* DIDN'T MAKE IT BACK TO HIS *BELFRY.*

HEY, YOU JOKERS WANTA KEEP IT *DOWN?* ME AN' HIM ARE GETTIN' ALONG *FINE.*

SEE...WE *UNNERSTAN'* EACH OTHER.

RIGHT?

RIGHT.

LET'S GET THIS *EL ZORRO BANDANA OFF* HIS HEAD 'N SEE WHO THIS MANGLER IS IN *REAL* LIFE.

DO YOU *KNOW* HIM, NOAH?

NOAH?

HEY, DOC... WHAT'S *UP?*

WHERE ARE YOU--

--GOING?

THE JUNKIE ANSWERS, TALKING TO THE *GRAFFITI CURSES.* HIS *BODY* ASKS WHERE THE NEXT FIX IS GOING TO COME FROM... AND HIS MIND IS *PUNCTURED* WITH A *PAINFUL NEED.* CAGE, NOAH, THE MANGLER... *NONE OF IT HAPPENED!*

QUENTIN CHASE **STUDIES** HIS REFLECTION. HE **APPEARS** RELAXED, AS IF HE HAS LEFT THE PRECINCT HOUSE **MOOD** BEHIND, BUT THE **TENSION** HAS TRAVELED WITH HIM TO HIS HOUSE ON **LONG ISLAND.**

YOU **KNOW** THIS MUSIC, DAD?

LISTEN, DAD. **LISTEN.**

UH HUT, UH HUT... THAT'S THE WAY... UH HUT, UH HUT... I LIKE IT.

THAT'S K.C. AND THE SUN-SHINE BAND.

K.C. AND THE **WHO?**

NOT K.C. AND **THE WHO,** QUENT.

WHOEVER. FOUR YEARS OLD AND MY DAUGHTER IS SINGING, "THAT'S THE WAY I LIKE IT."

THE SUN-SHINE BAND.

WHEN I WAS FOUR **MY** FAVORITE SONG WAS "YES, WE HAVE NO **BANANAS** TODAY!"

BIG LIBERAL, QUENTIN CHASE... EXCEPT WHEN IT COMES DOWN TO YOUR **OWN** LIFE.

AH, COME ON, CHRISTIE! I WAS MOSTLY KIDDING.

IT'S JUST THAT I'M BEGINNING TO FEEL LIKE **BILL COSBY** WHEN HE DOES HIS ROUTINE ABOUT **DAUGHTERS.** SHE'S ONLY FOUR AND **ALREADY** I FEEL LIKE THE NEIGHBORHOOD BOYS ARE COMING **AT** ME.

WE **LOVE** EACH OTHER, **DON'T** WE, DAD?

WE SURE **DO,** HONEY.

WE **DON'T** SO.

WE **DO** SO.

I KNOW, DAD. I WAS **FUNNIN'** YA.

CAGE HAS NOT SLEPT WELL. HE FELL ASLEEP WITH VISIONS OF NOAH BURSTEIN AND **SEAGATE** PRISON AS SURROGATE SHEEP--

--AND **AWAKES** THE NEXT AFTERNOON, WITH THE **SAME VISIONS** OF THE **EXPERIMENTS** THAT TRANSFORMED HIM INTO **POWER MAN** AND MADE HIM AN **ESCAPED CONVICT.**

ANOTHER DARK VISION TAKES **SHAPE** AT THE **NEW DOOR**--

--AND CAGE, **REMEMBERING** RENDING WOOD AND SPILLED COFFEE, ACTS **FIRST** THIS TIME.

IS THIS THE **OFFICE** OF ONE--

--LUCAS

CAAAGE!

WHO ARE YOU?

ARE WE...ARE WE UNDER **ATTACK?**

I SOME- TIMES WONDER.

SORRY ABOUT THE **ABRUPT** GREETING. I'M GOING TO TRY'N PULL MYSELF **TOGETHER.** I FEEL LIKE I'M COMIN' **UNGLUED.**

ANYHOW, WHAT CAN I DO FOR YOU?

MY NAME IS **OLIVER P. SNEAGLE,** MR. CAGE. AND I REPRESENT THE **I.R.S.**

THE INTERNAL REVENUE SERVICE...AND WE'D LIKE TO KNOW WHY YOU HAVEN'T FILED ANY **INCOME TAX** WITH US IN THE PAST **TWO YEARS,** MR. CAGE.

CAGE, LUKE

I'M SORRY, MR. CAGE. IS ANYTHING...**WRONG?**

CAGE ADDS ANOTHER *PHANTASM* TO HIS COLLECTION OF *DISTURBING VISIONS.* ALL THE WAY *UPTOWN* TO THE *STOREFRONT CLINIC,* OLIVER P. SNEAGLE'S SCARECROW COUNTENANCE *LEERS* AT THE FACES OF NOAH AND SPEAR.

CLINIC HRS.
7:00 A.M.–12:00 P.M.

HORA DI CLINICO...

HE WON'T BE ABLE TO PUT SNEAGLE OFF *FOREVER.*

COME ON, NOAH. *OPEN UP.* WE GOTTA *TALK,* MAN.

YOU GOTTA *LEVEL* WITH ME...TELL ME WHY YOU *SPLIT* AFTER SEEIN' THE *MANGLER'S* FACE... DO Y' HEAR...

THE MAN HAS A VERY *APPROPRIATE* NAME.

IT IS A PROFANE VERSION OF A *RAGGEDY ANDY DOLL,* SWAYING FROM THE LIGHT FIXTURES.

OH, YOU MOTHERLESS--

X-RAY

TECHN ONLY

LITTLE BLACK BUTTON EYES AND STRAW HAIR AND A POCKET HOLDING A CHILD'S STETHOSCOPE. ALL THE FACETS REGISTER BUT THE *IMPACT* COMES FROM THE SPEAR WHICH RUNS *THROUGH* ITS ADORABLE CHEST.

The time has come to end this charade, Noah Burstein. Come alone, else you will force me to hurt your friends, Claire Temple and Luke Cage. We will meet near Spuyten Duyvil, on the Hudson River. At the abandoned ferry docks. Be there, Dr. Noah Burstein, by 7:30. And don't be late!

INDIGO INTROSPECTION.

AMBER ACTION.

SKREE!

DISTANT MID-TOWN MANHATTAN LIGHTS *BEYOND* THE WATER.

2 QUARTERS AND 3 DIMES WON'T EVEN TAKE YOU A *CITY BLOCK.*

A *SILENT* CONFRONTATION.

116TH ST.

A *50¢ TOKEN* AND THE *LONG WAIT* FOR A TRAIN.

TWO PAIRS OF EYES GLARE AT EACH OTHER, AND THEY COMMUNICATE, WORDLESSLY. THOSE EYES LEAVE NOTHING *UNSAID.*

THE GUN *FIRES!* A BRIEF SOUND OF EJECTION ENDS WITH A *SICKENING* SOUND.

AND NOAH BURSTEIN IS LIFTED *OFF* THE BROKEN CEMENT DOCK...AND BACK INTO A WATERY *GRAVE.*

NEXT **MEMORIES BOTH VICIOUS AND HAUNTING!**
THE FATE OF NOAH BURSTEIN! THE VENGEANCE OF LUKE CAGE!

POWER-MAN
MARVEL COMICS GROUP
APPROVED BY THE COMICS CODE AUTHORITY
30¢
35 SEPT
02149
LUKE CAGE,
POWER MAN
54 WEST E
NO MATTER HOW THE TRIP ENDS, MANGLER--
--THIS IS YOUR LAST STOP!
BUT CAGE--AND A BUSLOAD OF INNOCENT PEOPLE--ARE STILL TRAPPED ON A:
ONE WAY RIDE TO REVENGE!
SEV. / ADKINS

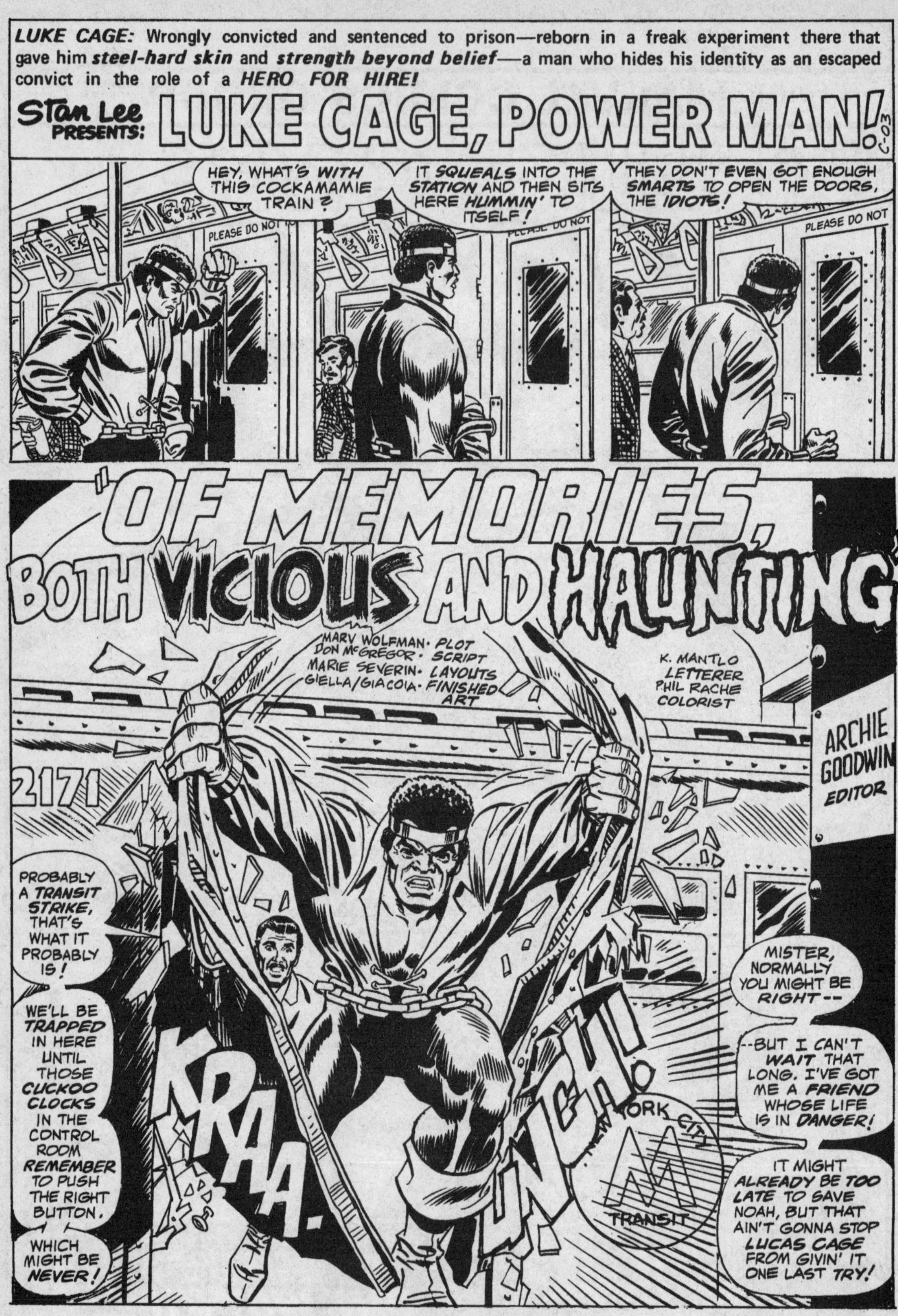
LUKE CAGE: Wrongly convicted and sentenced to prison—reborn in a freak experiment there that gave him steel-hard skin and strength beyond belief—a man who hides his identity as an escaped convict in the role of a HERO FOR HIRE!
STAN LEE PRESENTS: LUKE CAGE, POWER MAN!
C-03
HEY, WHAT'S WITH THIS COCKAMAMIE TRAIN?
IT SQUEALS INTO THE STATION AND THEN SITS HERE HUMMIN' TO ITSELF!
THEY DON'T EVEN GOT ENOUGH SMARTS TO OPEN THE DOORS, THE IDIOTS!
PLEASE DO NOT
"OF MEMORIES, BOTH VICIOUS AND HAUNTING"
MARV WOLFMAN · PLOT
DON McGREGOR · SCRIPT
MARIE SEVERIN · LAYOUTS
GIELLA/GIACOIA · FINISHED ART
K. MANTLO LETTERER
PHIL RACHE COLORIST
ARCHIE GOODWIN EDITOR
2171
PROBABLY A TRANSIT STRIKE, THAT'S WHAT IT PROBABLY IS!
WE'LL BE TRAPPED IN HERE UNTIL THOSE CUCKOO CLOCKS IN THE CONTROL ROOM REMEMBER TO PUSH THE RIGHT BUTTON.
WHICH MIGHT BE NEVER!
KRAAA-UNCH!
NEW YORK CITY TRANSIT
MISTER, NORMALLY YOU MIGHT BE RIGHT--
--BUT I CAN'T WAIT THAT LONG. I'VE GOT ME A FRIEND WHOSE LIFE IS IN DANGER!
IT MIGHT ALREADY BE TOO LATE TO SAVE NOAH, BUT THAT AIN'T GONNA STOP LUCAS CAGE FROM GIVIN' IT ONE LAST TRY!

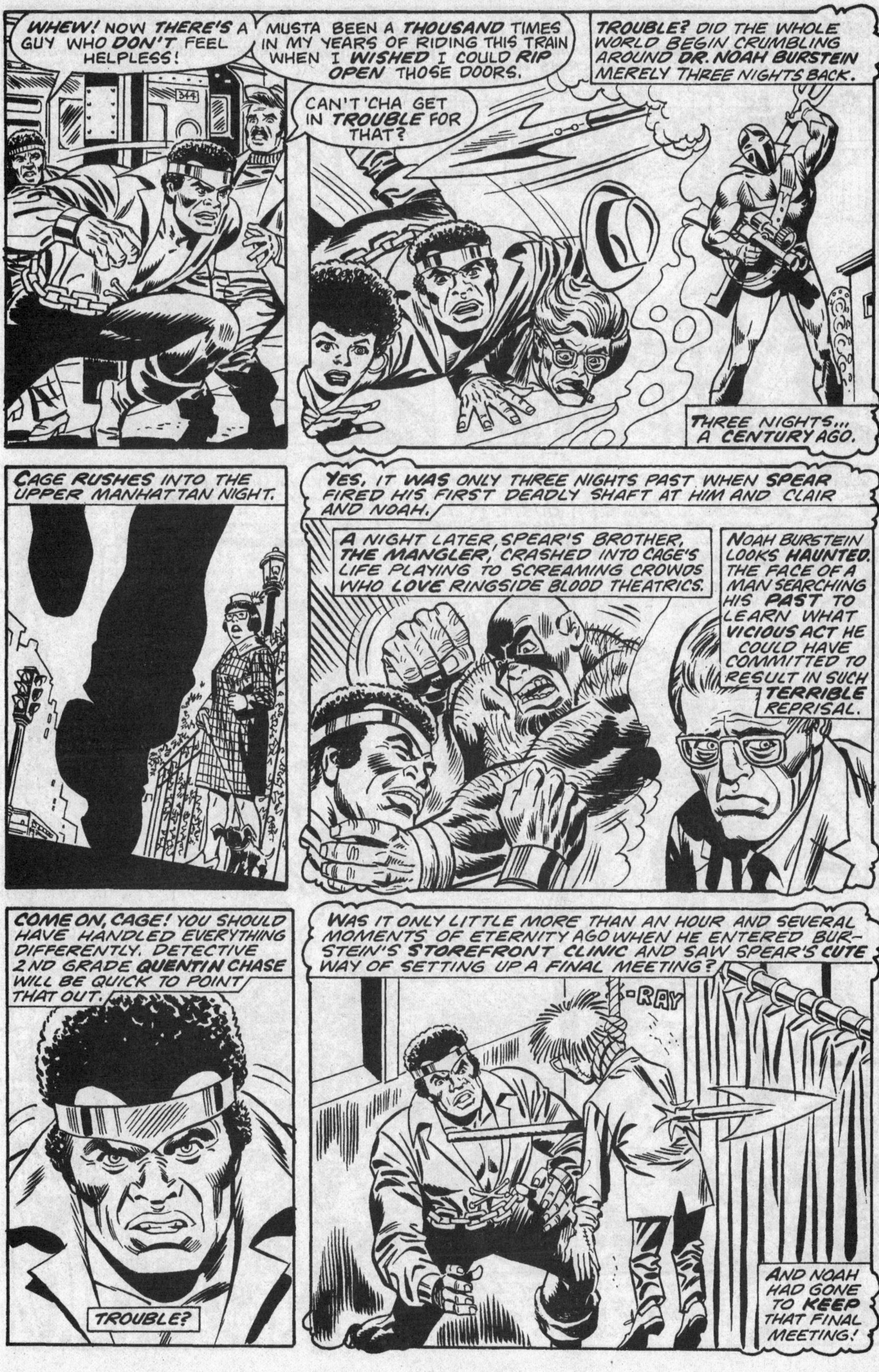

WHEW! NOW THERE'S A GUY WHO DON'T FEEL HELPLESS!
MUSTA BEEN A THOUSAND TIMES IN MY YEARS OF RIDING THIS TRAIN WHEN I WISHED I COULD RIP OPEN THOSE DOORS.
CAN'T'CHA GET IN TROUBLE FOR THAT?
344
TROUBLE? DID THE WHOLE WORLD BEGIN CRUMBLING AROUND DR. NOAH BURSTEIN MERELY THREE NIGHTS BACK.
THREE NIGHTS... A CENTURY AGO.
CAGE RUSHES INTO THE UPPER MANHATTAN NIGHT.
YES, IT WAS ONLY THREE NIGHTS PAST WHEN SPEAR FIRED HIS FIRST DEADLY SHAFT AT HIM AND CLAIR AND NOAH.
A NIGHT LATER, SPEAR'S BROTHER, THE MANGLER, CRASHED INTO CAGE'S LIFE PLAYING TO SCREAMING CROWDS WHO LOVE RINGSIDE BLOOD THEATRICS.
NOAH BURSTEIN LOOKS HAUNTED. THE FACE OF A MAN SEARCHING HIS PAST TO LEARN WHAT VICIOUS ACT HE COULD HAVE COMMITTED TO RESULT IN SUCH TERRIBLE REPRISAL.
COME ON, CAGE! YOU SHOULD HAVE HANDLED EVERYTHING DIFFERENTLY. DETECTIVE 2ND GRADE QUENTIN CHASE WILL BE QUICK TO POINT THAT OUT.
TROUBLE?
WAS IT ONLY LITTLE MORE THAN AN HOUR AND SEVERAL MOMENTS OF ETERNITY AGO WHEN HE ENTERED BURSTEIN'S STOREFRONT CLINIC AND SAW SPEAR'S CUTE WAY OF SETTING UP A FINAL MEETING?
-RAY
AND NOAH HAD GONE TO KEEP THAT FINAL MEETING!

CAGE REACHES THE *FERRY DOCKS.* THEY HAVE BEEN *CLOSED* SINCE THE 1930'S. THE OPENING OF THE GEORGE WASHINGTON BRIDGE *PUT TO REST* THE FERRIES WHICH CARRIED COMMUTERS ACROSS THE *HUDSON RIVER* TO AND FROM *NEW JERSEY.*

THE DOCKS SHOULD BE *DESERTED...* BUT THEY *AREN'T!*

SOMEBODY BETTER *HUSTLE* AN AMBULANCE OUT HERE FAST. THIS SPEAR HAS TO BE *CUT OUT!* HE'S ALREADY GONE INTO *SHOCK.*

GET YOUR HANDS *OFF* THAT THING! THEY'LL INVENT *MALPRACTICE* SUITS FOR COPS... AND MAKE YOU AN EXAMPLE.

NOAH--

OKAY, HOLD IT RIGHT *THERE,* TOUGH GUY. WHAT ARE YOU *DOING* AROUND HERE?

HE *DID* IT. SPEAR GOT *AWAY* WITH IT... BUT IT DOESN'T *END* HERE, MAN.

NOT BY A LONG SHOT.

YOU *KNOW* THE VICTIM? THESE TWO KIDS, THEY *SAW* WHAT HAPPENED.

I'M TELLIN' YA THIS CITY'S *TOO MUCH*--

"CYNTHIA AN' I... WE WERE...UH..,WELL, WE HEARD SOME *SCREAMIN'*"... I'M TELLIN' YA, OFFICER... THERE'S A LOTTA *ANGRY* PEOPLE IN THIS CITY--

"-- BUT USUALLY, WELL, THIS PLACE IS PRETTY DESERTED... IF YOU KNOW WHAT I MEAN.

"IT'S FUNNY HOW *DESERTED* PLACES CAN BE KINDA *HAIRY* IN THE CITY... AND WHEN WE *SAW* THIS FIGURE DECKED OUT LIKE THE *SHADOW,* I'D WISHED I'D NEVER READ 'HELTER SKELTER.'

"THE MAN HAD THESE *HUGE* SPEARS, BELIEVE IT OR NOT, AND HE'D FIRED ONE OF THEM RIGHT INTO THE OLD GUY THERE.

THAT'S SPEAR.

NO, I MEAN THE MAN'S *NAME* IS SPEAR.

THAT'S WHAT THE KID *SAID.*

I THINK YOU BETTER COME DOWN TO THE *PRECINCT HOUSE* WITH US.

IT'S A GOOD THING YOU GUYS GAVE ME A *LIFT*... SEEIN'S HOW I DIDN'T HAVE *FARE* BACK TO *MIDTOWN* MANHATTAN.

WE'RE NOT DOING THIS OUT OF THE KINDNESS OF OUR HEARTS.

YEAH... I KINDA *FIGURED* YOU WEREN'T.

SEVERAL PRECINCT HOUSES AND UNKIND INTERROGATIONS LATER, CAGE STANDS BEFORE QUENTIN CHASE.

CAGE, YOU *CAN'T* GO RUNNIN' AROUND THIS CITY LIKE A *ONE-MAN VIGILANTE COMMITTEE.*

I *HEAR* YA, CHASE... AND WHILE WE STAND HERE THROWIN' *INSULTS* BACK AND FORTH AT EACH OTHER... A *GOOD MAN* IS GOIN' UNDER THE SURGEON'S KNIFE.

NOAH'S A *FRIEND*... AND THAT'S A TERM THAT STILL *MEANS* SOMETHING TO ME.

I DON'T *SELL IT OUT* WHEN IT BECOMES *INCONVENIENT.*

PEOPLE ARE ONLY SUPPOSED TO *TALK* THAT KIND OF SENTIMENT, LUKE... NOT *LIVE* THAT WAY. I'M PUTTING YOU ON, BY THE WAY.

WELL, HELLO, MANGLER. LUKE, I BELIEVE YOU TWO HAVE *MET.*

I WAS THE ONE WHO INTRODUCED YOU TWO, REMEMBER?

HEY, I AIN'T SAYIN' *NUTHIN'* TO YOU GUYS... SO'S YOU CAN TAKE YOUR *BUGS* AND *ONE-WAY MIRRORS* AND SHOVE 'EM TO *TIM-BUCK TWO.*

THIS ISN'T A *MODERN-DAY TORTURE CHAMBER*, MANGLER. WE JUST WANT TO ASK YOU ABOUT YOUR *BROTHER*--THE ONE WITH THE *CLEVER* PSEUDONYM--SPEAR?

CRINSK!

CHRISTMAS, THE VANDALS THESE DAYS ARE REALLY GETTIN'...

SMUSK!

YOU WANTA KNOW *WHERE* MY BROTHER IS... THAT'S *HIM!* RIGHT OUTSIDE YOUR *WINDOW!*

HEY, BROTHER, YOU DID THAT *BETTER'N* THEY DO IN THE *COMIC BOOKS.*

TEAR GAS! NOW WHERE IN THE HELL DID A CREEP LIKE SPEAR GET AHOLD OF TEAR GAS? FROM AN ARMY SURPLUS STORE OR WHAT?

UNEMOTIONAL TEARS BURN AT CAGE'S EYES, THE WAY NOAH'S LIMP BODY BURNS IN HIS MEMORY.

COME ON, YOU MORON! I DON'T BELIEVE IN COINCIDENCES LIKE THIS--

--BUT AS LONG AS IT'S HAPPENED, WE'RE GOING TO MAKE THE MOST OF IT. I'M NOT LOSING ANOTHER BROTHER TO THE SYSTEM.

CAGE CRASHES INTO THE TELEPHONE AND MA BELL SOUNDS HER ANNOY-ANCE. DON'T MESS AROUND WITH THE GOODS, FRIEND, OR WE'LL UNPLUG YOU FROM THE ELECTRONIC UMBILICAL CORD.

CAGE IGNORES MA BELL'S CHAS-TISEMENT, AND GLARES THROUGH WATERY EYES AT THE TWO FIGURES HANGING HIGH OVER THE CITY STREETS.

SPEAR, I DON'T KNOW WHAT YOUR HANG-UPS ARE... BUT YOU MADE YOURSELF A BIG MISTAKE!

YOU HURT A FRIEND OF LUKE CAGE'S... AND I'M GONNA MAKE SURE YOU PAY FOR IT.

HEY, LEGGO, CAGE! THAT HOLD AIN'T FAIR!

SO GO COMPLAIN TO THE REFEREE... BUT KEEP HOLDIN' ONTO THE ROPES WHILE YOU DO IT!

THEY GOT ENOUGH POTHOLES IN THE STREETS WITHOUT ADDIN' US TO THE NUMBER.

THE CITY *SWAYS* BELOW THEM. IT LOOKS *LONELY*, A THOUSAND ISOLATED PEOPLE FENDING FOR THEMSELVES, AND HEADING TOWARD THEIR HIGH-RISE APARTMENT DUNGEONS.

THEY DON'T NEED *ACROBATS* OVER MANHATTAN.

CAGE, I *TOLD* YOU WAY BACK IN THE BEGINNING, TO STAY *OUT* OF THIS.

ACCOUNTS HAVE BEEN *SETTLED*. DON'T *MAKE* ME HAVE TO TAKE YOU OUT THE WAY I DID WITH BURSTEIN.

SNAP

AW, C'MON MANGLER, YOU DON'T *REALLY BELIEVE* YOU CAN MAKE IT *OUTTA* A BIG CITY POLICE STATION 'LESS YOU GOT *CONNECTIONS* OR BIG MONEY.

GIVE IT UP BEFORE YOU GET *BOTH* OF US--

WASTED!

SPLUSK-USH!

CAGE, THIS IS A NIGHT FOR *UNBELIEVABLE EVENTS*. YOU'RE LUCKY THE SANITATION DEPARTMENT IS *BEHIND SCHEDULE*, ELSE YOU'D'VE HIT AN *EMPTY* TRASH BIN.

YOU CALL *THIS* LUCKY.

NOT FOR *ME*... NOT FOR THE *MANGLER* THERE...

...AND CERTAINLY NOT FOR *NOAH*. IF TOMORROW'S GONNA BE *ANYTHING* LIKE TODAY ...*DON'T* WAKE ME UP FOR IT.

NKO 37

SPRINGTIME, AND DESPITE THE *DIRE NEWS* THAT FLASHES IN NEAT, ELECTRONIC COMPUTER LETTERING AROUND THE ALLIED CHEMICAL BUILDING, *7TH AVENUE* IS ALIVE.

CLAIRE TEMPLE HAS RETURNED FROM THE HOSPITAL, AND SHE TRIES TO *COMMUNICATE* WITH LUKE. SHE HAS SOME *COMPETITION*-- PAN-HANDLERS; HAWKSTERS, VARIOUS ZEALOUS RELIGIOUS GROUPS, CAUSES AND DELUSIONS *THRUST* INTO THE WAYFARER'S LIFE AS HE PASSES BY.

THEY VANISH DURING THE WINTER AND RE-APPEAR *MIRACULOUSLY* WITH THE WARM WEATHER.

YOU LOOK *WORRIED.* IS IT BECAUSE YOU THINK SPEAR WILL TRY TO *GET* TO NOAH WHEN HE *LEARNS* NOAH HASN'T *DIED?*

TAKE A TICKET? BEST *MASSAGE* IN TOWN.

PLEASE *PERUSE* OUR PAMPHLETS ... THEY WILL SHOW YOU THE WAY TO *INNER PEACE.* A SMALL DONATION, PLEASE.

THEY *STILL* DON'T KNOW HOW NOAH WILL *TURN OUT...* AND I'VE BEEN THINKIN' 'BOUT *ALEX SIMMONS* AND HIS DAUGHTER, *LITTLE BETH.* THEY'VE DECIDED TO MOVE *OUTTA* THEIR HOUSE.

ALEX SAYS *MEMORIES* OF THEIR SON, AUGGIE, *HAUNT* 'EM THERE... I GUESS THE WAY MY MEMORIES OF MY DAYS AS A *PRISONER* AT SEAGATE PRISON HAUNT ME... OR THE WAY *SPEAR* HAUNTS NOAH.

HOW'S BETH?

WHO KNOWS? WHATTA YOU *TELL* A KID SO THAT SOMETHING THAT *ISN'T* HER FAULT DOESN'T END UP SCREWING UP HER *WHOLE* LIFE?

SHE'LL GET TO BE 15, I S'POSE, AND BE LOST AND HURT AND SPENDIN' A *FORTUNE* ON SHRINKS. AN NEVER UNDER-STAND WHAT'S HANGIN' HER *UP...*

...LESS SHE LEARNS HOW TO *FORGIVE* HER-SELF... AND, CLAIRE, MAN, I SWEAR, THAT'S SOME-TIMES *HARD* TO DO.

UM-HUM, I KNOW. C'MON LET'S HAVE SOME *WOR SHEW OPP?* I'LL PAY.

CAGE RETURNS TO THE *GEM THEATER. IT SEEMS LIKE HE LEFT SEVERAL LIFE-TIMES AGO, BUT SHANE IS STILL ON THE SCREEN, AWAITING HIM. SHANE LEAVES BUT ALWAYS COMES BACK. ALAN LADD'S AND JEAN ARTHUR'S VOICES ARE REASSURING, AND CAGE HEARS MORE THAN THE WORDS.*

HE HEARS THE UNSPOKEN HONOR AND DIGNITY BEHIND THE WORDS. AND SOMETHING SEEMS TO BE *MISSING* OUT THERE IN THE WORLD.

HEY, LUKE, WANTA SEE SOME OF THE FIRST *OUT-TAKES* FROM MY FILM?

DON'T'CHA NEED A *LICENSE* TO SHOW A *DOG* LIKE THAT? IF YOU DON'T... YOU *SHOULD.*

BERTHA HAS NO TASTE FOR *ART.* SEE, A PART OF THE FILM'S *INSPIRED* BY "ONE FLEW OVER THE COOKOO'S NEST." A STUDY IN *INSENSI-TIVITY.* THE *NURSE RATCHET* MENTALITY...

THE NURSE *WHO* AND *WHAT*?

NURSE RATCHET. PEOPLE WHO REFLECT THAT KINDA *ATTITUDE* AND NEVER *REALIZE* IT, SEE, AND--

CLICK!

--AND YOU'RE GIVIN' THAT *SODA MACHINE* ANOTHER CHANCE.

KKLUP!

I'DA THOUGHT'T YOU'D *GIVE UP* ON THAT *MON-STER.* IT KEEPS GIVING YOU THE *SHAFT.*

ZLURP!

YEAH, BUT, D.W., IT'S GOTTA RUN *OUTTA* THINGS IT CAN *DO* TO ME. MACHINE'S *COOL* THIS...

CLICK!

UHHH... *WHAT'S* IT DOIN', D.W.?

KKLUP!

IS IT *DOIN'* WHAT I *THINK* IT'S DOIN'?

ZLURP!

WELL, *TWO FOR THE PRICE OF ONE...* HUH? ... MORE? HEY, *HOLD IT UP!*

CLICK! ZLURP! KKLUP!

ZLURP! CLICK! KKLUP! CLICK!

YOU GOT TO *GIVE IT* TO THE MACHINE FOR *IMAGINATION,* LUKE!

CLICK! KKLUP! CLICK! ZLURP!

THAT'S NOT ALL I'D LIKE TO GIVE IT.

THE SOUNDS OF THE HOSPITAL ARE NOT AS REASSURING AS THE VOICES OF JEAN ARTHUR OR ALAN LADD, BUT THERE IS A SENSE OF *RECKONING* IN THE HALLWAYS.

CAGE LOOKS AT QUENTIN CHASE AND REALIZES HE KNOWS *NOTHING* ABOUT THE MAN EXCEPT THAT HE IS A *COP.*

YOU *READY* TO GO IN?

WE BETTER NOT *WAIT* FOR THAT.

HEY, DOC... YOU'RE NOT, UH, *NOT LOOKIN BAD.*

LUCAS, DON'T TRY TO BE *TRITE* ... YOU'RE NOT MADE OUT FOR IT. YOU FORGET, I'M A DOCTOR... I *KNOW* WHAT I LOOK LIKE.

YEAH, WELL YOUR *DISPOSITION* HASN'T CHANGED ANY. YOU WALKED OUT ON ME THE NIGHT I *CAUGHT* THE MANGLER, WASN'T *NICE,* DOC.

"YES, AND YOU WANT TO KNOW *WHY.* AND SO DOES YOUR FRIEND, THE LIEUTENANT. *WHO IS SPEAR?* A *LUNATIC?* PERHAPS. THERE IS *MADNESS* IN THE AIR. IT INFECTS ALL OUR *PASTS.* BEFORE I USED YOU IN MY *CELL REGENERATION* EXPERIMENTS, LUKE, I WORKED ON INMATES AT SEAGATE PRISON WHO HAD TERMINAL DISEASES.

"*JACK DANIELS* WAS ONE OF THOSE PATIENTS NO, JACK *ISN'T* SPEAR, AND HE'S *CERTAINLY* NOT THE MANGLER. JACK WAS *DYING* OF A BRAIN TUMOR. THIS WAS NO "LOVE STORY" MELODRAMA. THE MAN *WAS DYING,* AND HE WAS DYING *PAINFULLY.* I OFFERED HIM A CHANCE THAT I'D HOPED WOULD *SAVE* HIS LIFE.

"HE SIGNED ALL THE LEGAL FORMS. I WAS IMPASSIONED BY MY *THEORIES,* YET ALL OF THE PROCEEDINGS IN THAT ROOM WERE *UNDRAMATIC* ... ALMOST IMPERSONAL.

"WE BEGAN THE *TREATMENTS.* I WANTED IT TO WORK SO *DESPERATELY.* I THINK I *DELUDED* MYSELF AT THE TIME INTO THINKING IT WAS FOR HIM, FOR JACK, AS WELL AS MYSELF.

"BUT THEN, I SUPPOSE I AM OVERLY *SUSPICIOUS* OF ALL MY *MOTIVES,* ESPECIALLY SINCE THAT DAY.

"ALL THE CLICHES CAME TO MIND. I'D SEEN 'FRANKENSTEIN' AND 'DR. JEKYLL AND MR. HYDE.'

"DON'T TAMPER WITH FORCES BEYOND THE SCOPE OF MAN. DON'T TRY TO BE GOD.

"ALL THAT STUFF FILLS YOUR MIND ALONG WITH ALL THE KNOWLEDGE YOU LEARN THROUGH YEARS OF STUDY AND PRACTICE.

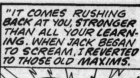

"IT COMES RUSHING BACK AT YOU, STRONGER THAN ALL YOUR LEARNING. WHEN JACK BEGAN TO SCREAM, I REVERTED TO THOSE OLD MAXIMS.

"YOU BERATE YOURSELF, YOU PROBE AT YOUR REASONS. I HADN'T THOUGHT I'D HAD ANY GOD COMPULSIONS. IT WAS A DESIRE TO GIVE SOMETHING TO THE WORLD. BUT AFTER THAT EXPERIMENT WENT WRONG, I WASN'T SURE OF THAT ANYMORE.

"WE NOTIFIED HIS FAMILY, AND IT WASN'T IMPERSONAL ANY LONGER. YOU LOOK INTO A DYING HUMAN'S EYES... AND THEY STRIP ALL THE PRETENSES WE SPEND A LIFETIME FABRICATING. IT'S BASIC AND REAL, AND PEOPLE ARE UNEASY ABOUT IT.

YOU SEE WHAT THEY DID TO HIM? COMMIT A CRIME AND THEY TREAT YOU LIKE YOU'RE A GUINEA PIG.

AIN'T RIGHT, MA. AIN'T!

IT WASN'T LIKE THAT, MRS. DANIELS. JACK WAS DYING, THERE WAS NOTHING WE COULD DO FOR HIM. THIS EXPERIMENT MIGHT HAVE GIVEN HIM A CHANCE. HE MADE THE CHOICE.

JACK DIDN'T HAVE NO CHOICE.

MAYBE HE WAS RIGHT, LUKE. FOR A GUY WHO DRESSES UP IN GAUDY TIGHTS AND MAKES HIS LIVING ON THE WRESTLING CIRCUIT, MAYBE HE TAGGED IT RIGHT. DID JACK HAVE A CHOICE?

DO ANY OF US, DOC?

I SEE YOUR POINT. THE CHOICES AREN'T SO WELL DEFINED THESE DAYS, ARE THEY, LUCAS? WHAT ARE OUR OPTIONS?

MANY AS YOU WANT, LONG AS YOU PLAY THE GAME.

YOU REST EASY, DOC.

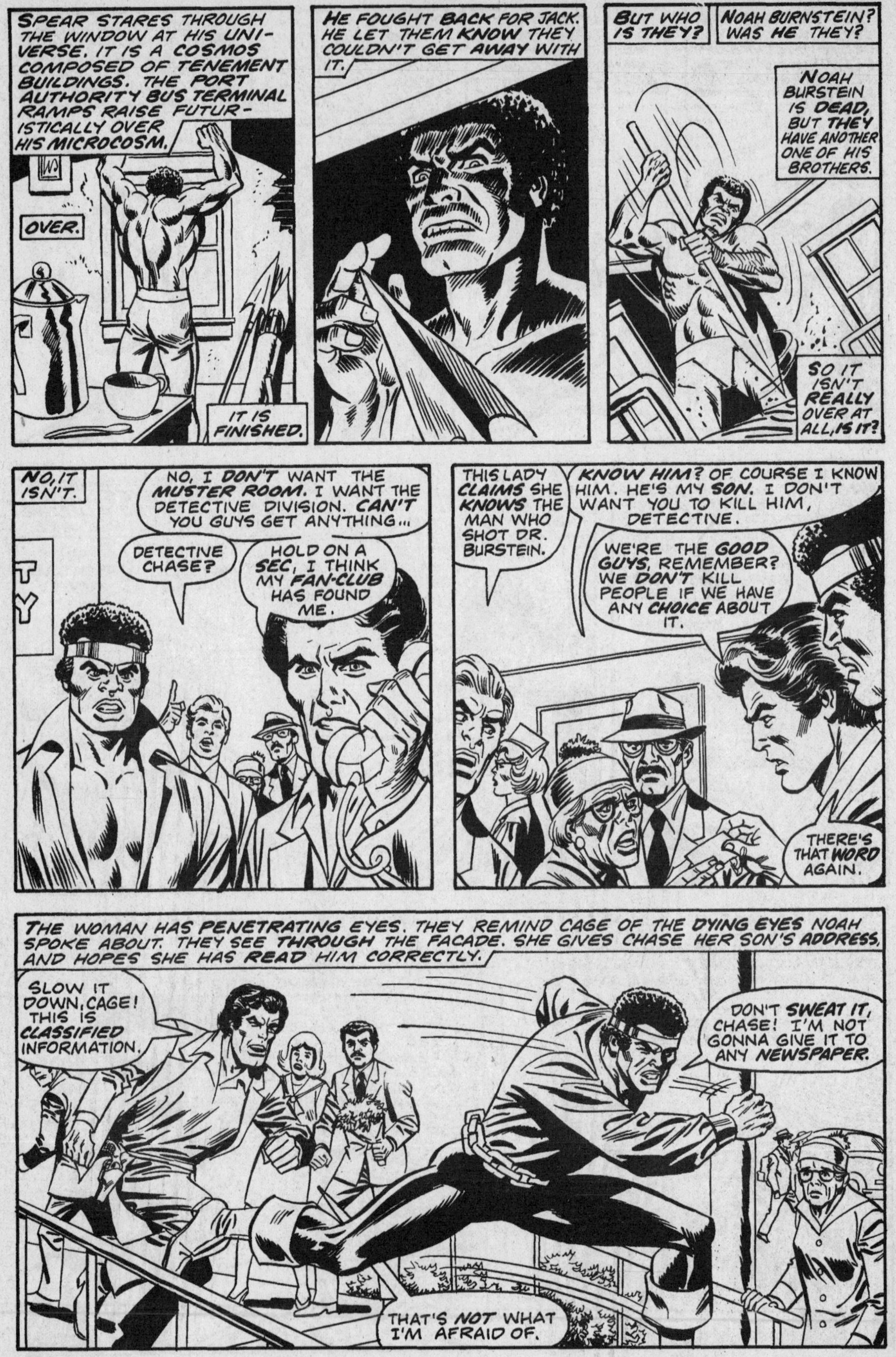
SPEAR STARES THROUGH THE WINDOW AT HIS UNIVERSE. IT IS A COSMOS COMPOSED OF TENEMENT BUILDINGS. THE PORT AUTHORITY BUS TERMINAL RAMPS RAISE FUTURISTICALLY OVER HIS MICROCOSM.
OVER.
IT IS FINISHED.
HE FOUGHT BACK FOR JACK. HE LET THEM KNOW THEY COULDN'T GET AWAY WITH IT.
BUT WHO IS THEY?
NOAH BURNSTEIN? WAS HE THEY?
NOAH BURSTEIN IS DEAD, BUT THEY HAVE ANOTHER ONE OF HIS BROTHERS.
SO IT ISN'T REALLY OVER AT ALL, IS IT?
NO, IT ISN'T.
NO, I DON'T WANT THE MUSTER ROOM. I WANT THE DETECTIVE DIVISION. CAN'T YOU GUYS GET ANYTHING...
DETECTIVE CHASE?
HOLD ON A SEC, I THINK MY FAN-CLUB HAS FOUND ME.
THIS LADY CLAIMS SHE KNOWS THE MAN WHO SHOT DR. BURSTEIN.
KNOW HIM? OF COURSE I KNOW HIM. HE'S MY SON. I DON'T WANT YOU TO KILL HIM, DETECTIVE.
WE'RE THE GOOD GUYS, REMEMBER? WE DON'T KILL PEOPLE IF WE HAVE ANY CHOICE ABOUT IT.
THERE'S THAT WORD AGAIN.
THE WOMAN HAS PENETRATING EYES. THEY REMIND CAGE OF THE DYING EYES NOAH SPOKE ABOUT. THEY SEE THROUGH THE FACADE. SHE GIVES CHASE HER SON'S ADDRESS, AND HOPES SHE HAS READ HIM CORRECTLY.
SLOW IT DOWN, CAGE! THIS IS CLASSIFIED INFORMATION.
DON'T SWEAT IT, CHASE! I'M NOT GONNA GIVE IT TO ANY NEWSPAPER.
THAT'S NOT WHAT I'M AFRAID OF.

MIDTOWN BETWEEN 9th AND 10th AVENUE. CAGE LIVED CLOSE TO THE GEM THEATER. ALL THE TIME, SPEAR LIVED CLOSE TO THE GEM THEATER.

HOW MANY TIMES HAD HE BEEN ON THIS STREET, GOING TO JOE'S PLACE TO SEE "B" WESTERNS AND CLIFF-HANGING SERIALS?

BOMP BOMP BOMP

THIS IS A BIT *UNORTHODOX* PROCEDURE, CAGE, BUT I DON'T WANT YOU BUSTING DOWN DOORS OR HEADS.

A FAINT *CLICK*, BARELY AUDIBLE.

HE'S HEARD THAT *SOUND* BEFORE. IT WAS FOLLOWED BY A PROJECTILE THAT NEARLY KILLED HIM.

THE MAN HAS *RIGHTS*, CAGE, REMEM--

CHUG! **ZONG!**

I'M *THROUGH* PLAYIN' THE GAME, CHASE. THAT'S *MY* CHOICE, AN' I GUESS I MADE IT *SOME* TIME AGO.

IT'S STARTIN' TO *CATCH UP* TO ME, TRUE... BUT THEY AIN'T *NAILED ME* YET... AN' SPEAR AN' I GOT US SOME THINGS TO SETTLE.

HEY! WHAT'S GOING ON? YOU JUST KILLED MY CAT, SYLVESTER.

CAGE DOESN'T CHARGE AT THE *DOOR*, HE CRASHES RIGHT THROUGH THE *CHEAP* PLASTER WALL.

KERUMPH!

AREN'T'CHA GONNA SAY *HELLO*, SPEAR?

THAT'S BETTER. YOU'VE MADE ME FEEL *WANTED*.

YOU WON'T STAY OUT OF *THIS*, WILL YOU, CAGE? ALL THE WAY *THROUGH*, YOU HAD TO *COMPLICATE* EVERYTHING.

CHUNK

WELL, THIS IS FOR MY *BROTHER*, WHO'S STARING AT *BARS* BECAUSE OF YOU! AND DON'T *WORRY*, CAGE, I'M *LEAVING* THIS TOWN.

THERE'S GOT TO BE ANOTHER UNIVERSE *SOMEWHERE*. MAYBE KANSAS, HUH? MAYBE *THERE*.

WHAT IN THE NAME OF HELL ARE YOU *BABBLIN'* ABOUT?

FORGET I *ASKED.* THE HECK WITH YOU IF YOU CAN'T TAKE A *JOKE.*

HEY, MAN, *WATCH* WHERE YOU'RE JUMPIN' 'FORE I RAP YOU *UPSIDE* YOUR HEAD.

DON'T GET 'IM *MAD.*

HEY, HE DON'T *SCARE* ME *NONE.* I'LL THROW HIM RIGHT OFF THIS *STOOP.*

CHASE, IF YOU'RE STILL *OUT* THERE CHECKIN' THE *LINO-LEUM DESIGN,* MAYBE YOU CAN MAKE SOME *TIME* DOWN THE STAIRS.

AND AFTER I GET MY *HANDS* ON SPEAR, I WANT THAT GUY WHAT SOLD HIM ALL THIS *TEAR GAS.*

AND THEN I WANT NOAH TO COME ACROSS WITH SOME *BREAD* TO PAY FOR THE *FANCY SHIRT* GONE THE WAY OF ALL *THINGS.*

SHAASHH!

YOU GUYS ARE REALLY *TRASHING* THE PLACE, I'LL SAY THAT.

THEY OUGHTTA *LOCK* YOU AWAY FOR A *PUN* LIKE THAT KID.

MAN, I FELT THAT LANDIN' ALL THE WAY UP TO MY *ARMPITS.*

NOW *WHERE* DID HE--? WELL THAT'S NOT *HARD* TO SEE.

COME BACK HERE, YOU *MANIAC!* I'VE ONLY GOT FOUR PAY-MENTS *LEFT* ON THIS *JUNK!*

FOUR! ONLY FOUR! MY WIFE IS GOING TO KILL ME!

GROCERY

PDQ271

I DON'T EXPECT YOU TO UNDERSTAND WHAT I'M TALKING ABOUT, *CAGE!*

I REALLY DON'T *CARE* WHETHER YOU UNDERSTAND OR NOT.

YOU'LL UNDERSTAND *THIS* THOUGH, OR AT LEAST THINK YOU KNOW WHY I'M *FIRING* AT YOU.

WHUSH!

PORT AUTHORITY TERM

I UNDERSTAND, SPEAR. I UNDERSTAND THOSE *SPIKES* OF YOURS CAN MAKE PEOPLE *DEAD!*

THIS AIN'T A *GAME,* AND YOU HAVEN'T THOUGHT IT *THROUGH,* SPEAR. BURSTEIN'S NOT YOUR *TARGET.*

YOU BEEN AIMIN' AT THE *WRONG* THING.

FOLKS, YOU PEOPLE ARE *LUCKY* YOU'RE GETTING OUT OF THIS PLACE. IT'S GETTING MORE *BERSERKO* ALL THE TIME.

TAXI

SANDY, IS *THAT--*?

YES, ALEX. THAT'S *LUKE.*

CAGE *GLIMPSES* THEM FROM THE CORNER OF HIS EYE, AND HE KNOWS THEY ARE *LEAVING.*

THAT *ISN'T* THE ANSWER. LEAVING IS NOT THE *ANSWER.*

AND THEN HE SEES LITTLE BETH'S *WOUNDED* EYES AND REALIZES HE DOES NOT *KNOW* WHAT THE ANSWER IS ... *IF* THERE IS ANY.

THEY ARE LOST IN EXHAUST FUMES AND VEHICLES. NOT EVEN A CHANCE FOR A GOODBYE, FOR SOME LAST INADEQUATE WORDS.

SPEAR!

HE'S LEAVING FOR THE TERMINAL AND HEADING FOR THE EXIT RAMPS.

HEY, YOU *IDIOT!* ARE YOU OUT OF YOUR *GOURD?*

THAT'S *TRUER* THAN YOU *SUSPECT.*

THAT'S *TRUER* THEN I EVEN *IMAGINED.*

SPEAR TAKES A DEEP BREATH, AND CARBON-MONOXIDE FLOODS HIS LUNGS AS HE LEAPS.

EXIT 40th EAST

SPEAR, THIS IS GONNA SOUND *TIRED*, AN', I GOT A FEELIN', *OBSOLETE...*

N.Y. - NEWARK 3477

-- BUT NOAH BURSTEIN AND I WERE *FRIENDS*, AN' THAT MEANS THIS COMES DOWN TO YOU--

--'AN ME!

STAR
PETER
THE

'SIDES, WHATTA YOU THINK YOU CAN FIND IN *NEWARK, NEW JERSEY*?

THE ROAD TO *OZ*? LET ME CLUE YOU, IT'S NOT *THERE*!

SPARE ME THE EMERALD CITY *ALLUSIONS*, CAGE.

I'M NOT EVEN SURE I KNOW *WHATEVER* YOU SAID, IS.

MAN, YOU KEEP GETTIN' ALL THE BREAKS, SPEAR.

STANDIN' ON TOPPA THIS *BUS* IS LIKE TRYIN' TO KEEP YOUR BALANCE ON A *WATER BED* IN THE MIDDLE OF A *DISCO PALACE*.

YOU'LL STILL FEEL THIS, MAN. *RIGHT*?

THE HUGE BUS LURCHES. THE TWO STRUGGLING FIGURES ARE THROWN FROM THE ROOF--

--AND HURTLE THROUGH THE WINDSHIELD!

KRASH!

HOLD YOUR FIRE, PATROLMAN! THERE'S NO WAY WE'RE GOING TO HIT THE RIGHT MAN!

CRANCHH!

HAROLD WOSNOSKI IS DRIVING THROUGH THE MIDDAY TRAFFIC, AWAITING AN EVENING'S ENTERTAINMENT OF ENDLESS CAR CRASHES ON THE TUBE.

HE WILL WATCH THEM WITH A BORED EYE, FALLING ASLEEP AS THE HUNDRETH CAR MAKES THE HUNDRETH HAIRBREADTH TURN.

THE BUS IS A TERRIFYING MONSTER THAT FILLS HIS VISION. TWENTY-FIVE-MILES-AN-HOUR SUDDENLY SEEMS TO BE A ROCKETING SPEED.

SPLINTER!

SPLACK!

LIKE A PREHISTORIC BEHEMOTH, THE BUS CRASHES THROUGH THE DOCKSIDE AREA--

--HOVERS FOR ONE FINAL DYING MOMENT, AS IF IT MIGHT SAVE ITSELF--

--AND THEN PLUMMETS INTO THE HUDSON RIVER! HAROLD WOSNOSKI HOLDS ONTO HIS STEERING WHEEL WITH SHAKING HANDS, AND RETURNS TO THE RELIGION HE LEARNED AS A CHILD.

THEY SEEK THE EXITS LIKE REFUGEES FROM "THE POSEIDON ADVENTURE."

THE DIFFERENCE IS THAT THEIR IMPENDING DEATHS DO NOT HAVE ANY POIGNANT MEANING OR DRAMATIC CONFRONTATION.

THEY ARE REDUCED TO IMPULSES OF SURVIVAL. RIP AT THE WINDOWS! CLAW AT THE DOORS!

AND THE SURVIVORS ARE LEFT WITH MEMORIES, UNLIKE THE MARIONETTES ON THE T.V. SHOW. THEY WILL RELIVE THIS DAY TO THEIR ACTUAL END.

YOU'RE NOT GOIN' ANYWHERE, SPEAR!

AT LEAST NOT ANYWHERE I DON'T SEND YOU.

CAGE!

WHAT'S YOUR PROBLEM ...QUENT?

CAGE!!

OH, YOU MEAN SPEAR. I ALMOST FORGOT.

YOU DIDN'T THINK I'D LET ANYTHING HAPPEN TO HIM, DID YOU?

WELL, THERE WAS A MOMENT THERE...

HEYYYY!

YOU MIND TELLING ME WHAT THAT WAS ALL ABOUT?

THAT'S-- --FOR DOUBTING ME.

THE TWO MEN LAUGH, A SOUND THAT WILL LEAVE A PLEASANTER MEMORY THAN THE REST OF THE DAY.

NEXT: CHEMISTRO IS BACK!

AND CAGE HAS GOT HIM!

POWER-MAN
MARVEL COMICS GROUP
APPROVED BY THE COMICS CODE AUTHORITY
30¢
36
OCT
02149
LUKE CAGE, POWER MAN
YOU'VE TURNED THE GROUND INTO QUICKSAND!
AND HERE'S WHERE CHEMISTRO MAKES SURE YOU DROWN IN IT!
WATCH OUT, CAGE!
CHEMISTRO IS BACK!
AND DEADLIER THAN EVER!

POWER MAN ANNUAL
1
1976
02433
50¢
CC
MARVEL COMICS GROUP
ALL NEW!
KING-SIZE ANNUAL!
APPROVED BY THE COMICS CODE AUTHORITY
LUKE CAGE, POWER MAN
TOO LATE, CAGE! YOU'VE DESTROYED MY MACHINE--
--BUT THE QUAKE IT'S STARTED WILL DESTROY YOU!!
Cockrum
EARTH SHOCK!
DOUBLE THE ACTION! DOUBLE THE THRILLS!

LUKE CAGE: Wrongly convicted and sentenced to prison—reborn in a freak experiment there that gave him steel-hard skin and strength beyond belief—a man who hides his identity as an escaped convict in the role of a HERO FOR HIRE!
Stan Lee PRESENTS: LUKE CAGE, POWER MAN!
EARTHSHOCK!
JAPAN...
ONCE UPON A TIME, THIS ISLAND KINGDOM HAD ISOLATED ITSELF FROM THE WORLD AROUND IT-- NO JAPANESE WAS ALLOWED TO LEAVE THESE ISLANDS, NO FOREIGNER ALLOWED TO ENTER-- THE PENALTY IN BOTH CASES WAS DEATH.
THEN, IN MAY OF 1853, COMMODORE MATTHEW CALBRAITH PERRY ARRIVED OFF THE JAPANESE COAST WITH FOUR WARSHIPS, DETERMINED TO THRUST JAPAN BACK INTO THE MAINSTREAM OF "CIVILIZED" SOCIETY... BY PERSUASION. OR BY FORCE.
HE SUCCEEDED.
AND EVER SINCE THAT TIME, JAPAN HAS BEEN A MAJOR POWER IN THE WESTERN PACIFIC. TO HER SHORES HAVE COME SOLDIERS AND STATESMEN, BUSINESSMEN AND SCHOLARS, CROOKS AND TOURISTS...
HEY, LUCAS, IF SOMEONE TOLD YOU THREE DAYS AGO THAT YOU'D BE DOIN' A JOB IN TOKYO, JAPAN--YOU'D HAVE LAUGHED IN HIS FACE...
...SO WHY AIN'T YOU LAUGHIN', CAGE?
AND FINALLY, IN THE SUMMER OF 1976, A SUPER-HERO...
...WHO FEELS SOMEWHAT OUT OF PLACE!
CHRIS CLAREMONT AUTHOR / LEE ELIAS & DAVE HUNT ARTISTS / DENISE WOHL LETTERER / B. WILFORD COLORIST / ARCHIE GOODWIN EDITOR

CHERRY BLOSSOM LANE-- A QUIET PLACE. ELEGANT, WELL-TO-DO HOUSES LINE WINDING, NARROW STREETS THAT MAKE *NO* CONCESSION TO THE *AUTOMOBILE.*

IT'S A *PRE-WAR* DISTRICT, ONE THAT SOMEHOW MANAGED TO *ESCAPE* THE FIREBOMB RAIDS THAT *DECIMATED* THE REST OF *TOKYO.*

A FINE AND *PRIVATE* PLACE, THIS, WHERE EACH HOUSE IS AN *ISLAND* UNTO ITSELF, *SCREENED* FROM THE UGLY REALITY THAT IS MODERN TOKYO BY HIGH, STATELY *WALLS.*

SCREENED, PERHAPS-- BUT *PRO-TECTED?*

NO.

THE MEN ARE *GATHERED,* SIR.

THANK YOU, *SAGAWAKA.*

YOU'VE ALL BEEN *BRIEFED;* YOU ALL KNOW WHAT TO DO.

I WANT *NO* MISHAPS AND NO *WITNESSES* -- AND I WANT THE WOMAN TAKEN *UNHARMED.*

YOU MEN HAVE YOUR *ORDERS.*

--NOW *CARRY* THEM OUT!

THEY MOVE IN SILENCE...

...DRESSED LIKE FUTURISTIC COMMANDOS, BUT SLIPPING THRU THE BALMY NIGHT AIR LIKE THE FEARSOME LEGENDARY NINJAS OF OLD.

WHY D' YOU THINK WE'RE OUT HERE, SHIRO?!

NO TRES-PASSING

BLESSED IF *I* KNOW.

MAYBE, THIS AMERICAN WOMAN IS THE COMMISSIONER'S *GIRLFR--*

=WHUH!=

SHIK

SHUK!

IT'S OVER IN THE BLINK OF AN EYE--

PHUT!

--*THREE MEN DONE TO DEATH BEFORE THEY'D EVEN REALIZED THEY WERE UNDER ATTACK.*

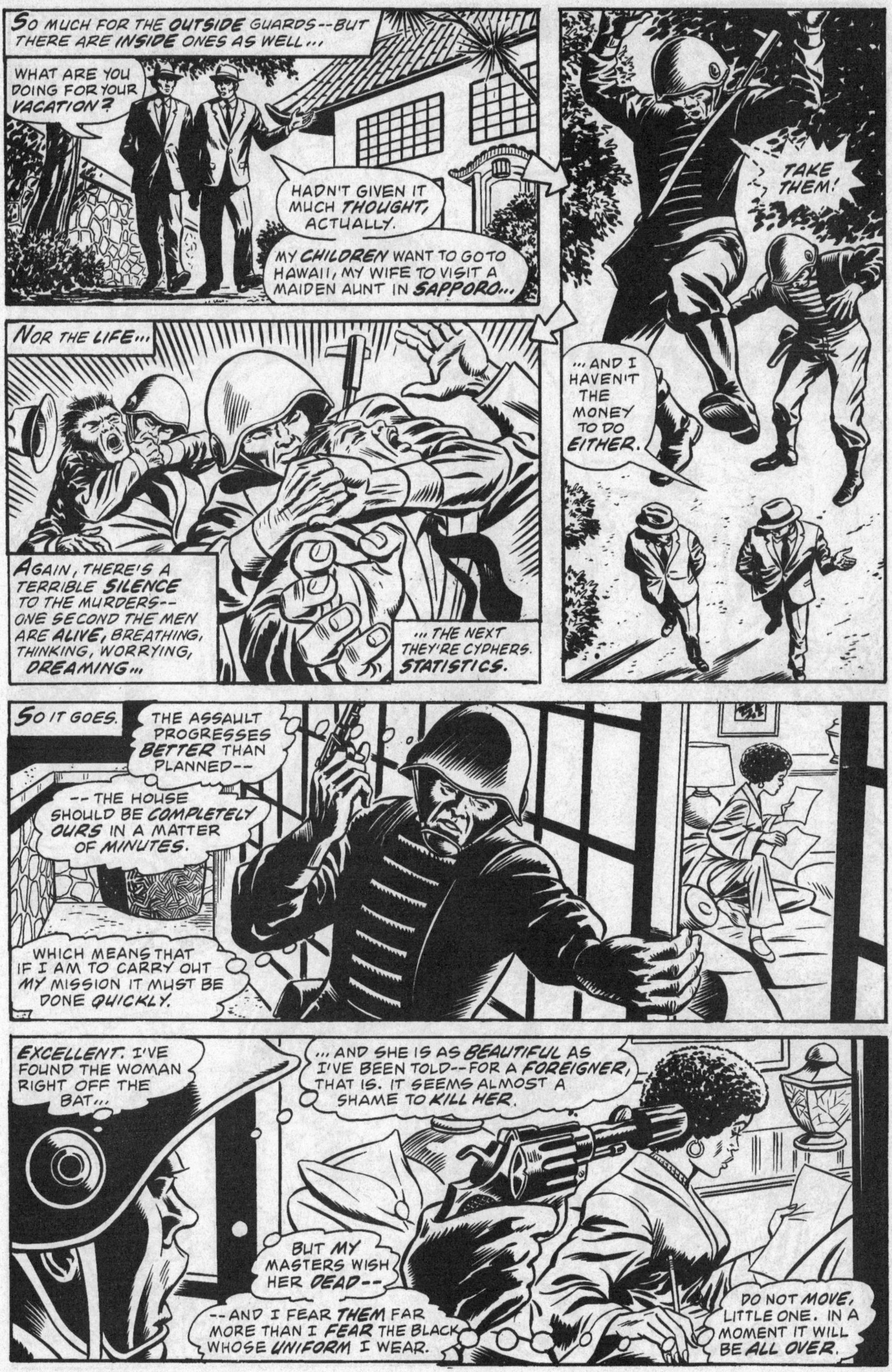
SO MUCH FOR THE OUTSIDE GUARDS--BUT THERE ARE INSIDE ONES AS WELL...
WHAT ARE YOU DOING FOR YOUR VACATION?
HADN'T GIVEN IT MUCH THOUGHT, ACTUALLY.
MY CHILDREN WANT TO GO TO HAWAII, MY WIFE TO VISIT A MAIDEN AUNT IN SAPPORO...
TAKE THEM!
...AND I HAVEN'T THE MONEY TO DO EITHER.
NOR THE LIFE...
AGAIN, THERE'S A TERRIBLE SILENCE TO THE MURDERS--ONE SECOND THE MEN ARE ALIVE, BREATHING, THINKING, WORRYING, DREAMING...
...THE NEXT THEY'RE CYPHERS. STATISTICS.
SO IT GOES.
THE ASSAULT PROGRESSES BETTER THAN PLANNED--
--THE HOUSE SHOULD BE COMPLETELY OURS IN A MATTER OF MINUTES.
WHICH MEANS THAT IF I AM TO CARRY OUT MY MISSION IT MUST BE DONE QUICKLY.
EXCELLENT. I'VE FOUND THE WOMAN RIGHT OFF THE BAT...
...AND SHE IS AS BEAUTIFUL AS I'VE BEEN TOLD--FOR A FOREIGNER, THAT IS. IT SEEMS ALMOST A SHAME TO KILL HER.
BUT MY MASTERS WISH HER DEAD--
--AND I FEAR THEM FAR MORE THAN I FEAR THE BLACK WHOSE UNIFORM I WEAR.
DO NOT MOVE, LITTLE ONE. IN A MOMENT IT WILL BE ALL OVER.

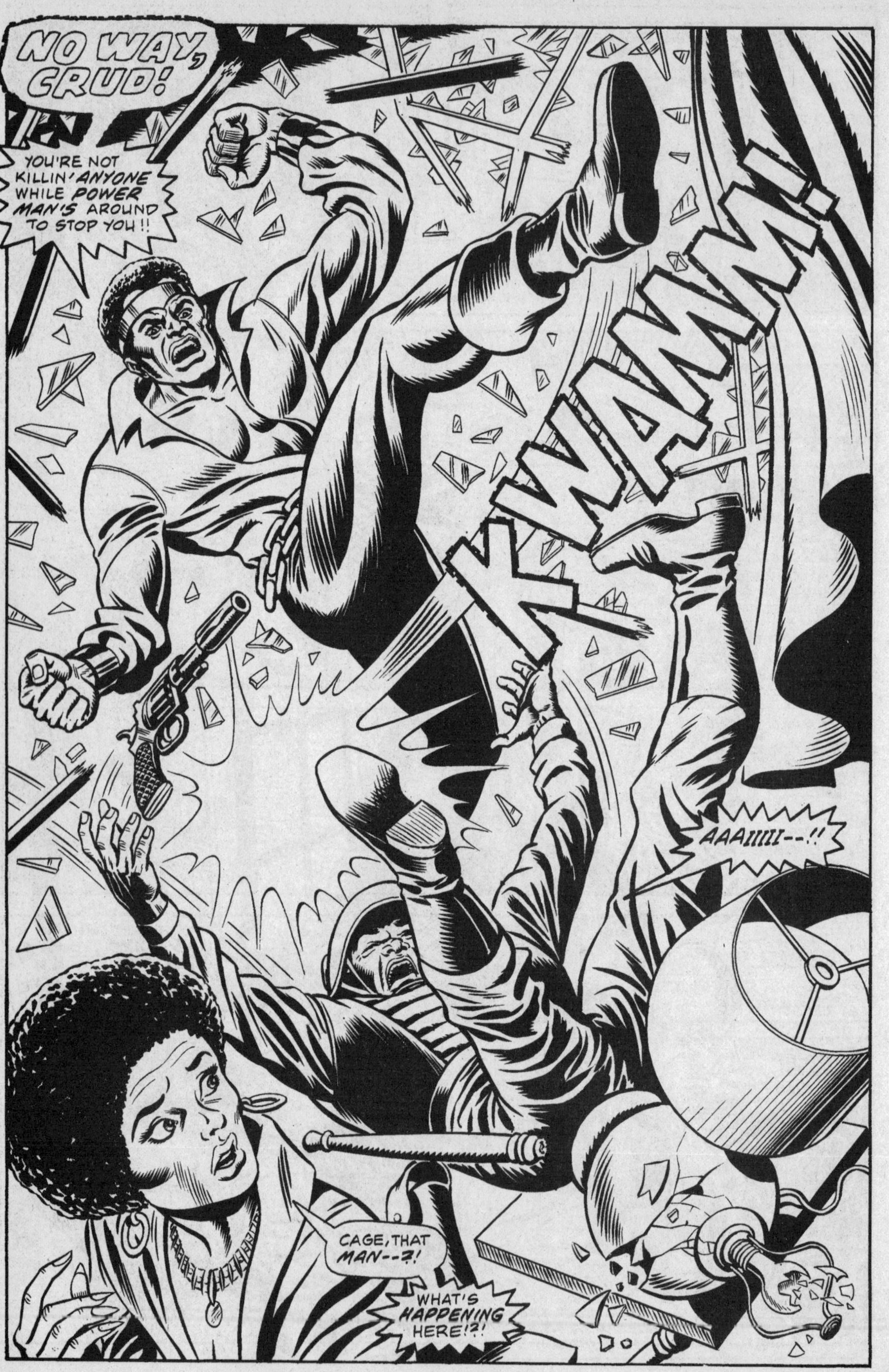
NO WAY, CRUD!
YOU'RE NOT KILLIN' ANYONE WHILE POWER MAN'S AROUND TO STOP YOU!!
K-WAMM!
AAAIIIII--!!
CAGE, THAT MAN--?!
WHAT'S HAPPENING HERE!?!

WHAT YOUR GRAN'MA WAS AFRAID OF, SAM--

--SO KEEP YOUR HEAD DOWN -- 'CAUSE IT LOOKS LIKE SOMEONE WANTS YOU DEAD AWFUL BAD.

AND NOT JUST THE WOMAN, FOOL--!

TWO CAN BE KILLED AS EASILY AS ONE!

DON'T BET ON THAT, SUGAR!

BROW

IZAWA-- ALL OF YOU! LOOK!

THE WOMAN HAS YET ANOTHER BODY-GUARD.

HEY, DOES THAT MEAN THIS CREEP'S A FRIEND OF YOURS--?

'CAUSE IF HE IS, THEN YOU CLOWNS CAN HAVE HIM BACK--

-- WITH INTEREST!!

WATCH THE ONE ON THE LEFT, LUCAS -- YOU MISSED HIM!

YOUR POWER IS INCREDIBLE, AMERICAN ...

.... BUT STRENGTH MATTERS LITTLE WHEN MATCHED AGAINST A WEAPON!

YOU JIVIN' ME, BABY--

--IT'LL TAKE MORE'N THAT POPGUN O' YOURS TO FAZE POWER MAN!

I DO NOT INTEND TO "FAZE", FOOL-- I INTEND TO KILL!

KBAM!

CHRISTMAS-- THAT HURT!

WHAT'S HE GOT THERE ANYWAY-- A PINT-SIZE ATOMIC CANNON?

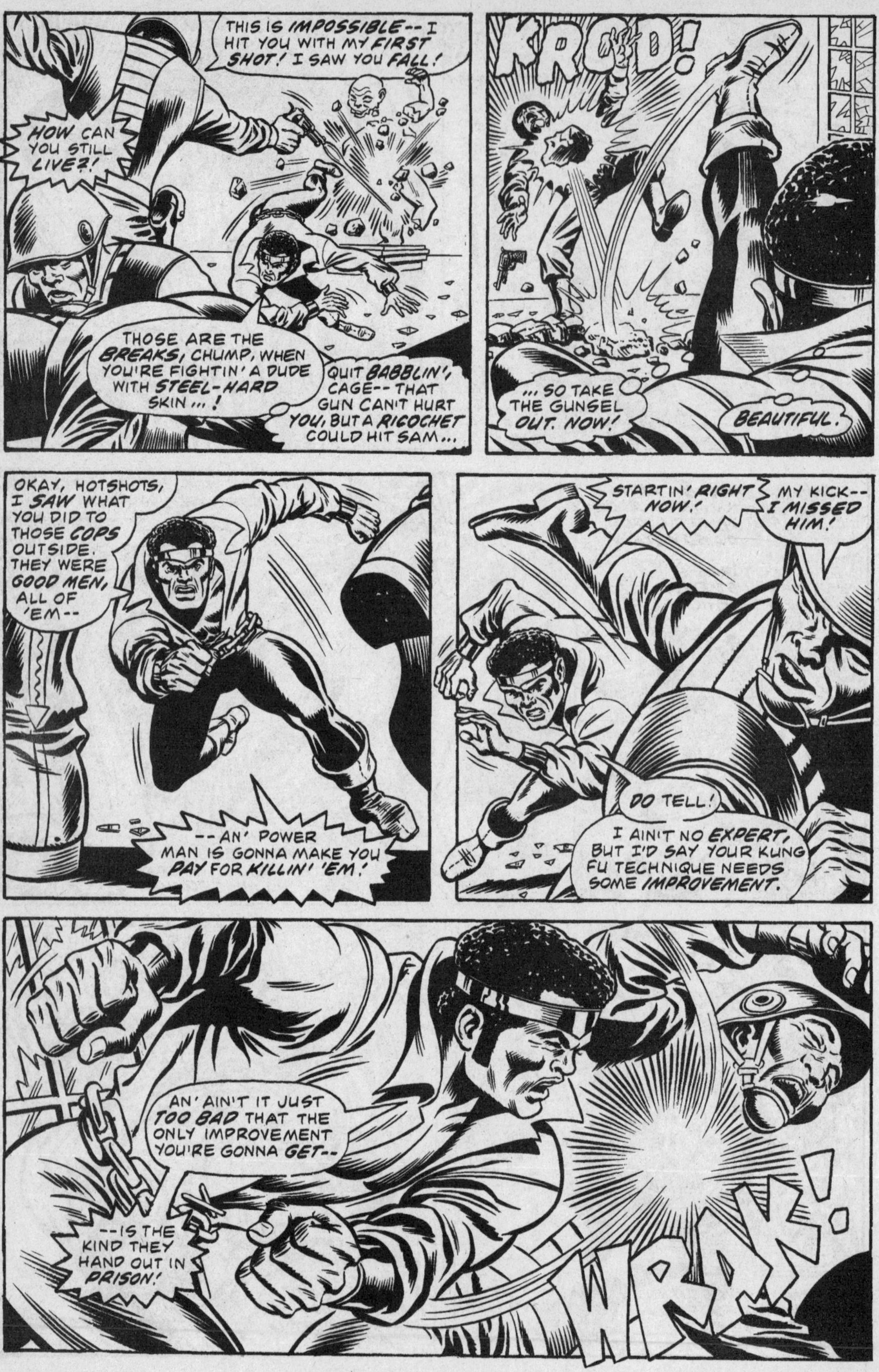
THIS IS IMPOSSIBLE-- I HIT YOU WITH MY FIRST SHOT! I SAW YOU FALL!
HOW CAN YOU STILL LIVE?!
THOSE ARE THE BREAKS, CHUMP, WHEN YOU'RE FIGHTIN' A DUDE WITH STEEL-HARD SKIN...!
QUIT BABBLIN', CAGE-- THAT GUN CAN'T HURT YOU, BUT A RICOCHET COULD HIT SAM...
KROD!
...SO TAKE THE GUNSEL OUT. NOW!
BEAUTIFUL.
OKAY, HOTSHOTS, I SAW WHAT YOU DID TO THOSE COPS OUTSIDE. THEY WERE GOOD MEN, ALL OF 'EM--
--AN' POWER MAN IS GONNA MAKE YOU PAY FOR KILLIN' 'EM!
STARTIN' RIGHT NOW!
MY KICK-- I MISSED HIM!
DO TELL!
I AIN'T NO EXPERT, BUT I'D SAY YOUR KUNG FU TECHNIQUE NEEDS SOME IMPROVEMENT.
AN' AIN'T IT JUST TOO BAD THAT THE ONLY IMPROVEMENT YOU'RE GONNA GET--
--IS THE KIND THEY HAND OUT IN PRISON!
WRAK!

DOG OF AN AMERICAN! WE ARE ALL *MASTERS* OF THE MARTIAL ARTS...

...NOT EVEN *IRON FIST*, THE DRAGON SON OF *K'UN-LUN* COULD STAND AGAINST OUR *COMBINED SKILL*--

--MUCH LESS AN *UNTUTORED AMATEUR* LIKE YOURSELF!

ARE YOU GUYS FOR *REAL*?

YOU'RE JUST *TWO-BIT PUNKS* DOIN' THE TOWN IN *BUCK ROGERS* MONKEY SUITS AND FIGURIN' THAT MAKES YOU *SOMETHIN'!*

MAN, YOU TURKEYS WOULDN'T LAST *TWO* MINUTES ON *8th* AVENUE.

BDOK

AND *YOU* WILL NOT LAST *ONE* MINUTE HERE!

THOD!

THE MAN HAS A *POINT.* EVEN *MY* POWER HAS A LIMIT-- AND, GIVEN THE *CHANCE...*

...THESE JOKERS *MIGHT* BE ABLE TO *WEAR ME DOWN!*

SO I GUESS I'D BETTER NOT *GIVE 'EM* THAT CHANCE.

SHOK

YOU WANT SOME *DOWN HOME KUNG FU,* FELLA-- THEN I'LL BE MORE'N GLAD TO *OBLIGE.*

BRAM!

AND I HAVE HAD MORE THAN I *CARE* TO STAND!

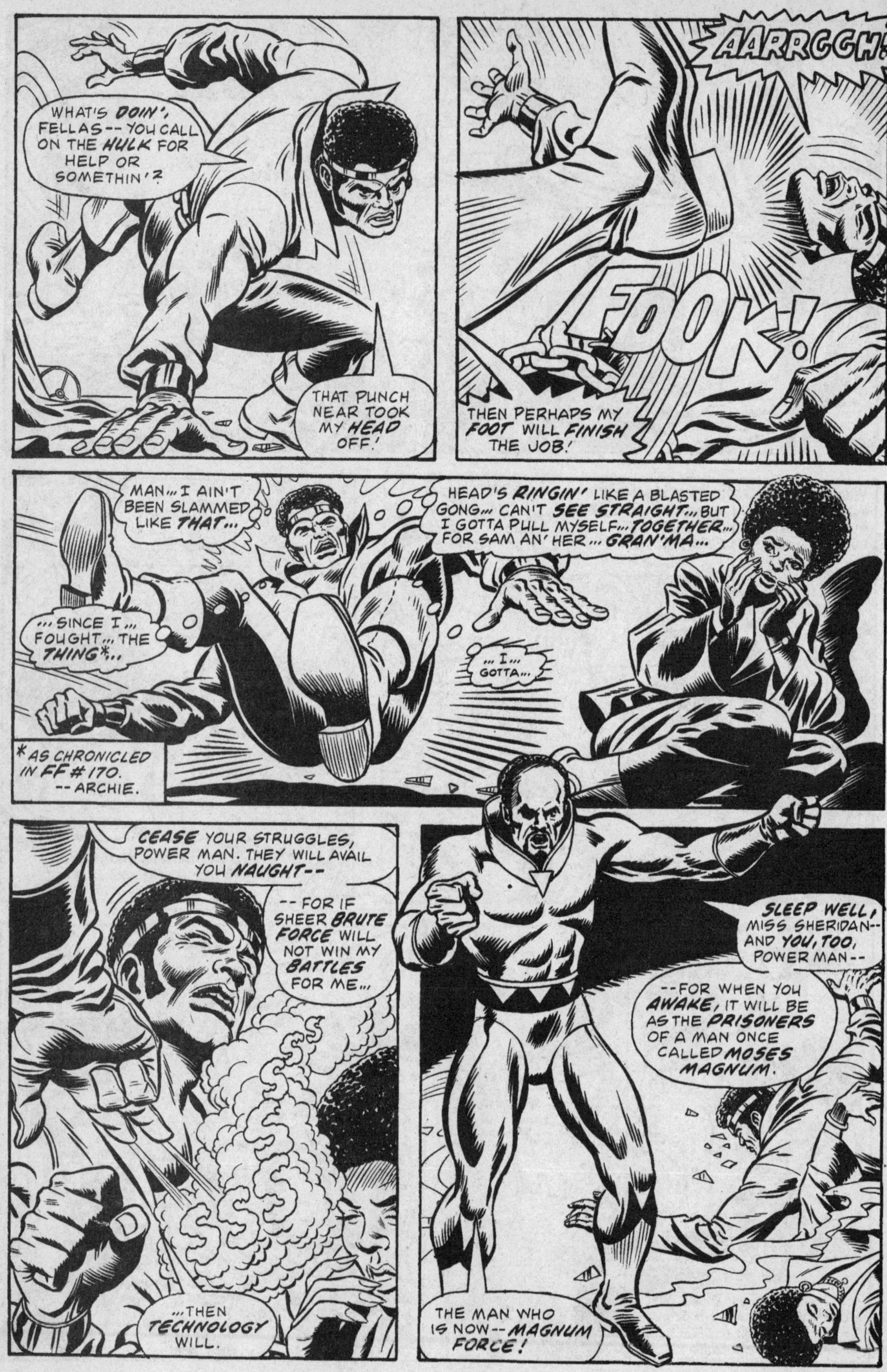
WHAT'S DOIN', FELLAS-- YOU CALL ON THE HULK FOR HELP OR SOMETHIN'?
THAT PUNCH NEAR TOOK MY HEAD OFF!
AARRGGH!
FDOOK!
THEN PERHAPS MY FOOT WILL FINISH THE JOB!
MAN... I AIN'T BEEN SLAMMED LIKE THAT...
...SINCE I... FOUGHT... THE THING*...
HEAD'S RINGIN' LIKE A BLASTED GONG... CAN'T SEE STRAIGHT... BUT I GOTTA PULL MYSELF... TOGETHER... FOR SAM AN' HER... GRAN'MA...
...I... GOTTA...
*AS CHRONICLED IN FF #170. --ARCHIE.
CEASE YOUR STRUGGLES, POWER MAN. THEY WILL AVAIL YOU NAUGHT--
--FOR IF SHEER BRUTE FORCE WILL NOT WIN MY BATTLES FOR ME...
...THEN TECHNOLOGY WILL.
SLEEP WELL, MISS SHERIDAN-- AND YOU, TOO, POWER MAN--
--FOR WHEN YOU AWAKE, IT WILL BE AS THE PRISONERS OF A MAN ONCE CALLED MOSES MAGNUM.
THE MAN WHO IS NOW-- MAGNUM FORCE!

TAKE THEM TO THE CARS-- *QUICKLY!*

THIS PHASE OF THE OPERATION HAS ALREADY TAKEN *TOO LONG!*

SOMEONE MAY HAVE *HEARD* THE FIGHT AND SUMMONED THE *POLICE.*

WHAT-- *STILL* STRUGGLING POWER MAN? I'M *IMPRESSED.*

GIVE HIM *ANOTHER* SHOT OF GAS AND GET HIM *OUT OF HERE.*

DARKNESS-- AND THEN, A *FINAL* SILENCE...

...AND IN THAT SILENCE, MEMORIES.

TWO DAYS AGO-- ONLY *TWO,* WAS THAT ALL--? FIFTH AVENUE IN THE MID-NINETIES.

THE DAY HAD BEEN MUGGY--HOT-- MORE AUGUST THAN JUNE-- AND CAGE'S *GEM THEATRE* OFFICE HAD BEEN LIKE AN *OVEN* WHEN THE MESSAGE ARRIVED.

"COME TO MY *RESIDENCE* THIS AFTERNOON AT 3," IT SAID. " I WILL MAKE IT WORTH YOUR WHILE."

IT WAS SIGNED, AMANDA SHERIDAN.

CAGE KNEW THE NAME-- AND HE NEEDED THE *MONEY.* SO HE WENT.

THE HOUSE WAS *OLD,* HEARKENING BACK TO TIME WHEN BEING RICH *MEANT* SOMETHING. BUT CAGE DIDN'T KNOW ABOUT *THAT...*

...HE'D NEVER BEEN RICH.

MRS. SHERIDAN WILL... *SEE* YOU NOW, MR. CAGE.

AMANDA SHERIDAN, A MOST FORMIDABLE WOMAN. SHE'D STARTED WITH *NOTHING--* HER MOTHER BORN A *SLAVE--* AND BUILT HERSELF A GREAT *FORTUNE.*

I'LL BE BRIEF AND *TO THE POINT,* MR. CAGE--

--I WISH YOU TO *KILL* A MAN.

THEN YOU *DON'T* WANT *ME.*

YOU WANT *HIRED GUNS,* I CAN GIVE YOU SOME *GOOD NAMES* -- BUT IF YOU WANT *POWER MAN* --

-- THEN IT'S ON *MY* TERMS OR *NOT AT ALL.*

YOU'RE IN NO POSITION TO REFUSE A *PAYING JOB,* MR. CAGE.

I GUESS NOT.

EXCEPT THAT I'M A *SUPER-HERO,* LADY -- AN' IF WE DON'T PLAY BY THE *RULES* ...

... WHY SHOULD *ANY-BODY?*

A GOOD POINT.

BUT BEFORE YOU TELL ME -- *POLITELY,* I'M SURE -- WHERE I CAN *STUFF* MY OFFER, WHY NOT *HEAR* ME OUT?

THE MAN CONCERNED IS *MOSES MAGNUM!*

THEN YOU'RE *WASTING* YOUR TIME.

MY *STREET SOURCES* TOLD ME THAT MAGNUM WAS KILLED BY THE *PUNISHER* MONTHS AGO.

YOUR SOURCES ARE *WRONG!*

MAGNUM IS VERY MUCH *ALIVE* AND IS NOW WORKING ON A PROJECT OF LITERALLY *EARTH-SHAKING* MAGNITUDE.

I ALSO HAVE REASON TO BELIEVE THAT HE INTENDS TO *INVOLVE* MY GREAT-GRAND-DAUGHTER, *SAM-ANTHA,* IN THIS PROJECT!

I WANT SAMANTHA *PROTECTED* -- AND I WANT MAGNUM *STOPPED!*

STOPPED?

ANY WAY YOU CAN.

IN OTHER WORDS, STOPPED *"DEAD."*

NO DEAL, MRS. SHERIDAN.

PROTECTING YOUR GRAN'DAUGHTER IS *ONE THING* -- KILLING A MAN -- *ANY MAN* -- IN *COLD BLOOD* IS SOMETHING ELSE.

MAYBE *YOU'VE* GOT WHATEVER IT TAKES TO DO THAT WITHOUT A *SECOND THOUGHT;* I HAVEN'T. AND I *WON'T.*

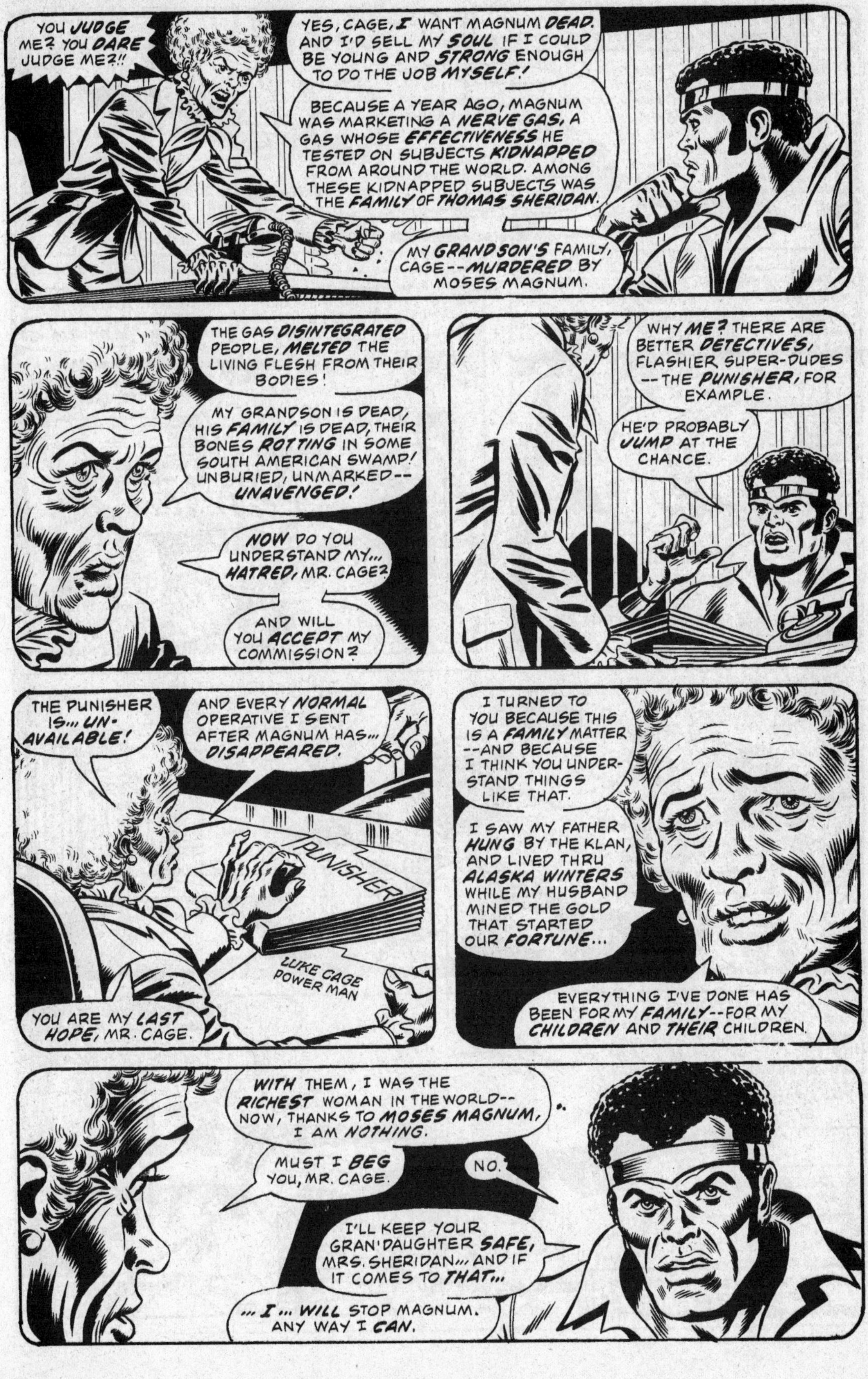

YOU JUDGE ME? YOU DARE JUDGE ME?!!
YES, CAGE, I WANT MAGNUM DEAD. AND I'D SELL MY SOUL IF I COULD BE YOUNG AND STRONG ENOUGH TO DO THE JOB MYSELF!
BECAUSE A YEAR AGO, MAGNUM WAS MARKETING A NERVE GAS, A GAS WHOSE EFFECTIVENESS HE TESTED ON SUBJECTS KIDNAPPED FROM AROUND THE WORLD. AMONG THESE KIDNAPPED SUBUECTS WAS THE FAMILY OF THOMAS SHERIDAN.
MY GRANDSON'S FAMILY, CAGE--MURDERED BY MOSES MAGNUM.
THE GAS DISINTEGRATED PEOPLE, MELTED THE LIVING FLESH FROM THEIR BODIES!
MY GRANDSON IS DEAD, HIS FAMILY IS DEAD, THEIR BONES ROTTING IN SOME SOUTH AMERICAN SWAMP! UNBURIED, UNMARKED--UNAVENGED!
NOW DO YOU UNDERSTAND MY... HATRED, MR. CAGE?
AND WILL YOU ACCEPT MY COMMISSION?
WHY ME? THERE ARE BETTER DETECTIVES, FLASHIER SUPER-DUDES --THE PUNISHER, FOR EXAMPLE.
HE'D PROBABLY JUMP AT THE CHANCE.
THE PUNISHER IS... UN-AVAILABLE!
AND EVERY NORMAL OPERATIVE I SENT AFTER MAGNUM HAS... DISAPPEARED.
PUNISHER
LUKE CAGE POWER MAN
YOU ARE MY LAST HOPE, MR. CAGE.
I TURNED TO YOU BECAUSE THIS IS A FAMILY MATTER --AND BECAUSE I THINK YOU UNDER-STAND THINGS LIKE THAT.
I SAW MY FATHER HUNG BY THE KLAN, AND LIVED THRU ALASKA WINTERS WHILE MY HUSBAND MINED THE GOLD THAT STARTED OUR FORTUNE...
EVERYTHING I'VE DONE HAS BEEN FOR MY FAMILY--FOR MY CHILDREN AND THEIR CHILDREN.
WITH THEM, I WAS THE RICHEST WOMAN IN THE WORLD-- NOW, THANKS TO MOSES MAGNUM, I AM NOTHING.
MUST I BEG YOU, MR. CAGE.
NO.
I'LL KEEP YOUR GRAN'DAUGHTER SAFE, MRS. SHERIDAN... AND IF IT COMES TO THAT...
...I... WILL STOP MAGNUM. ANY WAY I CAN.

BIG TALK, CAGE-- TOO BAD YOU COULDN'T PUT YOUR *MONEY* WHERE YOUR *MOUTH* WAS.

HANEDA AIRPORT, TOKYO-- ONE OF THE *LARGEST* AIR TERMINALS IN THE WORLD, HANDLING OVER *EIGHT MILLION* PASSENGERS AND *ONE HUNDRED TWENTY MILLION* FLIGHTS A YEAR...

TECHNOTICS PROGRAMMING CORPORATION

NC 375525

...A VAST, *SPRAWLING COMPLEX* OF PASSENGER AND *FREIGHT* OPERATIONS --BOTH COMMERCIAL AND (VERY) *PRIVATE*--

--THE KIND OF PLACE WHERE IT'D BE VERY *EASY* TO HIDE A *BODY*...

...OR *TWO.*

THERE'S *MAGNUM'S SIGNAL,* CAP'N--

--LET'S GET THIS SHOW ON THE *ROAD.*

MAY THAT ACCURSED *SUPER-HERO* BE DAMNED TO *TEN THOUSAND HELLS*--

--IF NOT FOR *HIM,* THE SHERIDAN WOMAN WOULD BE *DEAD* BY NOW, AND MY MISSION *ACCOMPLISHED.*

I MUST CONTACT THE *COUNCIL*--REQUEST FURTHER *INSTRUCTIONS.*

WHAT ARE YOU *DOING,* SAKURA? DO YOU WANT TO GET *LEFT BEHIND?*

SORRY, MAGNUM... I WAS JUST CHECKING SOME *EQUIPMENT!*

DO IT WHEN WE'RE *AIR-BORNE*--THE *GROUND CREW* WILL HANDLE WHAT WE'VE *LEFT BEHIND.*

NOW, *GET ABOARD!*

IN THE MOVIES, THIS IS USUALLY THE TIME THE HERO MAKES HIS *MOVE, BUSTING* UP THE PLANE AS *SCORES* OF POLICE CARS CONVERGE ON THE KIDNAPPERS --THE VILLAINS ARE *BEATEN,* THE HEROINE RESCUED, ALL ENDS WELL.

NO ONE KNOWS CAGE AND SAM ARE ABOARD AND--TRUTH TO TELL-- ALMOST *NO ONE REALLY CARES.*

BUT OUR HERO'S UNCONSCIOUS...

NC 375521

...AND THE KIDNAP PLANE IS OWNED AND OPERATED BY AN *UPSTANDING REPUTABLE FIRM.*

AND BY THE TIME THE *TOKYO POLICE* RUMBLE TO THE FACT THAT A NUMBER OF THEIR MEN HAVE BEEN *BRUTALLY MURDERED*--

--THE *PERPE-TRATORS* WILL HAVE BEEN LONG GONE.

POOR CAGE--HE'D ONLY JUST ARRIVED, TOO...

JAPAN AIRLINES ANNOUNCES THE ARRIVAL OF ITS FLIGHT ONE FROM NEW YORK!

TWELVE HOURS, NON-STOP--AND THAT'S A DRAIN ON ANY MAN--

--EVEN A *SUPER-HERO.*

CUSTOMS

LUCAS, YOU HADDA BEEN *CRAZY* TO SAY YES TO THAT *OLD WOMAN.*

I MEAN, WHAT *BUSINESS* YOU GOT BEING IN *JAPAN?*

YOU DON'T SPEAK THE *LANGUAGE* --YOU DON'T KNOW THE PEOPLE, THE *STREETS*--

YOU'RE A FISH OUTTA WATER JUS' *BEGGIN'* TO BE CAUGHT--*HUH?*

MR. CAGE?!

MR. *LUKE* CAGE?!

I'M CAGE. AN' *YOU* MUST BE *SAMANTHA SHERIDAN.*

RIGHT THE *FIRST TIME,* HANDSOME--

--SO FOLD YOURSELF INTO THIS *BOMB* AND LET'S TRY TO BEAT THE *RUSH HOUR* HOME.

Y'KNOW, MISS SHERIDAN ...

CALL ME *SAM.*

SAM, THEN. I'M *LUKE.* THAT PHOTO YOUR *GRAN'MA* GAVE ME DOESN'T DO YOU *JUSTICE.*

FLATTERY WILL GET YOU *EVERYWHERE,* LUKE--EXCEPT THRU *DOWNTOWN TOKYO.*

YOU REMEMBER THAT *RUSH HOUR* I TOLD YOU ABOUT ?

WELL, *GUESS WHAT!*

MIGHT AS WELL SIT BACK AND *RELAX,* OL' BUDDY-- WITH ANY *LUCK,* WE'LL GET TO MY PLACE IN *LESS TIME* THAN IT TOOK YOU TO FLY HERE FROM THE *STATES.*

I'LL TELL YOU-- WHEN YOUR GRAN'MA *HIRED* ME, I DIDN'T EVEN HAVE A *PASS-PORT*...

...AN' IN *ONE DAY* SHE GOT ME THAT, A FIRST-CLASS TICKET TO TOKYO, A CLEARANCE THROUGH JAPANESE *CUSTOMS*--

AMANDA DOESN'T USE HER *CLOUT* VERY OFTEN--BUT WHEN SHE DOES SHE GETS *RESULTS*.

SHE'S *QUITE* A WOMAN, THAT OLD LADY.

SO ARE *YOU*.

THANK YOU-- TOM FOSTER, MY *FIANCE* WILL LIKE THAT.

HE'S A *GEOPHYSICIST*-- LIKE *ME*-- WORKING AS AN ENVIRONMENTAL CONSULTANT ON THE *ALASKA PIPELINE*.

THAT FIGURES.

YOU KNOW WHAT THIS IS ALL *ABOUT*?

ONLY THAT IT HAS TO DO WITH MY PARENTS' *MURDER*--AND THAT I'M IN *DANGER*!

YEAH, WELL THAT ABOUT *SUMS IT UP*.

OH, SOMETHING AMANDA SAID I WAS TO *TELL YOU*. SHE CAN BE TERRIBLY *RUTHLESS* AT TIMES, NOT ABOVE *BLACKMAIL* TO GET WHAT SHE WANTS.

SHE SAID THAT YOU COULD HAVE BEEN HERS FOR A *WORD*, BUT THAT SHE *RESPECTED* YOU TOO MUCH FOR THAT. AND YOUR...*HM, SECRET* WILL ALWAYS BE *SAFE* WITH HER YOU HAVE HER WORD OF HONOR ON THAT.

WHAT'S THE WORD?

SEAGATE.

OH.

SEAGATE, AS IN *PRISON*. AS IN THE *"LITTLE ALCATRAZ"* THAT *LUKE CAGE* BUSTED *FREE* OF A LONG, LONG TIME AGO'...

MAN, EVEN WHEN YOU'RE INNOCENT, YOU PAY AND YOU PAY AND YOU PAY.

YOU'RE LOOKING VERY *GRIM*, LUKE-- WHAT IS IT?

NOTHING, SAM-- --NOTHIN' AT ALL.

LATER...

NO WAY, SAM-- THERE'S NO WAY ON GOD'S EARTH PEOPLE CAN *EAT* USIN' THESE KING-SIZED *TOOTHPICKS!*

HEY, I'M NOT EATIN' *OCTOPUS* OR ANY- THIN' LIKE *THAT*, AM *I?*

NO.

YOU'RE EATING HIBACHI STEAK AND A *FISH TEMPURA*-- THAT'S A BATTER-FRIED FISH-- ALMOST *SOUL FOOD*...

...AND THE *CHOP STICKS* ARE VERY EASY TO USE. *REALLY.*

FINE! *YOU* USE 'EM!

I'M STICKIN' TO A *KNIFE* AN' *FORK!*

AN' *WHAT* ARE YOU *LAUGHIN'* AT, WOMAN?

WAIT A MINUTE-- LEMME *GUESS*...

I SUPPOSE I AM ACTIN' KINDA *SILLY*. WHAT THE *HECK*, YOU CAN'T WIN 'EM *ALL.*

I'M HEADIN' FOR THE *ROOF* FOR AWHILE-- AFTER HALF-A- DAY SITTIN' ON A PLANE, I GOT *NO USE* FOR SLEEPIN' JUST YET.

DO YOU THINK SOME- THING WILL *HAPPEN* TONIGHT?

COULD BE.

THEN BE CAREFUL. *PLEASE.*

"DON'T SWEAT IT, SISTER-- I'M ALWAYS CAREFUL."

SUCCESSFUL IS SOMETHING ELSE AGAIN. BUT LIKE THE MAN SAID, "YOU CAN'T WIN 'EM ALL."

YEAH-- BUT AN *OCCASIONAL* ONE'D BE NICE...

PLAY IT COOL, BROTHER-- SOMEONE'S *TALKIN'.*

...ALREADY, MAGNUM'S *ABDUCTION* OF HER IS CAUSING THE *COUNCIL* GREAT INCONVENIENCE-- ABOVE ALL, THE *SHERIDAN* WOMAN MUST *NOT* REACH THE DRILL SITE ALIVE.

...ANOTHER *FAILURE* IN THIS REGARD WILL NOT BE *TOLERATED!*

TERMINATE THE WOMAN, SAKURA. DO IT *NOW,* WHATEVER THE *RISK!*

AND SHOULD YOU *FAIL,* YOUR *OWN* WORTHLESS LIFE WILL BE *FORFEIT.*

THE COUNCIL HAS *SPOKEN!*

THE COUNCIL WILL BE *OBEYED,* MY LORD.

CURIOUSER AND CURIOUSER --THIS JOB'S GETTIN' SO YOU CAN'T TELL THE PLAYERS WITHOUT A *PROGRAM.'*

MAGNUM'S *RUNNIN'* THE SHOW AN' HE WANTS SAM *ALIVE*--

--WHILE ONE OF HIS *GOONS* IS WORKIN' FOR SOME *BOZO COUNCIL* THAT WANTS HER *DEAD!*

WHICH MEANS IT'S TIME YOU STARTED *EARNING* YOUR PAY, BLOOD.

"'CAUSE THE GOON IS MAKIN' HIS MOVE."

IT WILL BE A *SIMPLE* MATTER TO *GARROTE* THE WOMAN--

KDOW!

STUFF THEM *OTHERS,* DUDE--

--YOU GOT *ENOUGH* TO WORRY ABOUT *RIGHT NOW!*

THIS IS THE *SECOND* TIME YOU'VE KEPT ME FROM MY *TARGET,* AMERICAN--

--THERE WILL BE *NO THIRD!*

BABY, *TIED UP,* I'M TEN TIMES THE MAN YOU'LL *EVER BE!*

--DEALING WITH *MAGNUM* AND THE *OTHERS* WILL BE *SOMETHING ELSE* AGAIN.

WHAT'S GOING *ON* HERE?!

MAGNUM!

IN A *NUTSHELL*, BIG MAN, YOU GOT A *ROTTEN APPLE* IN YOUR BARREL!

LIAR!

I SEE...

BTHOK!

THIS CLOWN WAS TRYIN' TO *KILL* SAMANTHA!

I'VE HAD MY *DOUBTS* ABOUT YOU FOR QUITE A WHILE, SAKURA--

--NOW SEEMS AS *GOOD* A TIME AS ANY TO *DEAL* WITH YOU!

MAGNUM, *PLEASE!* I AM *LOYAL!!*

I'M AFRAID IT'S *TOO LATE* FOR SECOND THOUGHTS.

MY *ONLY* REGRET IS THAT I MUST THROW THE *GOOD* OUT WITH THE *BAD.* MY *APOLOGIES,* POWER MAN!

LUKE-- OH MY *GOD!!*

LUKE!

HE'S OPENING THE *DOORS!*

AAAAAAAAAA

AAA

CHRISTMAS--!!

NO *TWO WAYS* ABOUT IT, CAGE--

--THIS TIME YOU'VE *HAD IT!*

CHAPTER 2

A *PITY* IT HAS TO END LIKE THIS--A ONE-MILE FALL TO *OBLIVION*--

--BUT AS YOU *AMERICANS* SAY, THOSE ARE THE *BREAKS.*

HAPPY LANDINGS, POWER MAN!

IT'LL BE *OVER* BEFORE YOU *KNOW IT!*

YOU *MURDER* TWO MEN IN *COLD BLOOD...*

...AND YOU CAN STAND THERE MAKING *JOKES* ABOUT IT?

WHAT KIND OF *MONSTER* ARE YOU?

SO, OUR *EARTHQUAKE SPECIALIST* REVEALS UNEXPECTED *COURAGE...*

...AND *CLAWS* TO MATCH, TOO, I'LL WAGER.

BUT THEY'LL DO YOU *NO GOOD* HERE, LITTLE ONE.

I HAVE *POWER* ENOUGH TO SLAY AN *ARMY!*

HANDLING *ONE* LONE WOMAN IS NO PROBLEM AT ALL.

HOWEVER, I'D ADVISE YOU NOT TO *PUSH YOUR LUCK!*

OH!

BECAUSE I'M A MONSTER WITH A VERY *SHORT TEMPER,* MISS SHERIDAN...

...AND WHEN I *LOSE* IT, THINGS CAN GET MOST *...UNPLEASANT.*

YOU'VE KILLED MY *FAMILY*, MY FRIENDS--THERE'S *NOTHING* YOU COULD DO TO *HURT* ME, MAGNUM.

IF I HAD THE *STRENGTH* I'D *KILL* YOU!

THAT'S BEEN *TRIED BEFORE...*

...BY THOSE *FAR DEADLIER* THAN *POWER MAN*

THE *PUNISHER*--!

"QUITE *CORRECT*, MY DEAR--GO TO THE *HEAD* OF THE CLASS. HE AND *SPIDER-MAN* BOTH WERE RESPONSIBLE FOR THE *DESTRUCTION* OF MY *NERVE GAS PROJECT*.

"I WAS HOLDING MY OWN AGAINST THE WALL CRAWLER--

"--IN FACT, I ALMOST HAD HIM *BEATEN*--

"--WHEN THE ACCURSED *PUNISHER* STEPPED IN.

PUNISHER! NO!

THAT *TANK'S FULL* OF NERVE GAS!

"THE TANK EXPLODED IN MY HANDS, FLOODING THE LABORATORY IN *SECONDS*...

MOVE IT, MAN!

WE'VE GOT TO GET OUT!

"I WAS CUT OFF FROM THE *DOOR* BY THE GAS....

DANGER DANGER

"...AND *SEALED INSIDE* A MOMENT LATER.

"THEY THOUGHT ME DOOMED BY MY OWN CREATION--TO A *HORRIBLE DEATH*--

"--*NEVER* REALIZING THAT MOSES MAGNUM PLANS FOR *EVERY EVENTUALITY!* I WAS WEARING A SELF-CONTAINED *ANTI-GAS BODY SUIT* UNDER MY CLOTHES.

"AND SO, I SURVIVED. AND ESCAPED, SWEARING *VENGEANCE* ON THOSE WHO HAD TRIED TO *DESTROY* ME.

"BUT FIRST, I HAD TO *RECOUP* MY SOMEWHAT *SUBSTANTIAL* LOSSES...

...WHICH IS WHERE YOU COME IN, MY DEAR-- BUT THE *DETAILS* NEED NOT *CONCERN* YOU.

TAKE HER AWAY-- AND *PREPARE* FOR *LANDING*.

UNFORTUNATELY -- THANKS TO THE *LAWS OF GRAVITY* -- THE *HERO* OF THIS BOOK WILL BE LANDING *FIRST.*

AND TAKE *OUR WORD* FOR IT, THAT THOUGHT WEIGHS *HEAVILY* ON HIS MIND.

IN SHORT, POWER MAN'S... *WORRIED!*

OKAY, BIG SHOT, HOW'RE YOU GONNA BEAT *THIS* RAP?

YOU AIN'T *IRON MAN* -- SO YOU CAN'T *FLY* -- AN' YOU SURE AIN'T *SPIDER-MAN,* SO YOU CAN'T WHIP UP SOME FANCY *WEB-KITE* OR PARACHUTE OR SOMETHIN'.

ALL YOU GOT IS *THREE HUNDRED POUNDS* O'FALLIN' BODY!

BUT IF MY *NUMBER'S UP,* I MIGHT AS WELL GO OUT *FIGHTIN'.*

FIRST OFF, I *SLOW* MY FALL AS MUCH AS POSSIBLE BY *SKY DIVIN'* -- REMEMBERIN' ALL THE BULL *D.W.'S* FRIEND, *EDELMAN,* TOLD ME ABOUT THIS LOUSY *SPORT.*

TROUBLE IS, HE HAD A 'CHUTE!

HOLD ON A MINUTE, CAGE -- WILL YOU LOOK AT *THAT!*

THAT SLOPE -- IT'S *SNOW* ON TOP O'*ICE!*

STEEP ENOUGH SO I DON'T GO *SPLAT* RIGHT OFF!

LONG ENOUGH TO MAYBE *SLOW* ME DOWN.

AN' WITH MY *STEEL HARD BODY,* THAT MIGHT BE *ALL I NEED* TO COME OUTTA THIS MESS *ALIVE.*

WHO'RE YOU *JIVIN'* LUCAS? YOU HAVEN'T GOT A *PRAYER.*

BUT ON THE OTHER HAND, THIS LOOKS LIKE THE *ONLY GAME IN TOWN.* SO --

--*GERONIMO!*

IMPACT!

Not bad, really--it's a lot like getting totalled by a forty-foot semi moving at top speed--

--except maybe worse.

The world goes crazy, spinning, bouncing, jarring, thudding--

--arms and legs slap/flapping all over the place, trying their level best to shatter themselves to bloody flinders.

Cage tries to scream, but he can't! There's no air in his lungs!

And every time he tries to breathe a new, even more-vicious tumble slams the air out of him!

It's pretty funny, when you think about it, surviving the fall and dying of suffocation.

No thoughts, now--nothing at all that isn't scrambled hell-bent towards oblivion.

He's in snow, flashing a rooster tail fifty feet high and triggering tiny avalanches all across the face of the glacier-- he's beginning to slow down, too...

...too little. And too late.

He's barely conscious when he goes off the edge...

AND, YET, SOMETHING INSIDE HIM JUST WON'T QUIT--

--HAZY, INSTINCT-BORN COMMANDS STRAIGHTENING HIS BODY--

--TURNING A PROBABLY FATAL BELLY FLOP--

--INTO A PASSABLE DIVE.

AFTER ALL, IF YOU'VE GOTTA GO, IT MIGHT AS WELL BE WITH STYLE...

...AND LUKE CAGE MAY HAVE GONE FOR GOOD.

ONE MINUTE. THE DIVE IS DEEP, MAYBE TOO DEEP.

TWO MINUTES. THE RIPPLES BEGIN TO FADE AWAY, THE LAKE SMOOTHING ITSELF OUT.

AND THEN...

AIR!!

MAN-OH-MAN, DOES THAT TASTE GOOD! I COULDN'T HAVE LASTED MUCH LONGER!

BUT YOU AIN'T ...DONE YET, LUCAS.

YOU STILL GOTTA GET TO SHORE.

THIS ICE COLD WATER MAY HAVE SHOCKED YOU AWAKE WHEN YOU HIT...

...BUT NOW IT'S WORKIN' AGAINST YOU, SUCKIN' THE STRENGTH OUTTA YOU LIKE A LEECH!

HECK, I MADE IT THIS FAR. I AIN'T GIVIN' UP -- NO MATTER HOW MUCH I HURT.

I'M POWER MAN...

...'AN I DON'T GIVE UP TO...NO ONE!

...NO... ONE...

THE SUN RISES TWO HOURS LATER, BUT CAGE ISN'T *CONSCIOUS* TO SEE IT.

AND THE DAY MOVES ON AND THE SUN SETS.

BUT AS FAR AS THE PEOPLE WORKING ON MAGNUM'S *PROJECT* ARE CONCERNED, IT COULD JUST AS EASILY BE NOON TOPSIDE AS MIDNIGHT...

THIS IS A TWENTY-FOUR HOUR OPERATION. WHEN ONE SHIFT *SACKS OUT*, ANOTHER STARTS WORK--AS HARD A LIFE FOR THE JAILERS--

--AS IT IS FOR THE JAILED.

AND YET, DESPITE ALL THAT'S *HAPPENED*, SAMANTHA SHERIDAN HASN'T GIVEN UP HOPE.

NOR HAS SHE GIVEN UP LOOKING FOR A WAY OUT.

CREEEK

HUH--?!

SOMEONE'S AT THE *DOOR*!

CAN'T TELL FOR *SURE*... ...BUT IT LOOKS LIKE ONE OF MAGNUM'S *GOONS.*

HE'S *ALONE*-- AND HE LEFT THE DOOR *OPEN*!

THIS IS YOUR *CHANCE*, WOMAN!

MOVE IT!

SHE TAKES THE MAN BY *SURPRISE*, STIFF-ARMING HIM INTO THE WALL AS SHE *LUNGES* FOR HER FREEDOM.

SHE ALMOST MAKES IT...

HEY, FOX. WHERE YOU *GOIN'*?!

LEMME GO! LET-ME-

YOU!

WHO WERE YOU *EXPECTIN'*? JOHN SHAFT?

CAGE? IS IT *REALLY* YOU?

CAGE?!

YOU'RE ALIVE!!

YEAH, MAN!

AFTER A *GREETING* LIKE THIS, LADY--

--YOU *BETTER BELIEVE* IT!

BUT HOW--? I SAW YOU FALL FROM THE AIRPLANE--WITHOUT A PARACHUTE! HOW COULD YOU HAVE SURVIVED?

I'M A SUPER-HERO, AIN'T I?

HUSH NOW, SAM--I'LL GIVE YOU THE GORY DETAILS LATER.

MEANTIME, I GOT WORK TO DO.

WHAT DO YOU MEAN?

I MEAN, WE'RE NOT OUTTA THE WOODS YET.

LIE ON THE COT, HON, AN' MAKE LIKE YOU'RE ASLEEP. COMPANY'S COMIN'!

ALL DAY I'VE WAITED FOR AN OPPORTUNITY TO GET AT THE WOMAN.

IT'S NOW OR NEVER!

THE COUNCIL WILL REWARD ME GREATLY FOR THIS SANCTION IF I SUCCEED ...

...AND WILL PAY ME WITH DEATH IF I FAIL.

BUT HOW CAN I FAIL? THIS IS LIKE SHOOTING FISH IN A BARREL ...

HATE TO TELL YOU, FLASH...

...BUT THEM FISH JUST UP AN' BIT YOU ON THE GOOD OL' BUTT.

WHA--! WHO--?!

NAME'S POWER MAN, CRUD!

SWEET DREAMS.

BTHAM!

MAN, WHATEVER THIS COUNCIL IS, THEY SURE ARE PERSISTENT.

BUT AT LEAST THIS CLOWN WON'T BOTHER US ANY MORE.

LET'S SPLIT, SAM!

CAGE, WE CAN'T LEAVE!

WHAT'RE YOU *TALKIN'* ABOUT, LADY-- I GOT A *BOAT* WAITIN' AN' EVERY- THIN'. WITH ANY *LUCK* WE'LL BE OFF THIS ROCK IN *NO TIME.*

MARVELOUS, BUT WE *STILL* CAN'T LEAVE.

NOT YET, ANYWAY.

OKAY, SAM, I'M *LIST'NIN'* -- BUT IT BETTER BE *GOOD.*

HOW DOES THE *END* OF THE WORLD STRIKE YOU?

I CAN TAKE IT OR LEAVE IT.

WHAT KIND'A *QUESTION* IS THAT, ANYWAY?

NEVER MIND-- I FIGURE YOU'LL *TELL* ME SOONER OR LATER.

COAST IS *CLEAR,* SO LET'S GET *GOIN'.*

I'M NOT *JOKING,* LUKE. MAGNUM IS PLAYING WITH FORCES THAT COULD *DESTROY* US ALL!

HE'S *MINING,* TRYING TO *TAP* THE MINERAL AND ENERGY POTENTIAL OF THE EARTH'S *MAGMA* -- ITS MOLTEN *CORE.*

YOU SEE, THIS ISLAND, *KATSYU SHIMA,* IS LOCATED OVER AN EXTREMELY *THIN* LAYER OF THE EARTH'S *CRUST.*

THAT FACT, COMBINED WITH THE ISLAND LYING *OUTSIDE* ANY NATION'S *JUR- ISDICTION,* MAKE MINING HERE WELL WORTH THE *VAST EXPENSE...*

...*BUT NOT THE RISK!*

ABOUT TWO MONTHS AGO, I DISCOVERED A *HAIR LINE FAULT* RUNNING ABOUT A MILE OFF THIS ISLAND--

--ONE THAT *CONNECTS* THE ALASKAN AND JAPANESE FAULT SYSTEMS, WHICH, IN TURN, MAKE UP *MAJOR* ELEMENTS OF THE *PACIFIC RIM.*

WHEN MAGNUM'S *LASER DRILL* BLASTS THRU TO THE EARTH'S CORE, THERE'S GOING TO BE A *HUGE PRESSURE EXPLOSION,* ONE THAT WILL TEAR THE KATSYU FAULT *WIDE OPEN.*

AND THAT WILL *TOPPLE* THE ENTIRE PACIFIC RIM LIKE A LINE OF *DOMINOS,* TRIGGERING *EARTHQUAKES* ALONG THE JAPANESE FAULT THE ALASKAN *SAN ANDREAS--!*

IT'LL BE *DISASTER* ON AN *APOCALYPTIC SCALE!*

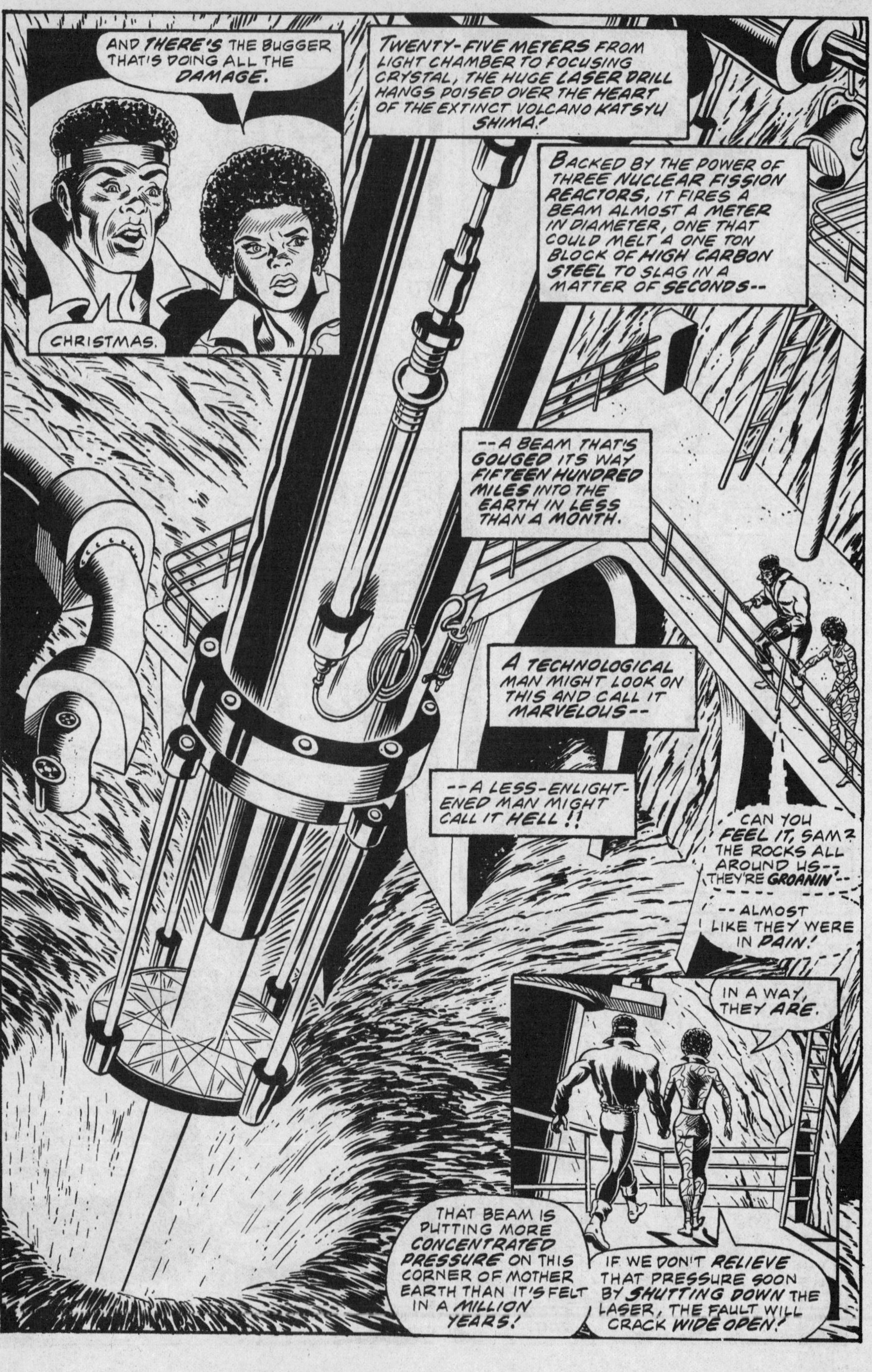
AND THERE'S THE BUGGER THAT'S DOING ALL THE DAMAGE.
CHRISTMAS.
TWENTY-FIVE METERS FROM LIGHT CHAMBER TO FOCUSING CRYSTAL, THE HUGE LASER DRILL HANGS POISED OVER THE HEART OF THE EXTINCT VOLCANO KATSYU SHIMA!
BACKED BY THE POWER OF THREE NUCLEAR FISSION REACTORS, IT FIRES A BEAM ALMOST A METER IN DIAMETER, ONE THAT COULD MELT A ONE TON BLOCK OF HIGH CARBON STEEL TO SLAG IN A MATTER OF SECONDS--
--A BEAM THAT'S GOUGED ITS WAY FIFTEEN HUNDRED MILES INTO THE EARTH IN LESS THAN A MONTH.
A TECHNOLOGICAL MAN MIGHT LOOK ON THIS AND CALL IT MARVELOUS--
--A LESS-ENLIGHTENED MAN MIGHT CALL IT HELL!!
CAN YOU FEEL IT, SAM? THE ROCKS ALL AROUND US-- THEY'RE GROANIN'--
--ALMOST LIKE THEY WERE IN PAIN!
IN A WAY, THEY ARE.
THAT BEAM IS PUTTING MORE CONCENTRATED PRESSURE ON THIS CORNER OF MOTHER EARTH THAN IT'S FELT IN A MILLION YEARS!
IF WE DON'T RELIEVE THAT PRESSURE SOON BY SHUTTING DOWN THE LASER, THE FAULT WILL CRACK WIDE OPEN!

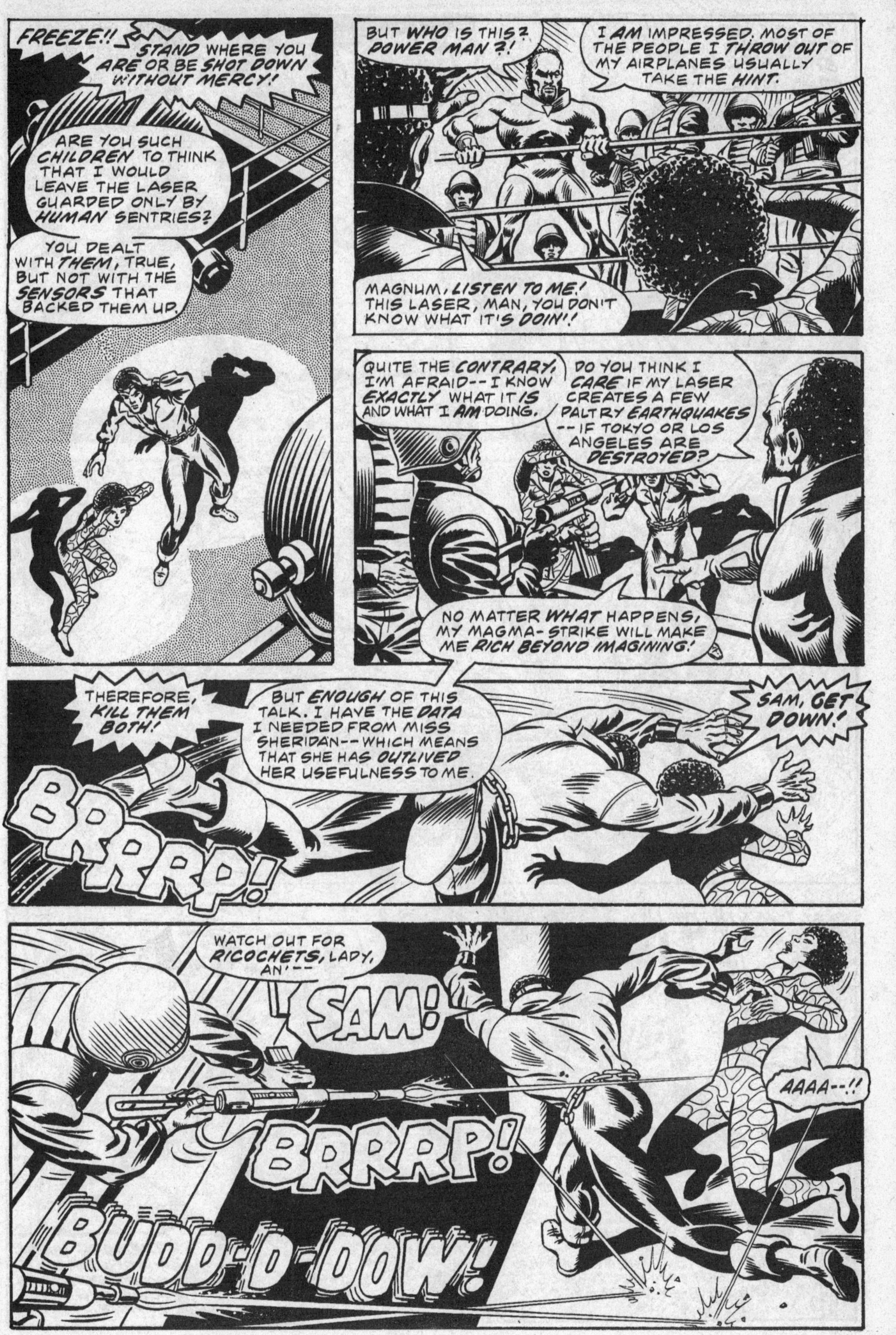

FREEZE!!
STAND WHERE YOU ARE OR BE SHOT DOWN WITHOUT MERCY!
ARE YOU SUCH CHILDREN TO THINK THAT I WOULD LEAVE THE LASER GUARDED ONLY BY HUMAN SENTRIES?
YOU DEALT WITH THEM, TRUE, BUT NOT WITH THE SENSORS THAT BACKED THEM UP.
BUT WHO IS THIS? POWER MAN?!
I AM IMPRESSED. MOST OF THE PEOPLE I THROW OUT OF MY AIRPLANES USUALLY TAKE THE HINT.
MAGNUM, LISTEN TO ME! THIS LASER, MAN, YOU DON'T KNOW WHAT IT'S DOIN'!
QUITE THE CONTRARY, I'M AFRAID-- I KNOW EXACTLY WHAT IT IS AND WHAT I AM DOING.
DO YOU THINK I CARE IF MY LASER CREATES A FEW PALTRY EARTHQUAKES -- IF TOKYO OR LOS ANGELES ARE DESTROYED?
NO MATTER WHAT HAPPENS, MY MAGMA-STRIKE WILL MAKE ME RICH BEYOND IMAGINING!
BUT ENOUGH OF THIS TALK. I HAVE THE DATA I NEEDED FROM MISS SHERIDAN-- WHICH MEANS THAT SHE HAS OUTLIVED HER USEFULNESS TO ME.
THEREFORE, KILL THEM BOTH!
SAM, GET DOWN!
BRRRP!
WATCH OUT FOR RICOCHETS, LADY, AN'--
SAM!
AAAA--!!
BRRRP!
BUDD-D-DOW!

YOU MOTHERIN' SCUM! YOU SHOT HER!!

CHUMP, THE BIGGEST *MISTAKE* YOU EVER MADE WAS BRINGIN' THE FIGHT DOWN TO MY *LEVEL!*

AIN'T YOU *HEARD?* POWER MAN IS THE DUDE WITH THE *STEEL HARD SKIN--*

AND WE WILL SHOOT *YOU* DOWN AS WELL, DOG OF AN *AMERICAN!*

BRRRP!

--AN' HE'S GOT STEEL HARD FISTS TO MATCH!

THWAM!

HOW'S IT *FEEL,* KILLERS, BEIN' ON THE *RECEIVIN' END* FOR A CHANGE?

OKAY, THAT'S *THREE* GOONS ACCOUNTED FOR---

---BUT THOSE *OTHERS* UP ON THE BALCONY ARE STILL *SCATTERIN'* LEAD!

THEY AIN'T HURTIN' *ME* NONE. BUT THERE'S NO WAY I CAN GET SAM OUTTA HERE SO LONG AS THEY KEEP SHOOTIN' AT US!

SKRA-A-AK!

SO I GUESS I'LL HAVE TO MAKE 'EM *STOP!*

SONUVA-GUN--*I* DID IT!

TREMOR--MINOR, UNNOTICED, LIKE A CAT ABSENTLY RIPPLING ITS FUR...

ATTACK HIM!

IF *ALL* OF US HIT HIM *AT ONCE*, WE CAN FORCE HIM INTO THE *DRILL PIT!*

HEY, COME ON, GUYS--

--WHO'RE YOU *KIDDIN'?*

BOY, ARE *YOU* ALL IN FOR A *SURPRISE!*

THE *THREE* OF YOU ARE GONNA *SHOVE ME* INTO THAT *PIT?*

IT WEIGHS A *HUNDRED KILOS*-- AND HE *THROWS* IT AS IF IT WEIGHS *NOTHING!*

SEE WHAT I *MEAN?*

WHUUUFF!

BTHOD!

YOU DO *VERY WELL* AGAINST MY MEN, CAGE.

LET'S SEE HOW YOU *FARE* AGAINST THEIR MASTER--*MAGNUM FORCE!*

BRK

FINE WITH *ME*, BLOOD--

--BUT WHAT'S THE *DIFFER-ENCE?*

A *SECOND* TREMOR--STILL *UNNOTICED*, BUT STRONG ENOUGH TO THROW CAGE'S PUNCH OFF A *FRACTION...*

CRETIN! *ONE PUNCH* DOES NOT *WIN* THE FIGHT...

...AND MAGNUM FORCE HAS *NEVER* BEEN DEFEATED!

WHOM!

THERE'S ALWAYS A *FIRST TIME,* FLASH.

LOOK ON THE *BRIGHT SIDE*--

BRAK!

--AT LEAST *I'M* WILLING TO BRING YOU BACK *ALIVE.*

THOSE ARE *WAY BETTER* ODDS THAN THE *PUNISHER* WILL GIVE YOU.

TRUE ENOUGH. THE PUNISHER KNOWS ME FOR WHAT I *AM*--

--A MAN WHO *CLAWED* HIS WAY TO THE *TOP* OF THE DIRTIEST PROFESSION IN THE WORLD, A *RUTHLESS* MAN--

--A MAN WHO *ALWAYS HAS* AN *ACE* UP HIS SLEEVE.

VZZZT

SLAM!

CASE IN POINT: MY *FINGER-MOUNTED FORCE BLASTERS!* FIRING A BEAM THAT CAN STOP A *CHARGING RHINO* DEAD IN ITS *TRACKS!*

THREE TREMORS, IN TWICE AS MANY MINUTES, THIS ONE STIRRING SAMANTHA SHERIDAN AWAKE, HER HEAD *THROBBING* WHERE THE BULLET *CREASED* HER, HER EYES WIDENING IN HORROR AS SHE *RECOGNIZES* THE TREMORS FOR WHAT THEY *ARE...*

YOU ARE INDEED A *REMARKABLE* MAN, MY FRIEND ... AND A *HEAVY* ONE TO BOOT.

MY *BLASTERS* WERE SET TO *KILL*--

--YET THEY ONLY *STUNNED!*

NO MATTER. WHERE MY *BLASTERS* FAILED...

...THE *LASER PIT* WILL *SUCCEED.*

IT'S A *TWELVE HUNDRED MILE* DROP, POWER MAN-- TO THE VERY *CENTER OF THE EARTH!*

ENJOY YOUR *TRIP!*

WHA--WHA'S *HAPP'NIN'?*-- MIND ALL FOGGED-- *CRIPES!* I'M GOIN' INTO THE *PIT!*

GRAB FOR THE *FLOORING,* CAGE, IT'S YOUR *ONLY* HOPE.

MADE IT!

NEVER SAY DIE, EH, POWER-MAN?

I *ADMIRE* THAT IN A MAN.... ...AND I'LL *SALUTE* YOUR MEMORY AS I *WATCH* YOU *FALL.*

IF *ANYONE'S* DOIN' ANY *FALLIN'* AROUND HERE, BLOOD-- --IT'S *YOU!*

MY FOOT! WHAT ARE YOU *DO*--?!

JUST THROWIN' YOU *BACK* SOME-- --AN GIVIN' ME *TIME* TO GET BACK ON THIS *BALCONY.*

'CAUSE I AIN'T *DONE* WITH YOU, MAGNUM. NOT BY A *LONG SHOT.*

VERY WELL, FOOL-- I'LL *BURN YOU DOWN* IN *SILENCE!*

UH-UH, BIG MAN!

YOU CAUGHT ME ONCE AN' *BLEW IT!*

AN' IN *THIS* LINE O' WORK--

--ONE CHANCE IS ALL YOU GET!

MAKE IT *GOOD*, CAGE, 'CAUSE THIS IS *YOURS*, MESS IT UP AN' MAGNUM'LL HAVE YOU PLAYIN' *HARPS* IN NO TIME AT ALL.

READY OR NOT, MAGNUM--

--POWER MAN'S COMIN' AT' CHA!!

NO!!

YOU GOT A LOT O' LIVES TO *PAY FOR*, BUTCHER!

--A LOT OF *GOOD* PEOPLE CRYIN' OUT FOR *VENGEANCE!*

BHAM

BUT LET'S DO THIS *RIGHT*--

--NO MORE FUNNY *ZAP* BEAMS--

DRAK

--NO MORE GAS!

NOTHING BUT *TWO GUYS* SETTLIN' THINGS LIKE MEN *SHOULD*--

--WITH THEIR *FISTS!!*

NEVER!

ONCE I GET TO A WEAPON--

OKAY, MAGNUM, HAVE IT *YOUR* WAY!

KD AM!

I CAN HANDLE YOU *ON MY OWN*, OR HAND YOU OVER TO THE *INTERNATIONAL COURT*--

--IT'S ALL THE *SAME* TO ME!

THE FLOOR JUMPS TO MEET MAGNUM'S CHIN! SAM ALONE NOTICES THIS LATEST TREMOR--AND SHE SCRAMBLES TOWARDS CAGE, PRAYING SHE'S WRONG AND KNOWING SHE ISN'T...

NO, CAGE! I'LL *NOT* LET MYSELF BE *TAKEN!*

IS THE MAN A *CONSUMMATE FOOL,* THINKING ME *BEATEN* SIMPLY BECAUSE I'VE TAKEN A FEW *PUNCHES?*

CAGE--!"

SAM, WHAT'RE *YOU* DOIN' OUT HERE--GET BACK *UNDER COVER!*

TOO LATE, POWER MAN!

YOU *FORGOT* ABOUT ME FOR AN *INSTANT,* AND THAT MOMENTARY *CARELESSNESS* WILL COST YOU AND THE WOMAN YOUR *LIVES!*

NOT EVEN YOUR *STEEL SKIN* CAN SAVE YOU FROM THIS *HAND LASER!*

IT'S THEN THAT CAGE REALIZES HOW QUIET IT'S BECOME. THE EARTH, GROANING AND SCREAMING IT'S *AGONY* THROUGHOUT THE FIGHT, SUDDENLY GOES *SILENT,* THE AIR HOT AND OPPRESSIVELY STILL --

--VERY MUCH LIKE THE *CALM BEFORE THE STORM.*

AND THEN, THE *STORM BREAKS!*

HEY--THIS *BALCONY* --THE WHOLE *CAVE!* EVERY THING'S *SHAKIN'!*

DEAR GOD IN HEAVEN, I THOUGHT WE HAD *MORE TIME--*

WHAT *IS* IT, SAM? WHAT'S *HAPPENING?*

WHAT THE *PRE-SHOCKS* TOLD ME WAS *ABOUT* TO HAPPEN, LUKE--WHAT I WAS MOST *AFRAID* OF--

EARTHQUAKE!

FIRST SHOCK: JARRING, RIPPING--STEAM PIPES RUPTURING AS MOVING ROCK *TEARS* THEM APART, THE BALCONY JUMPING LIKE SOMETHING *COME ALIVE...*

LOOKS LIKE YOU *CALLED IT,* LADY--

--AN' IF *THIS* AIN'T OUR CUE TO *LEAVE--*

--I *DON'T KNOW WHAT IS!*

THEY DON'T LOOK BACK AS THEY RUN. IT WOULDN'T HAVE MATTERED IF THEY HAD; THERE WAS NOTHING THEY COULD HAVE DONE...

SECOND SHOCK: RICHTER SIX, MASSIVE DESTRUCTION, THE DRILL CAVE SHAKING LIKE SOME GIANT WAS SLAPPING ITS WALLS AS HARD AS HE COULD...

MAGNUM TRIES FOR THE EXIT TUNNEL, BUT HIS FEET CAN'T GET PURCHASE ON THIS BALCONY-GONE-MAD.

...AND THEN, THE BOLTS FUSING THE GANTRY ASSEMBLY TO THE CAVE WALLS RIP FREE--THE WALLS THEMSELVES, SHATTERING, CRUMBLING-- ALL THE WORKS OF MAN FALLING BENEATH THOSE OF NATURE.

THE DRILL GOES, THE GANTRY GOES, THE BALCONY GOES, THEN MAGNUM GOES.

HE SCREAMS -- BUT HE'S DROWNED OUT BY THE ROAR OF THE QUAKE AND BESIDES, THERE'S NO ONE TO HEAR HIM.

ON THE UPPER LEVELS, PANIC RULES, MAGNUM'S MERCENARIES KILLING EACH OTHER IN THEIR FRENZY TO ESCAPE.

AND THOSE THE MEN LEAVE ALIVE, THE QUAKE KILLS...

...SAVE TWO.

HOW THEY GET OUT, THEY'LL NEVER KNOW. BUT THEY GET OUT JUST THE SAME. BATTERED, BRUISED, TORN AND BLEEDING, HURTING -- BUT ALIVE.

THIRD SHOCK: RICHTER SEVEN AND THE QUAKE'S NOT DONE YET, GREAT FISSURES OPENING KATSYU SHIMA TO THE SEA, WATER PLUNGING DOWN COUNTLESS MILES TO HIT THE UPRUSHING MAGMA AND EXPLODE INTO STEAM...

THERE'S MY BOAT!

MOVE IT, WOMAN! THE SOONER WE'RE OFF THIS ROCK, THE BETTER!

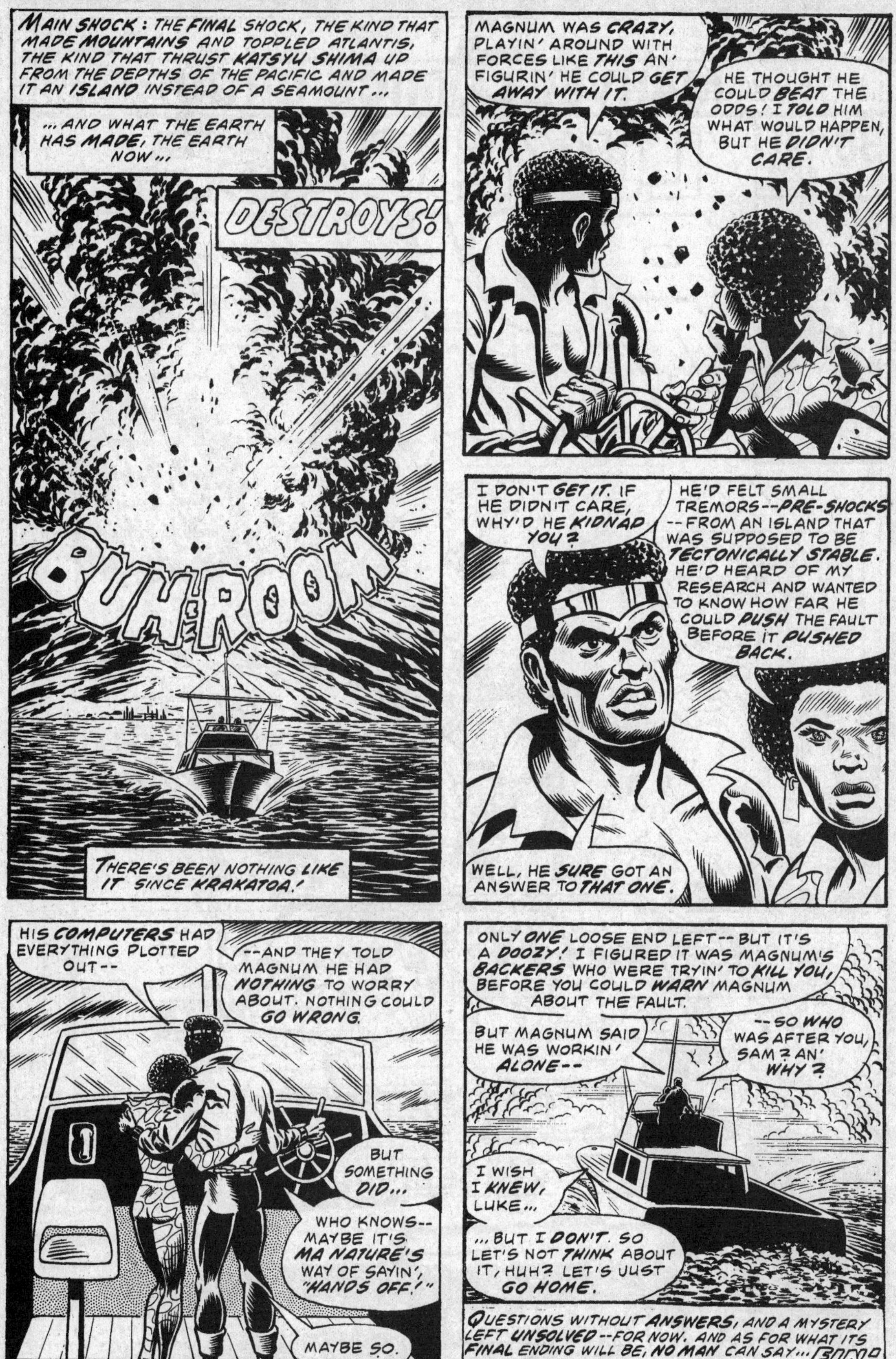
MAIN SHOCK: THE FINAL SHOCK, THE KIND THAT MADE MOUNTAINS AND TOPPLED ATLANTIS, THE KIND THAT THRUST KATSYU SHIMA UP FROM THE DEPTHS OF THE PACIFIC AND MADE IT AN ISLAND INSTEAD OF A SEAMOUNT...
...AND WHAT THE EARTH HAS MADE, THE EARTH NOW...
DESTROYS!
BUH-ROOM
THERE'S BEEN NOTHING LIKE IT SINCE KRAKATOA!
MAGNUM WAS CRAZY, PLAYIN' AROUND WITH FORCES LIKE THIS AN' FIGURIN' HE COULD GET AWAY WITH IT.
HE THOUGHT HE COULD BEAT THE ODDS! I TOLD HIM WHAT WOULD HAPPEN, BUT HE DIDN'T CARE.
I DON'T GET IT. IF HE DIDN'T CARE, WHY'D HE KIDNAP YOU?
HE'D FELT SMALL TREMORS--PRE-SHOCKS--FROM AN ISLAND THAT WAS SUPPOSED TO BE TECTONICALLY STABLE. HE'D HEARD OF MY RESEARCH AND WANTED TO KNOW HOW FAR HE COULD PUSH THE FAULT BEFORE IT PUSHED BACK.
WELL, HE SURE GOT AN ANSWER TO THAT ONE.
HIS COMPUTERS HAD EVERYTHING PLOTTED OUT--
--AND THEY TOLD MAGNUM HE HAD NOTHING TO WORRY ABOUT. NOTHING COULD GO WRONG.
BUT SOMETHING DID...
WHO KNOWS--MAYBE IT'S MA NATURE'S WAY OF SAYIN', "HANDS OFF!"
MAYBE SO.
ONLY ONE LOOSE END LEFT--BUT IT'S A DOOZY! I FIGURED IT WAS MAGNUM'S BACKERS WHO WERE TRYIN' TO KILL YOU, BEFORE YOU COULD WARN MAGNUM ABOUT THE FAULT.
BUT MAGNUM SAID HE WAS WORKIN' ALONE--
--SO WHO WAS AFTER YOU, SAM? AN' WHY?
I WISH I KNEW, LUKE...
...BUT I DON'T. SO LET'S NOT THINK ABOUT IT, HUH? LET'S JUST GO HOME.
QUESTIONS WITHOUT ANSWERS, AND A MYSTERY LEFT UNSOLVED--FOR NOW. AND AS FOR WHAT ITS FINAL ENDING WILL BE, NO MAN CAN SAY...
FIN!

POWER-MAN

MARVEL COMICS GROUP ™

APPROVED BY THE COMICS CODE AUTHORITY

30¢ 37 NOV 02149

LUKE CAGE, POWER MAN ™

ALL-NEW PULSE-POUNDING ACTION!

CAGE ENRAGED LIKE YOU'VE NEVER SEEN HIM!

LUKE CAGE: Wrongly convicted and sentenced to prison—reborn in a freak experiment there that gave him *steel-hard skin* and *strength beyond belief*—a man who hides his identity as an escaped convict in the role of a *HERO FOR HIRE!*

STAN LEE PRESENTS: LUKE CAGE, POWER MAN!

NEW YORK AND 42ND STREET! A NICE PLACE TO WALK THROUGH... VERY QUICKLY!

AIN'T HAD MUCH *TIME* TOGETHER, CLAIRE...

...GLAD WE COULD GRAB SOME *NOW.*

SOME- THIN' HAPPENED THESE PAST MONTHS...

HIYA, LUKE, MISS TEMPLE.

OH, HELLO, BERTHA.

...WE SORTA DRIFTED 'PART THERE FOR AWHILE--

CHEMISTRO IS BACK! DEADLIER THAN EVER!

LUKE!

SWEET SISTER! WHA--??

MY OFFICE-- IT'S ALL TURNED TO GLASS!

KRASH!

MARV WOLFMAN
WRITER / EDITOR

RON WILSON & A. BRADFORD
ARTISTS

MICHELE WOLFMAN
COLORIST

KAREN MANTLO
LETTERER

HOLY **CHRISTMAS!** CRASHED RIGHT THROUGH TO THE **PROJECTION ROOM!**

WHAT IN SWEET **BLAZES** IS HAPPENING?

HUH?

YOU'RE **SMASHIN'** MY BEAUTIFUL ROOM TO **PIECES**, THAT'S WHAT'S HAPPENING, MR. **LUKE CAGE, HERO-MAN!**

WHY DON'T YOU STAY **UPSTAIRS** WHERE YOU **BELONG?**

WHY, YOU **CRUMMY...**

DON'T START WITH THE WISE **REMARKS**, MISTER, 'CAUSE I GOT YOU **DEAD TO RIGHTS!** YOU **INVADED** MY PRIVATE ROOM HERE.

I **TOLD** MAX HE SHOULDN'T LET **YOU** RENT THAT ROOM UPSTAIRS!

NOW **LOOK** WHAT YOU'VE DONE TO THE PROJECTOR!

SNIFKINS, I OUGHTTA--

--I SAID **LOOK** AT WHAT YOU'VE **DONE.**

NOW, YOU TELL ME JUST HOW I'M SUPPOSED TO SHOW A MOVIE LIKE **THAT!**

I OUGHTTA CALL THE **UNION** ON YOU, CAGE. THEY **KNOW** HOW TO DEAL WITH **TROUBLE-MAKERS!**

SNIFKINS, I -- AW, **FORGET IT!**

OOPS, SOMETHING TELLS THIS LITTLE **MOVIE BUFF** THERE'S **TROUBLE** UPSTAIRS!

BETTER **CHECK** IT OUT. UNCLE MAX PUT **ME** IN CHARGE OF THIS THEATER WHILE **HE'S** ON VACATION, AND I **DON'T** WANT TO LET HIM DOWN.

BLAST! I'VE BEEN WAITING TO SEE "LAST OF THE FAST GUNS" FOR **MONTHS** NOW!

OH, WELL, THERE'S **ALWAYS** TOMORROW'S SHOW!

YOU OKAY, LUKE?

YEAH! BUT I **CAN'T** SAY THE SAME FOR SNIFKINS!

CAGE? I **SHOULD'VE GUESSED!**

I **WAS** GONNA CHECK ON THE **PRINT**, BUT I HAVE A **HUNCH** UNCLE MAX WOULD **PREFER** FINDING OUT WHAT **HAPPENED** TO YOUR... **OFFICE**?

WHICH **ALSO** MEANS I **KNOW** THE DUDE WHO DID IT TO ME.

I ASSUME YOU REALIZE THAT IT'S--

YEAH, D.W., WE **KNOW** IT'S TURNED INTO **GLASS**.

ONLY ONE **CREEP** HAS THOSE POWERS, AND HIS NAME'S--

--CHEMISTRO!

GOT HIS **ALCHEMY GUN** WHICH CAN TURN **ANYTHING** INTO ANYTHING ELSE.

LIKE A **LAMPSHADE** INTO **STEEL**!

WE GOT INTO A **HASSLE** A FEW MONTHS BACK* ONLY **HE** WINDED UP **DISINTEGRATIN'** HIS **FOOT** WITH THAT GIZMO OF HIS!

*CAGE #12--MARV.

YEAH, I REMEMBER YOU **TELLING** ME ABOUT HIM. BUT **WHY** IS HE AFTER YOU **NOW**?

DON'T KNOW, D.W. MAYBE HE THOUGHT I'D **CUT** MYSELF ON THOSE GLASS SHARDS AN' **BLEED** TO DEATH!

BUT I **MEAN** TO FIND OUT WHAT HE'S UP TO.

LUKE--?

LOOK, CLAIRE, I GOTTA GO NOW. I **REALLY** GOTTA.

I'LL **MAKE** IT UP TO YOU. I **PROMISE**!

LUKE CAGE LEAVES HIS SLIGHTLY ALTERED OFFICE AND **TURNS** INTO THE MID-MANHATTAN TRAFFIC.

DON'T LOOK AT **ME** THAT WAY, CLAIRE, HE'S **YOUR** MAN-FRIEND.

WAY HE'S BEEN ACTING THESE PAST WEEKS, HE'S GONNA BE MY **EX**-FRIEND REAL FAST!

I **HARDLY** SEE HIM ANYMORE.

THEN CLAIRE AND D.W. LEAVE AS WELL, ALL FAILING TO NOTICE A SMALL CRAYON-SCRAWLED WARNING DRAWN ONTO A GLASS FRAME.

DON'T GET INVOLVED WITH ME CAGE! BIG BROTHER

...A **WARNING** WHICH SIMPLY **HERALDS** THAT DANGER THAT LUKE CAGE, **POWER MAN**, IS SOON TO FACE.

HEY, C'MON DOWN FOR AN *ORANGE JULIUS.*

I DON'T THINK I CAN *CALL* UNCLE MAX ON AN EMPTY STOMACH.

DON'T MIND IF I DO, DW.

Y'KNOW, DW, I JUST DON'T *UNDERSTAND* THAT MAN. CAGE IS HARD, SOMETIMES CRUEL...

...YET, HE'S GOT A *HEART* BIGGER THAN *EVEREST.*

YOU KNOW, HE COLLECTED THE *REWARD* FOR CAPTURING *SPEAR**, AND HE TURNED IT ALL OVER TO THE SIMMONSES. DIDN'T KEEP A *PENNY* FOR HIMSELF.

YEAH, THAT'S, CAGE: PART SAINT, PART SINNER!

* POWERMAN #35 -- M.W.

DON'T ASK WHAT MOVIE THAT OLD CLICHÉ CAME FROM, CLAIRE, 'CAUSE I THINK IT WAS IN ALMOST *EVERY* CRIME FLICK MADE IN THE THIRTIES.

BUT CAGE *ISN'T* A MOVIE ROLE, DW.

CAGE IS REAL, AND SOMEHOW *I'M* CAUGHT UP IN HIS LIFE. ONLY I *DON'T* KNOW WHAT PART I'M PLAYING IN IT.

I GET THE *SAME* FEELING SOMETIMES, CLAIRE --WE'RE *ALL* PLAYERS WITHOUT A SCRIPT TO KNOW WHAT'S GOING ON.

BUT, I GUESS THAT'S WHAT MAKES LIFE *EXCITING.*

SAY, HOW ABOUT A *TOAST* TO THE HOLLY-WOOD SCREEN WRITERS AND THEIR SCRIPTS!

AT LEAST *THEY* KNOW IF PEOPLE ARE GONNA WIND UP HAPPILY EVER AFTER!

CHEERS, DW.

TO **REAL LIFE** AS OPPOSED TO **REEL** LIFE!

CHEERS, CLAIRE.

AND **PRAYERS**, D.W.

I THINK WE'RE GONNA **NEED** THEM.

MANHATTAN CAN BE A **LONELY** PLACE WHEN YOU'RE TRYING TO UNCOVER **ONE MAN** HIDING IN THE SHADOWS OF NINE MILLION OTHERS. **POLICE RECORDS** ARE OFF LIMITS TO LUKE CAGE, SO HE IS **REDUCED** TO SIMPLY ASKING QUESTIONS.

OF COURSE, WHEN YOU ARE **POWER MAN**, HERO FOR HIRE, **ASKING** QUESTIONS IS ACTUALLY NOT **THAT SIMPLE** AT ALL.

TAKE "TATTLER" MARTIN. LUKE ASKED HIM WHERE HE COULD FIND **CURTIS CARR**, ALIAS **CHEMISTRO**, AND MARTIN **REFUSED** TO ANSWER, SAID HE DIDN'T **HAVE** TO.

SO LUKE ASKED HIM **AGAIN**, ONLY **NOT** QUITE SO POLITELY.

IT TOOK **SIXTEEN MINUTES** FOR LUKE TO CONVINCE "APPLES" SMITH TO TELL HIM WHERE CARR HAD MOVED TO. OF COURSE, LUKE FINALLY **DID** GET THE ANSWER.

UNFORTUNATELY THAT DIDN'T PAN OUT, EITHER.

IN SHORT, IT TAKES LUKE CAGE THE **BETTER** PART OF A **DAY** TO GET THE INFORMATION HE WANTS.

AFTER ALL, NO ONE SAID BEING A **PAID** HERO WAS EASY WORK. IF IT **WERE**, THERE WOULD BE A HELLUVA LOT **MORE** PEOPLE POUNDING THE PAVEMENT ALONGSIDE LUKE.

FORTUNATELY FOR LUKE CAGE, MOST FOLKS DON'T HAVE THE STAMINA HE HAS.

STAMINA AND **PERSISTENCE**, FOR INSTANCE...

CHECKED THAT PAD OUT AND CARR **DOES** LIVE HERE ...ON THE **FOURTH** FLOOR.

ONLY I DON'T WANNA **ALERT** HIM TOO SOON.

SO I'LL CLIMB ON THE *OUTSIDE*... MAKE MY OWN *HANDHOLDS* AS I MOVE UP.

NOT AS *EASY* AS TAKING THE *STAIRS*, BUT I *DON'T* WANNA HAVE 'IM GRABBIN' FOR THAT *GUN* OF HIS.

SKAM

CHRISTMAS! BEING *SHOT* AT

BLAM

BAM

NOTHIN' MY SUPER-HARD *SKIN* CAN'T *STOP!*

BLAM

SLAP

--BUT I *STILL DON'T* LIKE THE *GREETIN'* I'M GETTIN' HERE!

BAM

BAM

BAM

EH? GANGLAND STYLE SHOOTIN'! A *HIT AND RUN!*

CRIPES! THE BULLETS ARE *BOUNCIN'* OFFA HIM!

WHY DIDN'T *BIG BROTHER* TELL US HE WAS A BLASTED SUPER HERO!

DON'T *RECOGNIZE* THOSE DUDES... 'COURSE WHEN I GET *DONE* WITH 'EM, THEY WON'T RECOGNIZE *THEMSELVES!*

BIG BROTHER 757

BIG BROTHER? I *HEARD* A' HIM! SUPPOSED TO BE SOME *NEW CREEP* IN TOWN... TAKIN' OVER THE *RACKETS*, THEY SAY.

GOTTA PUT AN *END* TO THAT...*QUICK!*

WOULDN'T'VE *BOTHERED* WITH HIM IF HE *HADN'T* SHOT AT ME, BUT ALL-UVASUDDEN HE AN' ME GOT A *PERSONAL* THING!

HEY-- HOLD ON, PUNKS...

...CAN'TCHA SEE LUKE CAGE IS *COMIN'* THRU!

GOT THE *BUMPER*... NOW TO *HOIST* MYSELF *OVER!*

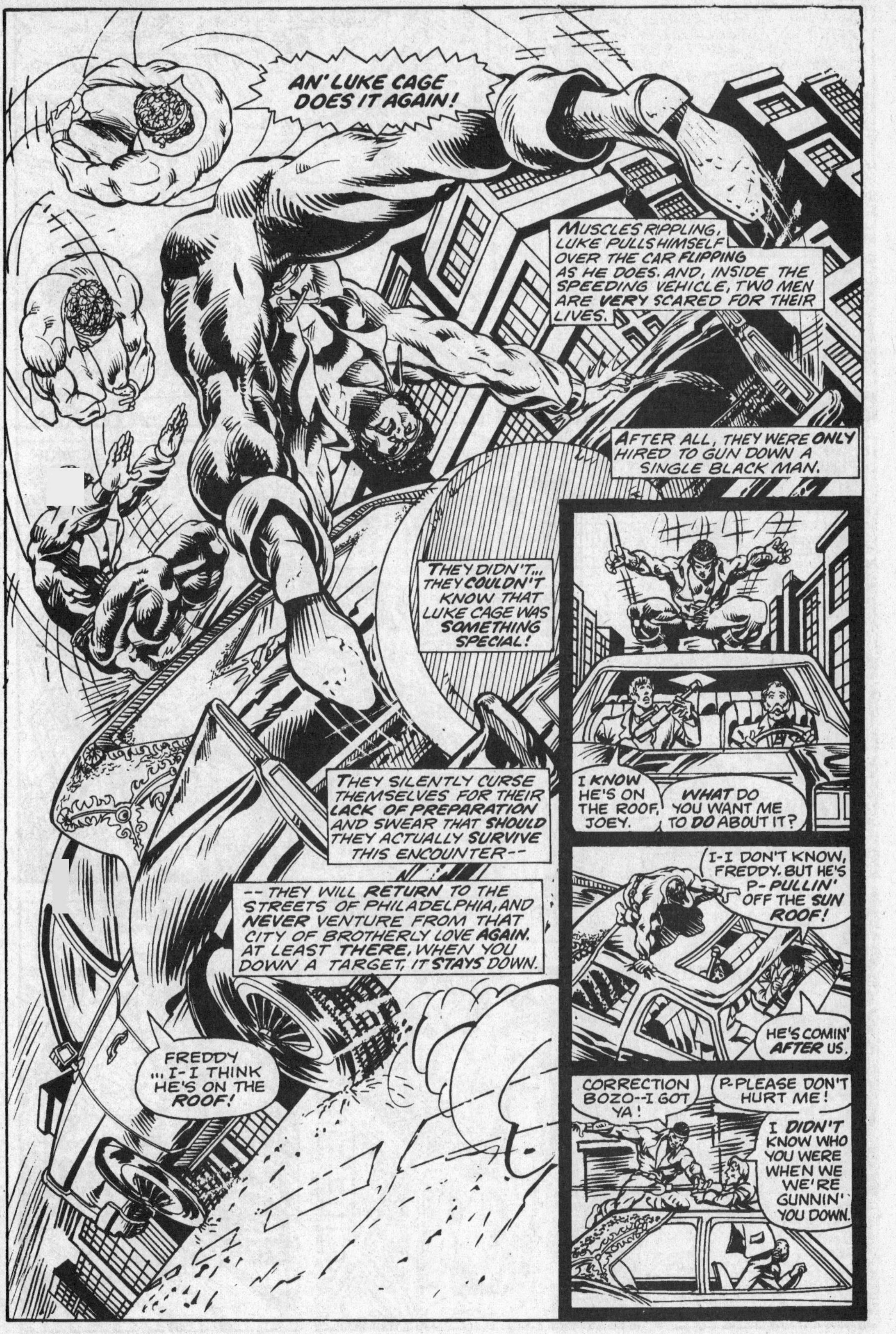
AN' LUKE CAGE DOES IT AGAIN!
MUSCLES RIPPLING, LUKE PULLS HIMSELF OVER THE CAR FLIPPING AS HE DOES. AND, INSIDE THE SPEEDING VEHICLE, TWO MEN ARE VERY SCARED FOR THEIR LIVES.
AFTER ALL, THEY WERE ONLY HIRED TO GUN DOWN A SINGLE BLACK MAN.
THEY DIDN'T... THEY COULDN'T KNOW THAT LUKE CAGE WAS SOMETHING SPECIAL!
THEY SILENTLY CURSE THEMSELVES FOR THEIR LACK OF PREPARATION AND SWEAR THAT SHOULD THEY ACTUALLY SURVIVE THIS ENCOUNTER--
--THEY WILL RETURN TO THE STREETS OF PHILADELPHIA, AND NEVER VENTURE FROM THAT CITY OF BROTHERLY LOVE AGAIN. AT LEAST THERE, WHEN YOU DOWN A TARGET, IT STAYS DOWN.
FREDDY ...I-I THINK HE'S ON THE ROOF!
I KNOW HE'S ON THE ROOF, JOEY.
WHAT DO YOU WANT ME TO DO ABOUT IT?
I-I DON'T KNOW, FREDDY. BUT HE'S P-PULLIN' OFF THE SUN ROOF!
HE'S COMIN' AFTER US.
CORRECTION BOZO--I GOT YA!
P-PLEASE DON'T HURT ME!
I DIDN'T KNOW WHO YOU WERE WHEN WE WE'RE GUNNIN' YOU DOWN.

AN' NOW THAT YOU KNOW I CAN CREAM YA-- YOU'RE APOLOGIZIN' FOR WHAT YOU DONE.

THAT REALLY MAKES MY HEART FEEL FOR YA, PUNK. ONLY IT DON'T STOP ME FROM LAYIN' YA OUT COLD!

JUST TO TEACH YOU NOT TO POINT GUNS AT FOLKS.

SPEAKIN' A WHICH, GIMME THAT PIECE.

YOU WON'T BE NEEDIN' IT NO MORE!

NOT WHERE I'M SENDIN' YA.

COURSE, YOU CAN GET OFF WITH ONLY A BROKEN FACE IF YOU ANSWER SOME QUESTIONS--

--LIKE WHERE DO I FIND YOUR BOSS --BIG BROTHER.

I-I DON'T KNOW! HE NEVER TOLD US.

SORRY, PUNK, BUT I DON'T THINK YOU PASSED MY LITTLE TEST.

MAYBE YOUR BUDDY DOWN BELOW HAS SOME BETTER ANSWERS.

SKUD

ULP! I KNEW HE'D BE GETTIN' TO ME!

BETTER STOP THIS JOB AN' RUN!

HEY, CREEPIE-- YOU AIN'T GOIN' NOWHERE TILL I FINISH WITH YOU.

I-I WASN'T GOIN' ANYWHERE, I SWEAR I WASN'T

THAT'S BEIN' A GOOD BOY, CREEPIE.

NOW, MOVE OVER AN' I'LL TAKE THIS WHEEL FROM HERE ON.

S-SURE...

I LIKE YOU, PUNK-- YOU'RE COOPERATIN' WITH ME.

NOW, JUST TELL ME WHERE I CAN FIND BIG BROTHER.

UNNHHHH...

I-I DON'T HAVE TO TELL YOU *NOTHIN'*! I--

AWW, YOU HADDA GO AN' *SPOIL* EVERY-THIN'! JUST WHEN I SAID YOU WERE *COOPERATIN'* WITH ME.

PUMF!

MAYBE I GOTTA TEACH YA A *STRONGER* LESSON, EH?

NO! I'LL TALK! I'LL *TALK!*

YOU BETTER, AN' MAKE SURE IT'S ALL *STRAIGHT!*

BIG BROTHER DOESN'T WANT YOU GETTIN' *INVOLVED* WITH 'IM, CAGE-- THAT'S WHY HE SENT *CHEMISTRO* TO YOUR OFFICE!

GET INVOLVED WITH *WHAT*, PUNK? I DIDN'T EVEN *KNOW* 'BOUT BIG BROTHER TILL TODAY!

D-DON'T KNOW NOTHIN' MORE, CAGE. I GOT MY *ORDERS*, AN' THAT'S ALL.

WE'LL SEE 'BOUT THAT *LATER*, PUNK... ...*AFTER* I BRING THIS CRATE A' YOURS TO A *HALT!* 'FORE WE *CRASH* INTO THAT CON ED FENCE!

DANG?

NO! THE BRAKE'S *GONE*... THREE HUNDRED *POUNDS* A' ME JUMPIN' ON THIS BABY PROB'LY *BUSTED* IT! ONLY GOT *ONE OPENIN'* LEFT TO ME.

DRIVE MY FOOT *THROUGH* THE BOTTOM...

...AN' *DRAG* THIS MOTHER-HUGGIN' DETROIT REJECT TO A *STOP* BY MYSELF!

C'MON BABY--SLOW DOWN...*SLOW DOWN!*

IT'S WORKIN' -- *WORKIN'!* ONLY IT *AIN'T STOPPIN'* FAST ENOUGH!

GONNA *CRASH!* HOLD ON *TIGHT*, PUNK!

SMASH

WILSON MUSIC STORE

MADE IT THROUGH WITHOUT A *SCRATCH* BUT PIN-HEAD'S *UNCON-SCIOUS!*

NOTHIN' A REST BEHIND *BARS* FOR *ATTEMPTED MUR-DER* WON'T CURE, THOUGH.

LANDGRAFTS

SAYONARA, BABY!

SEE YA IN *TRACTION!*

AND *THAT* STILL LEAVES ME BACK WHERE I STARTED FROM...

...NAMELY VISITIN' CURTIS CARR--*CHEMISTRO!*

AUB'S SHOP

WHILE, WATCHING OVER THE ENTIRE SCENE...

CHECKPOINT CHARLIE TO THE BARON.

WE GOT THE INFO YOU WANTED TO CAGE, AND HE BOUGHT IT ALL!

HE'S GOING AFTER BIG BROTHER STRAIGHT-AWAY!

JUST AS WE WISHED HIM TO DO, MY FRIEND.

FOLLOW CAGE, AND BEFORE WE ARE DONE, WE WILL WITNESS THE VALIANT "POWER MAN FOR HIRE" BATTLE BIG BROTHER FOR US.

AND WHEN HE DEFEATS OUR ARCH RIVAL, I WILL BE CRIME BOSS OF NEW YORK!

OVER, BARON. I'LL KEEP MY EYES WIDE!

UNAWARE THAT HE IS BEING SET UP, LUKE CAGE CONTINUES HIS INVESTIGATION... ONE WHICH BRINGS HIM BACK TO THE CRUMBLING APARTMENT HOUSE WHERE CURTIS CARR LIVES...

NO NEED TO PLAY GAMES THIS TIME. IF THOSE GUNSHOTS DIDN'T SEND 'IM RUNNIN', ME COMIN' THROUGH THE DOOR WON'T BOTHER 'IM NONE.

HMMM... DOOR'S UN-LOCKED!

CAGE? WHAT ARE YOU DOIN' HERE?

I'VE BEEN STRAIGHT SINCE MY RELEASE... I DON'T INTEND TO CAUSE TROUBLE.

NOT THAT I COULD ANYMORE, EVEN IF I WANTED TO.

YEAH! I CAN SEE THAT, CARR.

KNEW YOU DISINTERGRATED YOUR LEG DURING OUR LAST FREE-FOR-ALL, BUT I SORTA THOUGHT YOU MIGHT'VE FOUND YOURSELF ANOTHER BY NOW.

THAT TAKES MONEY, CAGE AND I DON'T HAVE A LARGE SUPPLY OF READY CASH AVAILABLE RIGHT NOW.

BUT NOW YOU'VE SEEN I'M A CRIPPLE, HOW ABOUT MARCHING RIGHT OUT OF HERE... THE WAY YOU CAME IN.

I DON'T WANT TO BE REMINDED OF THE PAST, CAGE.

HECK, I'M HAVING A HARD ENOUGH PROBLEM FORGETTING THE PRESENT!

YEAH! I CAN *SEE* I MADE A MISTAKE, CARR. *NATURAL* 'NOUGH THOUGH.

CONSIDERIN' ANOTHER *CHEMISTRO* JUST POPPED HIS HEAD UP.

CHEMISTRO?

YEAH, CARR-- LIVIN' OFF *YOUR* REP.

LOOK, I CAN SEE YOU'RE *NOT* THE DUDE I'M LOOKIN' FOR, WHICH MEANS I GOTTA *START* ALL OVER AGAIN.

I'LL SEE YA *LATER*, CARR.

A *NEW* CHEMISTRO. I WAS *AFRAID* OF THAT!

IT'S *GOT* TO BE HIM! THERE CAN BE *NO OTHER* ANSWER.

BLAST!

OUTSIDE, HIDING IN THE *SHADOWS* OF CURTIS CARR'S BUILDING...

HEY, BABY-- CHESHIRE CAT TO *BIG BRO!*

CAGE WENT STRAIGHT TO THE *MAN* HIMSELF.

AN' HE JUST *SPLIT*, MAN--ANGRY AS YOU KNOW *WHAT!*

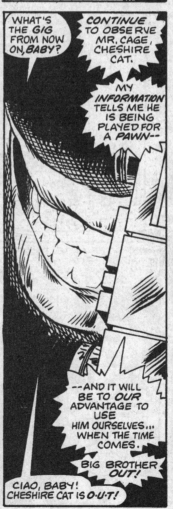

WHAT'S THE *GIG* FROM NOW ON, *BABY?*

CONTINUE TO *OBSERVE* MR. CAGE, CHESHIRE CAT.

MY *INFORMATION* TELLS ME HE IS BEING PLAYED FOR A *PAWN*--

--AND IT WILL BE TO *OUR* ADVANTAGE TO *USE* HIM OURSELVES... WHEN THE TIME COMES.

BIG BROTHER OUT!

CIAO, BABY! *CHESHIRE CAT* IS *O·U·T!*

CONFUSING? YOU NEEDN'T *WORRY. ALL* WILL *SOON* BE MADE *CLEAR.* BUT FIRST, LET'S TAKE A SHORT *TRIP* TO THE *NEW YORK HOSPITAL,* AND VISIT...

NOAH BURSTEIN, NURSE.

SORRY, MR. CAGE-- BUT *VISITING* TIME ISN'T FOR THREE MORE HOURS, YET.

SWEET *SISTER!* I *AIN'T* GOT THE TIME *LATER,* LADY. GOTTA SEE HIM *NOW!*

YOU'LL HAVE TO RETURN *LATER!*

MR. CAGE! MR. CAGE! *DON'T GO IN THERE!*

HOSPITAL

WHY DID I *EVER* BECOME A NURSE? *SOMEONE* TELL ME WHY?

HADDA **SEE** YOU, NOAH. SEE IF YOU'RE **STILL** AS ORNERY AS EVER.

I'LL **LIVE**, LUKE. I'M A DOCTOR. I **KNOW** WHAT'S WRONG WITH ME, AND I **KNOW** HOW LONG IT WILL BE BEFORE I **HEAL**.

SO, **DESPITE** MY IMPATIENCE, I **STAY** HERE AND **REST**.

MR. CAGE, **PLEASE** DON'T LEAN ON THE **EQUIPMENT**. IT'S RATHER **FRAGILE**.

SURE, SISTER. I'LL **MOVE**.

I'M **NOT** YOUR SISTER, MR. CAGE, IF YOU DON'T MIND.

IS **THIS** ANY **BETTER**, LADY?

NO, MR. CAGE, NOT THERE EITHER.

CAN'T YOU **STAND** STRAIGHT INSTEAD OF **LEANING** MISTER CAGE?

DIDN'T YOU LEARN **ANYTHING** ABOUT PROPER **POSTURE**?

HUH? LADY IF I WANNA **SLOUCH**, I'LL SLOUCH. SO **BUG OFF**, WILLYA?

LUCAS... **TEMPER**!

I'LL BE OUT IN ANOTHER **WEEK** LUCAS...ENOUGH TIME FOR THEM TO TAKE THE **STITCHES** OUT.

SURE **HOPE** SO, NOAH. THE CLINIC'S GETTIN' **LONELY** WITHOUT YOU.

YOUR **PATIENTS** DON'T KNOW WHAT TO DO WITH-OUT YOUR DAILY **TIRADES**.

THAT **HIM**, NURSE WINTERS?

YES, MA'AM.

MISSS-TER CAGE. THISSS IS A **HOSSS**-PITAL, AND **NOT** A GYMNASIUM. WE WANT **QUIIII**-ET HERE. I **SUGGESSST** YOU LEAVE **NOWWW**, WHILE YOU STILL **CANNNN**!

LOOK, LADY, I--

NOAH....?

DON'T LOOK AT **ME**, LUCAS. I CAN'T HELP YOU FROM **BED**.

GOODBYE, **MISSS**-TER CAGE. AND, GOOD **RIDDANCCCE**!

BLASTED WOMAN THINKS SHE OWNS *EVERYTHING!* I OUGHTTA...

HEY! WHAT'S THAT *SMELL--?*

...*LIKE...*

CHRISTMAS! THE WALLS ARE TURNIN' TO *MOLASSES!*

WHICH MEANS *CHEMISTRO'S* GOTTA BE HERE!

CORRECT, *CAGE.* I *AM* HERE. *BEHIND* YOU!

BEEN *WAITIN'* FOR YOU TO SHOW YOUR *UGLY* FACE, CREEP.

BUT I *DON'T* SEE YOUR FANCY GUN-GIZMO. WHAT *HAPPENED* TO IT?

I NO LONGER *NEED* THE ALCHEMY GUN, CAGE. THE *POWER* TO CHANGE MATTER NOW RESTS IN MY *HAND!*

WHICH MAKES ME TOTALLY *INVINCIBLE* AGAINST THE LIKES OF *YOU!*

BUT, I'M *NOT* HERE TO BATTLE YOU NOW--THAT WILL COME *LATER,* IF YOU HAVEN'T LEARNED YOUR *LESSON!*

RATHER, I'M HERE TO GIVE YOU A *WARNING.*

EAT YOUR WARNIN', PUNK. OR BETTER WHEN I *FREE* MYSELF FROM THIS *GUNK,* I'LL BE GLAD TO STUFF IT *SIDEWAYS* RIGHT UP YOUR FAT MOUTH!

I WILL *IGNORE* YOUR RATHER ILLITERATE THREAT, CAGE, WHILE I *FINISH* WHAT I STARTED.

YOU ARE TO LAY OFF BIG BROTHER'S OPERATIONS, OR, WHEN *NEXT* WE MEET, I WILL *NOT* TURN MY BACK TO YOU AND LEAVE.

I WILL *DESTROY* YOU ONCE AND FOR ALL!

IT IS *YOUR* DECISION, MR. CAGE. CONSIDER IT *WISELY.*

YOU AIN'T GOIN' *NOWHERE*, SWEETUMS.

NOT WHILE LUKE CAGE CAN *STOP* YA.

BLAST! FOOT'S *STUCK* IN THIS GUNK!

HARD AS *BLAZES* TO RIP IT FREE.

BUT I GOTTA-- I *GOTTA!*

THERE! IT'S COMIN' *LOOSE!*

DID IT!

NOW TO *FIND* THAT CHEMISTRY LAB *REJECT* AN' STUFF THAT SPECIAL *FIST* O' HIS WHERE THE *SUN* DON'T SHINE.

EH? WALLS'VE BEEN CHANGED TA *ICE?*

WHAT'S THAT *CREEP* UP TO *NOW?*

STEP *FASTER,* MR CAGE. *QUICKEN* YOUR PACE SO YOU *WON'T* HAVE ANY CONTROL AS I TURN THE *TILE* FLOORINGS FROM LINOLEUM TO--

ICE!

CAN'T KEEP MY BALANCE!

SLIPPING!

CHRISTMAS! I'M DOWN AN' THAT BLASTED BUNSEN BURNER'S *GONE!*

BUT, I *THINK* I KNOW WHERE TO FIND THAT FINK!

AN' *CURTIS CARR'S* GONNA FIND OUT THAT LUKE CAGE *DOESN'T GIVE UP WITHOUT A FIGHT!*

HEY, WHAT *HAPPENED?*

ABSOLUTELY *NOTHIN',* SWEETY-PIE! *EVERY* HOSPITAL SHOULD HAVE A WARD COVERED OVER WITH *ICE.*

LETS THE *PATIENTS* GO SKATING 'TWEEN OPERA-TIONS!

?

CARR DOESN'T LIVE TOO *FAR* FROM HERE...

...SO *ALL* I GOTTA DO IS GET THERE *BEFORE* HE DECIDES TO LAM OUT.

WHICH SOMEHOW I DON'T THINK HE'LL --HUH?

WHA? YOU'RE IN *BED?*

WHERE DID YOU *THINK* I'D BE, *CAGE?* I *TOLD* YOU I DON'T GO ANYWHERE.

I DON'T GET IT. I JUST *FOUGHT* YOU IN THE HOSPITAL.

UNLESS ... IT *IS* TRUE, AND THERE *IS* ANOTHER CHEMISTRO.

YOU *DON'T* HAVE TO PLAY TOUGH WITH ME, CAGE. I'LL TELL YOU *EVERYTHING!*

LISTEN.

BETTER MAKE IT *GOOD,* CARR.

I WAS CARTED OFF TO *PRISON* AFTER OUR *LAST* ENCOUNTER, AND WHILE SERVING MY *TIME* THERE, I DECIDED TO GO *STRAIGHT.*

"SEEMED THE ONLY *SENSIBLE* THING TO DO.

"ONLY, THERE WAS THIS GUY NAMED ARCH MORTON.

"SOMEHOW HE *HEARD* WHO I WAS, AND HE *DEMANDED* TO KNOW HOW MY ALCHEMY GUN WORKED.

"I *REFUSED* TO ANSWER. MY CRIMINAL PAST WAS *BEHIND* ME, AND *DIDN'T* WANT TO COMPROMISE MYSELF AGAIN.

"BUT, HE STARTED *BEATING* ME, CAGE-- FORCING ME TO TALK.

"CAGE, I'M NOT A *STRONG* MAN.

AND FINALLY, YOU *HAD* TO TELL HIM HOW THE GUN OPERATED?

YEAH, I CAN *UNDER-STAND* THAT, CARR. GO ON.

"MORTON WAS RELEASED A FEW WEEKS BEFORE ME, AND FROM WHAT I *HEARD,* HE IMMEDIATELY BEGAN BUILDING HIS *OWN* ALCHEMY GUN.

"ONLY HE *WASN'T CAREFUL*, AND THE GUN *EXPLODED* IN HIS HAND -- *SPRAYING* HIM WITH ITS SPECIAL *CHEMICAL PROPERTIES!*

AND SOMEHOW THE *POWER* THAT WAS IN THE GUN, SUDDENLY WAS *TRANSFERRED* INTO HIS *HAND*.

SO HE *DOESN'T NEED* A GUN AS I DID -- HE ONLY HAS TO *TOUCH* AN OBJECT FOR IT TO *CHANGE*.

LOOK, CAGE, I'M *WILLING* TO HELP YOU. I'VE *REFORMED*. I KNOW MOST FOLKS *CAN'T* BELIEVE CONS CAN COME CLEAN, BUT I *HAVE*.

BELIEVE ME, CAGE. I'M PLAYING *STRAIGHT* WITH YOU.

YEAH, CURTIS, I CAN *BELIEVE* YOU.

'SPECIALLY SINCE *I'VE* GONE THRU THE *SAME MILL*.

MEANWHILE, ACROSS THE STREET FROM CARR'S APARTMENT...

THERE HE *GOES*. YOU *READY*, CHEMISTRO?

YEAH, CHECK-POINT!

READY AND WILLING TO *MURDER*.

THEN -- *GO!*

CAGE!

I WAS 'SPECTIN' YOU TO *SHOW*.

I'VE BEEN GIVEN MY *ORDERS*, CAGE -- SEEMS BIG BROTHER IS *THROUGH* GIVING YOU WARNINGS.

HE DOESN'T WANT YOU *MESSING UP* HIS GAME PLANS.

YOU WANNA *KNOW* WHAT YOU CAN *DO* WITH YOUR BOSS, CREEP?

LANDGRAF

"I'LL SHOW YA!"

"WHAT? YOU'VE GRABBED MY WRIST! I CAN'T USE MY POWER!"

"YOU'RE A BRIGHT BOY, MISTER--"

"NOW GO TO THE HEAD OF THE CLASS!"

"NICE TRY, CAGE--BUT YOU JUST CAN'T EXPECT TO THROW ME THIS WAY--"

"--WITHOUT MY TURNING THIS BRICK WALL TO RUBBER..."

"...WHICH LETS ME REBOUND--"

"CHRISTMAS! DIDN'T EXPECT THAT--WASN'T READY!"

SWAK

"--RIGHT BACK INTO YOU!"

"JUST AS YOU WON'T BE READY FOR A STAINLESS STEEL FIST ACROSS YOUR MUG, CAGE!"

"I'VE ALTERED THE PROPERTIES OF MY SPECIAL SKIN-COLORED GLOVES JUST FOR YOU!"

SKAMM

"THANKS, SLIMY, ONLY KEEP IT TO YOURSELF, WILLYA!"

"DON'T NEED NO FAVORS FROM YOU--JUST THE DIRECTIONS TO YOUR BOSS' HEADQUARTERS!"

KRUNCH

YOU GONNA *TALK*, OR DO I HAVETA *BEAT* THE INFO FROM YA--LIKE YOU BEAT CURTIS CARR?

NO, FRIEND...

...I'M SAYING *NOTHING!*

AND *YOU* WILL DO NOTHING TO ME.

OBSERVE: I JUST *TOUCH* THE GROUND--

--*ALTER* ITS PROPERTIES, AND...

WHAA? I'M *SINKIN'!*

INTO QUICK-SAND, CAGE, I'VE TURNED THE VERY GROUND INTO YOUR *DEATH TRAP!*

AND, SPEED YOUR *DESCENT* INTO THE MIRE--

--I'LL *CHANGE* YOUR SHIRT FROM CLOTH INTO--

--HEAVY *LEAD!*

CHRISTMAS! I'M SINKIN' --NOTHIN' TO GRAB HOLD ON.

CAN'T *STRUGGLE*... CAN'T DO NOTHIN'!

GOODBYE, CAGE, I'M FINALLY *RID* OF YOU!

YOU STINKIN' *MOTHER-HUGGIN' SKUNK!*

I'LL *GET* YA--

I *DOUBT* THAT, CAGE...

ONLY YOUR *HEAD* SHOWS NOW, CAGE,... AND, IN MOMENTS, EVEN *THAT* WILL BE SUBMERGED.

AND *THAT* MEANS CAGE--

--IN SECONDS YOU WILL BE *DEAD!*

HA HA HA HA

NEXT: BIG BROTHER WANTS YOU

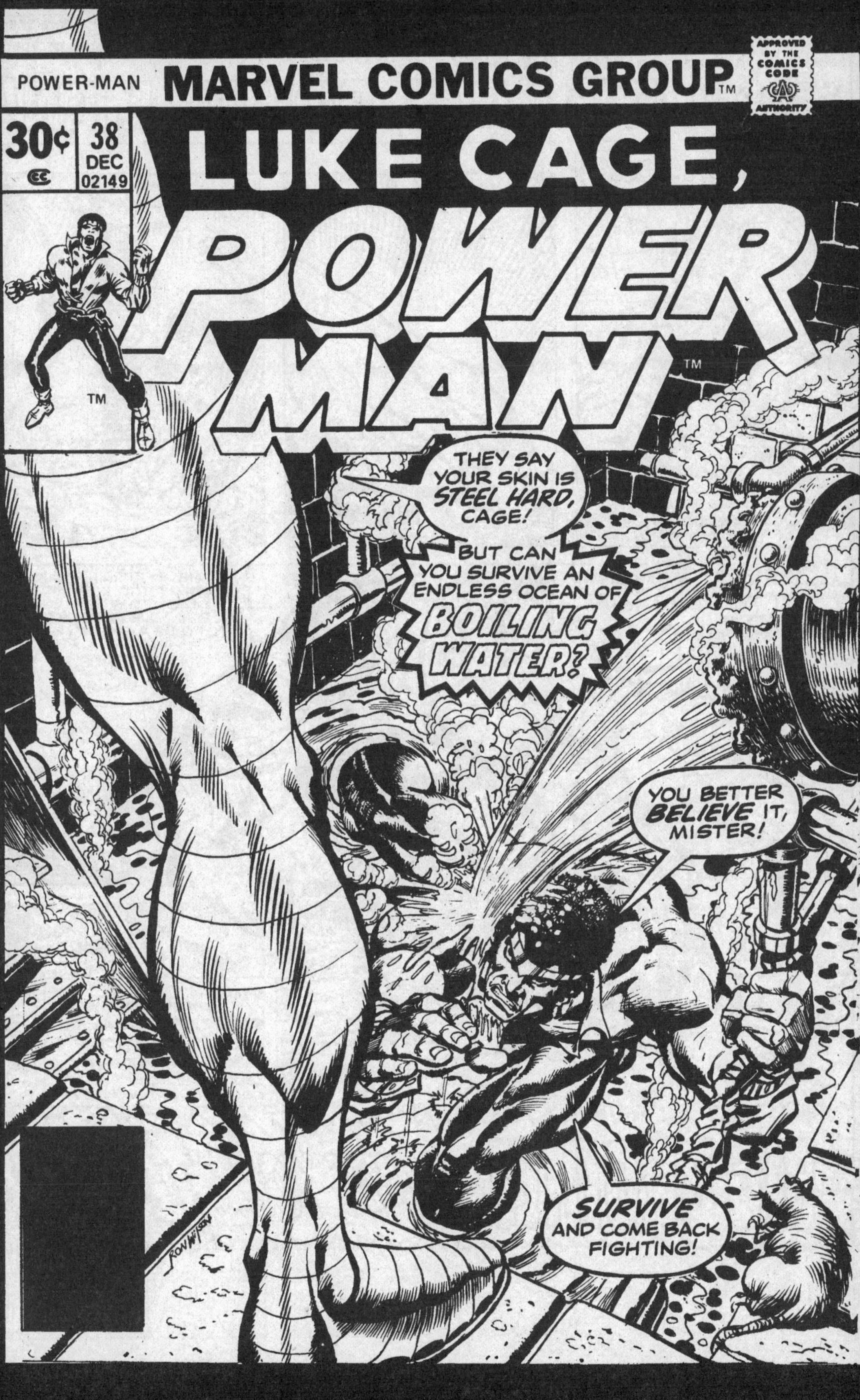

POWER-MAN
MARVEL COMICS GROUP™
APPROVED BY THE COMICS CODE AUTHORITY
30¢
38
DEC
02149
LUKE CAGE,
POWER MAN™
THEY SAY YOUR SKIN IS STEEL HARD, CAGE!
BUT CAN YOU SURVIVE AN ENDLESS OCEAN OF BOILING WATER?
YOU BETTER BELIEVE IT, MISTER!
SURVIVE AND COME BACK FIGHTING!
RON WILSON

LUKE CAGE: Wrongly convicted and sentenced to prison—reborn in a freak experiment there that gave him *steel-hard skin* and *strength beyond belief*—a man who hides his identity as an escaped convict in the role of a *HERO FOR HIRE!*

STAN LEE PRESENTS: LUKE CAGE, POWER MAN!

INSTANT REPLAY: THIS SCENE TOOK PLACE *FIFTEEN SECONDS* AGO.

YOU *CAN'T WIN,* CAGE--

--NOT WHEN ALL *CHEMISTRO* HAS TO DO IS *TOUCH THE GROUND--*

--ALTER ITS PROPERTIES, AND--

WHAA? I'M *SINKIN'!*

INTO *QUICK-SAND,* CAGE!

THE VERY *GROUND* HAS BECOME YOUR *DEATH TRAP!*

AND BY TURNING YOUR *SHIRT* INTO *HEAVY LEAD,* I'M SURE YOU'LL FIND YOUR *DESCENT* TO BE A *SWIFT ONE!*

BECAUSE, YOU *SEE,* MR. *CAGE--*

STORY & EDITING... MARV WOLFMAN
SCRIPT... BILL MANTLO
ART.... BOB BROWN
INKS...JIM MOONEY
LETTERS....JOE ROSEN
COLORS.....JAN COHEN

"BIG BROTHER *WANTS YOU...* DEAD!"

AND I'VE PROMISED TO *GIVE HIM* WHAT HE *WANTS!*

SILENCE.

LUKE CAGE IS *BEYOND ANSWERING.*

BUT NOT BEYOND *STRUGGLING...*

...TO *SURVIVE!*

BLASTED *LEAD SHIRT* IS DRAGGIN' ME *DOWN!*

FIGHTIN' IT'S TAKIN' TOO MUCH O' MY *AIR!* GOTTA *RELAX--*

--LET MYSELF GO *LIMP--*

--AN' *FLOAT DOWN* THROUGH THIS *MUCK* THAT USEDTA BE THE *SIDEWALK!*

ODDS ARE CHEMISTRO FIGURED I'D TRY TO FIGHT MY WAY *OUT!* HE WON'T BE *EXPECTIN'* ME TO DO JUST THE *OPPOSITE--*

--AN' *SWIM* FOR *BOTTOM!*

IF THERE *IS* ONE!

THERE *IS!*

PRAISE THE LORD FOR *SEWER PIPES!*

NOW, IF ONLY I GUESSED *RIGHT--*

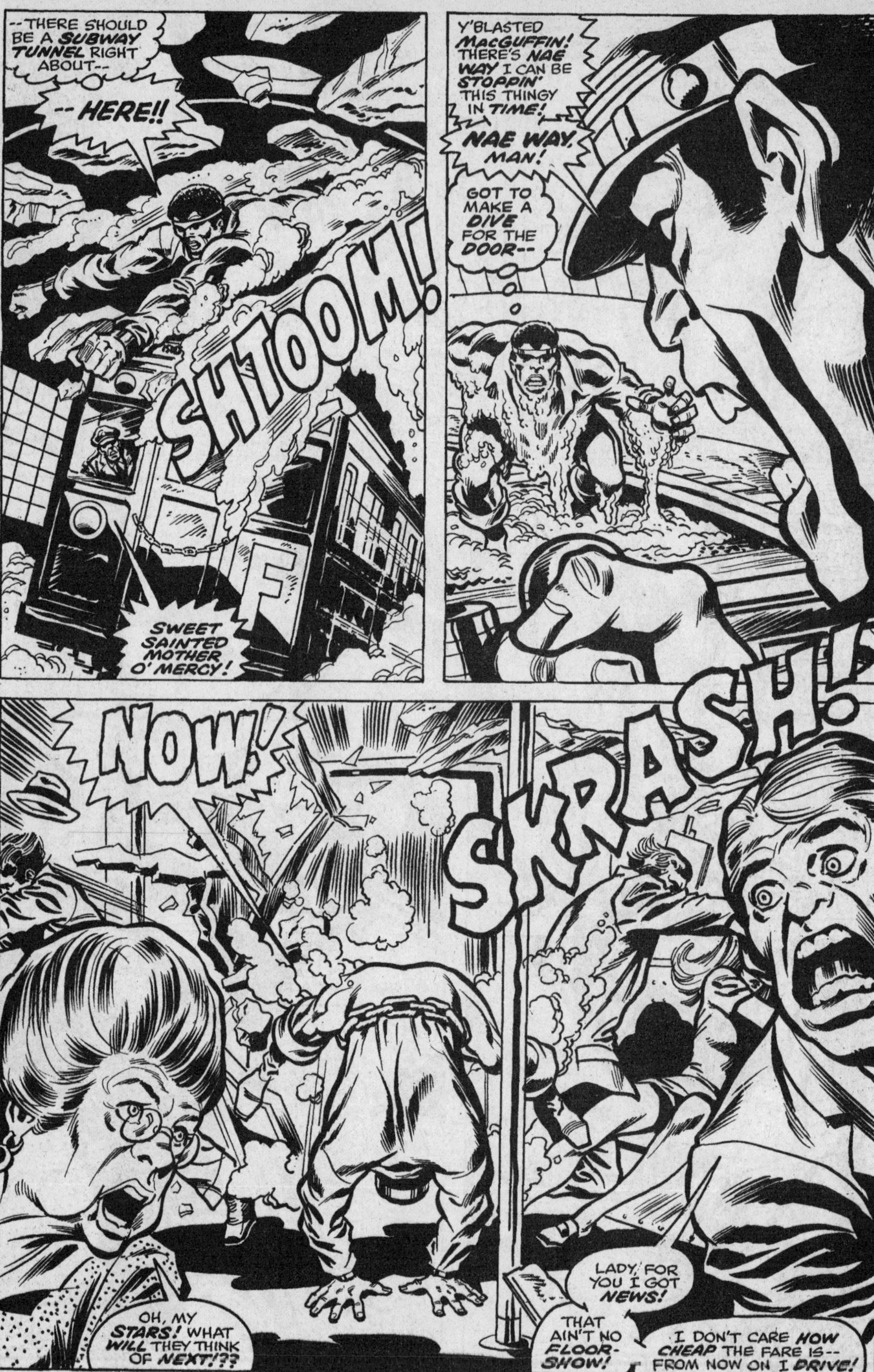

--THERE SHOULD BE A SUBWAY TUNNEL RIGHT ABOUT--
--HERE!!
SHTOOM!
F
SWEET SAINTED MOTHER O' MERCY!
Y'BLASTED MacGUFFIN! THERE'S NAE WAY I CAN BE STOPPIN' THIS THINGY IN TIME!
NAE WAY, MAN!
GOT TO MAKE A DIVE FOR THE DOOR--
NOW!
SKRASH!
OH, MY STARS! WHAT WILL THEY THINK OF NEXT!??
LADY, FOR YOU I GOT NEWS!
THAT AIN'T NO FLOOR-SHOW!
I DON'T CARE HOW CHEAP THE FARE IS--FROM NOW ON I DRIVE!

AND, IN TRUE NEW YORK *STYLE*-- NO ANSWERS ARE *OFFERED*, AND NO QUESTIONS ARE *ASKED*.

YOU *OWN* THIS POLE, LADY? OR CAN *ANYBODY* HANG?

WHY, OF ALL THE *NERVE!*

YOU'RE *DRIPPING* ALL OVER MY BEST *CHINCHILLA!*

WHILE, *UNOBSERVED*, A FEW YARDS *AWAY...*

C.C. TO *BIG BROTHER*-- OUR MAN *CAGE* IS A-*LIVE* AN' *JIVIN'!*

THE BRO'S GOT MORE LIVES THAN-- YOU'LL *EXCUSE* ME FOR SAYIN'-- --A *CHESIRE CAT!*

FOLLOW HIM, CAT! DON'T *LOSE* HIM!

AND, A FEW YARDS BEYOND *THAT...*

CHECKPOINT CHARLIE TO THE *BARON*-- I'VE GOT BOTH *CAGE* AND A GRINNING *WEIRDO* ON THE BEAM!

FUNNY LITTLE GUY-- *SHADES* AND A *SMILE* A MILE WIDE!

GOOD, *GOOD!* ALL GOES AS WE HAD *HOPED!* MONITOR THE *TRANSMISSION* COMING OVER YOUR *BELT-SCREEN*, CHECKPOINT!

WILL DO, BARON!

YEAH-- I READ YOU *LOUD* AN' *CLEAR!* THAT'S CAGE'S *SHADOW*, ALRIGHT!

HE IS KNOWN AS *CHESIRE CAT*-- OUT OF LOS ANGELES! *BIG BROTHER* MUST HAVE *IMPORTED* HIM TO DEAL WITH *CAGE!*

WHICH MEANS HE DOES NOT YET ANTICIPATE *OUR ROLE* IN THESE MANEUVERINGS!

WELL, WE SHALL LET THEM *BATTLE* EACH OTHER, AND WHEN *BOTH* ARE DOWN--

--IT WILL BE THE *BARON* WHO EMERGES AS *CRIME BOSS* OF NEW YORK!

"SINGIN' IN THE RAIN-- JUST *SINGIN'* IN THE RAIN--"...HEY, CAGE!

YOU'RE USING ALL MY *HOT WATER!*

NOT TO MENTION WHAT *QUICK-SAND'LL* DO TO MY *DRAINS!*

BETTER CHEMISTRO'S GUNK IN YOUR *DRAINS* THAN ON *ME!*

THE ONLY SERIOUS DAMAGE DONE WAS TO MY *SHIRT!*

GLAD TO *HEAR* IT... I *THINK!*

COFFEE?

BLACK, THANKS.

THEN, DRINK *UP* AND WE'LL HEAD OVER TO THE *THEATER!* YOU CAN BUY A NEW SHIRT ON THE WAY!

SURE! THINK YOU COULD LEND ME *FIVE BUCKS?*

SO THIS GUY *CARR*-- THE *ORIGINAL* CHEMISTRO-- HAS GOT AN *IMITATOR?**

*LAST ISH--MARV.

SHANE
ALAN LADD

YEH, HE *SAYS* HE'S STRAIGHT-- AN' I *BELIEVE* HIM!

BE KINDA *HARD* FOR A MAN WITH *ONE LEG* TO PULL OFF--

--THE KIND O' STUFF THE *NEW CHEMISTRO'S* BEEN GETTIN' *AWAY* WITH!

YOU MEAN--

--LIKE TURNING YOUR *OFFICE* TO *GLASS?*

SWEET CHRISTMAS!

I *FORGOT!**

*DITTO-- MARV.

AND SINCE THERE'S OBVIOUSLY *NOTHING* HE CAN DO THERE...

...CAGE HEADS FOR THE APARTMENT OF --

CURTIS CARR!

BACK SO SOON, CAGE?

BUT I GUESSED YOU WOULD BE! I HEARD ABOUT THAT FRACAS YOU HAD WITH MY DOUBLE! GLAD TO SEE YOU MADE IT!

YEAH, LUCKY ME.

LOOK, MAN -- WHY DON'T YOU RUN THROUGH YOUR STORY AGAIN, JUST SO I GET IT STRAIGHT?

"SURE, CAGE. WHY NOT?"

"WHILE FIGHTING WITH YOU, MY OWN ALCHEMY GUN TOOK MY LEG OFF -- LEFT ME A CRIPPLE --

"-- AND PRISON SET ME STRAIGHT. I'M OUT OF THE BAD GUY GAME, CAGE, FOR GOOD!"

AN' THIS PEN-MATE OF YOURS -- ARCH MORTON! YOU THINK HE'S THE NEW CHEMISTRO?

HAS TO BE, CAGE! HE BEAT THE SECRET OF THE ALCHEMY GUN OUTTA ME --

-- BUT IT EXPLODED -- TRANSFERRING ITS POWER DIRECTLY INTO HIS HAND!*

WHAT ABOUT THAT LITTLE "TRICK" YOU TOLD ME YOU WERE WORKIN' ON?

YOU'LL HAVE IT, CAGE -- BUT I CAN'T WORK MIRACLES! ANOTHER DAY, MAYBE.

HAVE TO DO, THEN, CARR! ALL RIGHT -- I'LL BE --

*P-M #36 -- MARV.

-- SEEIN' YOU!

RIIPPP!

WHAT! THE STAIRS'VE TURNED TO PAPER!!

DROPPIN' ME INTO THE *BASEMENT*-- --WHERE I GOT A *HUNCH* YOU-KNOW-*WHO'LL* BE COUNTIN' THE *SECONDS* 'TIL I *ARRIVE!*

CHEMISTRO!

OF *COURSE,* CAGE! DID YOU TRULY *BELIEVE* THAT YOUR CONVERSATIONS WITH *CARR* HAD GONE *UNOBSERVED?*

BIG BROTHER KNOWS *ALL,* CAGE-- AND THIS IS HIS *LAST WARNING!*

GET OFF THE *SCENT* OR YOU'LL DEAL WITH *HIM*-- INSTEAD OF *ME!*

MISTER-- JUST WHAT THE *BLAZES* YOU THINK I BEEN *SHOOTIN'* FOR??!

WHAT THE--??!

YOU ARE AN *IDIOT,* CAGE! I CAN AVOID YOUR *LEAP* MERELY BY TURNING THE FLOOR TO *RUBBER*--

--AND WHILE I AM THE MASTER OF *ANY ELEMENT*-- THE *SAME,* ALAS, CANNOT BE SAID FOR *YOU!*

JUST WAIT 'TIL I STOP *BOUNCIN'*--!

SPROING

AND *THEN* WHAT, CAGE? YOU'LL ONLY FIND THE WALLS HAVE ONCE *AGAIN* BEEN TURNED TO *GLASS!*

SKAAATTTRASH!

THOUGH *NOT,* UNFORTUNATELY, THE *STORAGE LOFT* AND THE *PRODUCE* THEREON!

THAT HAS *RETAINED* ITS ORIGINAL *PROPERTIES*-- INCLUDING ITS *MASS!*

YOU JUST WAIT 'TIL I DIG CLEAR, YOU BLASTED, WALKIN' TEST TUBE! YOU--

--STUFF! HE'S GONE!!

AN' CARR'S UPSTAIRS-- ALONE!

I BROUGHT THE MAN INTO THIS-- I AIN'T ABOUT TO LET CHEMISTRO TAKE 'IM--

--OUT!! BLAZES!!

CHEMISTRO'S DONE IT AGAIN! SYRUP!!

I HOPE THAT CRAZY LOONY TOON'S PAID UP ON HIS LIFE INSURANCE-- 'CAUSE I AIM TO SIGN AS THE BENEFICIARY--

--AN' THEN I MEAN TO COLLECT! IN SPADES!!

THIS DOOR! MUST LEAD TO THE ALLEY!

SWEET CHRISTMAS!

YOU'RE A LITTLE EARLY, CAGE! IT'S ONLY SEPTEMBER!

STILL-- I THINK MY TEMPERED STEEL CLOTHESLINE--

--IS PROBABLY THE NEXT BEST THING TO GIFT WRAPPING!!

I DON'T BELIEVE IT-- PJ'S SHARP AS SPEARS!!

BUT I ONLY GOTTA *DUCK 'EM* GARBAGE-MOUTH-- AN' HIT YOU WITH *ONE ELEMENT* I *KNOW* YOU'RE USED TO!

CRASH!

THIS ISN'T *WORKING OUT* THE WAY WE *PLANNED* IT!

CAGE IS TOO *STUBBORN* TO KNOW HE'S *BEATEN!*

I'D BETTER REPORT TO *HOME BASE* UNTIL THE *SUGGESTION IMPLANTS* ITSELF IN HIS THICK *SKULL*--

--AND HOPE *THE BARON* DOESN'T LOOK UPON MY ACTION AS A *RETREAT!*

HEY, *BRO'!* YOU *GOIN'* SOMEWHERE?

YOU'LL LEARN *SOON ENOUGH,* CAGE!

UNH-UNH, MAN! *NO WAY!*

I ASKED A *QUESTION*--AN' I FIGURE ON GETTIN' AN *ANSWER*--

--*NOW!!*

WHAM!

LORD, HE'S COMING AT ME *AGAIN!* BUT THERE'S STILL *TIME* TO--

GO *ON,* CHEMICAL MAN! WHAT'S IT GONNA BE *THIS* TIME, BABY?

MORE GLASS? MAYBE SOME MAPLE SYRUP?

NO, CAGE-- *TAR!!*

GLUP!

OH, *MAN,* LUCAS! YOU *WALKED* INTO IT *NOW!*

AN' I HOPE YOU GOT *IDEAS* ON HOW TO *WALK OUT!*

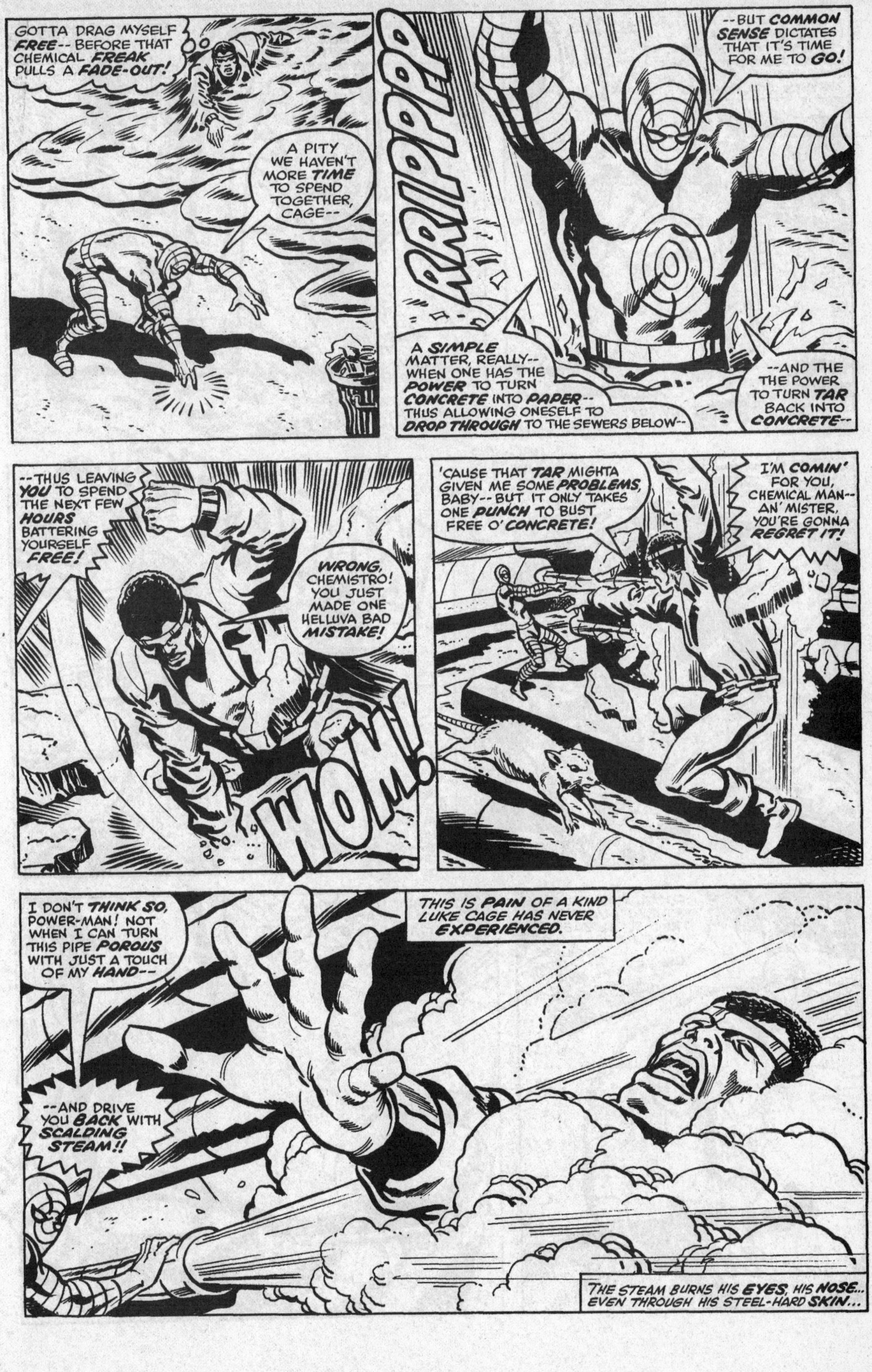
GOTTA DRAG MYSELF FREE-- BEFORE THAT CHEMICAL FREAK PULLS A FADE-OUT!
A PITY WE HAVEN'T MORE TIME TO SPEND TOGETHER, CAGE--
RRRIPPPP
--BUT COMMON SENSE DICTATES THAT IT'S TIME FOR ME TO GO!
A SIMPLE MATTER, REALLY-- WHEN ONE HAS THE POWER TO TURN CONCRETE INTO PAPER-- THUS ALLOWING ONESELF TO DROP THROUGH TO THE SEWERS BELOW--
--AND THE THE POWER TO TURN TAR BACK INTO CONCRETE--
--THUS LEAVING YOU TO SPEND THE NEXT FEW HOURS BATTERING YOURSELF FREE!
WRONG, CHEMISTRO! YOU JUST MADE ONE HELLUVA BAD MISTAKE!
WOM!
'CAUSE THAT TAR MIGHTA GIVEN ME SOME PROBLEMS, BABY-- BUT IT ONLY TAKES ONE PUNCH TO BUST FREE O' CONCRETE!
I'M COMIN' FOR YOU, CHEMICAL MAN-- AN' MISTER, YOU'RE GONNA REGRET IT!
I DON'T THINK SO, POWER-MAN! NOT WHEN I CAN TURN THIS PIPE POROUS WITH JUST A TOUCH OF MY HAND--
THIS IS PAIN OF A KIND LUKE CAGE HAS NEVER EXPERIENCED.
--AND DRIVE YOU BACK WITH SCALDING STEAM!!
THE STEAM BURNS HIS EYES, HIS NOSE... EVEN THROUGH HIS STEEL-HARD SKIN...

...BUT YOU DON'T GET TO BE A PART-TIME *DEFENDER* AND TEMPORARY MEMBER OF THE *FANTASTIC FOUR* BY GIVING IN JUST BECAUSE THE ODDS ARE *AGAINST* YOU.

DIE, CAGE! DIE!!

SSSSS

SHOOT! FORGET ALL *THAT*, BABY...

...YOU WOULDN'T LAST A DAY OUT ON THE *STREET* IF THAT'S ALL IT TOOK TO *WASTE* YOU!

I... HOPE... YOU'RE... *DIGGIN'* THIS... CHEMISTRY MAN!

I... HOPE... YOU'RE... DIGGIN' EVERY... *SECOND*!

'CAUSE IT'S GONNA BE THE *LAST THING* YOU'LL *EVER* DIG, BROTHER--

WUK

WUK WUK

WHAT ARE YOU--??

KTLANG!

DOIN'? WHY, BABY-- I'M *ENDIN'* THIS LITTLE *WEIRDO WALTZ* OF YOURS!

DO YOU *DIG* IT YET, *BRO*? YOU TRIED TO *SET ME UP*--

--BUT YOU *BLEW* IT--AN' NOW YOU'RE GONNA TAKE THE *FALL*!!

CRUNCH!

MY--MY **HANDS!** I THINK YOU **BROKE** THEM!

SAVE IT FOR THE **DISTRICT ATTORNEY!**

ME--ALL **I** WANT FROM YOU IS THE **INFO** ON **BIG BROTHER!** YOU GONNA **SPILL**-- OR DO I PUT ON THE **WEIGHT?**

I--I **CAN'T,** CAGE! HE'D **KILL ME!**

YOU DON'T **BETRAY** BIG BROTHER-- AND **LIVE!**

WHAT MAKES YOU THINK YOU CAN HOLD OUT ON LUKE CAGE AN' **LIVE,** PUNK? 'SPECIALLY AFTER ALL YOU **PUT ME** THROUGH?

I--OKAY, **OKAY!** I'LL **TALK!** BIG BROTHER'S HOLED UP IN AN OLD OFFICE BUILDING OFF **LENOX** AND **145TH STREET!**

IT'S A **FORTRESS** CAGE! HE'S SURROUNDED BY **ARMED HOODS!**

ALRIGHT, BABY! YOUR HANDS AIN'T BUSTED--JUST HURTIN'-- SO TAG ALONG AN' I'LL DELIVER YOU TO THE **BOYS IN BLUE!**

YOU'LL SEE I'M **PROTECTED**--FROM **BIG BROTHER?**

HUH? OH, **SURE.** JUST ONE MORE **THING** THOUGH, BEFORE I CAN LET BYGONES BE **BYGONES...**

AN' THAT'S **THIS,** BABY!

KA-STRAM!

DON'T YOU EVER MESS WITH LUKE CAGE **AGAIN!** DIG??

LATER, AFTER CHEMISTRO HAS BEEN SAFELY PUT AWAY BEHIND **BARS**...

GO **ON**, MR. LUKE CAGE--**HERO** FOR HIRE! WHAT KIND OF **JIVE** ARE YOU GOING TO LAY ON ME **THIS** TIME?

OR AM I SUPPOSED TO **UNDERSTAND** AND GO HOME AND BAKE THE **BREAD** EVERYTIME YOU LEAVE ME **STANDING** ON A STAIRCASE?*

*LAST ISH-- MARV.

I MEAN, WHAT KIND OF A **LIFE** ARE WE GOING TO HAVE, LUCAS?

ARE WE GOING TO HAVE ONE **AT ALL**?

YOU **KNOW** WE ARE, CLAIRE.

IT'S JUST THAT IT AIN'T GONNA BE AN **EASY** ONE! NOT WITH **MY** LINE OF **WORK**!

I...THOUGHT I **UNDER-STOOD** THAT, LUKE--

--BUT UNDERSTANDING IS **ONE THING**--

--WAITING... WONDERING IF YOU'RE **ALIVE** OR **DEAD**...

IS **ANOTHER**, YEAH, SWEET LADY--

--I CAN **DIG** THAT. LOOK, NEXT TIME I'M IN A **FIGHT** I PROMISE I'LL TRY AN' BE NEAR A **PHONE BOOTH** SO'S I CAN DROP IN A **DIME** AN'--

I'M AFRAID YOU **WON'T**, MR. LUKE CAGE!

HUH? WHO?

YOU KNOW VERY **WELL** WHO, MR. CAGE! OLIVER P. SNEAGLE, OF THE **INTERNAL REVENUE SERVICE**--*

*SEE POWER-MAN #34--MARV.

SNEAGLE!! WHAT IN BLAZES DO YOU THINK YOU'RE *DOIN'*, FOLLOWIN' ME *AROUND!?*

AUDITING YOU, MR. CAGE-- AND MAKING SURE YOU *DON'T* SPEND ANY *DIMES* UNTIL YOU PAY *UNCLE SAM* EVERY CENT YOU *OWE* HIM!

OH, YOU THINK YOU'RE *CLEVER,* DON'T YOU, MISTER *HERO FOR HIRE?*

YOU THOUGHT WE WOULDN'T SEE *THROUGH* YOUR LITTLE "CHARITABLE GESTURE" OF GIVING THE *REWARD MONEY* FOR THE CAPTURE OF *SPEAR* TO THE SIMMONS FAMILY! BUT WE *DID,* MR. CAGE--

--AND WHILE REAGAN MIGHT GET AWAY WITH *ZERO TAXES*-- YOU, SIR, ARE NOT *HIM!*

NOW YOU JUST *HOLD ON,* MAN--

I WILL *NOT.* HERE IS A *SUBPOENA*-- I TRUST YOU WILL *HONOR* IT AND SHOW UP AT OUR OFFICES. TILL *TUESDAY,* THEN?

YEAH, TUESDAY... OF THE *TRI-CENTENNIAL!*

LUKE! WHAT ARE YOU GOING TO *DO?*

CLAIRE, HONEY-- I'M GONNA TRY AN' *FORGET* I EVER HEARD THE NAME *OLIVER P. SNEAGLE*--

--AN' FEED MY *HARD-EARNED CHANGE* INTO THIS *ONE-ARMED BANDIT* OF A *SODA MACHINE*--

--AN' HOPE *THIS* TIME I GET A *COKE!*

CLOP!

TSHISH

GLUG

PTOOEY

CHRISTMAS! CHICKEN SOUP!!

MIDNIGHT.

SOMEHOW I DON'T THINK MY THREE-HUNDRED POUNDS WAS *MADE* FOR THIS ROOF-JUMPIN' *SCENE!*

LIKE, IT'S *MURDER* ON MY *HEELS!*

SO MAYBE I'LL GIVE 'EM A *REST*--

--AN' MAKE LIKE *DAREDEVIL!*

WHOO-EEE! IT AIN'T AS *HARD* AS IT *LOOKED*--

--LONG AS YOU LEAVE YOUR *STOMACH* ON THE *GROUND!*

BUT I AIN'T GONNA BE *UP* HERE ALL THAT *LONG*--

--'CAUSE THIS IS THE *OFFICE BUILDIN'* CHEMISTRO TOLD ME ABOUT--

SKRASH

--AN' I FIGURED ON MY *ARRIVAL* BRINGIN' OUT THE *WELCOME WAGON!*

IT'S *CAGE!*

DRILL HIM!!

BAM

BAM

DRILL ALL YOU *WANT*, PUNKS--

-- --BUT POWER-MAN'S COMIN' THROUGH ALL THE SAME!!

WHAM

CRIPES! WHO THE BLAZES ARE YOU? THE HULK?

THE BULLETS IS BOUNCIN' RIGHT OFF!

PTOW!

BLAM

HEY, MAN! AIN'T YOU GOT NO CLASS?

I MEAN, I DIDN'T SNEAK UP ON YOU CREEPS--

CRUNCH

GULP!

--SO I DON'T SEE WHERE YOU GET OFF SNEAKIN' UP ON ME!

YOU CAN SEE WHERE I'M COMIN' FROM, CAN'T YOU, CREEPO?

UHH-- SURE! YEAH! RIGHT! 'COURSE I CAN!

NOW, YOU BE REAL NICE AND CO-OPERATIVE LIKE AND TELL ME WHERE BIG BROTHER'S HOLED UP, OKAY?

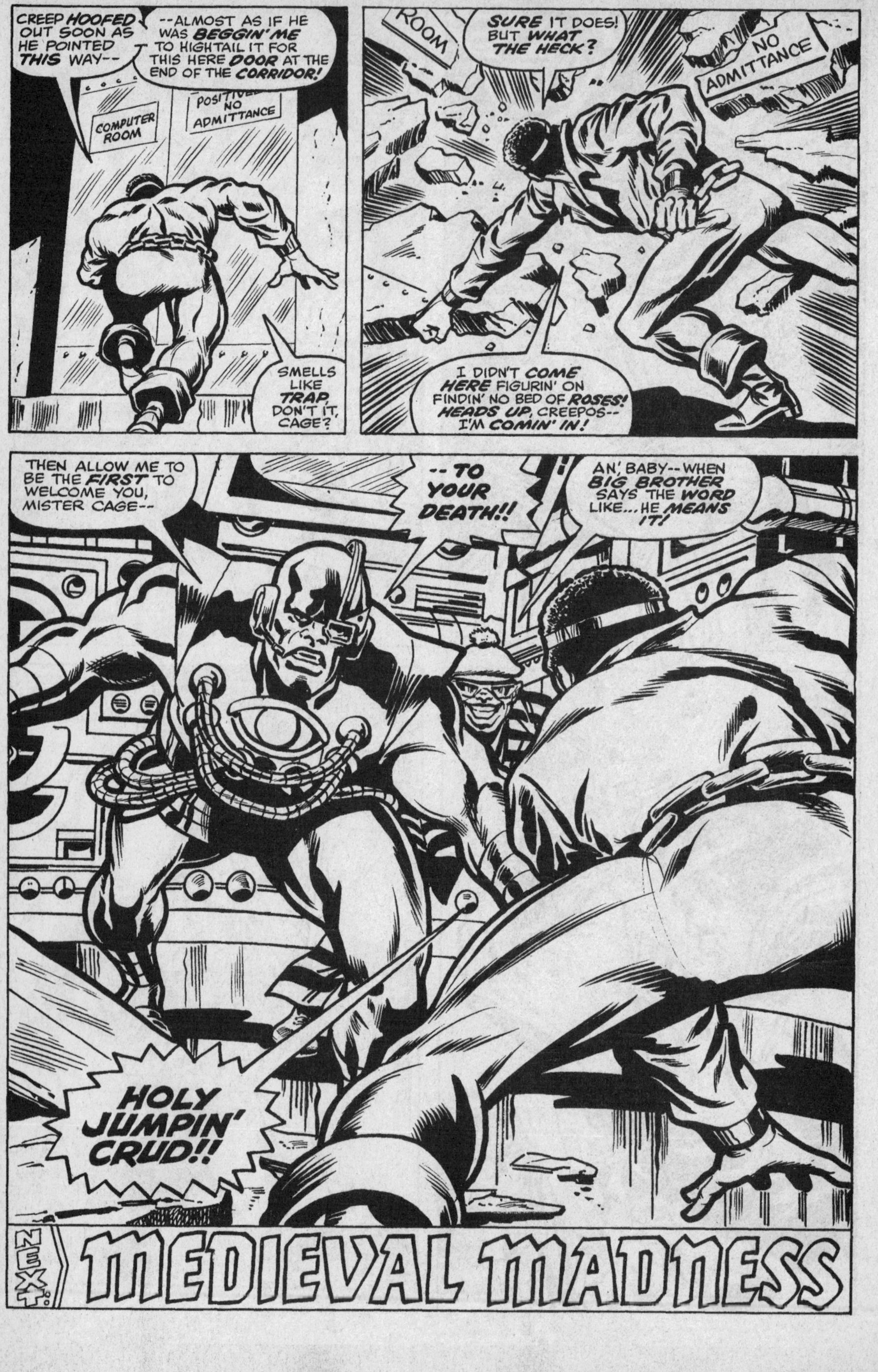
CREEP HOOFED OUT SOON AS HE POINTED THIS WAY--
--ALMOST AS IF HE WAS BEGGIN' ME TO HIGHTAIL IT FOR THIS HERE DOOR AT THE END OF THE CORRIDOR!
COMPUTER ROOM
POSITIVELY NO ADMITTANCE
SMELLS LIKE TRAP, DON'T IT, CAGE?
ROOM
SURE IT DOES! BUT WHAT THE HECK?
NO ADMITTANCE
I DIDN'T COME HERE FIGURIN' ON FINDIN' NO BED OF ROSES! HEADS UP, CREEPOS-- I'M COMIN' IN!
THEN ALLOW ME TO BE THE FIRST TO WELCOME YOU, MISTER CAGE--
--TO YOUR DEATH!!
AN', BABY--WHEN BIG BROTHER SAYS THE WORD LIKE...HE MEANS IT!
HOLY JUMPIN' CRUD!!
NEXT: MEDIEVAL MADNESS

POWER-MAN

MARVEL COMICS GROUP™

30¢ **39** JAN 02149

LUKE CAGE, POWER MAN™

MAYHEM AT MILEHIGH KEEP!

LUKE CAGE: Wrongly convicted and sentenced to prison—reborn in a freak experiment there that gave him *steel-hard skin* and *strength beyond belief*—a man who hides his identity as an escaped convict in the role of a HERO FOR HIRE!

Stan Lee PRESENTS: LUKE CAGE, POWER MAN!

M. WOLFMAN STORY ★ B. MANTLO SCRIPT ★ B. BROWN PENCILS ★ K. JANSON INKS ★ D. WOHL LETTERS ★ SLIFER & SHOOTER COLORS ★ A. GOODWIN EDITING

YOU *WANTED* ME, *BIG BROTHER*-- YOU *GOT* ME.!! AND, MISTER, YOU'RE GONNA *REGRET* THE DAY YOU EVER MESSED WITH *POWER MAN*!

I'M AFRAID YOU'VE BEEN *MISLED*, MISTER CAGE! I'VE *NEVER* "MESSED" WITH YOU--BUT I CAN SEE YOU'RE NOT READY TO HEAR THE *TRUTH* OF THAT!

HEY, BABY, THIS IS GONNA BE ONE *WILD GIG!* AN' THE *CHESHIRE CAT'S* GOT THE RINGSIDE SEAT!

BATTLE WITH THE BARON!

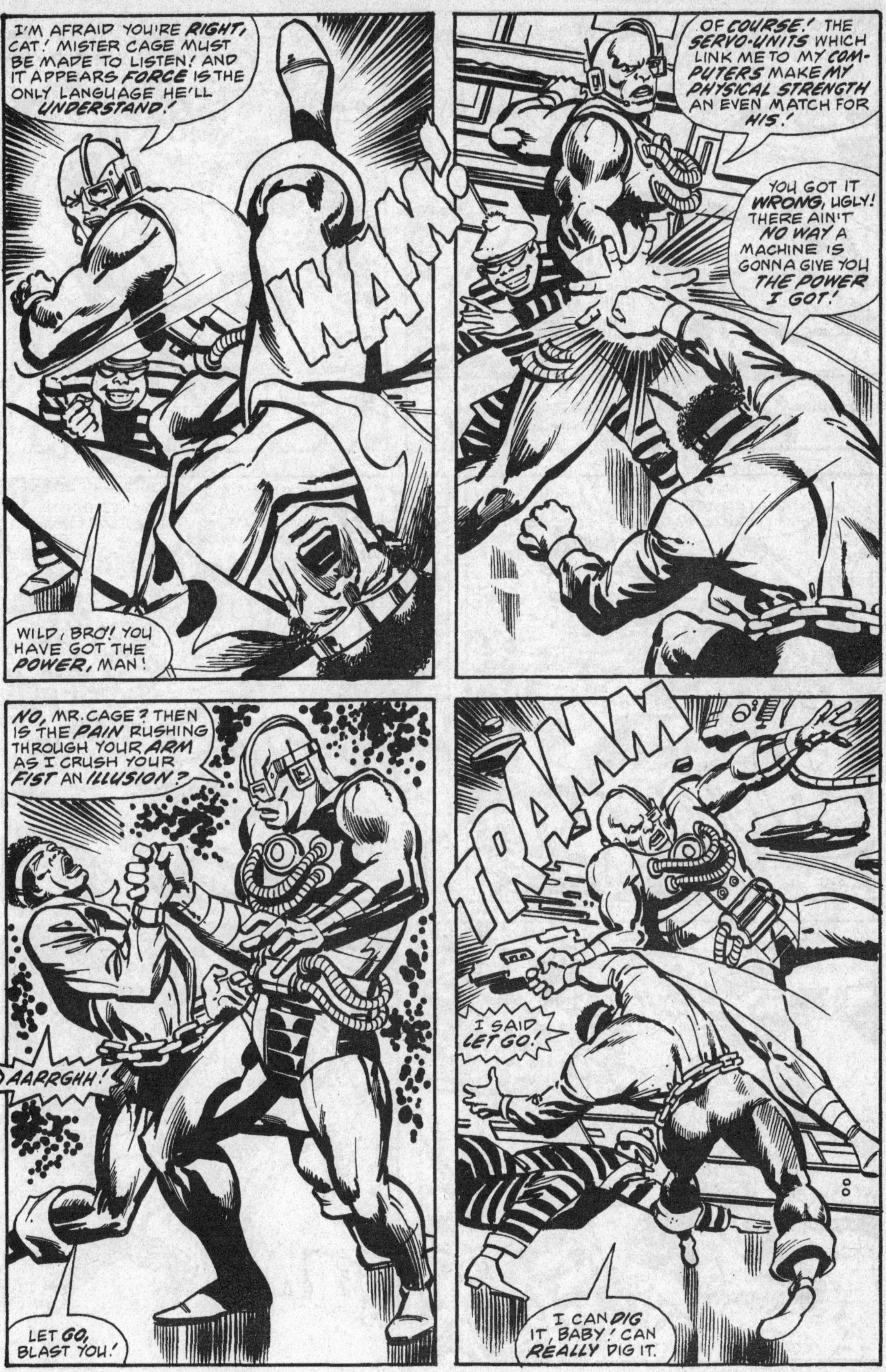
I'M AFRAID YOU'RE RIGHT, CAT! MISTER CAGE MUST BE MADE TO LISTEN! AND IT APPEARS FORCE IS THE ONLY LANGUAGE HE'LL UNDERSTAND!
WAM!
WILD, BRO! YOU HAVE GOT THE POWER, MAN!
OF COURSE! THE SERVO-UNITS WHICH LINK ME TO MY COMPUTERS MAKE MY PHYSICAL STRENGTH AN EVEN MATCH FOR HIS!
YOU GOT IT WRONG, UGLY! THERE AIN'T NO WAY A MACHINE IS GONNA GIVE YOU THE POWER I GOT!
NO, MR. CAGE? THEN IS THE PAIN RUSHING THROUGH YOUR ARM AS I CRUSH YOUR FIST AN ILLUSION?
AARRGHH!
LET GO, BLAST YOU!
TRAMM
I SAID LET GO!
I CAN DIG IT, BABY! CAN REALLY DIG IT.

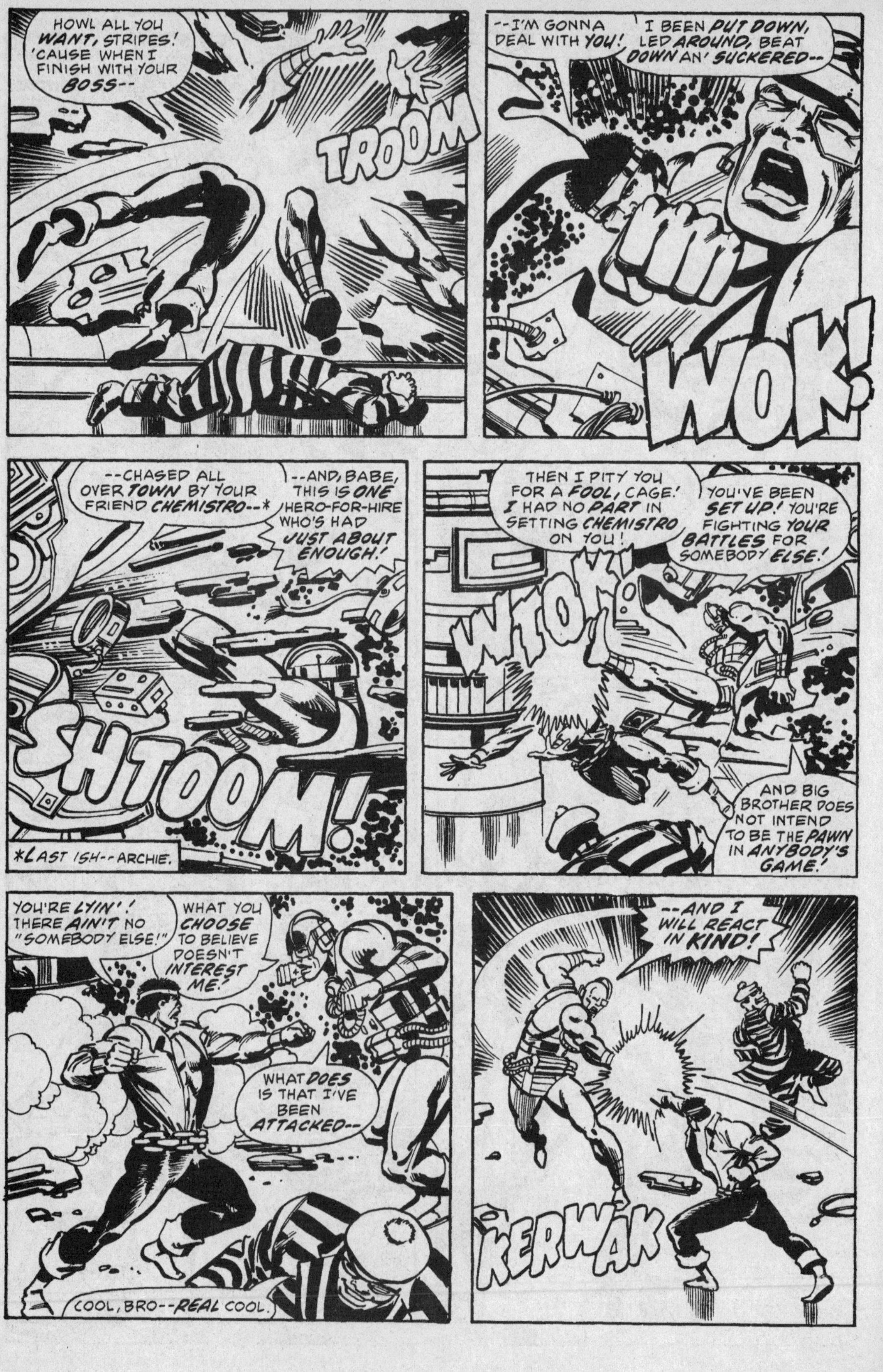
HOWL ALL YOU WANT, STRIPES! 'CAUSE WHEN I FINISH WITH YOUR BOSS--
TROOM
--I'M GONNA DEAL WITH YOU!
I BEEN PUT DOWN, LED AROUND, BEAT DOWN AN' SUCKERED--
WOK!
--CHASED ALL OVER TOWN BY YOUR FRIEND CHEMISTRO--*
--AND, BABE, THIS IS ONE HERO-FOR-HIRE WHO'S HAD JUST ABOUT ENOUGH!
SHTOOM!
*LAST ISH--ARCHIE.
THEN I PITY YOU FOR A FOOL, CAGE! I HAD NO PART IN SETTING CHEMISTRO ON YOU!
YOU'VE BEEN SET UP! YOU'RE FIGHTING YOUR BATTLES FOR SOMEBODY ELSE!
WTOM
AND BIG BROTHER DOES NOT INTEND TO BE THE PAWN IN ANYBODY'S GAME!
YOU'RE LYIN'! THERE AIN'T NO "SOMEBODY ELSE!"
WHAT YOU CHOOSE TO BELIEVE DOESN'T INTEREST ME!
WHAT DOES IS THAT I'VE BEEN ATTACKED--
COOL, BRO--REAL COOL.
--AND I WILL REACT IN KIND!
KERWAK

ARRHH! MY HAND!

YOURS?!

WHAT THE BLAZES YOU THINK *MINE* FEELS LIKE?!

THAT *CHECKS IT,* MAN! YOU BEEN DOIN' A LOT OF HEAVY *TALKIN'*, BUT ALL *I* DIG IS THE *POWER* YOU BEEN *THROWIN'* AROUND.

NOW MAYBE I *HAVE* BEEN *JIVED*, LIKE YOU BEEN SAYIN'--BUT *YOU* THREW THE *FIRST PUNCH,* JACK!

THEN, IF POSSIBLE, ALLOW ME TO *WITHDRAW* IT, CAGE!

WE HAVE *BOTH* BEEN USED AND, IN MY *ANGER,* I REACTED TOO *HASTILY!*

PROOF, MAN! CAN THE *WORDS* AND GET DOWN TO *CASES!*

AS YOU *SAY!* SEAT?

PROOF, *REMEMBER?*

YEAH, YEAH! I'M *IMPRESSED!*

YOU SHALL *HAVE* IT!

FIRST, THOUGH, AS YOU HAVE NO DOUBT ALREADY *ASCERTAINED* -- MY BUSINESS IS *CRIME,* MISTER CAGE! OR RATHER--TOTAL *DOMINATION* OF CRIME IN THIS *CITY!*

AN' I'M S'POSED TO *TRUST* WHAT YOU'RE GONNA *TELL* ME WHEN YOU START LIKE *THAT?*

YES, MISTER CAGE, YOU *ARE*--

--BECAUSE IF YOU DO *NOT*, THEN WE TWO WILL BE AT EACH OTHER'S *THROATS*--

--WHILE NEW YORK IS *TAKEN* AND *LOOTED* BY OUR *COMMON ENEMY!*

IN CASE YOU AIN'T *DUG* IT YET, BIG BROTHER--THE ONLY *ENEMY* I SEE IS *YOU!*

INACCURATE, MISTER CAGE--

--FOR AS THIS *VIDEOTAPE PLAYBACK* SHOWS, YOU HAVE ALREADY MET AND DEFEATED *ONE* OF OUR OPPOSITION'S *LACKEYS*--

--IN THE FORM OF ...*CHEMISTRO!*

I WAS *AWARE* OF YOUR BATTLES WITH THE CHEMICAL-MAN AS I AM AWARE OF *EVERYTHING* WHICH TRANSPIRES IN THIS *CITY!*

MY *COMPUTERS* FEED ME ANY AND ALL RELEVANT DATA, WHILE MY *AGENTS,* SUCH AS *CHESHIRE CAT,* SUPPLY ME *ADDITIONAL* INFORMATION I MAY *REQUIRE!*

DON'T *KNOCK* IT, BABY! IT'S THE *ICIN'* ON THE *CAKE!*

I *NEVER* "KNOCK IT," CAT--

--NOR DO I UNDERESTIMATE THE POWER OF OUR *OPPONENT!* WITNESS, MR. CAGE, *MILEHIGH KEEP!* THE *FORTRESS STRONGHOLD* OF OUR *MUTUAL FOE*--THE BARON.

CAGE LOOKS, HE CAN ALMOST HEAR THE *WIND* SCREAMING AROUND THE CRAGS AND PEAKS BELOW THE *CASTLE.*

HE CAN ALMOST SEE THE *GLINT* OF SUNLIGHT ON THE *WEAPONS* OF THE ARMED MEN AT EACH *PORTAL.*

HE CAN ALMOST *TASTE THE DANGER.*

DON'T LET THE "MEDIEVAL" TRAPPINGS *FOOL* YOU, CAGE! UNDER THAT ANACHRONISTIC VENEER THE *BARON* HAS HIDDEN THE *LATEST* IN WEAPONRY AND DEFENSES!

HIS SCIENTIFIC SKILL RIVALS MY *OWN!*

AND I TRUST YOU HAVE NOTED THE IDENTITY OF HIS *CHIEF VASSAL.*

CHEMISTRO!

EXACTLY! THE BARON'S PLAN WAS FOR HIS *AIDE,* CHEMISTRO, TO *DUPE* YOU INTO ELIMINATING *ME!*

THEN, WITH HIS COMPETITION *GONE,* HE INTENDED TO *TAKE OVER* THE *ENTIRE UNDERWORLD* AND, SECURE IN HIS *IMPREGNABLE FORTRESS,* RULE A *KINGDOM OF CRIME* WITH AN *IRON FIST!*

ENOUGH PROOF?

MAYBE, MAYBE NOT!

ALL THESE *WIRES* AND *CONTRAPTIONS* ARE S'POZED TO MAKE ME BELIEVE YOU CAN *TUNE IN* ON *ANYWHERE,* HUH? JUST LIKE THAT?

MY MIND IS *LINKED* TO THESE COMPUTERS, MR. CAGE, AND HENCE I AM AS IRREVOCABLY *LOGICAL* AS YOU ARE *SUSPICIOUS.*

KNOWLEDGE IS *POWER,* ERGO IT WAS LOGICALLY *ESSENTIAL* FOR ME TO DEVELOP METHODS TO LEARN ANY INFORMATION I NEEDED. I *DID*--

--BUT IT DID NOT HAPPEN "JUST LIKE THAT."

"I BEGAN LIFE AS A POOR URCHIN FROM *BROWNSVILLE*-- WEAK, SICKLY, ALMOST *ILLITERATE*--

"--AND TOO *SLOW* TO GET AWAY WITH A *STOLEN TIRE!*

"FIRST TIME I GOT SENT HOME! FIFTH TIME I WAS SIXTEEN --"

"...AND I CAN NO LONGER USE YOUR AGE AS AN EXCUSE! I MUST, UNDER LAW, SENTENCE YOU TO--"

"-- A YEAR IN REFORM SCHOOL WHICH STRETCHED INTO FIVE IN PRISON FOR ARMED ROBBERY!"

"BUT PRISON TAUGHT ME THAT I WANTED OUT OF A CELL, CAGE --AND THAT ONLY BRAINS WOULD GET ME THERE.

"I VOLUNTEERED FOR A PROGRAM IN COMPUTER TECHNOLOGY--"

"--AND SOON THE TEACHERS WERE LEARNING FROM ME!"

HE'S AMAZING! HE'S PROGRAMMED THAT ROBOT TO THINK AS IF IT'S ALIVE!

YES, AND HE'S EVEN MANAGED TO IMPROVE HIS OWN HEALTH THRU UNHEARD OF ADVANCES IN BIONICS.

"SOON AFTER I WAS PARDONED--"

-- AND I BEGAN TO MASTER MY SCIENCE IN EARNEST! IT HAS TAKEN MY ENTIRE LIFE, CAGE--BUT THE RESULT YOU SEE BEFORE YOU!

LISTEN, MAN-- I CAN LISTEN TO PRISON STORIES ANY DAY!

I'M STILL WAITIN' TO HEAR--

MORE ABOUT HOW THE BARON MADE A CHUMP OUTTA YOU? HEE-HEE!! RIGHT ON!

ONE MORE GIGGLE OUTTA YOU, AN' THE FIRE DEPARTMENT'S GONNA BE HAULIN' YOUR ASHES DOWN OUTTA SOME TREES!

ENOUGH! REMEMBER, WE HAVE A TRUCE, CAGE... BUT MY PATIENCE IS WEARING THIN!

I HAVE NO MORE TIME TO WASTE! IMPORTANT MATTERS AWAIT MY ATTENTION!

O.K., WE CALL IT A *DRAW* THIS TIME, BIG BROTHER--AN'IF THAT *BARON* DUDE *DID* SEND THAT *CHEMICAL FREAK* AFTER ME, THEN I GET *HIM* FIRST.

YOU'RE *NEXT!*

WATCH IT, *HERO-MAN!*

YOU *BET*, CAT! I'M *ALWAYS* CAREFUL!

SEE YOU BOYS *AROUND!*

WELL *PLAYED*, CAT! THE *PAWN* CONFRONTS THE *WHITE KING!*

THE BOARD IS *SET*--OUR *WAY!*

I CAN *DIG* IT, BB --BUT IF THE BARON *DON'T* KILL CAGE--

--I WANT '*IM!* DIG?

OF *COURSE!* BUT I THINK WE NEEDN'T *FEAR* THE OUT-COME! CAGE IS WALKING *BLIND* WITH A *MATCH* INTO A *POWDER KEG!* THE RESULTANT *EXPLOSION* SHOULD REMOVE *BOTH* OUR PROBLEMS BEFORE THE NIGHT IS *DONE!*

THE BIG *BANG* SOUND HEARD ROUND THE *WORLD*, BB! *OO-WEE*, MAN, WOULD I DIG HEAR-IN' DAT COOL PLATTER PLAY!

YOU *WILL* CAT! FOLLOW MR. *CAGE!* MAKE *SURE* THERE ARE NO *SLIP-UPS!*

YOU *WANT* IT, BIG BRO--

--YOU *GOT* IT!

MAN, Y'GOTTA FEEL *SORRY* FOR *CAGE*, 'CAUSE HE DIDN'T *NOTICE*--

--BUT HE MADE ME *MAD*--CRAZY *MAD*--

--*MEAN MAD!* AN' WHEN I GET LIKE *THAT*--

--BABY, I AM JUST NOT *ALL THERE!*

LATER, AT THE HOME OF DR. NOAH BURSTEIN...

HOW IN *BLAZES* DID YOU GET YOURSELF OUTTA THAT *HOSPITAL*, NOAH?*

I TOLD THEM I WANTED TO BE IN THE CARE OF MY *OWN* DOCTOR--

--ME!

*LAST ISH-- ARCHIE.

AND THEY *AGREED* THAT *SPEAR* HADN'T HURT ME ENOUGH TO WARRANT ANOTHER *MONTH* UNDER THE WATCHFUL EYE OF THE *HEAD NURSE*--

--AND THAT I MIGHT AS WELL RECUPERATE AT *HOME* WHERE AT LEAST I'D FEEL *COMFORTABLE!*

LET'S JUST CALL IT A *MUTUAL UNDERSTANDING.*

*POWER MAN #35 --ARCHIE.

I'M GLAD YOU'RE *ALL RIGHT*, MAN! SEEMS YOU CAME OUT THE *WORST* WITH THAT *SPEAR BUSINESS*--

--WHILE I WALKED AWAY *CLEAN!*

LOOK, IT'S *OVER*, LUKE! IT DIDN'T *STOP* ME--

--IT DIDN'T EVEN *HURT* ME AS BAD AS IT COULD *HAVE!* I'M PRETTY *TOUGH*, Y'KNOW!

WHATEVER HAPPENS, I THINK I'LL *LIVE!*

YEAH, WELL, I *HOPE* SO!

OUTSIDE...

NOAH'S *FINE!* BUT WHAT ABOUT *US*, LUKE?

LOOK, CLAIRE, WE WENT OVER THAT *YESTERDAY!*

WE ARE IMPORTANT-- BUT SO'S THE JOB I GOTTA DO!

THEN *DO* YOUR JOB, MY MAN-- --BUT AT LEAST LEAVE ME WITH A *KISS*, HUH?

YOU *GOT* IT, LADY!

CUT YET AGAIN, TO THE APARTMENT OF CURTIS CARR, THE ORIGINAL CHEMISTRO...

WHEN I BLEW MY OWN LEG OFF WITH MY ALCHEMY GUN, I KNEW MY DAYS AS CRIMINAL WERE OVER--

--BUT NOW A DUDE I MET IN PRISON IS CARRYIN' MY OLD HANDLE--

AN' HE GOT AWAY FROM ME AGAIN, CARR!*

CAGE!!

YOU GOT WHAT YOU PROMISED?

*LAST ISH --ARCHIE.

YES! IT'S ALL READY!

LOOK, IT SHOULD WORK! I GEARED IT TO THE PROPERTIES OF MY ORIGINAL GUN! BUT THE NEW CHEMISTRO HAS GOT THESE PROPERTIES ALL INSIDE HIS BIOLOGY! I DON'T KNOW!

WE'LL HAVE TO TAKE THAT CHANCE, CARR! I FIGURE ON SEEIN' THE MAN IN QUESTION TONIGHT!

THEN TAKE THE NULLIFIER--

--AND I'LL BE PRAYING THAT I HAVEN'T LET YOU DOWN, CAGE!

I MEAN THAT!

I BELIEVE YOU DO, CARR--

--AN' IF I COME OUT OF THIS, I WON'T FORGET WHAT YOU'VE DONE!

YOU NEED ANY-THING--ANYTIME, ANYPLACE--YOU CALL ON LUKE CAGE!

AND I MEAN THAT!

NIGHT.

GOTTA REMEMBER TO *THANK* THE DEFENDERS* FOR THE LOAN OF THE *BUS FARE* TO GET *UP* HERE!

THEN AGAIN, AFTER ALL I DONE FOR *THEM*-- MAYBE I'LL JUST LET IT *RIDE*!

*CAGE IS A PART-TIME *DEFENDER.* --ARCHIE.

BUT RIGHT NOW I JUST WANT TO SEE IF THIS *GRAPPLE-HOOK* I PICKED UP AT THE *ARMY-NAVY STORE* ON TIMES SQUARE--

--WILL DO THE *TRICK*--

SKRITT!

--OR WHETHER I HAVETA GO INTO *HOCK* FOR THE SUPER-EXPENSIVE *DELUXE MODEL!*

LOOKS LIKE I PICKED A *WINNER!* IT'S *HOLDIN'!*

SO FAR!

THE *BIG* TEST COMES WHEN THIS TWO-BIT CLOTHESLINE IS SUPPORTIN' MY SUPER-DENSE 300 POUND *BODY.*

IT'S A *LONG DROP!* I HOPE THIS RIG CAN TAKE IT!

OH, NO! THE ROPE'S *FRAYIN'* UP AHEAD! IT'S GONNA *SNAP!*

AN' I'M GONNA *DIE* 'CAUSE I DIDN'T HAVE $4.95 EXTRA FOR THE HEAVY-DUTY NUMBER.

SO CLOSE TO THE *CLIFF-FACE!* IF I COULD JUST *STRETCH*--!

MADE IT!

SO FAR, SO GOOD! GUESS THEY FIGURED NOBODY'D BE STUPID ENOUGH TO TRY AN' CLIMB THE CLIFF UP TO THE CASTLE!

BUT NOW COMES THE FUN PART! I DON'T INTEND TO CRAWL IN-- SNEAKY-STYLE--

--NOT WHEN I CAN LET 'EM KNOW I'M HERE WITH A BANG--

--POWER MAN STYLE!

CRASH!

CAGE!!

HERE! SEE HOW THIS FITS YOU 'FORE YOU TRY TURNIN' THE WHOLE WORLD TO MOLASSES AGAIN!

IT'S STICKING TO ME! SOMETHING'S WRONG! MY CHEMICAL POWERS AREN'T WORKING!!

YOU CAN THANK CURTIS CARR FOR THAT, CREEP--

--BUT YOU CAN THANK ME FOR THIS!

TRAM

SO MUCH FOR THE SMALL TRASH!

NOW TO FIND THE BIG GARBAGE WHOSE BEHIND ALL TH--

YOU HAVE ONLY TO TURN, LUKE CAGE!

HUH?

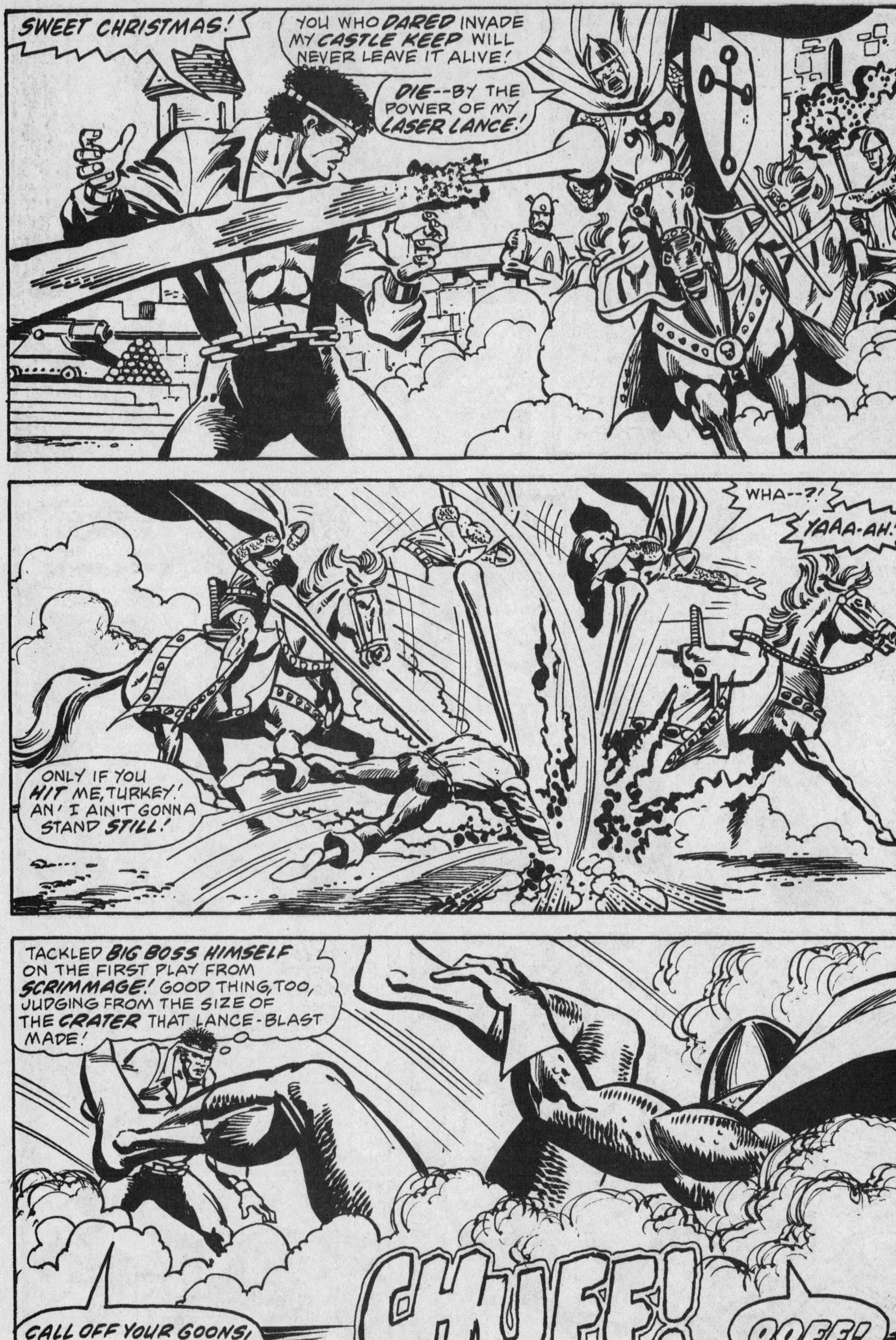

SWEET CHRISTMAS!
YOU WHO DARED INVADE MY CASTLE KEEP WILL NEVER LEAVE IT ALIVE!
DIE--BY THE POWER OF MY LASER LANCE!
WHA--?!
YAAA-AH!
ONLY IF YOU HIT ME, TURKEY! AN' I AIN'T GONNA STAND STILL!
TACKLED BIG BOSS HIMSELF ON THE FIRST PLAY FROM SCRIMMAGE! GOOD THING, TOO, JUDGING FROM THE SIZE OF THE CRATER THAT LANCE-BLAST MADE!
CHUFF!
OOFF!
CALL OFF YOUR GOONS, BARON, LESS YOU WANT AN INSTANT REPLAY!

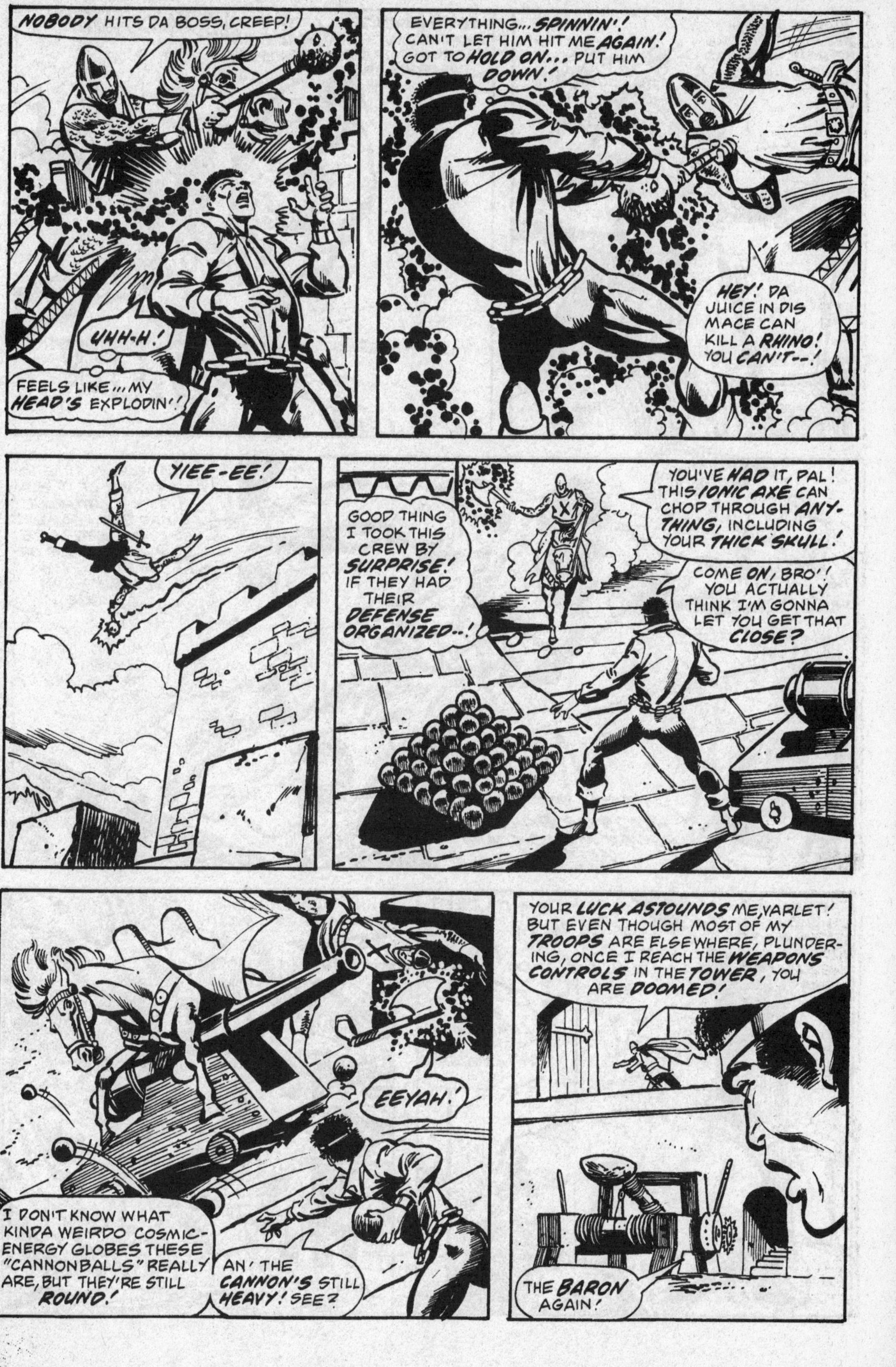
NOBODY HITS DA BOSS, CREEP!
UHH-H!
FEELS LIKE... MY HEAD'S EXPLODIN'!
EVERYTHING... SPINNIN'! CAN'T LET HIM HIT ME AGAIN! GOT TO HOLD ON... PUT HIM DOWN!
HEY! DA JUICE IN DIS MACE CAN KILL A RHINO! YOU CAN'T--!
YIEE-EE!
GOOD THING I TOOK THIS CREW BY SURPRISE! IF THEY HAD THEIR DEFENSE ORGANIZED--!
YOU'VE HAD IT, PAL! THIS IONIC AXE CAN CHOP THROUGH ANY-THING, INCLUDING YOUR THICK SKULL!
COME ON, BRO'! YOU ACTUALLY THINK I'M GONNA LET YOU GET THAT CLOSE?
EEYAH!
I DON'T KNOW WHAT KINDA WEIRDO COSMIC-ENERGY GLOBES THESE "CANNONBALLS" REALLY ARE, BUT THEY'RE STILL ROUND!
AN' THE CANNON'S STILL HEAVY! SEE?
YOUR LUCK ASTOUNDS ME, VARLET! BUT EVEN THOUGH MOST OF MY TROOPS ARE ELSEWHERE, PLUNDER-ING, ONCE I REACH THE WEAPONS CONTROLS IN THE TOWER, YOU ARE DOOMED!
THE BARON AGAIN!

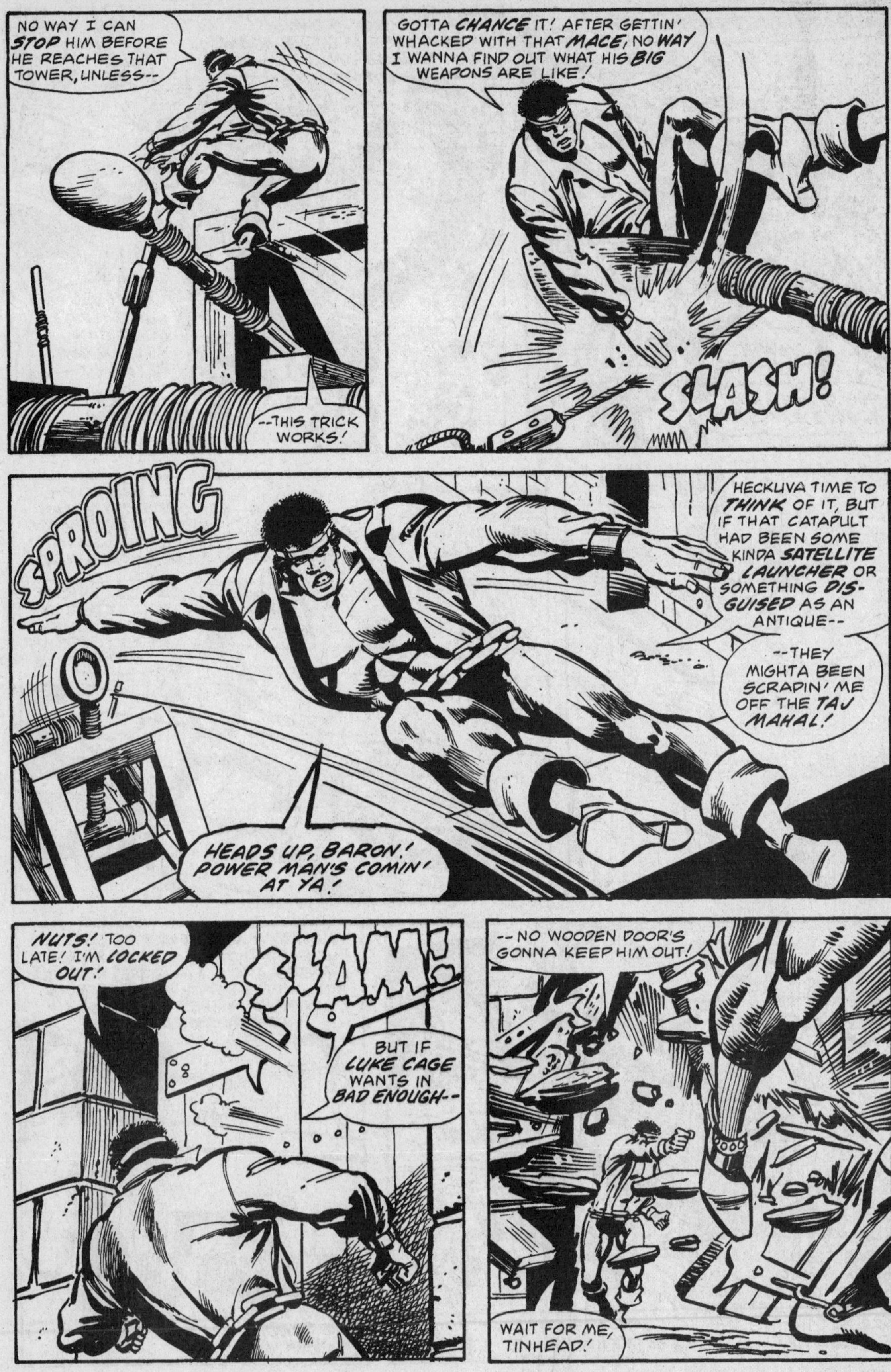
NO WAY I CAN STOP HIM BEFORE HE REACHES THAT TOWER, UNLESS--
--THIS TRICK WORKS!
GOTTA CHANCE IT! AFTER GETTIN' WHACKED WITH THAT MACE, NO WAY I WANNA FIND OUT WHAT HIS BIG WEAPONS ARE LIKE!
SLASH!
SPROING
HECKUVA TIME TO THINK OF IT, BUT IF THAT CATAPULT HAD BEEN SOME KINDA SATELLITE LAUNCHER OR SOMETHING DISGUISED AS AN ANTIQUE--
--THEY MIGHTA BEEN SCRAPIN' ME OFF THE TAJ MAHAL!
HEADS UP, BARON! POWER MAN'S COMIN' AT YA!
NUTS! TOO LATE! I'M LOCKED OUT!
SLAM!
BUT IF LUKE CAGE WANTS IN BAD ENOUGH--
--NO WOODEN DOOR'S GONNA KEEP HIM OUT!
WAIT FOR ME, TINHEAD!

HEY, MAN! CAN'T YOU SEE THE PARTY'S OVER?

NO! I CAN *STILL* REACH MY *CONTROLS.* YOU'LL BE *DEAD* IN *MINUTES,* KNAVE!

I *DOUBT* IT!

YOU I AIN'T SO SURE ABOUT, THOUGH!

AIEE-EE!

OKAY, YOU GOT ANY *LAST WORDS* BEFORE I PEEL THAT TIN SUIT OFFA YOU AND JAM IT DOWN YOUR *THROAT* FOR SENDIN' YOUR GOON *CHEMISTRO* AFTER ME?

I *HAD* TO! I HEARD THAT *BIG BROTHER* WAS PLANNING A *FULL-SCALE WAR* AGAINST MY OPERATION--

--A WAR I COULDN'T HOPE TO WIN!

SO I USED CHEMISTRO TO TRICK YOU INTO ATTACKING *BIG BROTHER,* HOPING YOU'D *ELIMINATE* HIM!

YOU--YOU'RE NOT... *WORKING* FOR BIG BROTHER, ARE YOU? YOU'RE NOT GOING TO TURN ME OVER TO--?!

--BIG BROTHER? NO WAY! I'M A *HERO-FOR-HIRE,* BUT I'M PARTIC'LAR ABOUT MY *CLIENTS!*

S'MATTER OF FACT, BOZO, IF IT MAKES YA *FEEL* BETTER, NOW THAT *YOUR* OPERATION'S KAPUT, I'M GOIN' AFTER *HIS* OUTFIT!

YOU MAY BE *TOO LATE,* CAGE! YOU MAY HAVE ALREADY WASTED TOO MUCH TIME HERE!

I *KNOW* WHAT BIG BROTHER'S PLANNING. FOR YEARS HE'S BEEN LINKING HIS *CONTROL CENTER* TO EVERY *COMPUTER* IN NEW YORK ...EVERY *COMMUNICATIONS* AND *ELECTRICAL SYSTEM!*

"SOON HE'LL BE ABLE TO JAM OR DISRUPT *EVERY ELECTRONIC DEVICE* IN THE CITY, AND CREATE *CHAOS* AT WILL, WRECKING MASS TRANSIT, STARTING *FIRES,* CAUSING *BLACKOUTS--!*"

THEN, HE'S GOING TO MAKE THE CITY ...THE WHOLE *COUNTRY...PAY!*

I WANTED *MONEY* AND *POWER--* TOTAL DOMINATION OF THE UNDERWORLD--BUT BIG BROTHER WANTS *DESTRUCTION!* HE'S GOING TO SQUEEZE NEW YORK TO *DEATH...* AND *ENJOY* THE *PAIN* HE CAUSES!

AND, MILES AWAY...

C.C. REPORTIN' IN, BRO'! THE BARON TOLD *ALL!* CAGE IS ON *OUR* CASE NOW!

HMM! I DIDN'T EXPECT HIM TO *SURVIVE,* BUT... NO MATTER! OPERATIONS WILL BEGIN ON SCHEDULE. HE'S *YOURS,* CAT. *KILL HIM!*

A *PLEASURE,* BABE! CAGE IS AS GOOD AS *WASTED!*

NEXT ISSUE: BIG BROTHER & LUKE CAGE-- IN FINAL BATTLE!

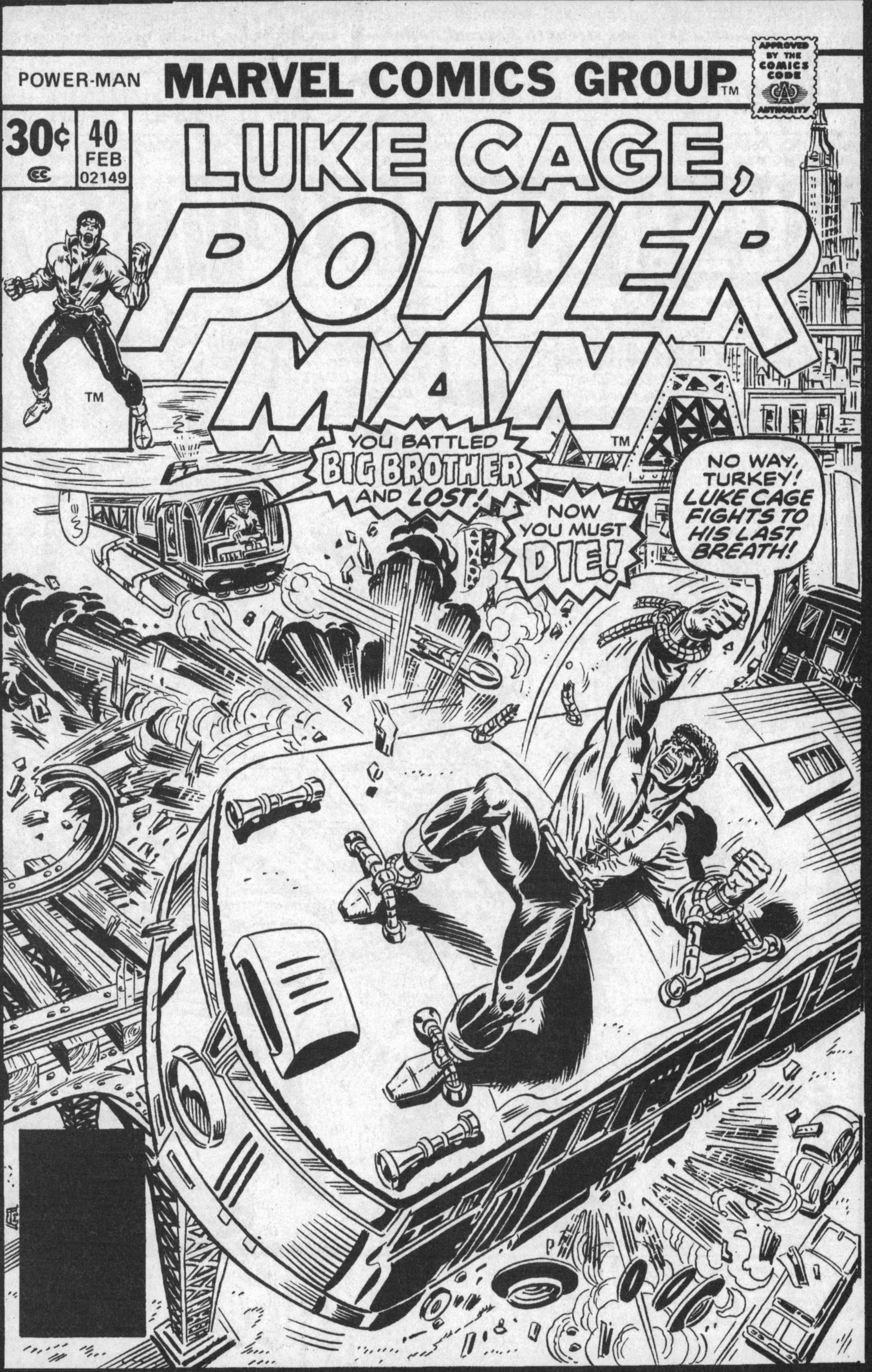
POWER-MAN
MARVEL COMICS GROUP™
APPROVED BY THE COMICS CODE AUTHORITY
30¢
40
FEB
02149
LUKE CAGE, POWER MAN™
YOU BATTLED BIG BROTHER AND LOST!
NOW YOU MUST DIE!
NO WAY, TURKEY! LUKE CAGE FIGHTS TO HIS LAST BREATH!

LUKE CAGE: Wrongly convicted and sentenced to prison—reborn in a freak experiment there that gave him *steel-hard skin* and *strength beyond belief*—a man who hides his identity as an escaped convict in the role of a HERO FOR HIRE!

STAN LEE PRESENTS: LUKE CAGE, POWER MAN!

MARV WOLFMAN WRITER/EDITOR / AND INTRODUCING LEE ELIAS·ARTIST / FRANK GIACOIA EMBELLISHER / DENISE WOHL LETTERER / JANICE COHEN COLORIST

RUSH HOUR to LIMBO!

WHAT HAS GONE BEFORE, DEPT.: LAST ISH, LUKE CAGE LEARNED FROM THE MEDIEVAL-MOTIFFED MOBSTER KNOWN AS THE BARON, THAT BIG BROTHER PLANNED TO BLACKMAIL THE ALREADY FINANCIALLY-TROUBLED CITY OF NEW YORK FOR BILLIONS!

THE THREAT? SHOULD THE CITY REFUSE TO PAY, BIG BROTHER'S COMPUTERS WOULD CREATE ELECTRONIC HAVOC.

GOT THAT? GOOD! NOW IT'S UP TO YOU!

THE GAME'S OVER, BIG BROTHER-- OVER FOR THE BARON, AN' OVER FOR YOU!

'CAUSE LUKE CAGE IS HERE--

--AN' HE'S NOT LEAVIN' WITHOUT YA!

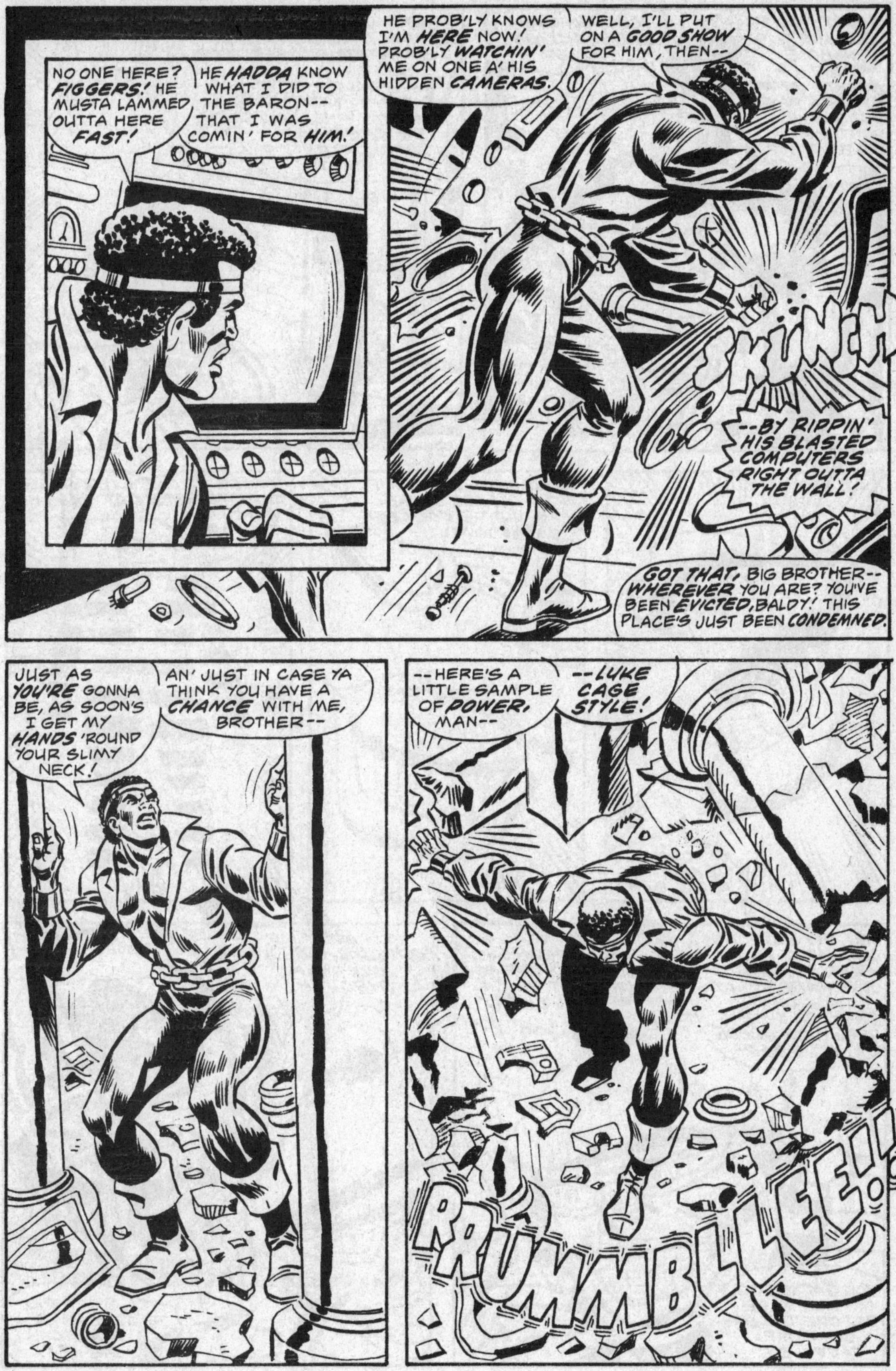
NO ONE HERE? FIGGERS! HE MUSTA LAMMED OUTTA HERE FAST!
HE HADDA KNOW WHAT I DID TO THE BARON-- THAT I WAS COMIN' FOR HIM!
HE PROB'LY KNOWS I'M HERE NOW! PROB'LY WATCHIN' ME ON ONE A' HIS HIDDEN CAMERAS.
WELL, I'LL PUT ON A GOOD SHOW FOR HIM, THEN--
SKUNCH
--BY RIPPIN' HIS BLASTED COMPUTERS RIGHT OUTTA THE WALL!
GOT THAT, BIG BROTHER-- WHEREVER YOU ARE? YOU'VE BEEN EVICTED, BALDY! THIS PLACE'S JUST BEEN CONDEMNED.
JUST AS YOU'RE GONNA BE, AS SOON'S I GET MY HANDS 'ROUND YOUR SLIMY NECK!
AN' JUST IN CASE YA THINK YOU HAVE A CHANCE WITH ME, BROTHER--
--HERE'S A LITTLE SAMPLE OF POWER, MAN--
--LUKE CAGE STYLE!
RRUMMBLLEE!!

SHOOT! SO I WRECKED THIS STINKHOLE WORSE'N A *BOOKIE JOINT* AFTER A RAID. BUT I STILL DON'T HAVE BIG BROTHER.

DON'T HAVE ANY *SATISFACTION*, EITHER.

FACT IS, DON'T HAVE MUCH OF *ANYTHING* THESE DAYS...

...NOT THAT I 'XPECTED A BARREL OF LAUGHS WHEN I *STARTED* MY "HERO-FOR-HIRE-GIG."

DIDN'T 'XPECT *NOTHIN'* THEN, AN' I'M *CERTAINLY* GETTIN' *PLENTY* OF THAT NOW!

DAMN!

BYE-BYE, CAGE...

COOL *EYEIN'* YA AGAIN, BABY.

'COURSE YA *COULDN'T* LAY A GLANCE ON ME, MAN. NOT THE *COOLEST* CAT IN TOWN.

'CAUSE *NO ONE* EVER SEES THE *CHESHIRE CAT* 'LESS HE WANTS 'EM TO, BABY.

HEY, BIG BRO--CAGE JUST SPLIT AND *FAST*, MAN. AND I JUST *HATE* TO LAY IT THICK ON YA, BABY, BUT HE IS DEFINITELY *DEEEE-STURBED!*

WE CAN *LIVE* WITH CAGE'S TEMPERMENT, CAT. JUST BE SURE TO *FOLLOW* HIM. I WANT A REPORT ON HIS *EVERY* MOVE.

YOU *GOT* IT, BRO. ANYTHIN' ELSE BEFORE THE *BIG* SIGN-OFF, DADDY-O?!

YOU HAVE YOUR *ORDERS*, CAT. JUST *SEE* THEM *THROUGH!*

I CAN DIG IT, MAN, I *SURE* CAN DIG IT!

TIME TO *BLOW* THIS GIG...

...TAG ALONG WITH THE *WILD ONE.*

AND, BROTHER, THAT MEANS IT'S *TEN-FOUR,* BABY--

--OVER AND *OH-YOU-TEE*...OUT!

TA TA!

NOT SURE IF I GOT IT ALL *STRAIGHT.* JUST BEEN *TOO MUCH* COMIN' DOWN LATELY.

HAVEN'T BEEN ABLE TO *THINK* IT ALL THROUGH.

ONLY I'M *SURE* IT BEGAN WITH THAT *CHEMISTRO* CREEP SAYIN' HE WORKED FOR BIG BROTHER-- WHILE HE WAS *REALLY* THE *BARON'S* HIT-MAN.

BIG BROTHER *TIPPED* ME OFF TO THAT *HIMSELF!*

THROUGH CHEMISTRO I FOUND THE BARON, AND *HE* TOLD ME 'BOUT THE *GAMES* BIG BROTHER WAS PLAYING!

WHICH *STILL* LEAVES ME NOWHERE--

--'CAUSE NOW *BB* BLEW OUT!

BUT I'VE *STILL* GOTTA FIND HIM.

JUST TO PROVE *NO ONE* MAKES A SUCKER OUT OF LUKE CAGE.

NO ONE!

HIGH ABOVE, *HELICOPTER BLADES* RAPIDLY BEAT. CAGE IGNORES THE SOUND TO CONCENTRATE ON HIS OWN THINKING...

UNFORTUNATELY, THAT IS A MISTAKE.

THE CHESHIRE CAT WAS *CORRECT* IN HIS ANALYSIS.

FROM HIS GAIT, CAGE IS *QUITE* ANGRY. AND *THAT* CAN ONLY BENEFIT *ME.*

CAGE IS A *STREET FIGHTER* WHO THINKS WITH HIS FISTS RATHER THAN HIS HEAD. ENRAGED, HE IS NOT LIKELY TO REASON *ANYTHING* OUT.

WHICH WILL MAKE *MY* PLANS, AND *HIS* DESTRUCTION, ALL THE MORE FEASIBLE, AND ALL ACCORDING TO *MY PROJECTED SCHEDULE!*

CAGE IS THE *ONLY* ONE WHO KNOWS MY PLANS. SOON HE'LL BE *DEAD...* THEN NEW YORK WILL *MEET* MY DEMANDS--OR I'LL *SHUT OFF ALL THEIR ELECTRICITY.*

PROPER REPROGRAMMING OF THEIR COMPUTER TAPES BY *MY* CENTRAL COMPUTER WILL CAUSE RAILWAY LINKINGS TO MALFUNCTION. THERE WILL BE *ENDLESS* MASS-TRANSIT ACCIDENTS. STREETLIGHTS WILL *CEASE* TO FUNCTION.

IN OFFICE BUILDINGS, *ELEVATORS* WILL *HALT* BETWEEN FLOORS. *BURGLAR ALARMS* WILL BE USELESS. AIR-TRAFFIC COMPUTERS GIVE INCORRECT CO-ORDINATES.

CHAOS WILL REIGN!

SOON, *FURTHER* MADNESS WILL ENSUE, AS THE STOCK MARKET *TICKER-TAPE* FEED OFF *INCORRECT* INFORMATION--SUPPLIED *BY ME!*

THE GOVERNMENT WILL BE *FORCED* TO INTERVENE, ESPECIALLY AFTER I THREATEN TO DO THE SAME TO THE *ENTIRE* COUNTRY.

THEY'LL PAY ME MY *BILLION* DOLLARS, OR I'LL SEIZE CONTROL OF THEIR *TACTICAL NUCLEAR NETWORK!*

NOTHIN' TO DO *HERE,* BETTER GET BACK TO CLAIRE... SEE IF I CAN *PATCH UP* THE MESS I LEFT BY WALKIN' OUT ON HER.

HEY, TAXI!!

HUNH!? PASSED ME *BY?*

ANOTHER ONE?

WHAT'S *GOIN' ON?* THERE A CON-SPIRACY AGAINST ME?

WELL, IF THAT'S SO, THE PLOT ENDS *NOW!*

HOLD ON THERE, BUDDY!

YOU'RE PICKIN' ME UP AS OF *NOW!*

BUT I'M ALREADY ON A RADIO *CALL!*

'LESS YOU WANT THAT *SQUAWK BOX STUFFED* SIDEWAYS, YOU GOT *NOTHIN'* BETTER TO DO THAN TAKE ME *DOWNTOWN--QUICK!*

GOT THAT?

I GOT IT, BUT I DON'T HAVE TO *LIKE* IT, MISTER.

FOR THE *MONEY* YOU GET--YOU DON'T HAVE TO LIKE *NOTHIN'!*

GET SET, CAGE--

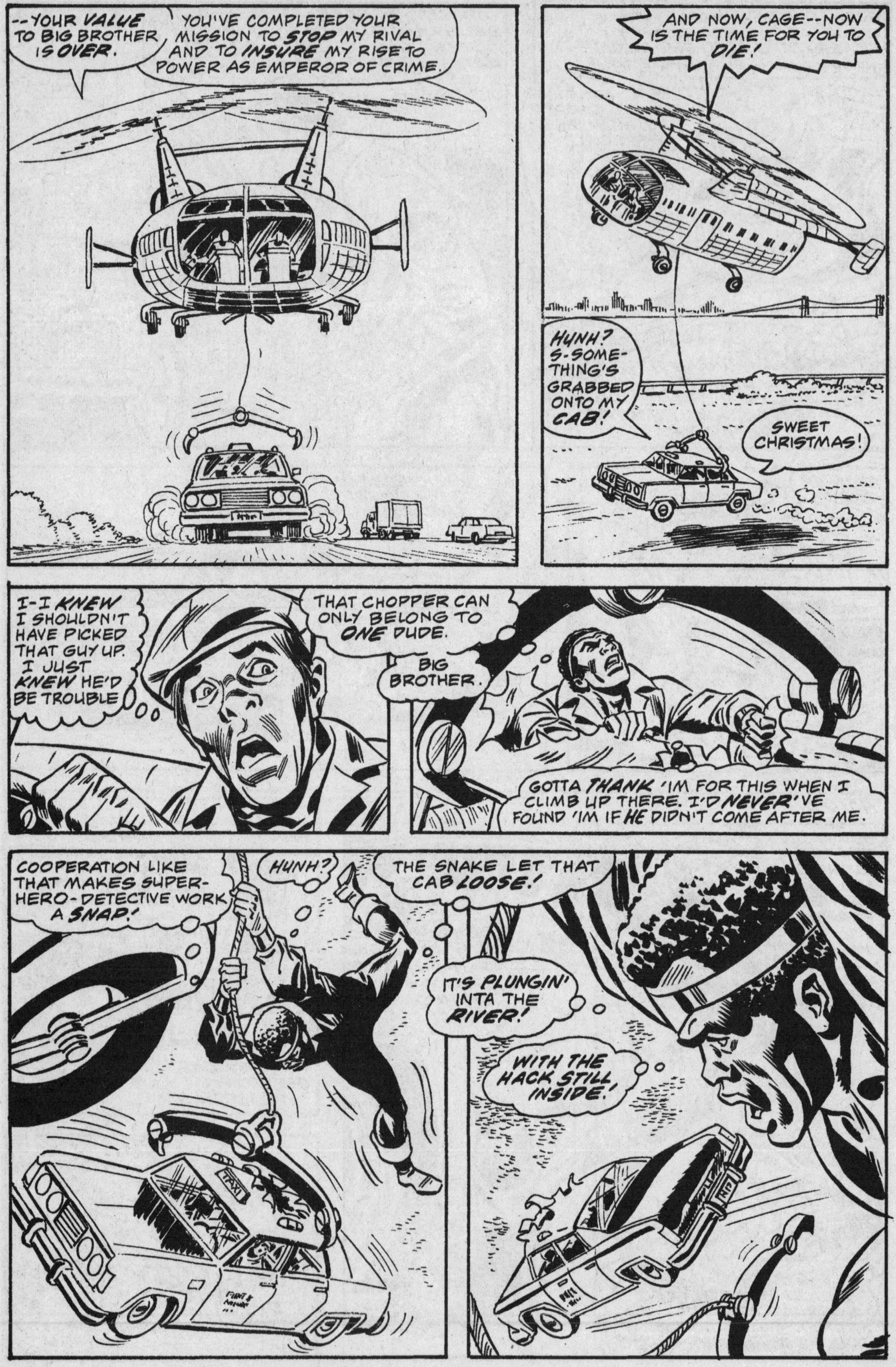
--YOUR VALUE TO BIG BROTHER IS OVER.
YOU'VE COMPLETED YOUR MISSION TO STOP MY RIVAL AND TO INSURE MY RISE TO POWER AS EMPEROR OF CRIME.
AND NOW, CAGE--NOW IS THE TIME FOR YOU TO DIE!
HUNH? S-SOMETHING'S GRABBED ONTO MY CAB!
SWEET CHRISTMAS!
I-I KNEW I SHOULDN'T HAVE PICKED THAT GUY UP. I JUST KNEW HE'D BE TROUBLE
THAT CHOPPER CAN ONLY BELONG TO ONE DUDE.
BIG BROTHER.
GOTTA THANK 'IM FOR THIS WHEN I CLIMB UP THERE. I'D NEVER 'VE FOUND 'IM IF HE DIDN'T COME AFTER ME.
COOPERATION LIKE THAT MAKES SUPER-HERO-DETECTIVE WORK A SNAP!
HUNH?
THE SNAKE LET THAT CAB LOOSE!
IT'S PLUNGIN' INTA THE RIVER!
WITH THE HACK STILL INSIDE!

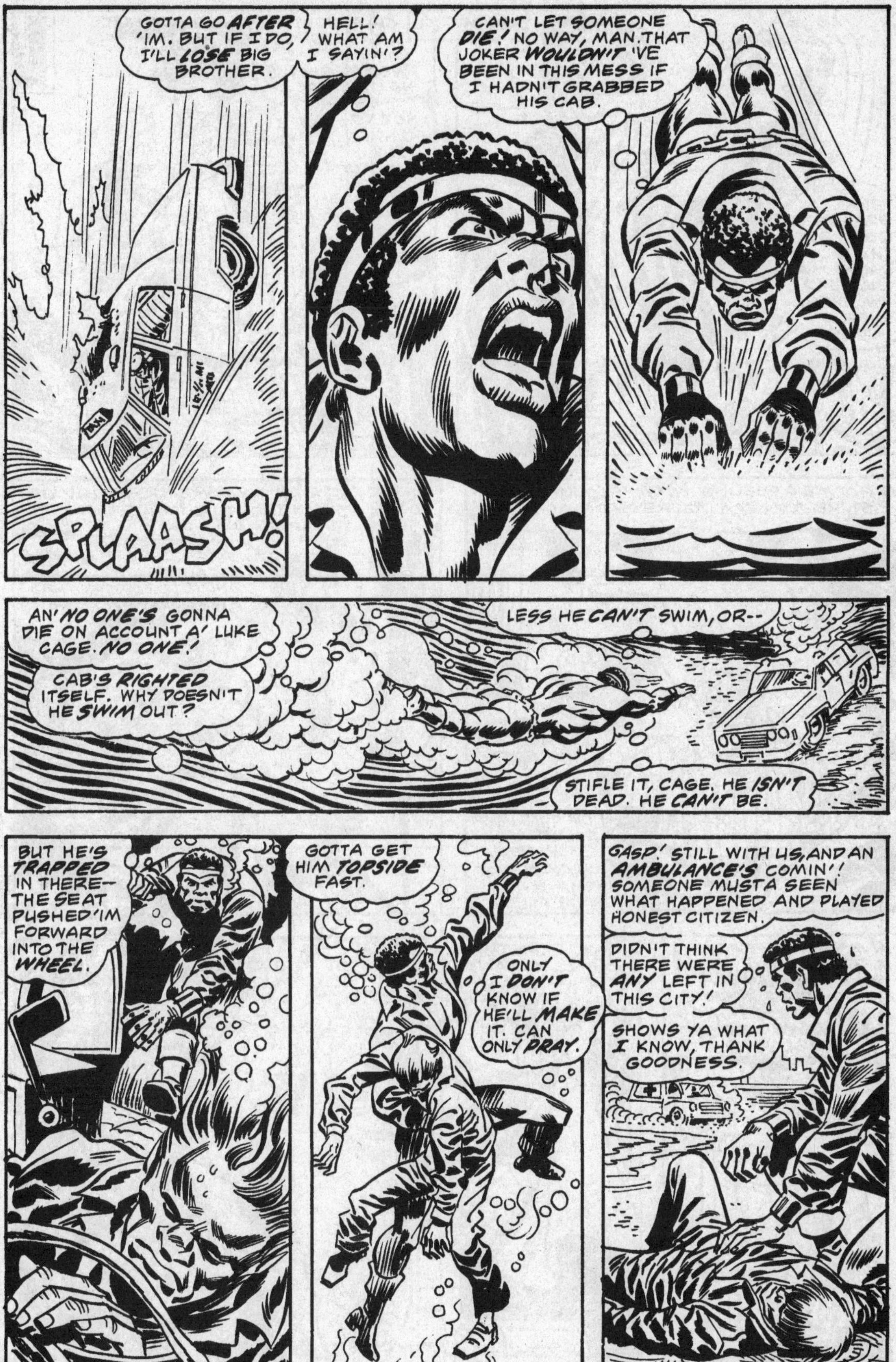
GOTTA GO AFTER 'IM. BUT IF I DO, I'LL LOSE BIG BROTHER.
HELL! WHAT AM I SAYIN'?
CAN'T LET SOMEONE DIE! NO WAY, MAN. THAT JOKER WOULDN'T 'VE BEEN IN THIS MESS IF I HADN'T GRABBED HIS CAB.
SPLAASH!
AN' NO ONE'S GONNA DIE ON ACCOUNT A' LUKE CAGE. NO ONE!
CAB'S RIGHTED ITSELF. WHY DOESN'T HE SWIM OUT?
LESS HE CAN'T SWIM, OR--
STIFLE IT, CAGE. HE ISN'T DEAD. HE CAN'T BE.
BUT HE'S TRAPPED IN THERE-- THE SEAT PUSHED 'IM FORWARD INTO THE WHEEL.
GOTTA GET HIM TOPSIDE FAST.
ONLY I DON'T KNOW IF HE'LL MAKE IT. CAN ONLY PRAY.
GASP! STILL WITH US, AND AN AMBULANCE'S COMIN'! SOMEONE MUSTA SEEN WHAT HAPPENED AND PLAYED HONEST CITIZEN.
DIDN'T THINK THERE WERE ANY LEFT IN THIS CITY!
SHOWS YA WHAT I KNOW, THANK GOODNESS.

BIG BROTHER'S GONE, BUT THAT'S OKAY, 'CAUSE MAN, I'LL *FIND* HIM WHEREEVER HE HIDES.

LUKE CAGE *SWEARS* TO THAT!

SHORTLY... CALM DOWN, LUCAS. YOU'LL WAKE UP THE *PATIENTS* IN THE NEXT WARD.

NOT TO MENTION ONE SLIGHTLY OVER-THE-HILL STOREFRONT MEDIC HERE.

I GOT ME A FEELING *NOTHIN'* COULD EVER DISTURB YOU NOAH. YOU'RE MADE A' *IRON!*

AND I'M FEELING A BIT *RUSTY* RIGHT NOW, LUCAS, ITCHING TO GET OUT OF THIS HOSPITAL BED AND BACK *HOME.* MY *WOUNDS* HAVE ALL HEALED!

AND, *YOU, CLAIRE.* YOUR WOUNDS HEALED, OR DO YOU *STILL* HATE ME FOR WALKIN' OUT ON YA THE OTHER NIGHT?

YOU GET A LITTLE *MORE* AFFECTIONATE, LUKE-- AND I'LL FORGET THAT OTHER DAY *EVER* EVEN EXISTED!

A MOMENTS PEACE AFTER A LONG, HECTIC NIGHT. *CHERISH* THAT OH-SO-BRIEF RESPITE, LUKE--'CAUSE THINGS ARE CHANGING RIGHT NOW!

LUKE-- BEHIND YOU!

CHRISTMAS! A *GAS CANNISTER.!!*

GOTTA BE...*CHOKE*... BIG BROTHER...*ONLY SKUNK* WHO'D...*CHOKE*...ATTACK ME ...IN THE HOSPITAL...*CHOKE*--

CLAIRE-- COUGH--GET NOAH...NOAH OUTTA HERE...HURRY...COUGH ...HU...

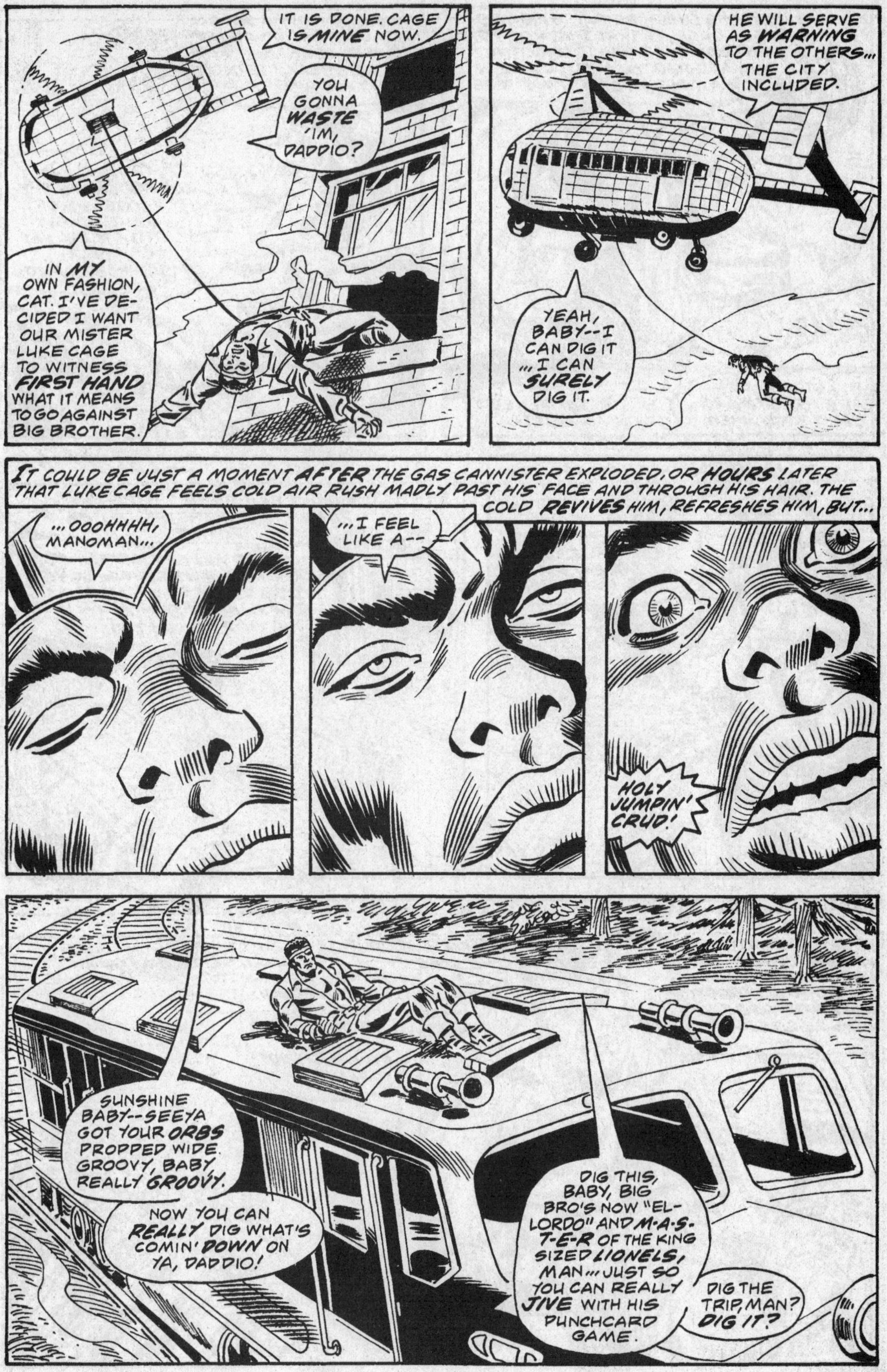
IT IS DONE. CAGE IS MINE NOW.
YOU GONNA WASTE 'IM, DADDIO?
IN MY OWN FASHION, CAT. I'VE DECIDED I WANT OUR MISTER LUKE CAGE TO WITNESS FIRST HAND WHAT IT MEANS TO GO AGAINST BIG BROTHER.
HE WILL SERVE AS WARNING TO THE OTHERS... THE CITY INCLUDED.
YEAH, BABY--I CAN DIG IT ...I CAN SURELY DIG IT.
IT COULD BE JUST A MOMENT AFTER THE GAS CANNISTER EXPLODED, OR HOURS LATER THAT LUKE CAGE FEELS COLD AIR RUSH MADLY PAST HIS FACE AND THROUGH HIS HAIR. THE COLD REVIVES HIM, REFRESHES HIM, BUT...
...OOOHHHH, MANOMAN...
...I FEEL LIKE A--
HOLY JUMPIN' CRUD!
SUNSHINE BABY--SEEYA GOT YOUR ORBS PROPPED WIDE. GROOVY, BABY, REALLY GROOVY.
NOW YOU CAN REALLY DIG WHAT'S COMIN' DOWN ON YA, DADDIO!
DIG THIS, BABY, BIG BRO'S NOW "EL LORDO" AND M-A-S-T-E-R OF THE KING SIZED LIONELS, MAN... JUST SO YOU CAN REALLY JIVE WITH HIS PUNCHCARD GAME.
DIG THE TRIP, MAN? DIG IT?

WHAT THE CHESHIRE CAT IS *TRYING* TO SAY, CAGE, IS THAT I'VE NOW *TOTAL CONTROL* OVER THIS LOCOMOTIVE YOU ARE TIED TO, AND YOU ARE IN FOR A MOST *INTERESTING* RIDE.

THIS IS SIMPLY A *SMALL* DEMONSTRATION OF MY POWER, CAGE. AND EVEN AS WE SPEAK, THE CITY OFFICIALS ARE --

--HELPLESSLY *WATCHING* THE PROGRESS OF YOUR *LONELY LITTLE RUNAWAY* ON THEIR SCANNER BOARDS.

BLASTED ROPES ARE *TOO STRONG*... CAN'T BREAK 'EM.

BUT I *GOTTA* KEEP TRYIN'! I GOTTA!

THEY NOW REALIZE THEY CANNOT *RESUME* CONTROL OVER THEIR OWN SYSTEM. PERHAPS THEY FINALLY REALIZE MY *THREATS* ARE QUITE, QUITE, *REAL*.

YOU'RE *NUTS*, CREEP. YOU KNOW THAT?

NOT SO, CAGE. I AM *CRAFTY*. THERE IS A *DIFFERENCE*. I UNDERSTAND HOW MUCH I CAN *PUSH* THE PEOPLE IN POWER. I UNDERSTAND MY *OWN* POWER.

AFTER ALL, I AM THE ONE WHO IS FREE, WHILE *YOU* ARE TIED WITH *UNBREAKABLE BONDS* TO THAT *OLD* RAILWAY CAR

A CAR I'VE *REROUTED* ONTO AN OLD AND PARTIALLY *DEMOLISHED* SECTION OF TRACK THE CITY FORSOOK *YEARS* AGO.

AND CAGE, AS YOU APPROACH THE BREAK, I'LL BUILD UP THE *SPEED* OF YOUR VEHICLE --

--UNTIL YOU FIND YOURSELF HELPLESSLY *SOARING OFF* A ONE HUNDRED FOOT CLIFF!

KEEP JABBERIN', CREEP, 'CAUSE YOU JUST GAVE ME MY *TICKET* OUTTA HERE. YOU SAID THESE METAL *BONDS* ARE UN-BREAKABLE--

--BUT YOU SAID *NOTHIN'* 'BOUT THIS TINKERTOY REJECT OF A RAILWAY CAR I'M STRAPPED TO.

YEAH ... IT'S *WORKIN'* ! I CAN *RIP* THE METAL WITH MY HANDS, BUT IT'S CUTTIN' TOO BLASTED *SLOW*!

YOU HAVE THIRTY FIVE SECONDS, CAGE ... ONE HALF A MINUTE BEFORE YOU *PLUNGE* TO YOUR DOOM!

KEEP COUNTIN', BALDY--SO YOU'LL KNOW 'XACTLY WHEN I COME AT YA WITH MY *HANDS* 'ROUND YOUR STINKIN' THROAT!

TWENTY SECONDS, CAGE. ARE YOU *SWEATIN'*, YET?

HANDS 'RE TAKIN' TOO *LONG*. GOTTA *KICK* MY WAY IN. GOT MORE *LEVER-AGE* USIN' MY FEET.

C'MON, YOU BLASTED MOTHER-LOVIN' SARDINE CAN-- *SPLIT WIDE* !

DID IT! BROKE THROUGH!

BUT I'M *NOT* OUTTA HOT WATER, YET.

STILL A LITTLE MATTER OF GETTIN' *OFFA* THIS TIN WHISTLE.

UNNY, I GOT INTO THIS HERO-FOR-HIRE RACKET FOR THE *MONEY*--

--NOW MAYBE I'M GONNA *DIE* WITHOUT EVEN A *CLIENT* TO FOOT THE FUNERAL EXPENSES.

FIGURES. PROBABLY EXPLAINS WHY I'VE ALWAYS COME UP THE *LOSER* IN LIFE--

I OUGHTTA JUST *SHUCK* --HEY!

TRACK'S COMIN' TO AN *END*!

BETTER *BLOW* THIS PRESSURE COOKER 'FORE IT BLOWS ME-- SEVEN WAYS TO SUNDAY!

WHICH MEANS 'LESS I'M *AWFUL* LUCKY, I'M *DEAD*! AND *THAT* REALLY CHEERS ME UP.

I HAVEN'T HAD ANY LUCK SINCE I FOUND THAT STORE WHERE I BUY ALL THESE CHEAP *YELLOW* SHIRTS I RIP TO SHREDS ALLA TIME.

C'MON, LUCAS, YOU UGLY MONKEY-- *JUMP*!

JEEZ! ANOTHER HALF-SECOND AND THAT'D BE ME PUSHIN' UP THE DAISIES DOWN THERE.

MAYBE THE LUCK'S CHANGIN', LUCAS. MAYBE I WON'T ALWAYS BE A LOSER.

SKARAK

AN' MAYBE THE SUN'LL SHINE GREEN IN JULY.

THIS MUSCLE-BOUND LIL BROTHER'S LUCK IS DEFINITELY A DOWNER.

HELL, I CAN'T CLEAR THE RECORD OF MY PRISON CONVICTION 'CAUSE THE ONLY ONES WHO KNOW I WAS INNOCENT ARE SIX-FEET UNDER...

...AND NOW THE FEDS ARE AFTER ME 'CAUSE A' MY TAXES.

KEEP QUIET NOW, CAGE--TIME FOR A LITTLE ACTION 'TWEEN THE SOAP-OPERA LIFE YOU LEAD, BIG BROTHER'S CHOPPER'S DESCENDING.... INSPECTIN' THE TRAIN WRECKAGE FOR MY BOD.

SOON'S THEY START CHECKIN' ME OUT CAREFULLY THEY'LL KNOW THERE REALLY AIN'T NO SUCH PERSON AS LUKE CAGE.

MAYBE I CAN DODGE THE HICKS DOWN SOUTH, BUT I'M IN NO LEAGUE TO PLAY GAMES WITH UNC'E SAM'S WATCHDOGS.

GUESS IT'S THE PERFECT TIME TO SPRING A LITTLE SURPRISE ON THE COMPUTER-IZED CREEP--

--NAMELY A CERTAIN THREE-HUNDRED POUND JIVIN' GHOST NAMED GUESS-WHO?

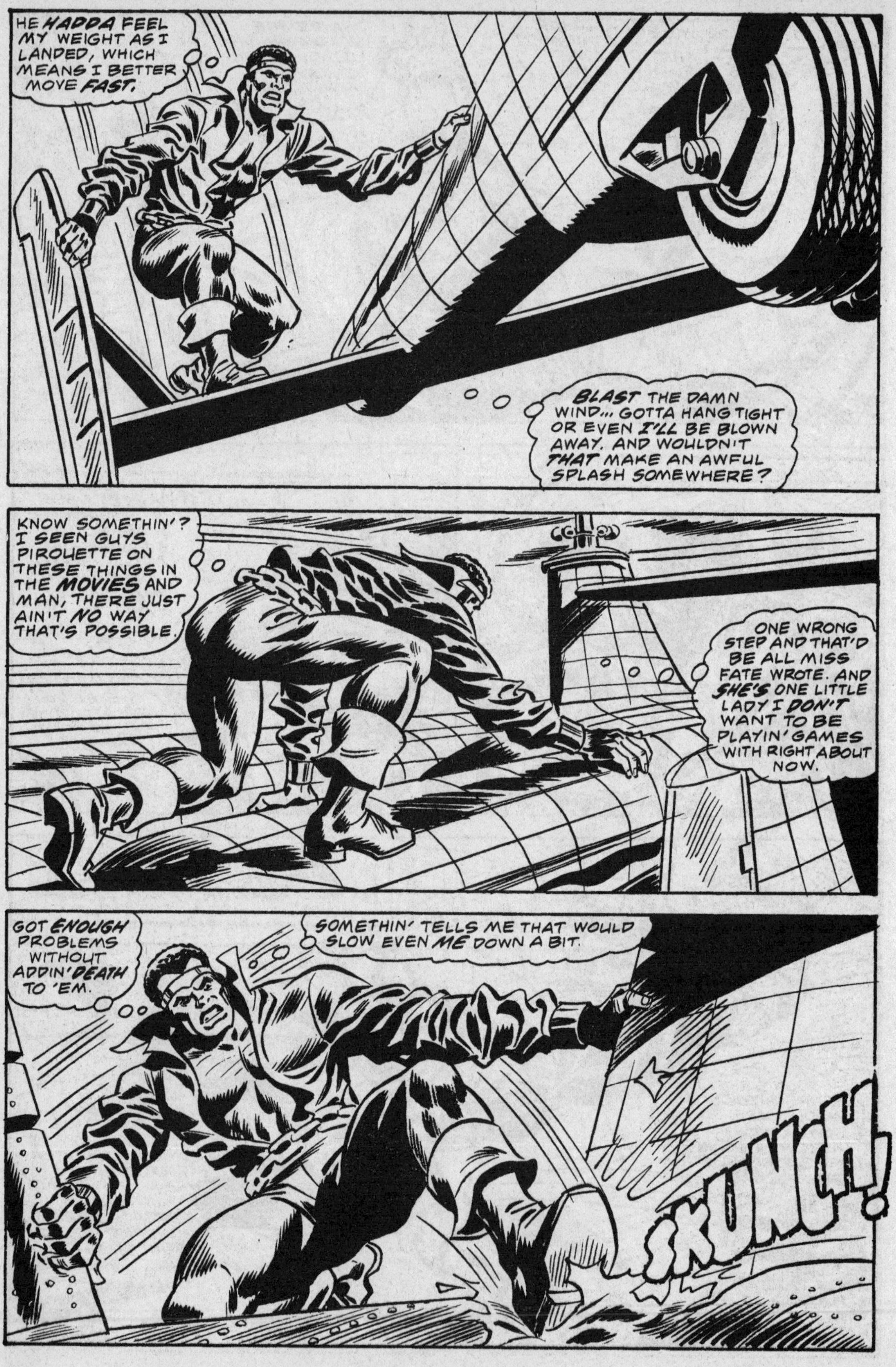
HE HADDA FEEL MY WEIGHT AS I LANDED, WHICH MEANS I BETTER MOVE FAST.
BLAST THE DAMN WIND... GOTTA HANG TIGHT OR EVEN I'LL BE BLOWN AWAY. AND WOULDN'T THAT MAKE AN AWFUL SPLASH SOMEWHERE?
KNOW SOMETHIN'? I SEEN GUYS PIROUETTE ON THESE THINGS IN THE MOVIES AND MAN, THERE JUST AIN'T NO WAY THAT'S POSSIBLE.
ONE WRONG STEP AND THAT'D BE ALL MISS FATE WROTE. AND SHE'S ONE LITTLE LADY I DON'T WANT TO BE PLAYIN' GAMES WITH RIGHT ABOUT NOW.
GOT ENOUGH PROBLEMS WITHOUT ADDIN' DEATH TO 'EM.
SOMETHIN' TELLS ME THAT WOULD SLOW EVEN ME DOWN A BIT.
SKUNCH!

LOOKIN' FOR ME, BROTHER? *CAGE?!* IT'S OBVIOUS YOU *SURVIVED* MY TRAP

RIGHT ON, BRIGHT BOY. SURVIVED AN' COMIN' RIGHT FOR YA!

SWAK

YOU'LL HAVE TO TRY *HARDER*, CAGE. I'M NOT *ONLY* A MASTER OF COMPUTERS --

-- BUT OF *PHYSICAL* COMBAT AS WELL!

SPOK

MAYBE SO, BALDY, BUT *YOU* DON'T HAVE LUKE CAGE'S *HATE BACKIN'* YOU UP, BABY.

SPOK

AN', MAN-- THAT COUNTS FOR SOMETHIN' *BAD!*

HEY DADDIO, THIS GIG IS GOIN' DOWN, DOWN DOWN.

NOT SO, CAT. I *ALLOWED* CAGE TO ATTACK FIRST BECAUSE I INSTANTLY COMPUTED THAT HE'D NOW BE IN THE *CORRECT* AREA FOR ME TO DO *THIS.*

POW

RIGHT ON, BRO-- *RIGHT ON!*

NEXT: THUNDERBOLT and GOLDBUG!!

POWER-MAN

MARVEL® COMICS GROUP

APPROVED BY THE COMICS CODE AUTHORITY

30¢ 41 MAR 02149

LUKE CAGE, POWER MAN

TM

IF THE **GOLDBUG** DOESN'T DESTROY YOU, CAGE—

—THEN **THUNDERBOLT** WILL!

SHOCKS! ACTION! DANGER! ALL IN THE MIGHTY MARVEL MANNER!

ERNIE CHAN 1976

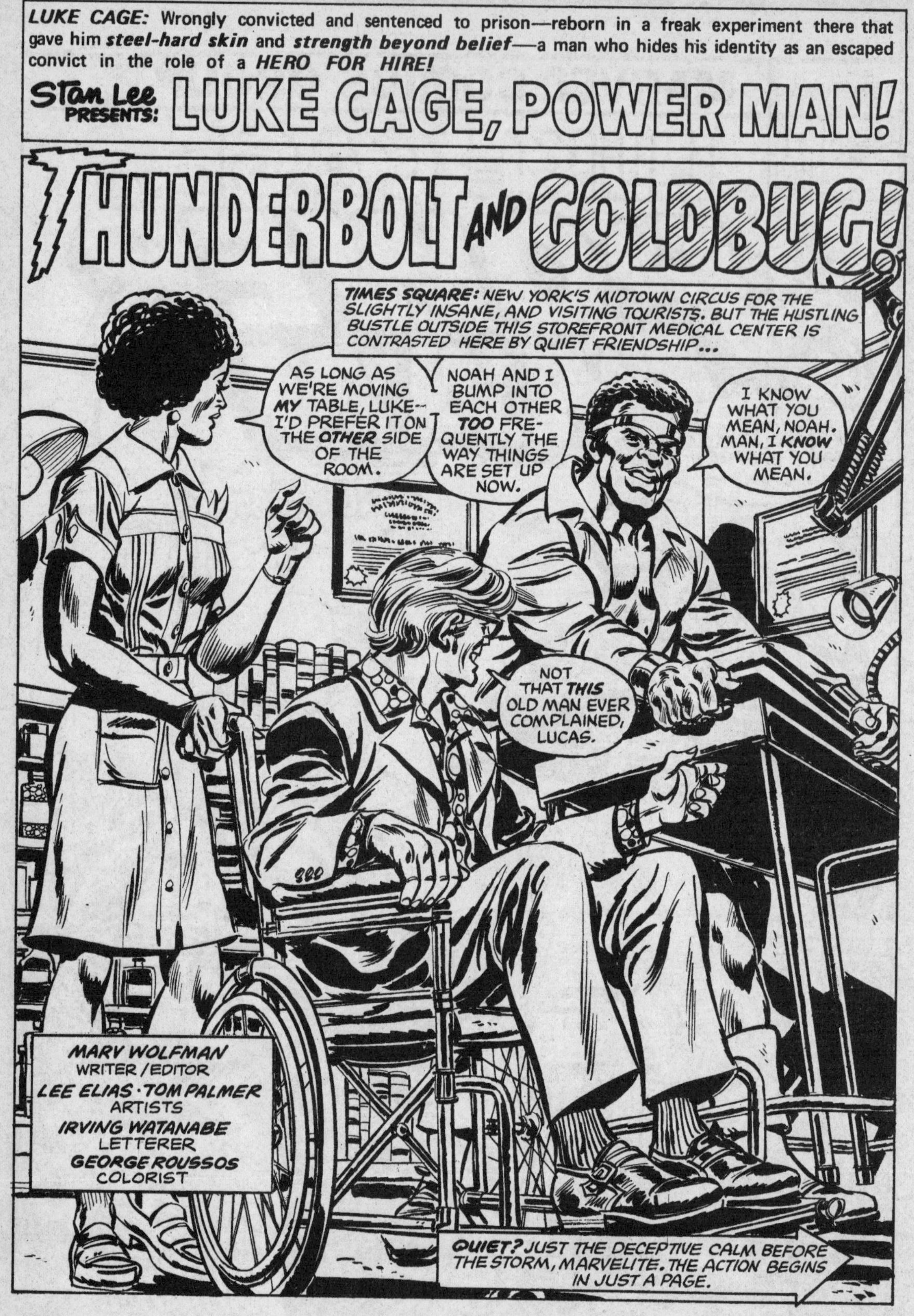
LUKE CAGE: Wrongly convicted and sentenced to prison—reborn in a freak experiment there that gave him steel-hard skin and strength beyond belief—a man who hides his identity as an escaped convict in the role of a HERO FOR HIRE!
STAN LEE PRESENTS: LUKE CAGE, POWER MAN!
THUNDERBOLT AND GOLDBUG!
TIMES SQUARE: NEW YORK'S MIDTOWN CIRCUS FOR THE SLIGHTLY INSANE, AND VISITING TOURISTS. BUT THE HUSTLING BUSTLE OUTSIDE THIS STOREFRONT MEDICAL CENTER IS CONTRASTED HERE BY QUIET FRIENDSHIP...
AS LONG AS WE'RE MOVING MY TABLE, LUKE-- I'D PREFER IT ON THE OTHER SIDE OF THE ROOM.
NOAH AND I BUMP INTO EACH OTHER TOO FRE-QUENTLY THE WAY THINGS ARE SET UP NOW.
I KNOW WHAT YOU MEAN, NOAH. MAN, I KNOW WHAT YOU MEAN.
NOT THAT THIS OLD MAN EVER COMPLAINED, LUCAS.
MARV WOLFMAN WRITER / EDITOR
LEE ELIAS · TOM PALMER ARTISTS
IRVING WATANABE LETTERER
GEORGE ROUSSOS COLORIST
QUIET? JUST THE DECEPTIVE CALM BEFORE THE STORM, MARVELITE. THE ACTION BEGINS IN JUST A PAGE.

SOMETHIN' TELLS ME THINGS ARE FINALLY *SETTLIN'* DOWN, CLAIRE.

NO PRESSIN' JOBS FOR THIS HERO-FOR-HIRE, AND NOAH'S BACK FROM THE *HOSPITAL.*

SEEMS LIKE WE'RE JUST ONE BIG *HAPPY* FAMILY.

LUKE--?

HUH?

SO *YOU'RE* IN MY DREAM, TOO, D.W.?

NEVER MIND, D.W.--WHAT'S UP?

SOMEONE *PINCH* ME. THIS'S *GOT* TO BE A DREAM. 'CAUSE MAN, *ANY* CALM IN MY LIFE *CAN'T* BE REAL.

CURTIS CARR DID A NEAT JOB FIXIN' UP YOUR *OFFICE,* LUKE. UNCLE MAX EVEN DECIDED NOT TO CHARGE YOU FOR THE *DAMAGES*...THIS TIME.

AS LONG AS YOU'VE GOT THIS SILVER LINING FLOATING OVER YOU, HOW ABOUT YOU AND CLAIRE LEAVING ME *ALONE* FOR AWHILE.

I WANT TO GET *RE-ACQUAINTED* WITH MY OFFICE BEFORE I OPEN UP AGAIN.

CRAFTY OLD FOX. HE *KNEW* WE'VE BEEN WAITING TO BE ALONE.

JUST WHAT THE DOCTOR ORDERED.

WHICH WILL PROBABLY PUT A *DAMPER* ON THIS PERFECT DAY, 'CAUSE CLAIRE--I KNOW YOU'VE BEEN *ANGRY* AT ME FOR RUNNIN' OUT ON YOU LATELY.

BUT I'M NOT ABOUT TO *GIVE UP* BEIN' WHAT I AM.

A BRAWLING *STREET-FIGHTER?* A HOT-TEMPERED BATTLER WHO FLIES OFF-THE-HANDLE AND USES *VIOLENCE* TO SOLVE EVERYTHING?

I'VE DONE A LOT OF *THINKING* LATELY, LUKE. I KNOW WHAT YOU ARE, I ACCEPT YOUR *JOB* AND YOUR *BIZARRE* POWERS--

--BUT, LUKE, LATELY YOU'VE BEEN LIVING LIKE YOUR *FISTS* CAN SOLVE EVERYTHING.

AND I DON'T *LIKE* IT, LUKE. NOT ONE BIT. BECAUSE SOMETIMES YOU ACTUALLY *FRIGHTEN* ME.

CLAIRE, I THINK YOU AN' ME'S GOT SOME *TALKIN'* TO DO. C'MON.

LET'S MOVE TO THE SOUTH AND WEST OF TIMES SQUARE, TO THE *DOCKS* LESS THAN TEN BLOCKS AWAY...

C'MON, WE HAVEN'T GOT ALL DAY.

YOUR FAULT, WILLIAMS. YOU SHOULDA *KILLED* THAT GUARD BEFORE HE SET OFF THE ALARM!

LOOK, HOW'D I KNOW HE'D-- EH, THAT *SOUND?*

I--IT CAN'T BE THE *COPS.*

DON'T WORRY-- LISTEN, IT'S ONLY THE WIND.

BARROOM!

WRONG!

PIER 54

IT'S A GUY!

WIND, MY FEDORA!

JUST NOT *ANY* "GUY," PUNKS.

CRACK

I--I DON'T BELIEVE IT! HE'S *OUTRUNNIN'* MY BULLETS!

A *SIMPLE* ENOUGH TASK, VERMIN--

--FOR THE MAN CALLED *THUNDERBOLT!*

TH-THUNDERBOLT?! I--I *HEARD* OF HIM!

K-POW!

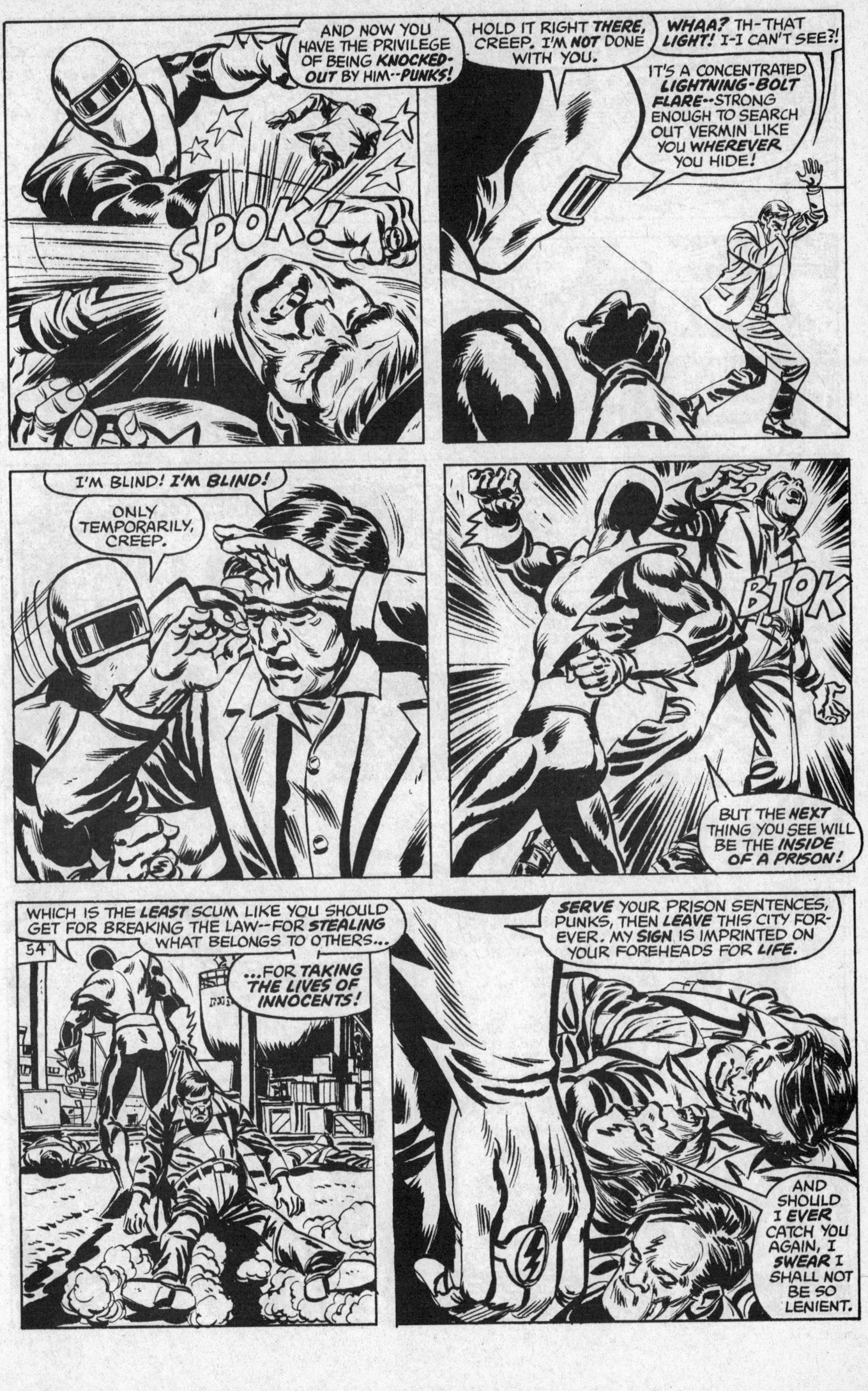

AND NOW YOU HAVE THE PRIVILEGE OF BEING KNOCKED-OUT BY HIM--PUNKS!
SPOK!
HOLD IT RIGHT THERE, CREEP. I'M NOT DONE WITH YOU.
WHAA? TH-THAT LIGHT! I-I CAN'T SEE?!
IT'S A CONCENTRATED LIGHTNING-BOLT FLARE--STRONG ENOUGH TO SEARCH OUT VERMIN LIKE YOU WHEREVER YOU HIDE!
I'M BLIND! I'M BLIND!
ONLY TEMPORARILY, CREEP.
BTOK
BUT THE NEXT THING YOU SEE WILL BE THE INSIDE OF A PRISON!
WHICH IS THE LEAST SCUM LIKE YOU SHOULD GET FOR BREAKING THE LAW--FOR STEALING WHAT BELONGS TO OTHERS...
...FOR TAKING THE LIVES OF INNOCENTS!
SERVE YOUR PRISON SENTENCES, PUNKS, THEN LEAVE THIS CITY FOREVER. MY SIGN IS IMPRINTED ON YOUR FOREHEADS FOR LIFE.
AND SHOULD I EVER CATCH YOU AGAIN, I SWEAR I SHALL NOT BE SO LENIENT.

THE *POLICE!* THEY FINALLY RESPONDED TO MY *CALL.* WHICH MEANS IT'S TIME FOR ME TO *LEAVE!*

BARROOM

LOOK AT THAT *LIGHTNING TATTOO.* THUNDERBOLT'S STRUCK *AGAIN!*

WHO IS HE? WHAT'S HIS *GAME?*

I WISH I KNEW, STANLEY. IT'S HARD ENOUGH FIGURING OUT IF HE'S ON *OUR* SIDE--OR IF HE'S JUST PLANNING SOME CRIMINAL CAPER OF HIS *OWN!*

C'MON! LET'S GET THESE PUNKS DOWNTOWN. I WANT TO GET OUT OF HERE *FAST!*

WHILE, IN QUEENS... RESTHAVEN CEMETERY

ANOTHER GANG OFF THE STREETS. MORE SCUM AND VERMIN WHO WILL NO LONGER PROWL THIS CITY.

IT STILL DOESN'T BRING *YOU* BACK, LONNIE. BUT, I *SWORE* WHEN YOU DIED, THAT THE UNDERWORLD WOULD *PAY* FOR WHAT THEY DID TO YOU, MY BROTHER....MY DEAR, DEAR BROTHER.

AND I *WILL* MAKE THEM PAY-- EVERY STREET-SCUM WHO INFESTS OUR CITY WILL SUFFER FOR YOUR DEATH.

LONNIE CARVER
1964-1976
REST IN PEACE

THUNDERBOLT SWEARS THAT!

QUESTIONS, MARVELITES? HANG IN THERE AS WE RETURN TO LUKE...

DON'T KNOW, D.W., BUT THIS PLACE IS *STILL* A JUNK-HEAP.

DON'T THINK IT'LL EVER CHANGE.

MR. CAGE? MR. LUKE CAGE?

YOU GOT MY NAME, BUD. DON'T USE IT UP.

MR. CAGE? THE NAME'S SMITH-- JACK SMITH OF SHANK'S ARMORED COURIERS.

MR. CAGE--?

YEAH? I'M *LISSENIN'*.

OH, I, UH... ER, MR. CAGE? W-WE HAVE A--UH--*PROBLEM.* YOU SEE, WE HAVE TO SHIP *TWO-MILLION* DOLLARS IN GOLD FROM HERE TO WASHINGTON.

TWO MILL? GO ON, I'M *INTERESTED* ALL OF A SUDDEN.

WELL, MR. CAGE, FRANKLY WE NEED *HELP* GUARDING THE MONEY.

HELP? YOU *GOTTA* HAVE YOUR OWN GUARDS. DON'T YA?

NORMALLY WE HAVE *MORE* THAN ENOUGH. BUT, MR. CAGE, AS I SAY, WE HAVE A SERIOUS PROBLEM.

PLEASE *LOOK* AT THIS. WE RECEIVED IT EARLIER THIS MORNING. AND, QUITE FRANKLY, MR. CAGE, WE'RE RATHER *WORRIED* ABOUT WHAT IT MEANS.

THAT LITTLE BUSINESS CARD? LEMME SEE.

THAT, MR. CAGE, IS THE CALLING CARD OF THE *GOLDBUG.* YOU'VE UNDOUBTEDLY HEARD OF THAT MASTER CRIMINAL?

CAN'T SAY THAT I *HAVE*, SMITH. 'COURSE, I DON'T READ THE PAPERS MUCH.

BUT I KINDA LIKE THIS LITTLE *DESIGN* HE HAS HERE.

THAT DESIGN, MR. CAGE, REPRESENTS HIS AIR-CRAFT. YOU SEE, HE IS A *GOLD-THIEF*, AND HE USES, WELL, SOME RATHER *BIZARRE* METHODS TO STEAL WHAT HE WANTS.

WHOOWEE. WHY DO THINGS SUDDENLY *CLICK* TOGETHER, SMITH?

MR. CAGE, ONE OF OUR TRUSTEES, A KYLE RICHMOND, RECOMMENDED YOU TO US, AND WE *DO* NEED YOU.

WE'LL PAY *TWO THOUSAND* DOLLARS, MR. CAGE. ONE THOUSAND NOW, THE OTHER ON DELIVERY TO THE FEDERAL RESERVE IN WASHINGTON.

TWO GRAND?

SMITH, YOU *BOUGHT* YOURSELF A SUPERHERO.

AND SHORTLY...

AS I SAID IN YOUR OFFICE, MR. CAGE, WE ARE WORRIED. AND THAT'S WHY WE'RE USING A SPECIAL *UNMARKED* VAN. THE DRIVER IS ALSO ONLY USING *BACKROADS* SO AS NOT TO CALL ATTENTION TO THE, UH, DELIVERY.

ONE MOMENT, SMITH.

YOU BOYS SEEM TO BE HAVING *TROUBLE*.

LET *ME* GIVE A HAND.

I-I DON'T *BELIEVE* IT!

THAT GOLD WEIGHS *TONS!*

GENTLEMEN, I BELIEVE WE HAVE MADE A *WISE* CHOICE IN HIRING MR. LUKE CAGE AS OUR GUARD. A WISE CHOICE, INDEED.

TAKE IT *EASY*, SMITH. *NO ONE'S* TAKING THIS LOAD AWAY FROM LUKE CAGE.

I'M *SURE* OF THAT, MR. CAGE. GOODBYE, AND GOOD LUCK.

JACK, THE "OLD MAN" WANTS TO SEE YOU.

THIS IS GONNA BE A PIECE OF *CAKE*, LUCAS. FIVE HOURS FROM NOW YOU'LL BE ROLLIN' INTO WASHINGTON AND MAKE ANOTHER *GRAND*.

EASIEST BUNDLE YOU'VE EVER MADE, BABY.

BUT--

SO THEY'VE HIRED LUKE CAGE TO PROTECT THE GOLD?

AN *INTERESTING* CHOICE, BUT HARDLY UNDEFEATABLE!

MR. CAGE, YOU'RE ABOUT TO HAVE SOME *COMPANY*--

--WHETHER YOU WANT ANY OR *NOT*!

AND...

MR. COYNE, THE SHIPMENT LEFT WITH CAGE *ABOARD* AS YOU REQUESTED.

VERY GOOD, SMITH. BUT I BELIEVE I'LL BREATHE A BIT *EASIER* ONCE HE'S REPORTED IN FROM WASHINGTON.

PRIVATE

THE GOLDBUG'S WARNING *STILL* BOTHERS ME.

BACK IN JACK SMITH'S OWN OFFICE...

YES, CAGE *IS* GUARDING THE GOLD--AS YOU DEMANDED, COYNE.

BUT *HE* WON'T BE GUARDING IT MUCH LONGER.

NOT ONCE HE'S BEEN *SLAIN*--

--BY THE GOLDBUG!

WHO WOULD EVER SUSPECT THAT JACK SMITH--THAT PANTY-WAISTED FOOL--COULD BE A MASTER CRIMINAL?

WHO WOULD KNOW THE YEARS I'VE SPENT CREATING SMITH'S IDENTITY AS A COVER-UP FOR THE GOLDBUG'S SCHEMES BECAUSE SMITH KNOWS OF EVERY GOLD SHIPMENT MADE IN THIS COUNTRY?

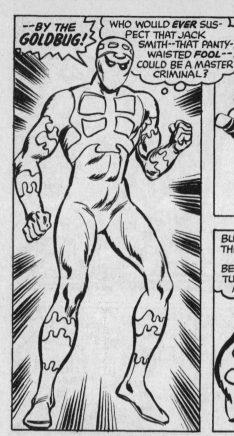

BUT THERE IS LITTLE TIME TO THINK OF THOSE THINGS NOW--FOR CAGE SHOULD JUST BE ENTERING THE NEW JERSEY TURNPIKE--AND I NEED MY GOLDBUG CRAFT.

ACROSS TOWN IN BROOKLYN, A SECLUDED GARAGE DOOR RESPONDS TO A SUPER-SONIC COMMAND SIGNAL, AND RISES...

INSIDE, A SMALL GOLDEN SHIP WHEELS ITSELF FROM ITS LOCKER THEN QUIETLY IS LAUNCHED INTO THE SKY AT EYE-BLURRING SPEED. NO ONE SEES ANY SIGN OF IT AS IT BECOMES AIRBORNE.

MOMENTS LATER...

THERE IT IS, RESPONDING TO MY COMMANDS--AS ALWAYS.

HOW LOVELY, A SILENT JET-SPEED HOVERCRAFT--FAR IN ADVANCE OF ANYTHING THE POLICE HAVE.

IT IS DEFINITELY A CRAFT BEFITTING THE MASTER CRIMINAL CALLED GOLDBUG!

RIGHT ON SCHEDULE. THE DRIVER IS FOLLOWING THE ROUTE I MARKED OUT FOR HIM *PRECISELY.*

A SHAME HE WILL *DIE* FOR HIS ACCURACY. EH? SOMEONE RUNNING *AFTER* THE VAN--AT *SUPER-SPEED?* WHO?

BAH! IT DOESN'T MATTER--NOT ONCE I'VE ACTIVATED THE *PRESSURE BOMB* ALREADY PLACED IN THE TRUCK.

SWEET CHRISTMAS! WHAT?!

SHWA-BAMM

WE'RE BEIN' *BOMBED!*

AN' THE *DRIVER* TOOK THE BRUNT OF IT!

CAGE--

YOU?! YOU GOTTA BE THE *MURDERER!* THE SCUM WHO SET OFF THAT *BOMB!*

YOU MISERABLE LITTLE *CREEP.* I--HUH?

HE'S DUCKING RIGHT *UNDER* MY FIST--

AND COMING UP *BEHIND* YOU, CAGE.

WE'LL TALK *AFTER* I'VE *DOWNED* YOU.

OOOFF!

YOU MADE *TWO* MISTAKES, MISTER. FIRST WAS KILLIN' THAT JOE IN THE TRUCK, AN' THE *SECOND* WAS THINKIN' YOU COULD TAKE *ME* ON.

NO, YOU'RE WRONG! WRONG!

THE *HELL* I AM PUNK.

ONLY THING WRONG HERE IS YOU THINKIN' YOU'LL COME *OUTTA* THIS IN *ONE PIECE!*

NO--YOU *ARE* WRONG...

AND I CAN *PROVE* IT--ONCE I'VE QUIETED YOU DOWN.

THAT *LIGHT!* MY *EYES!*

WHAT DID YOU *DO?*

JUST TRYING TO *STOP* YOU CAGE...LONG ENOUGH TO TALK.

NO TALKIN', CREEP.

I DON'T HAVE TO *SEE* YOU TO *SMELL* WHAT KIND OF SKUNK YOU ARE.

CAGE--!

SHUT UP, PUNK! YOU HEAR ME? SHUT UP!!

SKUNGE!

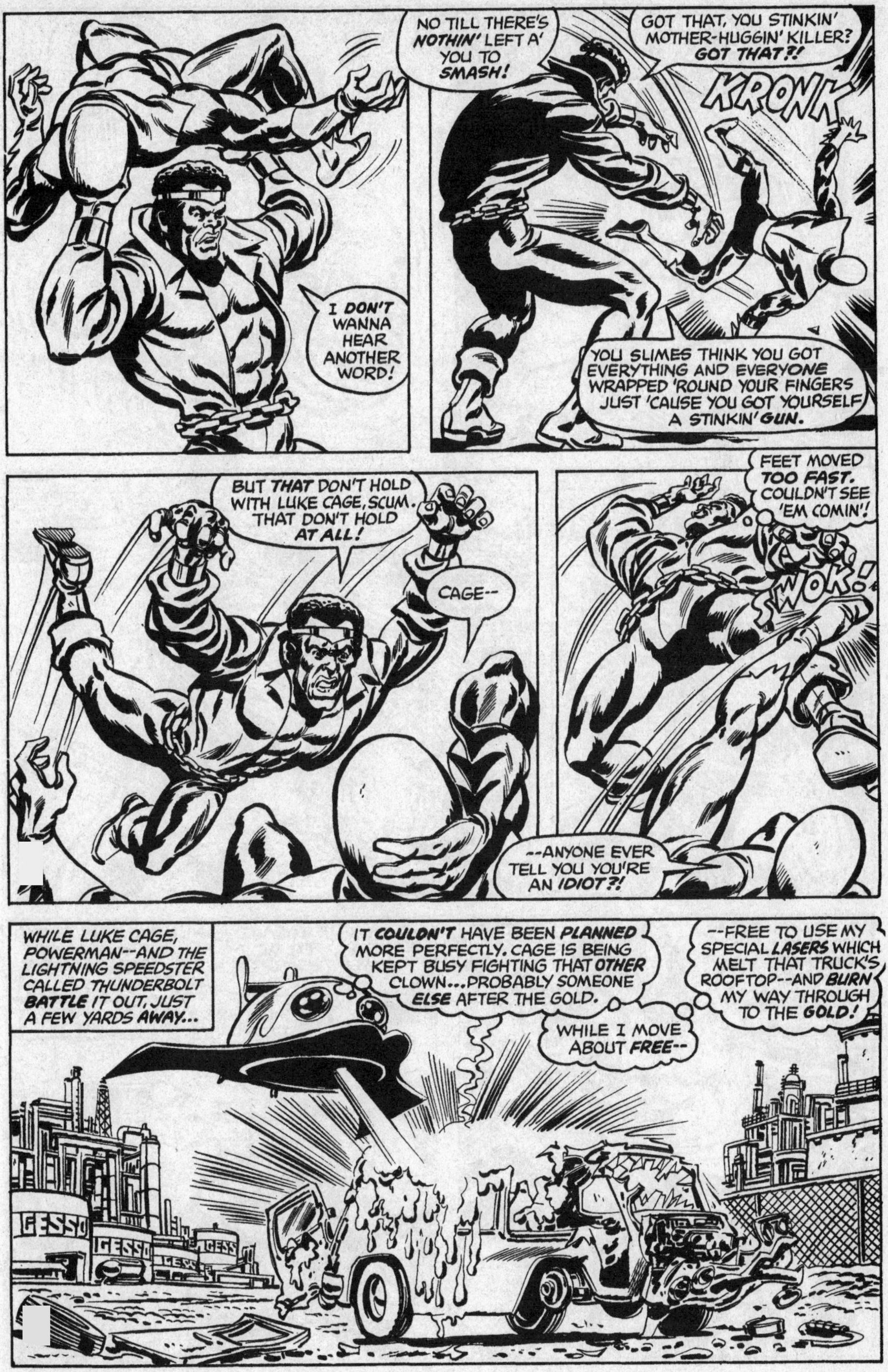
I DON'T WANNA HEAR ANOTHER WORD!
NO TILL THERE'S NOTHIN' LEFT A' YOU TO SMASH!
GOT THAT, YOU STINKIN' MOTHER-HUGGIN' KILLER? GOT THAT?!
KRONK
YOU SLIMES THINK YOU GOT EVERYTHING AND EVERYONE WRAPPED 'ROUND YOUR FINGERS JUST 'CAUSE YOU GOT YOURSELF A STINKIN' GUN.
BUT THAT DON'T HOLD WITH LUKE CAGE, SCUM. THAT DON'T HOLD AT ALL!
CAGE--
FEET MOVED TOO FAST. COULDN'T SEE 'EM COMIN'!
WOK!
--ANYONE EVER TELL YOU YOU'RE AN IDIOT?!
WHILE LUKE CAGE, POWERMAN--AND THE LIGHTNING SPEEDSTER CALLED THUNDERBOLT BATTLE IT OUT, JUST A FEW YARDS AWAY...
IT COULDN'T HAVE BEEN PLANNED MORE PERFECTLY. CAGE IS BEING KEPT BUSY FIGHTING THAT OTHER CLOWN... PROBABLY SOMEONE ELSE AFTER THE GOLD.
WHILE I MOVE ABOUT FREE--
--FREE TO USE MY SPECIAL LASERS WHICH MELT THAT TRUCK'S ROOFTOP--AND BURN MY WAY THROUGH TO THE GOLD!
GESSO

AIN'T GOT TIME 'TO PLAY FANCY WITH YOU, CREEP. STILL GOTTA STOP YOUR LITTLE PLAYMATE UP IN THAT SHIP.

SO YOU'LL PARDON ME IF I RUSH THINGS THROUGH JUST A BIT.

WON'TCHA, SWEETY?

CAGE, PLEASE-- I TOLD YOU-- YOU'RE MAKING A MISTAKE.

TELL ME ALL ABOUT IT, PUNK--

"AFTER YOU'RE SAFE AN' SOUND BEHIND THIS LITTLE GIFT I'M GIVIN' YA.

ALL RIGHT, CAGE-- I'M TRAPPED HERE, BUT PLEASE LISTEN.

SWUNG!

YOU REALLY 'XPECT ME TO BUY THAT GARBAGE, PUNK?

I'M NOT THE GOLDBUG...I DON'T EVEN KNOW HIM.

YOU'VE GOT TO, CAGE. LOOK AT ME AND TELL ME IF YOU HAVEN'T HEARD OF THUNDERBOLT.

I'VE BEEN WRITTEN UP IN ALL THE PAPERS LATELY.

THUNDERBOLT? THE GUY THE TV'S SAYIN'S STOMPIN' ON HOODS?

ONE AND THE SAME, CAGE. I WAS FOLLOWING YOU BECAUSE I KNEW GOLDBUG WOULD BE AFTER THAT SHIPMENT.

DON'T KNOW IF I SHOULD *BELIEVE* YOU, BOLT. BUT I KNOW IF YOU'RE *LYIN',* I COULD PULVERIZE YOU WITHOUT HALF TRYIN'!

SO I'LL LET YOU *FREE*--JUST IN CASE YOU ACTUALLY *ARE* TELLIN' THE TRUTH.

I *AM,* CAGE, BELIEVE ME!

I SORTA *DO,* BOLT-- 'CAUSE THE DUDE UP THERE'S BEEN *IGNORIN'* OUR LITTLE TIFF--

--GOIN' AFTER THE GOLD ALL BY HIS *LONESOME.*

IF HE WAS *YOUR* PARTNER, HE'D PROBABLY'VE *HELPED* YOU 'GAINST ME.

CAGE! WHAT ARE YOU DOING?

JUST GOIN' TO *GREET* THE GOLDBUG. YOU GOT ANY *OBJECTIONS?*

DIDN'T THINK YOU DID.

MAKE YOURSELF *USEFUL,* BOLT. HOW ABOUT TRY'N TO *STOP* BUGGY'S GIZMO FROM SUCKIN' UP ALL THE GOLD?

'CAUSE RIGHT NOW I GOT ME A FIGHT OF MY *OWN!*

A BATTLE YOU WILL *NOT* HAVE THE TIME TO WAGE, FOOL.

NOT AS LONG AS I STILL HOLD MY *GOLD-GUN!*

THEN GUESS WHAT, *BUG?*

YOU AIN'T GONNA BE HOLDIN' IT MUCH LONGER!

I SAID THERE WOULDN'T BE A FIGHT, CAGE--AND I MEANT IT. I'M TOO BUSY TO FOOL WITH YOU NOW.

I'VE ALREADY GOT ALL THE GOLD SIPHONED UP INTO MY SHIP.

--AND YOU'RE NOT NEEDED FOR ANY OF MY FUTURE PLANS. SO IT'S HAIL AND FAREWELL, CAGE.

FOR MY QUICK-HARDENING GOLD-DUST FORMS AN UNBREAKABLE COATING AROUND YOU-- PREVENTING YOU FROM ANY MOVEMENT--

--MAKING YOU AS HELPLESS AS A STATUE.

GOODBYE, CAGE!

CAGE!?

WE'LL NEVER MEET AGAIN. FOR, IN MERE MOMENTS, THE DUST WILL HARDEN TO THE POINT THAT ALL OXYGEN WILL BE CUT OFF!

AND YOU WILL SLOWLY, AND QUITE AGONIZINGLY, SUFFOCATE TO DEATH!

WHAM!

ONLY HAVE *SECONDS* BEFORE IT'S TOO LATE...WHICH MAKES IT *IMPERATIVE* I MOVE AT MY *FASTEST*...AND USE MY SUPER-SPEED *PUNCHES* TO SHATTER THE GOLD *BEFORE* IT CAN HARDEN.

HAVE TO SMASH EACH SECTION A *THOUSAND* TIMES IN THE TIME IT WOULD TAKE ANY *ORDINARY* MAN TO HIT IT *ONCE!*

NO! THE GOLD'S HARDENING EVEN *FASTER* THAN I THOUGHT. GOT TO *STRAIN*...PUSH MYSELF.

I *CAN'T* HAVE ANOTHER LONNIE CARVER EATING ON MY CONSCIENCE!

I-I THINK IT'S WORKING...THE GOLD'S BEGINNING TO *CRACK.* ONLY A MATTER OF MOMENTS-- BUT *CAN CAGE LAST THAT LONG?!*

WILL THE *AIR* RUN OUT *BEFORE* I CAN PULL HIM FREE?

AND AT LONG LAST...

CAGE... ARE YOU--

⸘GASP⸘...I-I'M FINE--⸘GASP⸘ JUST *FINE*...JUST GOT A LITTLE *CREAK* IN MY BACK...

...AN' SOME *GOLD DUST* AS A SOUVENIR.

THANKS BOLT... I *MEAN* THAT. I THOUGHT I WAS A *GONER!*

EPILOGUE:

YOU'RE OKAY, BUT GOLDBUG MADE OFF WITH THE GOLD.

MAKES NO DIFFERENCE, BOLT. 'CAUSE I'LL FIND 'IM NO MATTER WHERE HE'S HIDIN' HIS SCRAWNY BOD!

I WAS HIRED TO PROTECT THAT GOLD AND THAT MEANS NO MATTER WHAT, I GOTTA GET IT BACK.

'LLO, BERTHA.

HIYA, CAGE.

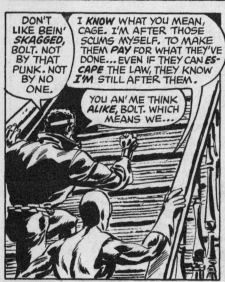

DON'T LIKE BEIN' SKAGGED, BOLT. NOT BY THAT PUNK. NOT BY NO ONE.

I KNOW WHAT YOU MEAN, CAGE. I'M AFTER THOSE SCUMS MYSELF. TO MAKE THEM PAY FOR WHAT THEY'VE DONE... EVEN IF THEY CAN ESCAPE THE LAW, THEY KNOW I'M STILL AFTER THEM.

YOU AN' ME THINK ALIKE, BOLT. WHICH MEANS WE...

CAGE, I-I DON'T THINK YOU SHOULD GO INTO YOUR OFFICES. THERE'S--

FORGET IT, D.W.. ANYONE IN THERE I'LL JUST GET RID OF. DON'T CARE WHO IT IS RIGHT NOW, 'CAUSE THIS HERO-FOR-HIRE IS MAD!

AN' THAT MEANS --HUNH!?!

THERE THEY ARE, GENTLEMEN-- THE MEN WHO STOLE OUR GOLD SHIPMENT!

ARREST THEM!

SWEET CHRISTMAS!

NEEDLESS TO SAY... TO BE CONTINUED!

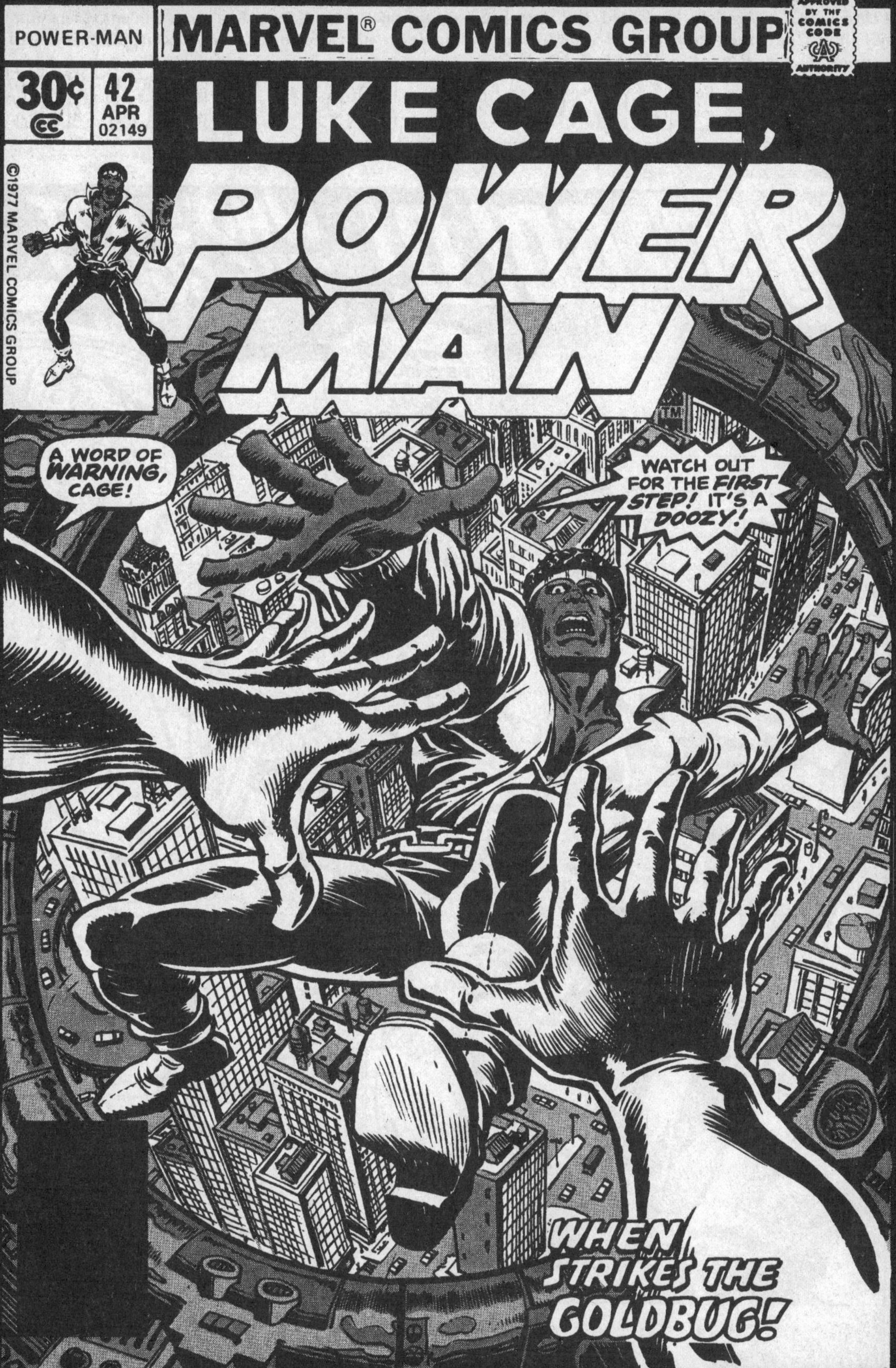
POWER-MAN
MARVEL® COMICS GROUP
APPROVED BY THE COMICS CODE AUTHORITY
30¢
42 APR 02149
LUKE CAGE,
POWER MAN
©1977 MARVEL COMICS GROUP
A WORD OF WARNING, CAGE!
WATCH OUT FOR THE FIRST STEP! IT'S A DOOZY!
WHEN STRIKES THE GOLDBUG!

LUKE CAGE: Wrongly convicted and sentenced to prison—reborn in a freak experiment there that gave him ***steel-hard skin*** and ***strength beyond belief***—a man who hides his identity as an escaped convict in the role of a ***HERO FOR HIRE!***

Stan Lee PRESENTS:

LUKE CAGE, POWER MAN!

MARV WOLFMAN WRITER / EDITOR / *LEE ELIAS* PENCILS / *ALEX NIÑO* INKS / *JOHN COSTANZA* letters / *DON WARFIELD* colors

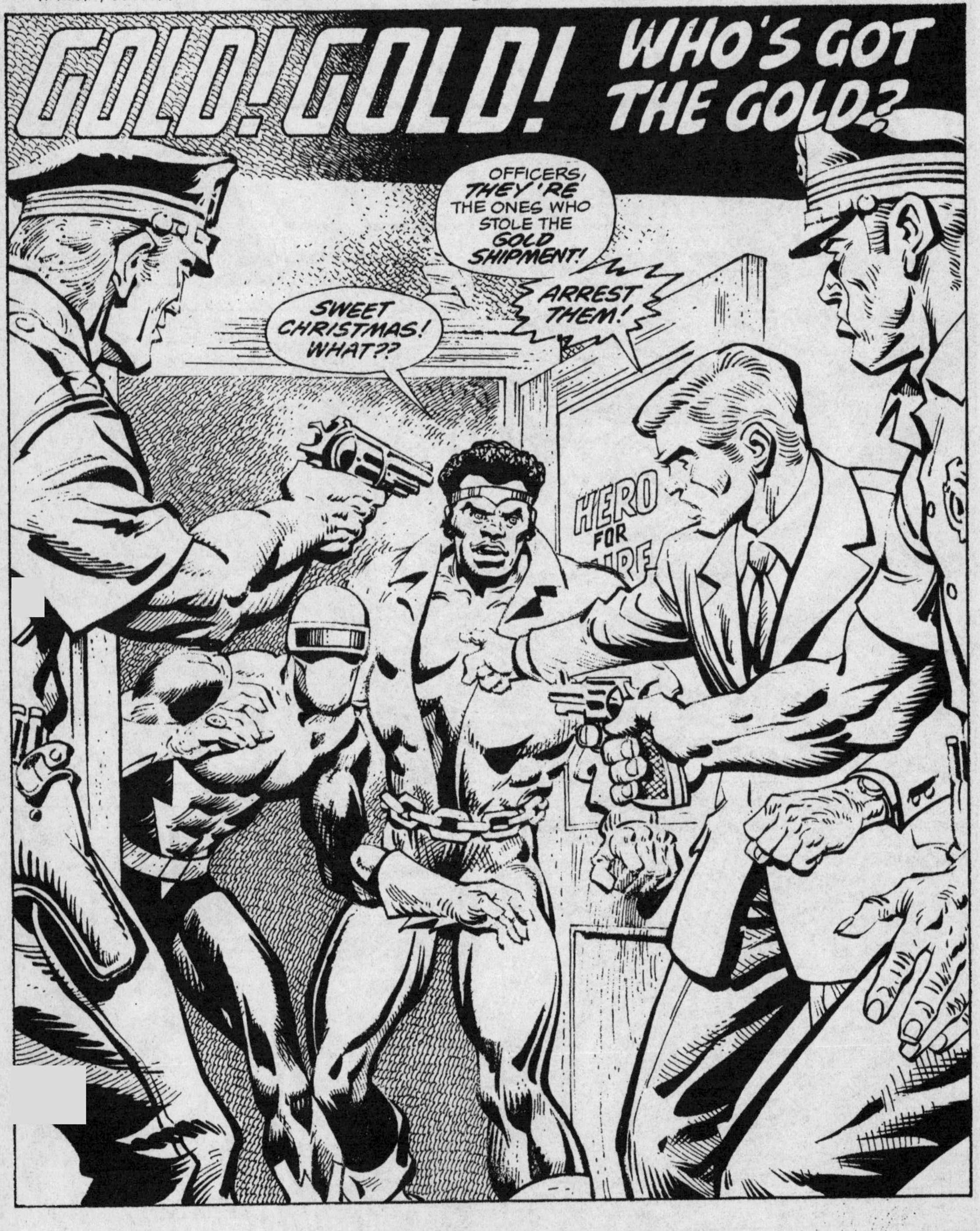
GOLD! GOLD! WHO'S GOT THE GOLD?
OFFICERS, THEY'RE THE ONES WHO STOLE THE GOLD SHIPMENT!
ARREST THEM!
SWEET CHRISTMAS! WHAT??
HERO FOR

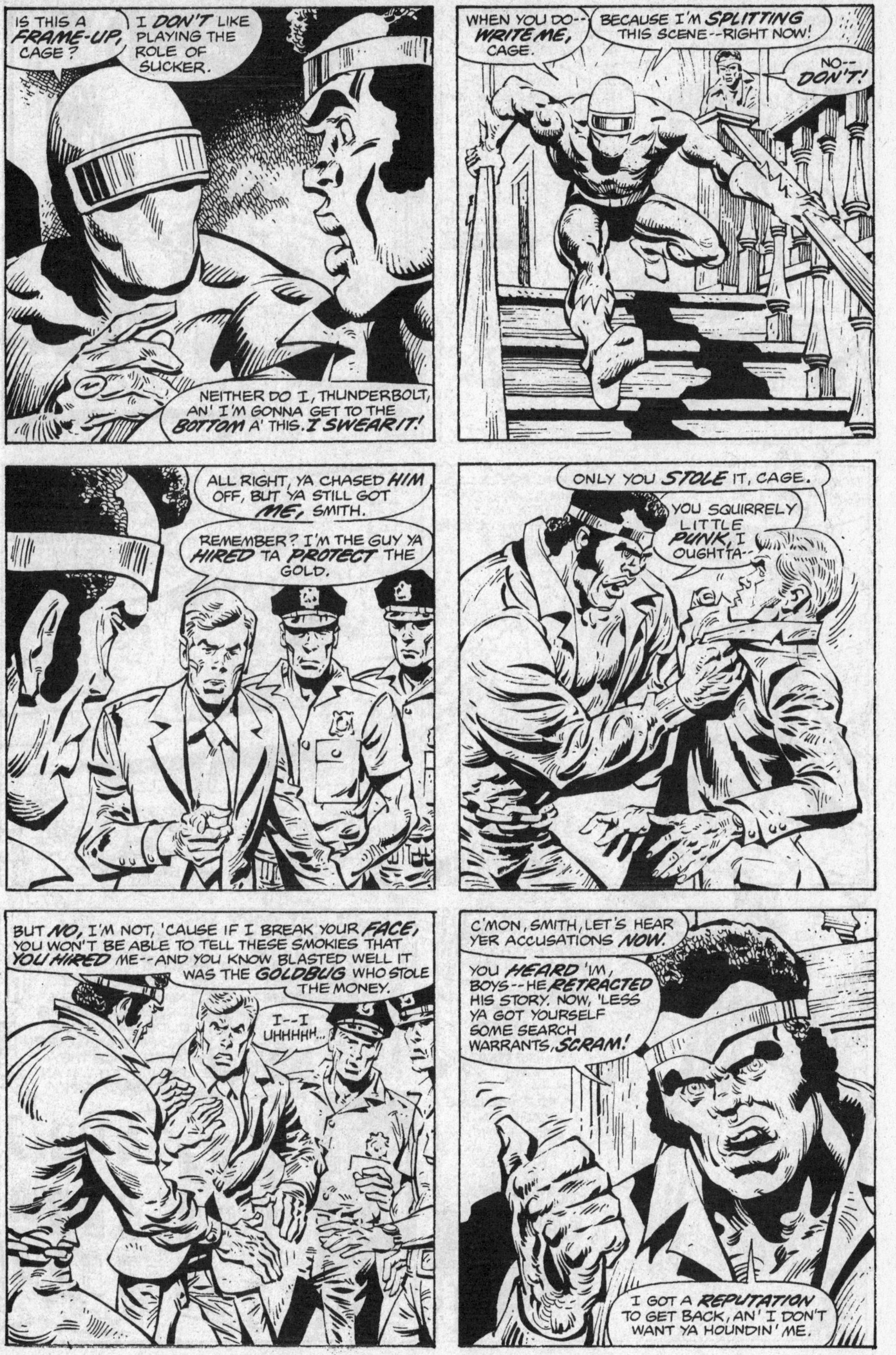
IS THIS A FRAME-UP, CAGE?
I DON'T LIKE PLAYING THE ROLE OF SUCKER.
NEITHER DO I, THUNDERBOLT, AN' I'M GONNA GET TO THE BOTTOM A' THIS. I SWEAR IT!
WHEN YOU DO-- WRITE ME, CAGE.
BECAUSE I'M SPLITTING THIS SCENE--RIGHT NOW!
NO-- DON'T!
ALL RIGHT, YA CHASED HIM OFF, BUT YA STILL GOT ME, SMITH.
REMEMBER? I'M THE GUY YA HIRED TA PROTECT THE GOLD.
ONLY YOU STOLE IT, CAGE.
YOU SQUIRRELY LITTLE PUNK, I OUGHTTA--
BUT NO, I'M NOT, 'CAUSE IF I BREAK YOUR FACE, YOU WON'T BE ABLE TO TELL THESE SMOKIES THAT YOU HIRED ME--AND YOU KNOW BLASTED WELL IT WAS THE GOLDBUG WHO STOLE THE MONEY.
I--I UHHHHH...
C'MON, SMITH, LET'S HEAR YER ACCUSATIONS NOW.
YOU HEARD 'IM, BOYS--HE RETRACTED HIS STORY. NOW, 'LESS YA GOT YOURSELF SOME SEARCH WARRANTS, SCRAM!
I GOT A REPUTATION TO GET BACK, AN' I DON'T WANT YA HOUNDIN' ME.

FIGURES I'D BE ACCUSED A' MAKIN' OFF WITH THE GOLD. SMITH NEEDED A *FALL GUY*.

HE HADDA PROTECT *HIMSELF*, 'CAUSE IT WAS *HIS* IDEA TA HIRE ME.

ONLY BOTH THUNDERBOLT AN' ME *KNOW* THE GOLDBUG HIGHTAILED IT OUTTA HERE WITH THE LOOT. ONLY BOLT *COULDN'T* HANG AROUND--

--NOT WHILE THE *POLICE* ARE AFTER 'IM FER PLAYIN' VIGILANTE.

DAMN, IT'S LIKE EVERYTHIN'S COMIN' DOWN ON ME AT *ONCE*.

I ESCAPE PRISON FOR A CRIME I *NEVER* COMMITTED, ONLY EVERYONE WHO *KNOWS* I'M STRAIGHT IS *DEAD*.

THE *FEDS* ARE BREATHING DOWN MY NECK ABOUT *TAXES*, AN' IF THEY START INVESTIGATIN' ME *TOO CLOSE* THEY'LL LEARN THERE AIN'T NO SUCH PERSON AS LUKE CAGE--

--'CAUSE THAT'S ONLY A *NAME* I TOOK WHEN I LAMMED OUTTA *SEAGATE PRISON*.

YEAH, MY WORLD'S BREAKIN' APART BAD AN' *FAST*, AN' I JUST WANNA RUN *OUTTA* HERE, MAKE FOR SOME *OTHER* PLACE AN' FORGET LUKE CAGE, POWERMAN, EVER EXISTED.

THERE'S *GOTTA* BE A BETTER LIFE OUT THERE SOMEWHERE.

HELL, WHAT AM I TALKIN' ABOUT? I DRAW *TROUBLE* LIKE CANDLES DO MOTHS. THERE'S *NO PLACE* I CAN HIDE WHAT I AM.

NO PLACE LUKE CAGE AIN'T GONNA STICK OUT LIKE A BLASTED *SORE THUMB*!

BUT... IF I *DON'T* FIND SOMEPLACE I CAN HOLE UP SOON, I'M IN FOR A *BAD* TIME, 'CAUSE FRIEND--

--THERE AIN'T NO WAY ON GOD'S GREEN EARTH THIS DUDE CAN DODGE THE FEDERAL GOVERNMENT ONCE THEY FIGURE OUT I'M AN *ESCAPED CON*!

ELSEWHERE, FOOT-STEPS RISE AND FALL WITH MACHINE-LIKE PRECISION...

MADE IT... NO ONE'S FOLLOWING ME.

WHICH MEANS I CAN FINALLY CHANGE BACK INTO BILL CARVER, DISTRICT ATTORNEY TOWER'S RIGHT-HAND ASSISTANT.

THE COPS WON'T BE HUNTING--

KRASH

SOMEONE BEHIND ME?!!

NO, A CAT... JUST A CAT.

CALM DOWN, CARVER. NEXT YOU'LL BE JUMPING AT YOUR OWN SHADOW.

"TAKE THINGS LIKE YOU USED TO--LIKE THE COOL-HEADED EX-GREEN BERET BACK FROM 'NAM THAT YOU ONCE WERE.

C'MON, BILL--JUST ONE MORE RIDE.

WHO'S ARGUING, SQUIRT? C'MON!

"LIKE THE MAN WHO RESCUED HIS BROTHER LONNIE FROM THE CLUTCHES OF THE THUNDERBOLT GANG AFTER JOINING THE D.A.'S OFFICE...*

"YEAH, WE WERE A FAMILY AGAIN, LONNIE AND ME, THE ONLY FAMILY WE EVER HAD WITH MOM AND DAD DEAD. AND I SHOULD'VE KNOWN THIS COULDN'T LAST FOR LONG...

*DAREDEVIL #69-- M.W.

"MY GREEN BERET TRAINING SHOULD HAVE ALERTED ME WHEN THE FERRIS WHEEL SUDDENLY JERKED TO A STOP THAT WE HAD BECOME THE CENTER OF A BULL'S EYE!

KRACK

LONNIE! LONNIE!!

MY GOD-- THEY SHOT HIM!

LONNIE!!

B...BILL... UHHHHHHHH

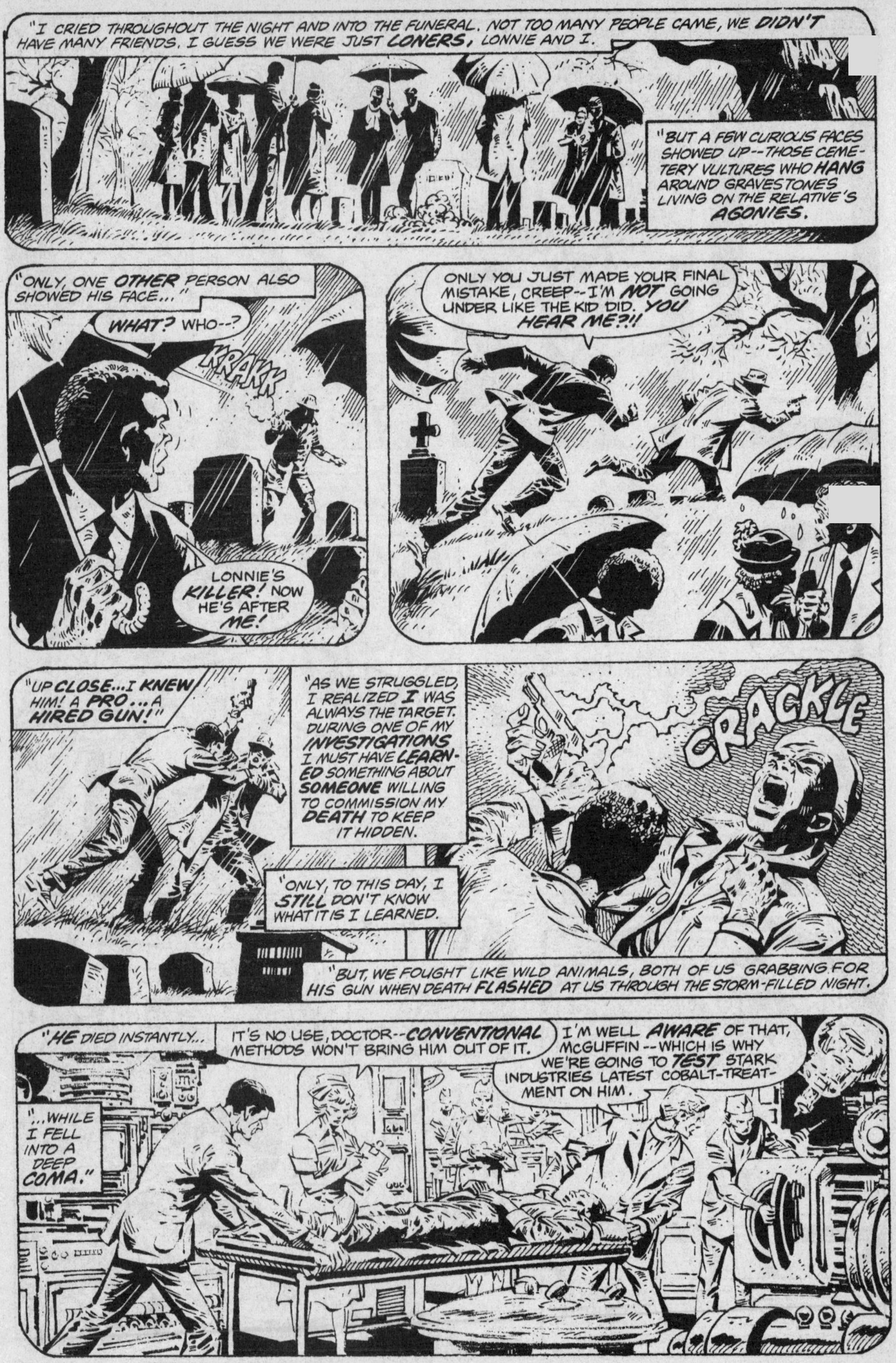

"I CRIED THROUGHOUT THE NIGHT AND INTO THE FUNERAL. NOT TOO MANY PEOPLE CAME, WE DIDN'T HAVE MANY FRIENDS. I GUESS WE WERE JUST LONERS, LONNIE AND I.
"BUT A FEW CURIOUS FACES SHOWED UP--THOSE CEMETERY VULTURES WHO HANG AROUND GRAVESTONES LIVING ON THE RELATIVE'S AGONIES.
"ONLY, ONE OTHER PERSON ALSO SHOWED HIS FACE..."
WHAT? WHO--?
KRAKK
LONNIE'S KILLER! NOW HE'S AFTER ME!
ONLY YOU JUST MADE YOUR FINAL MISTAKE, CREEP--I'M NOT GOING UNDER LIKE THE KID DID. YOU HEAR ME?!!
"UP CLOSE...I KNEW HIM! A PRO...A HIRED GUN!"
"AS WE STRUGGLED, I REALIZED I WAS ALWAYS THE TARGET. DURING ONE OF MY INVESTIGATIONS I MUST HAVE LEARNED SOMETHING ABOUT SOMEONE WILLING TO COMMISSION MY DEATH TO KEEP IT HIDDEN.
"ONLY, TO THIS DAY, I STILL DON'T KNOW WHAT IT IS I LEARNED.
CRACKLE
"BUT, WE FOUGHT LIKE WILD ANIMALS, BOTH OF US GRABBING FOR HIS GUN WHEN DEATH FLASHED AT US THROUGH THE STORM-FILLED NIGHT.
"HE DIED INSTANTLY...
"...WHILE I FELL INTO A DEEP COMA."
IT'S NO USE, DOCTOR--CONVENTIONAL METHODS WON'T BRING HIM OUT OF IT.
I'M WELL AWARE OF THAT, McGUFFIN--WHICH IS WHY WE'RE GOING TO TEST STARK INDUSTRIES LATEST COBALT-TREATMENT ON HIM.

IF IT WORKS, BILL CARVER WILL BE *CURED*. IF NOT, WE'RE *NO* WORSE OFF THAN BEFORE.

"BUT, IT *WORKED*, AND, A FEW DAYS *LATER*..."

YOU'RE LOOKING GOOD, MR. CARVER.

NEVER *FELT* BETTER, DOC. I'M *STRONGER* THAN I WAS BEFORE, AND MY *REFLEXES*, WELL--

BILL, WE MAY HAVE SOME *BAD NEWS* FOR YOU. YOU SEE, WE DISCOVERED A *RADIATION LEAKAGE* IN THE COBALT TREATMENT.

SOMETHING MAY HAVE *HAPPENED* AND WE JUST CAN'T LET YOU OUT OF HERE UNTIL WE'RE *SURE* YOU'LL BE ALL RIGHT.

FORGET IT, DOC. LONNIE'S *KILLER* MAY BE DEAD, BUT WHOEVER *HIRED* HIM IS STILL AROUND... AND STILL AFTER MY *HIDE*...

SO I'M LEAVING *TODAY*-- AND *DON'T* TRY TO STOP ME.

"SO I *LEFT* AND DISCOVERED THE RADIATION SPEEDED UP MY *REFLEXES*... GAVE ME THIS SUPER POWER."

BUT THAT ONLY *HELPED* ME, BECAUSE I WANTED THE ONE *RESPONSIBLE* FOR LONNIE BEING SHOT... AND SUDDENLY I'D DO *ANYTHING* TO GET HIM.

MAYBE THE RADIATION ALSO AFFECTED MY *MIND*-- MAYBE NOT. BUT I'M OUT FOR *BLOOD* NOW--

...AN' EVERY DAY, AFTER BILL CARVER'S DONE AT THE D.A.'S OFFICE, *THUNDERBOLT* PROWLS THE STREETS IN SEARCH OF THE NIGHT VERMIN.

AND I'LL *KEEP* PROWLING THE NIGHT --UNTIL I PAY BACK LONNIE'S KILLER-- *IN SPADES!*

CAB!

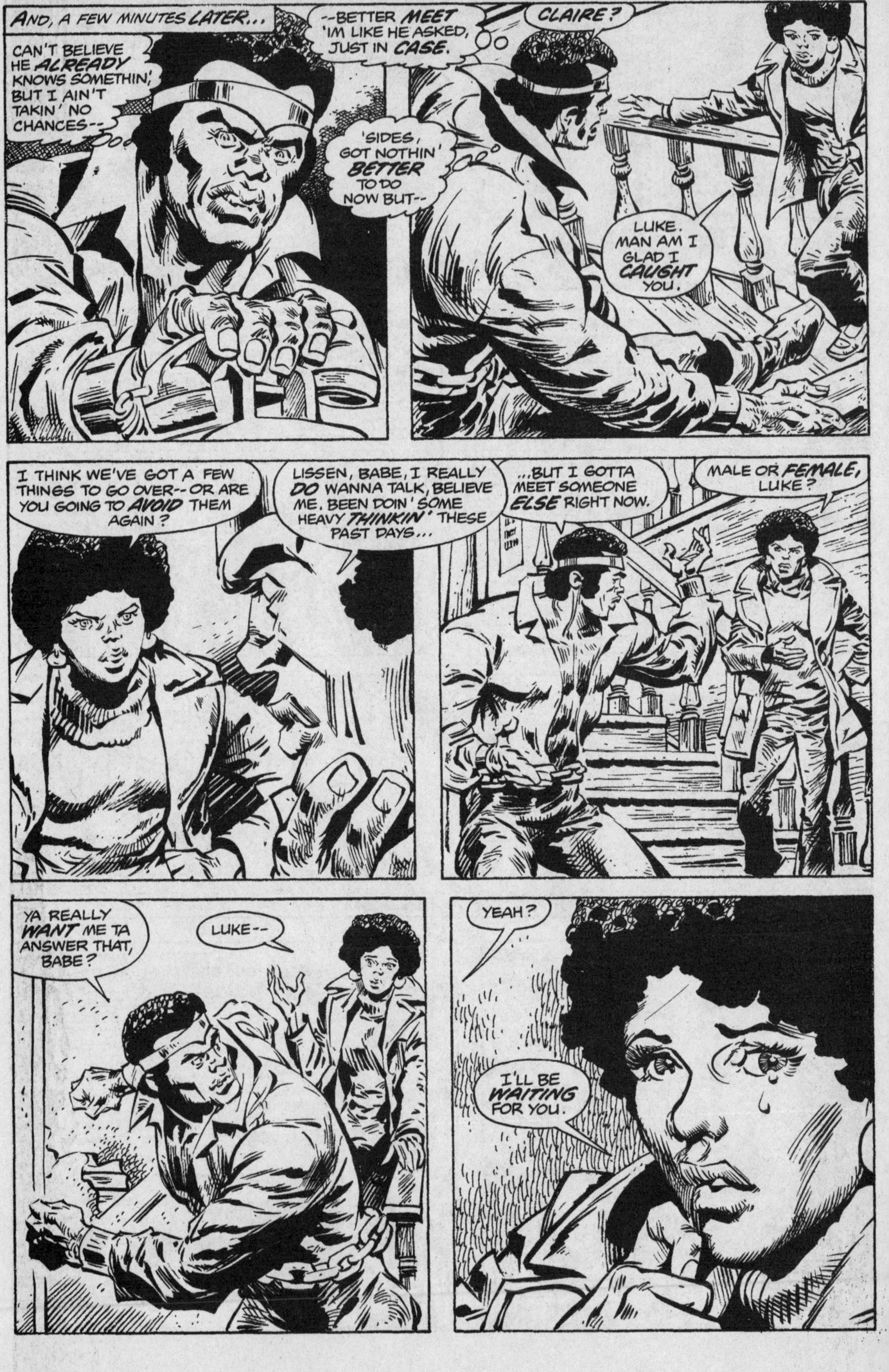

AND, A FEW MINUTES LATER...
CAN'T BELIEVE HE ALREADY KNOWS SOMETHIN', BUT I AIN'T TAKIN' NO CHANCES--
'SIDES, GOT NOTHIN' BETTER TO DO NOW BUT--
--BETTER MEET 'IM LIKE HE ASKED, JUST IN CASE.
CLAIRE?
LUKE. MAN AM I GLAD I CAUGHT YOU.
I THINK WE'VE GOT A FEW THINGS TO GO OVER--OR ARE YOU GOING TO AVOID THEM AGAIN?
LISSEN, BABE, I REALLY DO WANNA TALK, BELIEVE ME. BEEN DOIN' SOME HEAVY THINKIN' THESE PAST DAYS...
...BUT I GOTTA MEET SOMEONE ELSE RIGHT NOW.
MALE OR FEMALE, LUKE?
YA REALLY WANT ME TA ANSWER THAT, BABE?
LUKE--
YEAH?
I'LL BE WAITING FOR YOU.

HOW CAN I *REALLY* TELL HER WHAT'S COMIN' DOWN? DON'T THINK SHE'D *UNDERSTAND* THAT ANY MINUTE I MIGHT BE LOCKED UP FOR *LIFE* BEHIND PRISON BARS.

FACE IT, CAGE, CLAIRE'S A REAL *LADY*, AN' *YOU'RE* NOT WHAT A LADY SHOULD BE HANGIN' AROUND WITH.

SHE CALLED ME A *STREET FIGHTER* EARLIER.✱ SHE'S RIGHT, AN' MAYBE THAT'S *ALL* I'LL EVER BE. MAYBE I *CAN'T* BE MORE.

I AIN'T GOT *TIME* TO REASON THINGS OUT WITH THE SKUNKS AN' *SLIME* I USUALLY MEET. AN' I AIN'T EXACTLY *COLUMBO* PLAYIN' GAMES IN FANCY MANSIONS WITH MILLIONAIRES.

✱ LAST ISH. --MARV.

MY KINDA SPARRIN' PARTNERS ARE USUALLY LOWER 'N A *COCKROACH'S* BEHIND--THEY FESTER IN BACK ALLEYS AND SEWERS.

AN' MAYBE IT'S 'CAUSE I'M EXACTLY *LIKE* 'EM THAT I FIGHT THE WAY I DO.

EH? THIS IS *IT!* BUT *WHERE* THE HECK'S BOLT?

CAGE? YOU CAME?

I SAID I WOULD, BOLT. YOU GOT THAT *INFO* ABOUT THE GOLDBUG?

I SAID I DID, CAGE, DIDN'T I?

NOW, ARE WE FINISHED CROSS-EXAMINING EACH OTHER? BECAUSE, IF WE'RE *NOT*, I'LL LEAVE HERE JUST AS *FAST* AS I CAME.

PARTNERS, FOR NOW, CAGE?

SOLID.

FOR NOW.

"ALL RIGHT, THEN PLEASE *TRUST* ME. LET'S GO.

"AND IF ALL GOES WELL, THE GOLDBUG WILL BE *OURS* WITHIN THE HOUR."

THE 59TH STREET BRIDGE, SPANNING THE EAST RIVER FROM MANHATTAN'S RESIDENTIAL MIDTOWN TO--

--LONG ISLAND CITY'S DARK, DUSTY WAREHOUSE DISTRICT...

I GOT SOME REPORTS THAT THERE ARE *STRANGE* THINGS HAPPENING IN THAT GARAGE. THE DOOR SUDDENLY *OPENS* FOR NO APPARENT REASON--

--AND QUICK GLIMPSES OF BIZARRE LOOKING *AIR-CRAFT* CAN BE SEEN.

THE GOLDBUG'S CRAFT?

ON THE *BUTTON,* CAGE

ONE THING, BOLT--JUST *HOW* DID YOU GET THE INFO? I GOT MY BEST *STOOLIES* WORKIN' OVERTIME AN' THEY LEARNED *NOTHIN'*!

I'VE GOT *BETTER* STOOLIES THEN, CAGE. C'MON!

SOMETHING TELLS ME THE GOLDBUG IS *INSIDE!*

SKRUNCH!

WHO?

LOOK! IT'S *THUNDERBOLT!*

SWELL! *YOU* THEY RECOGNIZE, ME THEY--EH?

WE HAVE *INTRUDERS,* MEN. *STOP THEM!*

YOU *HEARD* THE BOSS. C'MON!

GRAB A *WRENCH!*

NO WAY, UGLY. I'M NOT GIVING YOU SCUM A CHANCE TO GRAB *ANYTHING!*

YOU'VE PREYED ON *INNOCENT* PEOPLE LONG ENOUGH, PUNK. YOU'VE TAKEN *ADVANTAGE* OF THOSE WHO COULD NOT HELP THEMSELVES.

NO! HE MOVES TOO *FAST!*

SOK

BUT NOW YOU'VE BEEN *BRANDED* WITH THE SIGN OF THUNDERBOLT! AND *WHEREVER* YOU RATS HIDE, THUNDERBOLT WILL BE ABLE TO *FIND* YOU.

BOK

SPID!

FOR *NOTHING* WILL EVER REMOVE MY MARK-- *NOTHING!*

BOLT, YOU DEAL WITH *THOSE* CREEPS. I GOT A FEW RUNAWAYS OF MY *OWN!*

HEY, PUNK, YA *FORGET* SOMETHIN'? I THINK YA LEFT YER *TIRE* BEHIND!

HERE, *TAKE* IT! YA KNOW HOW EXPENSIVE IT IS TO *REPLACE* THESE THINGS!

UNGGHHH!

SOMEONE MOVIN' UP *BEHIND* ME!

SKRONK!

SHAME YA COULDN'T BE MORE *QUIET*, PUNK-- OR I'D NEVER WOULD 'A BEEN ABLE TA DO *THIS!*

NOO!

AN' JUST IN CASE *YOU* FEEL LEFT OUTTA THIS, CREEP? *HERE!*

HOLD THIS AN' MAKE YOURSELF *USEFUL!*

BIK

C'MON, BOLT-- THESE TWO-BIT THUGS ARE *NOTHING!*

IT'S THE *BIG MAN* WE'RE AFTER.

HE MUST BE *BEHIND* THIS DOOR, CAGE.

SO GET *OUTTA* THE WAY, BOLT-- --WHILE I OPEN THIS LOCKED DOOR *CAGE STYLE!*

KUNGGG

HUNH? SOMEONE SITTIN' IN THE *SHADOWS!*

WHAT?

YOU ARE *GOOD,* MISTER CAGE, BUT *NOT* GOOD ENOUGH FOR THE *ADVANCED TECHNOLOGY* OF THE *GOLDBUG.*

SOME KINDA *BUBBLE* FORMIN' 'ROUND HIS CHAIR!

NOT BUBBLE, CRETIN-- *CAPSULE.* ONE DESIGNED TO PROTECT ME AS MY *JETS* WHISK ME FROM YOUR SIGHT.

NOW, *FAREWELL,* FOOL. FOR YOU SEE, THE GAMES HAVE *ENDED,* AND NOW IT IS TIME FOR YOU TO *SUFFER.*

GOODBYE, CAGE-- THUNDERBOLT!

A SHAME WE WILL *NEVER* MEET AGAIN!

PARKING

GONE! BUT AT LEAST WE KNOW WE WERE *RIGHT.* HE *WAS* HERE.

LOOK AT THESE *PAPERS* HE LEFT BEHIND, CAGE.

WOOWEEEE! THEY SPILL THE BEANS 'BOUT *EVERYTHIN'* HE'S BEEN UPTA.

MORE IMPORTANTLY, LOOK AT THAT *ADDRESS.* C'MON!

HEY, EVERYTHIN'S STARTIN' TA *SHAKE?* WHAT IN SWEET CHRISTMAS IS GOIN' *ON?*

CAGE! STEEL WALLS ARE SLIDING INTO PLACE--

BETTER *BELIEVE* IT, BOLT. BUGGY'S GOT US ENCASED IN A *SHELL!*

AND I THINK I KNOW WHAT WE'RE *IN FOR.* LISTEN, WE'LL HAVE TO ACT *QUICKLY!*

BUT, LESS THAN A *MINUTE* LATER...

...A SILVER CYLINDER SLIDES INTO THE LONG ISLAND CITY SKIES. ITS DESTINATION: *OBLIVION.* ITS PURPOSE: *DEATH!*

FOR, JUST A HEARTBEAT AFTER IT LIFTS ONE THOUSAND FEET SKY-WARD--

PARKING GARAGE

BARROOOM

PERFECT! CAGE AND THUNDERBOLT ARE *DEAD*--

BAWAM!

--AND NOW THERE IS *NO ONE* WHO CAN LINK THE GOLD-BUG TO JACK SMITH.

AND, A FEW MINUTES LATER, A SLEEK GOLDEN CRAFT SKIMS LOW ACROSS THE HORIZON...

I STILL HAVE *MORE* GOLD TO AMASS BEFORE THE GOLDBUG WILL RETIRE.

BUT, FOR NOW, IT IS TIME TO RETURN TO MY BROOKLYN HEADQUARTERS --TO PLAN MY NEXT LITTLE CAPER--MY *FINAL* CRIMINAL ACT...

...THE ONE WHICH WILL MAKE ME THE *WEALTHIEST HUMAN BEING ON EARTH!*

THINK A' THE *TAXES* YOU'LL HAVE TO *PAY* ON THAT, BUGGY.

BELIEVE ME, IT'LL BE A *WHOPPER!*

YOU? BUT *HOW?*

THE ROCKET *EXPLODED!* YOU MUST HAVE *DIED!*

ASSUMIN' WE WERE ON IT IN THE FIRST PLACE, HANDSOME.

WHICH YA *CAN'T* ASSUME, CONSIDERIN' WE POUNDED OUR WAY *OUTTA* IT JUST BEFORE YOUR LITTLE ROMAN CANDLE WENT BYE BYE.

YOU'RE *CLEVER*, CAGE, BUT NOT CLEVER ENOUGH TO *STOP* ME.

NO WAY, FILTH-- YOU CAN'T OUTRUN THUNDERBOLT--

...AND YOU CAN'T ESCAPE *RETRIBUTION!*

YOU'RE TRAPPED HERE, BUG. YOU MAY AS WELL *GIVE UP!*

GO, OR YOU'LL BE TRAPPED HERE IN MY SHIP WHEN WE TAKE OFF!

AND *YOUR* SENSE OF SELF-IMPORTANCE IS *LAUGHABLE,* THUNDERBOLT. I FEAR YOU ALMOST AS MUCH AS I DO A CATER-PILLAR.

OUTSIDE...

CHRISTMAS! AIN'T NO WAY I'M LETTIN' GO A' THIS LITTLE PLEASURE CRUISER *NOW*-- NOT WITHOUT DIGGIN' MY OWN GRAVE AS I *LAND!*

'SIDES, I *CAN'T* LEAVE--NOT WHILE THE BUG'S STILL ON THIS FLYING RAT-TRAP--'CAUSE I WANNA GET *MY* HANDS ON 'IM--

--WHETHER HE'S IN *ONE* PIECE, TWO--OR HOW-EVER MANY--HE'LL BE IN *MORE* WHEN I'M THROUGH WITH 'IM.

DIDN'T YOU HEAR ME, YOU CONTEMPTIBLE FOOL? I SAID GET *AWAY* FROM ME-- AND I *MEANT* IT!

THE GOLDBUG'S PLANS MUST *NOT* BE INTERFERED WITH, NOT BY *YOU!* NOT BY ANYONE!

POK!

BOLT!

HE'S FALLIN' TOO FAST-- NO WAY TA GRAB *HOLD* A' HIM!

JUST GOTTA *STRETCH* AN' PRAY...

C'MON, BOLT-- C'MON, YA UGLY BABOON! GOT YA!

THANKS, BUDDY-- NOW GIVE ME A BOOST BACK *INSIDE*-- WHERE I CAN *FINISH* WITH THIS WORTHLESS *TRASH!*

SOK

FOOL! YOU'VE THROWN ME INTO THE *CONTROLS.*

NOW AIN'T THAT JUST TOO BAD, PUNK?

YOUR LITTLE AIRPLANE'S JUST GONNA GO ALL TO *PIECES!*

LOOK FOR YOURSELF IF YOU'RE TOO *THICK* TO BELIEVE ME.

WITH ALL OF US *ON* IT, YOU MORON, WE'RE *STUCK* HERE, AND THE SHIP'S OUT OF *CONTROL!*

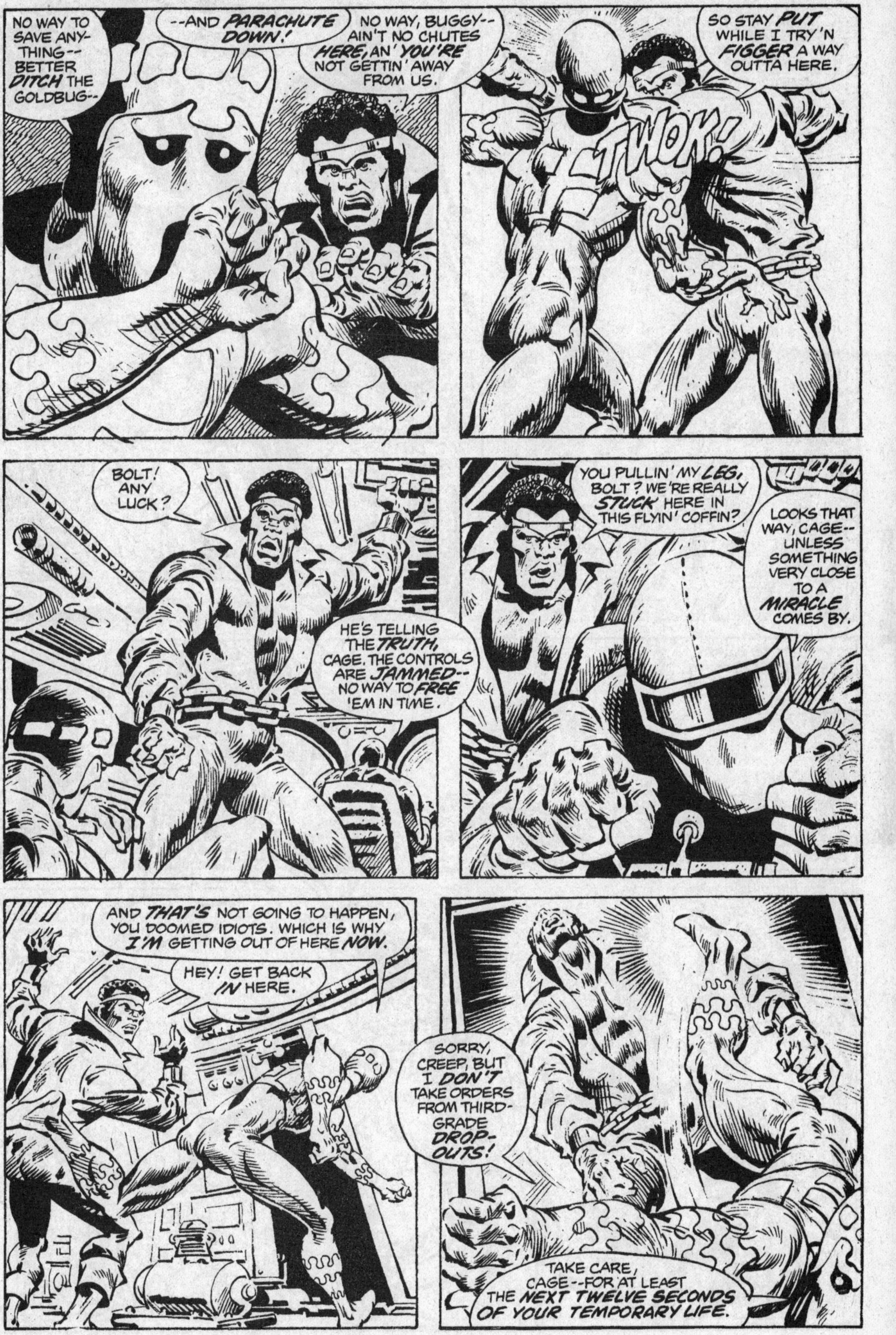
NO WAY TO SAVE ANY-THING-- BETTER DITCH THE GOLDBUG--
--AND PARACHUTE DOWN!
NO WAY, BUGGY-- AIN'T NO CHUTES HERE, AN' YOU'RE NOT GETTIN' AWAY FROM US.
SO STAY PUT WHILE I TRY'N FIGGER A WAY OUTTA HERE.
TWOK!
BOLT! ANY LUCK?
HE'S TELLING THE TRUTH, CAGE. THE CONTROLS ARE JAMMED-- NO WAY TO FREE 'EM IN TIME.
YOU PULLIN' MY LEG, BOLT? WE'RE REALLY STUCK HERE IN THIS FLYIN' COFFIN?
LOOKS THAT WAY, CAGE-- UNLESS SOMETHING VERY CLOSE TO A MIRACLE COMES BY.
AND THAT'S NOT GOING TO HAPPEN, YOU DOOMED IDIOTS. WHICH IS WHY I'M GETTING OUT OF HERE NOW.
HEY! GET BACK IN HERE.
SORRY, CREEP, BUT I DON'T TAKE ORDERS FROM THIRD-GRADE DROP-OUTS!
TAKE CARE, CAGE--FOR AT LEAST THE NEXT TWELVE SECONDS OF YOUR TEMPORARY LIFE.

NEXT ISSUE:
THE MAN CALLED MACE!

POWER-MAN
MARVEL® COMICS GROUP
APPROVED BY THE COMICS CODE AUTHORITY
30¢ CC
43 MAY 02149
LUKE CAGE, POWER MAN™
©1977 MARVEL COMICS GROUP
HE'S BACK--AND DEADLIER THAN EVER BEFORE! THE MAN CALLED MACE!
YOU WON'T BELIEVE IT, BUT IT'S TRUE-- THE DEATH OF LUKE CAGE!

LUKE CAGE: Wrongly convicted and sentenced to prison—reborn in a freak experiment there that gave him *steel-hard skin* and *strength beyond belief*—a man who hides his identity as an escaped convict in the role of a *HERO FOR HIRE!*

Stan Lee PRESENTS: **LUKE CAGE, POWER MAN!**

MARV WOLFMAN / LEE ELIAS & ALEX NINO / JOHN COSTANZA / JANICE COHEN
WRITER / EDITOR   PENCILS   INKS   letters   colors

IF YOU LIVE IN NEW YORK, AND YOU WALK THROUGH THE MID-TOWN AREA KNOWN AS *TIMES SQUARE,* YOU CAN EXPECT TO SEE ALMOST ANYTHING.

THE **DEATH** OF **LUKE CAGE!**

AND A NEW *BEGINNING* FOR *POWER MAN!*

BUT NOT EVEN THE MOST *JADED* RESIDENT OF THE *BIG APPLE* COULD POSSIBLY HAVE EXPECTED TO WATCH IN *MUTE HORROR* AS A *GIANT GOLDEN AIR-SHIP PLUMMETS DIRECTLY TOWARDS THE CITY'S BUSIEST INTERSECTION!*

BRYANT PARK

C'MON, BOLT--YA GOTTA *STOP* THIS PIECE A' *JUNK!*

YA GOTTA DO *SOMETHIN'!*

I'M *TRYIN'*, CAGE--

--BUT IT'S *USELESS!* WE'RE HEADIN' RIGHT INTO THE *FIFTH AVENUE LIBRARY!*

WHEN WE CRASH, *HUNDREDS* OF PEOPLE WILL BE KILLED!

NOT TO MENTION *US,* HANDSOME.

BUT I CAN'T LET THAT HAPPEN, BABY, COULDN'T *LIVE* WITH MYSELF IF IT DID.

SO I GUESS I GOTTA BE THE ONE TA DO SOMETHIN'-- AND I GOT ME AN *IDEA.*

THREE HUNDRED POUNDS A' LUKE CAGE POUNDIN' ON THIS TIN LIZZIE CAN'T DO MUCH--

--BUT MAYBE I DON'T *NEED* MUCH ...JUST GOTTA *TIP* THIS THING A LITTLE... CHANGE THE ANGLE ENOUGH--

BAMM · BADAMM

--SO IT SKIMS RIGHT *OVER* THE LIBRARY AND LANDS IN *BRYANT PARK!*

C'MON, YA MISERABLE PANCAKE--*MOVE!*

BTAM BDAM!

JUST *TILT* YER FLAMIN' WINGS AN *INCH* A'SO!

JUST 'NUFF TA MAKE IT *OVER* THE LIBRARY.

IT'S *WORKING* ...CAGE'S *ANGLED* THE SHIP JUST *ENOUGH.*

BUT HE'LL STILL BE *SACRIFICING* HIMSELF UNLESS *I* CAN PITCH IN.

AND MAYBE *THUNDERBOLT* IS THE ONLY GUY IN TOWN WHO *CAN* DO THIS! HAVE TO WORK UP MY SUPER-SPEED TO IT'S *FASTEST!*

SET UP AN *UP-DRAFT* TO SLOW DOWN THAT THING ENOUGH SO IT *DOESN'T* SCATTER ITSELF FROM HERE TO *BROOKLYN!*

NO WAY TO KNOW FOR SURE... IT'S STILL COMING IN *TOO FAST.* WHICH MEANS I'D BETTER GET *OUT* OF THE WAY AND *PRAY.*

YOU'VE *GOT* TO MAKE IT THROUGH, CAGE! *YOU'VE GOT TO!*

BARAMMM!

CAGE? *CAGE?*

NOTHING, DAMN! I WAS HOPING AGAINST HOPE...EVEN THOUGH I *KNEW* HE COULDN'T SURVIVE.

BLAST IT, CAGE-- BECAUSE OF *ME*-- YOU'RE *DEAD!* I LED YOU INTO THAT *TRAP!*

...HEY...KEEP IT DOWN, BOLT...

...YER WAKIN' UP THE *DEAD!*

CAGE? I-I--*UHHHH*...

OBOY! THE *COPS* ARE COMING, CAGE--

YOU WANT TO WASTE TIME ANSWERING *QUESTIONS?*

NOT *ME*, BUDDY. LET'S *SCRAM!*

MY *OFFICE* IS DOWN THE BLOCK--*MOVE IT!*

HUNH? I *SWEAR* I SAW SOMEONE STANDING HERE? I'M *SURE* OF IT.

AT LEAST I *THINK* I'M SURE.

CAGE, I'LL SEE YOU *LATER.*

BUT WHAT ABOUT THE GOLDBUG? WE STILL GOTTA *FIND* 'IM--?

WE *WILL*, BUT I *DON'T* WEAR THIS MASK FOR MY *HEALTH*, CAGE--

HERO 'FOR HIRE

--AND THE GUY *UNDER* IT STILL HAS A *JOB* TO GET BACK TO.

I'LL GIVE YOU A *CALL* TONIGHT. OKAY?

SURE, BOLT. SEE YOU *THEN.*

NO, LUKE--YOU *WON'T* BE SEEING THE MAN CALLED *THUNDERBOLT* TONIGHT, OR *ANY-TIME* IN THE NEAR FUTURE, FOR--

-- JUST A FEW MINUTES LATER, AN EVENT WHICH WILL *DRASTICALLY* CHANGE YOUR LIFE CHURNS INTO OPERATION, IN THE GUISE OF--

SNEAGLE? WHAT IN THE NAME A' *SCROOGE* DO *YOU* WANT?

WHAT I'VE *ALWAYS* WANTED, CAGE--*YOU!*

THE INTERNAL REVENUE DEPARTMENT MAY MOVE SLOWLY, CAGE-- BUT WE *MOVE!*

AND I NOW HAVE *DEFINITE* PROOF THAT YOU, MR. LUKE CAGE--*IF* THAT IS YOUR REAL NAME--*HAVE NEVER PAID TAXES IN YOUR LIFE!*

SNEAGLE, I OUGHTTA--

YOU TRY *ANYTHING,* CAGE--AND THE FULL WEIGHT OF THE U.S. GOVERNMENT WILL BEAR DOWN ON YOU.

NOW, LISTEN CAREFULLY, CAGE-- YOU *WILL* BE IN MY OFFICE *TOMORROW MORNING...*

...OR YOU WILL BE *BEHIND BARS* TOMORROW *NIGHT!* DO YOU UNDERSTAND THAT, MR. *HERO-FOR-HIRE?*

YEAH, I GOT IT, SNEAGLE. BUT I *DON'T* LIKE IT.

I DON'T GIVE A BLOODY HOOT *WHAT* YOU LIKE, CAGE.

YOU WILL DO *WHAT* I SAY BECAUSE YOU HAVE *NO* OTHER CHOICE.

GOOD DAY, MISTER CAGE. HAVE A *PLEASANT* AFTERNOON.

SLA M!

WELL, LUCAS, THIS IS WHAT YOU'VE BEEN *DREADIN'* EVER SINCE YA BUSTED OUTTA SEAGATE.

YER COVER'S GONNA BE *BLOWN*-- SKY-HIGH!

AND YA GOT ONLY *YERSELF* TA BLAME, BUDDY.

YOU COULDA *STAYED* IN SEAGATE, TAKEN THE RAP YOU WERE SET UP FOR AND THEN BEEN *FREED.*

BUT BECAUSE I *DIDN'T,* I GOT THIS *CLOUD* HUGGIN' ME WHEREVER I TURN, AN' I CAN'T ESCAPE IT 'CAUSE IT'S INSIDE MY *HEAD.*

I WAS *INNOCENT,* BUT THERE AIN'T NO WAY TO PROVE THAT NOW. SO I GOTTA KEEP *PAYIN'* FOR SOMETHING I DIDN'T EVER DO.

AN' NOW SNEAGLE AN' HIS EAGER-BEAVER DESIRE TA SEE ME *HANG* IS CAUSIN' TROUBLE. HECK, NON-PAYMENT OF TAXES! I NEVER *MADE* ENOUGH DOUGH TO PAY 'EM IN THE FIRST PLACE.

'SIDES, I WAS AFRAID A' *PUTTIN'* IN A *CLAIM* 'CAUSE THEN THE GOVERNMENT WOULDA' CHECKED-- FOUND OUT LUKE CAGE *DON'T* EXIST-- NEVER DID EXIST, AN' IT WAS ONLY A MADE-UP NAME FOR A *RUNAWAY CON!*

MAYBE I'VE BEEN A FOOL. IF I'M *BLAMED* FOR A CRIME, I SHOULDA JUST *COMMITTED* IT. CAN'T GO TO JAIL TWICE FOR THE *SAME THING.*

HECK, WHAT AM I TALKIN' ABOUT? I'M NO CRIMINAL, *NEVER* WAS. JUST A GUY CAUGHT UP IN SOMETHIN' THAT'S BIGGER'N 'IM, THAT'S ALL.

AN' I CAN'T EVEN GO TO THE *DEFENDERS* FOR HELP-- 'CAUSE *THEY* WOULDN'T BELIEVE ME--*NO ONE* WOULD.

GEM GEM

SHANE ALAN LADO

CLASSIC WESTERN
JACK PALANCE · ALAN LADO

IT'S MY WORD AGAINST THE WORLD'S. AN', BLAST IT, *THIS* TIME I'M THE ONE WHO'S RIGHT, AND THERE JUST *AIN'T* NO WAY IN HEAVEN OR HELL FOR ANYONE BUT ME TO KNOW IT!

WHICH MEANS THERE'S ONLY *ONE* COURSE LEFT OPEN TO ME.

AN', MUCH AS I HATE TA THINK ABOUT IT, NOTHIN' ELSE FOR ME TO *DO.*

OLIVER P. SNEAGLE-- YOU *WANTED* ME... BUT YER GONNA HAVE TO *FIND ME!*

'CAUSE FROM THIS MOMENT ON-- *LUKE CAGE IS DEAD!*

SEVERAL BLOCKS AWAY FROM CAGE'S LESS-THAN-LUXURIOUS OFFICE...

ALL RIGHT, JIMMY, I THINK WE'RE GOING TO BE *FINE*.

YOU SURE, DOC?

WELL, IN *TWENTY* YEARS OF *DOCTORING,* I'VE NEVER LOST A PATIENT TO A *SPRAINED* WRIST!

LUKE?

WHY ARE YOU DRESSED LIKE *THAT?*

I'M *LEAVING,* CLAIRE, RIGHT NOW. ONLY CAME TO SAY *GOODBYE.*

WHAT ARE YOU *TALKING* ABOUT, LUKE?

WHAT'S *WRONG,* LUKE? PLEASE-- *TELL ME!*

LOOK, BABY, I CAME *INTA* YOUR LIFE BECAUSE 'A *TROUBLE,* LET ME GET *OUTTA* IT 'FORE I CAUSE SOME MORE.

I DON'T WANT *NOTHIN'* TO HURT YOU, CLAIRE, YOU TOO, NOAH.

YOU *WON'T* TELL ME WHAT'S WRONG--AFTER *ALL* WE MEAN TO EACH OTHER?

BECAUSE WE MEAN SO MUCH TO EACH OTHER, CLAIRE. *THAT'S* WHY I'M SAYIN' *NOTHIN'* MORE.

CLAIRE, I WANT TO SPEAK WITH LUKE--*ALONE.*

PLEASE TAKE JIMMY BACK TO HIS MOTHER.

IT'S ABOUT SEAGATE, LUKE?

ISN'T *EVERYTHIN',* NOAH?

THE I.R.S. IS RUNNIN' A CHECK ON ME. THEY'LL *DISCOVER* WHO I AM.

THEY'LL FIND OUT WHO I AM, AND WHEN THEY DO, THEY'LL CONNECT ME WITH *YOU*.

THEY'LL FIND OUT YOU *KNEW* WHO I WAS-- THAT YOU WERE THE DOCTOR WHO *GAVE* ME THESE FREAKISH POWERS.

YOU'LL BE *ARRESTED* FOR PROTECTIN' A CRIMINAL, NOAH. YOU AN' CLAIRE.

BUT WITH ME GONE, YOU COULD SAY I *FORCED* YOU TO SAY NOTHIN'. THEY'LL *QUESTION* YOU, THEY'LL BE SUS-PICIOUS, BUT THEY WON'T HAVE ANYTHIN' TA *HANG* ON YOU.

Y'KNOW, IF I THOUGHT I COULD *BEAT* THIS RAP, I WOULDA TRIED. BUT I KNOW I *CAN'T*--NOT WITH-OUT HURTIN' MY *ONLY* FRIENDS.

SO THAT MEANS I GOTTA *GO*.

YOU'LL CALL US, TELL US *WHERE* YOU ARE, LUKE?

BETTER IF YOU *DON'T* KNOW, NOAH. LESS CHANCE ANYONE *ELSE'LL* FIND OUT.

SO LISTEN, OLD MAN-- TAKE CARE, WILLYA? I DON'T WANNA HEAR NOTHIN' *BAD*!

LUCAS, I'M *NOT* SAYING GOODBYE.

ONLY GOOD *LUCK*.

AND, A FEW MINUTES LATER...

WAS LUKE SERIOUS, NOAH? IS HE REALLY LEAVING?

HE'S *GONE*, CLAIRE, HE *HAD* TO GO.

BUT HE *CAN'T* DO THIS TO ME, NOAH. I *LOVE* HIM, HE'S MY *MAN*.

BUT HE HAS TO BE HIS *OWN* MAN, FIRST, CLAIRE.

HE HAS *NO* OTHER CHOICE.

GRAND CENTRAL STATION: SOME CALL IT THE *CROSSROADS* OF LIFE, THE *ENTRY* POINT TO NEW YORK.

BUT, TO THE MAN WHO CALLED HIMSELF LUKE CAGE FOR *FOUR* LONG YEARS, THIS WILL BE HIS *LAST* REMINDER OF THE CITY WHICH TOOK HIM IN, MADE HIM ONE OF ITS VERY OWN, AND IN A *STRANGE* WAY KNOWN ONLY TO ITS DEDICATED CITIZENS-- *LOVED* HIM AS NO OTHER CITY COULD.

THIS IS *GOODBYE*, LUCAS. YOU MADE THIS CITY YOUR OWN. NOW TAKE *PART* OF IT WITH YOU-- *WHEREVER* YOU GO.

HELL, I'M LATE--THE TRAIN'S ALREADY PULLIN' *OUT*!

TRACK 2

FIGGERS, CAN'T EVEN *LEAVE* THIS PLACE WITHOUT HAVIN' *TROUBLE* FOLLOW ME.

BUT THEN, TROUBLE AIN'T NO STRANGER TO LUKE--

WHAT AM I SAYIN'? LUKE CAGE IS *DEAD* AN' BURIED. FROM NOW ON I'M, UH--

--*MARK LUCAS.* YEAH! THAT NAME SOUNDS *GOOD.* MARK LUCAS IT *IS*!

TICKET, MISTER?

AIN'T GOT NONE, BUT HERE'S THE BREAD.

SHOULD PAY FOR A ONE WAY, DON'T IT?

TO CHICAGO? VERY GOOD, SIR.

THAT VOICE? IT'S HIM!

STILL HOUNDING ME...EVEN AFTER ALL THIS TIME.

BUT, HOW DID HE KNOW?

BAH! IT MAKES NO DIFFERENCE. IF CAGE IS HERE, ABOARD THIS TRAIN--

--THEN HE MUST DIE!

AND ONLY I AM ABLE TO ACCOMPLISH THAT LITTLE FEAT!

THERE'LL BE A NEW LIFE IN CHICAGO-- PEOPLE I DON'T KNOW...WHO DON'T KNOW ME.

I'M THROUGH WITH THAT POWER MAN, HERO-FOR-HIRE STUFF.

ONLY, CAN I BE THROUGH WITH CLAIRE? THAT'S THE ONLY QUESTION I GOT.

I DON'T KNOW HOW I'M GONNA MAKE IT WITHOUT YA, BABY.

I REALLY DON'T KNOW HOW.

BUT SOMEHOW I GOTTA TRY... FOR THE BOTH OF US.

FOR THE BOTH OF US...

A GOOD SOLDIER KNOWS *NOT* TO GIVE HIMSELF AWAY, CAGE.

OR ELSE THE *ENEMY* WILL MOVE FIRST.

SP—**AD!**

OBVIOUSLY, FOOL, YOU *NEVER* LEARNED THE CORRECT METHODS OF *WARFARE!*

CHRISTMAS!

IT'S BEEN A *LONG* TIME, HASN'T IT, CAGE? YOU MUST HAVE THOUGHT ME IN *CUSTODY* AFTER THAT SECURITY CITY FIASCO!*

BUT *NO ONE* IMPRISONS GIDEON MACE. *NO ONE!*

SWEET SISTER! YOU?!

LISSEN, MACE, I AIN'T—

* *POWER MAN* #23. — MARV W.

YOU'RE *NOT* GETTING THE CHANCE TO SPEAK, PIG.

YOU'RE *WEAK* NOW... I WON'T GIVE YOU THE CHANCE TO OFFSET THE *SURPRISE* OF MY ATTACK!

A GOOD GENERAL KNOWS WHEN TO STRIKE—WHEN HIS ENEMY IS AT HIS *WEAKEST*—AND YOU, CAGE...

...YOU ARE READY TO BE *SLAUGHTERED!*

DON'T *BET* ON THAT, SWEETS.

I AIN'T DOWN TILL I'M *OUT!*

THUK!

THAT WILL ONLY TAKE A MOMENT *MORE*, CAGE.

KRASH!

HE'S AFTER ME, AN' I CAN'T EVEN *TELL* 'IM HE CAN GO *WHISTLE* FOR ALL I CARE.

I DON'T *WANNA* FIGHT-- BUT HE AIN'T GIVIN' ME NO *CHOICE* HE'S *FORCED* ME INTA THIS.

HE'S MAKIN' ME TAKE UP BEIN' *POWER MAN* AGAIN!

SPOK!

BLAST YOU, MACE, IF I DIDN'T HATE YER *SLIMY* GUTS BEFORE--

--I'M *SICK* UP TA MY *ARMPITS* OF YOU NOW!

MACE'S EYES *GLIMMER* MADLY WITH EVERY ATTACK HE MAKES.

AGAIN AND *AGAIN* HE *LASHES* OUT.

UNTIL... YOU'RE *THROUGH*, CAGE.

YOU'RE *OUT* OF MY *HAIR--* FOREVER!

DON'T BE SO *SURE* A' THAT, DARLIN'!

YOU EVER HEAR 'BOUT THE *BAD PENNY* WHICH KEEPS TURNIN' UP?

WELL, *THIS* LITTLE ONE-CENT PIECE IS COMIN' FOR YA, GRUESOME--

--AN' HE'S GONNA *SQUEEZE* CHANGE OUTTA YA. HE'S GONNA *SQUEEZE* CHANGE, BABY!

EVER THE *BRAGGART*, CAGE? EVER THE ARROGANT *PUP!*

BUT GIDEON MACE DOESN'T *NEED* TO REVEL IN SELF-GLORY.

ONE OF THE MOST *GLORIOUS* MILITARY CAREERS IN U.S. HISTORY STANDS *BEHIND* ME...

...AND AN *UNSHATTER-ABLE* TITANIUM STEEL *MACE* AFFIXED TO MY WRIST WILL *SPEAK FOR ME!*

SHOK!

BTOK!

AN' A *JAW* MADE A' TAPIOCA PUDDIN' IS WAITIN' TA BE *SMASHED* FROM HERE TA *CLEVELAND*, SWEETY.

YER A POMPOUS JACKASS. YA *KNOW* THAT, CREEP?

AND *YOU'RE* AN INCOMPETENT *FOOL*, CAGE.

SNOK!

UNGGHHH!

WASN'T *BRACED*... COULDN'T *ROLL* WITH IT.

CHICAGO CENTRAL

YOU'D *HAD* YOUR WARNING NOW, CAGE. STAY *OUT* OF MY AFFAIRS.

MAYBE I WASN'T AFTER YOU *BEFORE*-- BUT NOW *NOTHIN'* CAN KEEP LU--ER, MARK LUCAS OFF YOUR SLIMY TAIL!

CHICAGO, HERE I COME!

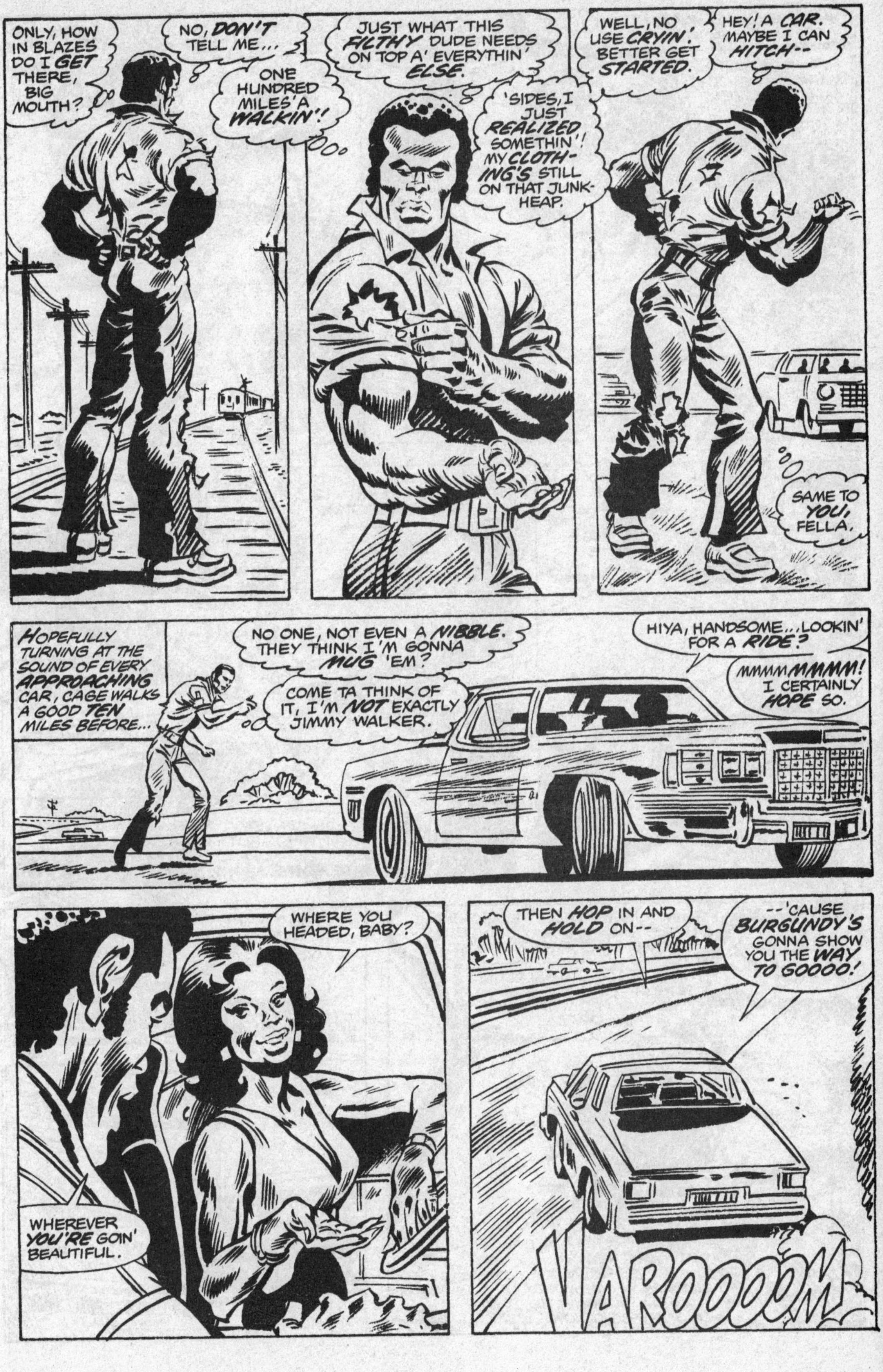

ONLY, HOW IN BLAZES DO I GET THERE, BIG MOUTH?
NO, DON'T TELL ME...
ONE HUNDRED MILES'A WALKIN'!
JUST WHAT THIS FILTHY DUDE NEEDS ON TOP A' EVERYTHIN' ELSE.
'SIDES, I JUST REALIZED SOMETHIN'! MY CLOTHING'S STILL ON THAT JUNK-HEAP.
WELL, NO USE CRYIN'. BETTER GET STARTED.
HEY! A CAR. MAYBE I CAN HITCH--
SAME TO YOU, FELLA.
HOPEFULLY TURNING AT THE SOUND OF EVERY APPROACHING CAR, CAGE WALKS A GOOD TEN MILES BEFORE...
NO ONE, NOT EVEN A NIBBLE. THEY THINK I'M GONNA MUG 'EM?
COME TA THINK OF IT, I'M NOT EXACTLY JIMMY WALKER.
HIYA, HANDSOME... LOOKIN' FOR A RIDE?
MMMMMMMM! I CERTAINLY HOPE SO.
WHERE YOU HEADED, BABY?
WHEREVER YOU'RE GOIN' BEAUTIFUL.
THEN HOP IN AND HOLD ON--
--'CAUSE BURGUNDY'S GONNA SHOW YOU THE WAY TO GOOOO!
VAROOOOM

DON'T SEE MANY *HIKERS* OUT THESE DAYS, MISTER--?

LU--ER, *LUCAS!* MARK LUCAS. JUST CALL ME *MARK,* BABY.

GOTCHA, MARK BABY. WHERE YOU *FROM?*

THE EAST... JERSEY. EVERYPLACE, I SORTA GUESS.

WELL, BABY, NOW YOU'RE HEADIN' TO THE BIG TOWN-- *CHICAGO!*

AN' MACE, BABY. HE'S GOTTA BE HOLED UP THERE.

GOOD. I GOT ME MY *SCORE* TO SETTLE.

WOOOWEEEE! SHE'S PACKIN' A PIECE!

OH, YOU *SAW* THE GUN, EH, MARK?

DON'T WORRY ABOUT IT, HANDSOME-- I ONLY USE IT FOR *PROTECTION.*

BUT YOU SUDDENLY GOT A *HAUNTED* LOOK ABOUT YOU, BABY. YOU *RUNNIN'* FROM SOME- THIN'?

YOU CAN *SAY* THAT, BABY. BUT NOTHIN' BIG 'NUFF TO WRITE *HOME* ABOUT.

HMMM. SOMETHING TELLS THIS LITTLE BIRD YOU MAY BE NEEDIN' A *JOB.* AM I *RIGHT,* HANDSOME?

WHAT'VE YOU STUMBLED INTO NOW, CAGE? SHE'S *GOT* TO BE INVOLVED WITH SOME- THIN' *SHADY.*

BUT I *DO* NEED A JOB...NEED *SOMETHIN'*-- MY CLOTHES AN' MY MONEY IS PROBABLY SOMEWHERE IN CHICAGO RIGHT NOW.

IF IT AIN'T *TOO* ILLEGAL, BABY, YOU *GOT* ME.

SOMEHOW, HANDSOME, I JUST THOUGHT I *MIGHT.*

STOWN 8
VILLE 15
RBORO 21

THIS IS MY *PAD*, HANDSOME.

NOT BAD, BUT AIN'T IT *EXPENSIVE?*

YOU PAY FOR THIS ALL *YOURSELF*, BABY?

I LIVE *ALONE*, IF THAT'S WHAT YOU'RE GETTIN' AT, BUT IT'S *PAID* FOR BY MY EMPLOYE

YOURS, TOO-- IF THINGS GO WELL, AND WOULDN'T *THAT* BE COZY?

C'MON, GET YOURSELF *CLEANED* UP.

AN' BY THE WAY, HANDSOME, THERE'S A PAIR OF *PANTS* IN THE BATHROOM CLOSET. SHIRT, TOO.

SHOULD BE *YOUR* SIZE.

IT *IS*, BURGUNDY. YOU *ALWAYS* KEEP MEN'S STUFF AROUND?

NEVER CAN TELL WHEN IT'LL COME IN *HANDY*, SWEETS.

NOW, C'MON. I TOLD MY BOSS ABOUT YOU, AND HE'S *WAITING.*

LET'S *GO!*

NEXT ISSUE: MURDER IS THE MAN CALLED MACE!

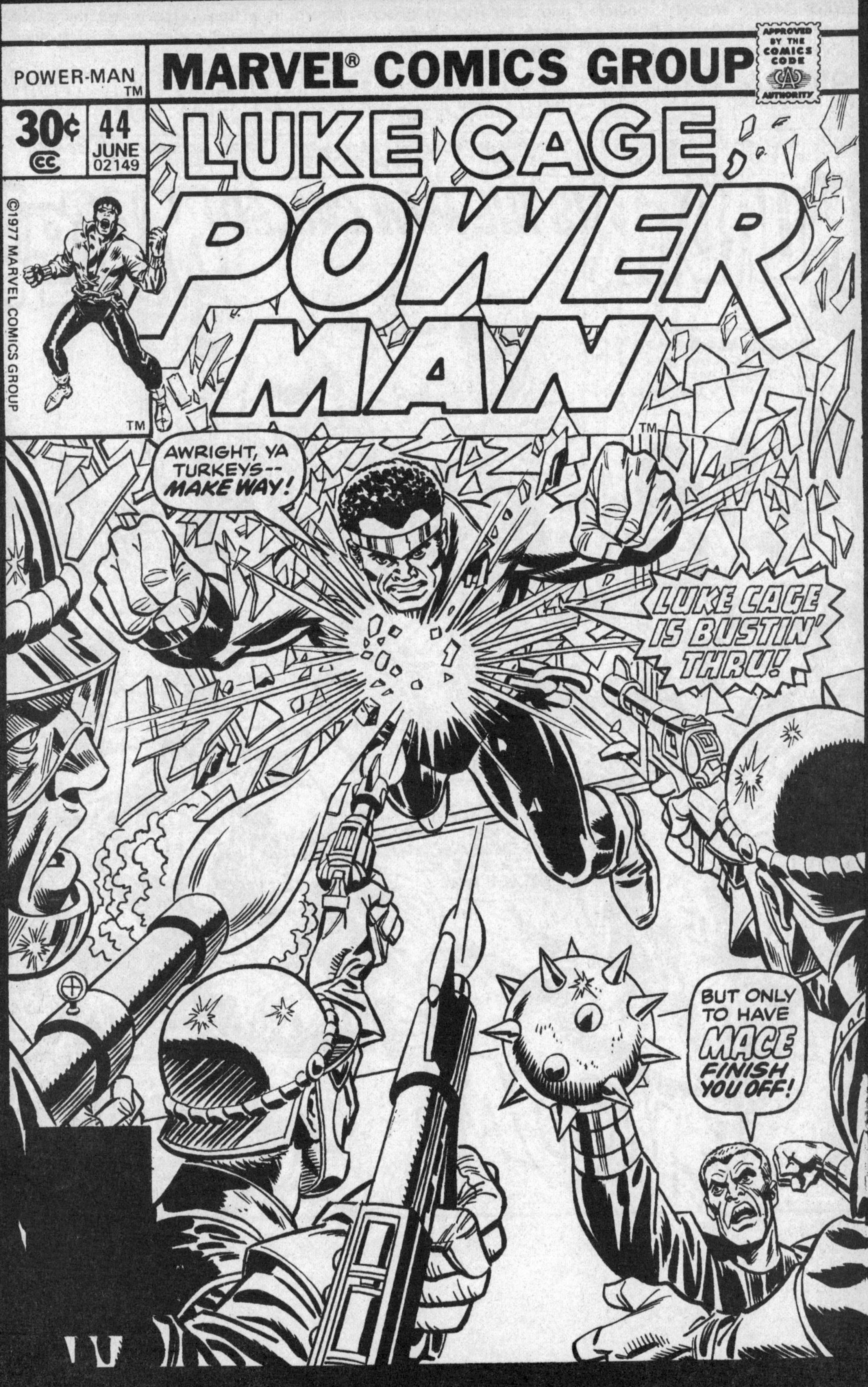

POWER-MAN ™
MARVEL® COMICS GROUP
APPROVED BY THE COMICS CODE AUTHORITY
30¢
CC
44
JUNE
02149
©1977 MARVEL COMICS GROUP
LUKE CAGE,
POWER MAN ™
AWRIGHT, YA TURKEYS-- MAKE WAY!
LUKE CAGE IS BUSTIN' THRU!
BUT ONLY TO HAVE MACE FINISH YOU OFF!

LUKE CAGE: Wrongly convicted and sentenced to prison—reborn in a freak experiment there that gave him *steel-hard skin* and *strength beyond belief*—a man who hides his identity as an escaped convict in the role of a *HERO FOR HIRE!*

STAN LEE PRESENTS: LUKE CAGE, POWER MAN!

MARV WOLFMAN EDITOR/PLOT / **LEE ELIAS & TOM PALMER** PENCILS / INKS / **ED HANNIGAN** GUEST SCRIPTER / **JOE ROSEN** LETTERER / **J. COHEN** COLORS

MURDER IS THE MAN CALLED MACE!

YOU'RE *CRAZY*, MACE! WAIT'LL I GET MY--

SHUT-UP, CAGE, AND STOP *STRUGGLING*, THOSE BONDS WHICH HOLD YOU ARE TITANIUM-STEEL *CABLES*. YOU'LL *NEVER* GET FREE.

SEE THESE *GUNS*, PRISONER--? THEY'RE MY SPECIAL *ANTI-PERSONNEL* BAZOOKAS, WITH EXPLOSIVE *PROXIMITY* ROCKETS.

YOU NEEDN'T SCORE A *DIRECT HIT* TO KILL YOUR TARGET.

MY SOLDIERS' *RIFLES* ARE SIMILARLY EQUIPPED!

WHY'S THAT? CAN'T THEY *SHOOT STRAIGHT*?

LISTEN, SWEETIE, YOU CAN *RANT* ALL YOU WANT, AN' IT DON'T MEAN *NOTHIN'* TO ME. WHY'NCHA SET ME FREE AN' SEE *HOW LONG* YER TIN SOLDIERS'LL LAST 'GAINST *POWER MAN*--POP-GUNS AN' ALL?

ENOUGH!

I'M BEING VERY *PATIENT* WITH YOU, CAGE-- BUT, PERHAPS YOU NEED A *DEMONSTRATION* TO CURB YOUR *ARROGANCE*.

HNNNH--

WATCH WHAT I DO TO THAT *STEEL WALL*...

DO YOU *COMPREHEND*, CAGE?

BWAM!

I CAN *DESTROY* YOU ANYTIME I *WANT* TO, SUCH IS THE *STRENGTH* OF THE *INVINCIBLE MACE* REPLACING MY *RIGHT HAND*.

BUT MY *TRUE* STRENGTH IS THE *WILL*-- THE *RESOLVE* TO FACE AND *DESTROY* MY *ENEMIES*.

THAT'S THE STRENGTH *AMERICA* NEEDS TO REGAIN ITS LOST *STATUS* IN THE EYES OF THE *WORLD*!

AND SINCE THIS COUNTRY NOW IS RUN BY *WEAKLINGS*-- I *WILL* DO IT, AND THEN AMERICA WILL BE *MINE*!

ON YET ANOTHER FLOOR OF THE VAST BUILDING...

THIS IS HOW SOLDIERS WERE MEANT TO BE TRAINED--

--WITH UNRELENTING DISCIPLINE-- TRAINED TO USE ALL FORMS OF THE MARTIAL ARTS--

--AND TO KILL, MERCILESSLY-- NOT LIKE AMERICA'S MOLLY-CODDLED VOLUNTEER ARMY.

I'M PROUD OF MY MEN.

LEAST HE'S GIVIN' ME THE TIME I NEED TO STRAIN THESE BLASTED BONDS--

WHERE'DJA GET THESE POWDER-PUFFS, ANYWAY?

THESE SPLENDID SOLDIERS, CAGE, ARE ALL DISILLUSIONED VETERANS OF WAR, AND MEN WHO WERE REJECTED FOR BEING WHAT THE ARMY CALLS OVER-ZEALOUS--

WOK!

KAAII!

--EVEN AS I WAS DISCHARGED BY THE SAME WITLESS FOOLS.

IT'S SHAMEFUL HOW WEAK AND GUTLESS THE GOVERNMENT OF THIS NATION HAS BECOME. THEY REFUSE TO TAKE A STAND ANYWHERE IN THE WORLD-- INSTEAD, ALL OVER THE GLOBE, OUR ONCE-PROUD MILITARY BASES ARE BEING SHUT DOWN--

--BLEEDING HEARTS ARE CUTTING BACK THE DEFENSES OF AMERICA, WHILE OUR MIGHTIEST ENEMY SPENDS SIX TIMES AS MUCH PREPARING FOR WAR!

IT'S IN ALL THE PAPERS.

I ONLY READ THE FUNNIES, BABY.

YOU SCOFF, BUT I HAVE SYMPATHIZERS AND CADRES THROUGHOUT THE COUNTRY. YOU COULD HAVE BEEN ONE OF MY OFFICERS, BUT YOU WERE TOO HARD-HEADED--

--LIKE ALL YOUR KIND!

COMBAT TRAINING AREA-D

AUTHORIZED PERSONNEL ONLY

YEAH, SWEETUMS-- WE'RE TOO BUSY SHUFFLIN' ABOUT TO START WARS.

IMPUDENT FOOL! I'LL NOT BE MOCKED!

SWAK!

MACE, I'LL--

DON'T TRY IT, MR. CAGE. MY GUARDS WILL SHOOT YOU DOWN BEFORE YOU EVEN GET *NEAR* ME!

AND *BELIEVE* ME, THEIR *EXPLOSIVE* BULLETS CAN PENETRATE EVEN *YOUR* STEEL HIDE!

HOWEVER, I WANT TO KEEP YOU *HEALTHY* FOR *YOUR* PART IN MY TRIUMPHANT COUP.

EVERYTHIN' *ALL RIGHT* HERE, BOSS?

BURGUNDY, COME IN, EVERYTHING'S *FINE!*

I WAS JUST ABOUT TO *EXPLAIN* TO MR. CAGE WHAT HIS ROLE IN THE *HISTORY BOOKS* WILL BE!

WELL, WELL, IF IT AIN'T LITTLE MISS *TURNCOAT!*

YOU GOT IT *ALL* WRONG, LUKE, HONEY. I'M ON MACE'S SIDE 'CAUSE HE'S *RIGHT.*

WHY CAN'T YOU *SEE* THAT?

OH, YEAH! I *KNOW* HOW RIGHT HE IS. ME AN' YOUR *MURDERIN'* BOSS GO WAY BACK.

LUKE, *LUKE.* YOU REMIND ME OF MY HUSBAND, JAIME. I *LIKED* YOU WHEN I MET YOU ON THE *HIGHWAY.** I DIDN'T EVEN KNOW WHO YOU *WERE* UNTIL I CALLED COL. MACE FROM MY *APARTMENT.* C'MON, WHY DON'T YOU *JOIN* US?

I'M SURE IT'S NOT TOO LATE.

STAY *AWAY* FROM ME, LADY. YER MAKIN' ME *SICK.*

*LAST ISH--MARV.

SSNAP!

IN FACT, I'M SICK'A *ALLA* YOU *CRUDS,* AN' I'M GONNA START *MESSIN'* UP THIS BEAUTY PARLOR--

--RIGHT NOW!

OHH...

LOOK OUT! HE'S FR-- UHHN!

PWAK!

OUTTA MY *WAY,* SOLDIER BOY.

CAPTURE HIM! YOU DID IT BEFORE, AND YOU CAN DO IT AGAIN! THAT'S AN ORDER!

I NEED HIM FOR OPERATION: CAGE!

NO WAY, ATTILA-- YER CADETS TOOK ME BY SURPRISE LAST TIME. NOW I GOT THE JUMP ON 'EM.

SWEET DREAMS, GRUNT!

POW!

CAN'T FIRE, HE'S TOO CLOSE TO TH' OTHER GUYS.

WE CAN TAKE 'IM WITH TEAMWORK, JUST LIKE THE COLONEL TAUGHT US.

OWW! HIS SKIN-- IT'S HARDER'N STEEL!

WHAM

GOTTA ADMIT-- THESE GUYS KNOW THEIR STUFF.

BUT THEY AIN'T NO MATCH FOR 300 LBS. OF MADDER'N'HELL POWER MAN--!

YEOWW!

SLAM!

--RETIRED OR NOT.

IN THE CLEAR. NOW, IF I CAN JUST GET TO MACE, AN' END THIS LITTLE TURKEY-TROT!

GOT A BEAD ON 'IM...

BUT THE BOSS WANTS 'IM ALIVE, SO...

OOOF! NO DICE.

BLAAM!

ALRIGHT-- HALT! STOP RIGHT THERE!

SIT ON IT, PAL -- I GOT BUSINESS WITH YER C.O.

BLAM!

NO GOOD! THEY GOT ME BOXED IN WITH THOSE BLASTED GUNS!

CAN'T TAKE MUCH MORE!

THAT WINDOW! I'LL GET OUTTA HERE, AN' GET ME SOME REINFORCEMENTS.

GO, LUCAS-- GO!

GET HIM! HE'S TRYING TO ESCAPE!

REMEMBER YOUR TRAINING, YOU LITTLE FOOLS!

NUTS. I FORGOT HOW FAR UP THIS FLOOR IS.

CAN'T GO OUT HERE. HAFTA TRY SOME OTHER--

--THEN, AGAIN...

SINCE YER SUCH AN EAGER SOUL, JUNIOR...

--I'LL TWIST AROUND AN' LET YOU LAND FIRST.

NOOOOO

WUMMPH! ROOF SLOWED US DOWN, PROB'LY SAVIN' BOTH OUR LIVES.

G. I. JOE HERE'LL BE TOO BUSTED UP FOR TARGET PRACTICE IN THE NEAR FUTURE, THOUGH.

I'LL TRY NOT TO LAND ON 'IM... TOO HARD!

CRASH!

YEAH, HE'S *BREATHIN'.* THAT'S COOL.

STOP THAT MAN. HE'S A DANGEROUS *CRIMINAL!*

UH, OH! THANKS FER *REMINDIN'* ME THAT I'M S'POSED TO BE ON THE *RUN* FROM THE *I.R.S.*

AN', IN THIS COUNTRY, *TAX EVASION'S* A WORSE CRIME'N *MURDER!*

BETTER *SPLIT* 'TIL I FIGGER OUT WHAT TO *DO!*

HEY, WE SHOULD TRY TO *STOP* HIM!

BE MY *GUEST,* LADY, *I'M* NOT TACKLIN' *HIM!*

BLAST IT! WE HAVE TO CATCH HIM. IF HE GOES TO THE *AUTHORITIES,* IT COULD *RUIN* EVERYTHING!

GET OUT THERE AND STOP HIM, EVEN IF YOU HAVE TO *KILL* HIM!

MACE! PLEASE DON'T LET THEM *HURT* LUKE! *PROMISE* ME!

THINK, BURGUNDY, IF THE POLICE FIND OUT WHAT WE'RE PLANNING--

--THEY'LL COME IN HERE WITH *GUNS BLAZING!*

I'M TRYING TO PREVENT A *BLOOD-BATH!*

I CAN'T LET THAT *HAPPEN* -- DO YOU *UNDERSTAND?*

Y-YES.

BASH!

GOOD. LET'S NOT SEE ANYMORE *WEAKNESS!*

I HAVE MANY *SUPPORTERS,* SOME OF WHOM ARE QUITE WEALTHY. I'M *PLEDGED* TO A *BLOODLESS* COUP D'ETAT!

THERE WON'T BE ANY *UNNECESSARY* DEATHS!

BUT *CAGE MUST BE STOPPED!*

SOME HOURS LATER...

LUKE, MY MAN, YOU DONE IT *NOW.* GOTTA STOP *MACE,* BUT *HOW?*

TOO *WEAK,* HAVE TO *REST.*

CAN'T GO TO THE *POLICE,* OR EVEN LET 'EM *FIND* ME, 'CAUSE IF THEY RUN A *CHECK,* THEY'LL KNOW WHO I AM-- AN *ESCAPED CON!*

'N WHO'S GONNA *BELIEVE* ME? THEY DON'T EVEN KNOW I'M *INNOCENT.*

I CAN'T *PROVE* IT, EITHER. *DAMN* SNEAGLE AN' HIS BLASTED *TAX AUDIT!*

I DON'T EVEN KNOW *ANYBODY* IN CHICAGO TO HIDE ME OUT!

HEY, PAL... YOU NEW 'ROUND HERE?

YEAH, I'M FROM OUTTA TOWN.

WELCOME TO THE *WINDY CITY!* S'MATTER-- MAYOR FORGET T'GIVE YA THE *KEY?*

HEH, HEH. *BLURP*

HERE, HAVE A HIT O' *THISH--* LIF'Y *SPIRITS.*

NO, *THANKS*-- COULDN'T DROWN *MY* HASSLES WITH *TEN* BOTTLES A *THAT* MEDICINE.

HEY-- THISH 'SH *GOOD STUFF.* BESHT *BURGUNDY* MONEY CAN BUY--!

BURGUNDY..?

--NOT THAT I *BOUGHT* IT, ZACKLY.

SEE YA 'ROUND, OLD TIMER.

FOLK JUSHT AIN' *P'LITE* ANYMORE. LET'S SEE-- WHERE WAS WE?

OH, YEAH...

...TRY'NA SEE IF I DRINK ENUFFA THISH *BURGUNDY,* I CAN READ TH' *FRENCH* ON TH' LABEL!

BLURP

SOON, AT THE APARTMENT OF--

BURGUNDY, HONEY, PULL YOURSELF *TOGETHER.*

SURE, THE HERO FOR HIRE IS *CUTE*, BUT YOU'VE WORKED *TOO HARD* FOR *MACE*, TO BLOW IT NOW.

BESIDES THE FACT THAT LUKE HATES YOUR *GUTS.*

WELL, BY TOMORROW, IT'LL BE ALL *OVER.*

WE'LL BE *RUNNIN'* THE CITY...

...AN' JAIME'S *DEATH* WON'T HAVE BEEN FOR *NOTHING.* WHAT'S THAT--?

DON'T MAKE A *SOUND*-- I WON'T HURT YA

CAGE?!

YER BOSS PROB'LY HAS MORE *BUGS* IN HERE THAN A 10TH AVENUE *FLOP HOUSE*-- SO JUST TALK LOW AN' NATURAL.

WHY TALK AT ALL...

WHEN WE CAN DO *THIS,* INSTEAD?

...MMMMM!

NOW, THAT AIN'T *BAD*, IS IT, HONEY?

CLICK--

RINNGGGG!

WHA--

THAT'S THE ALARM FROM *BURGUNDY'S* APARTMENT.

WELL, WELL-- WHAT A *GOOD* LITTLE GIRL!

KLIK!

LOOKS LIKE WE'RE STILL ON *SCHEDULE*, GENTLEMEN.

LET'S GET *OVER* THERE.

ON THE *DOUBLE!*

WHILE...

ALRIGHT, LADY, THAT'S *NOT* WHAT I CAME HERE FOR--

OHH!

SURE, LONE RANGER-- YOU'D RATHER KISS YOUR *HORSE*, RIGHT?

FIGGERS YOU'D THINK THAT WAY!

I-I'M *SORRY*, LUKE. I *DO* LIKE YOU-- *REALLY.*

FORGET IT, LADY-- I *CAME* HERE 'CAUSE I COULDN'T GO TO THE *POLICE.*

YER *BOSS* PROB'LY HAS ALL THE PRECINCTS COVERED ANYWAY-- HOPIN' TO *KILL* ME 'FORE I CAN BLOW THE *WHISTLE* ON 'IM!

HE'S *NOT* A KILLER-- HE'S A *HERO!*

YEAH? TELL ME ALL ABOUT IT.

IF YOU'LL *LISTEN*, CAGE. THOUGH I *DOUBT* IT. MY HUSBAND, JAMIE, HE WAS A SOLDIER IN 'NAM--

-- WORKING UNDER *MACE*.

"JAIME WAS AN *IDEALIST*, CAGE. HE FELT THE CONG WERE HURTING *FREEDOM*. HE WANTED TO FIGHT, AND HE MANAGED TO GET INTO MACE'S OUTFIT.

"YOU SEE, HE HEARD MACE WAS A *GOOD* SOLDIER. THE BEST.

"IT WAS IN 1968, DURING THE *TET OFFENSIVE* THAT MACE LED HIS NEW TROOPS INTO BATTLE.

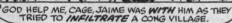

"GOD HELP ME, CAGE, JAIME WAS *WITH* HIM AS THEY TRIED TO *INFILTRATE* A CONG VILLAGE.

"JAIME WAS TOO EAGER, HE THOUGHT HE SAW A SNIPER. GUN IN HAND, HE STALKED FORWARD--

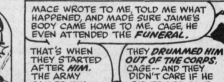

"--ONLY MACE TRIED TO CALL HIM BACK, TRIED TO *WARN* HIM.

"BUT JAIME DIDN'T HEAR THE SHOUTS, ALL HE HEARD WAS AN *EXPLOSION*, AND IT ENDED HIS LIFE--

"--EVEN AS IT *RIPPED* MACE'S HAND FROM HIS WRIST AS MACE TRIED TO PULL JAIME FREE."

MACE WROTE TO ME, TOLD ME WHAT HAPPENED, AND MADE SURE JAIME'S BODY CAME HOME TO ME. CAGE, HE EVEN ATTENDED THE *FUNERAL*.

THAT'S WHEN THEY STARTED AFTER *HIM*. THE ARMY CALLED HIM *UNFIT* BECAUSE OF HIS SEVERED HAND.

THEY *DRUMMED HIM OUT OF THE CORPS*, CAGE-- AND THEY DIDN'T CARE IF HE DID TRY TO SAVE JAIME. THEY DIDN'T CARE AT ALL.

AND THAT'S WHEN YOU STARTED WORKIN' FOR 'IM?

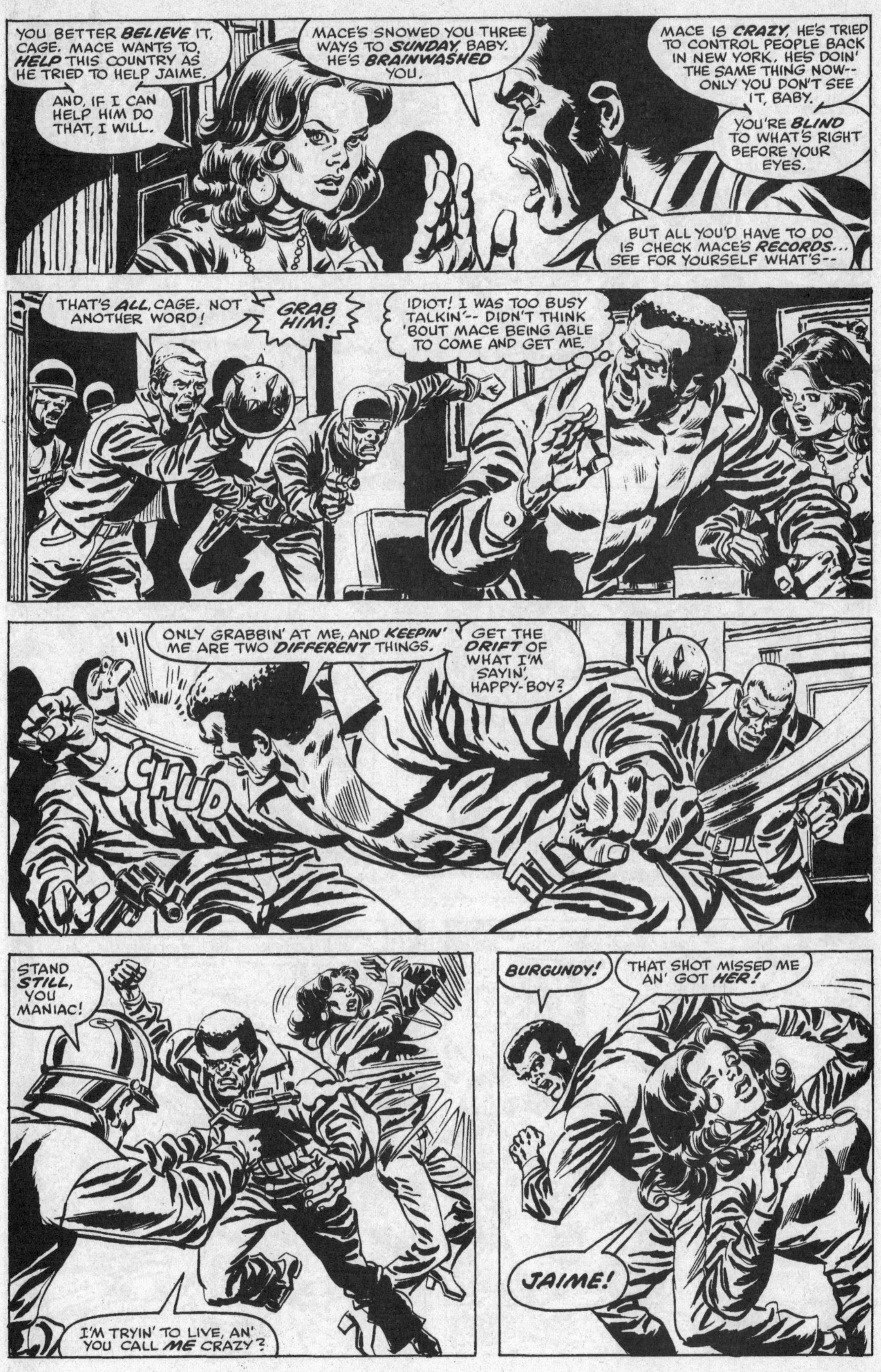
YOU BETTER BELIEVE IT, CAGE. MACE WANTS TO HELP THIS COUNTRY AS HE TRIED TO HELP JAIME.
AND, IF I CAN HELP HIM DO THAT, I WILL.
MACE'S SNOWED YOU THREE WAYS TO SUNDAY, BABY. HE'S BRAINWASHED YOU.
MACE IS CRAZY, HE'S TRIED TO CONTROL PEOPLE BACK IN NEW YORK. HE'S DOIN' THE SAME THING NOW-- ONLY YOU DON'T SEE IT, BABY.
YOU'RE BLIND TO WHAT'S RIGHT BEFORE YOUR EYES.
BUT ALL YOU'D HAVE TO DO IS CHECK MACE'S RECORDS... SEE FOR YOURSELF WHAT'S--
THAT'S ALL, CAGE. NOT ANOTHER WORD!
GRAB HIM!
IDIOT! I WAS TOO BUSY TALKIN'-- DIDN'T THINK 'BOUT MACE BEING ABLE TO COME AND GET ME.
ONLY GRABBIN' AT ME, AND KEEPIN' ME ARE TWO DIFFERENT THINGS.
GET THE DRIFT OF WHAT I'M SAYIN', HAPPY-BOY?
CHUD
STAND STILL, YOU MANIAC!
I'M TRYIN' TO LIVE, AN' YOU CALL ME CRAZY?
BURGUNDY!
THAT SHOT MISSED ME AN' GOT HER!
JAIME!

YOU MOTHERLESS CREEPS, YOU COULDA KILLED--

WE ONLY *NICKED* HER, FOOL. BUT YOU WILL NOT BE SO LUCKY!

THWOK

ALL RIGHT, MEN, CART THIS ONE AWAY, ATTACH HIM TO PROJECT *ALPHA!*

CAGE WANTED TO SEE WHAT I WAS UP TO--

--HE WILL, *CLOSE UP!*

AND I AM SURE WHAT HE SEES--*WILL BE THE FINAL THING LUKE CAGE WILL EVER SEE!*

YOU DID A FINE JOB, BURGUNDY. YOU WILL BE RICHLY REWARDED.

AND WHAT WILL HAPPEN TO *CAGE?*

HE WILL DIE, AS *ALL* WHO GET IN MY WAY WILL FALL.

I CAN'T ALLOW MY PLANS TO BE *SLOWED UP!*

NOW, NOW, MY DEAR, DON'T FRET. THINGS WILL WORK OUT VERY WELL...

...ONCE YOU'VE SEEN THAT *DEATH* IS A NORMAL PART OF LIFE.

MACE, I-I'LL JOIN YOU LATER.

I WANT TO C-CLEAN UP THE MESS HERE.

VERY WELL, BURGUNDY. TONIGHT.

YOU... *LIED* TO ME, MACE. YOU LIED ABOUT... *LUKE*, AND NOW, HE'S GOING TO DIE!

NOT... SURE WHAT I SHOULD *DO*.

MAYBE CAGE WAS *RIGHT!* *JAIME* NEVER WANTED TO *TAKE OVER* ANYTHING! HE WAS JUST TRYING TO *PROTECT* HIS COUNTRY, HIS *PEOPLE*.

184 MEMORIAL DRIVE, PLEASE.

MAYBE I CAN *FIND OUT* BEFORE IT'S TOO *LATE*...

...MAYBE I CAN *FIND OUT*, MACE--

-- *HOW BIG* IS YOUR *LIE?!*

U.S. ARMY ADMINISTRATION BUILDING

HELP YOU, MA'AM?

Y-YES. MY *HUSBAND*... DIED IN *VIET NAM!* HERE'S HIS *I.D.*

INQUIRIES

DEPT. OF THE ARMY PERSONNEL RECORDS

I WONDER IF YOU COULD GIVE ME ANY *INFORMATION* ON HIS COMMANDING OFFICER-- *COL. GIDEON MACE*. HE WAS QUITE *CLOSE* TO JAIME.

IN FACT, COL. MACE TRIED TO SAVE MY HUSBAND'S *LIFE*.

WELL, I'M NOT SUPPOSED TO *DO* THIS, BUT-- HERE'S COL. MACE'S *FILE!* HOPE IT HELPS YOU *FIND* HIM.

RETIRED

THANK YOU, CORPORAL.

OH... *NO!*

COL. GIDEON M

UNITED STATES DEPT. OF THE ARMY

SERIAL NO. A01372712

NAME: Mace, Gideon
RANK: Colonel
DISCHARGE: Medical
REASON FOR DISCHARGE: Insubordination, mental incompetence, suspicion of combat activity independent of orders
NOTE: The attitude of this officer was consistently one of violent disregard of standard Army operational procedures. Unfit to command or serve in the Armed Forces of the United States.
Signature *General William Westmoorland*
General William Westmoorland

SAY, IS ANYTHING WRONG, MA'AM?

NO... NOTHING.

JAIME... LUKE-- BOTH MURDERED... BY *MACE!*

SOON--AT MACE'S HEADQUARTERS...

THIS **WON'T** JUST BE FOR YOU AND ME, JAIME...

ALL RIGHT, YOU MEN HAVE YOUR ORDERS-- I EXPECT **PERFECT** PERFORMANCE! **NO SCREW-UPS!**

MACE... **YOU MURDERING SCUM!**

WHY, **BURGUNDY**--!

YOU... **LIAR!** YOU DIDN'T TRY TO SAVE **JAIME'S** LIFE! **HE** DIED SAVING **YOURS!** I READ IT IN YOUR **DISCHARGE RECORDS!**

HE DIED ON AN **UNAUTHORIZED MISSION!** THEY KICKED YOU OUT 'CAUSE YOU'RE **CRAZY!**

YES...THAT'S HOW THE **ARMY** SAW IT, TOO--AND THEY WERE **WRONG!**

WRONG, BECAUSE THEY WERE **WEAK**-- AND TODAY'S ARMY IS EVEN **WEAKER!**

MY PEOPLE ARE **STRONG!** THEY KNOW HOW TO FOLLOW **MY** ORDERS!

THAT'S WHY THE CITY OF **CHICAGO,** **EVANSTON,** AND THE **SOUTHERN PORTS** OF LAKE **MICHIGAN...**

FWAM!

...WILL ALL BE **MINE** BY THIS TIME **TOMORROW!**

I DON'T **CARE** HOW YOU INTERPRET THE ARMY'S FILES, MY DEAR--

--BY TOMORROW, AMERICA'S **REMAINING** WEAKLINGS WILL BE **QUAKING** WITH FEAR!

THE ONES IN **THIS** SECTOR WILL ALL BE **DEAD!**

DEAD?!

YOU SAID YOUR *TAKEOVER* WOULD BE *PEACEFUL*-- YOU SAID THERE WOULD *BE* NO--

--*UNNECESSARY* DEATHS, MY DEAR--!

UNFORTUNATELY, MILITARY *STRATEGY* REQUIRES THAT THIS AREA BE *DEPOPULATED*... TO MAKE A SLUMBERING AMERICA *AWARE* OF MY POWER.

OBSERVE.

KLIK!

LUKE-- *ALIVE!* THEN THERE'S STILL *HOPE.*

HOPE? *I* AM THE ONLY HOPE FOR THIS NATION. MR. CAGE WILL DIE A *SYMBOLIC* DEATH--

--AN *EXAMPLE* TO THOSE *FOOLISH* ENOUGH TO *OPPOSE* ME, AND AMERICA'S *DESTINY!*

THAT DEVICE CAGE IS LASHED TO IS A *COBALT BOMB.* IT'S DESIGNED TO UNLEASH A *RADIATION BLAST* CAPABLE OF KILLING *ALL* HUMAN AND ANIMAL LIFE IN THIS CITY.

THE *GENIUS* OF IT IS THAT THE BOMB PRODUCES *NO* SHOCK-WAVES. THE *INFRA-STRUCTURE*, THE BUILD-INGS OF THE CITY, WILL REMAIN INTACT!

BUT THE *PEOPLE* WILL ALL BE *DEAD!*

YES-- *EXACTLY!*

MY FORCES ARE EQUIPPED WITH *RADIATION SUITS!* THUS IMMUNE TO THE EFFECTS OF THE COBALT BLAST--

--THEY WILL *SECURE* THE CHICAGO AREA AGAINST THE POSSIBILITY OF *INVASION* FROM WITHOUT. IT WILL BE MY SOVEREIGN *FORTRESS!*

NO, *NO!* MURDERER!

THIS IS *WAR*, MY DEAR. THE *STRONG* AMERICANS, THE *SMART* AMERICANS, WILL SUPPORT MY *CAUSE!*

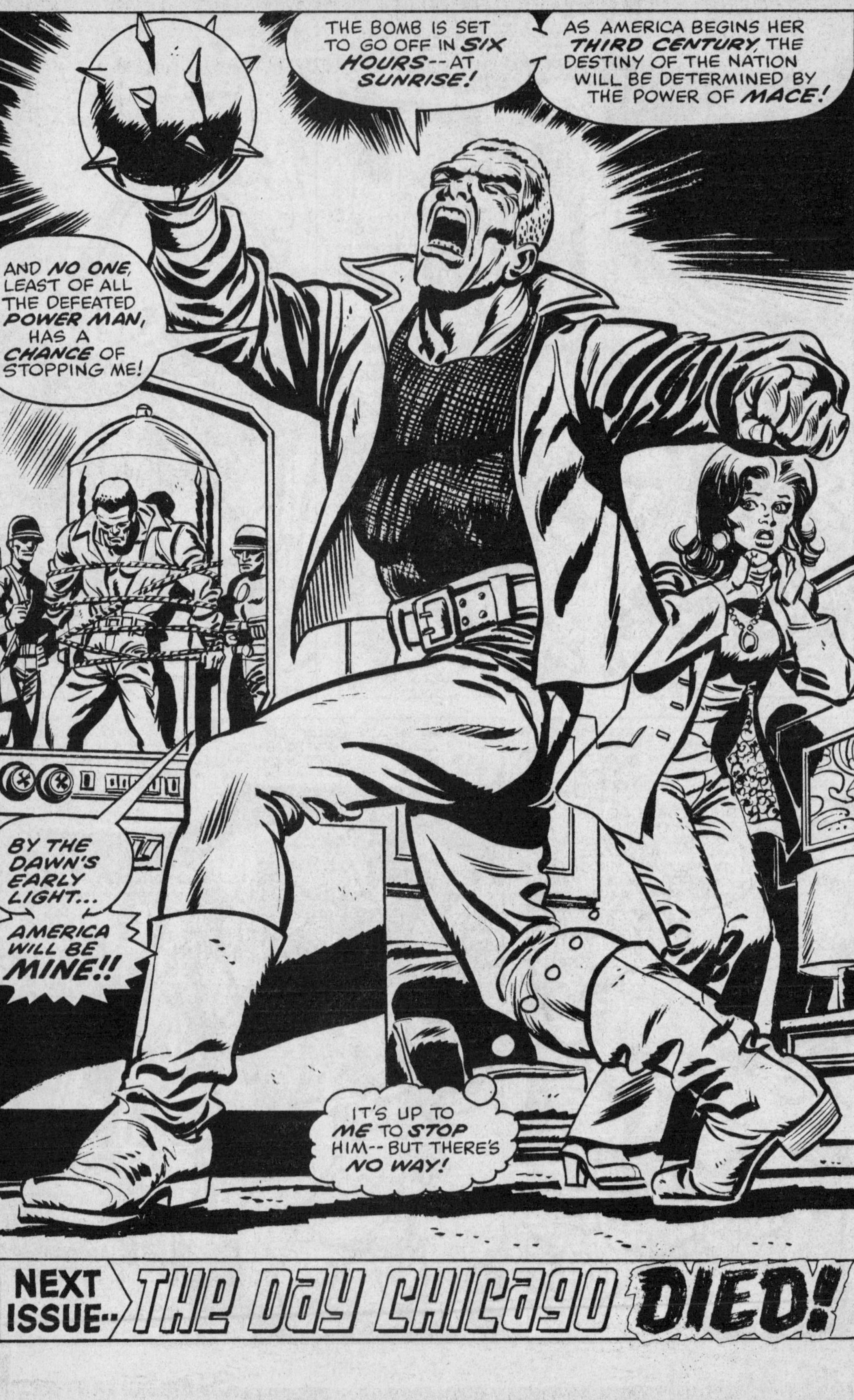
THE BOMB IS SET TO GO OFF IN SIX HOURS--AT SUNRISE!
AS AMERICA BEGINS HER THIRD CENTURY, THE DESTINY OF THE NATION WILL BE DETERMINED BY THE POWER OF MACE!
AND NO ONE, LEAST OF ALL THE DEFEATED POWER MAN, HAS A CHANCE OF STOPPING ME!
BY THE DAWN'S EARLY LIGHT...
AMERICA WILL BE MINE!!
IT'S UP TO ME TO STOP HIM--BUT THERE'S NO WAY!
NEXT ISSUE-- THE DAY CHICAGO DIED!

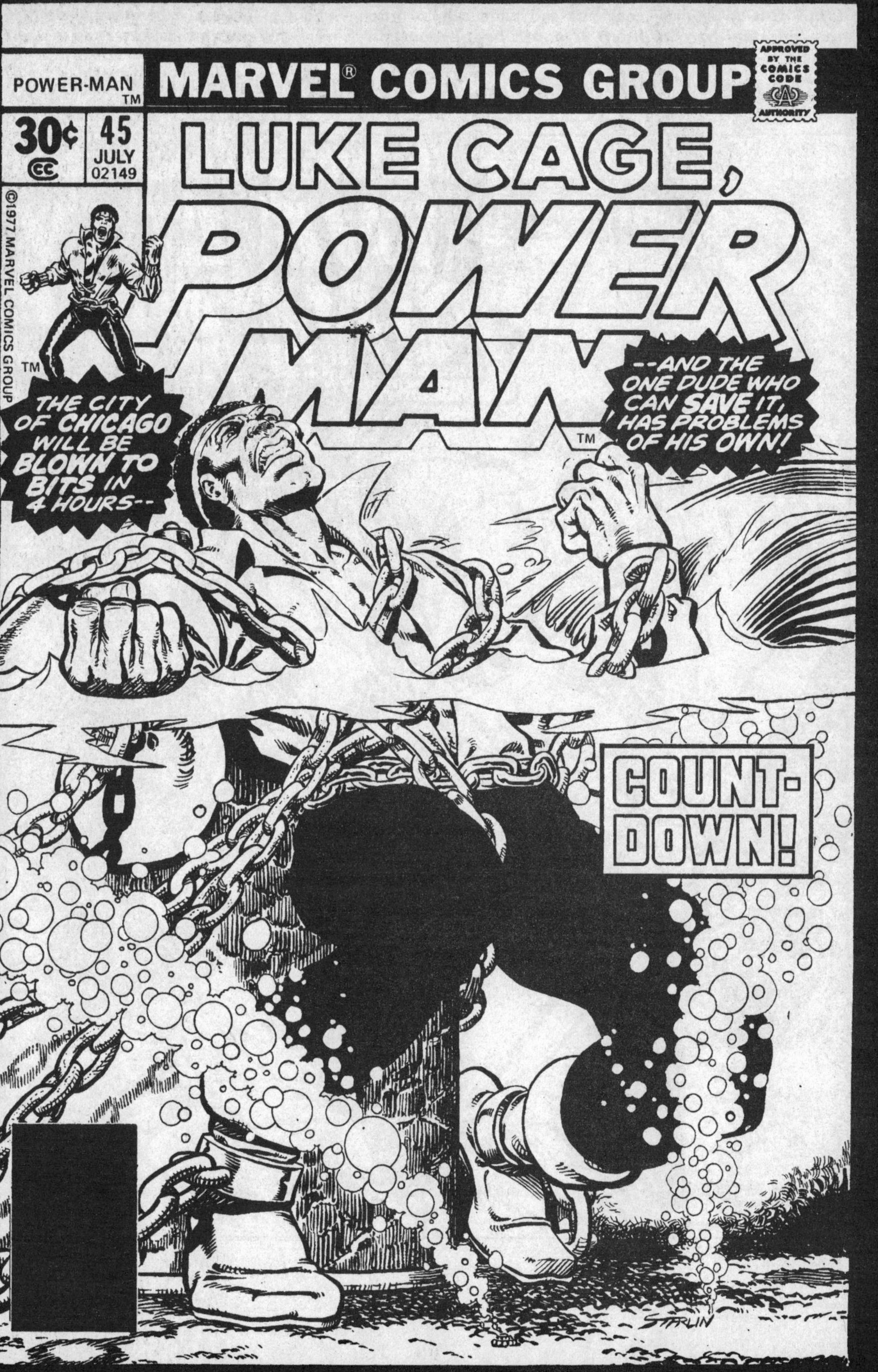

POWER-MAN TM
MARVEL® COMICS GROUP
APPROVED BY THE COMICS CODE AUTHORITY
30¢ CC
45 JULY 02149
©1977 MARVEL COMICS GROUP
LUKE CAGE, POWER MAN TM
THE CITY OF CHICAGO WILL BE BLOWN TO BITS IN 4 HOURS--
--AND THE ONE DUDE WHO CAN SAVE IT, HAS PROBLEMS OF HIS OWN!
COUNT-DOWN!
STARLIN

STAN LEE PRESENTS: LUKE CAGE, POWER MAN!

MARV WOLFMAN
WRITER / EDITOR

LEE ELIAS
ARTIST

IRV WATANABE
LETTERER

DON WARFIELD
COLORIST

THE DAY CHICAGO DIED!

C'MON, MAN-- YOU JUST GOTTA GET OFF OF THIS THING--

--BEFORE YOU AN' EVERYTHIN' ELSE IS BLOWN-- SKY-HIGH!

UHHHN! NO USE, THESE *TITANIUM* CABLES AIN'T BUDGIN'!

LAST ISSUE WE SAW LUKE CAGE BOUND TO A COBALT BOMB SET TO EXPLODE. NEED WE SAY MORE?

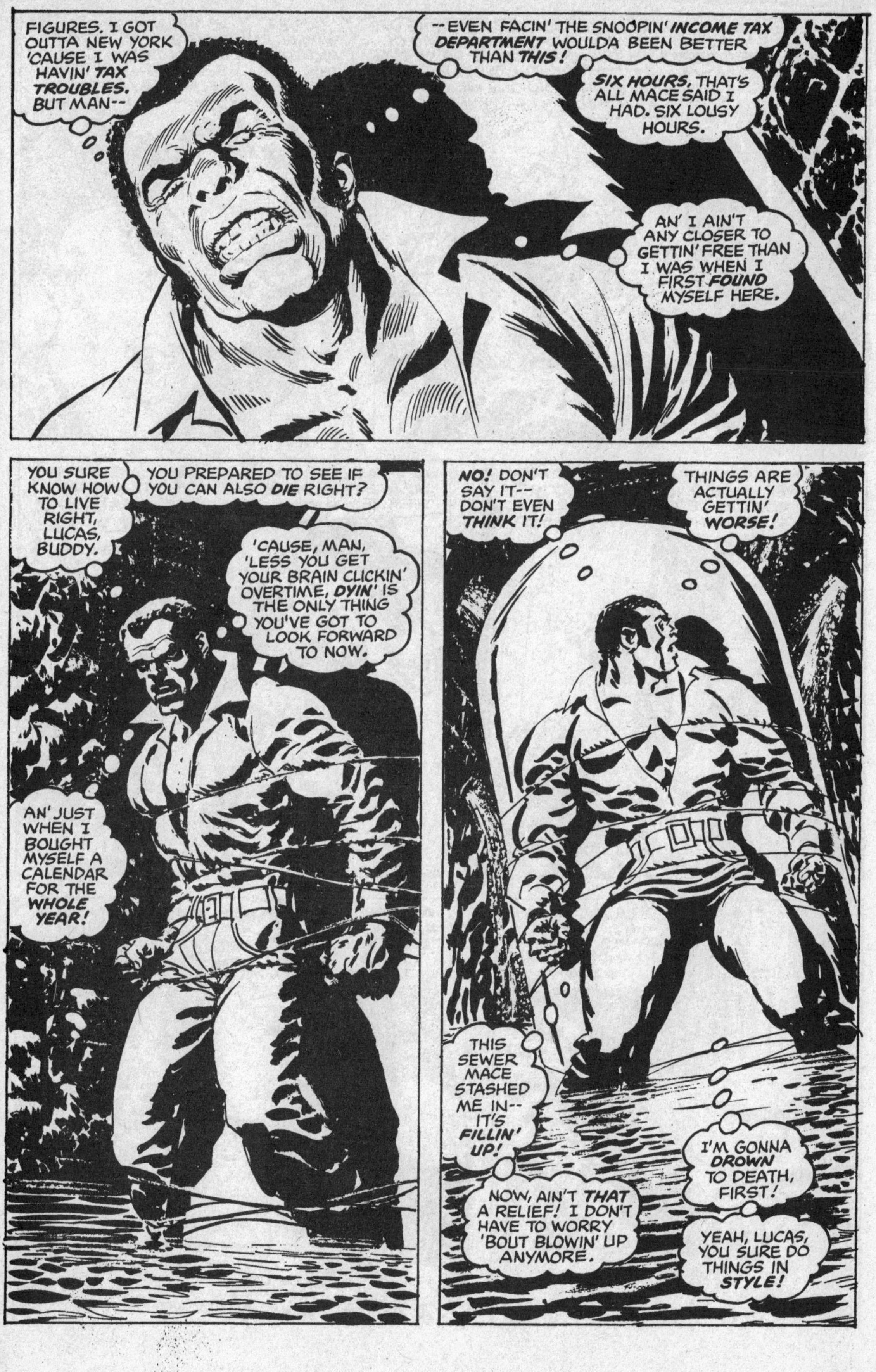
FIGURES. I GOT OUTTA NEW YORK 'CAUSE I WAS HAVIN' TAX TROUBLES. BUT MAN--
--EVEN FACIN' THE SNOOPIN' INCOME TAX DEPARTMENT WOULDA BEEN BETTER THAN THIS!
SIX HOURS. THAT'S ALL MACE SAID I HAD. SIX LOUSY HOURS.
AN' I AIN'T ANY CLOSER TO GETTIN' FREE THAN I WAS WHEN I FIRST FOUND MYSELF HERE.
YOU SURE KNOW HOW TO LIVE RIGHT, LUCAS, BUDDY.
YOU PREPARED TO SEE IF YOU CAN ALSO DIE RIGHT?
'CAUSE, MAN, 'LESS YOU GET YOUR BRAIN CLICKIN' OVERTIME, DYIN' IS THE ONLY THING YOU'VE GOT TO LOOK FORWARD TO NOW.
AN' JUST WHEN I BOUGHT MYSELF A CALENDAR FOR THE WHOLE YEAR!
NO! DON'T SAY IT-- DON'T EVEN THINK IT!
THINGS ARE ACTUALLY GETTIN' WORSE!
THIS SEWER MACE STASHED ME IN-- IT'S FILLIN' UP!
NOW, AIN'T THAT A RELIEF! I DON'T HAVE TO WORRY 'BOUT BLOWIN' UP ANYMORE.
I'M GONNA DROWN TO DEATH, FIRST!
YEAH, LUCAS, YOU SURE DO THINGS IN STYLE!

MEANTIME, ACROSS CHICAGO...

YOU'RE *INSANE*, MACE. YOU CAN'T POSSIBLY GET AWAY WITH THIS. THE GOVERNMENT WILL *STOP* YOU!

AND RISK SETTING OFF THE BOMB *AHEAD* OF SCHEDULE? NO, MY DEAR OUTRAGED BURGUNDY-- NO ONE WILL *DARE* HUNT ME DOWN. *MILLIONS* OF LIVES ARE AT STAKE.

YOU SEE, WOMAN, I *DID* THINK THIS OUT, TO ITS FINAL DETAIL.

AS THE *MASTER PLANNER* I AM, AS THE MILITARY *GENIUS* I HAVE ALWAYS BEEN--*NO MINOR DETAIL* ESCAPES MY ATTENTION.

THE GOVERNMENT WILL TURN OVER CHICAGO TO ME, OR *RISK* THE DEATH OF UNTOLD MILLIONS!

I'LL *TELL* THEM. THEY'LL COME *AFTER* YOU!

WE SHALL SEE. GO-- YOU ARE FREE. *WARN* THEM, IF YOU WILL.

I TELL YOU IT WILL *NOT* MATTER.

CHICAGO IS MINE! *MINE!*

AT LAST I'LL HAVE A CITY TO RULE, A PEOPLE TO *DICTATE* TO, AND *BILLIONS* TO LOOT!

AND THERE IS NOTHING ANY MAN ON EARTH CAN DO TO *STOP ME!*

HE'S *CRAZY*, AND TO THINK I *BELIEVED* HE ACTUALLY TRIED TO *SAVE* MY HUSBAND...

...INSTEAD, HE *CAUSED* HIS DEATH!

JUST AS HE WANTS TO DESTROY EVERY-ONE HERE.

ONLY...I *CANNOT* ALLOW THAT...I CAN'T!

DESPERATELY, BURGUNDY RACES FROM MACE'S IRON SKYSCRAPER...

OFFICER! YOU'VE GOT TO HELP!

THE MAN IN THAT BUILDING --HE'S GOT A BOMB!

CALM DOWN, LADY, AND TAKE IT FROM THE BEGINNING!

WHAT KIND OF BOMB?

HE CALLED IT A COBALT BOMB...SAID IT WAS EVEN MORE POWERFUL THAN AN ATOM BOMB!

LOOK, LADY, I DON'T KNOW WHAT YOU'RE PULLING. A SMALL PIPE BOMB, OR EVEN A LETTER BOMB, THEM I CAN BELIEVE. BUT AN A-BOMB?

WHERE'D HE GET FROM --THE SEARS CATALOGUE?

IT SEEMS BURGUNDY IS HAVING A DIFFICULT TIME CONVINCING THE MINIONS OF THE LAW.

A SHAME!

...NEEDED ...WORD OF MY THREAT TO BE RELEASED QUICKLY.

SIR? YOU WANT EVERYONE TO KNOW?

BUT WON'T THEY TRY TO STOP YOU?

I WANTED

NO, SERGEANT, AND THAT IS THE BEAUTY OF MY SCHEME. IF BURGUNDY DID NOT INFORM THE ARMY OF MY INTENT--

--MY THREAT, WHEN IT COMES, WOULD NOT BE TAKEN AS SERIOUSLY.

YOU SEE, SERGEANT, BURGUNDY IS MY MESSENGER, MY CLARION CALL, SO TO SPEAK.

AND ELSEWHERE...

WHERE'S YOUR CAPTAIN?

IN THE BACKROOM, MISS. BUT--

HEY! YOU CAN'T GO IN THERE.

TOO LATE. I ALREADY HAVE!

CAPTAIN, I'VE GOT TO SPEAK WITH YOU. IT'S URGENT!

THERE'S A COBALT BOMB READY TO BLOW CHICAGO OFF THE FACE OF THE MAP, AND NO ONE WANTS TO BELIEVE ME.

WHAT?

I'M **SORRY**, SIR. SHE RAN IN TOO FAST FOR ME TO STOP.

THAT'S ALL RIGHT, SERGEANT. GO BACK TO YOUR DESK

NOW THEN, MISS. WHAT **ABOUT** THE COBALT DEVICE?

AND PLEASE, SIT DOWN. I BELIEVE YOU.

MY EX-BOSS, GIDEON MACE--HE SAID HE **FOUND** A BOMB YOU PEOPLE LOST NEAR **BERMUDA** A FEW WEEKS BACK.

AND HE SAYS UNLESS HE GETS HIS WAY, HE'LL **DESTROY THIS CITY!**

WE'VE GOT TO DO SOMETHING, CAPTAIN. AND WE'VE GOT TO DO IT **FAST!**

WHILE BURGUNDY COMPLETES HER STORY, LET'S LOOK IN ON THE BOMB IN QUESTION...

ALMOST **TOO LATE** ...CAN'T BREATHE MUCH LONGER!

ONLY HOPE IS THAT THE **POUNDIN'** I'VE BEEN DOIN' ON THE PIPES FINALLY **DOES SOMETHIN'!**

EH? A **CREAKIN'** SOUND...IT'S **WEAKENIN'!**

I'M **FALLIN' THROUGH!**

KRASH

AN' DOWN HERE THERE'S **FRESH AIR**, THANK THE LORD.

AN' EVER BETTER'N THAT, THE CABLES FINALLY TORE LOOSE.

WHICH MEANS I CAN GET *OUTTA* HERE--

--PROVIDIN' I CAN FIGURE OUT A WAY TO *STOP* THIS TICKIN' DOOMSDAY DEVICE!

ONLY *I* DON'T KNOW WHICH IS EVEN THE *FRONT* END.

BETTER CALL THE *COPS* AN' LET 'EM SEND AN *EXPERT* DOWN HERE-- FAST!

HOWEVER, THE POLICE ARE *ALREADY* STORMING INTO ACTION...

YOU *HEARD* ME! I NEED THE *AUTHORITY* TO CALL OUT OUR RESERVES, AND *DON'T* GIVE ME ANY BLASTED LIP ABOUT *BUDGETS!*

HELL, IF WE DON'T MOVE FAST, THERE WON'T BE *ANY* BUDGETS, THERE WON'T BE ANY *CITY!*

CAPTAIN, WE JUST HAD A *PHONE MESSAGE*...SOMETHING ABOUT THE BOMB.

THE MAN SAID TO TURN ON CHANNEL SIX RIGHT AWAY!

THEN, BY THUNDER, WHAT ARE YOU *WAIT*-ING FOR?

MOVE IT, MAN.

GREETINGS, MY FELLOW OFFICERS. MY NAME IS MACE, *GIDEON MACE*, U.S. ARMY, RETIRED.

SIT BACK, GENTLEMEN. I HAVE A *PROPOSI-TION* TO DISCUSS WHICH YOU MAY FIND *INTERESTING!*

AS YOU WELL KNOW, YOU PEOPLE LOST A COBALT DEVICE OFF BERMUDA SEVERAL WEEKS AGO.

NEEDLESS TO SAY, IT IS NOW IS MY POSSESSION.

FURTHERMORE, IT IS SET TO EXPLODE, IN HOURS.

YOU HAVE ONE HOUR TO DECIDE, GENTLEMEN. OTHERWISE THE TOTAL POPULATION OF THIS CITY--DIES!

MACE! I HAVEN'T THE POWER TO--

BLAST! HE CUT ME OFF!

SERGEANT, GET THE MAYOR ON THE LINE--

--THEN GET ME THE PRESIDENT!

BUT BEFORE YOU DO ANYTHING, GET ME AS ASPIRIN!

LORD, I NEED ONE NOW.

ELSEWHERE...

IF I GO IN THERE, I MAY NEVER BE FREE AGAIN!

LUCAS, YOU GOT YOURSELF TO THINK ABOUT.

ONLY, IF YOU DON'T DO WHAT YOU KNOW IS BEST, YOU'LL NEVER BE ABLE TO LIVE WITH YOURSELF AGAIN!

POLICE HO

SERGEANT--?

CHAPTER 2: CHICAGO TRACKDOWN!

IT TAKES ONLY FIFTEEN MINUTES FOR THE **NATIONAL GUARD** TO BE CALLED INTO ACTION, ONE QUARTER OF AN HOUR FOR **TANKS** TO BE MOBILIZED, FOR **LOUDSPEAKERS** TO WARN WINDY CITY RESIDENTS TO **VACATE** THE STREETS.

THERE IS **BALKING**, OF COURSE, BUT THE CITY HAS HAD A **LONG** HISTORY OF OBEYING ITS LAW OFFICIALS, AND EVEN AFTER THE RECENT **DEATH** OF ITS POWERFUL LONG-TIME MAYOR, THE CITIZENS **RESPOND** ALMOST INSTINCTIVELY TO ORDERS.

THEREFORE, WITHIN ONE HALF AN HOUR, THE STREETS ARE VIRTUALLY **EMPTY**, SAVE FOR THE EXPECTED **STRAGGLERS** WHO GAWK IN WONDER.

SIR, THIS WOMAN **INSISTED** ON COMING IN HERE.

LUKE! YOU'RE **SAFE!**

BURGUNDY!?

I WAS **FRANTIC** WITH WORRY, LUKE. BUT NOW, IN YOUR ARMS, SUDDENLY I FEEL **SAFE!**

THAT'S **COOL,** BABY.

BUT DON'T FEEL **TOO** RE-LAXED, 'CAUSE MACE'S BOMB IS STILL OUT THERE, BABY, AND IT'S **STILL A THREAT!**

SPEAKING OF WHICH, MR. CAGE--?

HOLD YOUR *STARS*, GENERAL. I'D TELL YA WHICH SEWER I *LEFT* IT IN--

-- BUT THE *WATER* CAME SPLASHIN' DOWN AFTER ME. AND *WHO KNOWS* WHERE IT FLOATED TO BY NOW?

THE *NATIONAL GUARD* WILL FIND IT, CAGE.

AND MY *POLICE* ARE ALREADY CHECKING ALL CONDUITS.

WE'LL *FIND* THE BOMB, BELIEVE US.

YEAH, AN' I BELIEVE IN *TINKERBELL*, TOO.

MEANWHILE... BY NOW THE ARMY WILL BE SURVEYING THE AREA, SEARCHING FOR OUR BOMB. BUT THEY *WON'T* HAVE TIME TO STOP IT, AS IF THEY *COULD!*

MEANWHILE, LET US *WAIT* HERE IN COMFORT...UNTIL CHICAGO IS *OURS!*

BUT, SIR, WHAT IF THEY *DON'T* GIVE IT TO US? SHOULDN'T WE FIND A *SAFE* PLACE TO HIDE IF THE BOMB GOES OFF?

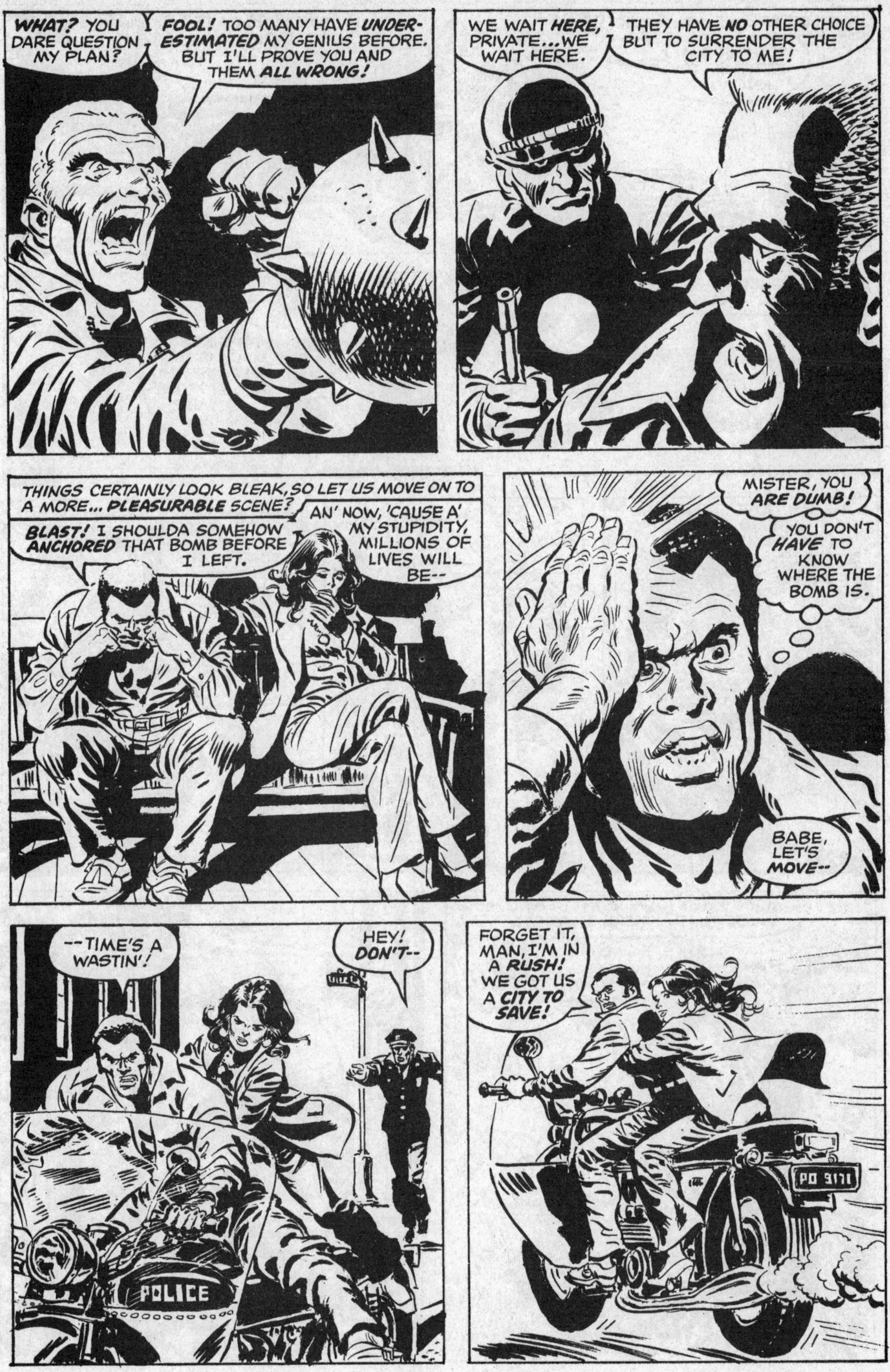
WHAT? YOU DARE QUESTION MY PLAN?
FOOL! TOO MANY HAVE UNDER-ESTIMATED MY GENIUS BEFORE. BUT I'LL PROVE YOU AND THEM ALL WRONG!
WE WAIT HERE, PRIVATE... WE WAIT HERE.
THEY HAVE NO OTHER CHOICE BUT TO SURRENDER THE CITY TO ME!
THINGS CERTAINLY LOOK BLEAK, SO LET US MOVE ON TO A MORE... PLEASURABLE SCENE?
BLAST! I SHOULDA SOMEHOW ANCHORED THAT BOMB BEFORE I LEFT.
AN' NOW, 'CAUSE A' MY STUPIDITY, MILLIONS OF LIVES WILL BE--
MISTER, YOU ARE DUMB!
YOU DON'T HAVE TO KNOW WHERE THE BOMB IS.
BABE, LET'S MOVE--
--TIME'S A WASTIN'!
HEY! DON'T--
POLICE
FORGET IT, MAN, I'M IN A RUSH! WE GOT US A CITY TO SAVE!
PO 9171

WHERE ARE WE GOING, LUKE? I THINK I'M ENTITLED TO KNOW!

WHERE *ELSE*, BABE? MACE'S PLACE!

MAYBE THE *COPS* ARE TOO FRIGHTENED TO *STORM* IT, BUT THAT DOESN'T COUNT *US* OUT!

AN' SINCE MACE IS THE *ONLY* ONE WHO CAN STOP THE BOMB SAFELY--

--ALL WE GOTTA DO IS FIND HIS *TRIGGERIN'* DEVICE, AND WORK IT *OURSELVES!*

GET BACK, I HAVE ORDERS TO KILL!

SO WHO'S STOPPIN' YOU FROM *TRYIN'*, SMILEY?

FIRE WHENEVER YOU WANNA--BUT ALL THE *BULLETS* IN THE WORLD AIN'T STOPPIN' LUKE CAGE!

DIG IT?

WHOMP

MACE'S GOT TO BE RIGHT BEHIND HERE, 'CAUSE THAT'S WHERE I LAST LEFT 'IM.

SO MAKE WAY, WORLD, I'M *BUSTIN'* MY WAY THROUGH!

SPOK

YEAH, TALL, DARK AN' *CRAZY'S* HERE, ALL RIGHT!

CAGE? *YOU* ESCAPED THE BOMB?

NOT THAT IT *MATTERS*, OF COURSE.

SOLDIERS! DECIMATE CAGE!

SORRY, FELLAS, BUT I'M NOT READY TO GO--LEAST NOT TILL YOUR TIN-PLATED HITLER *JOINS* ME!

BOP

SOK

SO IF I HAPPEN TO *FRACTURE* YOUR SKULL A LITTLE SO I CAN *GET* TO YOUR BOSS-MAN DON'T TAKE IT TOO PERSONAL. DIG?

BLAM

I SEE ALL MY *TRAINING* IS *WASTED.* IT TAKES A TRUE *MAN* TO OVERPOWER YOU!

A *SOLDIER* TO *STOP* YOU!

AND GIDEON MACE TO *DESTROY* YOU!

AN' A FULL-FLEDGED *GOOBER* TO STAND THERE WHILE A BOMB'S SAYIN' BYE-BYE TO US ALL!

YOU GOTTA *STOP--*

:CHOKE:

I HAVE TO DO *NOTHING*, CAGE. OR DID YOU FORGET THE *FULL POWER* OF MY *IRON-HAND?*

I CAN SPRAY *CHEMICAL MACE* WHEN I NEED TO *STOP* MY ENEMY DEAD IN HIS TRACKS.

N-NO, MACE, I DIDN'T FORGET.

I NEVER DO!

ELEPHANTS DON'T FORGET *EITHER*, CAGE-- AND YOU'RE AS *DUMB* AS THEY ARE!

YOU CAME TO MY HEADQUARTERS, TO FIGHT ME ON MY *GROUND*. THEREFORE YOU WILL *DIE!*

X-SQUAD-- MOBILIZE *NOW!*

I BUILT WEAPONRY INTO EVERY CORNER OF MY HEADQUARTERS. THERE IS NOWHERE HERE YOU CAN HIDE WITHOUT *ONE* ONE OF MY MEN FERRETING YOU OUT--

--AND *ATTACKING* YOU WITH ONE OF MY HIGHLY-ADVANCED WEAPONS.

UNGGHH!

YOU SEE, CAGE? YOU UNDERSTAND NOW HOW I AM GOING TO DEFEAT YOU, AND TAKE OVER THIS CITY AS *MINE?!*

I UNDERSTAND YOU'RE LOONIER 'N *DAFFY DUCK*. NOTHIN' ELSE!

AN' I UNDERSTAND HOW YOU JUST WASTED ONE A' BURGUNDY'S *SHIRTS*--

--AN' I CERTAINLY UNDERSTAND HOW I'M GONNA WASTE *YOU!*

YOU *ARE A FOOL*, CAGE!

MISTER, I'LL TAKE THAT LITTLE *LAUGH* A' YOURS AND SHOVE IT RIGHT BACK UP YOU!

THESE AIN'T NO ARMY MANEUVERS YOU'RE PLAYIN' NOW.

SKAK

MILLIONS OF LIVES HANG IN THE BALANCE, HERE.

AN', BABY, THAT MEANS THE *KID GLOVES ARE OFF!*

FOR ONCE I *AGREE* WITH YOU, CAGE. THIS *IS* SERIOUS BUSINESS. WAR ALWAYS IS--

--AND THAT'S WHY IT MUST BE LEFT TO *PROFESSIONALS* SUCH AS MYSELF...

...AND NOT TO THE NAMBY-PAMBY *WEAKLINGS* THEY NOW HAVE IN THE PENTAGON!

HOW MANY OF THEM COULD *HURL* A *CONCUSSION-MISSLE* WITH SUCH ACCURACY, CAGE?

BL*AMMO*

THE ANSWER IS: *NONE OF THEM!* ONLY *MACE* CAN!

AND *THOSE* INSIPID FOOLS DRUMMED ME OUT OF THE ARMY BECAUSE I WAS *BETTER* THAN THEY WERE!

WH*OOSHHH*

STOP IT, BOTH OF YOU. STOP EVERYTHING!

HASN'T THIS FIGHT GONE ON LONG *ENOUGH?*

WE'RE HERE TO *STOP* CHICAGO FROM BLOWING UP--

--NOT TO *FIGHT.*

BURGUNDY--

SHUP UP, MACE--

--OR I'M LIABLE TO REMEMBER HOW YOU *TRICKED* ME INTO WORKING FOR YOU.

SORRY YOU *BELIEVE* THAT, BURGUNDY. BUT I MAY AS WELL TELL YOU--

--THAT *EVEN* THOSE SPECIAL FLAME THROWERS WON'T STOP ME...NOT NOW.

STAND STILL, CAGE--*CORPSE STILL!*

OR MY MACE WILL GLADLY *RIP* THIS LOVELY GIRL'S HEAD--RIGHT OFF!

NO WAY, BUDDY, 'CAUSE WITH THAT HEAVY IRON HAND, YOU CAN'T MOVE FAST AS I CAN.

SCATTER, BABY, I GOT MACE!

AN' THIS TIME I AIN'T STOPPIN' TILL HE'S DOWN AN' OUT!

BDAM

FORGET IT, CAGE--THAT WILL NEVER HAPPEN.

SWAMM

GIDEON MACE WILL NEVER BE STOPPED!

KRASH

GOTTA ROLL WITH IT... TAKE THE BRUNT OF THAT KICK ON MY SIDE...

...AN' THEN GET BACK UP BEFORE HE LAMS OUTTA HERE.

BURGUNDY! MOVE, FIND THOSE BLASTED BOMB CONTROLS!

BAM

TIME'S RUNNIN' OUT ON US, GIRL--RUN!

IT ISN'T RUNNING OUT, CAGE--

--IT'S OVER!

FOR YOU AND FOR BURGUNDY ...AND THIS TIME, CAGE, I MEAN STAND BACK!

IF YOU EVEN TWITCH, BURGUNDY HAS HAD IT!

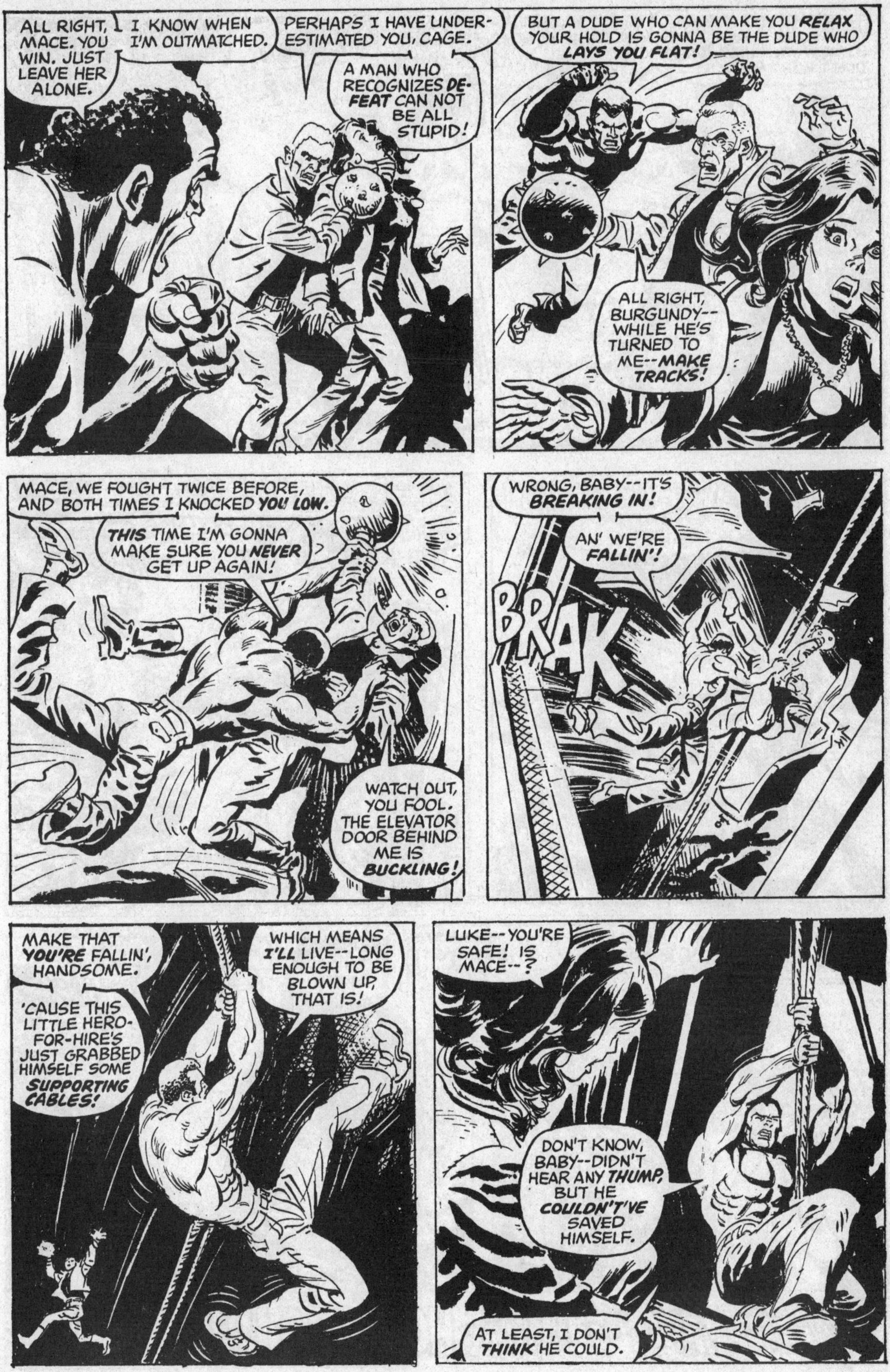
ALL RIGHT, MACE. YOU WIN. JUST LEAVE HER ALONE.
I KNOW WHEN I'M OUTMATCHED.
PERHAPS I HAVE UNDER-ESTIMATED YOU, CAGE.
A MAN WHO RECOGNIZES DE-FEAT CAN NOT BE ALL STUPID!
BUT A DUDE WHO CAN MAKE YOU RELAX YOUR HOLD IS GONNA BE THE DUDE WHO LAYS YOU FLAT!
ALL RIGHT, BURGUNDY-- WHILE HE'S TURNED TO ME--MAKE TRACKS!
MACE, WE FOUGHT TWICE BEFORE, AND BOTH TIMES I KNOCKED YOU LOW.
THIS TIME I'M GONNA MAKE SURE YOU NEVER GET UP AGAIN!
WATCH OUT, YOU FOOL. THE ELEVATOR DOOR BEHIND ME IS BUCKLING!
WRONG, BABY--IT'S BREAKING IN!
AN' WE'RE FALLIN'!
BRAK
MAKE THAT YOU'RE FALLIN', HANDSOME.
'CAUSE THIS LITTLE HERO-FOR-HIRE'S JUST GRABBED HIMSELF SOME SUPPORTING CABLES!
WHICH MEANS I'LL LIVE--LONG ENOUGH TO BE BLOWN UP, THAT IS!
LUKE--YOU'RE SAFE! IS MACE--?
DON'T KNOW, BABY--DIDN'T HEAR ANY THUMP, BUT HE COULDN'T'VE SAVED HIMSELF.
AT LEAST, I DON'T THINK HE COULD.

ALL RIGHT, YOU JOKERS. YOUR BOSS IS *DEAD.* AN' BY NOW YOU KNOW *BULLETS* DON'T HURT ME NONE.

SO, IF YOU WANNA *JOIN* YOUR BIG HONCHO, FINE. BUT IF YOU WANNA *LIVE,* DO AS I SAY.

AN' BABY, DO IT FAST. 'CAUSE THE FIRST GUY WHO EVEN SAYS "HUH," IS GONNA WISH HE WAS BORN *MUTE!*

YOU TIN-PLATED SOLDIER BOYS ARE GONNA *SCATTER*-- AN' IF I EVER FIND ONE A' YOU EVEN HOLDIN' A *FLYSWATTER,* I'LL DECK YOU OUT.

BUT, BEFORE YOU SPLIT, YOU GOTTA TELL ME *ONE* THING.

LIKE WHERE YOUR LITTLE NAPOLEON PUT THE *CONTROLS* TO HIS BOMB?

I-I DON'T KNOW, CAGE. NO ONE DOES... BUT MACE.

HE WOULDN'T TELL US *ANYTHING.*

THAT TRUE, BURGUNDY?

YOU BETTER *BELIEVE* IT. HE TRUSTED NO ONE.

SO, ONLY MACE KNOWS HOW TO TURN OFF THAT BOMB--

--AND *MACE* IS DEAD!

BABY, HAVE WE GOT TROUBLE!

YOU BETTER BELIEVE IT, CAGE. AS YOU'LL LEARN IN OUR *NEXT* EPIC, CALLED-- **THREE HOURS TO DOOMSDAY!**

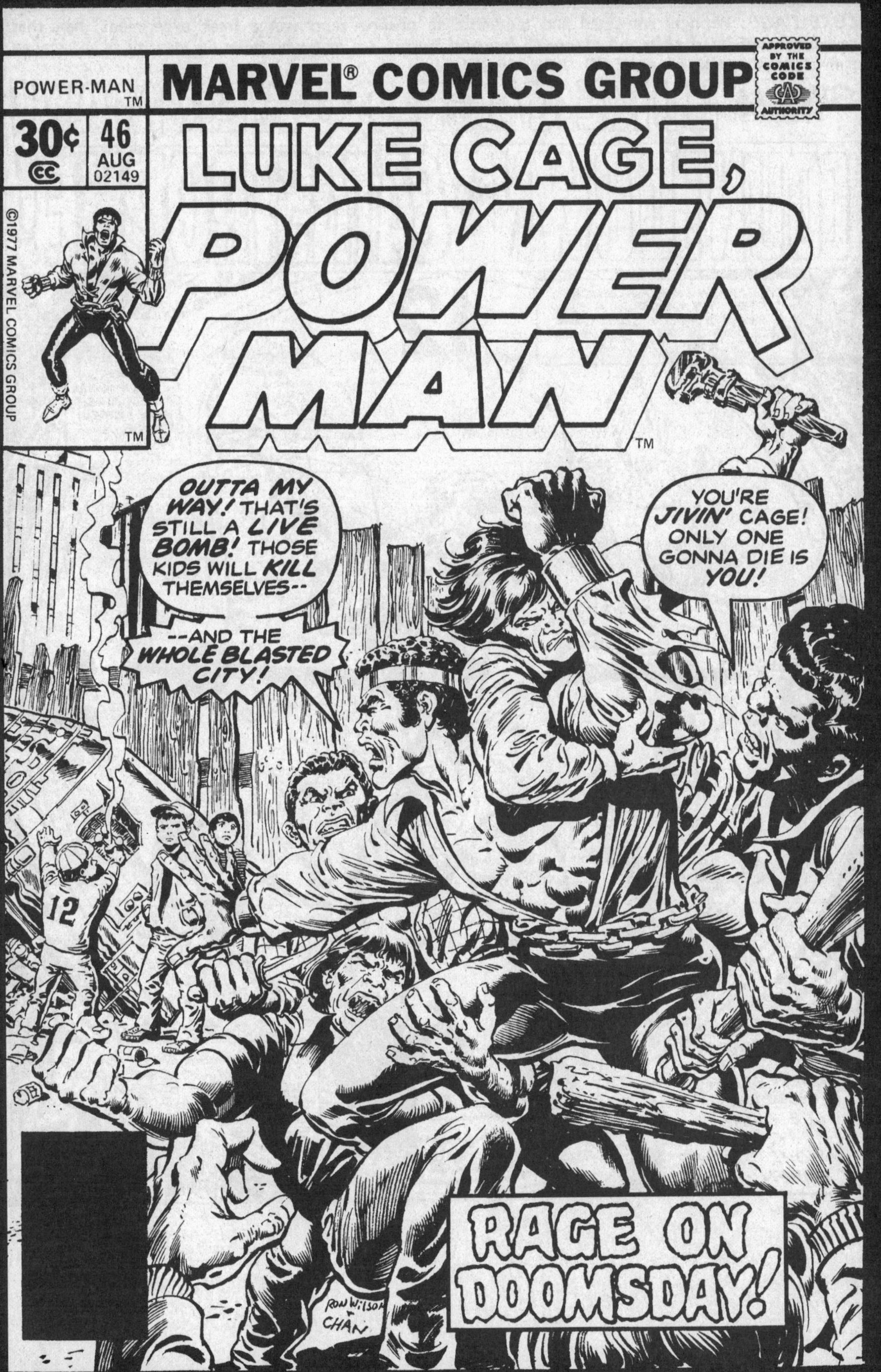
MARVEL® COMICS GROUP
POWER-MAN TM
30¢ CC
46 AUG 02149
LUKE CAGE, POWER MAN TM
©1977 MARVEL COMICS GROUP
APPROVED BY THE COMICS CODE AUTHORITY
OUTTA MY WAY! THAT'S STILL A LIVE BOMB! THOSE KIDS WILL KILL THEMSELVES--
--AND THE WHOLE BLASTED CITY!
YOU'RE JIVIN' CAGE! ONLY ONE GONNA DIE IS YOU!
12
RAGE ON DOOMSDAY!
RON WILSON + CHAN

STAN LEE PRESENTS: LUKE CAGE, POWER MAN!™

COUNTDOWN TO CATASTROPHE!

TIME: WHEN HE EXPERIENCED IT FROM THE INSIDE OF A *CELL* AT SEAGATE PRISON, LUKE CAGE FELT ITS PASSAGE WAS *SLUGGISH*, ALMOST UNMOVING.

YET NOW, BECAUSE OF THE MACHINATIONS SET IN MOTION BY THE MADMAN CALLED MACE, EVERY MOMENT SEEMS ELUSIVE, PRECIOUS.

FOR SOMEWHERE IN THE TEAMING CITY OF CHICAGO, CAGE KNOWS A COBALT TIME-BOMB WAITS... FOR SUNRISE... AND ITS SCHEDULED DETONATION!

MARV WOLFMAN
PLOTTER / EDITOR
ROGER SLIFER
SCRIPTER
LEE ELIAS
ARTIST
D. WOHL •LETTERER
J. COHEN • COLORIST

AT MACE'S HEADQUARTERS...

LOOKS LIKE THIS IS *IT*, BURGUNDY.

DISASTER ALWAYS SEEMS TO HAVE A WAY OF CUTTIN' *SHORT* LONG GOOD-BYES.

OH, LUKE, PLEASE...LET ME COME *WITH* YOU. I WANT TO *HELP* FIND THE BOMB.

SORRY, BABY. YOU'VE ALREADY HELPED ME *PLENTY*-- AGAINST *MACE*--

AN' WITH HIM *DEAD*, THE WHOLE CITY DE-PENDS ON THAT BOMB BEIN' FOUND--*QUICK*.

NOTHIN' PERSONAL, BABE--

"--BUT I JUST DON'T THINK YOU CAN *KEEP UP* WITH MY STYLE OF TRAVELIN'!"

NOW WHAT? THE POLICE ARE ALREADY SEARCHING THROUGH THE CITY'S *SEWER* SYSTEM TRYIN' TO FIND MACE'S BOMB.

GUESS MY BEST BET'S TO HOOK UP WITH *THEM*. CAPTAIN HUMMEL SAID THEY'D BE STARTIN' THEIR SEARCH UNDER THE *LOOP*--

--SINCE *THAT'S* WHERE I BUSTED THE BLASTED THING LOOSE FROM ITS BRACES.* *SHOOT!* WISH I'D HAVE THOUGHT TO RE-ANCHOR IT *THEN*...

UH-OH. THIS JUMP IS GOIN' TO BE A LITTLE *TOUGH*.

*LAST ISH.--M.W.

BUT NOT *TOO* TOUGH. NOT FOR A GUY WITH *STEEL-HARD* LEGS.

CAN'T AFFORD TO GET DELAYED *NOW*-- NOT BY ANYTHING!

BUT RARELY, IF EVER, DO EVENTS IN OUR LIVES DEVELOP ACCORDING TO OUR *DESIRES*.

NO SOONER DO WE ADDRESS OUR ACTIONS TO *ONE* PROBLEM...

...THAN *NEW* ELEMENTS UPSET THE EQUATION.

ONE DOWN.

PERFECT! SO ALL THIS TIME IN CHICAGO AIN'T *SPOILED* MY AIM NONE. I'M STILL SHARP AS *EVER!*

--ON THE *LOCAL* FRONT, POLICE CHIEF DANIELS HAS ISSUED A STATEMENT DESCRIBING THE COBALT BOMB THREAT TO THE CITY AS *"ENDED."* HE URGES THE CITIZENS TO REMAIN *CALM...*

SPASH! SPASH!

TWO...THREE!

ATTABOY, CHIEF! KEEP *TELLIN'* 'EM THAT THE BOMB THREAT IS OVER. MAYBE *THEY'LL* BELIEVE YA-- BUT CHARLIE BENNETT *WON'T!*

I OVERHEARD TWO OF YOUR *"FINEST"* NOT A HALF-HOUR AGO *TALKIN'* ABOUT IT.

AN', TOP COP, THEY WUZ *SCARED.* 'CAUSE YOU STINKIN' BLUECOATS DON'T EVEN KNOW WHERE THAT BOMB IS!

I HEARD IT'S GONNA GO OFF AT *DAWN!*

NO WAY ANYBODY'S GONNA FIND THAT THING BEFORE SUN-UP. CHI-TOWN'S TOO BIG A PLACE.

SO WE'RE ALL GONNA *DIE!*

"NOT THAT IT REALLY *MATTERS* MUCH. GOTTA DIE SOMETIME.

"THE HELL OF IT IS THAT MOST FOLKS WILL *BELIEVE* YOUR BULL. THEY WON'T FIGURE OUT YOU'RE JUST TRYIN' TA KEEP THE PANICKED ANIMALS FROM *BOLTIN'* WHILE THE FOREST *BURNS* DOWN.

"AN' BEFORE THE SUCKERS FIGURE IT OUT, THEY'LL BE *DEAD!* QUICK AND *PAINLESS.*

CRACK!

RAWK

"THAT JUST WON'T *DO.* NO, SIR, THERE'S A FEW PEOPLE THAT DESERVE TO STARE DEATH IN THE *FACE* BEFORE IT SWALLOWS THEM UP!

MEANWHILE, IN THE HEART OF THE CITY'S SEWER SYSTEM...

STEP IT UP, DONALDSON. ACCORDING TO THE *CHARTS*, THE PLACE WHERE THAT BIG GUY LEFT THE BOMB WAS RIGHT AROUND *HERE*.

B-BUT IT'S NOT HERE *NOW*, SIR. IT COULD HAVE BEEN CARRIED *ANYWHERE* BY THE WATER THAT CAME *FLOODING* IN AFTER HIM.

S-SIR? WHAT HAPPENS IF WE CAN'T *FIND* THE BOMB? WHAT IF IT GOES OFF?

THAT'S NOT OUR WORRY, SON. OUR JOB IS JUST TO *FIND* THE BOMB SO IT ISN'T ANYONE *ELSE'S* WORRY, EITHER.

B-BUT, SIR! HOW CAN I *IGNORE* THE CONSEQUENCES OF A *TIME BOMB*?! I-I JUST GOT *MARRIED*. I DON'T--

LOOK, DONALDSON... JERRY, I REALIZE YOU'VE ONLY BEEN ON THE FORCE FOR A *WEEK*--

--BUT YOU'RE *NEVER* GOING TO WORK OUT IF YOU DON'T CHANGE YOUR ATTITUDE!

I'M NOT ASKING YOU TO BE *CALLOUS*, SON...

...JUST TRY NOT TO LET YOUR *WORRY* OVERSHADOW YOUR *JOB*!

REMEMBER WHAT *HAS TO BE DONE*-- NOT WHAT *MIGHT* HAPPEN. YOU'LL NEVER GET ULCERS THAT WAY, SON.

ALL, RIGHT. I-I'LL TRY. AND THANKS, LIEU-TENANT.

ELSEWHERE...

GET OUT OF THE *WAY*, SANDY! LET *ME* CATCH IT!

NOT ON YOUR *LIFE*, BUSTER. I'VE--

--GOT OOPS!

AWW... GEEZ! I KNEW YOU'D BLOW IT!

OH, SHUT UP, SCHEELE. AND C'MERE. LOOKIT WHAT I FOUND!

WHILE THE ASTONISHED YOUTHS CROWD ABOUT THE STRANGE STEEL OBJECT, LET'S SHIFT OUR ATTENTION TO...

MAKIN' PRETTY GOOD TIME TRAVELLIN' THIS WAY. ANOTHER FIFTEEN MINUTES AND I SHOULD BE-- CRIPES!

WHAT A TIME TO STUMBLE ACROSS A MUGGIN'!

Y'HEAR ME? I SAID, LET'S HAVE THE POCKETBOOK, GRAN'MA--

NO...YOU CAN'T...!

LADY, WE CAN, AND BELIEVE IT-- WE WILL--

--ANY WAY WE HAFTA!

HEY, HEY, SUGAR! AIN'T ANYONE EVER TOLD YOU THE PROPER WAY TO USE A GUN?

WHA--?

YOU GRAB IT BY THE BUTT--

--AN' SQUEEZE!

SPAK!

NOW...WHOSE BUTT GETS SQUEEZED NEXT?

NOT BAD, SUPERDUDE. BUT D'YOU THINK YOU CAN TAKE US ALL ON?

WITHOUT EVEN HALF *TRYIN'*, JIVE-MOUTH.

URK!

OOLPH!

KRAK!

TRYIN' OUT FOR THE *BEARS*, JIVE MOUTH?

IF SO, I'M CALLIN' FOR A *TIME OUT--*

--TO DROP KICK TRASH LIKE *YOU* WHERE YOU *BELONG!*

HOLD ON THERE A SECOND, MA'AM. AN' I'LL HELP YOU WITH YOUR BAG.

CAN'T UNDERSTAND WHY YOU PICKED *THIS* TIME A NIGHT TO GO GROCERY SHOPPIN' THOUGH. PUNKS LIKE THOSE ARE *ALWAYS* PROWLIN' THIS HOUR.

OH, I DON'T MAKE A *HABIT* OF IT, YOUNG MAN. BUT MY POOR LITTLE *BUMPER* WAS OUT OF FOOD.

BUMPER?

MY *KITTEN.* I COULDN'T HARDLY LET HIM *STARVE* NOW, COULD I?

NO. GUESS YOU COULDN'T AT THAT. C'MON.

AND, AS A TIME-PRESSED CAGE HELPS THE ELDERLY WOMAN ACROSS THE WIDE CHICAGO AVENUE TO HER HOME...

...THOSE UNHAMPERED BY ALTRUISTIC AIMS SPEED TOWARD THEIR *OWN* DESTINIES.

SUDDENLY...

MRRROW!

BLAM!

WHA--?!

OH. A *CAT!* BLASTED THING *SPOOKED* ME!

DIDN'T MEAN TO FIRE--!

BUT IT DON'T MATTER! *NOTHIN'* MATTERS! THIS WHOLE CITY'S GONNA WAKE UP *DEAD* TO-MORROW--AND THE COPS ARE SO BUSY TRYIN' TO PREVENT IT, THERE AIN'T NOBODY AROUND TO WORRY ABOUT *ME!*

BUT, NOT FAR AWAY...

WHAT THE HECK WAS *THAT*--? A *GUNSHOT?*

WHY WOULD SOMEBODY BE TAKIN' *TARGET PRAC-TICE* AT THIS TIME OF NIGHT?

MAYBE... IT WAS A *TRUCK* BACKFIRIN'!

WHO ARE YOU TRYIN' TO KID, LUCAS? THAT WAS NO *TRUCK*--UNLESS DIAMOND-REO'S IN-STALLIN' *THIRTY-AUGHT-SIX* MUFFLERS NOWADAYS!

IT CAME FROM DOWN HERE!

LUKE CAGE RACES IN THE DIRECTION OF THE NOISE, UNAWARE THAT THE GUNMAN IS HIGH *ABOVE* HIM...

THIS IS A GOOD ANGLE... GOT TO PLACE THIS SLUG *SQUARE!*

EH? THAT IDIOT IN THE YELLOW SHIRT MUSTA *HEARD* MY SHOT BEFORE--

"--BUT *NOTHIN'S* GONNA KEEP ME FROM OFFIN' YOU MR. HIGH-AND-MIGHTY JEROME HAGEN! SO, JUST KEEP *SITTIN'* THERE, SUCKER!

I HOPE YOU'RE FEELIN' ALL HAPPY AND SAFE AND SECURE, JEROME... 'CAUSE THAT MEANS IT'LL *HURT* THAT MUCH MORE WHEN YOU FEEL YOUR *LIFE* OOZIN' AWAY!

CRACK!

HOLY MOTHER OF --! A SNIPER -- TRYIN' TO PICK ME OFF!

STEEL-HARD SKIN OR NOT--

-- BEING ON THE RECEIVIN' END OF POTSHOTS FROM SOME P.O.'D PUNK AIN'T MY IDEA OF FUN!

STAYIN' CLOSE TO THE BUILDING SHOULD KEEP THE ROOF LEDGE BE-TWEEN ME AN' HIM...

... AN' WITH THE SNOW MUFFLIN' MY FOOT-STEPS, MAYBE I CAN GET UP THERE REAL QUICK AND QUIET-- TAKE HIM BY SURPRISE.

HUH-UH. NO GOOD. THE GUY'S TOO SLICK. HE'S ALREADY SPLIT.

CAN'T FIGURE IT OUT. WHO'N CHICAGO WOULD BE OUT FOR LUKE CA--

WAIT! OVER THERE--! FROM THE GROOVE HIS RIFLE LEFT IN THE SNOW, HE WASN'T AIMIN' AT THE STREET--

--BUT AT THAT APARTMENT BUILDING!

SWEET CHRISTMAS! LOOKS LIKE HIS REAL MARK WAS BEHIND THAT WINDOW! HE MUST'VE JUST BEEN GOIN' AFTER ME FOR BONUS POINTS...

IT TAKES A FULL TWO-MINUTES FOR LUKE CAGE TO DETERMINE INTO WHICH APARTMENT THE BULLET WAS FIRED. BUT IT TAKES ONLY ONE GLANCE FOR HIM TO REALIZE HE IS ...

TOO LATE! AIN'T NUTHIN' CAN SAVE THAT POOR JOKER NOW.

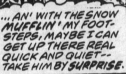

BLAST! THIS AIN'T THE *FIRST* DEATH I'VE SEEN, BUT IT NEVER GETS ANY SWEETER. THE NEAT ONES SEEM EVEN *WORSE*, SOMEHOW. MORE *DELIBERATE*... GUESS IT'S BECAUSE THEY *ARE*.

STASH THE MOURNIN', LUCAS, FOR A *QUIETER* TIME.

JUST PUT IN YOUR CALL TO THE PRECINCT-- HOPE THERE'S SOME BODY *LEFT* THAT AIN'T OUT BOMB CHASIN' AN' KICK YOUR TAIL INTO *HIGH GEAR*!

THE *LIVIN'* DESERVE SOME CONSIDERATION, TOO!

AN' BABY, THEY AIN'T GONNA GET THAT OR ANY-THING *ELSE*--

"--'LESS YOU *FIND* THAT *BOMB*!

WHAT *IS* IT?

AWW, WHO *CARES*? LET'S GET BACK TO THE *GAME*!

GARY, DON'T YOU HAVE *ANY* CURIOSITY AT *ALL*? I WANT TO *LOOK* AT IT A MINUTE.

ARTHUR, YOU'VE BEEN *STALLING* ALL NIGHT! WHY DON'T YOU JUST *ADMIT* THAT YOUR TEAM'S *LOST* THE GAME SO WE KIN GO HOME!?

I *SAID* I WANTED TO *LOOK* AT THIS, AN' I'M *GONNA*!

LET US DEPART THIS SCENE OF ADOLESCENT ANTAGONISM FOR NOW...

...AND TURN OUR ATTENTION TO A MORE *AMIABLE* PAIR...

YES, BUMPER, I'M GOING TO *FEED* YOU NOW--

--BUT I HOPE YOU WON'T MIND WAITING WHILE AN OLD WOMAN PUTS ON SOME *TEA*, WOULD YOU?

PRRRR

I THOUGHT NOT.

THERE! *NOW* THE SWEET LITTLE KITTY WILL HAVE HER SUPPER!

AS SOON AS I CAN GET THE CAN OPEN--

OH ,,,, OH MY ,,,, !

SPICES

MY HEART ,,,, !

A PAPERBAG SLIPS ONTO AN OPEN RANGE.

SPICES

FRUMP!

MEEOW

AND SUDDENLY, HUNGRILY, FLAMES DEVOUR THE TOPPLED GROCERY BAG...

WEEE!

CRACKLE!

...AND EVERY RISING FIERY SLIVER PROMISES THE ROOM WILL SOON BE A BLAZING INFERNO!

BUT THE HEAT IS ON IN MORE WAYS THAN ONE...!

ONLY AN HOUR TILL DAWN! AN' I'M STILL NO CLOSER TO FINDING THE BOMB!

BLAST IT! I'M NOT EVEN SURE I'M HEADED IN THE RIGHT DIRECTION!

SNOWSTORM'S MAKIN' IT HARDER TO SEE! THINK I MAY HAVE MADE A WRONG TURN. I DON'T KNOW CHICAGO LIKE I DO NEW YORK!

BUT HE NEVER GIVES UP, AND SO LUKE CAGE TRUDGES ONWARD, TO THIS GRIM STALKER, EACH FOOTFALL SOUNDS LIKE THE TICK OF A CLOCK.

AT LAST! NO MORE STUPID ARGUMENTS! NOW MAYBE WE CAN SEE WHAT THIS--

GEE, ARTHUR, ARE YOU SURE WE SHOULD? MAYBE--

OH, CRIPES! DON'T TELL ME YOU'RE TURNIN' CHICKEN, TOO?

WHO ELSE IS A CHICKEN, BUCK-TEETH?

TEMPERS ERUPT!

AND SOON, SOFT SNOW-MISSILES YIELD TO A MORE PERSONAL MEANS OF AGGRESSION.

WHILE ELSEWHERE, FLAMES CREEP EVER CLOSER, THEIR CRACKLE DROWNING OUT THE SOUNDS OF RASPING LABORED BREATHS AND FRIGHTENED MEWLING.

AND, BACK AT MACE'S ALL-BUT-DESERTED HEAD-QUARTERS...

I... I CAN'T STAY HERE JUST WAITING ANY LONGER! I'LL GO CRAZY!

THERE'S BEEN NO WORD FROM LUKE, NOTHING ON RADIO AND T.V. BROADCASTS.

LUKE TOLD ME WHERE THEY'RE STARTING THE SEARCH. I'LL GO THERE!

GOOD THING MACE ALWAYS KEPT A FLEET OF VEHICLES ON HAND. THERE SHOULD BE SOMETHING DOWN IN THE GARAGE I CAN DRIVE.

WAIT A MINUTE! I CAN MAKE A LOT BETTER TIME WITH MACE'S HELICOPTER THAN BY CAR, AND SINCE MACE WAS CERTAIN HE COULD KEEP HIS REAL INTENTIONS FROM ME, HE EVEN TAUGHT ME HOW TO OPERATE IT.

MOMENTS LATER, BURGUNDY USES HER SKILL TO LIFT THE CRAFT FROM THE HELIPORT ROOF...

HER INTENTIONS ARE VAGUE AT BEST.

WHILE CLOSE BY, ANOTHER REACHES A VERY SPECIFIC GOAL. HIS INTENT: DEADLY!

REVENGE IS SWEET. PUTTIN' THAT SLUG IN HAGEN ALMOST MAKES UP FOR HIM LURIN' TINA HERE FROM VERMONT-- FOR ALL HIS PROMISES OF GIVIN' HER ALL THE FAME AN' ATTENTION OF A "TOP FASHION DESIGNER"!

"WHY HIDE YOURSELF AWAY IN VERMONT," HE SAYS. "YOU'VE GOT A LOT OF TALENT FOR DESIGN. COME TO CHICAGO, I'LL INTRODUCE YOU TO ALL THE RIGHT PEOPLE! C'MON, KID, WHY NOT GIVE IT A SHOT?"

'CAUSE WE WUZ CONTENT IN VERMONT, THAT'S WHY. SHE WUZ HAPPY TO JUST BE MY WIFE--AN' TEND TO ME LIKE A GOOD WIFE SHOULD!

THE CONSORT ROOM AT THE CONTINENTAL PLAZA....

COULD I INTEREST YOU IN A DRINK ON THE TERRACE?

NO.

HONESTLY, RICHARD, DO YOU REALLY THINK THE LACROSSE FASHION HAS A PLACE IN TODAY'S MARKET?

WHY NOT, TINA?

IT'S SLEEK, IT APPEALS TO A WOMAN'S FEMININITY AS WELL AS HER NEED FOR A LOOK OF INDEPENDENCE, AND--

WHILE, ON THE CITY STREETS...

REALLY GOTTA MAKE TRACKS NOW! I AIN'T EVEN TO THE STARTIN' GATE SO I CAN BEGIN LOOKIN' FOR THE BOMB, AN' IT'S ALMOST SUNUP!

BUT UNFORTUNATELY FOR OUR HARRIED HERO, A MOVING FIGURE CATCHES THE CORNER OF HIS EYE...

IT'S HIM!

LUKE SPIES THE SNIPER--AND WISHES HE HADN'T.

FOR THOUGH THE BOMB HE SEEKS THREATENS THE ENTIRE POPULACE OF CHICAGO...

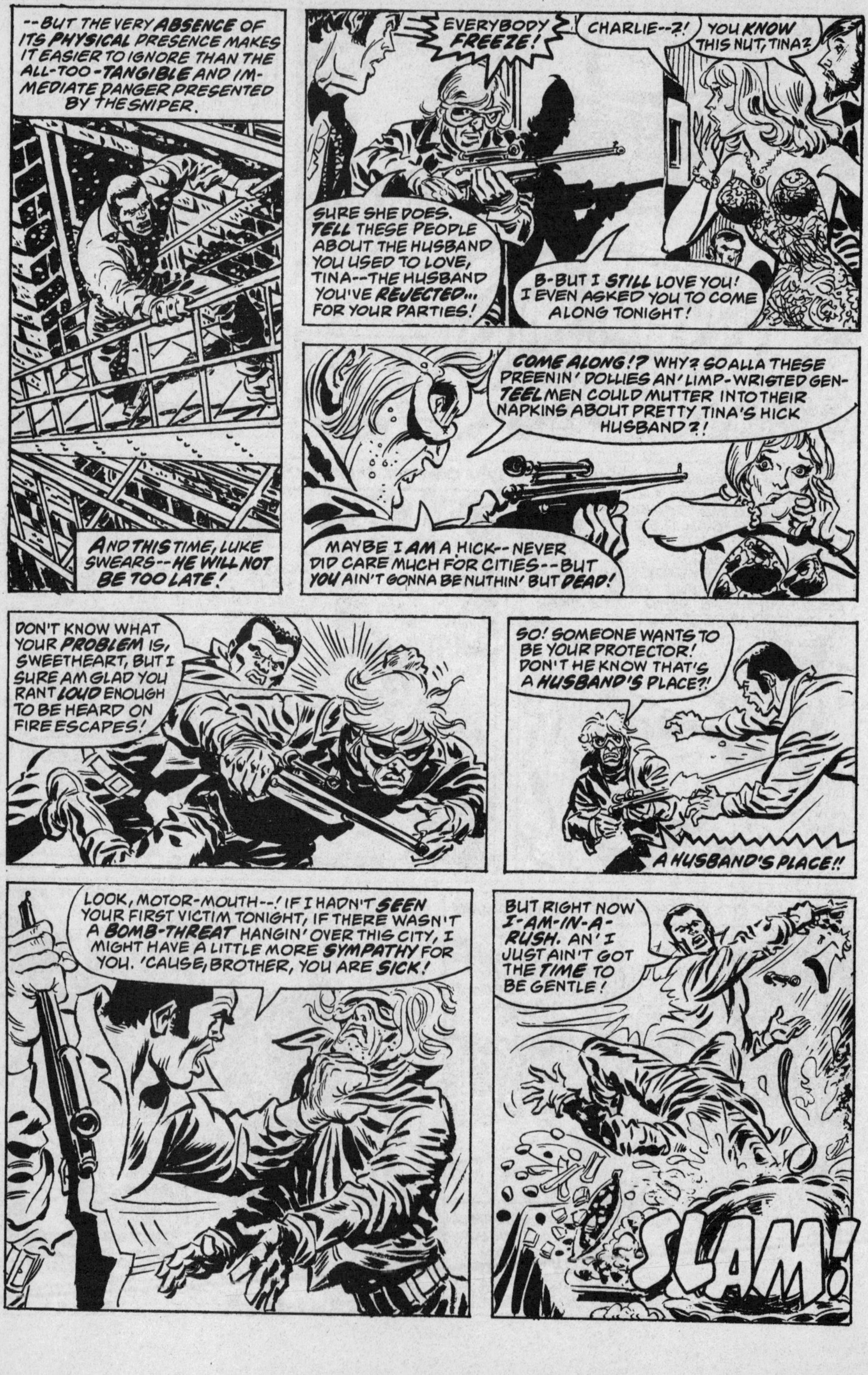

--BUT THE VERY ABSENCE OF ITS PHYSICAL PRESENCE MAKES IT EASIER TO IGNORE THAN THE ALL-TOO-TANGIBLE AND IMMEDIATE DANGER PRESENTED BY THE SNIPER.
AND THIS TIME, LUKE SWEARS--HE WILL NOT BE TOO LATE!
EVERYBODY FREEZE!
CHARLIE--?!
YOU KNOW THIS NUT, TINA?
SURE SHE DOES. TELL THESE PEOPLE ABOUT THE HUSBAND YOU USED TO LOVE, TINA--THE HUSBAND YOU'VE REJECTED... FOR YOUR PARTIES!
B-BUT I STILL LOVE YOU! I EVEN ASKED YOU TO COME ALONG TONIGHT!
COME ALONG!? WHY? SO ALLA THESE PREENIN' DOLLIES AN' LIMP-WRISTED GENTEEL MEN COULD MUTTER INTO THEIR NAPKINS ABOUT PRETTY TINA'S HICK HUSBAND?!
MAYBE I AM A HICK--NEVER DID CARE MUCH FOR CITIES--BUT YOU AIN'T GONNA BE NUTHIN' BUT DEAD!
DON'T KNOW WHAT YOUR PROBLEM IS, SWEETHEART, BUT I SURE AM GLAD YOU RANT LOUD ENOUGH TO BE HEARD ON FIRE ESCAPES!
SO! SOMEONE WANTS TO BE YOUR PROTECTOR! DON'T HE KNOW THAT'S A HUSBAND'S PLACE?!
A HUSBAND'S PLACE!!
LOOK, MOTOR-MOUTH--! IF I HADN'T SEEN YOUR FIRST VICTIM TONIGHT, IF THERE WASN'T A BOMB-THREAT HANGIN' OVER THIS CITY, I MIGHT HAVE A LITTLE MORE SYMPATHY FOR YOU. 'CAUSE, BROTHER, YOU ARE SICK!
BUT RIGHT NOW I-AM-IN-A-RUSH. AN' I JUST AIN'T GOT THE TIME TO BE GENTLE!
SLAM!

ALL RIGHT, FOLKS, YOU CAN GO BACK TO YOUR PARTYIN'. THE EXCITEMENT'S OVER.

I-I DON'T KNOW WHAT *HAPPENED* TO HIM. HE WAS *FINE* BEFORE WE MOVED TO CHICAGO. THEN HE BEGAN TO BE *JEALOUS* OF THE TIME I SPENT WITH MY CAREER.

I TRIED TO *TALK* TO HIM-- LET HIM *KNOW* I STILL LOVED HIM. I GUESS HE JUST DIDN'T *UNDERSTAND*.

STILL AN' ALL, LADY, IT AIN'T NO EXCUSE FOR *KILLIN'*...NO EXCUSE AT ALL.

AND OUTSIDE, THE TWO ARE SPOTTED BY SOMEONE WHOSE SEARCH HAS BEEN AMPLY *REWARDED!*

THAT MAN BELOW. IT *LOOKS* LIKE...IT *IS*, IT'S--

LUKE! IT'S ME, BURGUNDY! I THINK I *FOUND* THE BOMB!

YOU READY FOR A 'COPTER RIDE, SNIPER-MAN 3? 'CAUSE ME AN' THE WINDY CITY DON'T HAVE NO TIME TO *WASTE!*

I SAW SOME KIDS PLAYING WITH SOMETHING *LARGE* NEAR THE RIVER! I WAS HURRYING TO FIND THE POLICE!

HOPE YOU'RE *RIGHT*, LADY, 'CAUSE WE'VE GOT LESS THAN A *HALF-HOUR* TO SUN-UP!

HOWEVER, NO SOONER ARE THEY IN THE AIR, THEIR PRISONER FIRMLY BOUND, THAN...

TAKE IT *DOWN* AGAIN, BURGUNDY.

BUT--?!

NO TIME TO TELL BURGUNDY THAT THIS IS THE *SAME* *APARTMENT* I WALKED THAT OLD WOMAN TO EARLIER TONIGHT!

AN' THERE AIN'T NO TIME TO BE SHY 'BOUT *ENTERIN'* EITHER!

SPLAM!

WHEW! JUST IN TIME! FLAMES WERE JUST GETTIN' READY TO *FRY* HER!

THOUGHT I MIGHT BE ABLE TO PUT OUT THE FIRE WITH THESE *DRAPES.* BUT-- *NO GOOD.* IT'S GOIN' TOO *STRONG!*

WH-WHAT *IS* IT? WHAT'S HAPPENED?

GET ME A FIRE EXTINGUISHER-- *QUICK!* BEFORE THERE AIN'T NUTHIN' BUT *CINDERS* LEFT OF THIS PLACE!

THE MAN OBEYS LUKE'S COMMANDING TONE...

BE CAREFUL, YOUNG MAN. YOU'LL *BURN* YOURSELF!

DON'T WORRY ABOUT ME. JUST *STAY* BACK!

SOON, THE BLAZE IS EXTINGUISHED...

I'VE GOTTA GET GOIN'! CAN YOU TAKE CARE OF HER?

YES. I'M FAMILIAR WITH HER CONDITION AND WHERE SHE KEEPS HER MEDICINE. SHE SHOULD BE ALL RIGHT.

AND THANK YOU SO MUCH FOR YOUR HELP. IT'S SO RARE THAT YOUNG PEOPLE WILL TAKE TIME OUT FOR OLDER FOLKS THESE DAYS.

ASSURED THAT THE SITUATION IS WELL IN HAND, CAGE WASTES NO TIME--

--AND IN MOMENTS IS AIRBORNE ONCE AGAIN...

THERE, LUKE! DO YOU SEE IT? IS THAT THE BOMB?

ATTABOY, GARY! GIVE IT TO HIM!

HEY, COOL IT, GUYS! WE'RE BEIN' WATCHED!

CAGE, WAIT! LET ME LAND THIS THING!

NO TIME, BURGUNDY! IF THAT BOMB'S GONNA BE STOPPED, IT'S GOTTA BE NOW!

SCATTER, MEN! THAT EGG YOU'RE NUZZLIN' IS A BOMB!

A-A BOMB!

LET'S GET OUTTA HERE!

CRUD! I JUST REALIZED--! I BEEN SO UPTIGHT 'BOUT FINDIN' THIS HUNKA ARMY SURPLUS, I NEVER CONSIDERED-- HOW IN BLAZES AM I GONNA SNUFF IT?!

TIK TIK TIK

GREAT. IF THINGS WEREN'T BAD ENOUGH ALREADY --IT JUST STARTED TICKING!

AN' THAT'S A *SURE* SIGN THERE'RE ONLY *SECONDS* LEFT 'FORE IT BLOWS!

SWEET MOTHER .... WHAT AM I GONNA DO?!

STOP HOLDIN' YOURSELF BACK, CAGE. CONSIDERIN' THE CIRCUMSTANCES, THERE'S ONLY ONE THING YOU *CAN* DO--

HIT THIS MOTHER WITH ALL YOU GOT--AN' HOPE TO HARLEM YOU CAN *SMASH* THE TIMING DEVICE!

HOLD IT, FELLA!

TIK TIK TIK

HUH--?

NO TIME FOR INTRODUCTIONS, BUT BEFORE YOU DO ANYTHING *RASH*, TAKE A LOOK AT THE *BUTTON* ON THE SIDE-- SEEMS TO BE A *DEACTI-VATING* MECHANISM!

GEE, LIEUT. ARE YOU *SURE*?

NOT AT *ALL*, DONALDSON, BUT IT SURE DESERVES TO BE CHECKED OUT BEFORE WE TRY *PUNCHING OUT* THE BOMB!

GOTTA AGREE WITH YOUR PARTNER, SON. CAN'T AFFORD *NOT TO TRY!*

TIK TIK TIK

CLICK!

IT- IT *WORKED!* THE TICKING STOPPED!!

WE'LL TAKE OVER NOW, LIEUTENANT.

MEET THE CHICAGO *BOMB SQUAD*--TRIMBLE AND JEFFERSON.

BY THE WAY, I'M LIEUTEN-ANT LAW-RENCE.

YOU CAN CALL ME ...UH, *MARK.* MARK LUCAS.

THE FOLLOWING DAY, AT A VERY PRIVATE ARMY BRIEFING SESSION...

I'M SORRY TO INFORM YOU PEOPLE --ESPECIALLY AFTER YOUR HEROIC EFFORTS --BUT THIS BOMB IS A *FAKE.*

WHAT?!

THIS CASING IS *HOLLOW*--ALL IT CONTAINS IS A FIRING MECHANISM AND A TIMER--NO *COBALT* MATERIALS.

APPARENTLY THEN, MACE'S SOURCES ONLY TOLD HIM A COBALT BOMB WAS *MISSING.* THEY WEREN'T ABLE TO *RETRIEVE* IT.

MACE MUST HAVE FELT THE NEXT BEST THING TO HAVING A BOMB WAS *CONVINCING* PEOPLE HE HAD ONE.

THE *REAL* BOMB IS STILL OFF THE COAST OF *BIMINI.* MY *SUPERIORS* HAVE ALREADY MADE ARRANGEMENTS FOR ITS *RECOVERY.* *

*SEE THE RESULTS OF THAT RECOVERY MISSION IN MARVEL TWO-IN-ONE #34 --MARY.

IT WAS NOTHING BUT A LOUSY *BLUFF!* THEN TONIGHT WAS A *WASTE--* A *TOTAL WASTE!*

A *WASTE,* LIEUTENANT? ALL DEPENDS ON YOUR POINT OF VIEW I GUESS.

YEAH ... IT SURE MUST DEPEND ON THAT--!

NEXT: WOULDJA BELIEVE-- ZZZZAX! THE LIVING DYNAMO!

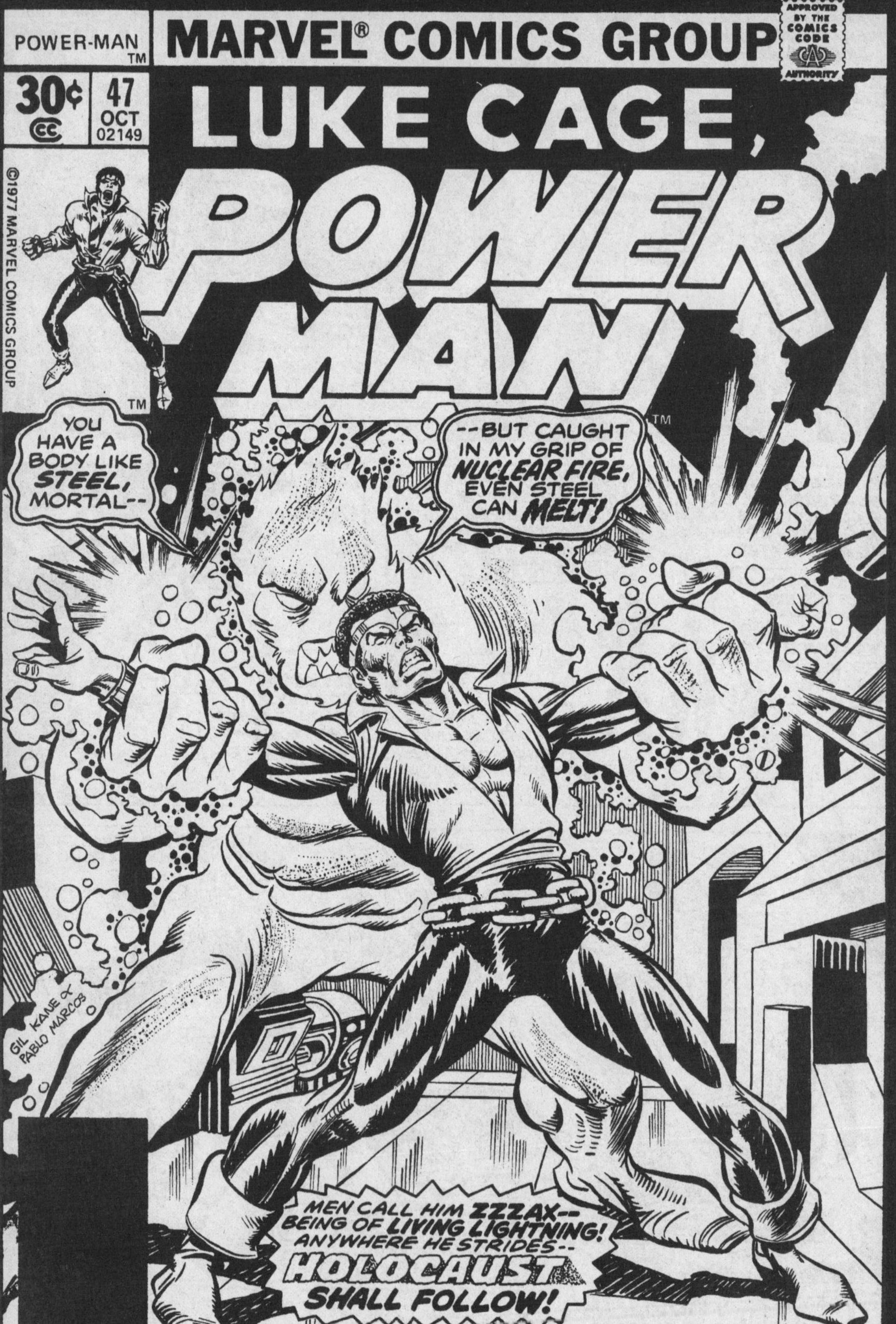
POWER-MAN TM
MARVEL® COMICS GROUP
APPROVED BY THE COMICS CODE AUTHORITY
30¢
47 OCT 02149
LUKE CAGE,
POWER MAN TM
©1977 MARVEL COMICS GROUP
YOU HAVE A BODY LIKE STEEL, MORTAL--
--BUT CAUGHT IN MY GRIP OF NUCLEAR FIRE, EVEN STEEL CAN MELT!
GIL KANE & PABLO MARCOS
MEN CALL HIM ZZZAX-- BEING OF LIVING LIGHTNING! ANYWHERE HE STRIDES-- HOLOCAUST SHALL FOLLOW!

LUKE CAGE: Wrongly convicted and sentenced to prison—reborn in a freak experiment there that gave him ***steel-hard skin*** and ***strength beyond belief***—a man who hides his identity as an escaped convict in the role of a ***HERO FOR HIRE!***

STAN LEE PRESENTS:

LUKE CAGE, POWER MAN!

C. CLAREMONT AUTHOR / G. TUSKA ARTIST / B. SMITH INKER / H. BENDER LETTERER / J. COHEN COLORIST / A. GOODWIN EDITOR

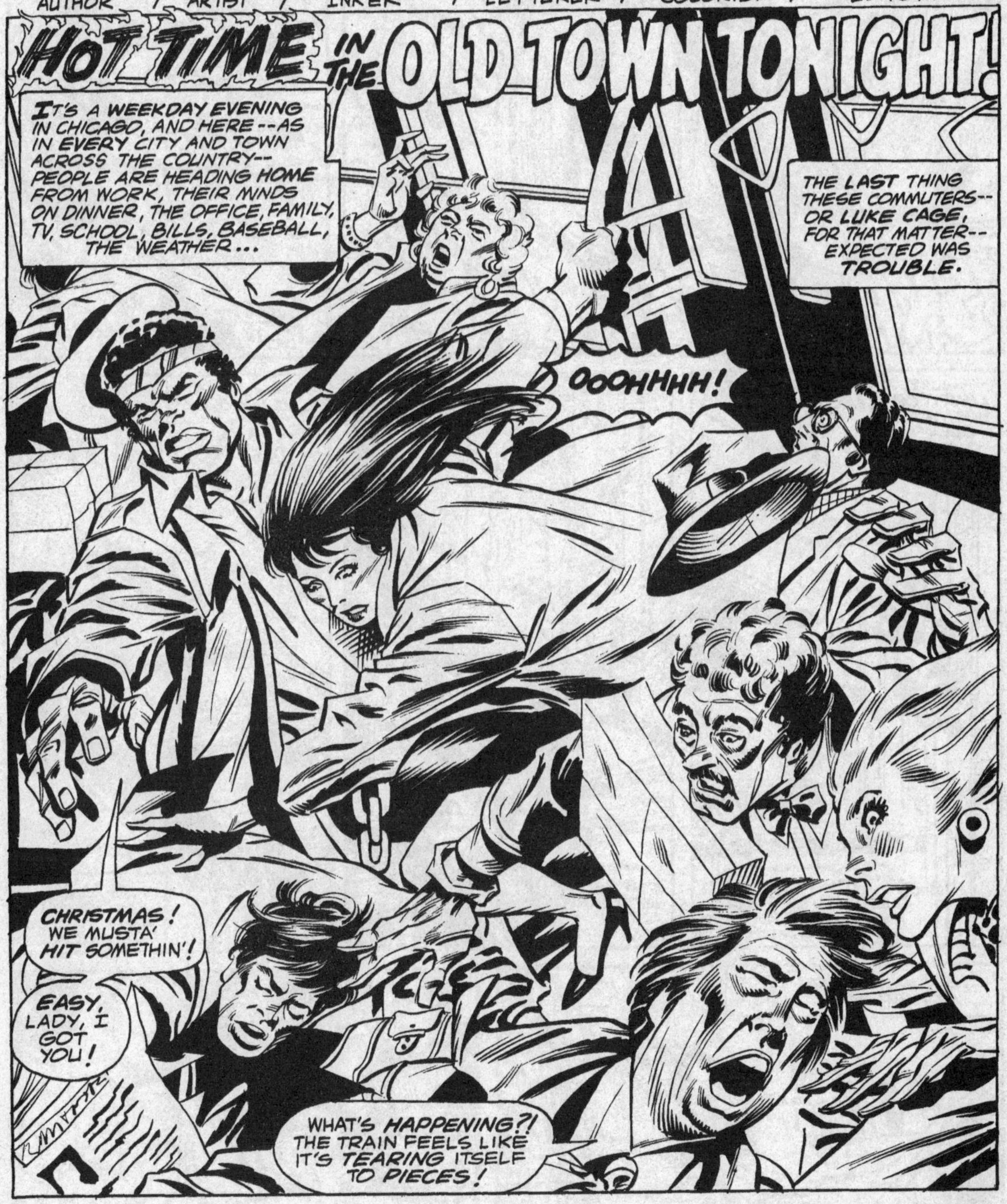
HOT TIME IN THE OLD TOWN TONIGHT!
IT'S A WEEKDAY EVENING IN CHICAGO, AND HERE--AS IN EVERY CITY AND TOWN ACROSS THE COUNTRY--PEOPLE ARE HEADING HOME FROM WORK, THEIR MINDS ON DINNER, THE OFFICE, FAMILY, TV, SCHOOL, BILLS, BASEBALL, THE WEATHER...
THE LAST THING THESE COMMUTERS--OR LUKE CAGE, FOR THAT MATTER--EXPECTED WAS TROUBLE.
OOOHHHH!
CHRISTMAS! WE MUSTA' HIT SOMETHIN'!
EASY, LADY, I GOT YOU!
WHAT'S HAPPENING?! THE TRAIN FEELS LIKE IT'S TEARING ITSELF TO PIECES!

IT DIDN'T TAKE MUCH TO START IT-- A FLAWED STRETCH OF TRACK, A MOTORMAN GOOSING THE THROTTLE TO MAKE UP SOME TIME...

...AND ALL OF A SUDDEN, THE TRAIN'S DERAILING AT 30 MILES PER HOUR!

THE FRONT CAR HITS HARD, GOUGING WOODEN TIES AND STEEL SUPPORTS AS IT SKIDS TO A RELUCTANT STOP.

GIRDER'S RIPPIN' THE CAR LIKE A GIANT CAN OPENER. TRAIN'S PITCHIN' OVER, TOSSIN' THE GAL AN' ME TOWARDS THE HOLE--!

HOLD ON TO ME TIGHT, GIRL--

SKRREEERRAKK!

--'CAUSE, LIKE IT OR NOT, WE'RE GOIN' OUT!

OH NO! NO!

C'MON, CAGE! KEEP YOU'RE STEEL-HARD BODY BETWEEN THE WOMAN...

...AN' ANYTHIN' YOU HIT ON THE WAY DOWN!

CAN'T SLOW US, BLAST IT! NOTHIN' TO HOLD ON TO!

NO TIME TO TRY ANYTH-- UNNNGNH!

WHAM!

ANYONE ELSE WOULD HAVE DIED ON IMPACT...

...BUT ANYONE ELSE ISN'T POWER MAN.

MY CAR! MY BEAUTIFUL CADILLAC! YOU KILLED IT!

BE COOL, MAN, YOU'RE LUCKY YOU'RE STILL BREATHIN'!

GOOD LORD-- LOOK!

THE TRAIN--!!

"IT LOOKS LIKE IT'S HANGIN' BY A THREAD!"

SRRRRRRR

FROM THE GROUND, YOU CAN HEAR THE GROAN OF TORTURED METAL, THE CRIES OF THE TRAPPED PASSENGERS...

EVERYONE, PLEASE, STAY CALM! HELP IS ON THE WAY!

MEANTIME, NO ONE MOVE! DON'T EVEN BREATHE HARD.

MAN, ONE O' THOSE PEOPLE EVEN SNEEZES, AN' IT'S ALL OVER.

EVEN WHEN THE COPS GET HERE, THERE'S NO GUARANTEE THEY CAN HELP.

BUT I'M HERE, AN' I GOT THE POWER-- I HOPE!

ANYWAY, I CAN'T JUST WALK AWAY.

LET'S SEE IF STRENGTH ALONE'LL DO THE TRICK!

UHHHRRRR

HEY! THAT BLACK BUCK IN THE HALLOWEEN COSTUME-- THE SLIME'S TRYIN' TO PITCH US OVER!

BELT UP, MISTER. HE'S TRYING TO HELP.

PASTE CHES

FORGET IT, PAL! YOU'RE ONLY MAKING THINGS WORSE!

SO MUCH FOR THAT IDEA.

BUT I AIN'T DONE YET. NO WAY.

THE GIRDER GIVES ME AN IDEA. MAYBE I DON'T HAVE THE RAW STRENGTH TO HEFT THAT CAR BACK ONTO ITS TRACKS...

...BUT IF I USE THIS GIRDER AS A LEVER...

HO-BOY, THIS MAMA IS *HEAVY*. BUT THAT'S WHAT I *NEED*.

ANYTHIN' LESS'LL *BUCKLE* UNDER THE *PRESSURE*. GOTTA WATCH OUT FOR THE *ELECTRIC RAILS*, TOO. IF THEY'RE *LIVE*, I DON'T WANNA FIND OUT THE *HARD WAY*.

I'LL *BRACE* THIS THING ON THAT PILE OF *WRECKAGE* NEXT TO THE *TRAIN*.

NOW TO *SLIP* THE GIRDER *UNDERNEATH*... STEADY, LUCAS, DON'T *BOTCH* THINGS NOW.

OKAY, SO FAR, SO GOOD.

DON'T WANNA RISK THE CAR *SLIPPIN'* FREE BEFORE I'M DONE, SO I'LL *LASH* IT TO THE GIRDER WITH MY *BELT*.

ALWAYS *FIGURED* THESE STEEL LINKS'D COME IN *HANDY* SOMEDAY.

ALL SET. BETTER GET IT RIGHT THE *FIRST* TIME!

HEAVE!

NOTHIN'! IT AIN'T *WORKIN'!*

PUT YOUR *GUTS* INTO IT, MAN-- OR ARE YOU GONNA *FOLD* RIGHT OFF THE BAT...

...LIKE *BOBICK* DID AGAINST NORTON? YOU'RE S'POSED TO BE A *SUPER-HERO*, MISTER.

PROVE IT!!

HALLELUJAH!

SHRREAKK!

IT'S MOVIN'!!

EASY, BRO', NICE-AN'-EASY DOES IT--*SHOOT!* THAT BRACE IS STARTIN' TO *GIVE!*

STRAIN'S... *INCREDIBLE.* CAN'T HOLD MUCH *LONGER.*

17643

BUT I'M ALMOST... *HOME FREE.*

WAY TO GO CAGE!

SHE'S DOWN ON THE *TRACKS* AGAIN!

NOW IT'S SAFE FOR THE FOLKS INSIDE TO HEAD ON OUT THE *BACK* OF THE TRAIN!

B'OMM!

WHERE'S THE MAN WHO SAVED US? I WANT TO *SHAKE HIS HAND!*

LATER, OKAY, FRIEND?

LIKE, WHEN EVERYONE'S *ON THE GROUND?*

I AM JUST ABOUT *DONE IN.*

AIN'T FELT THIS *ROCKY* SINCE I TOOK A *HEADER* DOWN THAT *JAPANESE GLACIER* *

*POWER MAN ANNUAL #1 --ARCHIE.

I THINK I'LL *SLEEP* FOR A WEEK. WONDER IF *BURGUNDY*--

--*CRIPES!*

THE *EL'S* GIVIN' WAY UNDER ME.'

DON'T MOVE! I'M A *DOCTOR,* I CAN HELP YOU!

DON' SWEAT IT MAMA--

--I AIN'T MOVIN'.

SOON...

YOU NEED A *HOSPITAL,* MR...?

AH, *LUCAS...* MARK LUCAS...

OH, YEAH? MISTER, YOU'RE COMING WITH *ME.*

...AN' *NO HOSPITALS,* DOC, I'LL BE *ALL RIGHT* SOON AS I'VE HAD A CHANCE TO *REST UP* A BIT.

INTERLUDE: ABOUT TEN MILES UP *LAKE MICHIGAN* TO ILLINOIS EDISON'S BRAND-SPANKING-NEW *BREEDER REACTOR* POWER STATION...

...A TRIBUTE TO MODERN *NUCLEAR TECHNOLOGY,* A SHOWPIECE FOR THE NATION, DESIGNED TO OPERATE BOTH AS *RESEARCH CENTER* AND MULTI-MEGAWATT *POWER STATION.*

ONLY TROUBLE IS, SOMETHING'S *GONE WRONG.*

IT'S *CONFIRMED,* WILL--

--AN *UNSTABLE* REACTION IN CORE #2. OUR CONTROL SYSTEMS *FAILED* TO DAMP IT, AND IT'S GOING *WILD.*

SHUT DOWN THE *PLANT,* THEN.

I'LL *DAMP* THE RUNAWAY CORE BY *HAND.*

YOU'RE *CRAZY!* LOOK AT THE *RADIATION LEVELS,* MAN!

"EVEN WEARING A *PROTECTIVE* SUIT--TWO MINUTES IN THAT HELL...

"...AN' YOU'LL BE A *WALKING DEAD MAN!*"

TOO TRUE, MARTY. BUT THOSE ARE THE *RISKS*--MY LIFE VERSUS THE *HUN-DREDS OF THOU-SANDS* WHO MIGHT DIE IF THE CORE GOES WILD.

THE FOOLS, I *TOLD* THEM NOT TO *CUT CORNERS* DURING CONSTRUC-TION.

RADIATION DEADLY NO ADMITTAN[CE]

SHODDY MATERIALS AND WORKMANSHIP--AND NOW I'M PAY-ING THE PRICE.

A REACTOR ALLOWS *NO MARGIN FOR ERROR.* IT'S EITHER *PERFECT,* OR IT'S A *KILLER.*

MY *TWO MINUTES* ARE UP. I GUESS I'M *DEAD.*

ALMOST *FINISHED!* FUNNY, SUDDENLY I HAVE THE FEELING I'M NOT *ALONE* IN HERE.

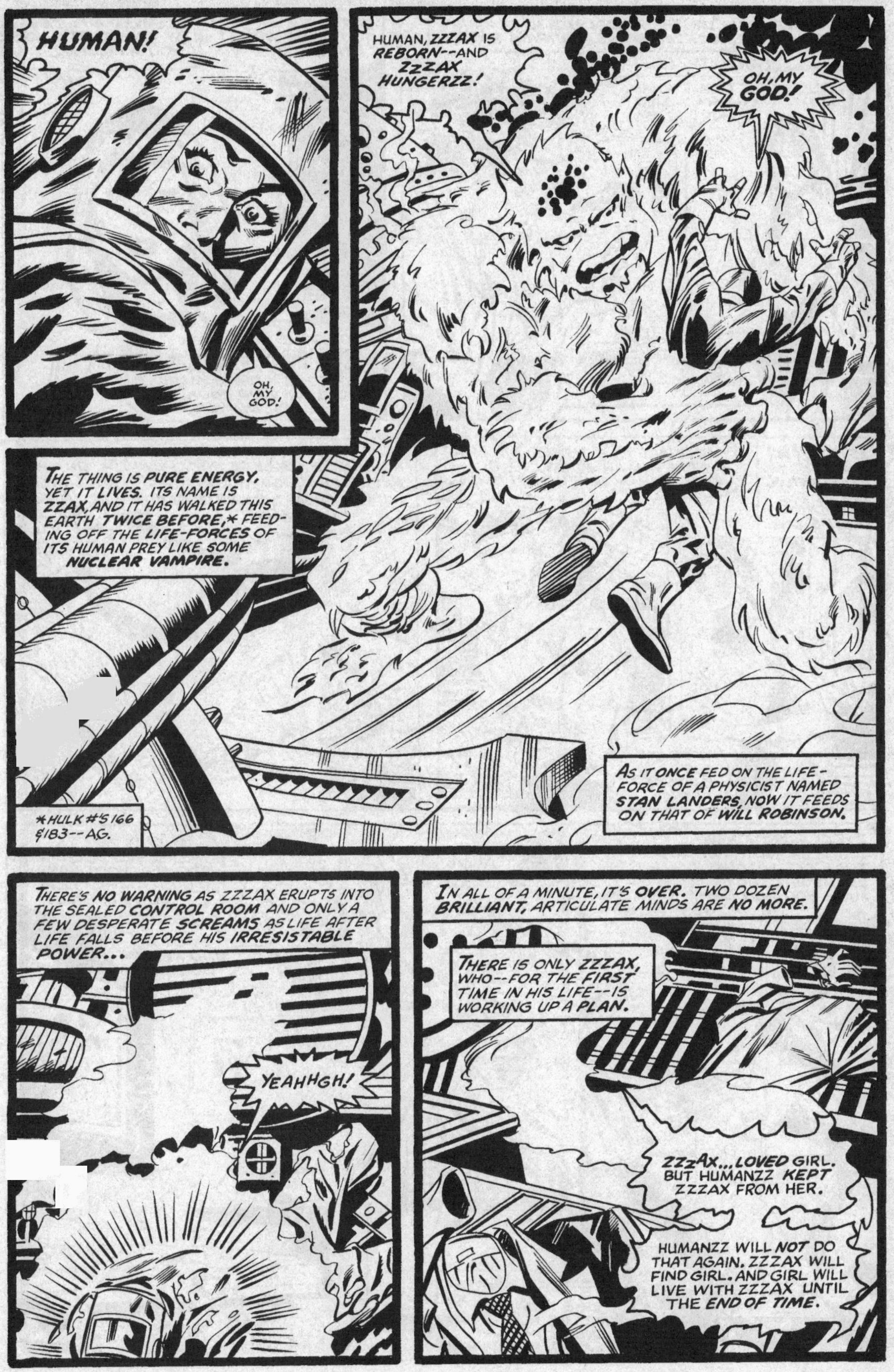
HUMAN!
OH, MY GOD!
HUMAN, ZZZAX IS REBORN--AND ZZZAX HUNGERZZ!
OH, MY GOD!
THE THING IS PURE ENERGY, YET IT LIVES. ITS NAME IS ZZAX, AND IT HAS WALKED THIS EARTH TWICE BEFORE,* FEEDING OFF THE LIFE-FORCES OF ITS HUMAN PREY LIKE SOME NUCLEAR VAMPIRE.
*HULK #'S 166 &183--AG.
AS IT ONCE FED ON THE LIFE-FORCE OF A PHYSICIST NAMED STAN LANDERS, NOW IT FEEDS ON THAT OF WILL ROBINSON.
THERE'S NO WARNING AS ZZZAX ERUPTS INTO THE SEALED CONTROL ROOM AND ONLY A FEW DESPERATE SCREAMS AS LIFE AFTER LIFE FALLS BEFORE HIS IRRESISTABLE POWER...
YEAHHGH!
IN ALL OF A MINUTE, IT'S OVER. TWO DOZEN BRILLIANT, ARTICULATE MINDS ARE NO MORE.
THERE IS ONLY ZZZAX, WHO--FOR THE FIRST TIME IN HIS LIFE--IS WORKING UP A PLAN.
ZZZAX... LOVED GIRL. BUT HUMANZZ KEPT ZZZAX FROM HER.
HUMANZZ WILL NOT DO THAT AGAIN. ZZZAX WILL FIND GIRL. AND GIRL WILL LIVE WITH ZZZAX UNTIL THE END OF TIME.

MEANWHILE, IN THE UNIVERSITY OF CHICAGO CAMPUS APARTMENT OF PROFESSOR ALEXANDRIA KNOX...

NICE COFFEE, MAMA.

I HAVE A NAME, MARK. WOULD IT HURT TO USE IT?

SORRY. I'M NOT TOO GOOD WITH STRANGERS.

YOU SAVED MY LIFE. IN MY BOOK THAT MAKES YOU A FRIEND.

LOOK, I'M STILL SHOOK FROM THAT WRECK, AND I REALLY HATE EATING ALONE. I HAVE SOME STEAKS, MARK, AND I'M A FAIR COOK. JOIN ME FOR DINNER?

IT TAKES A LITTLE PERSUASION, BUT IN THE END, CAGE YIELDS, AND...

HERE ARE THE DISHES. SAY, ARE YOU AN ACTOR OR ROCK STAR OR SOMETHING?

HMM? OH, MY THREADS.

NOPE. I'M JUST AN ORDINARY GUY.

AN' IF SHE BELIEVES THAT, SHE AIN'T NO GENIUS COLLEGE PROF. I WAS NEVER ANY GOOD AT LYIN.' THIS RUNNIN FROM THE LAW IS GETTIN' ME DOWN.

I'LL TURN ON THE LIGHTS, ALEX.

--HOLY!!

ZZZAX HAZZ FOUND YOU, ALEX KNOX--WOMAN THAT ZZZAX LOVEZZ. ZZZAZ HAZZ COME TO MAKE YOU HIZZ OWN.

NO!

WHAT IS THIS? A WALKIN', TALKIN' 'LECTRICAL STORM? SHOOT, MAMA, DIDN'T YOU PAY YOUR CON ED BILL?

I GOT A BAD FEELIN' 'BOUT ALL THIS--

--LIKE THIS TIME I MAY BE PLAYIN' OUTTA MY LEAGUE.

ANY HUMAN WHO TRIEZZ TO ZZTOP ZZZAX--

--WILL DIE!!

ZOT!

NICE FRIENDS YOU GOT HERE, LADY! ALEX.?.!?

SHE DOEN'T *HEAR* AS THE *NIGHTMARE* SHE'D THOUGHT *DEAD* AND BURIED *LONG AGO*, TOGETHER WITH THE *BODY* OF THE MAN SHE'D *LOVED*, TAKES SHAPE *AGAIN*...

AND *NOW*--AS THEN--ALL SHE CAN DO IS SCREAM.

DO NOT *FEAR* ZZZAX, ALEX. ZZZAX *LOVEZZ* YOU.

THAT *SO*, UGLY? SHE SURE DON'T LOOK LIKE SHE LOVES *YOU*.

HANG *ON*, ALEX! WE GOTTA FIND US SOME *RUNNIN'* ROOM--*FAST*!

INSIDE YOUR PLACE, ZZZAX IS HOLDIN' ALL THE *ACES*--

BRRASH!

--BUT *OUTSIDE*, ON THE STREET, MAYBE WE GOT A *CHANCE*.

ANYONE *ELSE* LIVE IN THIS *BUILDIN'*?

N-NO, I'M THE *FIRST* T-TENANT.

GOOD. 'CAUSE WE AIN'T GOT TIME T' *WARN* NOBODY!

SCANT SECONDS LATER...

SHKAM!

HUMAN!!

PERSISTENT DUDE, AIN'T HE? THE MONSTER WITH THE *ONE-TRACK MIND*.

OH, *LORD*, HE'LL STOP AT *NOTHING* TO GET ME. THE ONE OTHER TIME HE *TRIED*--

--IT TOOK THE *HULK* TO BEAT HIM!*

*HULK #183--A.G.

DO TELL? WELL, I AIN'T *BIG-AN'-GREEN*, DOC--

BRAK!

--BUT I AIN'T *HELPLESS*, EITHER!

WHAT D'YA KNOW? I THINK I *HURT* HIM.

HEY! WHAT HAPPENED TO THE *LIGHTS*?

UH... THAT *BLACK DUDE* JUST THREW OUR *UTILITY POLE* AT THAT *MONSTER* HE'S FIGHTIN'!

HARRY, CALL THE COPS-- *QUICK!*

MEN

HARRY WASTES NO TIME. UNFORTUNATELY, THE PRECINCT SERGEANT WHO TAKES THE CALL MERELY LAUGHS, MAKES A NUMBER OF RUDE COMMENTS AND HANGS UP. AFTER ALL MONSTERS? IN CHICAGO?!?

SHOOT! ZAKKO'S *TORCHIN'* THE POLE, IGNITIN' THE *TAR* SOAKED INTO THE WOOD--!

ZAP!

HEAT'S *BUILDIN' UP*-- REACHIN' THE *INSULATORS!* THE POLE'S GONNA--

KRAKOW!

YOU ARE *DOOMED*, HUMAN! *ZZZAX HAZZ* YOU NOW!

NOT FOR *LONG*, PLUG-PUSS!

ARRGH! INSIDE MY HEAD--*BURNIN'!* WHAT'S HE DOIN' T' MY *MIND*?!

IMPOZZ-ZZ'BLE. YOU ZZTILL *LIVE!*

YOU ZZHOULD HAVE *DIED* AT *ZZZAX'S TOUCH!*

I....ALMOST *DID*, UGLY. NEVER FELT *SO... WEAK* BEFORE...

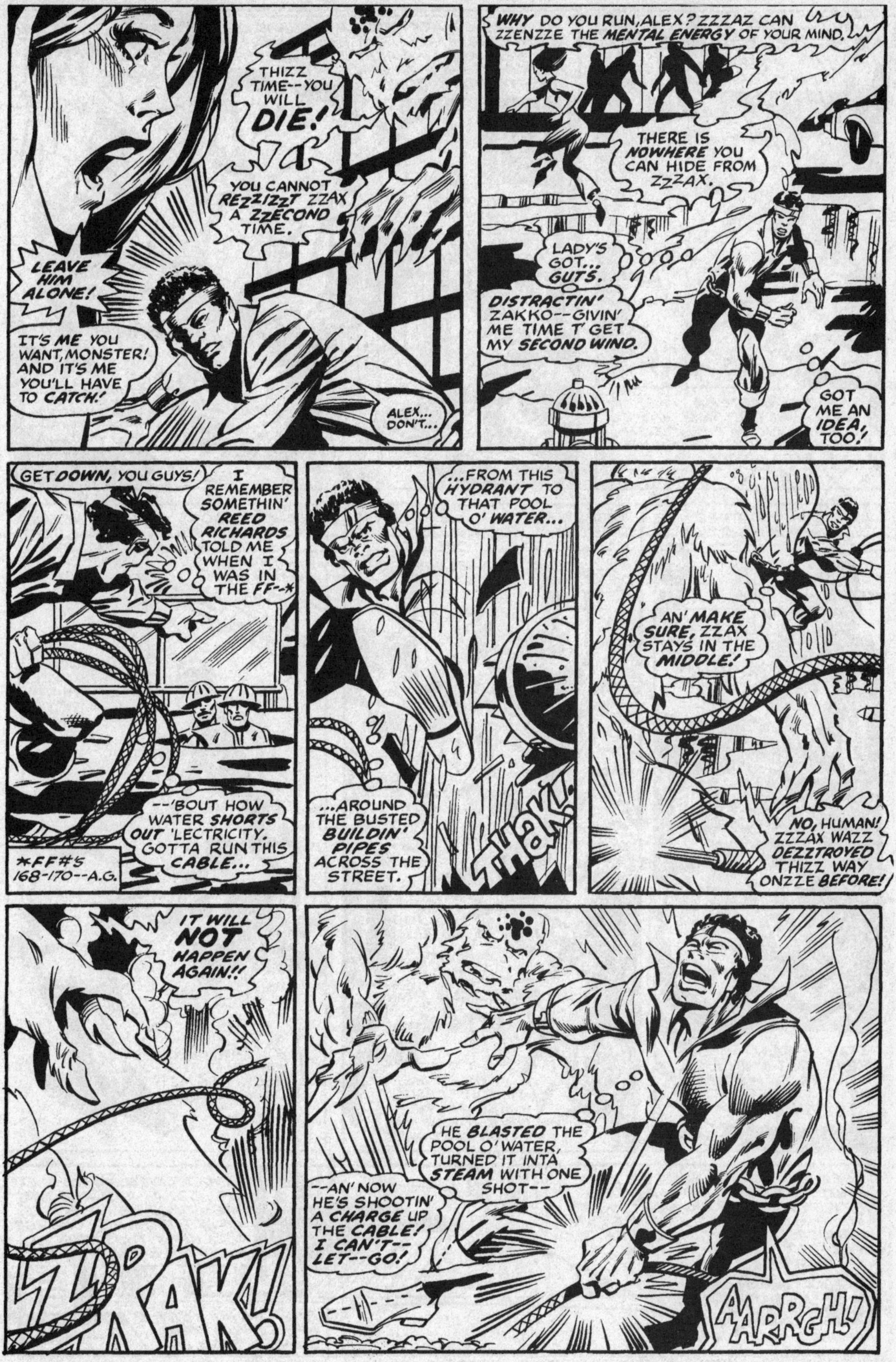
THIZZ TIME--YOU WILL DIE!
YOU CANNOT REZZIZZT ZZAX A ZZECOND TIME.
LEAVE HIM ALONE!
IT'S ME YOU WANT, MONSTER! AND IT'S ME YOU'LL HAVE TO CATCH!
ALEX... DON'T...
WHY DO YOU RUN, ALEX? ZZZAZ CAN ZZENZZE THE MENTAL ENERGY OF YOUR MIND.
THERE IS NOWHERE YOU CAN HIDE FROM ZZZAX.
LADY'S GOT... GUTS.
DISTRACTIN' ZAKKO--GIVIN' ME TIME T' GET MY SECOND WIND.
GOT ME AN IDEA, TOO!
GET DOWN, YOU GUYS!
I REMEMBER SOMETHIN' REED RICHARDS TOLD ME WHEN I WAS IN THE FF--*
--'BOUT HOW WATER SHORTS OUT 'LECTRICITY. GOTTA RUN THIS CABLE...
*FF#'S 168-170--A.G.
...FROM THIS HYDRANT TO THAT POOL O' WATER...
...AROUND THE BUSTED BUILDIN' PIPES ACROSS THE STREET.
THAK!
AN' MAKE SURE, ZZAX STAYS IN THE MIDDLE!
NO, HUMAN! ZZZAX WAZZ DEZZTROYED THIZZ WAY ONZZE BEFORE!
IT WILL NOT HAPPEN AGAIN!!
ZZRAK!
HE BLASTED THE POOL O' WATER, TURNED IT INTA STEAM WITH ONE SHOT--
--AN' NOW HE'S SHOOTIN' A CHARGE UP THE CABLE! I CAN'T--LET--GO!
AARRGH!

TIME PASSES...

IN THE BEGINNING, THERE'S DARKNESS...

...BROKEN, AFTER A TIME, BY FLASHES OF BRILLIANT COLOR... FLASHES THAT EVENTUALLY RESOLVE THEMSELVES INTO A FACE.

HIS NAME IS MARK REVEL, AND HE HAS LOVED ALEXANDRIA KNOX FROM THE MOMENT HE SAW HER. AND, LIKE ALEX, THIS NIGHT HE HAS COME FACE-TO-FACE WITH A NIGHTMARE REBORN.

WHICH MAKES HIM--AT THIS MOMENT--A VERY DESPERATE MAN.

BLAST YOU, WAKE UP!

EASE OFF, PAL, I... HEAR YOU. WHA'S HAPP'NIN' MAN... WHO'RE... YOU?

INTRODUCTIONS ARE QUICKLY MADE, AND THEN...

--ZZZAX HAS ALEX! WE'VE GOT TO RESCUE HER!

I DID MY BEST, REVEL, BUT I AIN'T NO MIRACLE WORKER. WHAT YOU NEED IS THE AVENGERS!

THERE'S NO TIME! IT MAY ALREADY BE TOO LATE!

YOU GUTLESS WONDER, I OUGHTTA...

SHUT YOUR MOUTH, BUDDY--'FORE YOU GET SOME INSTANT DENTAL WORK.

GO ON, HIT ME! IT WON'T CHANGE THE TRUTH-- THAT POWER MAN'S TURNED COWARD!

BLONDIE'S GOT A POINT. ALEX KNOX IS ONE FINE WOMAN. IF I WALKED OUT ON HER NOW...

...I'D NEVER BE ABLE TO LIVE WITH MYSELF.

OKAY, REVEL, WHICH WAY'D THEY GO?

AN' WHILE WE'RE TAILIN' 'EM YOU CAN TELL ME WHAT THE HECK THIS MESS IS ALL ABOUT!

THEY HEAD NORTH ALONG THE LAKE, AND--HALTINGLY--MARK REVEL TELLS OF A STORMY EVENING MONTHS AGO WHEN, ALONG WITH ALEX AND STAN LANDERS, HE UNWITTINGLY RE-CREATED THE LIVING DYNAMO NAMED ZZZAX.

LANDERS DIED SAVING ALEX' LIFE. ZZZAX ABSORBED HIS LIFE-FORCE, HIS MEMORIES, HIS FEELINGS, HIS LOVE FOR ALEX KNOX. THUS, THE MONSTER KIDNAPPED HER.

*IN HULK #183, AGAIN--A.G.

AND THE HULK SAVED HER. IT WAS THAT SIMPLE THEN. *

"NOW" MAY BE SOMETHING ELSE AGAIN.

SIGN OUT FRONT SAID *FERMI NUCLEAR POWER STATION.* YOU *SURE* THIS IS THE RIGHT PLACE?

MY *PORTABLE SENSORS* ARE RIGGED TO TRACK ZZZAX'S *UNIQUE ENERGY PATTERN,* HERO, AND THEY LED US *HERE.*

SEE FOR *YOURSELF,* BLONDIE.

GOOD LORD.

IT'S *ALEX!* BUT WHAT'S ZZZAX *DOING* TO HER?!

YEAH, I'M SURE. I ONLY HOPE WE'RE *NOT TOO LATE.*

DO NOT BE *AFRAID,* ALEX. THERE IZZ *NOTHING* HERE TO *HARM* YOU. ZZZAX WOULD NOT HARM THE WOMAN ZZZAX *LOVEZZ.*

TRY TO *UNDERZZTAND.* YOU ARE *HUMAN,* AT ZZZAX'S *TOUCH,* YOU WOULD BE *ABZZORBED* INTO ZZZAX'S BEING LIKE THE *OTHER* HUMANZZ. ZZZAX DOES NOT *WANT* THAT.

ZZZAX HAS *INTEL-LIGENZZ* NOW, ALEX, AND ZZZAX HAZZ *UZZED* IT TO DEZIGN THIZZ *MOLECULAR TRANZZFORMER.*

THE *TRANZZFORMER* AND THE *PARA-MAGNETRON GRID* WILL *REDUZZE* YOUR HUMAN FROM TO ITS *BAZZIC ATOMIC ZZTRUCTURE* AND THEN RECREATE IT IN *ZZZAX' IMAGE.* YOU, TOO, WILL BECOME A BEING OF *LIVING ENERGY.*

WE WILL BE TO-GETHER FOR ALL TIME.

NO! DEAR LORD-- NO!!

I'VE HEARD SOME *HORROR STORIES* IN MY *TIME,* ZAKKO--

--BUT THIS ONE *TAKES* THE CAKE!

HUMAN CALLED *POWER MAN!*

THAT'S ME, UGLY-- THE ONE-TIME *HERO-FOR-HIRE!*

DOIN' WHAT COMES *NATURALLY!*

MAN, I SURE HOPE THIS *CRAZY PLAN O' REVEL'S* WORKS.

"ON THE OTHER HAND, IF IT DON'T, THEN I GUESS ALL MY TROUBLES'LL BE OVER, AN' HOW!"

THE BATTLE BEGINS...

...WHILE THE PRIZE EVERYONE'S FIGHTING FOR WRITHES ON THE GLOWING PARA-MAGNETRON GRID, HER BODY OUTLINED BY ARCS OF RAW POWER PULLED OFF THE MID-AMERICA POWER NETWORK.

FOR HER, TIME IS QUICKLY RUNNING OUT.

WHA--?!? ANOTHER HUMAN--CARRYING A WEAPON!

NOT AN ORDINARY WEAPON, MONSTER!

A HOSE LINE--CONNECTED TO THE PLANT'S RESERVOIR OF LIQUID HELIUM!

LET'S SEE HOW WELL YOU STAND UP AGAINST A SPRAY THAT'S--

--FOUR HUNDRED-THIRTY DEGREES BELOW ZERO!

COLD SO INTENSE THAT IT CAN AFFECT A BEING MADE OF PURE ENERGY POURS FORTH.

THAT STUFF REVEL'S USIN'--ONE SQUIRT AN' THIS WHOLE LAB FEELS LIKE INSTANT WINTER.'

IT'S WORKIN', THOUGH, ZZZAX IS BACKIN' AWAY FROM IT. HE LOOKS SCARED. NOW'S MY CHANCE T' GET TO ALEX!

OR, MY CHANCE TO TRY, AT LEAST!
CHRISTMAS! WHO TOLD ZAKKO WE WAS PLAYIN' TACKLE?!

IT'S THAT HELIUM-STUFF REVEL'S USIN'--IT'S DOIN' SOMETHIN' T' THE FLOOR, MAKIN' IT SLICKER THAN ICE!

UNNOTICED IN THE SUDDEN CONFUSION, ALEX KNOX'S BODY BEGINS TO...GLOW...

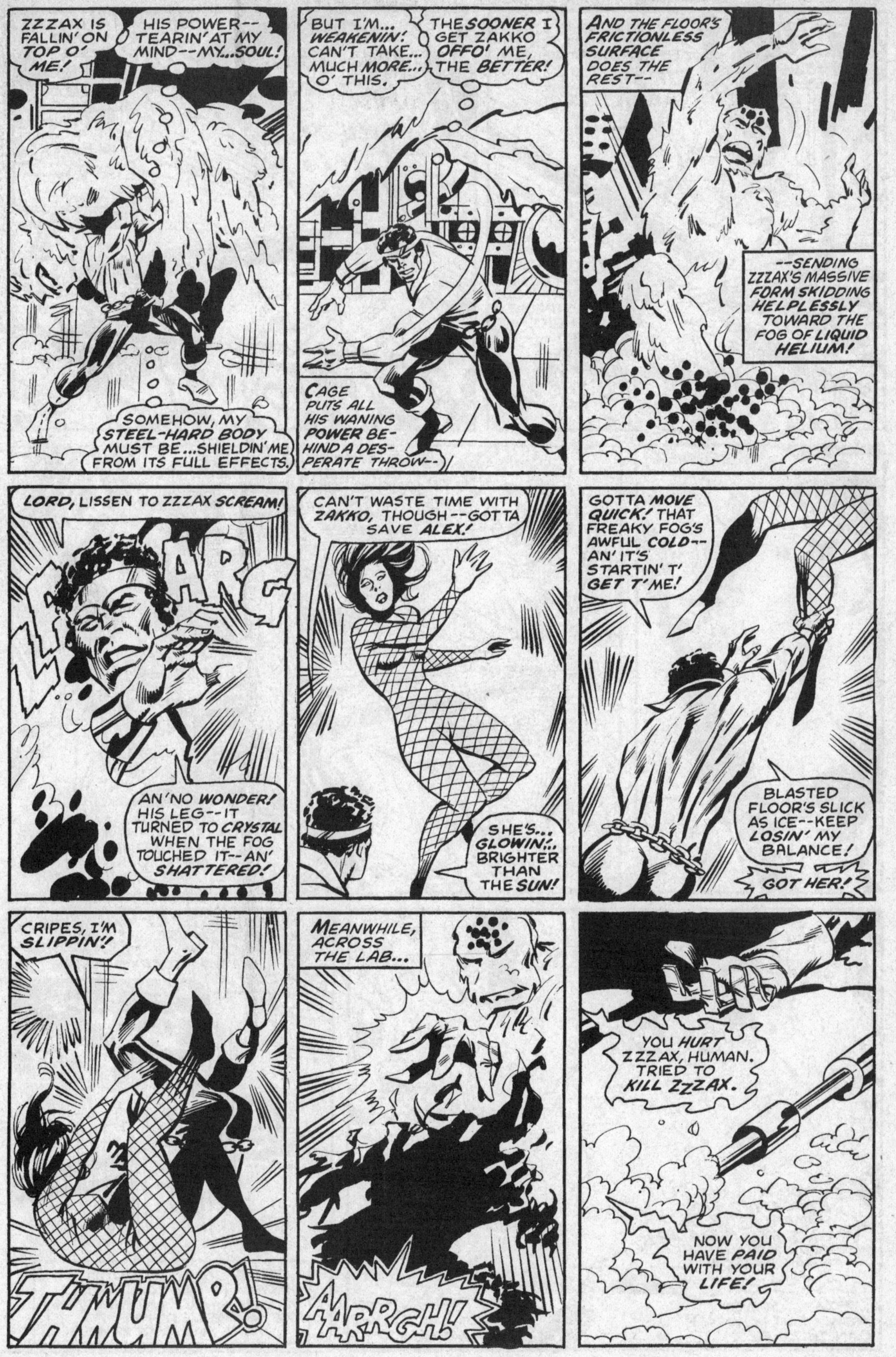
ZZZAX IS FALLIN' ON TOP O' ME!
HIS POWER-- TEARIN' AT MY MIND--MY...SOUL!
SOMEHOW, MY STEEL-HARD BODY MUST BE...SHIELDIN' ME FROM ITS FULL EFFECTS.
BUT I'M... WEAKENIN'! CAN'T TAKE... MUCH MORE... O' THIS.
THE SOONER I GET ZAKKO OFFO' ME, THE BETTER!
CAGE PUTS ALL HIS WANING POWER BE-HIND A DES-PERATE THROW--
AND THE FLOOR'S FRICTIONLESS SURFACE DOES THE REST--
--SENDING ZZZAX'S MASSIVE FORM SKIDDING HELPLESSLY TOWARD THE FOG OF LIQUID HELIUM!
LORD, LISSEN TO ZZZAX SCREAM!
ARG
AN' NO WONDER! HIS LEG--IT TURNED TO CRYSTAL WHEN THE FOG TOUCHED IT--AN' SHATTERED!
CAN'T WASTE TIME WITH ZAKKO, THOUGH--GOTTA SAVE ALEX!
SHE'S... GLOWIN'... BRIGHTER THAN THE SUN!
GOTTA MOVE QUICK! THAT FREAKY FOG'S AWFUL COLD-- AN' IT'S STARTIN' T' GET T' ME!
BLASTED FLOOR'S SLICK AS ICE--KEEP LOSIN' MY BALANCE!
GOT HER!
CRIPES, I'M SLIPPIN'!
THUMP!
MEANWHILE, ACROSS THE LAB...
AARRGH!
YOU HURT ZZZAX, HUMAN. TRIED TO KILL ZZZAX.
NOW YOU HAVE PAID WITH YOUR LIFE!

REVEL!! HE--HE'S DEAD!

AN' HIS HOSE IS STILL SPRAYIN'! THAT FOG'S CUTTIN' OFF THE ONLY EXIT!

BUT-- I AIN'T GONNA WORRY 'BOUT BUSTIN' OUTTA HERE--

WRENCH!

--UNTIL I STOP ZZZAX!

YOU HEAR ME, ZAKKO? YOU'RE GONNA PAY FOR KILLING REVEL!

B'THOW!

OH, BROTHER.

WELL, IF AT FIRST YOU DON'T SUCCEED...

YOU'RE GOIN' IN STYLE, ZAKKO--LIKE EVERY ENERGY VAMPIRE SHOULD--

--WITH A STAKE THROUGH THE HEART!!

I CAN TELL THAT AIN'T GONNA HOLD HIM LONG, MAMA--

--BUT ALL I NEED IS ENOUGH TIME T' BATTER A HOLE THROUGH THE WALL TO GET YOU TO SAFETY! AND THEN--

YOU WILL NOT EZZCAPE ZZZAX, HUMAN! AFTER ZZZAX HAZZ INZZINERATED YOUR PUNY ZZTEEL BAR, ZZZAX WILL...

...ZZZAX...CANNOT MOVE! BUT HOW CAN THIZZ BE?!?

OF COURZZE! THE TRANZZFORMER BEAM IZZ ZZTIL BUILDING UP POWER-- AND THE ENERGY ZZHACKLEZZ THAT HELD ALEX KNOX TO THE PARA-MAGNETRON GRID NOW HOLD ZZZAX.

BUT ONLY FOR A MOMENT!

A MOMENT. SO LITTLE TIME IN THE SCHEME OF THINGS. YET TIME ENOUGH FOR THE FREEZING HELIUM FOG TO REACH ZZZAX'S POWER CONSOLES...

...SUBJECTING DELICATE MACHINERY TO MORE STRESS IN THAT SINGLE MOMENT THAN THEY WERE DESIGNED TO TAKE IN A LIFETIME!

THE PIERCING COLD TRANSFORMS THE METAL SHIELDING HIGH-VOLTAGE CONDUITS INTO A SUPER-CONDUCTOR, AND SUDDENLY THOUSANDS OF MEGAWATTS OF POWER POUR THROUGH RAVAGED COMMAND CIRCUITS, OVERLOADING ALL OF ZZZAX'S CONSOLES AT ONCE--

--AND, A HEARTBEAT LATER...

KAVOOOM!

MEANWHILE, OUTSIDE THE PLANT...

KEEP YOUR HEAD DOWN, GIRL.

I'LL PROTECT YOU!

THE EXPLOSIONS ARE TAPERIN' OFF. I THINK IT'S OVER.

THE TWO PEOPLE I LOVED MOST IN THIS WORLD ARE DEAD-- BECAUSE OF ZZZAX--BECAUSE OF ME!

AN' YOU'RE AFRAID-- 'CAUSE IF ZAKKO CAN COME BACK ONCE, HE CAN DO IT AGAIN-- AN' AGAIN.

I UNDERSTAND, BABE.

OH, GOD, I WISH I'D DIED WITH THEM.

YOU JUST HOLD ON TO LUCAS, HON, AN' HAVE YOURSELF A GOOD CRY. YOU'LL FEEL BETTER WHEN YOU'RE DONE.

I WISH I HAD A MAGIC WAND, ALEX-- ONE WAVE AN' NO MORE NIGHTMARES. BUT IT AIN'T THAT EASY. NEVER IS.

ANYONE CAN DIE, Y'KNOW? THAT DON'T TAKE NOTHIN' SPECIAL. BUT LIVIN'-- SOMETIMES THAT CAN BE THE HARDEST THING OF ALL.

NEXT ISSUE: THE BEGINNING OF A NEW ERA, AS POWER MAN MEETS IRON FIST IN A BATTLE THAT WILL CHANGE BOTH THEIR LIVES... FOREVER. BE HERE IN SIXTY DAYS FOR:

FIST OF IRON, HEART OF STONE!

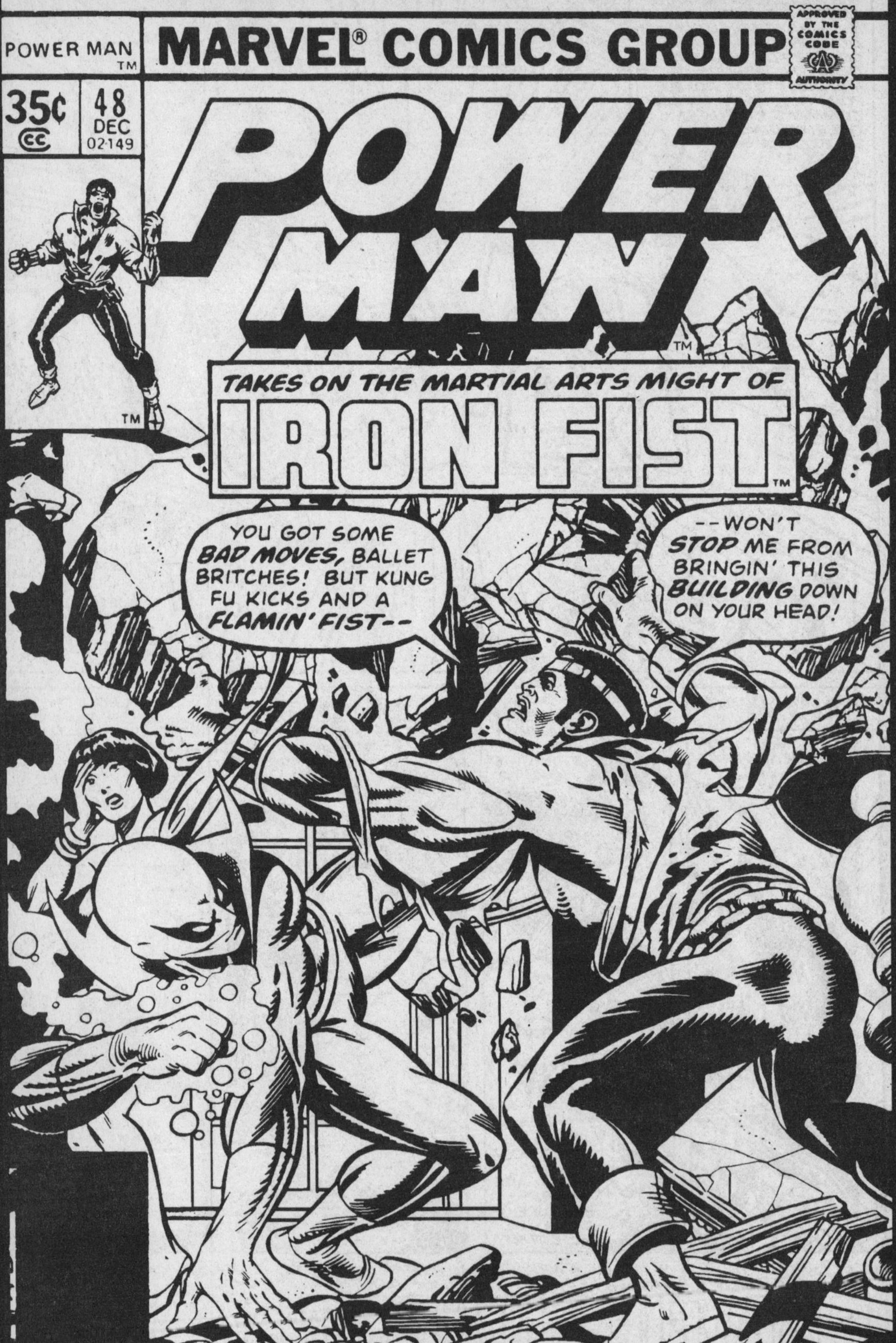
POWER MAN
MARVEL® COMICS GROUP
APPROVED BY THE COMICS CODE AUTHORITY
35¢
48 DEC 02149
POWER MAN
TAKES ON THE MARTIAL ARTS MIGHT OF
IRON FIST
YOU GOT SOME BAD MOVES, BALLET BRITCHES! BUT KUNG FU KICKS AND A FLAMIN' FIST--
--WON'T STOP ME FROM BRINGIN' THIS BUILDING DOWN ON YOUR HEAD!

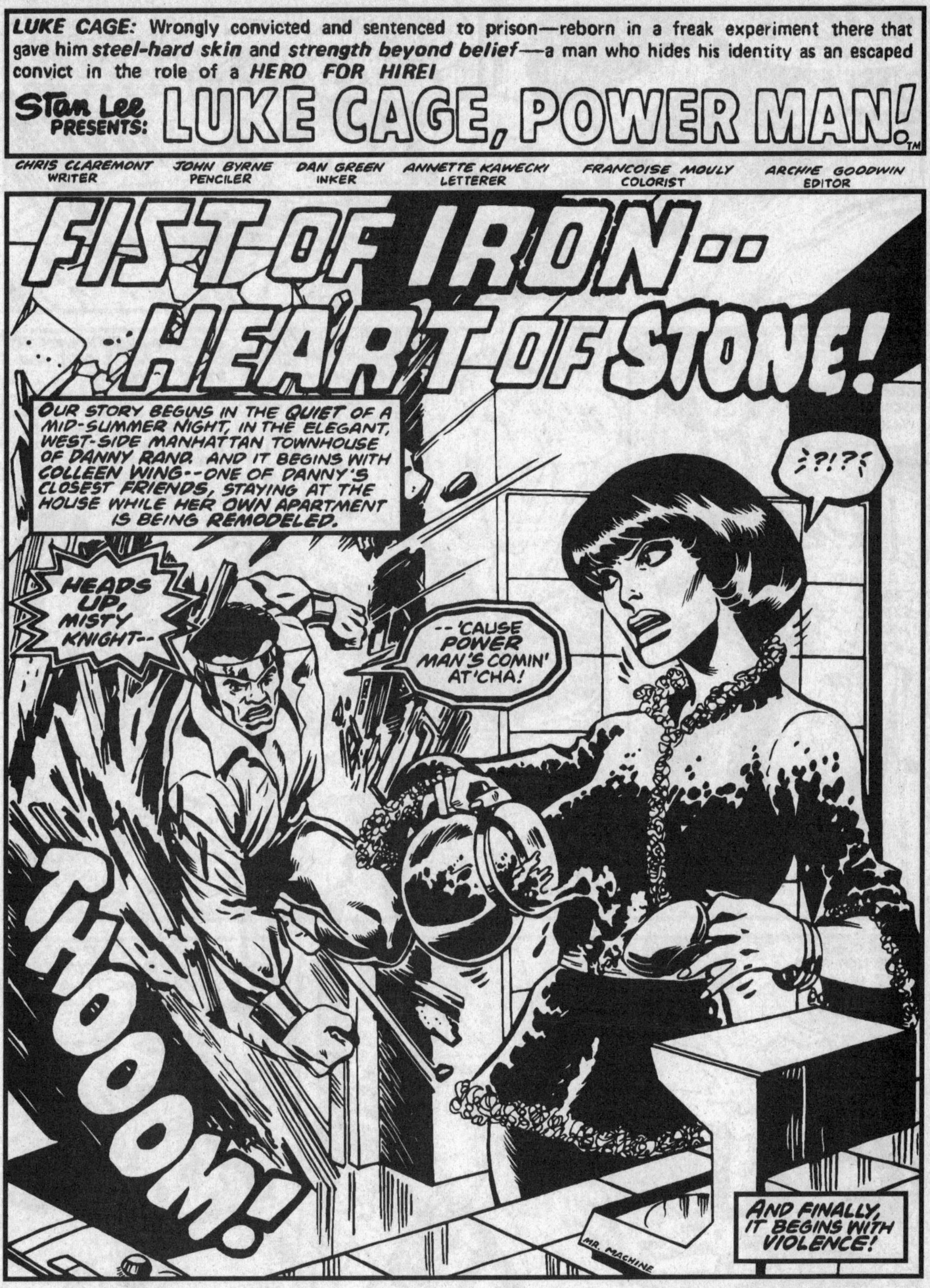
LUKE CAGE: Wrongly convicted and sentenced to prison—reborn in a freak experiment there that gave him steel-hard skin and strength beyond belief—a man who hides his identity as an escaped convict in the role of a HERO FOR HIRE!
Stan Lee PRESENTS: LUKE CAGE, POWER MAN! TM
CHRIS CLAREMONT WRITER
JOHN BYRNE PENCILER
DAN GREEN INKER
ANNETTE KAWECKI LETTERER
FRANCOISE MOULY COLORIST
ARCHIE GOODWIN EDITOR
FIST OF IRON-- HEART OF STONE!
OUR STORY BEGINS IN THE QUIET OF A MID-SUMMER NIGHT, IN THE ELEGANT, WEST-SIDE MANHATTAN TOWNHOUSE OF DANNY RAND. AND IT BEGINS WITH COLLEEN WING--ONE OF DANNY'S CLOSEST FRIENDS, STAYING AT THE HOUSE WHILE HER OWN APARTMENT IS BEING REMODELED.
?!?!
HEADS UP, MISTY KNIGHT--
--'CAUSE POWER MAN'S COMIN' AT'CHA!
THOOOM!
AND FINALLY, IT BEGINS WITH VIOLENCE!
MR. MACHINE

WAIT A MINUTE! YOU'RE NOT MISTY KNIGHT--

--HEY!!

THAT'S FOR SURE, BUSTER!

POWER MAN! HE'S THAT HERO-FOR-HIRE BUCK WHO WORKS OUT OF 42nd STREET.

BETTER MAKE TRACKS. THAT BOILING COFFEE ISN'T GOING TO DO MUCH GOOD...

...AGAINST CAGE'S STEEL-HARD SKIN.

NOT SO FAST, LI'L LADY!

WHOU-U-UFFF!

YOU AIN'T GOIN' ANYWHERE TILL YOU ANSWER SOME QUESTIONS.

I GOTTA FIND THIS KNIGHT WOMAN--AN' I GOT NO TIME T'WASTE.

SO BE COOL, MAMA, AN' TELL ME WHAT I WANT T' KNOW. I DON'T WANT TO HAVE TO GET ROUGH...

THIS IS INSANE-- I THOUGHT CAGE WAS ONE OF THE GOOD GUYS.

ROUGH DOESN'T FAZE ME, PAL--

--BECAUSE I'M NOT THE ONE WHO'S GOING TO GET HURT!

HAI-YAAHHH!!

SKRASH!

CHRISTMAS!

NOT BAD. SHE HEFTED MY THREE HUNDRED POUNDS LIKE I WEIGHED NOTHIN'.

NO WONDER THE MAN SAID I WAS THE ONLY ONE WHO COULD HELP HIM.

BUT *FANCY MOVES* OR NO, SHE'S *ONLY A WOMAN.*

AN' I'VE COME *TOO FAR* TO BACK OFF NOW. THERE'S TOO MUCH AT *STAKE.*

MAKE IT *EASY* FOR YOURSELF, FOX. I DON'T WANT TO *HURT* YOU. JUST GIVE ME A *LEAD* ON MISTY KNIGHT.

AND WHAT THEN? YOU'LL DO TO *ME* WHAT YOU DID TO THE *BACK DOOR*--? NO, THANK YOU, CAGE.

YOU'VE SURE COME A *LONG WAY,* BABY, FROM A TEMPORARY MEMBERSHIP IN THE *FANTASTIC FOUR.*

THAT'S RIGHT, MAMA. BUT A MAN'S *GOTTA* DO WHAT HE'S *GOTTA* DO.

I *WISH* THERE WAS SOME OTHER WAY! I WISH I COULD LET YOU *GO* ...BUT I *CAN'T.*

SO COME *GET* ME, HOTSHOT.

NICE. SHE KNOWS SHE'S WAY *FASTER 'N* ME--SO SHE STAYS *BEHIND* THE COUCH...

...FIGURIN' IF I COME *AROUND* OR *OVER* IT, SHE'LL HAVE AN *OPENIN'* TO THE *LIVIN'* ROOM DOOR.

TROUBLE IS, LADY, I'M *POWER MAN*--AN' I DON'T GO OVER, UNDER, OR AROUND *NOTHIN'*!

I GO *THROUGH!*

B THOW!

HAD *ENOUGH,* FOX?

FELLA, I'VE *JUST STARTED!*

CAN'T HANDLE THIS *ALONE!* IT'S TAKING ALL MY MARTIAL ARTS SKILL TO SIMPLY *STAY ALIVE.*

SOONER OR LATER, I'LL MAKE A *MIS-TAKE.*

CAN'T RISK HEADING *OUTSIDE*, THOUGH-- CAGE MAY HAVE BROUGHT *FRIENDS*.

WHAT'S HIS *INTEREST* IN MISTY? HE DOESN'T EVEN *KNOW* HER.

AND *NIGHTWING RESTORATIONS* HAS NEVER WORKED ON A CASE THAT IN-VOLVED *POWER MAN*.

WHATEVER IT IS, I'VE A FEELING IT ISN'T *LEGIT*-- WHICH MEANS POWER MAN'S TURNED *BAD*. I GUESS THE *HERO* FOR-HIRE RACKET DOESN'T *PAY* ENOUGH.

AND *CRIME DOES*.

OKAY, I MADE DANNY'S THIRD-FLOOR *STUDY* IN RECORD TIME, BUT CAGE'LL BE COMING *RIGHT BEHIND ME*.

LUCKILY, HE HAS *NO IDEA* WHICH FLOOR I'M ON, WHICH *ROOM* I DUCKED INTO. HE'LL HAVE TO CHECK 'EM *ALL* OUT.

UNFORTUNATELY, WHEN HE *DOES* GET HERE, THIS *DOOR* ISN'T EVEN GOING TO *SLOW HIM DOWN*.

THIS *BOOKCASE*, ON THE OTHER HAND, *MIGHT*.

IF I CAN *SHOVE* IT IN FRONT OF THE *DOOR*.

=UNNNNFFF=

NO GOOD. THE BLOODY THING MUST WEIGH A *TON!* CAN'T EVEN *BUDGE* IT.

CALM YOURSELF, COLLEEN, REMEMBER YOUR GRAND-FATHER'S *TEACHINGS*-- --*FOCUS ALL* YOUR STRENGTH...

...*ALL* THE POWER OF YOUR *WILL*. BE-COME AS *ONE* WITH YOUR PURPOSE...

...AND THEN LET YOUR POWER FLOW *THROUGH* YOU LIKE A *LIVING THING*.

IT *ISN'T* DANNY'S *IRON FIST*, BUT IT'LL HAVE TO DO THE *TRICK*.

KIA!!

SKRREEEK!!

THE QUESTION IS, COLLEEN, WAS IT DONE IN TIME?

CALL POLICE *SECOND*--IT'LL TAKE TOO LONG TO *CONVINCE* THEM OF WHAT'S GOING ON.

BESIDES, IT'LL TAKE *MORE* THAN A FEW *NYPD BLUE*-AND-WHITES TO STOP CAGE.

I NEED MISTY--AND *DANNY*, SHE SAID SHE WAS *COOKING* THEM DINNER AT HER APARTMENT.

BLAST-- I MIS-DIALED!

RELAX, WOMAN! HEART'S *RACING*--MOVING THAT CASE TOOK *MORE* OUT OF ME THAN I THOUGHT.

ESPECIALLY SINCE MY BODY'S BARELY *RECOVERED* FROM THAT *NIGHTMARE* JOB MISTY AND I TOOK IN *HONG KONG*. *

C'MON, MISTY! *ANSWER* THE PHONE!

* SEE *DEADLY HANDS OF KUNG FU* #'S 32 AND 33 --ARCHIE.

DOOR'S *LOCKED!*

KIK!

KLAK!

AN' FROM THE *SOUND* OF IT, THE FOX IS CALLIN' FOR *HELP*.

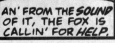

HANG IT UP, WOMAN!

'CAUSE AS OF *RIGHT NOW*, FUN-TIME'S *OVER!*

SKA-THAM!

KNIGHT-GREY APARTMENT. WHO'S CALLIN'?

MISTY!

OH, MY GOD-- NO!!

SCENE-SHIFT: A FEW MINUTES BACK IN TIME, AND ABOUT A HUNDRED BLOCKS DOWNTOWN, TO THE GREENWICH VILLAGE APARTMENT SHARED BY JEAN GREY AND MISTY KNIGHT...

THE PLACE LOOKS *NICE*, MISTY. YOU'D NEVER KNOW THE *X-MEN* AND I TURNED IT INTO A *WAR ZONE.**

SO JEAN *TOLD* ME. THAT MUST'VE BEEN SOME FIGHT, PAL.

IT HAD ITS... MOMENTS.

*IN IRON FIST #15 -- A.G.

I'LL BET. Y'KNOW, DANNY, AFTER THAT *BUSHMASTER FIASCO*--AN' THE HONG KONG CAPER WITH *COLLEEN*--IT'S GOOD TO BE *HOME.*

IT'S *GOOD* TO HAVE SOMEONE TO COME HOME *TO.*

I *KNOW* HOW YOU FEEL. I *MISSED* YOU. A *LOT.*

BORWWG!

DON'T *ANSWER* IT, MISTY.

SORRY, PAL, I'M A COMPUL-SIVE *PHONE ANSWERER.*

KNIGHT-GREY APART-MENT. *WHO'S CALLIN'?*

MISTY!

OH, MY GOD--*NO!*

KLIKT!

WHAT THE--?! THAT WAS COLLEEN'S VOICE.

SHE WAS *CUT OFF*--AN' NOW THE LINE'S GONE *DEAD.*

C'MON, DANNY! LET'S GET UP TO *YOUR* PLACE --*FAST!*

WHAT'S HAPPEN-ING?

I'M *NOT* SURE

COULD BE *NOTHIN'*, AN *ACCIDENT*, MAYBE.

OR IT COULD BE *TROUBLE.* I'VE GOT A *GUT* FEELING ABOUT THIS, PAL-- AN' IT'S *BAD.*

CAGE, WHAT'S **WRONG** WITH YOU, MAN?! YOU GONE **CRAZY**?!? YOU KEEP ON USIN' YOUR **MUSCLES** 'STEAD A' YOUR **BRAINS** AN' YOU AIN'T GOT A **PRAYER**.

I SHOULD A' **FIGURED** THE LADY'D **BARRICADE** THE DOOR.

AN IF SHE'S **HURT**-- OR **WORSE**--THEN WHAT DO I DO?

I'M A **PUPPET**, DANCIN' TO THE **BOSS MAN'S** TUNE. HE'S GOT ME **BOXED IN,** AN' THE HARDER I TRY T' CUT MYSELF **LOOSE**...

...THE **WORSE** EVERYTHING GETS.

THANK THE LORD FOR **SMALL** FAVORS, ANYWAY.

SHE'S **BREATHIN'!** SHE'S **ALIVE!!**

MEANWHILE, ACROSS THE STREET FROM THE **RAND HOUSE**...

HE'S BEEN IN THERE A **LONG TIME,** MAN--WHAT'S KEEPIN' HIM?

BE **COOL,** BRO'.

GOIN' FROM SUPER-HERO TO **KIDNAPPER** IN ONE NIGHT IS A **HEAVY** CHANGE FOR A **RIGHTEOUS** DUDE LIKE **LUCAS.**

YEAH? SUPPOSE HE'S SETTIN' UP A **DOUBLE-CROSS?**

NO WAY, **COMMANCHE!** WE BEEN RIDIN' **SHOT-GUN** ON HIM SINCE WE FLEW OUTTA **CHI.**

AN' WE **CUT** THE HOUSE'S **PHONES** THE MINUTE THE LADY INSIDE TRIED TO MAKE A **CALL.**

AND POWER MAN'S NO **FOOL**, M'MAN, HE KNOWS WHAT'LL **HAPPEN** IF HE STEPS OUTTA LINE,

HEADS UP, COM-MANCHE! LOOKS LIKE WE GOT **COMPANY.** AN' BLESS MY SOUL IF IT AIN'T **JUST** THE FOXY LADY WE BEEN **LOOKING** FOR.

STREET'S QUIET --HOUSE LOOKS **NORMAL.** SO WHY'S MY HEART **POUNDIN'** FIT T' BUST?

YOU'D THINK AFTER **ALL** THESE YEARS I'D BE OVER BEIN' **SCARED.**

GOOD THING THAT *DESK* TOOK MOST OF THE *IMPACT*--IF THOSE CASES HAD HIT SQUARE, SHE'D HAVE *DIED.* HOW'D SHE EVER *MOVE* THAT THING?! SHE DON'T LOOK THAT *STRONG.*

SHE GOT OFF LUCKY WITH A *BROKEN ARM.*

COLLEEN WING--MISTY KNIGHT'S PARTNER IN THEIR DETECTIVE AGENCY.

SHOULD'A *RECOGNIZED* HER, I GUESS, BUT THE *PHOTO* SHADES GAVE ME SHOWED HER WITH A *DIFFERENT* HAIR STYLE.

UNNH...

REST EASY, HON, I FIXED YOU UP *BEST* I COULD, BUT I'M NO *DOCTOR.*

THERE'S TIMES I THINK I'M NOT MUCH OF *ANYTHING.*

CUT IT OUT, LUCAS! YOU KEEP TALKIN' LIKE *THIS* AN' YOU'RE *BEATEN* BEFORE YOU--

--HOLD *IT!*

NOISE FROM *DOWN-STAIRS*--SO QUIET I ALMOST *MISSED* IT.

THE CLICK OF A KEY TURNIN' IN A LOCK--SOMEBODY COMIN' THROUGH THE *FRONT DOOR.*

WAY TO-NIGHT'S GOIN', IT'S PROB'LY THE *AVENGERS.*

HOPE I *KNEW* WHAT I WAS DOIN' WHEN I DROPPED *DANNY* OFF A COUPLE OF BLOCKS *BACK.*

TOO LATE FOR *SECOND THOUGHTS* NOW, BABE--SO HERE GOES *NOTHIN'.*

COLLEEN? YOU *HOME,* HON?

SHE *IS,* MISS KNIGHT, BUT SHE AIN'T SEEIN' *VISITORS*--AN' BY THE TIME SHE *WAKES UP,* YOU AND I ARE GONNA BE *LONG GONE.*

KLIK

POWER MAN?!?

YOU *GOT* IT...AN' I GOT MY *ORDERS,* LADY, AN' YOU'RE COMIN' WITH ME, EITHER *PEACEABLY...*

...OR IN *PIECES.* THE CHOICE IS *YOURS.*

MISTER, YOU JUST MADE THE BIGGEST *MISTAKE* OF YOUR EN-TIRE *MISBEGOTTEN* LIFE.

'CAUSE I'M GOIN' *NO-WHERE* WITH YOU--

--UNLESS IT'S TO THE *CITY MORGUE* TO IDENTIFY YOUR *BODY!*

B'LAM!

THAT'S A *LAUGH*, LADY! FOR ALL THE *GOOD* YOUR *COLT'S* DOIN', YOU MIGHT AS WELL BE THROWIN' *SPITBALLS* AT THE MAN.

BUT I'VE GOTTA KEEP HIM *OFF-BALANCE!*

AIN'T YOU *HEARD,* MAMA? I'M THE *DUDE* WITH THE *STEEL-HARD SKIN.*

THAT *TOY* YOU'RE PACKIN' MAY *BRUISE* ME A LITTLE--

--BUT THAT'S ABOUT *ALL.*

WE'LL SEE.

FIVE MORE SHOTS, TRIGGERED IN AS MANY SECONDS, EACH DEAD ON TARGET, EACH HAVING *NO* EFFECT ON CAGE AS HE MOVES DOWN THE STAIRS TOWARDS MISTY.

FINALLY, SHE RUNS OUT OF *BULLETS.*

OKAY, PAL, FIRST ROUND TO *YOU.*

BUT THIS FIGHT'S GOT A *WAYS* TO GO BEFORE IT'S *DONE.*

BIG TALK, LITTLE LADY. YOU GOT ME *SHAKIN'* IN MY BOOTS.

WHAT'RE YOU GONNA DO-- *PUNCH* ME?

SOMETHING LIKE THAT.

KWHAM!

I'M...*IMPRESSED.* I AIN'T BEEN HIT LIKE THAT IN QUITE A *WHILE.* YOU KEEP UP THE PRESSURE...

...AN' I GUESS I *MIGHT* BE IN TROUBLE.

YOU'RE IN TROUBLE *NOW,* BUCK!

AN' FOR *YOUR* SAKE, COLLEEN WING HAD BETTER BE *ALL RIGHT*--

--*HEY!!*

SHOK!

SHE'S *FINE,* LADY.

WHICH IS A LOT *MORE'N* I CAN SAY FOR *YOU* IF YOU DON'T LEARN YOUR *PLACE*--AN' *FAST!*

YOU CAUGHT ME *OFF-GUARD* WITH THAT FIRST SHOT, *MISTY*--

--BUT YOU'RE *NEVER* GONNA GET THAT LUCKY AGAIN. *DIG?*

BKASH!

OUT COLD.

I HEARD ON THE *STREET* THAT MISTY KNIGHT HAD SOME SORT'A *HYPED-UP* ARM--*BIONIC,* "THE PROFESSOR" TOLD ME ONCE...

DIDN'T FIGURE ON IT BEING THIS *POWERFUL,* THOUGH.

GUESS I OUGHTTA BE *PROUD* O' MYSELF --I MEAN, TWO *WO-MEN* PUNCHED OUT IN *ONE* NIGHT.

WHAT'S *NEXT--KIDS?*

YEAH, IT'S *LOUSY*--BUT MAN, I GOT *NO CHOICE.*

MR. CAGE --TURN AROUND.

THE NAME O' THE GAME IS *SURVIVAL,* AN' THE *ONLY RULE* IS THAT THERE *AIN'T* NO RULES.

HUH?!?

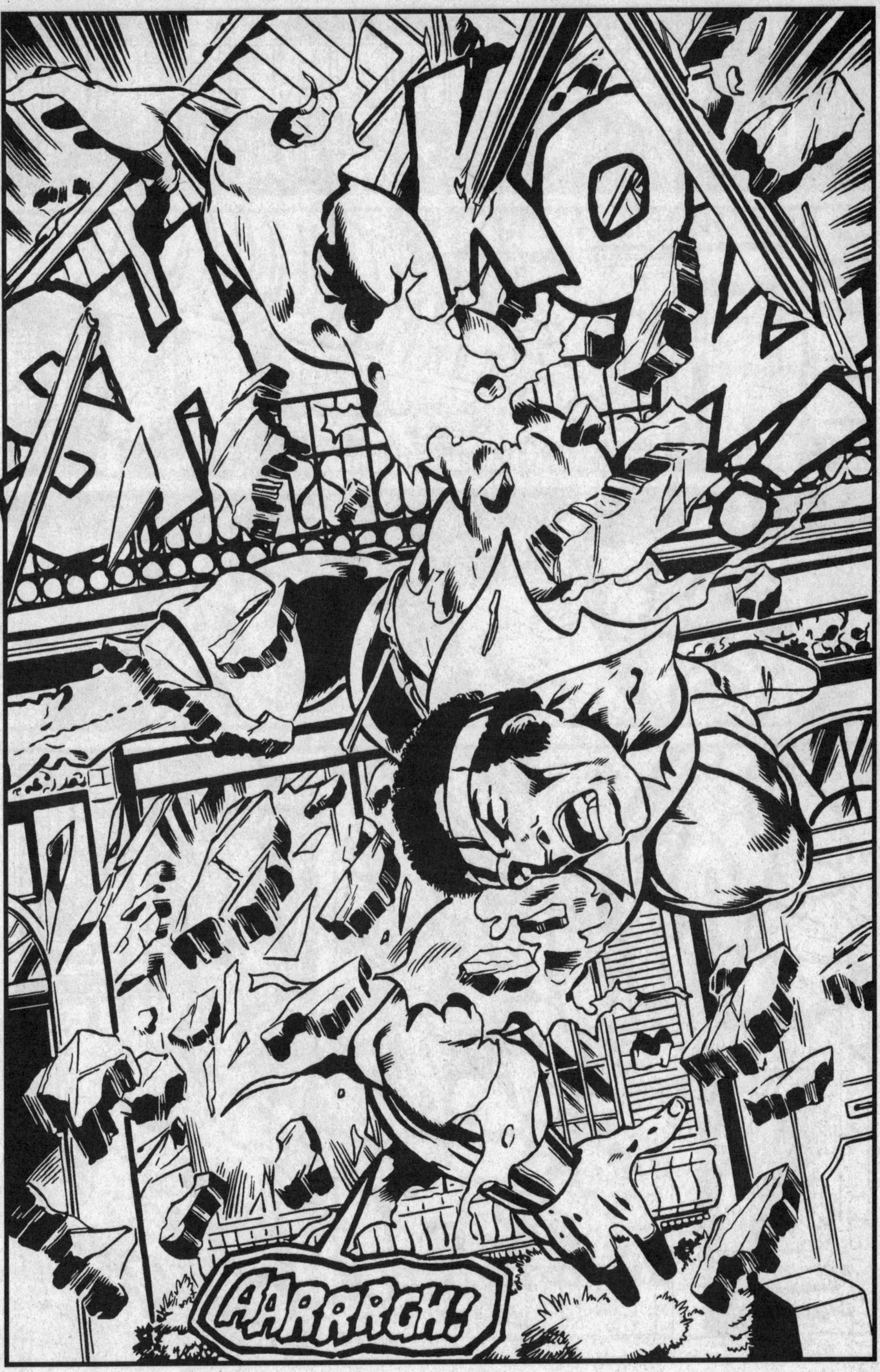
AARRRGH!

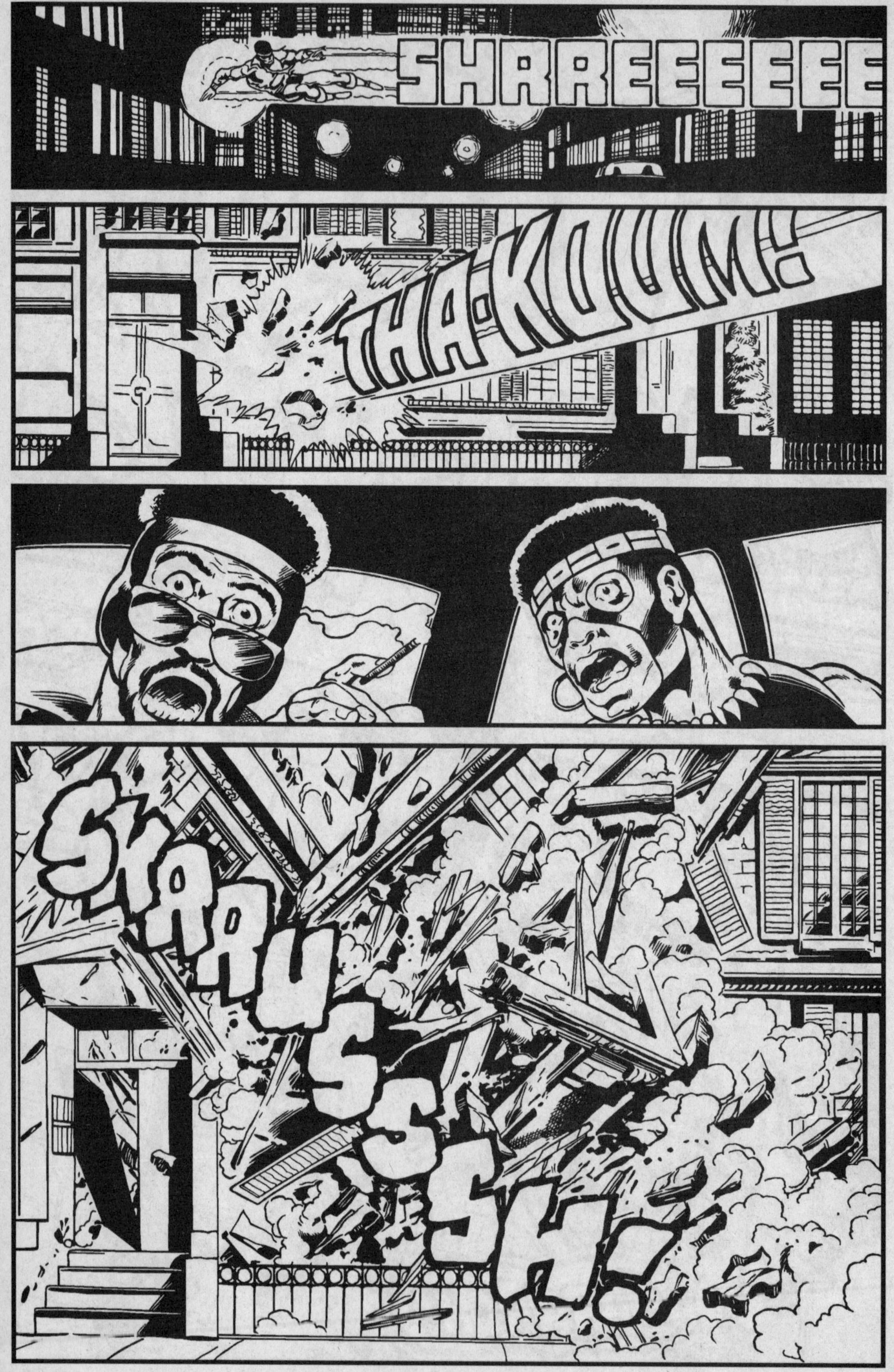
SHRREEEEEE
THA-KOOOM!
SKARUSSSH!

IT'S OVER SO QUICKLY, IT'S ALMOST IMPOSSIBLE TO BELIEVE WHAT'S HAPPENING--EXCEPT THAT WHERE A CONDEMNED BROWNSTONE STOOD A MOMENT AGO...

...THERE'S NOTHING LEFT BUT A PILE OF RUBBLE.

AND AS FAR AS SHADES AND COMMANCHE ARE CONCERNED, THAT'S A CLEAR SIGN.

FLOOR IT, BRO! GET US OUTTA HERE!

THE BOSS FIGURED LUCAS COULD HANDLE ANY OPPOSITION THIS SIDE O' THE FF--

-- BUT HE FIGURED WRONG!

NEITHER MAN LOOKS BACK AS THE CAR GUNS TOWARDS BROADWAY.

PERHAPS THEY SHOULD HAVE.

NO!!

SHADES, COMMANCHE-- THEY'RE BUGGIN' OUT!

THEY MUST'A FIGURED I WAS ZAPPED FOR GOOD!

THEY'LL CALL THE BOSS, TELL HIM WHAT WENT DOWN-- AN' THEN HE'LL-- HE'LL...

MY LIFE--MY FRIENDS' LIVES--WERE ON THE LINE TONIGHT, AN' I BLEW IT!

IT'S TOO LATE FOR THEM--TOO LATE FOR ME --BUT BEFORE LUKE CAGE GOES DOWN...

...SOMEONE'S GONNA PAY!!

HEART OF THE DRAGON!

MISTY, GET OUT OF HERE-- I'LL HOLD HIM OFF!

FOR ALL OF TWO SECONDS, FELLA-- 'FORE I BUST YOU WIDE OPEN!

HE MAY HAVE A *POINT.* WHAT'S THE MAN *MADE* OF, ANYWAY? I HIT HIM WITH THE *FULL FORCE* OF THE IRON FIST--

--YET HE'S AS FAST AND AS *POWERFUL* AS EVER.

HE HAS NO *FIGHTING TECHNIQUE*--BUT HE DOESN'T *NEED* ANY. *HITTING* HIM IS LIKE HITTING A CHUNK OF *CAST STEEL.*

BROM!

WORSE, ACTUALLY. I CAN *SHATTER* STEEL.

ALL I'M DOING WITH *POWER MAN* IS SMASHING MY *FEET.*

KROM!

YOUR PLAYIN' *JACK-RABBIT* AIN'T GONNA SAVE YOU *FOR-EVER,* PUNK!

FOREVER WILL TAKE CARE OF *ITSELF,* MR. CAGE--WHAT WORRIES *ME* IS THE NEXT FEW *MINUTES.*

OUCH!!

KRAK!

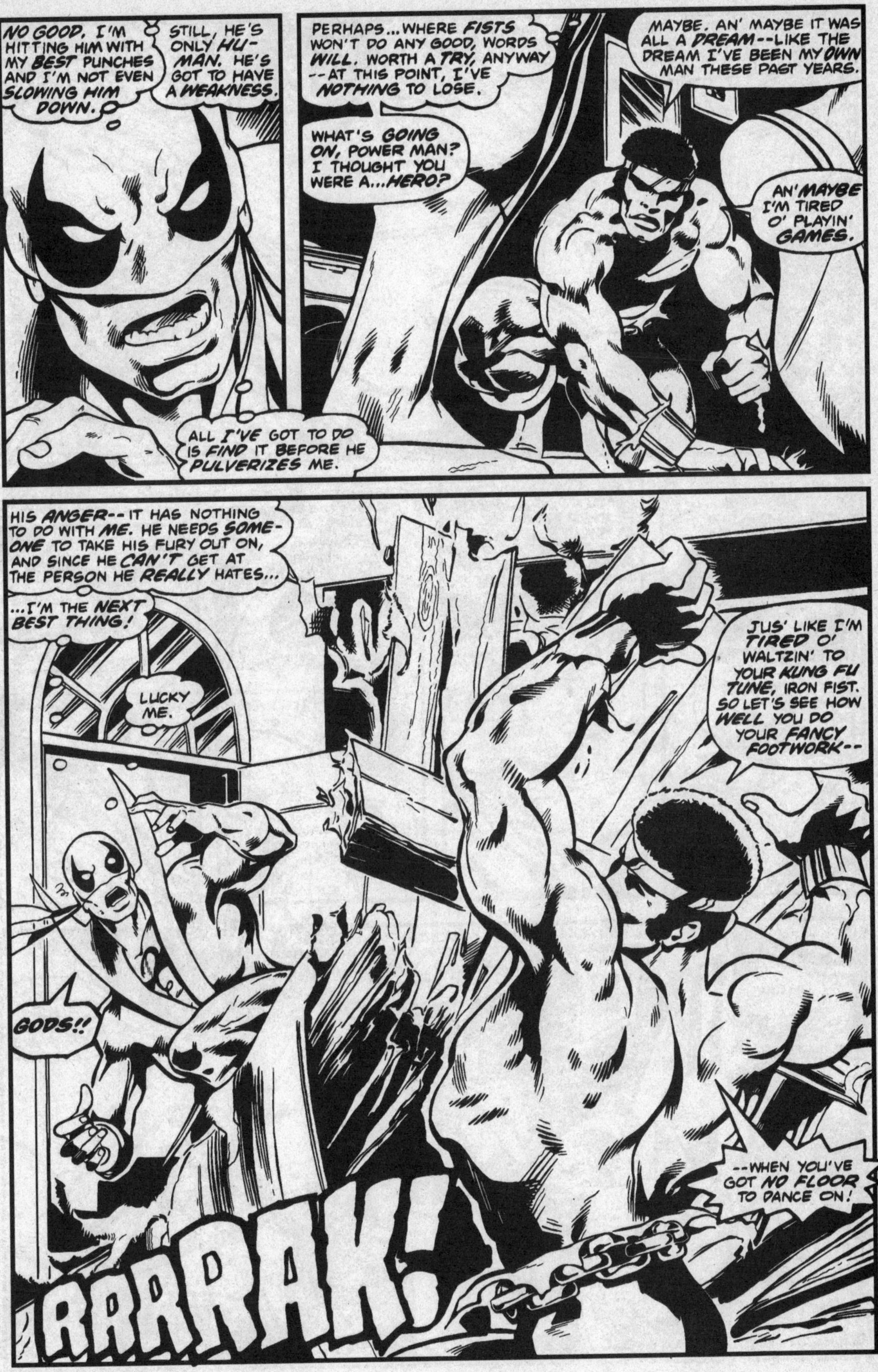
NO GOOD. I'M HITTING HIM WITH MY BEST PUNCHES AND I'M NOT EVEN SLOWING HIM DOWN.
STILL, HE'S ONLY HU-MAN. HE'S GOT TO HAVE A WEAKNESS.
ALL I'VE GOT TO DO IS FIND IT BEFORE HE PULVERIZES ME.
PERHAPS...WHERE FISTS WON'T DO ANY GOOD, WORDS WILL. WORTH A TRY, ANYWAY --AT THIS POINT, I'VE NOTHING TO LOSE.
WHAT'S GOING ON, POWER MAN? I THOUGHT YOU WERE A...HERO?
MAYBE. AN' MAYBE IT WAS ALL A DREAM--LIKE THE DREAM I'VE BEEN MY OWN MAN THESE PAST YEARS.
AN' MAYBE I'M TIRED O' PLAYIN' GAMES.
HIS ANGER-- IT HAS NOTHING TO DO WITH ME. HE NEEDS SOME-ONE TO TAKE HIS FURY OUT ON, AND SINCE HE CAN'T GET AT THE PERSON HE REALLY HATES...
...I'M THE NEXT BEST THING!
LUCKY ME.
JUS' LIKE I'M TIRED O' WALTZIN' TO YOUR KUNG FU TUNE, IRON FIST. SO LET'S SEE HOW WELL YOU DO YOUR FANCY FOOTWORK--
GODS!!
--WHEN YOU'VE GOT NO FLOOR TO DANCE ON!
RRRRAK!

POWER MAN, *LISTEN* TO ME! WHAT-EVER'S *HAPPENED*, IS IT *WORTH* THROWING YOUR *LIFE* AWAY FOR?!

I GOT *NO LIFE* ANYMORE, *KID!*

ALL I GOT IS *HATE!*

HANDS LIKE *VISE...* CAN'T BREATHE...

BUT...I...SENSE AT *HEART...* POWER MAN ISN'T... *KILLER.*

IT'S A DESPERATE, DANGEROUS GAMBLE, PLAYED FOR THE *ULTIMATE STAKES*-- AND AS THE SECONDS PASS, IT LOOKS LIKE IRON FIST HAS *LOST.*

I CAN TRY...*TIGER CLAW* TO EYES...LAST RESORT...*BLIND HIM...*

...THEN, *IF* THAT WORKS, IF I CAN SUMMON...STRENGTH ...*POP* HIS EARDRUMS ...KILLING BLOW, BUT *NOT YET.*

AND THEN, WHEN IT'S ALMOST *TOO LATE...*

LORD, NO-- WHAT AM I DOIN'?

≥WHEW!≤

FOR A *WHILE* THERE, YOU HAD ME *WORRIED.*

WELL, YOU DON'T NEED TO WORRY *NO MORE.* WHATEVER ELSE LUKE CAGE IS, HE'S *NO KILLER.*

CEPT OF HIS *CLOSEST* FRIENDS.

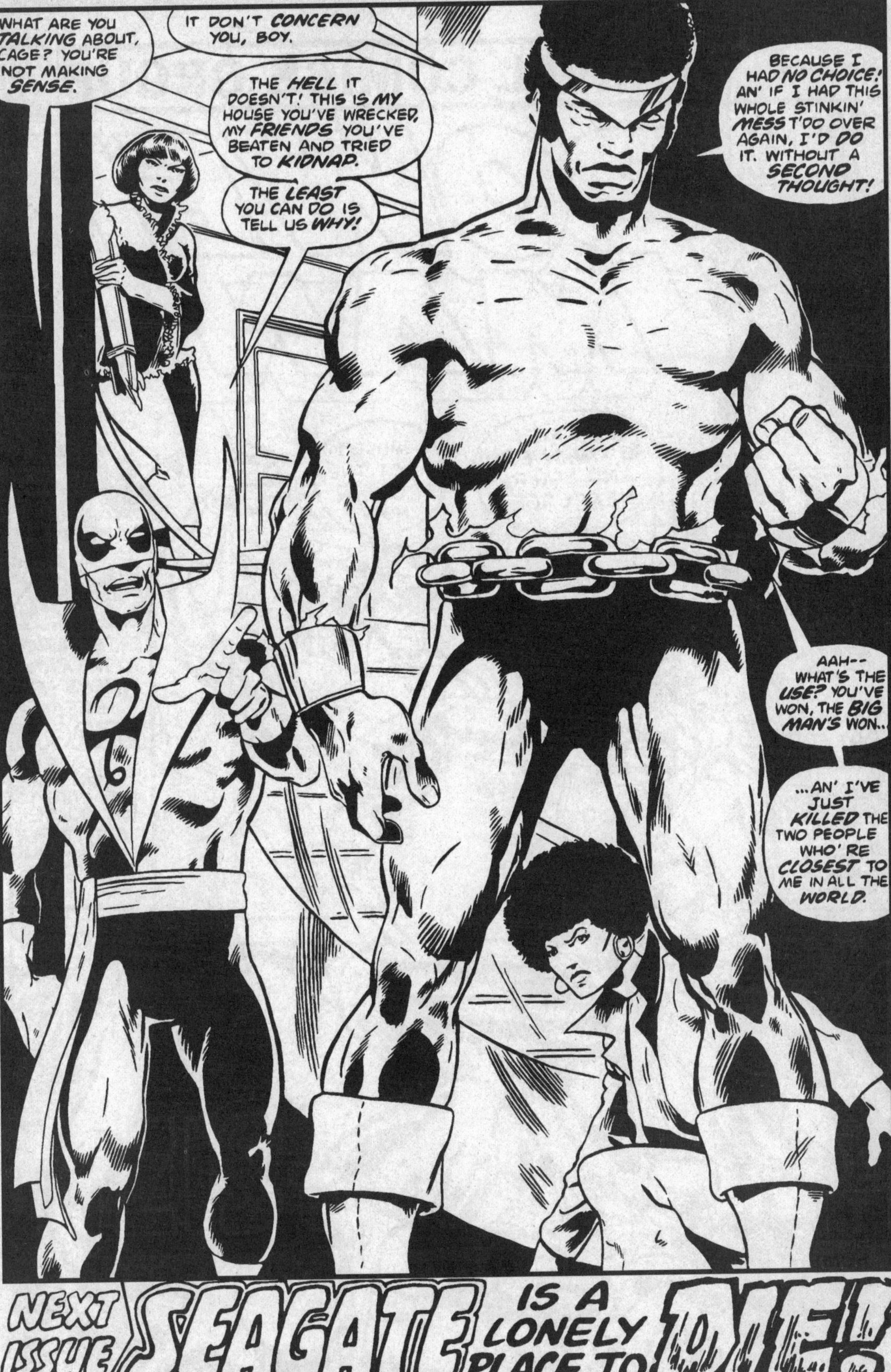
WHAT ARE YOU TALKING ABOUT, CAGE? YOU'RE NOT MAKING SENSE.
IT DON'T CONCERN YOU, BOY.
THE HELL IT DOESN'T! THIS IS MY HOUSE YOU'VE WRECKED, MY FRIENDS YOU'VE BEATEN AND TRIED TO KIDNAP.
THE LEAST YOU CAN DO IS TELL US WHY!
BECAUSE I HAD NO CHOICE! AN' IF I HAD THIS WHOLE STINKIN' MESS T'DO OVER AGAIN, I'D DO IT. WITHOUT A SECOND THOUGHT!
AAH-- WHAT'S THE USE? YOU'VE WON, THE BIG MAN'S WON..
...AN' I'VE JUST KILLED THE TWO PEOPLE WHO'RE CLOSEST TO ME IN ALL THE WORLD.

NEXT ISSUE / SEAGATE IS A LONELY PLACE TO DIE!

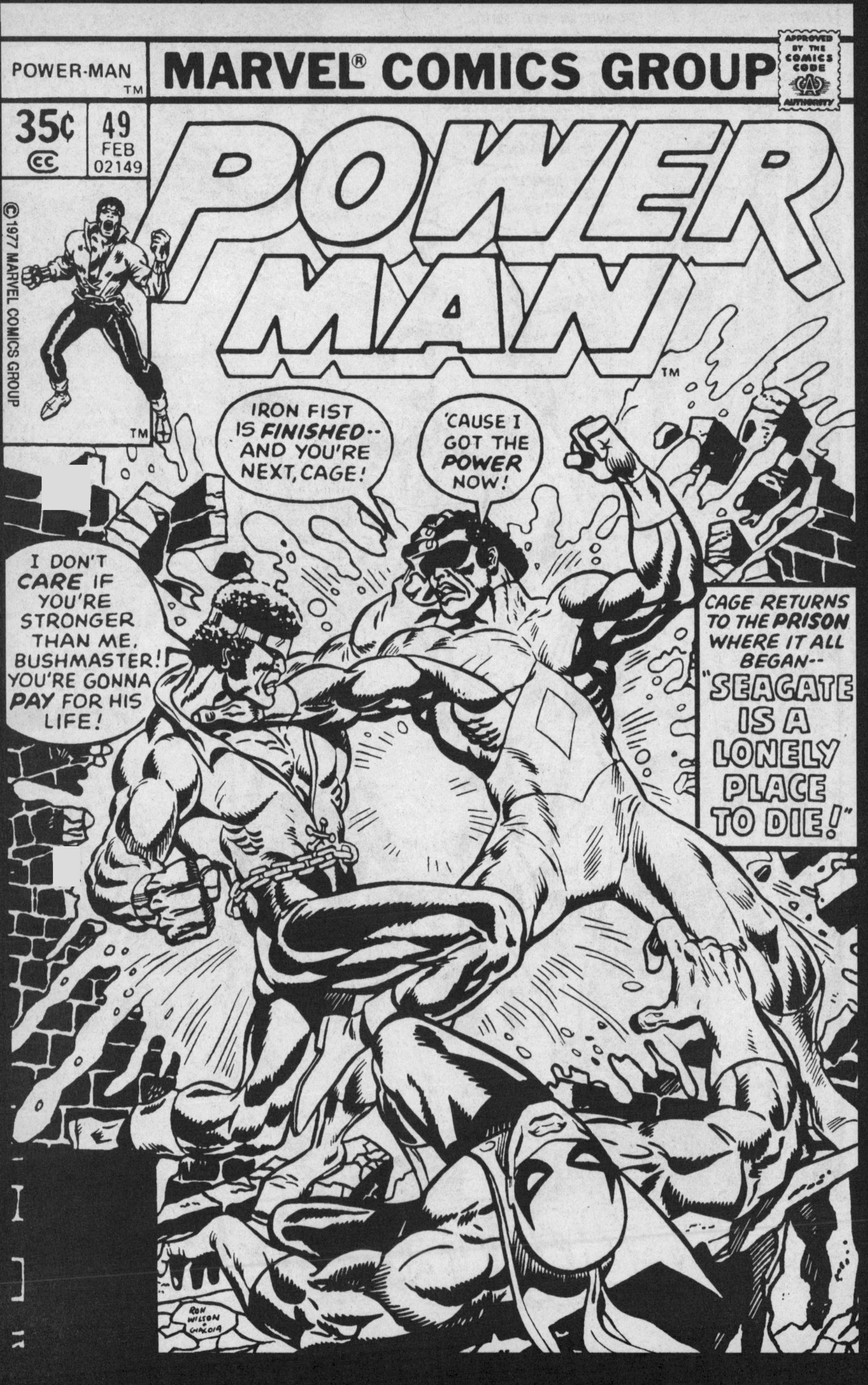

POWER-MAN
MARVEL® COMICS GROUP
APPROVED BY THE COMICS CODE AUTHORITY
35¢
49 FEB 02149
POWER MAN
© 1977 MARVEL COMICS GROUP
IRON FIST IS FINISHED-- AND YOU'RE NEXT, CAGE!
'CAUSE I GOT THE POWER NOW!
I DON'T CARE IF YOU'RE STRONGER THAN ME, BUSHMASTER! YOU'RE GONNA PAY FOR HIS LIFE!
CAGE RETURNS TO THE PRISON WHERE IT ALL BEGAN-- "SEAGATE IS A LONELY PLACE TO DIE!"

LUKE CAGE: Wrongly convicted and sentenced to prison—reborn in a freak experiment there that gave him *steel-hard skin* and *strength beyond belief*—a man who hides his identity as an escaped convict in the role of a HERO FOR HIRE!

STAN LEE PRESENTS: LUKE CAGE, POWER MAN!

CHRIS CLAREMONT — AUTHOR | JOHN BYRNE — ARTIST | DAN GREEN — INKER | ANNETTE K., LETTERER | MOULY & KLACZAK, COLORISTS | ARCHIE GOODWIN — EDITOR

Seagate IS A LONELY PLACE TO Die!

His name is *LUKE CAGE*, one-time *HERO FOR HIRE*, now called *POWER MAN*. A few minutes ago, he almost *MURDERED* the three people sitting around him in the living room of DANIEL RAND'S WEST-SIDE TOWNHOUSE:

IRON FIST, THE LIVING WEAPON, AND HIS TWO CLOSEST FRIENDS, *MISTY KNIGHT* AND *COLLEEN WING*.

UNDERSTANDABLY, NOW THAT THE BATTLE'S OVER, THEY'RE ALL WONDERING...

BROWLF!!!

WHY, CAGE?

THE ANSWER IS *SILENCE*, AND IN THAT SILENCE, CAGE'S MIND DRIFTS *BACK*...

...TO THE MOMENT HE SMASHED HIS WAY INTO THE RAND MANSION, HUNTING MISTY...

THOOM!

...AND FINDING COLLEEN, INSTEAD.

COLLEEN LED HIM A MERRY CHASE THROUGH THE VAST, EMPTY HOUSE, BUT ALL SHE MANAGED TO DO WAS DELAY THE INEVITABLE.

CAGE CAUGHT UP WITH HER, CORNERED HER, AND--WITHOUT MEANING TO--NEARLY KILLED HER.

BEFORE THAT HAPPENED, THOUGH, COLLEEN MANAGED TO PUT THROUGH A PHONE CALL TO MISTY.

B'LAM!

NOT THAT HER INTERVENTION DID MUCH GOOD. DESPITE HER COLT PYTHON AND HER BIONIC RIGHT ARM...

...CAGE HAD NO TROUBLE TAKING MISTY OUT.

UNFORTUNATELY FOR HIM, SHE HADN'T COME ALONE.

MR. CAGE-- TURN A- ROUND.

SHOW!

ANYONE ELSE WOULD HAVE BEEN PULVERIZED BY THE POWER OF THE IRON FIST, BUT CAGE JUST CAME BACK FIGHTING...

...CONSUMED BY A BERSERKER FURY THAT EVEN IRON FIST'S MARTIAL ARTS SKILLS COULDN'T WITHSTAND.

CAGE HAD COME WITHIN A HEARTBEAT OF KILLING HIM. *

LORD, NO-- WHAT AM I DOIN'?

*AS WE ALL SAW LAST ISH--ARCHIE.

WELL, CAGE?

AFTER WHAT'S HAPPENED, THE LEAST YOU OWE US IS AN EXPLANATION.

YOU SAID THAT THE *"BIG MAN'S WON,"* THAT YOU'D JUST *KILLED* THE TWO PEOPLE WHO'RE *CLOSEST* TO YOU IN ALL THE WORLD.

WHAT DID YOU *MEAN?*

WHAT I *SAID.*

I FEEL LIKE I'M DROWNIN'! IRON FIST WANTS TO HELP, BUT IF I TELL HIM THE WHOLE STORY--

--I GOTTA TELL HIM WHO I REALLY AM. AN' THIS MISTY-FOX IS AN EX-COP.

BUT THEY'RE THE ONLY HOPE I GOT TO SAVE CLAIRE AN' NOAH-- MAN, I'M DAMNED IF I DO, DAMNED IF I DON'T!

MORE COFFEE, CAGE?

NO. THANKS.

I GOTTA LEVEL WITH 'EM--AT THIS POINT, I GOT NO- THIN' LEFT TO LOSE.

HIS VOICE A LOW MONOTONE, CAGE BEGINS HIS STORY, AS MISTY SLIPS OUT OF THE ROOM BEHIND HIM...

...AND HEADS DOWN THE HALL TO A BOOK-LINED STUDY THAT HAD ONCE BEEN WENDELL RAND'S.

IT TAKES HER ONLY A MOMENT TO PRIME THE STUDY'S COM- PUTER TERMINAL AND PATCH IT INTO AN OUTSIDE LINE.

WHILE, BACK IN THE LIVING ROOM...

...I WAS MAKIN' THE ROUNDS THROUGH CHICAGO, HUNTIN' UP A CHEAP APARTMENT, WHEN THIS BLACK CADDY UP AN' CUTS ME OFF.

SNAPPY-DRESSIN' DUDE INSIDE SAYS HIS BOSS HAS A JOB ONLY I CAN DO, AND THAT I'LL BE WELL-PAID FOR MY TROUBLE.

"I FIGURED THE CAPER TO BE SHADY, BUT I WENT ALONG FOR THE RIDE. IF MY HUNCH WAS WRONG--AN' THE JOB TURNED OUT T' BE LEGIT--I'D TAKE IT. I NEEDED THE BREAD.

"IF IT WAS CROOKED, I'D SIMPLY WALK OUT--AN' TRASH ANY CLOWN FOOL ENOUGH T' GET IN MY WAY.

"IT WASN'T A LONG DRIVE. WE WERE JUST PAST EVANSTON WHEN THE LIMO PULLED UP IN FRONT OF A MILLION-DOLLAR SPREAD SET RIGHT ON LAKE MICHIGAN.

"THE MAN WAS WAITIN' FOR ME INSIDE...

GOOD EVENING, MR. CAGE. I AM BUSHMASTER.

I HAVE NEED OF YOUR...UNIQUE TALENTS.

THAT SO?

NEVERTHELESS, CAGE, YOU *WILL* DO THIS JOB FOR ME. BECAUSE, YOU SEE, *CLAIRE TEMPLE* AND *NOAH BURSTEIN* ARE MY..."GUESTS".

AND IF YOU *TURN ME DOWN...*

I *HEARD* O' YOU ON THE STREET, MAN. YOU'RE THE *EUROPEAN* BROTHER BEEN GIVIN' THE MAGGIA SO MUCH *GRIEF*-- WIPIN' THEM OUT SO YOU CAN *TAKE OVER.*

YOU GOT THE *WRONG* MAN, BUSHMASTER, I'M A *HERO* FOR HIRE.

AND *I* AM MOST DEFINITELY A *VILLAIN.*

...I'LL HAVE NO *ALTERNATIVE* BUT TO ORDER MY MEN TO *KILL THEM.*

THE ASSIGNMENT IS A *SIMPLE* ONE.

YOU'RE TO GO TO *NEW YORK,* FIND THIS *WOMAN...*

...AND BRING HER TO ME.

I...KNEW HER AS *MAYA KORDAY.* HER TRUE NAME IS *MISTY KNIGHT.*

AND *WHAT* HAPPENS AFTER SHE'S *HERE?!*

THAT NEED NOT *CONCERN* YOU.

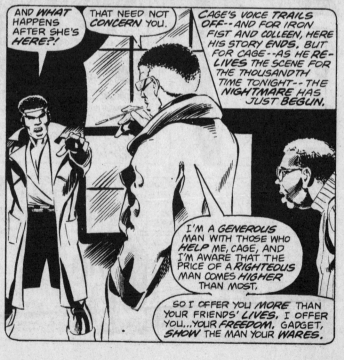

CAGE'S VOICE *TRAILS OFF*--AND FOR IRON FIST AND COLLEEN, HERE HIS STORY *ENDS.* BUT FOR CAGE--AS HE *RELIVES* THE SCENE FOR THE *THOUSANDTH* TIME TONIGHT-- THE *NIGHTMARE HAS JUST BEGUN.*

I'M A *GENEROUS* MAN WITH THOSE WHO *HELP* ME, CAGE, AND I'M AWARE THAT THE PRICE OF A *RIGHTEOUS* MAN COMES *HIGHER* THAN MOST.

SO I OFFER YOU *MORE* THAN YOUR FRIENDS' *LIVES,* I OFFER YOU...YOUR *FREEDOM,* GADGET, *SHOW* THE MAN YOUR *WARES.*

THE *GADGET-MAN* USED TO WORK FOR *WILLIS STRYKER*--I SEE YOU *KNOW* THE NAME. AS INSURANCE AGAINST WILLIS EVER *TURNING* ON HIM, GADGET SECRETLY *VIDEO-TAPED...*

...STRYKER PLANTING TWO KILOS OF *UNCUT HEROIN* IN YOUR APARTMENT.

THIS TAPE IS *PROOF* OF YOUR INNOCENCE, CAGE. IT'S *YOURS* --IN EXCHANGE FOR A WOMAN YOU DON'T EVEN *KNOW.*

SOME *EXCHANGE.* A WOMAN FOR A TAPE-- AN' A *CROOKED* DRUG BUST FOR A *FEDERAL KIDNAPPIN'* RAP, ONLY THIS TIME, I'LL BE *GUILTY AS HELL.*

CAN'T *PUNCH* MY WAY OUTTA THIS--GOTTA USE MY *BRAIN,* STRING THE MAN ALONG AN' TRY T' FIND SOME KIND'A *ANGLE...*

ALL RIGHT, BUSHMASTER, I'LL...*DO IT.*

EXCELLENT, CAGE. YOU'LL LEAVE *TONIGHT.* I'LL EXPECT YOU AT MY *AMERICAN BASE* OF OPERATIONS--WITH MISS KNIGHT--BY *DAWN.*

AND, ON THE *OFF-CHANCE* YOU SHOULD EVEN REMOTELY CONSIDER *BETRAYING* OUR AGREEMENT...

...I'VE PROVIDED SOME *OLD FRIENDS* OF YOURS TO INSURE THAT YOU *TOE THE LINE.*

BEEN A *LONG TIME,* BLOOD.

LIFE BEEN TREATIN' YOU *REAL GOOD,* EH, LUCAS?

SHADES! COMANCHE!

BUSHMASTER HAD ME *BOXED IN,* AN' HE KNEW IT. MAN, HE REALLY *DUG* WATCHIN' ME SQUIRM.

THE *ONLY* WAY I COULD FIGURE THIS CAPER WAS TO GO *THROUGH* WITH IT...

...AN' MAKE MY *MOVE* WHEN I GOT TO HIS BASE, PLAY IT BY *EAR* AN' HOPE FOR THE *BEST.*

GREAT PLAN, LUCAS. IT WOULD'VE GOTTEN ME *KILLED* FOR SURE AN' LEFT BUSHMASTER OWNIN' YOU *BODY AN' SOUL.*

IF HE DOESN'T *ALREADY.* WHAT'S HE *GOT* ON YOU THAT YOU'RE SO *AFRAID* OF, CAGE?

THIS IS *IT,* MAN--YOU ONLY TOLD 'EM *HALF* THE TRUTH BEFORE, DO YOU *LEVEL?* OR DO YOU *LIE?*

I... I'M A *CON.* I WAS DOIN' TWENTY YEARS *HARD TIME* FOR PUSHIN' *SCAG.* I *ESCAPED.*

I WAS *FRAMED,* Y'SEE, AN' BUSHMASTER HAS A *VIDEO-TAPE* THAT *PROVES* IT.

SCORE ONE FOR *YOU*, CAGE.

I PUNCHED THE *LATENT PRINTS* OFF YOUR COFFEE MUG THROUGH THE *NCIC*.* AND CAME UP WITH THIS FEDERAL *RAP SHEET*.

IF YOU'D *LIED* TO ME JUST NOW, I'D HAVE CALLED THE *COPS*. BUT SINCE YOU *TRUSTED* US...

* *NATIONAL CRIME INFORMATION CENTER -- A.G.*

...YOU'RE GONNA TRUST *ME*. I GUESS I'M *FLATTERED*. BUT BUSHMASTER STILL HOLDS ALL THE *CARDS*. HE KNOWS I'M A CON, TOO --HE'D TURN ME IN JUST FOR *SPITE*.

WE DON'T EVEN *KNOW* WHERE HE'S GOT NOAH AND CLAIRE--ASSUMIN' THEY'RE STILL *ALIVE*.

OH, BUT WE *DO* KNOW, Y'SEE, AS MAYA KORDAY, I WAS *WITH* HIM WHEN HE *SET UP* THE BASE.

TELL ME, CAGE-- DOES THE TERM *"LITTLE A"* MEAN ANYTHING TO YOU?

LITTLE A. AS IN LITTLE ALCATRAZ. AS IN SEAGATE PRISON. THE HARD CASES WERE SENT HERE --THE LIFERS, THE INCORRIGIBLES, THE TROUBLE-MAKERS--AND CAGE WAS THE HARDEST CASE OF ALL.

A YEAR OR SO AFTER HIS ESCAPE, THE GOVERNMENT CLOSED THE PRISON AND SOLD IT FOR A MODEST PROFIT. IN NO TIME AT ALL, MOST PEOPLE SEEMED TO FORGET THAT SEAGATE PRISON HAD EVER EVEN EXISTED.

MOST PEOPLE--BUT NOT LUKE CAGE. IF HE LIVES FOREVER, HE'LL NEVER FORGET SEAGATE. OR WHAT IT DID TO HIM.

THERE IT IS. I'VE BEEN *CLIMBIN'* THE WALLS THE PAST FEW DAYS, WHILE WE GOT *READY*. BUT NOW...

SKIN'S *CRAWLIN'*-- JUS' LIKE IT DID THE DAY I *ARRIVED*, THE DAY I MET *QUIRT* AN' *RACKHAM*...

I WASN'T IN STIR MORE'N AN *HOUR* 'FORE THEY STARTED *IN* ON ME--WORDS, FIRST OFF, THEN *FISTS*--

--KNOWIN' ALL THE TIME I COULDN'T *FIGHT BACK.*

WELL, I *COLLECTED* WHAT THOSE TWO OWED ME--WITH *INTEREST*--AN' TONIGHT, IT'S *BUSHMASTER'S* TURN.

HE WON'T BE EXPECTIN' *TROUBLE*--MISTY LEAKED WORD TO THE NEW YORK *PAPERS*...

...THAT I WAS *KILLED* WHEN THAT BROWNSTONE *FELL* ON TOP O' ME.*

*AGAIN, LAST ISH-- A.G.

OKAY, FOLKS, THIS IS AS *CLOSE* AS THE JET BOAT GOES WITHOUT *WAKIN'* ANY GUARDS.

FROM HERE ON, IT'S *YOUR* SHOW.

CHTIK!

GOOD *LUCK.*

AND, TWO MINUTES LATER...

NICE WORK, DANNY--LOOKS LIKE YOU GOT THE *ONLY* GUARD.

BLAST! I'M *OVERSHOOTIN'* THE WALL, GOTTA GRAB THIS *STANCHION* AS I GO BY--USE MY *BIONIC ARM* TO STOP ME--

--AN' HOPE THE *NON-BIONIC* REST O' ME CAN TAKE THE *STRAIN.*

BOO

ARE YOU *ALL RIGHT,* MISTY? YOUR APPROACH SEEMED A LITTLE *HIGH*--?

IT *WAS.* I HAD TO LAND THE *HARD WAY*--AN' I GOT THE *ACHES T'* PROVE IT.

LET'S GET *MOVIN',* HOTSHOT.

LIKE WRAITHS, THEY MOVE DEEP INTO THE OLD PRISON--AVOIDING TROUBLE WHEN THEY CAN, DEALING WITH IT SWIFTLY AND SILENTLY WHEN THEY HAVE TO.

PIECE O'CAKE, PAL!

IF YOU *SAY SO,* MISTY. I JUST HOPE YOU'VE *REMEMBERED* THE LAYOUT OF THIS BASE *CORRECTLY.*

TRUST ME. IF BURSTEIN AN' THE GIRL ARE STILL ALIVE, THEY'LL BE IN *THIS* SECTION.

OKAY, I'LL GET *DR. BURSTEIN.* YOU GET *CLAIRE* TEMPLE. AND *HURRY UP*--WE'RE FALLING *BEHIND* SCHEDULE.

I'M NOT SURE *WHY,* BUT I HAVE A *BAD* FEELING IN MY BONES,

DANNY'S *CHANGED* --INSIDE--EVER SINCE HE FOUGHT *STEEL SERPENT.** PART OF HIM *DIED* WHEN THE IRON FIST WAS *TORN* OUT OF HIM.

WELL-- HEL-LO, CLAIRE.

*MTU #'S 63 & 64--A.G.

THE POWER HE *TOOK BACK,* BUT THE... *INNOCENCE...*

DOC TEMPLE, NAME'S *MISTY KNIGHT.* I'VE COME TO *RESCUE* YOU,

I STARTLED HER--SHE'S TENSING TO *SCREAM!* NO TIME TO EXPLAIN THINGS.

I'LL HAVE TO KNOCK HER *OUT*--WITH A BIONIC *NERVE-PINCH.*

UNNNGNH!

MISTY, I *FOUND* BURSTEIN'S ROOM, BUT HE'S *NOT* THERE!

BEAUTIFUL,

WHAT DO WE DO *NOW?* OUR TIME'S UP--CAGE'LL BE MAKING HIS *MOVE!*

PLACE-CUT: TO SEAGATE'S MAIN GATE...

...WHERE A *BORED* GUARD, MARKING TIME UNTIL HIS *SHIFT* CHANGES...

...IS ABOUT TO GET...

...THE SURPRISE OF HIS LIFE!!

ON YOUR TOES, TURKEYS!

'CAUSE POWER MAN IS BUSTIN' THROUGH--

--AN' I AIN'T STOPPIN' 'TIL I GET MY HANDS ON BUSHMASTER!

KTHOOM!

SOUND THE ALARM! WE'RE UNDER ATTACK!

YOU GOT IT, YO-YO!

AN' YOU BETTER THANK YOUR LUCKY STARS IT'S YOUR BOSS I'M AFTER-- AN' NOT YOU!

I'M FEELIN' MEAN TONIGHT, SCUM, AN' WHEN POWER MAN FEELS MEAN--

--PEOPLE GET HURT!!

KRAM!

THAT CRASH OUTSIDE-- AND NOW, GUNSHOTS!

I THINK CAGE HAS MADE HIS ENTRANCE-- RIGHT ON CUE.

ANY MINUTE NOW, THIS ENTIRE ROCK WILL BE CRAWLING WITH BUSHMASTER'S MERCENARIES,

WE'VE GOT CAGE'S GIRL.

YOU WANT TO PLAY IT SAFE AND CALL IT QUITS WHILE WE'VE GOT THE CHANCE?

WE GAVE CAGE OUR *WORD*, MISTY--THAT WE'D HELP HIM *RESCUE* HIS FRIENDS, THEN TRY TO FIND GADGET'S *VIDEO-TAPES*.

YOU GET CLAIRE TO *SAFETY*. I'LL TRY TO FIND *BURSTEIN*.

DANNY'S *NERVOUS-NESS* MUST BE CATCHING-- NOW *I'M* ON EDGE.

I DIDN'T REALLY *EXPECT* TO FIND THESE TWO *ALIVE*.

IT ISN'T *LIKE* BUSHMASTER TO LEAVE *LOOSE ENDS* LYING AROUND--IF THEY'RE *HEALTHY*, IT'S ONLY BE-CAUSE HE *NEEDS* THEM.

QUESTION IS, FOR *WHAT*?!

I'D BETTER TAKE THE *PRESSURE* OFF CAGE SO ONE OF US CAN GO *FIND OUT*.

RUN FOR *COVER*, HERO! I'LL KEEP THESE JOKERS *OCCUPIED*!

WE'VE *FOUND* YOUR LADY FRIEND!

LITTLE MAMA, THAT'S *MUSIC* TO MY EARS!

SHE'S COMIN' TO, MISTY!

LUKE--?

EASY, HON, EVERYTHIN'S GONNA BE *JUS' FINE*.

FORGET...ABOUT ME! BUSHMASTER'S TAKEN NOAH TO THE *SOLITARY CONFINEMENT LEVELS*-- WORKING NIGHT AND DAY SINCE WE *ARRIVED*.

I WAS TRYING TO *TELL* YOUR GUN-TOTING *IDIOT* PARTNER THAT WHEN SHE KNOCKED ME *OUT*!

BEAUTIFUL.

IRON FIST IS *LOOKING* FOR HIM, CAGE.

OKAY, MISTY, I'LL HANDLE IT FROM HERE. YOU GET CLAIRE OUT TO THE *BOAT*.

NOAH'S WORKIN' IN *SOLITARY*--BUT THAT'S WHERE...

LUCAS, YOU BETTER *MOVE*!

"'CAUSE IF WHAT CLAIRE SAID *MEANS* WHAT I THINK IT MEANS, THAT *KUNG FU KID* IS AS GOOD AS DEAD!"

GET IN-SIDE, BRO'--

AT THAT VERY MOMENT, DOWN IN *SOLITARY*...

BYANG!

--THE DUDE'S MOVIN' TOO *FAST* FOR ME TO *HIT*!

SLAM!

KLIK!

FROM CAGE'S *DESCRIPTION*, THOSE TWO ARE *SHADES* AND *COMANCHE*-- *BUSHMASTER'S* LIEUTENANTS.

THEY'LL BE *EXPECTING* ME TO SMASH THROUGH THE *DOOR*--WITH THEM POISED TO CUT ME TO *PIECES* THE INSTANT I MAKE MY *ENTRANCE*.

GENTLEMEN, IT *ISN'T* GOING TO BE THAT *EASY*.

AFTER ALL, *WHY* SHOULD I USE THE *DOOR*, WHEN THE POWER OF THE *IRON FIST*--

--MAKES IT JUST AS EASY TO COME THROUGH THE *WALL ITSELF*?!

SHKOW!

DR. BURSTEIN, I PRESUME?

HEART OF THE DRAGON-- WHAT GOES *ON* IN HERE?!

MACHINERY STACKED TO THE CEILING, ENOUGH *COMPUTERS* TO RUN A SMALL PENTAGON-- ALL MANNER OF ADVANCED ELEC-TRONIC *HARDWARE*.

IT'S LIKE BARON *FRANKENSTEIN'S* LAB UPDATED TO THE *SPACE AGE*.

OH, LORD... NO...

Y-YOU'RE... IRON FIST...!

THE ONE-AND-ONLY, DOCTOR--WERE YOU EXPECTING THE AVENGERS?

I'M HERE WITH POWER MAN TO RESCUE YOU AND DR. TEMPLE.

LUCAS-- OH, NO! NO!

GET AWAY, IRON FIST--BEFORE IT'S TOO LATE!

IT'S ALREADY TOO LATE, LITTLE MAN!

SOMEONE BEHIND ME--! MOVING SO SILENTLY I DIDN'T HEAR HIM--BUT THAT'S IMPOSSIB--

BOK

OK

AAAGKKH!

BOTH HEROES' DAYS ON EARTH ARE NUMBERED!

THAK!

BROO!

IRON FIST!!

THAT KID WENT BY HERE LIKE HE WAS SHOT OUT OF A CANNON!

CHRISTMAS! IT'S BURSTEIN'S LAB-- BETTER EQUIPPED THAN EVER!

GREETINGS, MR. CAGE.

I'VE BEEN HOPING AGAINST HOPE THAT OUR PATHS WOULD CROSS AGAIN.

BUSH- MASTER!

IN THE FLESH.

YOU BROKE OUR AGREEMENT, CAGE-- AS I KNEW YOU WOULD--AND FOR THAT TRANSGRESSION, I AM GOING TO KILL YOU.

WITH MY BARE HANDS.

YOU--AN' WHO ELSE, CLOWN?!

IT'S GONNA TAKE MORE'N A BIG MOUTH AN' A FANCY COSTUME T'CASH IN POWER MAN'S CHIPS!

THAT WAS MY SUNDAY PUNCH. IF THAT DON'T DECK HIM, I DON'T KNOW WHAT WILL.

KROK!

ALL RIGHT, THEN--HOW ABOUT RAW POWER?

BRAK!

SWEET SISTER--I FELT THAT!

I AIN'T EVER BEEN HIT THIS HARD BEFORE!

SEAGATE, BURSTEIN, THE LAB-- IT ALL ADDS UP.

BUSHMASTER MUST'A BEEN FORCIN' NOAH T' TURN HIM INTO ANOTHER POWER MAN!

KTHOK!

FOR--FORGIVE ME, LUCAS --I'M AN OLD MAN, AND BUSHMASTER THREATENED TO TORTURE CLAIRE,

I HAD NO CHOICE!

I'M SO VERY, VERY SORRY-- BUT YOU HAVE NO CHANCE,

UNLESS... IRON FIST-- WAKE UP! PLEASE!

...OOOOHHHHH...

QUICKLY, YOUNG MAN! POWER MAN IS FIGHTING FOR HIS LIFE! YOU MUST HELP HIM!

STAY OUTTA THIS, KID! BUSH-MASTER'S ALL MINE!

I....UNDER-STAND, CAGE.

IRON FIST DOESN'T TRY TO EXPLAIN AS HE LEAVES, BURSTEIN HAM-MERING AT HIS CHEST, CURSING HIM FOR A COWARD. INSTEAD, HIS MIND FLASHES BACK ACROSS THE WEEKS, TO INWOOD PARK...

...AND HIS FINAL CONFRONTATION WITH STEEL SERPENT. * HE WAS HOPELESSLY OUTMATCHED, YET IT WAS A DUEL THAT--WIN OR LOSE--HE HAD TO FIGHT ALONE, TO PROVE--TO HIMSELF, MORE THAN ANYONE ELSE--THAT HE ALONE WAS WORTHY OF HIS NAME.

AND AS IT WAS FOR IRON FIST, SO IT IS--HERE AND NOW--FOR POWER MAN.

RRRRAK!

YOU'RE A FOOL, CAGE!

I AM THE ULTIMATE PRODUCT OF BURSTEIN'S EXPERIMENTS. IN ALL RESPECTS, MY POWER DWARFS YOURS!

*MTU #66--A.G.

YOU CAN NO MORE STAND AGAINST ME THAN AGAINST A TIDAL WAVE!

TONG!

THE MAN MAY HAVE A POINT THERE.

FOR EACH SHOT I GIVE HIM, I GET TWO BACK--WITH INTEREST.

AT MOST, I'M ANNOYIN' HIM. HE'S HURTIN' ME.

KRUNNCH!

HAD ENOUGH, BOY?

HE TALKS LIKE RACKHAM-- SO SURE OF HIMSELF, SO SURE I CAN'T TOUCH HIM, WORKIN' ON ME DAY IN, DAY OUT, TRYIN' T' BREAK ME--!

BE REAL EASY T' GIVE UP, TOO--SPARE MYSELF A LOT O' PAIN-- AS EASY NOW AS IT WAS THEN.

THAM!

ONLY I AIN'T GIVIN' UP!

YOU MAY *KILL* ME, BUSHMASTER, BUT IF I *DIE*--

--I DIE *FIGHTIN'!*

THEY COME TOGETHER LIKE TITANS-- AND, INDEED, THERE'S A *MYTHIC* QUALITY TO THEIR BATTLE, AS CAGE TRIES TO *TEAR* THE HALF-TON I-BEAM OUT OF BUSHMASTER'S GRASP...

...THEIR *SUPERHUMAN* STRUGGLE TAKING THEM *PERILOUSLY* CLOSE TO BURSTEIN'S *CHEMICAL VAT.*

SPLUTCH!

UNTIL, SUDDENLY, THE BEAM *PUNCHES* THROUGH THE CHEMICAL *CONTAINMENT* LIKE SOME MONSTROUS CAN-OPENER.

DOUSING BOTH MEN IN *BOILING* HOT LIQUID.

WHA--?!?

IT'S THE *GUNK* NOAH WAS DUNKIN' ME IN THE DAY I GOT TURNED INTO *POWER MAN*--IT'S BURNIN' LIKE *FIRE!*

FLOOOSH!

SWEET-MAMA, I CAN FEEL THE STUFF THROUGH MY *STEEL-HARD* SKIN-- LIKE IT'S BURNIN' *INSIDE* ME, TWISTIN' ME INSIDE-OUT! AND FROM THE *LOOKS* O' THINGS, IT'S HITTIN' BUSHMASTER THE *SAME* WAY!

GREAT, NOW WE'RE FIGHTIN' IN THE MIDDLE OF A *LAKE.*

CRIPES! THE CHEMICALS ARE WASHIN' TOWARDS THE LAB'S *MAIN POWER LINES!*

AN' IF THEY *CONNECT*--!

THEY DO, AND THE RESULTS ARE *PREDICTABLE.*

AAARGGH!

NOT TO MENTION EXPLOSIVE!

BUH-WHROOM

GODS OF K'UN-LUN!

THAT EXPLOSION-- FROM THE *LOWER LEVELS* WHERE CAGE WAS FIGHTING BUSH-MASTER, AND... *MISTY'S* SOMEWHERE INSIDE!

GET BURSTEIN INTO THE *BOAT*, DR. TEMPLE, AT THE FIRST SIGN OF TROUBLE-- *TAKE OFF!*

MISTY *CLOBBERED* MOST OF BUSHMASTER'S TROOPS ON HER WAY *OUT* WITH CLAIRE--BUT THEN, SHE WENT *BACK* INTO SEAGATE, IN THE DRAGON'S NAME--*WHY?!?*

NO *SIGN* OF HER-- OR CAGE.

MISTY! CAGE!

MISTY!!

MOVEMENT! IS THAT *HER?!?*

NO. IT'S ONLY *CAGE*, BUT-- *HOW???* THE EXPLOSION COL-LAPSED THIS WHOLE SECTION OF THE *PRISON*.

I'LL... BE. I'M *STILL*... *BREATHIN'*...

YOU'RE *ALL RIGHT*, CAGE! THAT'S... *INCREDIBLE!*

AND YOU'VE *WON*, TOO. YOUR FRIENDS ARE *SAFE*.

IT'S A FREAKIN' *MIRACLE*, KID.

YEAH, BUT *WITHOUT* THAT TAPE, I'M STILL NO MORE'N AN *ESCAPED CON*. BUSHMASTER DISCOVERED THE *TRUTH*; IT'S ONLY A MATTER OF *TIME* BE-FORE SOMEONE ELSE *DOES*.

BY THEN, CAGE, MAYBE IT **WON'T** MATTER.

MISTY?! YOU GONNA WAVE YOUR **MAGIC WAND**--

--AN' MAKE EVERYTHIN' **COOL**, MAMA?

SOMETHING LIKE THAT.

I BELIEVE YOU'VE ALREADY **MET** THE GADGET-MAN. HE'S GOT SOMETHING T' **GIVE** YOU, CAGE, OUT OF THE **KINDNESS** OF HIS HEART AN' A DESIRE T' SEE **JUSTICE** DONE.

WELL--ER, AH-- NOT EXACTLY... THAT IS, I MEAN I...ER...

RIGHT, LITTLE MAN?

KLIK!

HERE, MR. CAGE!

THIS IS THE **TAPE** YOU'RE AFTER! THE ONE THAT'LL **CLEAR** YOU!

WITH THAT, THEY'RE **ON** THEIR WAY-- WITH COMANCHE AND SHADES AND THE MERCENARIES LEFT **LOCKED** IN SEAGATE'S CELLS FOR THE **FEDS** TO DEAL WITH.

...NOT A **BAD** NIGHT'S WORK, FOLKS. COLLEEN'LL BE **FURIOUS** AT HAVING TO **MISS** IT.

I'VE ONLY **ONE** REGRET --THAT BUSHMASTER DIED BY **ACCIDENT.**

I WOULD HAVE **LIKED** TO HAVE DONE THE JOB **MYSELF.**

YOU THINK HE'S **DEAD**, MAMA? WE NEVER FOUND HIS **BODY.**

CAGE, I'LL SAY THIS **ONCE.** I AM **NOT** YOUR "MAMA", SWEET OR OTHERWISE. **DIG?**

AS FOR BUSHMASTER, HE'S PROBABLY **BURIED** UNDER TONS OF RUBBLE, MAN, **NO ONE** COULD HAVE SURVIVED THAT **EXPLOSION.**

I DID.

FIN

NEXT ISSUE: FREEDOM!

CAGE'S FIRST NIGHT AS A FREE MAN MAY TURN OUT TO BE HIS **LAST**--THAT IS, IF **STILETTO** AND **DISCUS** HAVE ANYTHING TO SAY ABOUT IT.

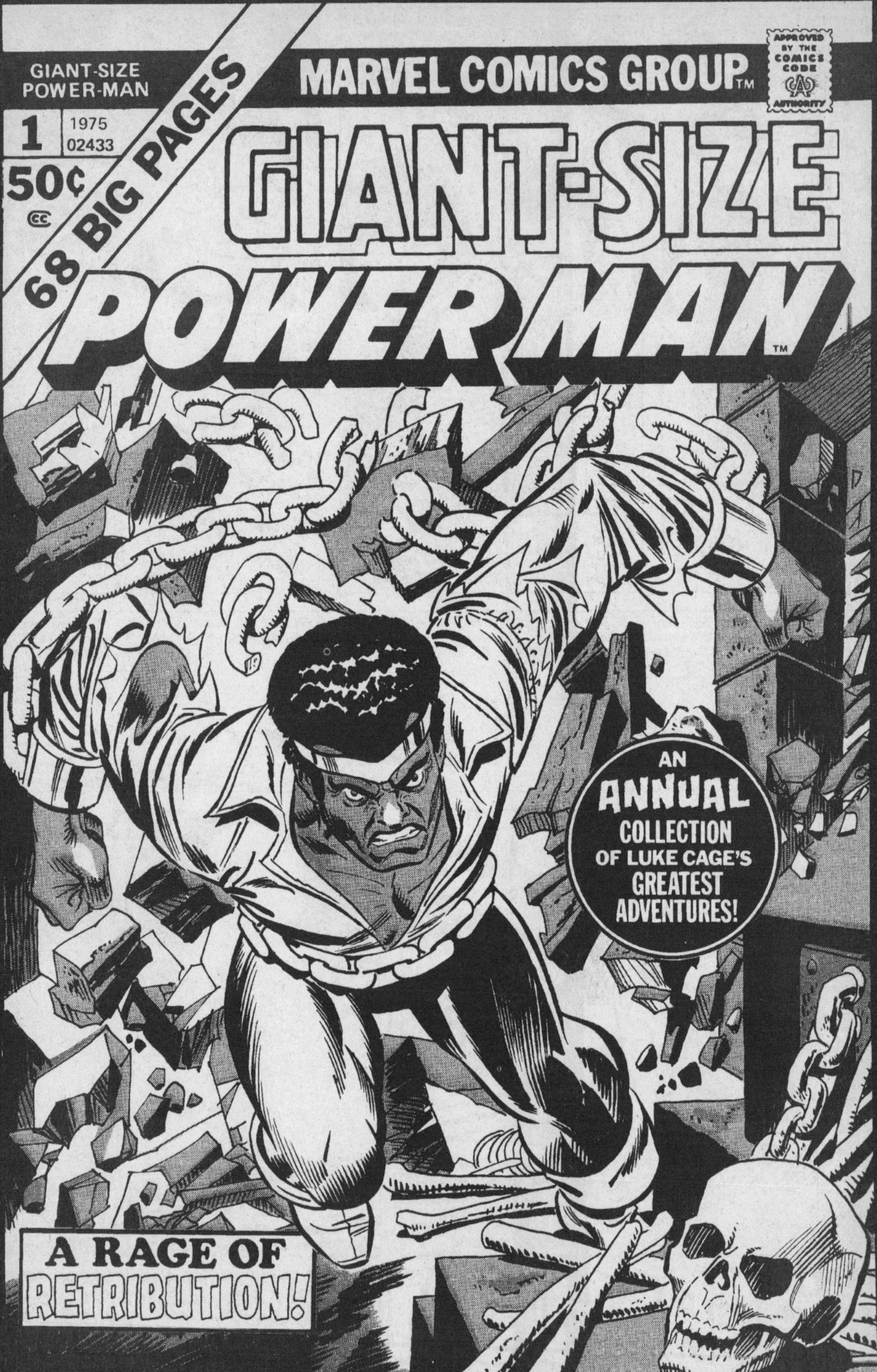
GIANT-SIZE POWER-MAN
1
1975
02433
50¢
CC
68 BIG PAGES
MARVEL COMICS GROUP
APPROVED BY THE COMICS CODE AUTHORITY
GIANT-SIZE
POWER MAN
AN ANNUAL COLLECTION OF LUKE CAGE'S GREATEST ADVENTURES!
A RAGE OF RETRIBUTION!